Softwar
Assessments,
Benchmarks, and
Best Practices

Addison-Wesley Information Technology Series

Addison-Wesley will provide film

Software Assessments, Benchmarks, and Best Practices

Capers Jones

Addison-Wesley

Boston • San Francisco • New York • Toronto • Montreal
London • Munich • Paris • Madrid
Capetown • Sydney • Tokyo • Singapore • Mexico City

The publisher offers discounts on this book when ordered in quantity for special sales. For more information, please contact:

Pearson Education Corporate Sales Division
One Lake Street
Upper Saddle River, NJ 07458
(800) 382-3419
corpsales@pearsontechgroup.com

Library of Congress Cataloging-in-Publication Data

Jones, Capers.
    Software assessment, benchmarks, and best practices / Capers Jones.
        p.   cm.
    Includes bibliographical references and index.
    ISBN 0-201-48542-7
    1. Computer software—Evaluation.   I. Title.

    QA76.76.E93 J66 2000
    005.1'4—dc21   00-023304

Visit AW on the Web: www.awl.com/cseng

ISBN 0-201-48542-7
Text printed on recycled paper
1 2 3 4 5 6 7 8 9 10–MA–0403020100
First printing, April 2000

To Eileen—for making all things possible

Contents

CHAPTER 8   **BENCHMARKS AND BEST PRACTICES**
             FOR OUTSOURCED SOFTWARE   235

CHAPTER 10   **BENCHMARKS AND BEST PRACTICES FOR COMMERCIAL SOFTWARE   399**

Contents

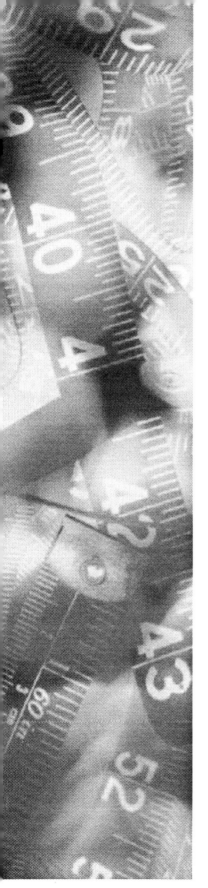

Preface

During my writing, this book evolved considerably from the first plan. Originally I intended to divide the book into two major sections. The first section was to discuss a number of assessment and benchmark methods used in the United States and Europe. The second section was to present an overview of software productivity and quality benchmarks, and associated "best practices" derived from benchmark studies. The benchmarks and best practices in this book cover six major kinds of software project: (1) management information system (MIS) projects, (2) outsource projects, (3) systems and embedded software projects, (4) commercial software projects, (5) military software projects, and (6) personal software projects developed by end users.

However, as the writing commenced, the focus of the book began to change. It soon became clear that a complete discussion of benchmarks and best practices for each of the six kinds of software would be about twice as large as initially planned. I had planned to devote approximately 30 pages to the benchmark and best-practice information for each type of software. But to do justice to the available data, almost 60 pages were needed for five of the six forms of software. Furthermore, a discussion of how assessment and benchmark studies operate and their technical differences may be of interest to those of us in the assessment and benchmark business, but it is not necessarily of great interest to those outside the limited circle of benchmark consultants.

As a result, the discussion of assessment and benchmark methods was cut back, and the sections devoted to information gathered during assessments and benchmark studies was expanded. Instead of a book with two sections of roughly equal size, the book now has a briefer introductory section and greatly expanded discussions of each type of software and the issues that confront each type.

This book also emphasizes assessments and benchmark data from the United States. Although my colleagues and I have gathered data in more than 24 countries, the issues of international benchmarks are quite complex. The international variations in working years and working days, how overtime is treated, and European restrictions on some kinds of data collection made me decide to concentrate on U.S. data.

Readers should note that this is a book about assessments and benchmarks written by someone who is in the assessment and benchmark business. Because my company has been performing assessments and benchmarks since 1985, we have an obvious interest in the topic. However, this is not a marketing book, nor is it a book about how my company's assessments and benchmarks work. The topics of software assessments and benchmarks are important ones, and this book attempts to include the general principles under which all assessment and benchmark consulting groups operate.

In my view, and also in the view of my competitors, assessments and software benchmarks are important to the global economy. Software has been the most labor-intensive product of the twentieth century, and the most error prone. Assessments, benchmarks, and empirical data are on the critical path to minimizing software project failures. Every software project manager, every software quality assurance specialist, and every software engineer should understand the basic concepts of software assessments and benchmarks. This is a view shared by all of the assessment and benchmark consulting groups.

The software industry has achieved a notorious reputation as being out of control in terms of schedule accuracy, cost accuracy, and quality control. A majority of large systems run late, exceed their budgets, and many are cancelled without ever reaching completion. Assessment and benchmarks followed by planned process improvement programs can aid in bringing software under management control. These are not "silver bullet" methods. Assessments, benchmarks, and process improvement programs require effort and can be expensive, but project failures are far more expensive.

This book discusses the kinds of complex software projects that benefit from assessments and benchmark studies. Small and simple projects are not the main focus of assessments and benchmarks. The proper focus of assessments, benchmarks, process improvements, and this book is on large and complex applications.

Chapter 1 provides an introduction to the topic of software assessments and benchmarks. This chapter discusses the kinds of data that should be collected. It also cautions against some common problems, such as depending on data without validating it, and using hazardous metrics such as *lines of code*. This chapter also discusses the need to keep client data protected, and suggests some coding methods that can be used to perform benchmarks without revealing proprietary client information.

Chapter 2 deals with the history of software process assessments and discusses some of the kinds of information that are gathered during software process assessments. Although more than a dozen forms of assessment exist, the form made popular by the Software Engineering Institute is the best known. Some recent and more specialized forms of assessment, such as those performed for the Y2K problem, have also been widely used since about 1998.

Chapter 3 deals with the related topics of software benchmarks and software baselines. *Benchmarks* collect and compare quantitative data against industry norms. *Baselines* measure the rate at which a company can improve productivity and quality when compared with an initial starting point. Of course, sometimes productivity and quality can get worse instead of better.

Chapter 4 discusses 36 key factors that should be recorded during assessment and benchmark studies. If these 36 key factors are recorded, the data gathered by almost any benchmark and assessment consulting group, or by any company or government agency, could be compared meaningfully.

Chapter 5 addresses an important topic that is somewhat ambiguous in the software literature. When we speak of "best practices" what exactly do we mean? Chapter 5 discusses some criteria for including or excluding tools and technologies from best-practice status. It is suggested that any technology considered a potential best practice needs empirical results from at least ten companies and 50 projects.

Chapter 6 discusses an important follow-on activity to assessment and benchmark studies. Both assessments and benchmark studies are diagnostic in nature, rather than therapeutic. These studies can identify problems, but they cannot cure them. Therefore, a natural follow-on activity to either an assessment or a benchmark analysis, or both, would be to implement a process improvement program.

Chapter 7 deals with benchmarks and best practices for MIS projects. These are software applications that companies and government agencies build for their own internal use. MIS applications are often keyed to large corporate database access, and their main purpose is to convert raw data into useful information. Although MIS projects are often fairly high in productivity for small projects, large MIS projects tend to experience more than average failure rates. Quality at the large end is often poor too.

Chapter 8 deals with benchmarks and best practices for outsource software projects. The emphasis in this chapter is on projects under contract for MIS, rather than for military or systems software outsourcing. The major outsource vendors such as Andersen, Electronic Data Systems, and IBM concentrate on the MIS market because it is the largest market for their services. In general, outsource projects have higher productivity and quality levels than in-house MIS projects; however, litigation between clients and outsourcers does occur from time to time.

Chapter 9 deals with benchmarks and best practices for systems and embedded software, which are applications that control physical devices such as computers, telephone switching systems, aircraft flight controls, or automobile fuel injection systems. The close coupling of systems software to physical hardware devices has led to very sophisticated quality control methods. The systems software community has the best track record for applications larger than 10,000 function points.

Chapter 10 deals with benchmarks and best practices for commercial software. Commercial software applications are intended for the mass market, and some of these applications are used by millions of customers on a global basis. The commercial and systems software domains overlap in the arena of operating systems because commercial products such as Windows 98 are both systems and commercial software. The commercial world needs to deal with special issues such as translation and nationalization of packages, piracy, and very extensive safeguards against viruses.

Chapter 11 deals with benchmarks and best practices for military software, with special emphasis on the U.S. armed services and the Department of Defense. The military software domain is fairly good at building large and complex applications, although military software productivity is lower than any other domain. The legacy of U.S. military standards has left the defense community with some very cumbersome practices. Plans and specifications in the military domain are approximately three times larger than equivalent civilian projects. The bulk is due primarily to military oversight requirements, rather than to the technical needs of the project.

Chapter 12 deals with benchmarks and best practices for end user software development. As the new century begins, there are more than 12,000,000 U.S. office workers who know how to write computer programs if they wish to do so.

By the middle of this century, the number of computer-literate workers in the United States will top 125,000,000. Indeed, there are some signs that computer literacy will actually pull ahead of conventional literacy in the sense of being able to read and write. End user applications are currently in a gray area outside the scope of normal assessments and benchmarks. More importantly, end user applications are also in a gray area in terms of intellectual property law. As end user applications become more and more numerous, it is important to set policies and guidelines for these ambiguous applications.

As this book is written, benchmarks based on function point metrics are dominant in the software world, except for military software, in which benchmarks based on lines of code still prevail. This book utilizes function point metrics and cautions against lines-of-code metrics for benchmarks involving multiple programming languages. Version 4.1 of the function point rules defined by the International Function Point Users Group is the standard metric used throughout.

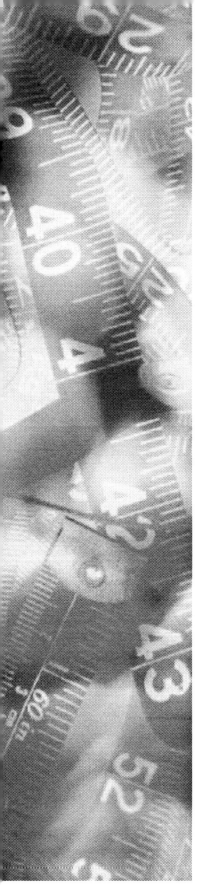

Acknowledgments

As always, special thanks to my wife, Eileen Jones, for her help. She makes all of my books possible. Eileen handles all of our publishing contracts, and by now knows the details of these contracts as well as some attorneys. Thanks also for her patience when I get involved in writing, even on holidays.

This manuscript is being finished approximately two years after the merger of Software Productivity Research (SPR) with Artemis Management Systems. Many thanks to Steve Yager, the president of Artemis, for his interest and support of SPR's assessment and benchmark studies. Thanks also to the many Artemis colleagues and distributors around the world.

Thanks also to Alec Gores and Vance Diggins of the Gores Group for including SPR in such an excellent organization.

Special thanks to Charles Douglis, SPR's president, for many years of leadership and friendship. Great appreciation is due to all of my colleagues at SPR for their aid in gathering data. Special thanks to the families and friends of the SPR staff, who have had to put up with lots of travel overtime. Thanks to Ed Begley, Chuck Berlin, Amy Bowers, Julie LeBaron, Michael Bragen, Doug Brindley, Jack Boyle, Tom Cagley, Sudip Charkraboty, Michael Cunnane, Gail Flaherty, Richard Gazoorian, Mike Griffin, David Gustafson, Bill Harmon, Bob Haven, Steve Hone, Jan Huffman, Peter Katsoulas, John Mulcahy, Joy Mohr, Donna O'Donnell, Mark Pinis, Mickie Prault, Tom Riesmeyer, Evelyn Rooney, Kathy Russell, Todd Santora, Keith Savage, Pam Simonvich, Bill Walsh, and John Zimmerman.

Special thanks to Allan Albrecht, the inventor of function points, for his invaluable contribution to the industry and for his outstanding work with SPR. Without Allan's pioneering work in function points, the ability to create accurate baselines and benchmarks would probably not exist. Thanks also to the International Function Point Users Group (IFPUG) for expanding the role of function points.

Thanks also to Mary O'Brien and her colleagues at Addison Wesley Longman. It is always enjoyable for an author to work with an excellent editorial and production team.

Much appreciation is due to the client organizations whose interest in software assessments, benchmarks and baselines, measurement, and process improvements have let us work together. These are the organizations whose data make estimation tools possible.

There are too many groups to name them all, but many thanks to our colleagues and clients at Andersen Consulting, AT&T, Bell Atlantic, Bell Northern Research, Bell Sygma, Bendix, British Air, CBIS, Charles Schwab, Church of the Latter Day Saints, Cincinnati Bell, CODEX, Credit Suisse, DEC, Dun & Bradstreet, DuPont, Electronic Data Systems, Finsiel, Ford Motors, Fortis Group, General Electric, General Motors, GTE, Hartford Insurance, Hewlett-Packard, IBM, Informix, Inland Steel, Internal Revenue Service, JC Penney, JP Morgan, Kozo Keikaku, Language Technology, Litton, Lotus, Lucent, Mead Data Central, McKinsey Consulting, Microsoft, Motorola, Nippon Telegraph, NCR, Northern Telecom, Bell Atlantic, Pacific Bell, Ralston Purina, Sapiens, Sears Roebuck, Siemens-Nixdorf, Software Publishing Corporation, SOGEI, Sun Life, Tandem, TRW, Unisys, U.S. Air Force, U.S. Navy surface weapons groups, US West, Westinghouse, and many others.

Thanks also to my colleagues and competitors in software assessments and benchmark studies. Without the pioneering work of researchers such as Howard Rubin, Watts Humphrey, Bill Curtis, Ron Radice, Mark Paulk, and Bob Park, the assessment and benchmark domains would not be widely known in the software world. Special thanks to the late Ted Climis and Jim Frame of IBM, who were pivotal in introducing assessments and benchmarks into the IBM software community.

Capers Jones

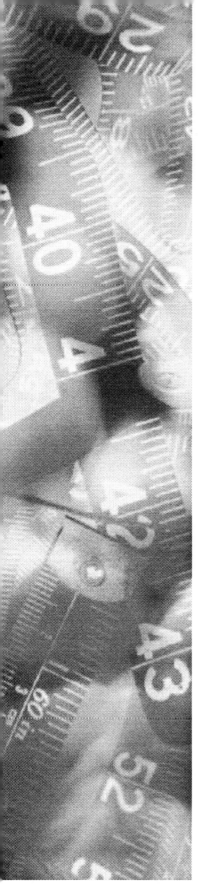

Abstract

Benchmarks are collections of quantitative data that compare an enterprise against other similar enterprises in the same industry. Software benchmarks are often used for productivity and quality comparisons, and also for comparisons of salaries and spending levels.

Baselines are collections of quantitative data used to mark the starting point of a process improvement program. Baselines and benchmarks are similar in that they both collect quantitative data. Baselines are often used with outsource agreements that serve as the starting point for contractual obligations to improve productivity and quality.

Software assessments are on-site reviews of the methods, tools, and processes used to develop software applications. Assessment data is qualitative in nature. Assessments are used to place organizations on a comparative scale and show relative levels of capability.

When assessment data, benchmark data, and baseline data are combined, a powerful synergy results. The combination of assessments, benchmarks, and baselines can identify best practices, average practices, and worst practices. The term *best practices* refers to methodologies, tool suites, and organizational structures that raise software quality and productivity levels above average by at least 15% in repeated trials within at least ten companies and 50 projects.

CHAPTER ONE

Introduction

Software has been a troubling technology for more than 50 years. Computers and software are the major tools of business, government, and military organizations, but computers and software can be troublesome, expensive, and error prone.

Developing large software applications is particularly troublesome. Software application development is more labor intensive than any other business artifact. Software projects are cancelled or run late, and exceed budgets more often than any other kind of project in modern business. Software applications are also highly error prone, and some of these errors can trigger major business expenses. For example, the year 2000 (Y2K) software problem is already the most expensive business problem in history, and the most widespread.

The troublesome nature of software and the many failures and delays associated with large software applications have been a source of concern and dismay to top executives throughout the world. Because software is so important to the modern world, finding ways to minimize failures and to optimize success would be valuable to all major corporations.

The most effective way of reducing the problems of software is to study all possible approaches for building and maintaining applications. From careful analysis of both quantitative and qualitative data, it is possible to separate beneficial practices from harmful practices. The current three primary forms of analysis utilized for exploring software construction are

1. Software process assessments to examine development practices
2. Software benchmarks against empirical industry data to rank performance
3. Software baselines against which progress can be measured

The term *process assessment* refers to formal and structured methods for examining the way software projects are built and maintained. Assessments can be performed by outside consultants or by in-house personnel. However, because in-house personnel may find it difficult to be objective, outside consultants are used more often.

The term *benchmark* refers to comparisons of quantitative data between specific companies. It also refers to a more general comparison of a company against industry norms. Benchmark studies are performed most often by consulting organizations that collect large volumes of data from hundreds of companies. Although benchmarks can be done between individual companies, if they are direct competitors it is not usually feasible to share proprietary information. Therefore, "blind" studies among multiple companies, with the sources of specific data points concealed, are more common.

The term *baseline* refers to quantitative data collected to indicate the starting point in a process improvement program. The rate of improvement is compared against the starting values of the baseline. If baselines are to be used for contractual purposes, such as outsource agreements, they need to be performed with great accuracy. Because few companies entering into outsource agreements have accurate productivity and quality data available at the start of the agreement, baselines are sometimes sources of later dispute and even litigation.

For any company that is prepared to invest in software process improvement programs, it would be prudent to establish an initial quantitative baseline. Because process improvement programs are fairly expensive and can run for three to five years, an accurate baseline of productivity, schedule, quality, and quality data is used to determine the return on investment (ROI) of the investments and hence demonstrate the value of the program. Without a quantitative baseline, software process improvement programs might founder because of corporate criteria that major investments must return a significant, positive ROI within a three- to five-year period.

Assessments, baselines, and benchmarks typically overlap in the forms of data collected. Process assessments gather a great deal of qualitative data on how well activities are performed. Benchmarks and baselines gather some qualitative data, but their main emphasis is on quantitative data. Project size, productivity levels, quality levels, schedules, salary levels, and staffing levels are normal quantitative factors.

Although the three activities of assessments, benchmarks, and baselines are often performed separately, combining the data from assessments, benchmarks, and baselines leads to the most effective results. Process assessments collect useful qualitative data, but without quantitative data it is hard to justify investments in process improvement programs. Benchmarks and baselines collect quantitative data, but without the qualitative data from assessments it is not possible to understand why productivity and quality levels might be less than desired. Data from assessments, benchmarks, and baselines combined are able to answer six important questions from top corporate and software executives.

1. Are our productivity and quality better or worse than our competition?
2. If we lag behind our competition in any key areas, what can we do to improve this?
3. If we invest in improvements, how large an investment is needed?
4. If we invest in improvements, how many years will have to be funded?
5. If we invest in improvements, what is the ROI?
6. After the improvement program, what will our productivity and quality be?

Although assessments, benchmarks, and baselines are useful individually, there is a strong synergy among them. Companies that perform only assessments or only benchmark studies have access to useful but only partial data. Companies that perform assessments and benchmarks are well positioned to fund software process improvement programs and set targets for results. However, the targets will be relative targets against an initial quantitative baseline.

As this book is written, most of the large corporations in the Fortune 500 class have undergone software process assessments of their major software groups. A smaller but growing percentage have undertaken benchmark and baselines studies. My company (Software Productivity Research [SPR]) has performed assessments and benchmark studies of approximately 150 of the companies in the Fortune 500 class. We have also worked with more than 100 smaller companies and quite a few government agencies and military organizations. Because many large enterprises have multiple software development locations and laboratories, we have gathered data from almost 600 sites all told.

Because assessments, benchmarks, and baselines are often performed by different companies using different methods, it is not easy to compare the results from one study with another. One of the recommendations of this book is to develop an international standard for key data elements in assessments, benchmarks, and baselines. This standard would allow assessment, benchmark, and baseline data to be compared, and would lead to eventual pooling of data from many different sources.

Protecting and Comparing Confidential Data

From collecting data and analyzing approximately 9,000 software projects from almost 600 sites, we have had to deal with practical issues associated with large-scale studies; for example, when portions of the data gathered are proprietary and confidential. We have also encountered situations in which a client has utilized two or more assessment and benchmark consulting groups simultaneously. Naturally the clients are interested in whether the data collections from both consulting companies are similar. Sometimes the benchmark results have differed widely, and this requires a great deal of study to understand why. The dual issues of preserving confidentiality and comparing data gathered by independent assessment and benchmark organizations will become more common during the twenty-first century as more and more data is gathered.

The SPR method for preserving confidential data uses standard industry codes, rather than identifying clients by name. We also have developed methods for identifying the specific kinds of software projects included in our database of projects.

In order for software comparisons to be meaningful, it is important that similar projects be compared. Furthermore, most companies are concerned with how their performance compares with direct competitors in their own industry. This means that to perform a meaningful assessment or benchmark for an organization such as a bank or insurance company, data must be available from other banks and other insurance companies. However, none of the banks and insurance companies want competitors to know their specific results.

Because most companies perceive information regarding their software schedules, productivity levels, and quality levels as proprietary and confidential, it is important for the assessment and benchmark consulting groups to conceal the specifics of their clients' identities. Usually the client cannot be identified to other companies, nor can the names of the projects that were examined or the personnel who were interviewed. Indeed, the consulting group doing the work usually has to sign a nondisclosure agreement, as we do at SPR.

The dual need for confidentiality plus the need to compare similar projects means that specific industries, project types, and other kinds of data need to be encoded rather than displayed openly. Also, to perform statistical analyses of hundreds or thousands of projects, it is useful to be able to aggregate projects that share common attributes. There are seven basic kinds of information that are common among assessments, benchmarks, and baseline studies for which encoding may be useful:

1. The country in which the client is located
2. The city in which the client is located (optional)
3. The industry of which the client is a part
4. The nature of each project being analyzed
5. The scope of each project being analyzed
6. The class of each project being analyzed
7. The type of each project being analyzed

Before discussing assessments, benchmarks, and baselines themselves, it is useful to consider how software project data can be recorded so that it is usable for statistical analysis but still preserves the confidentiality of client data.

Currently there is no industry-standard taxonomy for identifying projects studied during software assessments and benchmarks. Because the methods used by SPR have been fairly effective for more than 15 years, they are shared here in the hope that other assessment and benchmark organizations adopt similar methods or improve on ours. If methods better than SPR's should be developed, we would probably conform to them. The immediate problem that we face several times a year is when we and other companies are commissioned by the same client to perform assessments or benchmark studies. In this situation, how can the client be sure that the two samples are more or less equivalent?

We also face even more serious problems when we testify as expert witnesses. It is quite common in lawsuits for defendants or plaintiffs to want to compare a specific project with "industry averages." Thus, accuracy in gathering benchmark data may have significant legal implications.

The following is an example of how different benchmark data might appear unless it is gathered consistently. Four years ago, a financial services company commissioned benchmark studies by both SPR and another benchmarking group. When the two benchmark reports were presented to the client, our analyses of the client's own results were similar. However, background benchmark data for the financial services industry varied by approximately 50% between our data and the other company, with our data indicating lower productivity rates. Our sample showed productivity rates of roughly 9 function points per staff month compared with roughly 14 function points per staff month in the other sample of financial services software projects. This difference naturally raised questions by the client regarding how the two sets of benchmarks had been derived, and what they contained.

The answer in this case illustrates some of the problems of software benchmark studies. Our data is gathered by means of on-site interviews with managers and technical workers. The other benchmark company used mailed and telephone surveys, and had received data from a number of companies' internal cost tracking systems. As discussed later, it just so happens that most cost tracking systems "leak" and do not record accurately all of the effort that is expended on software projects. In this case, the data derived from mail and telephone surveys had not captured unpaid overtime, project management effort, and the technical work performed by clients.

The relative magnitudes of these missing data items were approximately 15% for unpaid overtime, 12% for project management effort, and 19% for technical work performed by clients. The client technical activities included participating in joint application design (JAD), attending design reviews, assisting in prototypes, preparing user manuals, and performing acceptance testing. In other words, approximately 46% of the total software effort was not recorded by corporate cost tracking systems, and hence did not show up in the other benchmark study.

It is interesting that both of the benchmark studies were "correct" in that both were accurate reflections of the data that had been collected. The problem was that the values were so different that our mutual client was distrustful of software benchmarks. The other benchmark recorded accurately the values submitted by their clients from their cost tracking systems. But software cost tracking systems leak so severely that the data they contain is unsafe to use for benchmarks.

The problem of "leakage" from cost tracking systems is quite common in the software industry but is not often discussed in benchmark studies. The need to correct leakage explains why we prefer to go on-site and actually interview managers and technical workers. One of the major purposes of "live" interviews is to correct omissions and errors in software cost tracking systems.

Another problem with normal cost tracking systems (not encountered in the example discussed here) is the fact that sometimes when budgeted money is running low on one project, time is charged to another project.

Incidentally, leakage from software cost tracking systems has been a factor in several contract lawsuits between outsource vendors and their clients. Under the terms of their agreements, the outsource vendors were required to demonstrate annual productivity gains using the last year prior to the start of the contract as the baseline against which improvement would be measured. Because the clients' cost tracking systems omitted many cost elements, the outsource vendors were presented with artificial baselines that were much higher than those actually achieved by their clients. Of course, it would have been useful for the contracts to include a data validation clause. This would have verified the accuracy of the baseline.

Another problem caused by leakage has been difficulty in calibrating software cost-estimating tools. When a client compares the output from a commercial software cost-estimating tool with historical data, the estimate often predicts higher costs and longer schedules than the historical data indicates occurred. The client may assume that the error is in the estimating tool, but very likely the error is because the historical data is incomplete and it omitted factors such as unpaid overtime, management effort, and early requirements definition before the tracking system was initialized.

Overall, the software industry has been neither consistent nor complete in recording software resource, schedule, and cost data. This means that surface studies using only data reported from corporate cost tracking systems are likely to understate effort and to overstate productivity, due to such missing factors as unpaid overtime, management effort, and other common omissions.

International Country and City Codes

The countries in which clients are located is not usually regarded as confidential or proprietary information. The cities may or may not be regarded as confidential. For example, assuming that the client wanted all data to be confidential, if the company is located in a small town in which there are no other major companies, then recording the city may be troublesome. On the other hand, for major cities such as London, New York, Los Angeles, and Tokyo, recording the city would usually not be a cause for concern because these major cities contain thousands of companies.

For studies performed in the United States, using the standard two-character abbreviation for states developed by the U.S. postal service is a useful compromise. Every U.S. state has hundreds or thousands of companies, so identifying a project down to the level of state probably will not reveal the specific company. Many international software studies simply identify the cities and countries by spelling them out. The only problem with identifying countries and cities by name is that if data is to be pooled from multiple sources, it is important to ensure that the same languages and spellings are used. For example, if international data is being pooled between studies done by U.S. and Italian consulting groups, it would be acceptable to use either "Rome" or "Roma" or "Paris" or "Parigi" but not both, assuming the data is to be sorted alphabetically.

It is also possible to use the numeric country and city codes assigned for telecommunication purposes, although these codes may become unstable as the world begins to run out of telephone numbers by about 2012. These codes are readily available from telephone companies, and even from many large municipal telephone directories. Unfortunately, area codes in the United States now have a life expectancy of less than three years before changing, so this method is no longer stable.

Using Standard Industry Classifications (SICs) for Software Studies

When data on thousands of software projects drawn from hundreds of companies has been collected, it needs to be organized in such a way that it can provide useful benchmark information to clients. The use of SIC codes allows data to be displayed by industry, and also allows specific company names to be protected and secured. For organizing assessment and benchmark studies by industry, I (and my company, SPR) utilize the SIC codes developed by the U.S. Department of Commerce for economic and statistical studies.

Many large-scale economic studies utilize SIC codes, so this is quite appropriate for software assessment and benchmark studies. There are several levels of SIC codes. The two-digit and four-digit versions of the SIC code are used most widely for benchmarks, with the four-digit form giving greater granularity. The full set of SIC codes and their definitions are available from the Government Printing Office in Washington, DC, or even as advertisements from companies such as Dun & Bradstreet.

The purpose of recording the SIC codes is to allow assessment and benchmark comparisons of projects with similar projects taken from the same industry or from related industries. In the absence of any better way of showing data by industry, I recommend that SIC codes become a standard feature of both software process assessments and software benchmarks. If the Software Engineering Institute (SEI) and all of the other assessment groups adopt the use of SIC codes, this would facilitate large-scale industry studies that might combine data from various sources such as SPR, SEI, International Standards Organization (ISO), Software Process Improvement and Capability dEtermination (Spice), Quantitative Software Management (QSM), Howard Rubin Associates, TickIT, and so forth.

There are too many SIC codes to include all of them here, but some of the two-digit forms of SIC codes that tend to have large populations of software personnel and hence large inventories of software applications for benchmark purposes include those listed in Table 1.1.

Table 1.1   Two-Digit SIC Codes Using Software Extensively

Code	Classification
13	Oil & Gas Extraction
20	Food & Kindred Products
21	Tobacco Products
27	Printing, Publishing, & Allied Industries
28	Chemicals & Allied Products
29	Petroleum Refining & Related Industries
33	Primary Metal Industries
35	Industrial & Commercial Machinery
36	Electronic, Electrical Equipment & Components
37	Transportation Equipment
40	Railroad Transportation
42	Motor Freight Transportation
44	Water Transportation
45	Transportation by Air
47	Transportation Services
48	Communications

continued

Table 1.1   *continued*

Code	Classification
49	Electric, Gas, & Sanitary Services
50	Wholesale Trade—Durable Goods
51	Wholesale Trade—Nondurable Goods
53	General Merchandise Stores
60	Depository Institutions
61	Nondepository Credit Unions
62	Security & Commodity Brokers & Dealers
63	Insurance Carriers
64	Insurance Agents & Broker Services
67	Holding & Other Investment Offices
70	Hotels & Lodging
73	Business Services
80	Health Services
87	Engineering, Accounting, & Research Services
91	Executive, Legislative, & General Government
92	Justice, Public Order, & Courts
93	Public Finance, Taxation, & Monetary Policy
94	Human Resource Programs
95	Environmental Programs
96	Economic Programs
97	National Security

Although the two-digit form of SIC code is useful for large-scale studies, it is often desirable to record data at a more granular level, so more SIC digits are often used. Examples of some of the four-digit SIC codes for industries that contain significant software personnel populations and large inventories of applications include those listed on Table 1.2.

Table 1.2   Four-Digit SIC Codes Using Software Extensively

Code	Classification
3571	Electronic Computers
3572	Computer Storage Devices
3575	Computer Terminals
3613	Switchgear & Switching Apparatus
3661	Telephone & Telegraph Apparatus
3711	Motor Vehicles & Car Bodies
3721	Aircraft
3724	Aircraft Engines & Engine Parts
3761	Guided Missiles & Space Equipment
4512	Air Transportation, Scheduled
4812	Radiotelephone Communication
4813	Telephone Communication
4911	Electric Services
5045	Computers, Peripherals, & Software
5311	Department Stores
6011	Federal Reserve Banks
6021	National Commercial Banks
6022	State Commercial Banks
6211	Security Brokers & Dealers
6311	Life Insurance
6321	Accident & Health Insurance
7371	Custom Computer Programming Services
7372	Prepackaged Software
7373	Computer Integrated System Design
7374	Data Processing & Preparation
7375	Information Retrieval Services
7376	Computer Facilities Management
8062	General Medical & Surgical Hospitals
8742	Management Consulting Services

Although the four-digit form of SIC encoding is more precise, usually the two-digit form is easier to use and provides an adequate basis for benchmark comparisons. Once SIC codes are associated with assessment and benchmark data, it then becomes possible to perform large-scale statistical studies within specific industries without revealing individual companies.

The SIC codes are not perfect by any means. They tend to be ambiguous for state and local government agencies, and do not fully support conglomerates and multidivisional corporations. However, as this book is written, there is no better substitute available. At the very least, SIC codes allow statistical analysis of data without revealing confidential factors such as client identity.

A Taxonomy of Software Projects for Benchmark and Assessment Studies

When performing assessment and benchmark studies, it is useful to be able to place a software project unambiguously among the universe of all possible kinds of software projects. This is much harder to do than one might think. We developed a hierarchical classification method based on project nature, scope, class, and type. Because these terms may not be well understood, it is useful to define and illustrate them. The structure of the SPR taxonomy has been in use since 1985 but has been expanded several times to accommodate new forms of software as they occur.

The initial aspect of the SPR taxonomy is the "nature" of the software project being examined. The term *nature* refers to the important topic of whether the project is a new project or whether it involves some form of maintenance and modification to an existing application. The nature factor is significant in assessment and benchmark studies, and for baselines too. Obviously the work involved with building a new application and the work of modifying an existing application overlap, but they also have many different characteristics. The nature parameter is also used in our commercial software estimating tools. Examples of project nature include

1. New development
2. Enhancement (new functions added to existing software)
3. Mandatory change (updates for new statutes or regulations)
4. Maintenance (defect repairs to existing software)

5. Performance updates (revisions needed to improve throughput)
6. Conversion or adaptation (migration to a new platform)
7. Nationalization (migration to a new national language)
8. Reengineering (reimplementing a legacy application)
9. Mass update (modifications for the Euro or Y2K)
10. Hybrid (concurrent repairs and functional additions)

If the project is a brand new one, in which an application is being developed for the first time, there is little chance for ambiguity. However, when existing projects are being updated, there are many different forms of updates that might occur. The hybrid form is the most common among our clients. Usually when new features are being added to an application, defect repairs occur at the same time.

When the updates are hybrid and involve multiple forms of modification, we record all of the kinds of work that are being done. Although it would be useful for benchmarks to know the percentage of effort and costs associated with each kind of update, our clients' data is seldom precise enough to show percentages. Even when we interview the managers and the development team, there still may be ambiguity, because fixing defects and adding new features may be carried out by the same team at the same time and they may neither record nor remember the specifics.

Another element of our taxonomy is the "scope" of the project. The term *scope* attempts to deal with the magnitude and importance of the project. In our benchmarks we also include the specific size of projects using both function points and lines-of-code (LOC) metrics, but for large-scale statistical analysis the scope factor is quite useful. For example, if an application is large enough to be a "system," it is usually more than 5,000 function points. Systems are comprised of many individual programs and therefore require extensive integration that would not be used on individual programs. Examples of project scope include

1. Subroutine of sub-element of a program
2. Module of a program
3. Reusable module or object
4. Disposable prototype
5. Evolutionary prototype
6. Stand-alone program
7. Component of a system

8. Release of a system
9. New system or application
10. Compound system (multiple linked systems)

Knowing the size of a project in terms of source code statements and function points is important, but size alone does not distinguish between a stand-alone program and a component of a system. If a stand-alone program of 1,000 function points is compared with a system component of 1,000 function points, their schedules, effort, and costs will not be identical. The component will usually take longer and have higher costs due to the need to define interfaces to other components, perform integration test, and in some cases include the component in system-level activities such as architecture and system test.

The next attribute of a software project is its "class." The term *class* is used to define the business arrangement that leads to a software application. The major class distinction is whether the application is to be developed internally or whether it is to be delivered to external clients. The use of a class factor for assessments and benchmarks is to ensure that similar projects are part of the comparison. Project comparisons within a class are more significant than comparisons between classes. The classes have been selected because the applications within each class share quite a few common attributes, so comparisons within a class are very interesting to our clients. As might be expected, the class of internal projects is often less rigorous than the class of projects intended for external clients. Military projects are the most rigorous of all. Examples of project classes include

1. Personal application for private use
2. Personal application to be shared by others
3. Academic program developed in an academic environment
4. Internal application to be installed at one location
5. Internal application to be accessed via an intranet or time-sharing
6. Internal application to be installed at many locations
7. Internal application developed by contract personnel
8. Internal application developed using military standards
9. External application, to be freeware or shareware
10. External application to be placed on the World Wide Web
11. External application leased to users
12. External application embedded in hardware
13. External application bundled with hardware
14. External application marketed commercially

15. External application developed under outsource contract
16. External application developed under government contract
17. External application developed under military contract

The class factor is quite important for large-scale statistical analysis of hundreds of applications and international studies. Even for benchmarks and baselines involving only a single company, if the company is large enough it may produce software in almost every class. For example, a large high-technology corporation such as IBM produces many external applications that go to customers. But IBM also produces large amounts of internal software for corporate use, such as payroll applications, human resource applications, production control, inventory management, and competitive analysis.

The next level of the SPR taxonomy concerns the *type* of the application. Although the class taxonomy has been fairly stable for more than ten years, the type taxonomy is updated almost every year as new kinds of software projects appear in the industry. There is an IEEE standard that overlaps our type parameter, but the IEEE standard does not handle the class, nature, and scope parameters. Examples of software types include

1. Nonprocedural (spreadsheet, query, generators, and so forth)
2. Web applet
3. Batch application
4. Interactive application
5. Batch database application
6. Interactive database application
7. Pen-based application
8. Client/server application (two tier)
9. Client/server application (three tier)
10. Enterprise resource planning (ERP) application
11. Scientific or mathematical application
12. Systems or hardware control application
13. Communications or telecommunications application
14. Process control application
15. Embedded or real-time application
16. Trusted system with stringent security
17. Graphics, animation, or image-processing application
18. Robotic or manufacturing control application
19. Expert system with substantial knowledge acquisition

20. Artificial intelligence application
21. Neural net application
22. Hybrid project (multiple types)

The type portion of the taxonomy is quite important in assessment and benchmark studies, and is also useful for baselines. Because baselines are usually done inside a single company, the type factor is used to set separate improvement targets for the kinds of software in which the company is interested. It would hardly be reasonable to assume that batch applications, embedded applications, and neural net applications would achieve the same productivity levels or even use many of the same technologies.

The combinations of nature, scope, class, and type indicate that the software industry produces no less than 37,400 different forms of software. (This value is derived by multiplying the numbers of choices in each factor of the SPR taxonomy.) Each of these 37,400 forms tends to have characteristic profiles of development practices, programming languages, and productivity and quality levels.

When comparing projects between different companies, it can be seen that the combination of SIC code, nature, scope, class, and type serve a useful purpose in ensuring like-to-like comparisons. For example, when showing benchmark or assessment data to clients, the following combination of factors "triangulates" the project and makes it clear to the client exactly what sort of project is under discussion, but does not reveal proprietary or confidential data about the other company that provided the information:

Country code	001	United States
State code	NY	New York
City code	212	Manhattan (optional)
SIC code	6021	National Commercial Bank
Nature code	1	New application development
Scope code	9	New system
Class code	6	Internal program for use at multiple locations
Type code	9	Client/server application, three tier

In this example, revealing the city—New York—would probably not reveal the specific client because New York has dozens of banks. However, if the study were done in a small town, such as Bedford, Massachusetts, then the city might not be identified because some small towns may have only one major company located there.

I am by no means maintaining that the SPR method of recording SIC code, nature, scope, class, and type is perfect. Indeed, it might be of value to the software industry to develop an improved taxonomy. However, as assessments and benchmarks become common in the software domain, some kind of formal taxonomy is necessary to ensure comparisons of similar kinds of applications while preserving the confidentiality of client organizations.

Because of the large number of more than 37,000 permutations of projects, when they are identified by the SPR taxonomy of nature, scope, class, and type, some combinations are fairly rare. Therefore it is not always possible to have statistically valid samples of every permutation.

For displaying data and for general aggregation of results, we use a simpler taxonomy that is discussed in detail later. We divide projects into six general classes and six discrete size ranges. The six general classes are

1. End-user applications—developed privately for personal use
2. Information systems—developed in-house for corporate use
3. Outsource or contract projects—developed under legally binding contract
4. Commercial software—developed to be marketed to external customers
5. Systems software—developed to control physical devices
6. Military software—developed using military standards

Each of these general classes share similar attributes and often have similar tendencies. For example, military software projects produce requirements and specifications that are approximately three times larger than civilian averages. Systems software projects are likely to have very stringent reliability criteria. Outsource projects often have contractually determined schedules and quality levels.

The six primary overall size plateaus are each an order of magnitude apart, starting with very small projects of 1 function point in size:

1. function point
2. 10 function points
3. 100 function points
4. 1,000 function points
5. 10,000 function points
6. 100,000 function points

Obviously, most projects are not exactly one of these six size ranges in size, so we normally aggregate projects to the closest size plateau. Here, too, the rationale is because projects in one of these six size ranges share common attributes. For example, projects at the 10,000-function point size plateau are invariably major systems. Therefore, activities such as architecture and system test are likely to be performed. By contrast, projects in the 100-function point range are often enhancements to legacy applications and are seldom new projects.

Using this combination of six general classes and six size ranges allows us to aggregate data in the form of a matrix with six rows and six columns. For example, the approximate numbers of projects on which we have gathered data can be illustrated using such a matrix, as depicted in Table 1.3.

Over the years, this six-by-six matrix has been very useful in illustrating interesting trends and differences among software projects. Of course this combination of six general classes and six general size ranges is merely used to simplify aggregation and presentation of overall results. For many kinds of projects we can perform comparisons using the actual size of the project and more detailed classification factors.

As this book is written, the software industry has no standard practices for how data should be aggregated and displayed when presenting assessment and benchmark results. As these activities become more common, it would be useful

Table 1.3   Distribution of SPR Project Benchmarks circa 1999

Function Points	End User	MIS	Out-source	Commercial	Sys-tems	Mili-tary	Total
1	50	50	50	35	50	20	255
10	75	225	135	200	300	50	985
100	5	1,600	550	225	1,500	150	4,030
1,000	0	1,250	475	125	1,350	125	3,325
10,000	0	175	90	25	200	60	550
100,000	0	0	0	5	3	2	10
Total	130	3,300	1,300	615	3,403	407	9,155
Percent	1.42	36.05	14.20	6.72	37.17	4.45	100.00

if the various organizations that collect benchmark and assessment data could agree on how to categorize projects in terms of size and similar attributes.

There are also no standard practices on how to deal with the normal "leakage" from software cost tracking systems. Here a possible solution would be to move toward activity-based analysis, with the data gathered during live interviews. However, because live interviews are more costly than mail or telephone surveys, there is definitely a need for improved methods of capturing historical data without omitting major topics such as unpaid overtime and management costs. Thus we must caution readers and benchmark organizations to be very careful of data taken from normal cost tracking systems because it may represent only a fraction of the total effort actually expended.

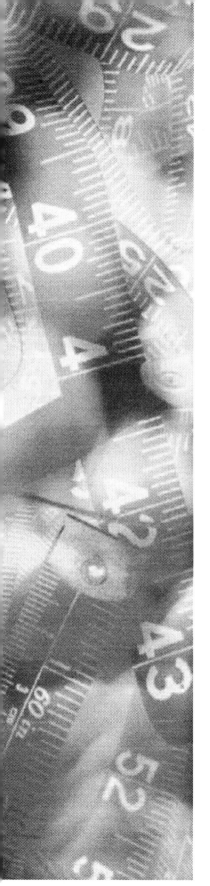

CHAPTER TWO

Software Process Assessments

Because software applications are built by human beings, the methods, tools, and practices used for software have become subject to study and analysis. Software process assessments are normally carried out on-site by independent assessors, although in-house assessments are not uncommon. The assessments consist of a series of scripted interviews with managers and technical personnel.

Formal software assessments appear to have originated within the IBM corporation in the early 1970s. The primary goal of software process assessments is to gather qualitative information about the practices, methods, tool suites, and organizational structures used for software. Some forms of assessments, such as SPR's, gather additional information on topics such as office space and ergonomic factors used by the organization undergoing the assessment.

Because software has become a worldwide business phenomenon, the need for software process assessments has become more and more important. Software is a very troublesome and difficult technology. For large systems, failures outnumber successes by a considerable margin.

Many consulting companies such as SPR, Howard Rubin Associates, QSM, Meta Group, and many nonprofit organizations such as the SEI have developed methods for studying and evaluating software development practices. As of 1999, no less than a dozen varieties of software process assessments have been noted in the literature.

Software process assessment data is normally gathered by means of structured interviews with managers and technical personnel. To ensure consistency among enterprises, standard questionnaires are utilized by most of the assessment methods, although the questions vary from method to method.

Scripts and questionnaires for data collection used by many of the major kinds of software assessments are now utilized throughout the world. Some of the more common forms of software process assessments now in use include

- The SPR assessment methodology
- The SEI assessment methodology
- The ISO assessment methodology
- The SPICE assessment methodology, used primarily in Europe
- The TickIT assessment methodology, used primarily in the United Kingdom
- The Trillium assessment methodology, used primarily in Canada
- The Howard Rubin Associates assessment method, developed by Dr. Howard Rubin
- The Gartner Group assessment method, used primarily for Y2K assessments
- The Information Technology Association of America (ITAA) assessment method, used primarily for Y2K assessments

Although many more forms of software assessment exist, these examples of assessment methods are sufficient to illustrate that software process assessments are now global undertakings.

Incidentally, the arrival of the Y2K problem created a temporary new subclass of software process assessments. These assessments were tightly focused on Y2K preparations and remediation. Their purpose was twofold: (1) to assist clients in anticipating all possible kinds of Y2K damages that might occur and (2) to gather supporting data that could be used in the event of lawsuits against the client for any missed Y2K problems. The increasing incidence of litigation involving software projects and the Y2K problem has caused a significant increase in these specialized assessments. Indeed, Y2K assessments were so common in 1999 that they interfered with the more general kinds of software process assessments and benchmark studies.

A software process assessment is somewhat equivalent to undergoing an annual medical examination. The annual physical examination is not intended to cure any specific disease. The main purpose is to find out about the health of the patient. If the physical examination finds any serious problems, then the physician can prescribe a therapy program. However, the examination itself is performed for diagnostic purposes, not for therapeutic purposes.

Unfortunately, this analogy of medical checkups is sometimes overlooked by clients of software process assessments. That is, companies regard the assessment as an end in itself, rather than a means to an end. Assessments by themselves will not improve software quality or productivity, or cure any specific problems that are found. But without the assessment, many problems would remain invisible. Assessments should be viewed as nothing more than annual checkups to ensure that no new problems have occurred and that progress is being made on curing problems found during the last assessment.

From studies that I have carried out, more than 250 factors have been identified that can affect the outcome of software development projects. This claim is based on all factors that have been noted that affect systems software, information systems, military software, commercial software, outsourced projects, and end user applications. However, any specific software project will probably have only 15 to 20 major factors that influence its outcome. Indeed, the major topics that are covered by software process assessment can be summarized by ten key process areas that are common among many of the various assessment methods. These ten areas are not specific to any individual kind of assessment, but are the topics examined by several forms of assessment because they have a very significant impact on software project schedules, productivity, and quality levels:

1. Project management methods such as estimating
2. Requirements-gathering and analysis methods
3. Design and specification methods
4. Coding methods
5. Reusability methods
6. Change control methods
7. User documentation methods
8. Pretest defect removal methods such as inspections
9. Testing methods and tools
10. Maintenance methods and tools

Because software projects start with a need to understand user requirements and end with the delivery of a software application, the stream of activities that must be performed is termed *the development process*. The word *process* implies that software development is a dynamic activity.

Software process assessments attempt to identify practices that can lead to successful outcomes on software projects. Conversely, process assessments also seek to identify harmful practices that might lead to delays or unacceptable outcomes.

Because software projects are very labor intensive and require exceptional skills on the part of technical and management personnel, software assessments may also examine the factors that are concerned with hiring and supporting software personnel. The following is a list of ten key personnel-related topics that may be examined during software process assessments:

1. Staff hiring practices
2. Staff training and education
3. Management training and education
4. Specialists and occupational groups
5. Compensation levels
6. Office ergonomics
7. Organizational structures
8. Morale surveys and results
9. Work patterns and overtime
10. Staff turnover rates

Because software development is still a largely manual activity performed by skilled craftsmen, it is obvious that success on software projects requires very capable personnel led by capable managers. However, good teams must also utilize methods and practices that are known to produce excellent results, and should avoid practices that have led to failures. In a nutshell, this is what assessments are all about.

You should always bear in mind that assessments are diagnostic studies and not therapies in themselves. Although assessments are an excellent precursor to a software therapy program, it should never be assumed that a software process assessment, by itself, will cure software problems. Assessments do not cure software problems, but they can identify and rank the problems that need to be cured, and hence lead to successful therapy programs.

The Origins of Software Process Assessments

Several common forms of software process assessments originated in the IBM Corporation in the 1970s, when IBM was the world's largest producer of both systems and applications software. Circa 1970, IBM had 26 software development laboratories throughout the world and was the first corporation to employ more than 25,000 software development personnel.

In the early days of the computer era, in the 1960s, computers such as the IBM 1401, 1410, and the 7090 series had so little memory and such limited storage that both systems software and application software were necessarily small scale. Both systems and application software were usually less than 1,000 function points or 100,000 source code statements in size.

Small software projects can be developed without significant process rigor, so long as the development team is capable and equipped with adequate tool suites, both of which were the norm within IBM. Therefore, IBM did not experience major problems with software for the first 20 years of the computer and software era.

However, the IBM 360 and 370 computer systems introduced permanent changes into the computing and software world. The advent of the operating systems that controlled these computers—OS/360 (later to become Multiple Virtual Storage [MVS]), TSO, VMS, and the other operating systems—were almost an order of magnitude larger than previous systems software. The IBM 360 architecture introduced a major change to the software domain. Before the IBM 360, the hardware of specific computers varied so much that software could only operate on one hardware platform. When clients moved from one kind of computer to another, all of the old software had to be replaced. The IBM 360 architecture introduced longevity into software applications by promising that software would continue to run on newer versions of IBM computers. Furthermore, an additional feature of the new IBM architecture was upward compatibility, so that the same software packages could run on entry-level computers with minimal storage and memory capacities, or on more sophisticated versions with extensive storage and memory capacities. Thus, the IBM 360 architecture transformed software from a disposable asset with a life expectancy of less than five years into a long-term asset with a life that may extend 20 years or more.

An unintended consequence of this architecture was the fact that certain problems could become surprisingly pervasive and last for many years. For example, the Y2K problem would not have been troublesome if the IBM 360 architecture had not allowed software to run, more or less, forever as older computers were replaced by newer and faster models.

IBM's MVS operating system was more than 10,000 function points or 1,000,000 source code statements in size at the first release, and rapidly grew to approach 100,000 function points or 10,000,000 source code statements in size. IBM's major application packages such as the Information Management System (IMS) database and data communication system began to exceed 5,000 function points or 500,000 source code statements.

In the 1970s, IBM's software labs and software executives soon experienced a series of embarrassing schedule delays in getting new software released, and also in making the announced dates of major enhancements. Even worse, the quality levels of large software systems and application packages fell far below the expectations of IBM customers, and IBM executives as well.

Dr. Fred Brooks was the senior executive of the IBM OS/360 operating system. His thoughtful analysis of the problems IBM experienced when software began to dominate hardware has become a literary classic: *The Mythical Man-Month* (Brooks 1995), the first edition of which was published in 1975. The book was recently revised and reissued with more than 20 years of additional experience. The fundamental observations are as valid today as they were in 1975: Quality control remains the top issue for successful large-system development.

Thomas J. Watson Jr. was the chairman of the board of IBM in the 360 era. Watson took a personal interest in software process improvement as a result of an IBM shareholder meeting during which major IBM shareholders, who were also users of IBM software, complained that IBM's software quality and reliability were not good enough to be satisfactory. As a result, Watson brought the major IBM software lab directors to Armonk and gave them a strong directive that software within IBM must be brought under control. Although these may not have been his exact words, the message to the IBM software directors was: If you can't fix the problems, I'll find someone who can.

Both myself and Watts Humphrey, who later described the framework of the SEI software process assessment method, worked at IBM during the 1970s, although on opposite coasts. Both Humphrey and I became part of the large-scale IBM initiatives to improve software development practices.

As a result of the chairman's directives, many software projects were examined and many of IBM's programming laboratories developed software process improvement programs. The software process assessments and improvement strategies within IBM circa 1975 were quite effective. For example, the quality levels of the IMS database product were improved by a rate of almost ten to one within a four-year period, whereas productivity improved by more than 15%. Similar results were achieved in other IBM labs.

The IMS example is a very good illustration of how once a diagnostic assessment is performed, it can lead to an effective therapy program. In the early 1970s, the IMS product had one of the highest levels of defects of any IBM product, coupled with very low levels of customer satisfaction. A detailed assessment of IMS practices noted several significant findings, including the presence of "error-prone modules" in the IMS product. It was also noted that formal design and code inspections had not been applied to early IMS releases. Once the assessment report was presented to the IMS director, an immediate therapy program was implemented. This program included the use of formal design and code inspections on existing error-prone modules, and on all new features to be added from that point forward.

Based on the results of the inspections, approximately 31 of 425 IMS modules were repaired or completely redeveloped to eliminate all error-prone modules. In the span of less than one year, customer-reported defects against the IMS product were reduced ten to one, and total maintenance costs were reduced by more than 45%. When customer satisfaction surveys were performed after the repairs, the levels of customer satisfaction climbed from "unacceptable" to "good." Although productivity had not been a major issue, it was interesting to note that productivity of IMS releases after the removal of error-prone modules was almost 15% higher than releases the year before their removal. The productivity gains occurred primarily during the testing stages, which were cut down by more than two to one in elapsed time.

The IBM corporation has long been a pioneer in improved software processes and tools. A significant percentage of the "best practices" for managing, building, and maintaining large software projects originated with the various IBM software labs. Some of the major IBM software innovations include

- Defect severity levels, circa 1960
- Automated configuration control, circa 1967
- Automated defect tracking, circa 1968
- Error-prone module analysis, circa 1970
- Defect removal efficiency measures, circa 1972
- Software quality estimation tools, circa 1973
- Activity-based cost estimation tools, circa 1973
- Software process assessments, circa 1974
- Structured walkthroughs, circa 1974
- Design and code inspections, circa 1974
- JAD, circa 1975
- Structured design, circa 1975
- Function point metrics, circa 1976
- Ergonomic programming offices, circa 1977

IBM continues to support software research and is still one of the most active software research companies in the world. For example, the new orthogonal defect classification method for analyzing software quality is a recent IBM innovation, circa 1997.

While IBM was performing internal software process assessments, other major corporations were experiencing the kinds of software problems that made assessments useful. Another large corporation with software problems was the ITT Corporation, which was chaired by Harold Geneen in the 1970s. ITT also employed Phil Crosby, who achieved international fame with the publication of his book *Quality Is Free* (Crosby 1979). This book and some of Crosby's concepts would later play a part in software process assessments. The ITT Corporation under Geneen, Crosby, and other executives had created a world-class quality program for manufacturing, but that program was not totally successful for software. By 1977 ITT had experienced so many problems with major software systems that Geneen initiated a national talent search to find a key executive who could bring software under management control. The executive selected was James H. Frame, who had been IBM's director of languages and data facilities, headquartered in IBM's Santa Teresa Programming Laboratory in San Jose, California. Frame and his team had applied software process assessments to many of the directorate's software packages, with considerable success.

Frame moved from IBM to ITT in 1978, and started a major software improvement initiative that served as a model for many other companies. He created the well-known ITT Programming Technology Center (PTC) in Stratford, Connecticut. This lab employed more than 150 software process researchers at its peak in 1984, and pioneered many innovations in software development and assessment technologies.

The five-level capability maturity model (CMM) that Watts Humphrey utilized at the SEI appears to have been derived in part from an ITT scale used as part of the quality maturity model Crosby developed. Not only did some of the principles of Crosby become part of the SEI process assessment method, but Dr. Bill Curtis, who succeeded Watts Humphrey as the manager of the SEI assessment program, worked at ITT during this era. Also at ITT was Dr. John Manley, who served as the first director of the SEI.

The ITT PTC employed a number of well-known software researchers such as Dr. Tom Love, Dr. Ted Biggerstaff, Dr. Claude Walston, and myself. The PTC software programs included not only software process assessments, but also original work in software reusability, object-oriented methods, measurement and metrics, and many other important topics.

The software process assessment approach that originated at IBM and was expanded at ITT provided some of the framework of two distinct software assessment methods. The first of these was the assessment method created by SPR in 1985, published in *Programming Productivity* in 1986 (Jones 1986). The second was the assessment method described by Watts Humphrey for the SEI, published in *Managing the Software Process* in 1989 (Humphrey 1989). Although these two assessment methods are different in many ways, both involved researchers who had been active in the internal software assessments performed by IBM.

Although the SPR and SEI methods developed in different years and in different cities, both used five-point scales for evaluating performance and both used a set of scripted questions for performing on-site analysis.

The term *assessment* is defined in a software context as a qualitative comparison of one company's methods, tool use, and processes against industry norms or practices used by similar companies. In the case of SEI assessments, the term also includes comparing an enterprise's pattern of software practices against a set of standard practices associated with each of the five levels of the CMM.

The SEI Assessment Approach

Both the SEI and SPR were incorporated in 1984. Both organizations independently developed assessment methodologies, and both methods are used internationally. It is significant to explore how these two assessment methods operate.

One of the early, major, and continuing activities of the SEI was the development of a formal assessment schema for evaluating the capabilities of defense contractors. Indeed Watts Humphrey's book on this topic, *Managing the Software Process* (Humphrey 1989), became a best-seller.

The SEI assessment data is collected by means of on-site interviews using both standard questions, observations, and informal data. Once collected, the assessment data is analyzed and used to place a software organization on one of the five plateaus of the well-known SEI CMM. Although the assessment and maturity-level concepts can be considered separately, most people regard the two as being a linked set.

Formal SEI software assessments are performed by the SEI and by a number of licensed consulting organizations. There are also less formal "SEI-style" assessments that companies perform on their own or that are done by consultants who are not licensed by the SEI but who use assessment approaches derived from the published SEI materials.

The SEI assessment approach is now very well documented and well covered in the software literature. Indeed, Addison Wesley Longman has an entire series devoted to SEI assessments. Some of the many titles dealing with SEI assessments include Kim Caputo's *CMM Implementation Guide* (Caputo 1998); Carnegie Mellon University's *The Capability Maturity Model* (Carnegie Mellon University, 1995); Curtis, Hefley, and Miller's *People Capability Model* (Maturity-Curtis, Hefley, and Miller 1995); Watts Humphrey's *Managing the Software Process* (Humphrey 1989); Humphrey's *A Discipline for Software Engineering* (Humphrey 1995); Humphrey's *Introduction to the Personal Software Process* (Humphrey 1997), and El Emam and Madhavji's *Elements of Software Process Assessment and Improvement* (El Emam and Madhavji 1999).

Because the amount of SEI assessment literature is so large, it is not necessary in this book to explain the SEI approach in great detail. Readers should examine some of the books or technical reports that are specific to SEI assessments for expanded discussions.

Because of the importance of very large systems to the Department of Defense (DoD), the SEI assessment approach originally dealt primarily with the software processes and methodologies used by very large companies that produced very large systems. The original SEI assessment approach was derived from the best practices used by large corporations such as Boeing, IBM, and ITT, which employ from 5,000 to more than 25,000 software professionals, and which could build systems safely in excess of 1,000,000 LOC or 10,000 function points.

Based on the patterns of answers to the SEI assessment questions, the final result of the SEI assessment process is to place the software organization on one of the levels of a five-point maturity scale. The five plateaus on the SEI maturity level are presented in Table 2.1.

Table 2.1   Five Levels of the SEI CMM

SEI Maturity Level	Meaning	Frequency of Occurrence, %
1 = Initial	Chaotic	75.0
2 = Repeatable	Marginal	15.0
3 = Defined	Adequate	8.0
4 = Managed	Good to excellent	1.5
5 = Optimizing	State of the art	0.5

It is immediately obvious that the distribution of software organizations is skewed toward the low end of the scale. A similar kind of skew would occur if you were to look at the distribution of candidates selected to enter the Olympics for events such as downhill skiing. Most ordinary citizens could not qualify at all. Very few athletes could make it to the Olympic tryouts, even fewer would represent their countries, and only three athletes from around the world will win medals in each event.

The U.S. Air Force commissioned several studies to explore a fundamental question: Are there measurable productivity and quality differences as the CMM levels get above CMM level 1? Due to the fact that SPR collects quantitative data, we were one of the companies commissioned to explore the SEI results.

As data began to be collected, it became evident that there is quite a bit of overlap among the various SEI maturity levels. For example, in terms of quality and productivity, the best software projects from level 1 organizations can be superior to the worst developed by level 3 organizations. For smaller companies that cannot afford some of the infrastructure and special departments assumed by level 3 of the SEI CMM concept, rather good results are possible even at level 1. Conversely, achieving levels 3, 4, and 5 on the SEI CMM scale does not guarantee that all software projects will be successful, although statistics do indeed favor the higher CMM levels.

There is now fairly solid evidence about the CMM from studies carried out by QSM in 1993 and SPR in 1994. When organizations move from CMM level 1 up to levels 2, 3, 4, and 5, their productivity and quality levels tend to improve based on samples at each level. These studies use quantitative benchmarks and calibrate SEI CMM levels against productivity and quality results.

The early versions of the SEI CMM assessment approach concentrated on software development process factors and did not deal with many other factors. Although software process factors are important, they are not the only factors that influence software projects. In fact the first publications of the SEI CMM only covered approximately 35% of the factors known to influence the outcomes of software projects. The initial SEI CMM approach more or less ignored the following:

- Project management tools
- Development tools
- Quality assurance tools
- Testing tools
- Programming languages

- Staff hiring practices
- Personnel appraisal methods
- Salaries and benefits
- Office environments and ergonomics

These early omissions before 1990 meant that a company could achieve SEI CMM level 3 status and still not be totally successful in building and maintaining software. The omissions explain the empirical observations that some software projects developed by level 3 organizations were defective and of poor quality after deployment.

Conversely, some smaller organizations still at level 1 on the CMM could produce exceptionally good software. This is because the personnel involved were very capable and the applications created were fairly small—less than 1,000 function points in size. Good teams with capable managers can produce smaller applications without formal processes, but this approach runs into a barrier near the 1,000-function point plateau. For larger applications in the 10,000-function point domain, process rigor is a critical factor leading to success, and informal methods are associated with delays and cancellations.

More recently, in the 1990s, the SEI has broadened the sets of factors included under the assessment and CMM umbrella. Indeed, the evolution of the SEI CMM has been continuous. Additional SEI factors dealing with personnel skills and human relations were added several years ago under the leadership of Dr. Bill Curtis (Curtis et al. 1995). It is a positive sign that the SEI is expanding assessment factors as the industry changes.

The SEI CMM has been quite successful in leading scores of companies in undertaking software process improvement programs. The CMM has divided the topics that need to be at state-of-the-art levels into sets, with each set associated with a particular level (Table 2.2).

Although some aspects of the CMM level structure have been debated and are sometimes misinterpreted, there is no doubt that this structure has been fairly successful in guiding companies through process improvement programs.

Software process improvements cannot be successful if they overlook key topics or emphasize one topic and ignore others. Thus the broad range of topics included under the CMM umbrella emphasize the fact that success in software requires being good in many activities.

Another area in which the SEI has been successful is in awakening the software industry to the need for software process assessments as a precursor leading to software process improvements. Before the creation of the SEI, assessments

Table 2.2   SEI CMM Key Focus Areas by Level

Level	Focus	Technologies Emphasized
Level 1, initial	None	None
Level 2, repeatable	Project management	Planning, estimating, oversight and tracking, contracting and subcontracting, quality assurance, change and configuration control, requirements gathering and analysis
Level 3, defined	Software engineering	Organization and infrastructure, peer reviews and inspections, team training, coordination and communication, project engineering, software management
Level 4, managed	Quality processes	Software quality management, software process management
Level 5, optimizing	Continuous improvement	Technology upgrading, process upgrading, defect prevention

were proprietary analyses performed only in a few very sophisticated companies such as IBM and ITT. Although assessments were performed by consulting companies such as Howard Rubin Associates and SPR, the number of such studies before the formation of the SEI was fairly small.

The publicity associated with the SEI CMM has expanded the use of process assessments significantly. By 1999 more than 250 Fortune 500 companies have commissioned software process assessments and are embarking on software process improvement programs of various kinds. The success of the SEI CMM has led to the creation of a large nonprofit group called the Software Process Improvement Network (SPIN). SPIN chapters are now located in many large cities throughout the world, and the SPIN organization has many conferences at local, national, and international levels.

The SEI assessment approach has also been the impetus leading to other assessment methods that utilize part of the CMM framework but add other topics or include other factors: The TickIT, Bootstrap, SPICE, Trillium, and ISO Audit approaches are all partly derived from the SEI assessment concept.

It is an interesting phenomenon that few of the assessment organizations collect quantitative benchmark data. Conversely, few of the benchmark organizations perform software process assessments. This sometimes leads to the curious situation that companies commission assessments and benchmarks at the same time, using two different vendors. The most efficient and cost-effective approach is to integrate the collection of software assessment information and software benchmark information so that both are collected at the same time.

The SPR Assessment Approach

My company, SPR, is one of several companies with a software assessment method that includes the collection of quantitative benchmark data as well as process assessment factors. The SPR method is slightly older than the SEI approach, and has been in continual use since 1985.

Since that time, SPR has performed assessments and benchmarks for nearly 350 corporations and 50 government organizations. Approximately 75 of our clients have been overseas, and we have collected data in more than 20 countries. Because many of our clients are conglomerates or multinational companies, the number of actual sites from which we have collected data is in excess of 600 locations. Because we usually have between two and five new assessment and benchmark clients each month, the number of studies continues to grow.

Approximately 90 of our commercial clients have also commissioned SEI assessments, and more than half of our government clients have also utilized SEI assessments. The SPR and SEI assessments complement each other in several ways. Indeed, one company, AT&T, has developed a proprietary in-house process assessment method that is based on joint SEI and SPR analysis using a merged set of assessment factors.

The basic SPR assessment questionnaire and some of the quantitative results derived from the SPR assessment method were first published in 1986 in *Programming Productivity* (Jones 1986). Another 11 books since the first have published additional SPR assessment and benchmark data. Normally, a book with new findings has been published every 18 months. The Appendix contains the basic SPR assessment and benchmark questionnaire.

One of the interesting differences between SPR and SEI assessments is the SPR focus on specific software projects. With the assistance of our clients' management teams, we perform individual project assessments on a sample of roughly 10 to 30 software projects. Once each project is analyzed, we then aggregate the results from these projects and show the ranges observed in all factors.

The combination of the SEI organizational focus and the SPR project-level focus is synergistic. In fact, the project-level data SPR collects on quality and productivity is very useful in demonstrating the value of moving up from level 1 on the SEI CMM to higher levels. For example, project-level productivity rates and defect removal efficiency both improve at higher SEI CMM levels.

The SPR assessment interview approach is a group activity for each project analyzed. The SPR consultant meets with the project manager and as many as seven technical staff members at the same time. All of the participants have seen the questionnaires ahead of time, so they know the kinds of information we are seeking. If the project is a huge one with multiple locations and teams, we may carry out more than one interview session for the project.

The "official" assessment questionnaire is filled out by the SPR consultant using the group consensus as the source of information. (See the Appendix for a sample questionnaire.) Sometimes there may be debate or polarized opinions among the team members, as can occur on any human activity. When there is polarization, we record the full set of responses. For example, some team members may feel that a particular approach such as rapid application development (RAD) is very useful, whereas other team members may feel that the approach is too informal. Usually, however, a group consensus soon becomes apparent.

The interview sessions run from approximately two hours up to a maximum of four hours. We try and schedule two project interview sessions during each business day. In a few instances there may be follow-up phone calls to gather additional facts that none of the participants had readily available during the session. The assessment interview sessions are not too intrusive, but they do take at least two hours for the project manager and several technical staff workers.

This method of gathering assessment data is surprisingly interesting and even enjoyable for the project team being interviewed, once they get over a few minutes of initial apprehension. For example, we ask questions about office space and ergonomics as part of our standard assessment approach. In some companies and government agencies, the assessment is the first time anyone has ever asked employees how they feel about their office space.

Because project teams talk to each other, once the first few interviews have taken place the other teams are usually no longer apprehensive. In fact, it happens frequently that projects not selected as part of the assessment sample request being added to the assessment. Whether the requests are granted is the responsibility of the corporate manager who is coordinating the assessment for the company.

Companies are not homogeneous in the way they go about software development and maintenance work. A typical sample of 20 projects will span a very broad range of sophistication and process rigor. In a single company, and sometimes in a single location, the best projects may use techniques that would be associated with level 4 or 5 on the SEI maturity scale, whereas the worst projects use methods that might be encountered far back in level 1. We try and examine a representative sample of the kinds of projects on which our clients normally work: some new projects, many enhancements, maintenance or defect repairs, and some package modifications. Some of the projects we examine are ongoing at the time of the assessment whereas others have been completed. A few may even have been cancelled.

It would not be a fair assessment if we only examined the best projects that the client has developed, so we seek out a representative sample that may be in the range of more than 30% of all projects in development or finished within the past year. Although we look at more than 100 factors on each project, and include more than 250 factors in all of our questionnaires summed together, it is useful to summarize the findings into broad categories to present the results to clients. We often divide our findings into five major themes:

1. Findings about the projects or software products assessed
2. Findings about the software technologies utilized
3. Findings about the software processes utilized
4. Findings about the ergonomics and work environments for staff
5. Findings about personnel and training for management and staff

Like the SEI, the SPR assessment approach uses structured interviews based on a set of scripted questions. The SPR questionnaires make use of sets of 100 to more than 200 multiple-choice questions. (Enhancement projects need more questions than new projects, for example. There are also special questions if user satisfaction is included as part of the assessment.)

Some of the SPR questions overlap the same topics as the SEI questions, although the forms are different. Multiple-choice questions allow a wide range of responses. They also make it easy to see trends when locations are revisited and reassessed after several years. One of the SPR questions associated with quality is

Software Quality Assurance Function (select one choice)
   1) Formal SQA group with adequate resources
   2) Formal SQA group but understaffed (<1 to 30 ratio)
   3) SQA role is assigned to development personnel
   4) SQA role is performed informally
   5) No SQA function exists for the project

This five-level structure is the normal mode for most of the questions asked during SPR process assessments. The structure somewhat resembles the Richter scale for earthquake severity. That is, the low end of the spectrum is the "safe" end whereas the larger values are more hazardous. All of the SPR five-point questions use the middle value (three) to indicate approximate U.S. averages.

Once a sample of projects has been analyzed using the questionnaires, the answers to the questions are input directly into a tool (CHECKPOINT) that performs a statistical analysis of the results and shows the mean values and standard deviations of all factors. This tool also sorts the answers to the assessment questions into three sets: topics in which the client is much better than industry norms (answer scores averaged below 2.5), topics in which the client's average indicated average performance (answer scores range from 2.5 to 3.5), and topics in which the client is worse than average (answer scores averaged higher than 3.5).

Like the SEI approach, the SPR assessment method is also used to place software development groups, contractors, and outsource vendors on a five-plateau excellence scale. However, the SPR scale runs in the opposite direction from the SEI scale (Table 2.3).

Table 2.3   Five Levels of the SPR Excellence Scale

SPR Excellence Scale	Meaning	Frequency of Occurrence
1 = Excellent	State of the art	3.0
2 = Above average	Superior to most companies	18.0
3 = Average	Normal in most factors	54.0
4 = Below average	Deficient in some factors	22.0
5 = Poor	Deficient in most factors	3.0

Another difference between the SEI and SPR evaluation scales is the overall distribution of results. The SPR scale results approximate a bell-shaped curve whereas the SEI scale is absolute, and hence has the bulk of results clustered at the low end of the scale.

When presenting the final results, topics in which the client is approximately average do not attract much interest. The clients are very interested in the polar opposites, or the topics in which they are either much better than average (which we term *strengths*) or much worse than average (which we term *weaknesses*).

Although strengths are very laudable, the real value of a process assessment for most clients is the discovery and objective analysis of areas in which the client is lagging and needs improvement. Identifying these areas of weakness is the key to a successful process improvement program. Once the areas of weakness have been analyzed and discussed, the client is in an excellent position to begin a successful improvement program.

Because companies have trouble seeing or studying their own areas of weakness, this explains why assessments are so often performed by external consulting groups. If companies wish to perform assessments using their own personnel, it is best to bring in assessment teams from other locations rather than trying to conduct a purely local assessment using local employees. For one thing, local employees report to local managers and therefore are not in a good position to record or report areas of weakness. There might be some risk that an assessment that turned up unfavorable data might lead to punitive actions against the assessors, if they report to the managers whose projects have been assessed. If the assessment team is from another location or from an outside company, it is easier to be objective.

We usually start our assessment reports to clients with a high-level overview that summarizes our key findings and discusses basic topics such as the numbers of projects that were examined during the assessment. We use various forms of graphical representation for presenting our results. One that has proved to be effective over the years is a "whisker diagram," which shows the average results as a block, and the ranges in both directions (Figure 2.1). The graphical illustrations are, primarily, to set the stage for a detailed analysis of the patterns of strengths and weaknesses that the assessment uncovered.

To illustrate the patterns of strengths, average performance, and weakness, the following contains some samples that were noted in an SPR assessment of a telecommunications company. The assessment covered 30 projects. The patterns of strengths and weaknesses were presented to the client, starting with areas of

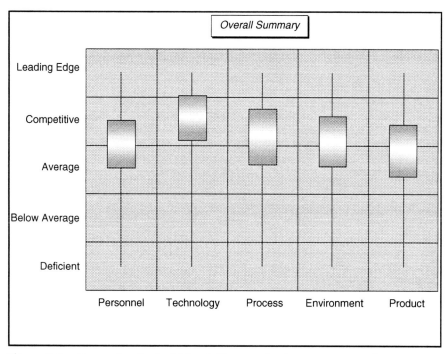

Figure 2.1   Example of a "whisker" diagram to show means and ranges

strength, then average performance, and then areas of weakness. Because areas of weakness are the most controversial and need the greatest amount of time to discuss, we like to get through the good news first before moving to the bad news. Incidentally, the pattern of strengths and weaknesses shown in this example occurs fairly often with many clients.

As background, the client was a large telecommunications company. The assessment results are for one software laboratory with a total employment of approximately 450 personnel. A sample of 30 projects was assessed. The projects were related to the core business of telecommunications switching and transmission. Because the client and the telecommunications industry have been building reliable software applications for more than 35 years, they know quite a lot about standard development practices. For example, the client had long recognized that change control was a key technology and had stepped up to fully automated change management tools augmented by a change control board for major projects.

Because the telecommunications industry has long had a need for very reliable equipment and very reliable software, telecommunications companies are often very sophisticated in software quality control. Techniques such as formal inspections, defect tracking, formal quality assurance, and testing specialists are more or less the norm in the telecommunications industry. The following are the major strengths we noted:

Pattern of Client Strengths (Better than Average Performance)

- Requirements analysis (quality function deployment [QFD])
- Change control methods (fully automated with traceable requirements)
- Project management: quality measurement and metrics
- Design methods, fully automated
- Customer support tools, fully automated
- Customer support methods, both hot-lines and Internet support
- Maintenance release testing
- Regression testing
- Development testing
- Performance modeling
- Performance testing
- Lab testing of hardware and software concurrently
- Support for telecommuting and remote employees
- Support for multisite projects

Incidentally, no company that we have assessed is uniformly good or uniformly bad. Most companies are "average" in more than 50% of every factor we assess. In the context of this example, the client was approximately "average" in the following factors:

Pattern of Average Results (Average Performance Within Industry)

- Staff experience with application types
- Staff experience with in-house development processes
- Staff experience with development tools
- Staff experience with programming languages
- Staff specialization: testing
- Staff specialization: quality assurance
- Staff specialization: maintenance
- Quality control: use of formal design inspections
- Quality control: use of formal code inspections

- Quality control: formal software quality assurance teams
- Unit testing by development personnel
- Office ergonomics: two-person cubicles of 60 square feet per worker

Note that in SPR assessments, the term *average* is used in specific contexts. Because this example illustrates a telecommunications company, the term *average* is weighed against the background of other major telecommunication manufacturing companies.

Turning now to weaknesses, we often find weakness in the domain of project management, in activities such as sizing, planning, estimating, and tracking. Indeed, project management failures are often much more common and also more serious than development technology failures as causes of missed schedules or outright cancellations of software projects.

Another very common weakness is failure to use formal design and code inspections prior to commencing testing, although we do not find this weakness among telecommunications companies. Failure to use inspections would be viewed as a weakness because inspections are about twice as efficient as most forms of testing in finding errors or bugs. Formal design and code inspections can each average more than 60% in terms of defect removal efficiency, whereas most forms of testing are less than 30% efficient. Furthermore, not only do inspections have an excellent record in terms of defect removal, but they also are synergistic with testing and raise the efficiency of standard test stages, such as new function test, regression test, and system test.

Another common weakness is in the software maintenance domain. Although software development is often funded and supplied with state-of-the-art tools, maintenance is not as "glamorous" as development, and hence may lag. In terms of our example, none of the more powerful maintenance support tools were deployed: complexity analysis tools, code-restructuring tools, reverse-engineering tools, reengineering tools, and so forth.

Yet another common weakness or gap in software development is failure to move toward a full software reusability program. An effective software reuse program entails much more than just source code reuse, and includes many other artifacts such as design specifications, test materials, and user documents and even project plans.

Although the client had a good track record for standard development practices and methods, there were some significant weaknesses visible in terms of project management, pretest defect removal, and software reuse:

Pattern of Client Weaknesses (Worse than Average Performance)

- Project management: annual training in state-of-the-art methods
- Project management: cost estimating
- Project management: quality estimating
- Project management: risk analysis
- Project management: value analysis
- Project management: schedule planning
- Project management: lack of productivity measurements
- Project management: lack of productivity metrics
- Project management: incomplete milestone tracking
- Maintenance: no use of complexity analysis
- Maintenance: no use of code-restructuring tools
- No reuse program: requirements
- No reuse program: design
- No reuse program: source code
- No reuse program: test materials
- No reuse program: documentation
- No reuse program: project plans

As can be seen from the patterns of strengths and weaknesses, the client organization was fairly solid in basic development practices but somewhat behind the state of the art in terms of project management and reusability. Maintenance was not unusually far behind, but neither was it at the leading edge.

A final weakness in this example is the failure to provide enough training for managers and technical personnel. Usually, a range of ten to 15 days per year is an optimal amount for teaching new skills and for refreshing current skills. See the interesting work by Curtis et al., *People Capability Model* (Curtis et al. 1995), for additional insights into training methods. This new work augments the SEI capability maturity model with a new dimension that deals with personnel topics.

No company is uniformly good or uniformly bad in all factors. Figure 2.2 illustrates typical patterns from leading, average, and lagging organizations.

It should be emphasized that neither SPR nor SEI assessments actually cure any problems that are found. Assessments are excellent tools for diagnostic purposes, but they are not therapy programs. However, once the areas of weakness have been discussed with client managers and executives, the next stage is for the client to undertake a therapy program for some or all of the areas of weakness.

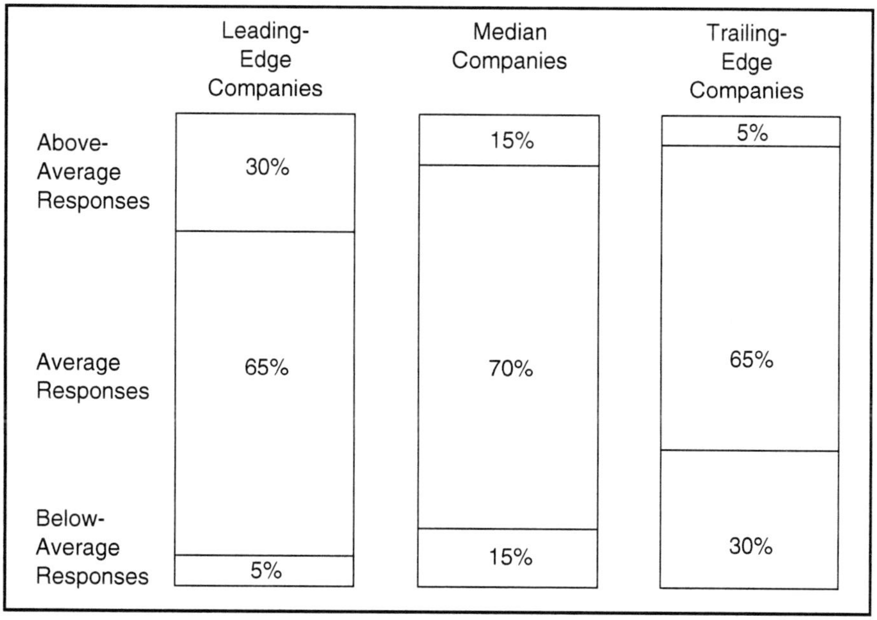

	Leading-Edge Companies	Median Companies	Trailing-Edge Companies
Above-Average Responses	30%	15%	5%
Average Responses	65%	70%	65%
Below-Average Responses	5%	15%	30%

Figure 2.2   Distribution of results of SPR assessments

One of the differences between the SPR and SEI assessment methods is the fact that SPR also collects quantitative productivity and quality data from each of the projects assessed. When we report our findings to clients, we discuss not only the assessment results, but also try to illustrate what those results might mean in terms of specific quality and productivity levels. Because this example is for a telecommunications company, Figure 2.3 illustrates "best-in-class" productivity rates for telecommunication projects compared with other classes of software.

During this assessment, the client asked for some information on how the telecommunications industry compared with other industries and classes of software in terms of quality, productivity, schedules, and costs. Unfortunately, the telecommunications industry is not at the top rung of productivity, although quality levels are better than most other industries.

It is interesting that coding productivity in the telecommunications industry is actually better than many other industries. However the telecommunications industry ranks second only to defense in the production of paperwork. The volumes of requirements, specifications, plans, and other paper documents supporting a telecommunications software project is approximately twice as large as

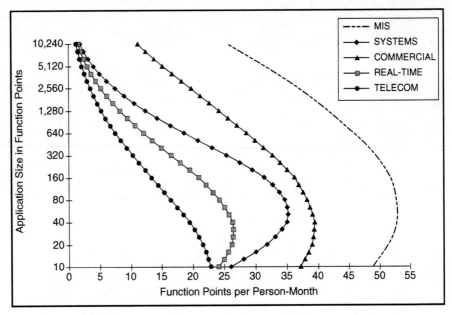

Figure 2.3   Example of quantitative results gathered during assessment studies

most civilian industries, although smaller than the amount of paperwork created for military software projects.

A mixture of qualitative assessment findings coupled with quantitative data on productivity and quality levels is very effective in leading clients to undertake software process improvement programs. The quantitative data allows clients to create specific productivity and quality targets, then monitor progress toward those targets, and the improvement program proceeds. Once enough data has been collected, it is somewhat easier to justify on a cost basis process improvement work by contrasting the client's observed productivity and quality levels with what they might expect after several years of process improvement work.

Our assessments tend to produce a more normal bell-shaped distribution of results than the SEI assessments. This is due in part to the fact that each industry is evaluated against its own norms. Also, small companies with less than 50 software personnel are compared against similar companies, rather than against major corporations with thousands of software personnel.

Correlating the SEI and SPR Scoring Systems

Because both Humphrey (of SEI) and myself (of SPR) worked at IBM during the same time period, both of our assessment approaches have some points in common. One of the shared attributes of both SPR and SEI assessment methods is the use of five-point scales for evaluating software capabilities. The ITT quality scale developed by Crosby also utilizes a five-point scale, as do the scoring methods of several other assessment approaches.

Unfortunately, because the SEI, SPR, and ITT scoring methods were developed independently, these three scoring methods do not utilize the same factors although they share the use of five points as part of their scales of merit. Table 2.4 presents the SPR, SEI, and ITT five-point scales.

The Crosby ITT scale is seldom used for software, although it has many uses in corporate quality programs. (As a matter of minor historical interest, the Crosby ITT scale can be traced back to an eight-level scale used by Tibetan Buddhists for showing the stages on the path to spiritual enlightenment. Other religions also describe various stages leading to some spiritual destination.)

Because both the SPR and SEI scales are widely used for software evaluations, it is of interest to establish a correlation between the two. It is not possible simply to invert the SPR or SEI scale and achieve equivalence with the other. The reason for this is because the SPR results take the form of a bell-shaped curve whereas the SEI results are absolute and are skewed toward the initial end of the spectrum.

The SPR assessment scale utilizes two decimal places of precision whereas the SEI CMM scale is normally expressed in terms of integer values. By inversion

Table 2.4   SPR, SEI, and ITT Five-level Evaluation Scales

The SPR Scale	The SEI CMM Scale	The Crosby ITT Scale
1 Excellent	1 Initial	1 Uncertainty
2 Above average	2 Repeatable	2 Awakening
3 Average	3 Defined	3 Enlightenment
4 Below average	4 Managed	4 Wisdom
5 Poor	5 Optimizing	5 Certainty

and mathematical compression of the SPR scores, it is possible to establish a rough equivalence between the SPR and SEI scales, as presented in Table 2.5.

I have developed a software tool that summarizes data from SPR assessments and converts the SPR score into an equivalent SEI CMM level. This tool provides two decimal places of precision for both the SPR and SEI results, which clients usually find interesting and useful.

Clients who are at level 1 on the SEI CMM scale are particularly interested in the use of two-decimal-place precision. The reason for this is that clients who are very far back in level 1 may opt to turn over software development to an out-source vendor rather than attempt to improve in-house development practices. On the other hand, clients that are approaching the boundary between levels 1 and 2 on the CMM may decide to continue with internal improvements. Because of the unequal distribution of results, the conversion between the two scales is not perfect, but is a good first-order approximation.

Regardless of whether clients utilize the SPR or SEI assessment scales, both methods, or some other method, the purpose of a process assessment is to provide a company with a diagnostic strength and weakness report. None of the software process assessment methods are curative, and it is important to realize the difference between a diagnostic study and a therapy program.

After the process assessment, any weak areas can be singled out and therapy programs can then be developed. During the therapy stages, companies minimize and eliminate the weak areas, and bolster strength areas. Companies starting improvement programs will also want to create both quality and productivity baselines to judge rates of future improvement. They also should perform a benchmark against industry norms, or against other companies within their industry.

Table 2.5   Approximate Conversion Between the SPR and SEI Software Scores

SPR Scoring Range	Equivalent SEI Score	Approximate Frequency, %
5.99–3.00, poor	1 Initial	75.0
2.99–2.51, below average	2 Repeatable	15.0
2.01–2.50, average	3 Defined	5.0
1.01–2.00, above average	4 Managed	3.0
0.01–1.00, excellent	5 Optimizing	2.0

Readings and References on Software Assessments

The literature on software process assessment has grown to be one of the most extensive fields of software engineering. The SEI approach alone has more than a dozen books and scores of monographs and articles that deal with aspects of the assessment method or the related SEI CMM.

Another form of assessment that is widely published is the variety of specialized Y2K assessments that exploded across the software world during 1998 and 1999. ISO quality assessments are also covered extensively in the literature. However, as the new century begins, almost every form of assessment has books and articles in print, including TickIT, SPICE, the SPR method, the Howard Rubin Associates method, and so on. Here are but a few:

Abdel-Hamid, Tarek, and Stuart Madnick. *Software Project Dynamics.* Englewood Cliffs, NJ: Prentice Hall, 1993. (ISBN 013-8220409)

Austin, Robert D. *Measuring and Managing Performance in Organizations.* New York: Dorset House Publishing, 1996. (ISBN 0-932633-36-6, 216 pages)

Brooks, Frederick P. *The Mythical Man-Month.* Reading, MA: Addison Wesley Longman, 1995. (ISBN 0-201-006502, 295 pages)

Caputo, Kim. *CMM Implementation Guide.* Reading, MA: Addison Wesley Longman, 1998. (ISBN 0-201-37938-4, 319 pages)

Carnegie Mellon University. *The Capability Maturity Model: Guidelines for Improving the Software Process.* Reading, MA: Addison Wesley Longman, 1995. (ISBN 0-201-54664-7, 464 pages)

Charette, Robert N. *Software Engineering Risk Analysis and Management.* New York: McGraw Hill, 1989. (ISBN 0-07-010719-X, 325 pages)

———. *Application Strategies for Risk Analysis.* New York: McGraw Hill, 1990. (ISBN 0-07-010888-9, 570 pages)

Crosby, Philip B. *Quality Is Free.* New York: Mentor Executive Library, 1979. (270 pages)

Curtis, Bill, William E. Hefley, and Sally Miller. *People Capability Maturity Model.* CMU/SEI-95-MM-02 Pittsburgh, PA: Software Engineering Institute, Carnegie Mellon University, 1995.

DeMarco, Tom. *Controlling Software Projects.* New York: Yourdon Press, 1982. (ISBN 0-917072-32-4, 284 pages)

DeMarco, Tom, and Tim Lister. *Peopleware.* New York: Dorset House Publishing, 1987. (ISBN 0-932633-05-6, 188 pages)

Department of the Air Force. *Guidelines for Successful Acquisition and Management of Software Intensive Systems.* Vols. 1 and 2. Hill Air Force Base, UT: Software Technology Support Center, 1994.

El Emam, Khaled, and Nazim Madhavji, eds. *Elements of Software Process Assessment and Improvement.* Los Alamitos, CA: IEEE Computer Society Press, 1999. (ISBN 0-8185-8523-9, 384 pages)

Garmus, David, and David Herron. *Measuring the Software Process: A Practical Guide to Functional Measurement.* Englewood Cliffs, NJ: Prentice Hall, 1995. (ISBN 0-13-349002-5)

Grady, Robert B. *Practical Software Metrics for Project Management and Process Improvement.* Englewood Cliffs, NJ: Prensice Hall, 1992. (ISBN 0-13-720384-5, 270 pages)

———. *Successful Software Process Improvement.* Upper Saddle River, NJ: Prentice Hall, 1997. (ISBN 0-13-626623-1, 314 pages)

Grady, Robert B., and Deborah L. Caswell. *Software Metrics: Establishing a Company-Wide Program.* Englewood Cliffs, NJ: Prentice Hall, 1987. (ISBN 0-13-821844-7, 288 pages)

Humphrey, Watts S. *Managing the Software Process.* Reading, MA: Addison Wesley Longman, 1989. (ISBN 0-201-18095-2)

———. *A Discipline for Software Engineering.* Reading, MA: Addison Wesley Longman, 1995. (ISBN 0-201-54610-8)

———. *Introduction to the Personal Software Process.* Reading, MA: Addison Wesley Longman, 1997. (ISBN 0201548097)

———. *Managing Technical People.* Reading, MA: Addison Wesley Longman, 1997. (ISBN 0-201-54597-7, 326 pages)

Jones, Capers. *Program Quality and Programmer Productivity.* IBM technical report TR07.764. San Jose, CA: IBM Santa Teresa, January 1977. (97 pages)

———. "Measuring Programming Quality and Productivity." *IBM Systems Journal* 1978: 17(1): 39–63.

———. *Programming Productivity: Issues for the Eighties.* Los Alamitos, CA: IEEE Computer Society Press, 1st ed., 1981; 2nd ed., 1986. (ISBN 0-8186-0681-9, IEEE Computer Society Catalog 681, 489 pages)

———. *Programming Productivity.* New York: McGraw Hill, 1986. (ISBN 0-07-032811-0, 280 pages)

———. *A Ten-Year Retrospective of the ITT Programming Technology Center.* Burlington, MA: Software Productivity Research, 1988.

————. *Assessment and Control of Software Risks*. Englewood Cliffs, NJ: Prentice Hall, 1993. (ISBN 0-13-741406-4, 711 pages)

————. *Critical Problems in Software Measurement*. Carlsbad, CA: Information Systems Management Group, 1993. (ISBN 1-56909-000-9, 195 pages)

————. *Software Productivity and Quality Today—The Worldwide Perspective*. Carlsbad, CA: Information Systems Management Group, 1993. (ISBN 156909-001-7, 200 pages)

————. *New Directions in Software Management*. Carlsbad, CA: Information Systems Management Group, 1994. (ISBN 1-56909-009-2, 150 pages)

————. *Patterns of Software System Failure and Success*. Boston, MA: International Thomson Computer Press, 1995. (ISBN 1-850-32804-8, 292 pages)

————. *Applied Software Measurement*. 2nd ed. New York: McGraw Hill, 1996. (ISBN 0-07-032826-9, 618 pages)

————. *Software Quality: Analysis and Guidelines for Success*. Boston, MA: International Thomson Computer Press, 1997. (ISBN 1-85032-876-6, 492 pages)

————. *Becoming Best in Class*. SPR technical report. Burlington, MA: Software Productivity Research, January 1998. (40 pages)

————. *Estimating Software Costs*. New York: McGraw Hill, 1998. (ISBN 0-07-9130941, 725 pages)

————. "Sizing Up Software." *Scientific American* 1998; 279(6): 104–111.

————. *The Costs, Schedule, and Value of Software Process Improvement*. SPR technical report. Burlington, MA: Software Productivity Research, January 1998. (27 pages)

————. *The Year 2000 Software Problem: Quantifying the Costs and Assessing the Consequences*. Reading, MA: Addison Wesley Longman, 1998. (ISBN 0-201-30964-5, 303 pages)

Kan, Stephen H. *Metrics and Models in Software Quality Engineering*. Reading, MA: Addison Wesley Longman, 1995. (ISBN 0-201-63339-6, 344 pages)

Marciniak, John J., ed. *Encyclopedia of Software Engineering*. New York: John Wiley & Sons, 1994. (ISBN 0-471-54002, in two volumes)

Multiple authors. *Rethinking the Software Process*. CD-ROM. Lawrence, KS: Miller Freeman, 1996. (This is a new CD-ROM book collection produced jointly by the book publisher Prentice Hall and the journal publisher Miller Freeman. This CD-ROM disk contains the full text and illustrations of five Prentice Hall books: *Assessment and Control of Software Risks* by Capers Jones, *Controlling Software Projects* by Tom DeMarco, *Function Point Analysis* by

Brian Dreger, *Measures for Excellence* by Larry Putnam and Ware Myers, and *Object-Oriented Software Metrics* by Mark Lorenz and Jeff Kidd.)

Oman, Paul, and Shari Lawrence Pfleeger, eds. *Applying Software Metrics*. Los Alamitos, CA: IEEE Computer Society Press, 1996. (ISBN 0-8186-7645-0, 336 pages)

Park, Robert E., et al. *Software Cost and Schedule Estimating: A Process Improvement Initiative*. Technical report CMU/SEI 94-SR-03. Pittsburgh, PA: Software Engineering Institute, May 1994.

Park, Robert E., et al. *Checklists and Criteria for Evaluating the Costs and Schedule Estimating Capabilities of Software Organizations*. Technical report CMU/SEI 95-SR-005. Pittsburgh, PA: Software Engineering Institute, January 1995.

Perry, William E. *Handbook of Diagnosing and Solving Computer Problems*. Blue Ridge Summit, PA: TAB Books, 1989. (ISBN 0-8306-9233-9, 255 pages)

Pressman, Roger. *Software Engineering: A Practitioner's Approach*. New York: McGraw Hill, 1982.

Putnam, Lawrence H. *Measures for Excellence: Reliable Software on Time, within Budget*. Englewood Cliffs, NJ: Prentice Hall, 1992. (ISBN 0-13-567694-0, 336 pages)

Putnam, Lawrence H., and Ware Myers. *Industrial Strength Software: Effective Management Using Measurement*. Los Alamitos, CA: IEEE Computer Society, 1997. (ISBN 0-8186-7532-2, 320 pages)

Rubin, Howard. *Software Benchmark Studies for 1998*. Pound Ridge, NY: Howard Rubin Associates, 1999.

Software Productivity Consortium. *The Software Measurement Guidebook*. Boston, MA: International Thomson Computer Press, 1995. (ISBN 1-850-32195-7, 308 pages)

Software Productivity Research. *Quality and Productivity of the SEI CMM*. Burlington, MA: Software Productivity Research, 1994.

Wiegers, Karl A. *Creating a Software Engineering Culture*. New York: Dorset House Publishing, 1996. (ISBN 0-932633-33-1, 358 pages)

Yourdon, Edward. *Death March: The Complete Software Developer's Guide to Surviving "Mission Impossible" Projects*. Upper Saddle River, NJ: Prentice Hall, 1997. (ISBN 0-13-748310-4, 218 pages)

Zells, Lois. *Managing Software Projects: Selecting and Using PC-Based Project Management Systems*. Wellesley, MA: QED Information Sciences, 1990. (ISBN 0-89435-275-X, 487 pages)

Zvegintzov, Nicholas. *Software Management Technology Reference Guide*. Release 2. New York: Software Maintenance News, 1994. (ISBN 1-884521-01-0, 240 pages)

CHAPTER THREE

Software Benchmarks and Baselines

Software benchmarks and baselines collect similar data. Benchmarks compare a company against industry norms. Baselines compare a company against its own history for several years in the past.

Benchmarks and baselines collect quantitative and qualitative data on a number of important topics, including investments, staffing levels, development schedules, staff effort, costs, quality, and customer satisfaction. Benchmark studies often include supplemental information on specific tool suites, programming languages, and formal methods utilized. Thus, benchmark studies and assessment studies overlap to a degree.

Benchmarks are primarily comparisons between a specific company and other companies in the same kind of business. Of course the word *company* is not quite accurate because benchmarks are also performed between military software groups, government agencies, and even the software organizations of associations and major churches.

Benchmark studies or comparisons of quantitative data are older than the software industry. Indeed, comparisons between companies have been taking place for hundreds of years. For example, studies of market shares, staff compensation levels, executive pay, and customer satisfaction have long been performed.

In a software context, software benchmarks can be traced back to the 1960s, when studies of data center performance and downtimes started to be performed. These were soon followed by corporate-level studies of investments in information technology, compensation studies of software personnel, and studies of software schedules and costs. Within the software industry, there are a number of levels of benchmark studies that have been noted to occur. It is interesting to consider these various kinds of benchmarks.

Macroeconomic benchmarks are concerned with very large-scale issues such as the impact of computers and information technology on the economic health of nations and industries. A recent topic of macroeconomic importance centers around the costs and risks associated with the Y2K problem. Obviously, nations and industries with heavy dependence on automation have spent more on Y2K repairs. Whether these nations and industries will experience more damage was a topic of considerable interest and debate as this book was written. Macroeconomic benchmarks are usually performed by national governments and sometimes by economists or universities.

Economic benchmarks are concerned with topics such as whether investments in computers, software, and factory automation benefit the profitability and market shares of companies that spend more than others. Some of the topics being researched are surprisingly contentious. For example there is some debate, as this book is written, on a topic called *the productivity paradox*. At least some data supports a hypothesis that investments in computers, software, and automation have not created tangible improvements in productivity, profits, or corporate performance.

Economic benchmarks are performed by economists, universities, and by management consulting groups. Some very interesting books on economic benchmarks have been produced by Paul Strassmann, the former chief information officer (CIO) of the DoD. His books on *The Squandered Computer* (Strassmann 1997) and *The Politics of Information Management* (Strassmann 1995) are excellent examples of economic benchmarks.

Corporate information technology benchmarks deal with a host of interesting comparisons among companies. Some of the comparisons that are studied under corporate benchmarks include

- Percent of corporate employees in information technology
- Number of users supported per staff member in information technology
- Annual corporate spending for computer hardware equipment
- Revenues per information technology employee
- Sales volumes correlated to information technology expenses

- Profitability correlated to information technology expenses
- Average salaries for information technology workers
- Numbers of specialist occupations employed within information technology
- Annual attrition or turnover among information technology employees
- Corporate revenues per information technology worker

Information technology benchmarks are produced by many universities, by consulting organizations, and sometimes by universities and consultants together. For example the Gartner Group, Meta Group, and Giga Group are all prominent in corporate benchmark studies. Dr. Howard Rubin's annual benchmark reports (Rubin 1998) are excellent examples of corporate benchmarks and are widely cited in the software literature. Corporate benchmarks are also produced by software journals such as the annual software compensation and salary levels published by ComputerWorld.

Corporate software benchmarks have been produced for more than 20 years, and some of the pioneering approaches to corporate benchmarks can be attributed to the work of Dr. Richard Nolan and David Norton, who realized the importance of benchmarks in the 1970s. The well-known Nolan and Norton consulting company gathered benchmark data as one of their primary services.

Compensation and personnel benchmarks predate the computer era and have been performed for more than 50 years. To avoid the risk of possible antitrust violations, compensation benchmarks are performed in a special way. Companies contribute data on occupations and compensation levels to an independent consulting group. The reports that are produced compare each client's data against the group, but do not reveal the specific ranges for any company. Some of companies producing compensation benchmark data include Culpepper and ComputerWorld.

Customer satisfaction benchmarks also predate the computer era and can be traced back more than 100 years. In the context of software applications, customer satisfaction surveys for specific products are often carried out by the vendors themselves. However, comparative benchmarks between classes of similar products, such as word processors or spreadsheets, require more extensive data.

Specialized benchmark companies such as Auerbach and International Data Corporation (IDC) have long produced interesting comparisons of mainframe software applications. The major software journals such as *PC World* and *PC Magazine* typically produce benchmarks of personal computer (PC) software applications, and of PCs themselves.

Project-level benchmarks for software have been carried out since the 1970s. A software "project" is not well defined in the software literature. In this book, a software project is defined as a computerized application that is developed to perform a specific technical or business function. A software project has its own budget, its own requirements, and a team of workers dedicated to its completion. Examples of typical software projects include an insurance claims handling system, a telephone switching system, a word processing application, or a manufacturing support application. A software project can also add features to an existing application. In fact, as this book is written, projects that enhance existing software packages are far more common than projects for building new applications.

Although benchmark studies cover a wide variety of topics, there are some significant gaps that have sparse coverage and little in the way of solid empirical data in the software literature. The major gaps as this book is written include lack of benchmark information on

- The numbers and sizes of corporate databases
- Delivered defects in commercial applications
- The reliability of commercial applications
- The usage patterns of the World Wide Web
- The usage patterns of e-mail

The gaps associated with database benchmarks reflect an interesting problem. As this book is written there are no metrics available for expressing the size or volume of information in a database. For software, both LOC metrics and function point metrics have long been available for performing benchmark studies. However, the database domain does not have any size metrics at all. Due to the lack of data metrics, there are no benchmarks on many critical topics in the database, data warehouse, and data mining domains.

As this book is written there are no published studies that explore how much data a corporation owns, the numbers of errors in the data, how much it costs to create a database, the value of the data, or the eventual costs of removing obsolete data. Thus, a topic of considerable economic importance is, essentially, a void in terms of benchmark studies.

Some of the other gaps should be filled too. For example, a question that occurs frequently in lawsuits is that of the number of bugs or defects still present when commercial software is delivered to clients. Although this kind of data is available for many kinds of software, it is not readily available for commercial applications released by major software vendors such as Microsoft and SAP. As far as can be determined, information on defect levels in commercial software is regarded as proprietary and is almost never released, except during litigation.

With hundreds of companies performing scores of benchmarks it is not surprising that there are many variations in how the work is performed. Benchmark studies can be carried out in a variety of ways, including

- Blind studies in which none of the participating companies are identified
- Hybrid studies with a mix of named and unnamed participants
- Open studies in which all participants are aware of one another
- Targeted studies between two specific companies
- General studies between one company and industry averages
- Benchmarks by means of mailed or e-mailed survey instruments
- Benchmarks by means of telephone surveys
- Benchmarks by means of on-site interviews

The most common form of benchmark up until the late 1990s consisted of mailed surveys, followed by telephone surveys. However, the explosion of the Internet and the World Wide Web are leading to new forms of data collection by means of Web-based surveys. Indeed, several commercial software companies have created special application packages for gathering data via the World Wide Web.

The major form of benchmark analysis performed by my colleagues and I consists of project-level benchmarks in which the data is collected by means of on-site interviews, rather than using mailed or e-mailed surveys. The standard SPR method of gathering benchmark data consists of on-site interviews with project managers and at least a core of the software technical staff members.

Among other purposes, the on-site interviews are used to correct "leakage" from software cost and effort data. Normal software cost tracking systems are usually incomplete, and leave out significant amounts of useful data such as unpaid overtime, management effort, and early work on requirements carried out before the cost system was initialized. Figure 3.1 illustrates the basic activities normally performed during a benchmark study.

The goal of a software benchmark analysis is to show clients exactly where they stand in the context of their own industry. Normally, clients care about the average results from their industry, but care more about best-in-class results. Simply placing the client against the background of their industry is not enough. A good benchmark should also uncover information on why the results are the way they are. Also, because benchmarks are precursors to process improvement programs, the benchmark should indicate some of the steps that might be

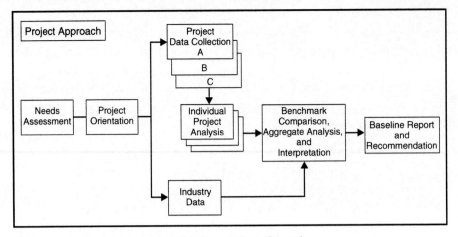

Figure 3.1   Basic sequence of software benchmarks

needed to improve the client's standing against industry data. Figure 3.2 illustrates how all of these topics interrelate. In short, benchmarks show clients where they are, why they are there, and how far they would have to go to reach best-in-class status within their industry.

Benchmarks are even more effective than assessments in causing companies to start software process improvement programs. If a company is well below average ranges in productivity and quality, this situation presents tangible data

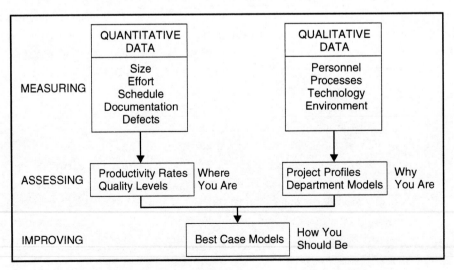

Figure 3.2   Benchmarking overview

that executives can understand easily. For example, the virtues of moving up from an SEI level 1 to a level 3 might be abstract and difficult to explain, but the need to improve productivity rates from five function points per staff month to ten to reach industry norms is fairly unambiguous.

Accurate benchmarking of software projects was difficult for many years due to problems with the LOC software metric, which was unreliable for studies involving multiple programming languages. For example comparisons between projects in unlike languages, such as COBOL and Visual Basic, can lead to invalid conclusions. The advent of the function point metric, since 1979, has opened a door to more accurate benchmark studies of software projects. In turn, the use of function point metrics has improved higher level benchmarks at the levels of countries, industries, and companies.

Benchmark studies can explore a number of different topics. At the level of corporations, gross factors such as annual software expenses and total software employment can be compared. However, corporate benchmarks are not granular enough to detect problems or lead to improvements in software development methods.

Very interesting software benchmarks can be carried out at the project level. These project-level benchmarks can generate very useful information. However, project-level benchmarks require a great deal of care to ensure an apples-to-apples comparison.

The most common questions our clients have asked about benchmark studies over the past 15 years have been

- What are best-in-class productivity rates in our industry?
- What are best-in-class development costs per function point in our industry?
- What are best-in-class development schedules in our industry?
- What are best-in-class maintenance assignment scopes in our industry?
- What are best-in-class quality levels in our industry?
- What are the best development processes for software like ours?
- What are the best development tools for software like ours?
- What does it cost to move from SEI CMM level 1 to SEI CMM level 3?
- What are the differences in results between SEI CMM level 1 and CMM level 3?

As can be seen from these very common questions, the most interesting topics from benchmarks are those associated with best practices and best-in-class results. Averages are interesting and useful, but benchmark studies are often commissioned by companies with goals that are to be much better than average.

This brings up an interesting observation about why and when benchmark studies are commissioned. Benchmark studies are often precursors to entering into outsource agreements. Some clients commission benchmarks to aid in the decision process of whether to outsource.

If the clients are well ahead of industry averages, they may decide to continue with in-house development. If the clients are average, they may decide to invest in a software process improvement program. If the clients are significantly below the industry average, they may seek outsource assistance. In this case, the benchmark data can also be used as a baseline to judge the performance of the outsource vendor after the contract is underway.

For benchmarks to be useful, or even for the comparisons to be valid, the projects that are compared during the benchmark have to be similar in size and in nature. This is not as easy as it might sound. Consider some of the types of software projects that are being constructed in the United States at the beginning of the twenty-first century:

- Expert systems
- Systems software controlling physical devices
- Embedded software contained within physical devices
- Monolithic information systems
- Two-tier client/server software
- Three-tier client/server software
- Distributed component-based software
- Web applets
- Entertainment and game software
- Pen-based applications
- Commercial software packages
- Military weapons software
- Military logistics software
- End user applications
- ERP applications

It would be appropriate to do benchmark studies within each of these types of software, but benchmark studies between types may not be considered valid by the participants. Some of our clients only care about the specific type of project on which they are working, and regard even closely related projects with suspicion as being "different." Even if the comparisons are valid, comparisons across multiple types of software require special care in order for the results to be useful.

For benchmarking purposes, it is not a normal practice to compare unlike software applications, such as comparing the productivity level of a small Web applet with the productivity level of a large military weapons system.

As discussed, we often aggregate project data into six large categories in which the software projects share similar attributes. Later in this book, data from each of these six major categories is discussed and illustrated. Here, the six are introduced and defined:

1. Systems software that operates physical devices
2. Military software that follows military standards
3. Commercial software developed for sale or lease to customers
4. Information systems developed in-house for corporate use
5. Outsourced projects developed under contract
6. End user applications developed privately for personal use

The unifying theme of *systems software* is that it controls a physical device. Thus, operating systems that control computers, switching systems that control telephone circuits, and embedded systems that control manufacturing equipment are all within the general type of systems software projects.

We are asked by some clients to break out embedded software that is contained within a physical device and treat this as a separate type. Sometimes embedded software is created as microcode using special languages and tools. Although we can and sometimes do benchmark embedded applications separately, these applications share many characteristics with other forms of systems software that control devices from outside, rather than from inside.

The unifying theme of *military software* is adherence to military standards such as DoD standard 498 or 2167A. In recent years, military software applications have been moving toward civilian practices and away from the unique criteria contained in the older DoD standards. However, old practices die hard, and military projects still tend to be more concerned with oversight and independent verification and validation (IV&V) than civilian projects.

One of the reasons why we classify military software separately is because during the 1970s through the early 1990s, military software had developed a unique set of software documentation criteria. Under military standards such as DoD 2167, specifications and planning documents for military applications were approximately three times larger than civilian norms. The mass of military paperwork and the extensive oversight requirements made military software project productivity the lowest of any industry. However, productivity of military programming using the specialized military languages of Ada83, CMS2, and Jovial compared favorably with civilian programming productivity.

Incidentally, it was not until function point metrics and activity-based cost studies were applied to military software that it was discovered that their documentation standards were so verbose. Benchmark studies using the older LOC metrics often showed low productivity for military and defense applications, but LOC studies did not measure documentation costs as separate activities because documents cannot be measured by means of LOC.

When function point analysis was applied to military software projects, it was discovered that the specification volumes were approximately three times larger than civilian norms. The effort associated with producing paper documents for military software projects required roughly twice as much effort as the code itself. Indeed, these discoveries were one of the reasons why the DoD has been moving toward adopting civilian standards and civilian best practices.

Military projects also utilized a number of activities seldom encountered in civilian projects. For example, military software projects utilized separate contractors for IV&V.

Military applications can be weapons systems, command and control systems, or logistical support systems. Some military applications are very similar to civilian information systems, such as the software used to control inventories in post exchanges. However, if these applications adhere to military standards, that fact is significant enough to classify them as military projects.

The unifying theme of *commercial software* is that it is intended to be sold to external clients, who may or may not have contributed to the requirements. The family of commercial software products overlaps systems software because Microsoft Windows NT is both systems software and a commercial product. However, many other commercial applications do not control physical devices, such as word processors, spreadsheets, games, and personal information managers.

Building software for hundreds or thousands of potential clients triggers many unique situations that justify classifying commercial software as a unique type. For example, many commercial applications are released in multiple languages (such as English, Japanese, and French), so these applications have nationalization expenses that are seldom encountered in other types. The maintenance of commercial software is also a special case, and sometimes features 24-hour-a-day hot-line support, Web sites, and the need to make patches and updates available for remote deployment via the Internet.

The unifying theme of *information systems* is that the applications are produced by companies for their own internal use, rather than being marketed to external customers. The traditional name for information systems is *management information systems* or MIS, because the primary purpose of many applications is to provide useful data to corporate or enterprise executives. Examples of MIS projects include insurance claims handling applications, banking systems, and payroll and human resource applications.

The unifying theme of *contracted or outsourced projects* is that they are covered by legally binding agreements that may include penalties if the projects are late, over budget, or below stated quality levels. Outsource projects can either be information systems, systems software, or even embedded applications. However, the serious prospect of litigation in case of failure justifies classifying outsource projects as a unique type. The chance of litigation brings with it special forms of oversight and management control seldom encountered in internal projects that are not under contract.

Software projects by major outsource vendors such as Andersen, Electronic Data Systems (EDS), and IBM are often more productive than similar projects produced by their client organizations. This appears to be due to the considerable experience of the outsource software personnel, by the availability of reusable materials, and by some fairly significant volumes of unpaid overtime by the outsource teams.

Many military software projects are also developed under contract or outsource agreements. In this situation, both the implications of military standards and the implications of potential litigation make such projects a fairly unique subtype. When presenting results to clients, we usually separate contracted military projects from military projects completed internally using the services with their own internal staffs.

The unifying theme of *end user applications* is that they are created by and for the users themselves. We don't actually get many requests to study end user applications because they are small and fairly inexpensive. However, the software press has tended to exaggerate the capabilities of end user applications. There are intermittent stories to the effect that, Company X avoids the software bottleneck by letting users build their own applications.

End user applications are invariably small, many are less than 10 function points. There are no known end user applications larger than 100 function points. End user applications are usually developed without any rigor or oversight, and may not be usable or maintainable by anyone but the original author. On the whole, end user applications are lots of fun for computer-literate personnel, but fairly hazardous in a corporate context. They are definitely not a safe replacement for professional software teams in a business context.

Because small software projects and large software applications are not developed in the same manner, SPR also aggregates software projects by size. We normally use function point metrics for size aggregation. A useful approach is to aggregate projects into six general size plateaus, each an order of magnitude apart:

1. 1 function point
2. 10 function points
3. 100 function points
4. 1,000 function points
5. 10,000 function points
6. 100,000 function points

Usually projects less than 100 function points are enhancements or updates to existing applications. Individual programs such as Microsoft Word or our own commercial estimating tools are normally larger than 1,000 function points. Many corporate systems such as payroll and accounting applications are in the 10,000-function point range. This size plateau constitutes a critical size range and hence is often subject to assessment and benchmark studies. Applications in the 10,000-function point range are very risky, and more than 50% of such projects run late or are cancelled. The top plateau of 100,000-function point projects is a fairly rare category. Some of the projects in this size range include IBM's MVS operating system, Microsoft Windows NT, and a number of specialized military applications.

Because applications in the 100,000-function point size range usually have staffs that number in the hundreds and schedules that can top five calendar years, it is obvious that only large corporations and government agencies can even attempt such projects. The top size plateau is only encountered in the largest and most sophisticated corporations in the world. Even here, producing 100,000-function point applications is a hazardous undertaking.

Because most projects obviously are not exactly one of these sizes, we round the raw data to the closest size plateau. For example, a project of 300 function points would be normalized to the 100-function point plateau, whereas one of 700 function points would be normalized to the 1,000-function point plateau. Table 3.1 illustrates the approximate average sizes of 15 kinds of software packages.

Table 3.1   Size Ranges of Software in Both Function Points and LOC

Application	Size, function points	Size, LOC	LOC per function point
Personal programs	25	1,625	65
Web applets	50	3,250	65
Computer games	3,000	195,000	65
Word processors	3,500	437,500	125
Spreadsheets	3,500	437,500	125
Client/server applications	7,500	675,000	90
Database packages	7,500	937,500	125
Telephone switching systems	7,500	937,500	125
Manufacturing applications	7,500	937,500	125
Large business applications	10,000	1,050,000	105
Major corporate applications	25,000	2,625,000	105
Major government applications	50,000	5,250,000	105
Operating systems	75,000	11,250,000	150
Enterprise systems	150,000	18,750,000	125
Major defense systems	250,000	25,000,000	100

As can be seen, the range of software application sizes is quite large. Readers may wonder why the last column, the ratio of LOC to function points, varies. There are approximately 600 programming languages in use as this book is written. Because these languages vary from low-level languages, such as Assembly, to very high-level languages, such as Smalltalk, the ratios in the table simply reflect the most common languages used for the applications in question.

For example, the nominal ratio for COBOL is approximately 105 source code statements per function point. The nominal ratio for the C programming language is approximately 125 statements per function point. The nominal ratio for Visual Basic is approximately 65 statements per function point, with the caveat that the visual languages don't use "statements" or LOC for many functions due to their graphical tools.

Table 3.2 illustrates the approximate productivity rates within the set of 36 cells that result when the size and classification factors are shown together. Table 3.2 uses data from a sample of 500 projects in the United States collected between 1997 and 1999.

Analysis of the data on Table 3.2 reveals some of the problems that confront benchmark organizations and their clients. Notice that some of the cells are blank because we have no data. For example end user applications larger than 100 function points are basically impossible, so we will never have data for the larger cells of end user development.

Another problem is not immediately apparent, but should be understood by readers and other benchmark organizations. This book is being written in 1999 and early 2000, and hence the function point data is based on Version 4.1 of the International Function Point Users Group (IFPUG) counting rules. One of my previous books, *Applied Software Measurement* (Jones 1996) was first published in 1991, and the second edition was published in 1996 but used data gathered up to 1995. Version 3.4 of the IFPUG counting rules were in effect at that time, and they differ from today's rules by approximately 20%. This means that long-range studies may require data conversion between older metrics and current metrics. Also, the averages in Table 3.2 are simply the arithmetic mean of each column of data. This method tends to inflate productivity rates somewhat because the larger projects—more than 1,000 function points—actually absorb more than 50% of all effort in major enterprises.

When actually doing benchmarks, other forms of statistical averaging present more accurate analysis. We also use modes, medians, weighted averages, harmonics, and geometric means as well as simple arithmetic means.

Consider a hypothetical example to understand why the arithmetic mean of productivity results is not always suitable. Suppose in one year a company had nine projects of 100 function points in size, which they completed at a rate of 20 function points per staff month. Suppose they had one large project of 10,000 function points, which they completed at a rate of 5 function points per staff month. What was their average productivity for the year?

The arithmetic mean of the productivity rates of these ten projects yields a result of 18.5 function points per staff month because the nine small projects pull up the overall average. But in the year in question, 2,000 months of effort went to the massive project of 10,000 function points whereas only 45 months went to the nine smaller projects. Thus a weighted average based on 10,900 total function points produced divided by 2,045 total staff months expended yields a

Table 3.2 United States Software Productivity Rates circa 1999

Size, function points	End User Software	MIS Projects	Outsource Projects	Commercial Projects	Systems Software Projects	Military Projects	Average
1	50.00	16.00	20.00	10.00	9.50	5.00	22.58
10	40.00	15.00	16.00	11.00	9.00	4.50	16.75
100	25.00	11.00	12.00	10.00	7.50	4.25	12.46
1,000	–	6.50	7.00	6.00	5.50	3.50	5.70
10,000	–	3.50	4.50	4.00	4.00	2.50	3.70
100,000	–	2.00	3.00	2.50	2.50	1.50	2.30
Average	38.00	9.00	10.42	7.25	6.33	3.54	12.42

Data is expressed in function points per staff month.

more realistic annual result of 5.33 function points per staff month. This result reflects the actual distribution of effort for the year far better than the arithmetic mean of the projects.

Although this example is hypothetical, it illustrates a common problem with benchmark studies. Small projects outnumber large systems by at least 50 to one in almost every major organization. If benchmarks or annual baseline results are based on simple arithmetic averages of project productivity rates, the results will indicate much higher productivity rates than would be produced using weighted averages.

As can be seen, the bulk of our benchmark studies has involved either information systems or systems software, followed by outsource projects. We have done fewer benchmark studies for military and commercial organizations. We have actually done no formal benchmarks at all for end user applications, but because many of my colleagues and friends and I develop such personal applications, the SPR methods have been applied informally.

Although Table 3.2 is interesting, it is obvious that a full benchmark requires a much more complete story to explain what is happening and why. We usually create more than a dozen charts and graphs of key topics. For example, when we perform benchmarks of maintenance and enhancement projects, we record the sizes of both the base application and the update. Maintenance and enhancement benchmarks are quite complex and need additional data gathered. When using our six-plateau size ranges, we often encounter updates of between 1 and 100 function points to base applications between 1,000 and 10,000 function points. Occasionally we encounter a major release, such as a 1,000-function point addition to a 10,000-function point base application.

The lesson to be learned from this is that benchmarks or assessments, by themselves, may raise more questions than they answer. This is why a combination of assessment data and benchmark data is more useful than either by itself. Data should be able to answer two key questions from clients and top executives:

1. How do our productivity and quality levels compare with others in our industry?
2. Why are our results better or worse than others in the industry?

The quantitative benchmark data answers the first question of how client productivity data compares with industry norms. The qualitative assessment data answers the second question of why the results are better or worse than industry norms. Both questions are important and therefore both assessments and benchmarks are needed to provide the full answers to questions that are vital to top executives.

Because we are more likely to be commissioned to study large projects rather than small, our benchmark data exhibits a skew toward the larger size ranges. Thus, although our benchmark data is fairly extensive, it is not a perfect replica of U.S. or global software project distributions. We have observed among our clients that small projects less than 100 function points outnumber large applications by several hundred percent, even though that pattern is not reflected in our benchmark database.

The six general software classes and six general size plateaus are useful for showing general trends. For example, it is possible to illustrate why small information systems projects less than 100 function points and large military systems greater than 10,000 function points have such different productivity levels and quality levels.

Benchmarks and the Problem of Size Metrics

As the twenty-first century begins, function points are now the major metric for software benchmarks and baseline studies. The function point metric was developed by A. J. Albrecht and his colleagues within IBM in the middle 1970s. The function point metric was put into the public domain by IBM.

A nonprofit organization, IFPUG has taken over responsibility for refining and publishing the counting rules. The data used in this book are based on Version 4.1 of the IFPUG counting rules (IFPUG 1999). IFPUG is headquartered in the United States in Westerville, Ohio. There are affiliated organizations that support function point metrics in more than 20 countries.

There are some serious problems with attempting to perform benchmark or baseline studies using LOC metrics. These problems are serious enough so that using LOC metrics for cross-language comparisons can be considered an example of professional malpractice.

As benchmark studies become more common in the software industry, it is important for both clients and researchers to understand the strengths and weaknesses of various size metrics that can be used for software artifacts. As this book is written, there are benchmark studies being performed using at least half a dozen variations in how LOC are counted, and half a dozen variations in how function points are counted. These variations may not be apparent to clients and even to the benchmark organizations, but they can distort benchmark results significantly when attempting large-scale comparisons between published benchmark data.

One of the fundamental benchmark issues for software that should be put on a firm and rational basis is how to measure the *size* of various software deliverables. Before turning to the available metrics for dealing with size, it is useful to step back and examine the kinds of items associated with software projects for which size information is needed. There are 20 software artifacts for which size information is important because the costs of creating or dealing with these deliverables is significant:

1. The functionality of the application
2. The volume of information in databases
3. The quantity of new source code to be produced
4. The quantity of changed source code, if any
5. The quantity of deleted source code, if any
6. The quantity of base code in any existing application being updated
7. The quantity of "dead code" no longer utilized but still present
8. The quantity of reusable code from certified or uncertified sources
9. The number of paper deliverables (plans, specifications, documents, and so on)
10. The sizes of paper deliverables (pages, words)
11. The number of national languages (English, French, Japanese, and so on)
12. The number of on-line screens
13. The number of graphs and illustrations
14. The size of nonstandard deliverables (for example, music, animation)
15. The number of test cases that must be produced
16. The number of bugs or errors in requirements
17. The number of bugs or errors in specifications
18. The number of bugs or errors in source code
19. The number of bugs or errors in user manuals
20. The number of secondary "bad fix" bugs or errors

The available metrics for quantifying the size of software deliverables include the following:

- Natural metrics such as counts of screens, pages, and words in paper documents
- Source code metrics using physical LOC
- Source code metrics using logical statements
- Function point metrics as defined by IFPUG
- Function point variants as defined by other organizations

- Object-oriented (OO) metrics of various kinds
- Counts of bugs or defects

A major omission from this list of metrics is the absence of any known size metric for databases, data warehouses, data quality, or repositories. As of early 2000, the database domain has no ability to estimate size, quality, or costs. This is a major benchmark deficiency that needs immediate research. Unfortunately the database vendors have not stepped up to this problem. When it is mentioned to database vendors, the usual response is, "It is not our responsibility."

When the software industry began in the early 1950s, the first metric developed for quantifying the output of a software project was the metric termed *source lines of code* or SLOC. The variant LOC has essentially the same meaning and is also widely used. However, almost at once some ambiguity occurred, because a LOC could be defined either as a physical line of code or a logical statement.

Physical LOC are simply sets of coded instructions terminated by pressing the Enter key of a computer keyboard. For some languages, physical LOC and logical statements are almost identical, but for other languages there can be major differences in apparent size based on whether physical lines or logical statements are used. Unfortunately, the differences between physical LOC and logical statements is often omitted from the software metrics literature.

Table 3.3 illustrates some of the code-counting ambiguity for a simple COBOL application using both logical statements and physical lines. This table

Table 3.3   Sample COBOL Application Showing Sizes of Code Divisions Using Logical Statements and Physical LOC

Division	Logical Statements	Physical Lines
Identification	25	25
Environment	75	75
Data	300	350
Procedure	700	950
Dead code	100	300
Comments	200	700
Blank lines	100	100
Total LOC	1,500	2,500

shows the sizes of the various divisions of typical COBOL applications, and how physical LOC counts and logical statement counts might vary.

As can be seen from this simple example, the concept of what actually comprises a LOC is surprisingly ambiguous. The size range can run from a low of 700 LOC if only logical statements in the procedure division are used, to a high of 2,500 LOC if a count of total physical lines is used. Almost any intervening size is possible, and most variations are in use for productivity studies, benchmarks, journal articles, and so forth.

I once interviewed six managers in the same company whose offices were all within 150 feet of one another. When the question, How do you define a line of code? was put to these six managers, four distinct counting methods were noted and the range between the most concise method and the most diffuse method was almost 500%.

Bear in mind that Table 3.3 is a simple example using only one programming language for a new application. The SPR catalog of programming languages (*SPR Table of Programming Languages and Levels* [SPR 1996]) contains approximately 600 programming languages and dialects, and more are being added on a monthly basis.

Furthermore, a significant number of software applications utilize two or more programming languages at the same time. For example, combinations such as COBOL and SQL or Ada and Jovial are very common. SPR has observed one system that actually contained 12 different programming languages.

There are other complicating factors too, such as the use of macro instructions, inclusion of copybooks, inheritance, class libraries, and other forms of reusable code. There is also ambiguity when dealing with enhancements and maintenance, such as whether to count the base code when enhancing existing applications. Obviously, with so many variations in how LOC might be counted, it would be useful to have a standard for defining what should be included and excluded. Here we encounter another problem. There is no true international standard for defining code-counting rules that encompasses all programming languages. Instead, there are a number of published informal standards that, unfortunately, often conflict with one another.

Citing just two of the more widely used but informal standards, the SPR code-counting rules was first published in 1991 in *Applied Software Measurement* (Jones 1996). The SPR method uses logical statements. The SEI code-counting standards published in 1992 by Robert Park uses physical LOC (Park 1992). Both of these standards are widely used and widely cited, but they differ in many key assumptions. Counts of the same COBOL application using the Park physical

LOC definitions can be as much as 50% larger than a count using the SPR logical statement definitions.

As an experiment, I carried out an informal survey of code counting practices in software journals such as *American Programmer, Byte, Application Development Trends, Communications of the ACM, IBM Systems Journal, IEEE Computer, IEEE Software, Software Development,* and *Software Magazine.* Approximately one third of the published articles using LOC data used physical lines, another third used logical statements, and the remaining third did not define which method was used and hence were ambiguous in results by several hundred percent. Although there may be justifications for selecting physical lines or logical statements for a particular research study, there is no justification at all for publishing data without stating which method is utilized!

Let us now consider the major strengths and weaknesses of common software metrics as used in the software literature and in benchmark studies. We will start with the strengths and weaknesses of physical LOC because this method is the oldest metric in continuous usage in the software literature. The main strengths of physical LOC are

- The physical LOC metric is easy to count.
- The physical LOC metric has been automated extensively for counting.
- The physical LOC metric is used in a number of software estimating tools.

The main weaknesses of physical LOC are

- The physical LOC metric may include substantial "dead code."
- The physical LOC metric may include blanks and comments.
- The physical LOC metric is misleading for mixed-language projects.
- The physical LOC metric is ambiguous for software reuse.
- The physical LOC metric is a poor choice for full life cycle studies.
- The physical LOC metric does not work for some "visual" languages.
- The physical LOC metric is erratic for direct conversion to function points.
- The physical LOC metric is erratic for direct conversion to logical statements.

When we turn our attention to the metric of logical statements, we find a slightly different pattern of strengths and weaknesses. The main strengths of the logical statements are

- Logical statements exclude dead code, blanks, and comments.
- Logical statements can be converted mathematically into function point metrics.
- Logical statements are used in a number of software estimating tools.

The main weaknesses of logical statements are

- Logical statements can be difficult to count.
- Logical statements are not automated extensively.
- Logical statements are a poor choice for full life cycle studies.
- Logical statements are ambiguous for some "visual" languages.
- Logical statements may be ambiguous for software reuse.
- Logical statements may be erratic for direct conversion to the physical LOC metric.

On the whole, logical statements are a somewhat more rational choice for productivity and quality data based on coding, but neither physical LOC nor logical statements are appropriate for exploration of noncoding work such as creation of specifications, user manuals, or project management tasks.

Indeed, when LOC metrics are utilized for productivity studies that include noncoding activities such as the creation of requirements, specifications, and user manuals, they, paradoxically, move backward and give invalid results. This problem was first published by me in the *IBM Systems Journal* in 1978 (Jones 1978), and has been discussed in more than a dozen books and 100 articles since the initial publication. The LOC results are so misleading that starting in 1995, I have been stating: "Using lines of code for productivity studies involving multiple languages and full life cycle activities should be viewed as professional malpractice."

An example can illustrate the paradoxical reversal of productivity when LOC metrics are used to perform productivity comparisons between two different languages. Assume that two versions of the same application are created, with one being programmed in Assembly language and the other version being programmed in the C++ language. Assume that the programming staffs are skilled equally in both languages and have exactly the same salary levels. Both versions of the application are functionally identical, and differ primarily in the use of two different programming languages. The version done in Assembly language required 1,000,000 logical source code statements whereas the version done in the higher level C language required only 500,000 source code statements to code the same feature set. The features in both versions of this application total 4,000 function points. The ratio of source code statements to function points for Assembly language in this example is 250 statements per function point. The ratio for C++ is 125 source code statements per function point.

In terms of real economic productivity, the C++ version is visibly superior because the C++ project cost only $11,500,000 whereas the version done in

Assembly language cost $20,000,000, or almost twice as much (Table 3.4). However, when the two projects are compared using "cost per source line" or "LOC per staff month," the Assembly version looks best! This reversal of real economic productivity is the basis for the assertion that using LOC metrics for cross-language comparisons constitutes professional malpractice.

Note how the use of LOC metrics in Table 3.4 violates standard economic assumptions and gives a distorted and misleading picture. Even though the Assembly language version required almost twice the effort, the huge volume of Assembly code yields much higher LOC productivity rates than the C++ version. The reason for this distortion has actually been understood for hundreds of years and is common knowledge among managers in every industry except software.

When a manufacturing process is impacted heavily by fixed costs and there is a reduction in the number of units produced, the cost per unit must go up. When LOC are considered to be an economic unit and there is a switch from a low-level programming language to a high-level programming language, it is obvious that the number of "units" will be reduced. However, the costs of producing paper documents such as specifications stay constant and act as though they were fixed costs. Thus, when two programming languages are compared using LOC metrics, the lower level language appears falsely to be superior to the higher level language.

Table 3.4   Productivity Paradox with LOC Metrics

Activity	Assembly Source Code (1,000,000 LOC), Staff Months	C++ Source Code (500,000 LOC), Staff Months	Difference (500,000 LOC total) Difference
Testing/debugging	650	250	400
Paper documents	600	550	50
Coding	550	250	300
Management	200	100	100
Total	2,000	1,150	850
Application cost	$20,000,000	$11,500,000	$8,500,000
LOC per staff month	500	435	65
Cost per LOC	$20.00	$23.00	–$3.00

Some researchers attempt to avoid this paradox by including only coding or core development activities in their measures, and excluding the activities that behave as fixed costs such as requirements, specifications, user manuals, and the like. Unfortunately, this approach excludes more than 50% of the total cost elements for large software projects and is not a valid solution to the distortions of using LOC. Benchmark studies using only coding may avoid the consequences of the LOC paradox, but they are not suitable for serious economic analysis.

The form of metric that allows noncoding work to be measured as effectively as coding work consists of function point metrics. Function points are not related to source code volumes at all, but rather to the external features of the application as defined in user requirements. Function points were developed within IBM and placed in the public domain in 1979. IBM, which in the 1970s was the world's largest developer of software applications, commissioned a team to develop a software metric that could be used for software economic studies regardless of the programming language, or combination of languages, utilized for the code itself.

The IBM metrics team was headed by Allan Albrecht, and the result of their research was termed *the function point metric*. Function points were used internally by IBM in the mid 1970s. They are developed from the requirements and specifications of a software application, and consist of the weighted and adjusted totals of five key elements:

1. Inputs (screens, signals, and so on)
2. Outputs (screens, reports, checks, and so on)
3. Inquiries
4. Logical files
5. Interfaces

The actual rules for counting and adjusting function points are fairly complex, so training is needed to count function points accurately. The counting rules have passed from IBM and are now controlled in the United States by the nonprofit IFPUG. IFPUG publishes function point counting rules (Version 4.1 as this book is written) and administers the certification exams that are a prerequisite for those who wish to become function point analysts.

Function points are now the preferred choice for software economic studies involving multiple programming languages and full life cycle costs. For example, function points actually match the real economic situation of the case study shown previously in Table 3.4.

In our previous example, if we assume that both the Assembly version and the C++ version perform the same functions, and both are 4,000 function points in size, then we can perform a valid economic comparison. The Assembly version cost $5,000 per function point whereas the C++ version only cost $2,875 per function point, for a savings of $2,125 per function point or an economic gain of 42.5%.

Many software researchers recognized the advantages of function points for software economic studies but were not completely satisfied with the form and structure of the function point metric as defined originally by the IBM team, and more recently defined by the IFPUG Counting Practices Committee.

In 1983, Charles Symons gave a presentation in London on an alternative function point variant that he termed the *Mark II function point*, which is now widely used in the United Kingdom and to a lesser degree in Hong Kong and Canada. Symons' Mark II function point is discussed in his book *Software Sizing and Estimating* (Symons 1991).

The Mark II function point alternative was only the first in a growing set of function point variants that now include at least 25 alternative functional metrics. It is fairly obvious that 25 variations in how the function point metric might be counted is too many. The ISO is attempting to develop a standard for function point sizing, but the complicated international politics of functional metrics are currently interfering with the pure technical issues. Adherents of various alternative function point methods are striving to have their method become the basis for the ISO standard.

In terms of usage, the IFPUG form of function point outnumbers all other forms put together by more than five to one on a global basis. The second-ranked function point variation would be the British Mark II version, which is used by approximately half the studies in the United Kingdom, and the IFPUG version is used by the other half. The Mark II version has essentially no usage in the United States.

Some of the other minor variants include *feature points, 3D function points,* and *full function points.* However, usage of these minor variants is so slight that none of them have been used for published benchmark studies with the exception of a book published in 1993 that was based on feature points. *Software Productivity and Quality Today: The Worldwide Perspective* (Jones 1993) used feature points for a large-scale international comparison.

Feature points were developed to solve a psychological problem of the 1980s. When function points were first introduced, much of the initial data was taken from information systems. The real-time and systems software community formed the incorrect impression that function points only work for information systems.

The feature point metric was first used in 1986 for telecommunication switching systems and real-time applications. This metric was successful in introducing the concept of functional metrics to the real-time and systems software community, but once standard IFPUG function points started to be applied to systems and real-time software, the need for the alternative feature point metric disappeared.

A common reason for developing alternative function point metrics is based on a misunderstanding of function point principles. Function points were developed as a unit of measure for expressing the *size* of software applications. Other factors, in addition to size, determine the *effort* required to build applications. Unfortunately, some of the alternative function point metrics were developed for dealing with software that is costly to construct, such as real-time and embedded software.

The reason for developing alternative function points for these difficult applications is that when productivity is measured using standard IFPUG function points, the productivity is rather low. Instead of exploring the reasons why real-time software productivity is often lower than information systems, some researchers preferred to develop alternative function points that gave real-time software larger apparent sizes than standard IFPUG function points, and hence artificially elevated the productivity of real-time development. The overall range of results across the many function point variants has not been studied in detail, but is probably in excess of $\pm$ 50% compared with standard IFPUG function points.

When we examine the patterns of strengths and weaknesses of functional metrics, we see that for economic studies and for studies that include noncoding work such as specifications, function points are clearly superior to LOC metrics. The main strengths of function point metrics are the following:

1. Function points stay constant regardless of the programming languages used.
2. Function points are a good choice for full life cycle analysis.
3. Function points are a good choice for software reuse analysis.
4. Function points are a good choice for OO economic studies.
5. Function points are supported by many software cost-estimating tools.
6. Function points can be converted mathematically into logical code statements for many languages.

The main weaknesses of function point metrics are the following:

1. Accurate counting requires certified function point specialists.
2. Function point counting can be time-consuming and expensive.
3. Function point counting automation is of unknown accuracy.
4. Function point counts are erratic for projects less than 15 function points in size.
5. Function point variations have no conversion rules to IFPUG function points.
6. Many function point variations have no "backfire" conversion rules.

Unfortunately when data is published using function point metrics, it is imperative that the authors identify which variety of function point is actually being used. Some of the major variants with published data include

- Function points as defined by IBM in 1979
- Function points as defined by IBM in the 1984 revision
- Function points defined by IFPUG
- Mark II function points, widely used in the United Kingdom since 1983
- 3D function points, which originated in the Boeing Corporation circa 1995
- Full function points, which originated in Canada circa 1997
- SPR function points, which originated in the United States in 1985
- SPR feature points, which originated in the United States in 1986
- Netherlands function points, which originated in the Netherlands circa 1996
- Engineering function points, which originated in the United States circa 1996
- DeMarco function points or "Bang points," which originated circa 1982
- Object points, which originated in the United States circa 1995

There are many metrics that have variants in use, but function point metrics have more variants than most. For example, it is necessary to distinguish between nautical and statute miles, between temperature measured in Fahrenheit or Celsius, and between three separate ways of calculating gasoline octane ratings. However, the competition among the function point variants has reached a point that unless a true international standard for function point metrics can be developed, there is some danger that the fragmentation of the metric into competing variants will damage its usefulness.

In the 1970s Allan Albrecht and his colleagues at IBM measured a number of projects using both logical source code statements and function point metrics. These pioneering studies found some interesting but not perfect correlations between source code size and function points for many programming languages.

Table 3.5 illustrates some typical ratios of logical source code statements and equivalent volumes of function points. This is a small excerpt from the main SPR table of languages with almost 600 entries.

Backfiring has become the most popular method for ascertaining function point size of aging legacy applications. In fact, for many legacy applications backfiring is the only convenient method for developing function point totals because the specifications are often missing and the original developers have departed.

Backfiring was quickly adopted by commercial software estimating vendors and is now a common feature among most of the well-known software estimating products such as CHECKPOINT, COCOMO II, GECOMO, KnowledgePlan, and SLIM. Backfiring was also adopted for benchmark studies by a number of well-known consulting companies such as Compass Group, Gartner Group's Real Decision subsidiary, Meta Group, QSM, Rubin Systems, and my company, SPR.

Table 3.5   Ratios of Logical Source Code Statements to Function Points for Selected Programming Languages Using Version 4.1 of the IFPUG Rules

Language	Nominal Level	Source Statements per Function Point		
		Low	**Mean**	**High**
Basic Assembly	1.00	200	320	450
Macro Assembly	1.50	130	213	300
C	2.50	60	128	170
FORTRAN	3.00	75	107	160
COBOL	3.00	65	107	150
Pascal	3.50	50	91	125
PL/I	4.00	65	80	95
Ada83	4.50	60	71	80
C++	6.00	30	53	125
Ada95	6.50	28	49	110
Visual Basic	10.00	20	32	37
Smalltalk	15.00	15	21	40
SQL	27.00	7	12	15

Because backfiring is used so often in commercial software estimating tools and also by management consultants and commercial benchmark companies, it is arguably the most widely used software metric in the world. The accuracy of backfiring is not claimed to be as high as normal function point counts. The accuracy of backfiring from logical statements is approximately ± 20%, whereas normal counting by certified function point counters has been measured to range by approximately ± 10% in a study commissioned by IFPUG and performed by Dr. Chris Kemerer (Kemerer 1993) when he was at MIT.

It is a curious situation that neither IFPUG nor any of the other major function point associations have evaluated backfiring, and the published literature on this method comes primarily from estimating tool vendors and software management consultants rather than the function point user community itself. It will be even more curious if the ISO creates a new standard for function point metrics that omits backfiring.

The main strengths of backfiring function points are the following:

1. Backfiring is extremely quick and easy to perform.
2. Backfiring automation is available commercially.
3. Backfiring is supported by many software cost-estimating tools.
4. Backfiring is used in many software benchmark studies.

The main weaknesses of backfiring function point metrics are the following:

1. Backfiring is of lower accuracy than normal function point counting.
2. Backfiring is ambiguous if the starting point is physical LOC.
3. Backfiring may be ambiguous for mixed-language applications.
4. Backfiring results may vary based on individual programming styles.
5. Backfiring is not endorsed by any of the major function point associations.

Backfiring is perhaps the most common technique for determining function point values for aging legacy applications. The accuracy of this approach is less than that of counts by certified personnel, but the speed and ease of generating results continue to make this approach popular.

As the OO paradigm began to spread throughout the software community, it was quickly apparent that OO projects needed to be estimated and measured just as procedural projects. Both LOC metrics and function point metrics have been utilized with OO projects with varying degrees of success.

The fundamental differences in the way OO projects are constructed compared with procedural projects led quickly to new kinds of software metrics aimed exclusively at OO projects. Some of the specialized OO metrics include those of Kemerer and Chidamber (Kemerer and Chidamber 1994) in the United States originally termed *metrics for object-oriented systems environments* or MOOSE, and Abrieu and colleagues in Portugal with their *metrics for object-oriented design* or MOOD metrics. Some of the specialized OO metrics constructs include weighted methods per class, depth of inheritance tree, number of children, coupling between object classes, and a number of others.

In the past, both LOC metrics and function point metrics have splintered into a number of competing and semi-incompatible metric variants. There is some reason to believe that the OO metrics community will also splinter into competing variants, possibly following national boundaries.

The main strengths of OO metrics are the following:

1. OO metrics are psychologically attractive within the OO community.
2. OO metrics appear to be able to distinguish simple from complex OO projects.

The main weaknesses of OO metrics are the following:

1. OO metrics do not support studies outside the OO paradigm.
2. OO metrics do not deal with full life cycle issues.
3. OO metrics have not yet been applied to testing.
4. OO metrics have not yet been applied to maintenance.
5. OO metrics have no conversion rules to LOC metrics.
6. OO metrics have no conversion rules to function point metrics.
7. OO metrics lack automation.
8. OO metrics are difficult to enumerate.
9. OO metrics are not supported by software estimating tools.

Unfortunately, OO metrics are totally unrelated to all other known software metrics. As far as can be determined, there are no conversion rules between OO metrics and any other, so it is difficult or impossible to perform side-by-side comparisons between OO projects and conventional projects using the current crop of available OO metrics.

Software metrics research is an important topic, but is not yet a well-formed or mature topic. Each of the major software metrics candidates has splintered into a number of competing alternatives, often following national boundaries. There is no true international standard for any of the more widely used software metrics. Furthermore, the adherents of each metric variant claim remarkable virtues for their choice, and often criticize rival metrics.

From a distance, the software metrics domain is fragmented, incomplete, and gives the appearance of being more influenced by "metrics politics" than by technical considerations. Unfortunately, all of the debates and disputes in the metrics domain impact necessarily the validity of benchmark and baseline studies. Before benchmarks can be useful to the participants, great care is needed in ensuring that the projects being compared are close enough in size and nature to draw meaningful conclusions. The purpose of benchmarking is to gain insight into ways of improving, and not to reach simplistic conclusions based on superficial project characteristics.

If data representing all size ranges and all classes of software is graphed, the ranges are too broad to draw meaningful conclusions. Figure 3.3 shows the ranges of software productivity from a sample of 1,500 projects between 10 and 100,000 function points.

Software productivity is a complex phenomenon with at least 250 known factors that can influence the outcomes of software projects, if you include all forms of software and all size ranges. The SPR knowledge base of roughly 9,000 software projects spans a range of productivity results that runs from a low of 0.13 function points per staff month to a high of near 165 function points per staff month. When the range of data is this broad, it is quite unsafe to use "averages" for any serious business purpose. This is why we segregate our benchmark results by size and type of software.

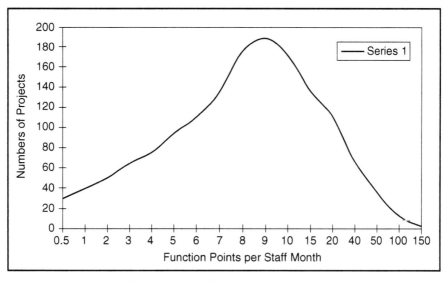

Figure 3.3   Distribution of productivity rates of 1,500 software projects

When the data is more focused, such as "systems software projects of 1,000 function points," then the results can be useful, although they are still broad enough to require an explanation. For example, the productivity range of systems software projects of 1,000 function points runs from approximately 1.5 to just more than 25 function points per staff month. The mean or average is approximately 5.5 function points per staff month for this combination.

As can be seen from Figure 3.3, the overall range of software productivity results is very broad. This brings up a key question that assessment and benchmark studies must answer to be of practical value: What causes productivity to be significantly better or worse than average results? Some of the factors that influence software productivity results are outside the control of the software project team. Although these factors are important, there is little ability to change them. For example,

- Large new systems of more than 10,000 function points have lower productivity rates than small projects of less than 100 function points.
- Military software projects that follow the older DoD standards such as DoD 2167 have lower productivity than similar civilian projects because of the huge volume of required paperwork.

There is little value in discussing factors that are outside the control of the software development team, although it is useful to know what these factors are. This book is concerned with the factors over which there is a measure of control, such as the choice of tools, programming languages, and development processes.

Assessment and benchmarks should generate enough solid data so that valid conclusions can be drawn from the results, rather than simplistic or flawed conclusions. An example of a simplistic and flawed conclusion that we encounter fairly often is: Because large software projects are hazardous, let us divide all large projects into smaller independent components.

Unfortunately, large software projects are large because there is no effective technology for decomposing them into smaller independent pieces. Consider another domain outside software. You cannot simplify the work of building a large 70,000-ton cruise ship by building 3,000 small boats instead. If you need to construct large cruise ships, then you must learn the technologies that work for large ships. If you need to build a large software application, then you need to master the technologies that work for large systems. You should not deceive yourself into thinking that simply dividing the system into lots of small pieces can solve difficult architectural and technical problems. Indeed, in the case of

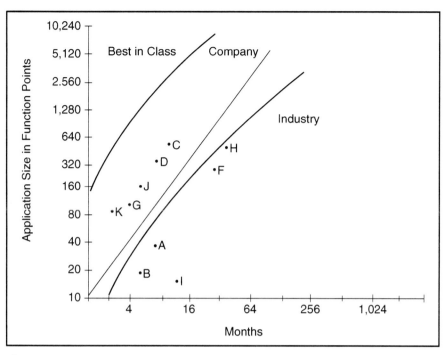

Figure 3.4   Benchmark sample

software, faulty decomposition into large numbers of small pieces can make the application harder to build rather than easier.

The most common question that clients ask from benchmark studies is how they compare against industry averages and against best-in-class results from their industry. In this case the phrase *best in class* can be defined as the quantitative results representing the top 5% of projects analyzed.

Our normal method of presentation is to plot the results of the client's projects against both industry and best-in-class curves, as shown in Figure 3.4. The data points, using letters of the alphabet, are the projects analyzed, shown against trend lines representing industry averages and the top 5%. The client's trend line or the curve showing the best fit through the client's projects is also displayed.

Benchmarking Software Costs

The single most frequently asked question of software benchmark companies is: What does it cost to build software? This is not an easy question to answer with accuracy. Software productivity measurements based on human effort in terms of work hours or work months can be measured with very good precision, but cost data is much more complicated than any other kind of benchmarks. Cost data is the most complex and difficult of any form of benchmarking.

There are major problems in the cost domain that have existed for years but have escaped notice so long as software used inaccurate metrics like LOC, which tended to mask a host of other important problems. These same problems occur for other industries besides software, incidentally. They tend to be more troublesome for software than for most other industries because software is so labor intensive.

There are seven interconnected sets of cost factors that need to be evaluated to determine software costs, and each one is an independent variable:

1. Variations due to inflation rates for studies spanning several years
2. Variations due to industry compensation averages
3. Variations due to company size
4. Variations due to geographic regions or locations
5. Variations due to merit appraisals or longevity
6. Variations due to burden rate or overhead differences
7. Variations due to work patterns and unpaid overtime

Most of the large applications that are included in benchmark and baseline studies have development cycles that span from three years to more than five years. This means that inflation has to be taken into account. Due to the current personnel shortage brought on by the need to handle the Euro and the Y2K problems, software salary inflation rates in 1998 and 1999 topped 10% for software personnel with critical skills.

When gathering software cost data, it is important to record the year in which the data is gathered. For personnel costs, it is important to record supplemental data such as the occupational groups included in the benchmark, the industry, the geographic location of the client organization, and the local assumption of the inflation rate.

When presenting benchmark and baseline cost data to clients, it is important to show the years and details of when the data was gathered. For example, in 1998

I published a book entitled *The Year 2000 Software Problem: Quantifying the Costs and Assessing the Consequences* (Jones 1998). This book contained some software salary and compensation rates using 1996 values.

It is interesting to compare some of the compensation figures from the 1996 data with 1999's data. For example, average compensation for software project managers in the banking industry has gone up by approximately $5,000 between 1996 and 1999. Average compensation for a software systems programmer has gone up from $60,000 to near $68,000, which is even more than management salaries have risen.

For the software industry as a whole, productivity gains and inflation rates have been more or less equal over fairly long periods. Thus, increases in salaries and compensation levels have been offset by improvements in tools, programming languages, and the availability of reusable materials. However, this phenomenon is not true for every industry and every kind of software project.

Between the years 1985 and 1999, software development productivity on new projects in the United States increased at an approximate average rate of near 4%. However, maintenance and enhancement productivity actually declined under the impact of client/server applications in the 1990s. Because maintenance and enhancement projects outnumber new development projects, the overall results in terms of national productivity levels have gone down slightly in 1997, 1998, and the first half of 1999. The increasing maintenance workloads brought on by the Euro, Y2K, and client/server maintenance loads have been the chief causative factors for this recent decline.

A significant problem with software cost measures is the fact that salaries and compensation vary widely from job to job, worker to worker, company to company, region to region, industry to industry, and country to country. For example, among SPR's clients in the United States, the basic salary of the occupation of "software project manager" ranges from a low of $45,000 per year to a high of more than $100,000 per year. When international clients are included, the range for the same position runs from less than $12,000 per year to more than $120,000 a year.

Table 3.6 shows 1999 averages and ranges for project management compensation for 20 U.S. industries taken from among SPR's client organizations. The table presents average results in the left column, and then shows the ranges observed based on company size and geographic region. In general, large corporations pay more than small companies. For example, large urban areas such as the San Francisco Bay area or the urban areas in New York and New Jersey have much higher pay scales than more rural areas or smaller communities. Also,

Table 3.6   1999 Annual Compensation Levels for Software Project Managers in 20 Industries in the United States

Industry	Average Annual Salary	Range by Company Size (+ or –)	Range by Geographic Region (+ or –)	Maximum Annual Salary	Minimum Annual Salary
Banking	$77,706	$20,000	$6,000	$103,706	$51,706
Electronics	$76,750	$15,000	$6,000	$97,750	$55,750
Telecommun-ications	$76,500	$15,000	$6,000	$97,500	$55,500
Software	$76,250	$15,000	$6,000	$97,250	$55,250
Consumer products	$75,929	$14,000	$5,500	$95,429	$56,429
Chemicals	$74,929	$13,000	$5,500	$93,429	$56,429
Defense	$70,828	$13,000	$5,500	$89,328	$52,328
Food/beverages	$68,667	$12,000	$5,000	$85,667	$51,667
Media	$65,125	$12,000	$5,000	$82,125	$48,125
Industrial equipment	$65,009	$12,000	$5,000	$82,009	$48,009
Distribution	$64,900	$11,000	$5,000	$80,900	$48,900
Insurance	$63,117	$10,000	$5,000	$78,117	$48,117
Public utilities	$61,120	$7,500	$4,500	$73,120	$49,120
Retail	$60,125	$7,000	$4,500	$71,625	$48,625
Health care	$57,880	$7,500	$4,500	$69,880	$45,880
Nonprofit organizations	$56,900	$7,500	$4,500	$68,900	$44,900
Transportation	$56,500	$7,000	$4,500	$68,000	$45,000
Textiles	$55,585	$7,000	$4,500	$67,085	$44,085
Government	$53,150	$6,000	$4,000	$63,150	$43,150
Education	$52,375	$6,000	$4,000	$62,375	$42,375
Average	$65,467	$10,875	$5,025	$81,367	$49,567

some industries such as banking and financial services, and telecommunications and manufacturing tend to have compensation levels that are far above U.S. averages, whereas other industries such as government service and education tend to have compensation levels that are significantly lower than U.S. averages. These basic economic facts mean that it is unsafe and inaccurate to use "U.S. averages" for cost comparisons of software. At the very least, cost comparisons should be within the context of the same or related industries, and comparisons should be made against organizations of similar size located in similar geographic areas.

Other software-related positions besides project management have similar ranges, and there are now more than 75 software-related occupations in the United States. This means that to perform software cost studies it is necessary to deal with very large differences in costs. These differences are based on industry, on company size, on geographic location, on the kinds of specialists that work on any given project, and on years of tenure or merit appraisal results.

Table 3.7 illustrates the 1999 ranges of basic compensation (exclusive of bonuses or merit appraisal adjustments) for 15 software occupations in the United States. As can be seen, the range of possible compensation levels runs from less than $30,000 to more than $100,000.

Over and above the basic compensation levels shown in Table 3.7, a number of specialized occupations are now offering even higher compensation levels than those illustrated. For example, programmers who are familiar with SAP R/3 integrated system and the ABAP programming language can expect compensation levels approximately 10% higher than average, and may even receive a signing bonus. Other key skills with bonuses or premiums include JAVA programming and Web-related skills.

Even if compensation for one occupation is considered, there are still wide ranges. Application programmers working in large companies in large cities such as New York and Los Angeles will have higher compensation rates than application programmers employed by small companies in smaller cities such as St. Petersburg, Florida, or Bismarck, South Dakota. Of course there are some local exceptions. For example Cambridge, Massachusetts, and Scotts Valley, California, are smaller towns located in software-intensive regions. These towns have very high salary and compensation levels for software workers.

Although the topic is not illustrated and the results are proprietary, there are also major variations in compensation based on merit appraisals and on longevity within grade. This factor can add about another ± $7,500 to the ranges of compensation for technical positions, and even more for executive and managerial

Table 3.7   1999 Variations in Compensation for 15 U.S. Software Occupation Groups

Occupation	Average Annual Salary	Range by Company Size (+ or −)	Range by Geographic Region (+ or −)	Range by Industry (+ or −)	Maximum Annual Salary	Minimum Annual Salary
Software architect	$81,000	$13,000	$4,500	$7,500	$106,000	$56,000
Senior systems programmer	$80,000	$13,000	$4,500	$6,000	$103,500	$56,500
Senior systems analyst	$73,000	$11,000	$4,000	$6,000	$94,000	$52,000
Systems programmer	$68,000	$12,000	$4,000	$5,500	$89,500	$46,500
Systems analyst	$60,000	$10,500	$3,750	$5,000	$79,250	$40,750
Process analyst	$57,000	$10,500	$3,750	$5,000	$76,250	$37,750
Programmer/analyst	$56,000	$11,000	$3,500	$5,000	$75,500	$36,500
Database analyst	$55,000	$12,000	$3,750	$6,000	$76,750	$33,250
Applications programmer	$55,000	$10,000	$3,500	$5,000	$73,500	$36,500
Maintenance programmer	$53,000	$10,000	$3,500	$5,000	$71,500	$34,500
Testing specialist	$52,500	$10,000	$3,500	$5,000	$71,000	$34,000
Metrics specialist	$52,000	$8,000	$3,750	$5,000	$68,750	$35,250
Quality assurance	$51,000	$7,500	$3,500	$5,000	$67,000	$35,000
Technical writer	$41,500	$5,000	$3,500	$3,000	$53,000	$30,000
Customer support	$38,500	$2,000	$3,500	$2,000	$46,000	$31,000
Average	$58,233	$9,700	$3,767	$5,067	$76,767	$39,700

positions. Unfortunately, the ranges of merit increases over average compensation is a difficult topic to explore because most companies regard this information as highly proprietary and don't wish to divulge it except under terms of strict confidentiality. As a result, this kind of information is seldom included in normal benchmark and baseline studies.

Also not illustrated are the bonus programs and stock equity programs that many companies offer to software technical employees and to managers. For example, the stock equity program at Microsoft has become famous for creating more millionaires than any similar program in U.S. industry.

Because small startup software companies have been creating new jobs while larger corporations such as Compaq and Computer Associates have been growing slowly or sometimes declining in overall personnel, there are some anomalies in software compensation levels. Small startup companies often have lower than average salaries, but offer equity as an inducement to key employees. Should these small startup companies prosper and go public, the value of the stock may be worth millions. If the companies fail, as many do, the stock may have no value at all.

Even more complex and difficult to analyze are the components of the *burden rate* or the overhead costs added to basic compensation to determine software billing rates. All companies apply some kind of burden rate to apportion the costs of taxes, medical benefits, rent, and other services across operating units. The components of the burden rate are highly variable. Expressed as a percentage of average staff compensation levels, the burden rates can run from less than 30% for small companies in rural locations to more than 300% for major defense contractors. Although software compensation levels are usually readily available, the inner structure of burden rates is extremely difficult to ascertain and indeed may be viewed as proprietary by the companies that commission the benchmark study. Even when companies such as SPR are commissioned to perform benchmark studies, we may be given the overall percentage that the client uses for burden or overhead purposes, but not the specifics. For example, we are usually not given the specific amounts set aside for depreciation, taxes, utility payments, medical and dental insurance, and so forth.

There are no industry standards for the components of burden and overhead rates, although there are some common practices such as including medical benefits, taxes, and office space costs. As a result of the lack of common overhead structures, companies of the same size and in the same industry can have overhead rates that vary from 50% to more than 250% of nominal average salaries.

To illustrate some of the variability of corporate burden rates, consider the variations in Table 3.8. This table expresses the percentages of average salaries for various overhead purposes. Table 3.8 depicts a large company with a nominal software staff totaling near 1,000 personnel, and a small company with a nominal software staff of ten personnel.

Table 3.8   Generic Components of Burden or Overhead Costs

Component	Large Company		Small Company	
	Cost	Percent	Cost	Percent
Average annual salary	$65,000	100.00	$55,000	100.00
Personnel burden				
Payroll taxes	$6,500	10.00	$5,500	10.00
Bonus	$6,500	10.00	$0	0.00
Benefits	$6,500	10.00	$2,750	5.00
Profit sharing	$6,500	10.00	$0	0.00
Subtotal	*$26,000*	*40.00*	*$8,250*	*15.00*
Office burden				
Office rent	$13,000	20.00	$5,500	10.00
Property taxes	$3,250	5.00	$1,100	2.00
Office supplies	$2,600	4.00	$1,100	2.00
Janitorial service	$1,300	2.00	$1,100	2.00
Utilities	$1,300	2.00	$1,100	2.00
Subtotal	*$21,450*	*33.00*	*$9,900*	*18.00*
Corporate burden				
Information systems	$6,500	10.00	$0	0.00
Finance	$6,500	10.00	$0	0.00
Human resources	$5,200	8.00	$0	0.00
Legal	$3,900	6.00	$0	0.00
Subtotal	*$22,100*	*34.00*	*$0*	*0.00*
Total burden	$69,550	107.00	$18,150	33.00

Note two significant differences in the overhead structures of the small and large companies. First, the larger company uses higher percentages for some of the cost elements. Second, the larger company has more cost elements, such as a bonus structure and profit sharing, that are not used by the smaller company. The net results of these two differences can lead to very large overall differences.

For benchmarking of software costs, the large variability in burden rates is a very complex issue. Incidentally, thus far only overhead structures in the United States have been discussed. If the benchmarks are between European and U.S. companies, the situation is even more complex. The social costs of European companies are often greater than U.S. companies. Thus, comparisons between countries such as Switzerland, Sweden, or Belgium and the United States must deal with some significant differences in overhead structures. Conversely, the overhead structures of countries such as India and Pakistan may be much less than the United States or Western Europe.

As you can see, the overhead costs for the large corporation are much higher than for the small corporation. Some companies include many more cost elements than those illustrated, or use larger percentages. Therefore, overhead structures remain one of the top sources of uncertainty in large-scale benchmark studies.

The net result is that successful software cost benchmarks need to include data on SIC codes, geographic locations, type of industry, company size, the occupational groups included, and the overhead rates. The following are examples of the kinds of information that should be included with benchmark data reports. This illustrative example is for a major national bank located in Manhattan:

Organization collecting benchmark	Software Productivity Research
Date of benchmark	October 15, 1999
Benchmark client (optional)	Not to be identified
SIC code	6021 (National Commercial Banks)
Country code	001 (United States)
State	NY
City (optional)	New York
Staff size	Large (1,000 software personnel in total)
Software occupations employed	15

Average monthly compensation	$8,000
Burden rate	100%
Fully burdened monthly compensation	$16,000
Number of projects benchmarked	25
Type of software benchmarked	Information systems
SPR excellence score	2.75 (slightly better than average)
SEI CMM score	1.35 (slightly better than average)
Average size of projects	750 function points
Largest project included	3,000 function points
Smallest project included	125 function points
Total size of sample	18,750 function points
Maximum productivity noted	30 function points per staff month
Minimum productivity noted	2 function points per staff month
Average productivity	12.0 function points per staff month
Standard deviation	8.17
Average productivity	13.3 work hours per function point
Standard deviation	11.5
Average schedule noted	14.5 calendar months
Longest schedule noted	24.5 calendar months
Shortest schedule noted	4.0 calendar months
Average defect potential	4.75 defects per function point
Average removal efficiency	87%
Average delivered defects	0.62 defects per function point
Cost per function point, unburdened	$666.66
Cost per function point, burdened	$1,333.33

As you can see from this small example, collecting benchmark data that can be used later for large-scale statistical analysis at the levels of industries and companies requires a great deal of rigor and many different kinds of information.

Hazards of Using Project-Level Data for Software Benchmark Studies

There are three major components of software benchmarking:

1. Collecting the data to be used for the benchmark
2. Analyzing the data statistically
3. Publishing the benchmark results

By far the most common way of expressing software benchmark results is simply to show the overall project results, without any detailed structure of which activities were performed. Unfortunately, restricting benchmark studies only to the level of projects, rather than getting down to the level of activities, tends to introduce significant errors. The most severe form of error is that productivity benchmarks that use only project-level data will usually seem to be higher than benchmarks that use activity-level data.

There are two reasons why project-level data is not sufficient for serious economic and benchmark analysis.

1. Different kinds of software projects do not perform the same sets of activities.
2. Software cost tracking systems "leak" and may omit more than 50% of all effort.

A similar and equally simplistic approach is to express productivity data in terms of "phases" such as requirements, design, coding, and testing. Phase-level data is inadequate as well because a number of significant activities span multiple phases, such as configuration control, preparation of user manuals, and project management.

My colleagues and I at SPR perform benchmark studies for many kinds of software companies and many kinds of software projects: information systems, systems software, military software, and so forth. We often *display* data at the level of projects, but our main data collection efforts and analyses are at the level of *activities*. For many years we have used a standard 25-activity "chart of accounts" for collecting software cost and resource data. There are significant variations in how many of these 25 activities are performed from project to project; however, unless we capture activity-based data, these differences in activity patterns are invisible.

Indeed, using only project-level data is a major barrier that makes cross-industry comparisons hazardous and frequently misleading. When data is collected and analyzed at the level of activities, otherwise mysterious findings can be understood. For example, the reason that military software projects have lower productivity rates than civilian projects of the same size is because military standards trigger far more activities (and much larger deliverable items) than civilian projects. Table 3.9 illustrates some of the variations in activity patterns found among various kinds of software development classes.

Table 3.9   Typical Activity Patterns for Six Software Domains

Activity Performed	End User	MIS	Out-source	Com-mercial	Systems	Military
01 Requirements		X	X	X	X	X
02 Prototyping	X	X	X	X	X	X
03 Architecture		X	X	X	X	X
04 Project plans		X	X	X	X	X
05 Initial design		X	X	X	X	X
06 Detail design		X	X	X	X	X
07 Design reviews		X	X	X	X	X
08 Coding	X	X	X	X	X	X
09 Reuse acquisition	X		X	X	X	X
10 Package purchase		X	X		X	X
11 Code inspections				X	X	X
12 IV&V						X
13 Configuration management		X	X	X	X	X
14 Formal integration		X	X	X	X	X
15 User documentation	X	X	X	X	X	X
16 Unit testing	X	X	X	X	X	X

Activity Performed	End User	MIS	Out- source	Com- mercial	Systems	Military
17 Function testing		X	X	X	X	X
18 Integration testing		X	X	X	X	X
19 System testing		X	X	X	X	X
20 Field testing				X	X	X
21 Acceptance testing		X	X		X	X
22 Independent testing						X
23 Quality assurance			X	X	X	X
24 Installation/ training		X	X		X	X
25 Project manage- ment		X	X	X	X	X
Activities	5	16	20	21	22	25

One of the basic reasons why productivity rates vary from project to project, industry to industry, and country to country is because the software development activity patterns are not the same. Table 3.9 shows common patterns of development activities for six kinds of software projects: end user applications, MIS, outsource contract projects, commercial software, systems software, and military software.

If you were to compare only project-level data for MIS projects with military projects, the MIS projects would average approximately twice the productivity of military projects. This fact is well known. However, only activity-based data can reveal *why* the rates vary. As can be seen from Table 3.9, MIS projects average only 16 software development activities whereas military projects perform all 25. Even activity-level data is not quite enough to explain all variations. Another reason why military projects have low productivity is that military software projects produce paper documents that average more than three times the volume of civilian projects of the same size.

The purpose of benchmark studies is to show not only the variations between software projects, but also to help clients understand why these variations occur. To meet this criteria of explaining why variations occur, it is necessary to get down below the level of projects and deal with specific activity patterns and deliverable volumes.

Hazards of Mailed Surveys for Software Benchmark Studies

A very common way of collecting benchmark data is to use survey forms and questionnaires that are mailed to various respondents, or sent via e-mail or the Internet. The usage of mailed questionnaires is hazardous because of the problems already discussed, or variances in activity patterns and leakage from standard cost tracking systems.

Both SPR and the SEI have found that on-site interviews of project managers and technical personnel is the most effective way to collect and validate software assessment and benchmark data, although it is certainly not the least expensive way. There are several related problems and limitations associated with the usage of mailed and networked survey instruments:

- Mailed surveys must be short (less than 15 minutes to complete) and hence are incomplete.
- Mailed surveys cannot reach the level of activity-based cost and resource data.
- Mailed surveys are difficult to validate and may have erroneous data reported.
- Mailed surveys may be misinterpreted by different respondents.
- Mailed surveys may be thrown away by more than 75% of those receiving them.

The full set of information necessary to explore software productivity and quality in a serious manner is roughly equivalent in volume to the information collected as part of a complete annual medical examination. Mail surveys are simply not complete enough and not thorough enough to be used for detailed economic analysis of software projects. This is not to say that mailed surveys are totally worthless. Indeed, for certain kinds of information such as user satisfaction surveys or statistical marketing studies of how many people use certain tools, mailed surveys can be very useful. Unfortunately, mailed surveys are not appropriate for full-scale assessment and benchmark studies.

A typical SPR assessment and benchmark analysis for a single software project will involve interviews with project team members that usually run from two to four hours in duration and may sometimes run even longer. During these interviews, 75 to more than 200 factors might be discussed. The specifics vary with the class, type, and size of the project being assessed. In addition, many questions by the respondents will come up and can be answered by the consultant. The live-interview method is obviously more time-consuming than mailed surveys but is also more complete, and the data is much more reliable than that amassed by mailed surveys.

SPR and the SEI agree that on-site interviews are desirable for achieving a detailed understanding of software development practices. In fact, all of the more serious assessment and benchmark methodologies depend on on-site interviews and analysis rather than mailed or e-mailed data: Baldrige Awards, ISO 9000–9004 certification, SEI assessments, SPICE assessments, SPR assessments, TickIt assessments, and so forth. Mailed surveys are useful for simple studies but far from adequate for detailed process improvement analysis.

Moving to Activity-Based Software Benchmark Data

The advent of function point metrics in the late 1970s opened up a new way of dealing with software economic research that allowed exploration of noncoding activities such as requirements, plans, specifications, user manuals, and change requests that could not be explored properly using LOC metrics. Indeed, it is now known that for some software projects such as large defense systems, the costs associated with paper document production are twice as expensive as the costs of the code itself.

The ability to explore the full set of activities associated with software production has led to the concept of activity-based cost studies of software projects. With activity-based costing, each one of a selected set of activities or tasks is measured individually to ascertain the number of work hours associated with it, as well as the sizes of various deliverable items. Many readers will no doubt realize that the concepts of activity-based costing are also used in several other domains, including automobile repair shops and the rate calculations that insurance companies use for common medical and dental procedures.

The concept of activity-based costing is a step in the direction of greater precision for dealing with software projects. Rather than considering the project only in its entirety, each activity is shown in terms of the normal amount of effort needed to perform it, and then the burdened and unburdened cost structures.

In our example, the standard set of 25 activities used by SPR during software cost studies serves as the base. The cost structures are based on the assumptions of an "average" monthly compensation for software personnel of $5,000 and an "average" burden rate of 100%. Note that any or all of these values should be replaced by specific values derived from your own company's data.

Although my colleagues and I use 25 activities for software cost and resource data collection, that does not imply that every project performs all 25 activities. For example, small end user applications might only perform one of the 25, and that would be "coding."

In general, the information system community performs between eight and 16 activities out of the 25 in the SPR activity set. The systems and real-time software domain performs between 15 and 20 of the activities. The military software domain is the only group that routinely performs all 25 of the activities listed. In fact, two of the activities (IV&V and independent testing) are almost never performed on civilian software projects but are routine in the military world.

To use Table 3.10, you need to know at least the approximate function point size of the application in question. Then select the set of activities that you believe will be performed for the application. After that you can add up the work hours per function point for each activity. You can do the same thing with costs, of course, but you should replace the assumed costs of $5,000 per staff month and the 100% burden rate with the appropriate values from your own company or organization.

The information shown in Table 3.10 illustrates the basic concept of activity-based costing. However, when used for international project benchmarking, additional activities may be needed, and some of the activities in the table may not be used at all. For example, international software projects need to collect cost and resource information on the following topics:

- Translation of documentation into various national languages
- Certification to ISO 9000–9004 standard, if required
- Possible extra costs for achieving Euro currency compliance
- Possible extra costs for achieving Y2K compliance

The important point is that for software to be amenable to serious economic study, methods such as project-based data and phase-based data must give way to the more rigorous methodology of activity-based data.

The use of activity-based charts of accounts for data collection and analysis does not mean that project-level data cannot be displayed or used in presentations to clients. However, to validate incoming data and to ensure that major elements such as unpaid overtime are not omitted, only activity-based information is sufficient. Also, for sophisticated regression analysis studies or understanding topics such as why military software productivity rates are lower than information systems, it is necessary to know the variations in activity patterns because these contribute to the overall differences in a significant way.

Once activity-based costing is started, it can be extended to include many other activities in a similar fashion. For example, the set of activities shown in Table 3.10 is common for development projects. If you are concerned with maintenance of aging legacy applications, with porting software from one platform to another, or with bringing out a new release of a commercial software package then you need to deal with other activities outside of those shown in Table 3.10.

Note that the productivity rates and work hours per function point are based on U.S. function points as defined by IFPUG Version 4.1. If you use British Mark II function points, feature points, the older IFPUG Version 3 function points, Boeing 3D function points, DeMarco function points, Cosmic function points, feature points, engineering function points, or some other variant, you need to make adjustments to the basic rates.

You should also be aware that over and above the cost variances that have already been discussed, there are also variances in the real productivity rates. These variances are based on many factors, including staff experience, tools used, programming languages, and the amount of unpaid overtime that might be part of the project but not tracked by resource tracking systems.

Activity-based cost analysis can also be used for estimating purposes. What is starting to occur in the software industry is the development of sets of activity *templates* based on specific companies or industries, on methodologies such as ISO 9000, and on other criteria such as the five levels of SEI's CMM. It can be predicted that activity-based cost studies will be increasing in number and rigor as we enter the twenty-first century.

Software Quality Benchmarks

Software quality is an issue of global concern. Achieving high levels of software quality is on the critical path to achieving short times to market and to achieving excellent market shares as well. The relationship between quality and productivity is well supported by empirical data, even if the topic is not well understood by the industry as a whole. As far back as the early 1970s, IBM discovered that software projects with the lowest levels of defects had the shortest development schedules and the highest development productivity. The reason for this situation

Table 3.10 Outsource Software Activities and Rates for 10,000 Function Points

Parameter	Value
Application size	10,000 function points
Application size	1,000,000 LOC
Source language	COBOL
Work hours per month	132
Monthly Compensation	$14,000

Activity Performed	Assignment Scope, function points	Production Rate, function points	Staff	Effort, Months	Schedule, Months	Cost	Percent
01 Requirements	500	85	20	118	5.88	$1,647,059	5.33
02 Prototyping	2,000	125	5	80	16.00	$1,120,000	3.63
03 Architecture	2,500	300	4	33	8.33	$466,667	1.51
04 Initial design	250	75	40	133	3.33	$1,866,667	6.05
05 Detail design	175	60	57	167	2.92	$2,333,333	7.56
06 Design reviews	175	125	57	80	1.40	$1,120,000	3.63
07 Coding	115	25	87	400	4.60	$5,600,000	18.14
08 Reuse acquisition	2,000	1,000	5	10	2.00	$140,000	0.45
09 Code inspections	115	100	87	100	1.15	$1,400,000	4.53

Activity Performed	Assignment Scope, function points	Production Rate, function points	Staff	Effort, Months	Schedule, Months	Cost	Percent
10 Configuraton management	1,500	500	7	20	3.00	$280,000	0.91
11 Formal integration	2,000	500	5	20	4.00	$280,000	0.91
12 Documen-tation	1,000	75	10	133	13.33	$1,866,667	6.05
13 Unit testing	125	45	80	222	2.78	$3,111,111	10.08
14 Function testing	150	60	67	167	2.50	$2,333,333	7.56
15 Integration testing	150	75	67	133	2.00	$1,866,667	6.05
16 System testing	200	100	50	100	2.00	$1,400,000	4.53
17 Acceptance testing	300	150	33	67	2.00	$933,333	3.02
18 Project management	1,200	45	8	222	26.67	$3,111,111	10.08
Totals/averages	166[1]	4.53[1]	60[1]	2,205[2]	36.57[1]	$30,875,948[2]	100.00[2]

Cost per function point, $3,088; Cost per LOC, $29.41
[1] Average
[2] Total

is because software defect removal is actually the most expensive and time-consuming form of work for software. Projects that were successful in preventing defects and removing them efficiently via inspections sailed through testing with few delays. By contrast, projects with marginal quality tended to enter testing early, but could not exit testing on schedule due to the large numbers of defects encountered.

One of the many serious problems with LOC metrics is the difficulty in measuring or exploring defects in noncode deliverables such as requirements and specifications. When measured carefully, noncode defects amount to more than half of all bugs or errors reported for many applications. Here, too, function point metrics have illuminated data that was previously invisible.

Based on a study published in *Applied Software Measurement* (Jones 1996), the average number of software errors in the United States is approximately five per function point. Note that software defects are found not only in code, but originate in all of the major software deliverables, in the approximate quantities presented on Table 3.11.

These numbers represent the total numbers of defects that are found and measured from early software requirements throughout the remainder of the life cycle of the software. The defects are discovered via requirement reviews, design reviews, code inspections, all forms of testing, and user-reported problem reports.

U.S. averages using function points lend themselves to graphical representation. Figure 3.5 is a graph that shows two critical software quality factors as the two axes: defect potentials and defect removal efficiency levels. Figure 3.5 also identifies three zones of significance.

Table 3.11   U.S. Averages in Terms of Defects per Function Point

Defect Origins	Defects per Function Point
Requirements	1.00
Design	1.25
Coding	1.75
Document	0.60
Bad fixes	0.40
Total	5.00

1. The central zone of average performance, where most companies can be found
2. The zone of best-in-class performance, where top companies can be found
3. The zone of professional malpractice, where companies that seem to know nothing about quality can be found.

It is very revealing to overlay a sample of an enterprise's software projects on this graph. Note that the Defects per Function Point axis refers to the total defect potential, which includes errors in requirements, specifications, source code, user manuals, and bad fixes. Complementing the function point metric are measurements of defect removal efficiency, or the percentages of software defects removed prior to delivery of the software to clients.

The U.S. average for defect removal efficiency, unfortunately, is currently only about 85%, although top-ranked projects in leading companies such as AT&T, IBM, Motorola, Raytheon, and Hewlett-Packard achieve defect removal efficiency levels well in excess of 99% on their best projects.

All software defects are not equally easy to remove. Requirements errors, design problems, and bad fixes tend to be the most difficult. Thus, on the day

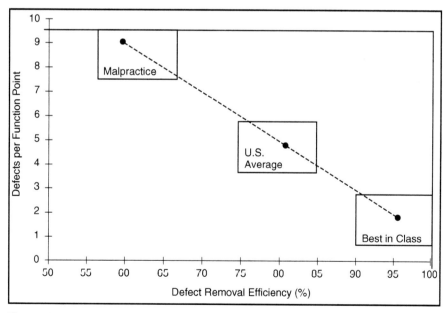

Figure 3.5   U.S. software quality performance ranges

when software is actually put into production, the average quantity of latent errors or defects still present tends to be approximately 0.75 per function point. Table 3.12 provides an overview of defect removal efficiency.

Note that at the time of delivery, defects originating in requirements and design tend to far outnumber coding defects. Data such as this can be used to improve the upstream defect prevention and defect removal processes of software development.

The best results in terms of defect removal are always achieved on projects that utilize formal pretest inspections of design, code, and other major deliverables, such as user manuals and even test cases.

The SPR approach to collecting quantitative data using function points has led to the creation of a table that shows quantitatively how the five levels of the CMM can affect software quality. Some of the data in Table 3.13 is derived from a study SPR was commissioned to perform by the U.S. Air Force in 1994.

As you can see, the combination of function point metrics and defect removal efficiency metrics are beginning to clarify quality topics that have long been ambiguous and intangible.

It is obvious that no single defect removal operation is adequate by itself. This explains why best-in-class quality results can only be achieved from synergistic combinations of defect prevention, reviews or inspections, and various kinds of test activities.

Table 3.12   U.S. Averages for Defect Removal Efficiency

Defect Origins	Defect Potentials	Removal Efficiency, %	Delivered Defects
Requirements	1.00	77	0.23
Design	1.25	85	0.19
Coding	1.75	95	0.09
Document	0.60	80	0.12
Bad fixes	0.40	70	0.12
Total	5.00	85	0.75

Data expressed in terms of defects per function point.

Table 3.13   Defect Potentials and Removal for the SEI CMM Levels

SEI CMM Level	Defect Potentials	Removal Efficiency, %	Delivered Defects
1	5.00	85	0.75
2	4.00	89	0.44
3	3.00	91	0.27
4	2.00	93	0.14
5	1.00	95	0.05

International data on defect removal efficiency using function point metrics is only just starting to become available. From preliminary data, countries such as Japan, Norway, Germany, Sweden, and Canada appear to be at or slightly better than U.S. norms.

Software Baselines

Software baselines are normally used as starting points when beginning process improvement programs. Another very common use of baselines is when outsource agreements include a contractual obligation for the vendor to improve quality or productivity over measured time intervals.

Baselines are technically very challenging and difficult to create with acceptable accuracy. The reason for this is because most companies do not routinely collect accurate quality and productivity data. In fact, many companies don't even collect accurate cost data on how much they spend on software projects. Unless internal software projects are charged out to the business units that commission them, accuracy in cost collection is very rare in the corporate world, and rare in government agencies as well. As a result, many baselines are so imperfect and inaccurate that they can eventually cause litigation between outsource vendors and their clients. The reason is that the client's initial baseline may accidentally exaggerate productivity levels, and hence give the outsource vendor artificially high starting points. If an outsource contract calls for something like a 15% annual improvement in productivity or quality levels compared with the starting baseline, the outsource vendor needs to have the baseline be extremely accurate.

Because most corporate software cost and resource data omits more than 35% of total effort, companies often think their productivity levels are higher than they really are simply because their cost tracking systems "leak" by such large amounts. Table 3.14 illustrates the typical leakage observed in corporate software effort tracking. This table uses the standard 25-activity chart of accounts used by SPR for benchmark and baseline studies.

In addition to the fact that the effort and costs for many activities are incomplete, there are several other significant cost elements that are seldom recorded at all. One of the most important missing pieces of information is the amount of unpaid overtime applied to software projects. Unpaid overtime is a very important factor for international software comparisons. For software projects in countries such as Japan, sometimes as much as 20% of the total effort is in the form of unpaid overtime. (This volume of unpaid overtime can also be found in some U.S. companies with intense work ethics, such as Microsoft and EDS.) Countries such as Canada and Germany have much lower amounts of unpaid overtime applied to software projects, on average. For example, in Germany, working on weekends is so uncommon that some companies turn off the electricity and shut down their computer centers on weekends.

Another missing piece of information is the work that software clients themselves perform during development cycles. For many (but not all) software projects, the clients are direct technical participants for activities such as requirements analysis, prototyping, design reviews, user documentation creation, and certain forms of testing such as acceptance testing. Indeed, here too almost 20% of a project's total effort can be performed by users who seldom record their time as part of standard cost tracking information.

Because leakage is so common, initial baselines are often very unrealistic. For example, if a software organization's actual productivity is 5.0 function points per staff month but their cost tracking system only captures low-level design, coding, and testing costs, their apparent productivity might look like 15.0 function points per staff month.

Many software cost tracking systems omit requirements, high-level design, project management, creation of user manuals and documents, and the work of specialists in areas such as software quality assurance, database administration, change control, and administrative support, such as secretaries and program librarians. Sometimes the activities omitted actually accumulate more costs than the activities that are tracked. The bottom line is that baselines are very challenging to create well and accurately. If they are going to serve a purpose in contracts between outsource vendors and clients without leading to litigation, then baselines need to be accurate and reliable.

Table 3.14   Missing Resource and Cost Data from Software Cost Tracking Systems

Activity Performed	Completeness of Historical Data
01 Requirements	Missing or incomplete
02 Prototyping	Missing or incomplete
03 Architecture	Incomplete
04 Project planning	Incomplete
05 Initial analysis and design	Incomplete
06 Detail design	Incomplete
07 Design reviews	Missing or incomplete
08 Coding	Complete
09 Reusable code acquisition	Missing or incomplete
10 Purchased package acquisition	Missing or incomplete
11 Code inspections	Missing or incomplete
12 IV&V	Complete
13 Configuration management	Missing or incomplete
14 Integration	Missing or incomplete
15 User documentation	Missing or incomplete
16 Unit testing	Incomplete
17 Function testing	Incomplete
18 Integration testing	Incomplete
19 System testing	Incomplete
20 Field testing	Incomplete
21 Acceptance testing	Missing or incomplete
22 Independent testing	Complete
23 Quality assurance	Missing or incomplete
24 Installation and training	Missing or incomplete
25 Project management	Missing or incomplete
26 Total project resources, costs	Incomplete

Readings and References on Software Benchmarks and Baselines

Many of the most interesting benchmark and baseline studies are proprietary reports that are not published in the general software literature. At least half of the Fortune 500 companies have commissioned benchmark studies of various kinds. However, the data from these studies is only available to the executives and technical personnel of the companies themselves.

The external literature on software benchmarks is often created by the consulting companies that perform benchmarks for their clients, such as the David's Group, Gartner Group, Howard Rubin Associates, SPR, Meta group, and the Standish Group. These companies may publish "sanitized" data that summarizes the results from a number of clients.

Because benchmark data is often used in designing and calibrating software cost-estimating tools, most of the vendors of commercial estimating tools such as SPR or QSM have also published books and articles on benchmarks and data analysis.

IFPUG is attempting to create a global database of software benchmarks using function point metrics. As this book is written, the volume of IFPUG data consists of several hundred projects. However, IFPUG plans to add projects continuously.

The relevant literature on benchmarks and baselines includes materials on metrics, on the application of metrics, and on studies that use metrics for comparative purposes.

Abran, A. and P. N. Robillard. "Function Point Analysis. An Empirical Study of Its Measurement Processes." *IEEE Transactions on Software Engineering* 1996; 22(12): 895–909.

Albrecht, Allan. "Measuring Application Development Productivity." Presented at the Proceedings of the Joint Share/Guide/IBM Application Development Symposium. Monterey, April, 1979 (10 pages)

———. *AD/M Productivity Measurement and Estimate Validation*. Purchase, NY: IBM Corporation, May 1984.

Austin, Robert D. *Measuring and Managing Performance in Organizations*. New York: Dorset House Publishing, 1996. (ISBN 0-932633-36-6, 216 pages)

Boehm, Barry. *Software Engineering Economics*. Englewood Cliffs, NJ: Prentice Hall, 1981. (ISBN 0-13-82212-7, 900 pages)

Bogan, Christopher E., and Michael J. English. *Benchmarking for Best Practices.* New York: McGraw Hill, 1994. (ISBN 0-07-006375-3, 312 pages)

Brooks, Frederick P. *The Mythical Man-Month.* Reading, MA: Addison Wesley Longman, 1995. (ISBN 0-201-00650-2, 295 pages)

Chidamber, S. R., and C. F. Kemerer. "A Metrics Suite for Object Oriented Design." *IEEE Transactions on Software Engineering* 1994; 20: 476–493.

Chidamber, S. R., D. P. Darcy, and C. F. Kemerer. "Managerial Use of Object Oriented Software Metrics." Working paper no. 750. Pittsburgh, PA: Joseph M. Katz Graduate School of Business, University of Pittsburgh, November 1996. (26 pages)

Conte, S. D., H. E. Dunsmore, and V. Y. Shen. *Software Engineering Models and Metrics.* Menlo Park, CA: The Benjamin Cummings Publishing Company, 1986. (ISBN 0-8053-2162-4, 396 pages)

DeMarco, Tom. *Why Does Software Cost So Much?* New York: Dorset House Publishing, 1995. (ISBN 0-932633-34-X, 237 pages)

———. *The Deadline.* New York: Dorset House Publishing, 1997. (ISBN 0-932633-39-0)

DeMarco, Tom, and Tim Lister. *Peopleware.* New York: Dorset House Publishing, 1987. (ISBN 0-932633-05-6, 188 pages)

Dreger, J. Brian. *Function Point Analysis.* Englewood Cliffs, NJ: Prentice Hall, 1989. (ISBN 0-13-332321-8, 185 pages)

Fenton, Norman, and Shari Lawrence Pfleeger. *Software Metrics: A Rigorous and Practical Approach.* 2nd ed. Los Alamitos, CA: IEEE Computer Society Press, 1997. (ISBN 0-534-95600-0, 416 pages)

Fetcke, Thomas, Alain Abran, and Tho-Hau Nguyen. *Mapping the OO-Jacobsen Approach into Function Point Analysis.* Montreal: Université du Quebec à Montreal, Software Engineering Management Research Laboratory, 1997. (11 pages)

Galea, R. B. *The Boeing Company: 3D Function Point Extensions.* V2.0, release 1.0. Seattle, WA: Boeing Information Support Services, June 1995.

Garmus, David, and David Herron. *Measuring the Software Process: A Practical Guide to Functional Measurement.* Englewood Cliffs, NJ: Prentice Hall, 1995. (ISBN 0-13-349002-5)

Grady, Robert B. *Practical Software Metrics for Project Management and Process Improvement.* Englewood Cliffs, NJ: Prentice Hall, 1992. (ISBN 0-13-720384-5, 270 pages)

————. *Successful Software Process Improvement.* Upper Saddle River, NJ: Prentice Hall, 1997. (ISBN 0-13-626623-1, 314 pages)

Grady, Robert B., and Deborah L. Caswell. *Software Metrics: Establishing a Company-Wide Program.* Englewood Cliffs, NJ: Prentice Hall, 1987. (ISBN 0-13-821844-7, 288 pages)

Howard, Alan, ed. *Software Metrics and Project Management Tools.* Phoenix, AZ: Applied Computer Research, 1997. (30 pages)

IFPUG. *IFPUG Counting Practices Manual.* Release 3. Westerville, OH: International Function Point Users Group, April 1990. (73 pages)

————. *IFPUG Counting Practices Manual.* Release 4. Westerville, OH: International Function Point Users Group, April 1995. (83 pages)

————. *IFPUG Counting Practices Manual.* Release 4.1. Westerville, OH: International Function Point Users Group, 1999. (95 pages)

Janulaitis, Victor M. *Information Systems, Communication and Data Processing Metrics HandiGuide.* Santa Monica, CA: Positive Support Review, 1993.

Jones, Capers. "Measuring Programming Quality and Productivity." *IBM Systems Journal* 1978; 17(1): 39–63.

————. *Programming Productivity: Issues for the Eighties.* Los Alamitos, CA: IEEE Computer Society Press, 1st ed., 1981; 2nd ed., 1986. (ISBN 0-8186-0681-9, IEEE Computer Society Catalog 681, 489 pages)

————. *Programming Productivity.* New York: McGraw Hill, 1986. (ISBN 0-07-032811-0, 280 pages)

————. *A Ten-Year Retrospective of the ITT Programming Technology Center.* Burlington, MA: Software Productivity Research, 1988.

————. *Assessment and Control of Software Risks.* Englewood Cliffs, NJ: Prentice Hall, 1993. (ISBN 0-13-741406-4, 711 pages)

————. *Critical Problems in Software Measurement.* Carlsbad, CA: Information Systems Management Group, 1993. (ISBN 1-56909-000-9, 195 pages)

————. *Software Productivity and Quality Today: The Worldwide Perspective.* Carlsbad, CA: Information Systems Management Group, 1993. (ISBN 156909-001-7, 200 pages)

————. *New Directions in Software Management.* Carlsbad, CA: Information Systems Management Group, 1994. (ISBN 1-56909-009-2, 150 pages)

————. *Patterns of Software System Failure and Success.* Boston, MA: International Thomson Computer Press, December 1995. (ISBN 1-850-32804-8, 292 pages)

————. *Applied Software Measurement.* 2nd ed. New York: McGraw Hill, 1996. (ISBN 0-07-032826-9, 618 pages)

————. *Table of Programming Languages and Levels.* Burlington, MA: Software Productivity Research, 1996. (Eight versions from 1985 through July 1996, 67 pages for Version 8)

————. *Software Quality: Analysis and Guidelines for Success.* Boston, MA: International Thomson Computer Press, 1997. (ISBN 1-85032-876-6, 492 pages)

————. *The Economics of Object-Oriented Software.* SPR technical report. Burlington, MA: Software Productivity Research, April 1997. (22 pages)

————. *Estimating Software Costs.* New York: McGraw Hill, 1998. (ISBN 0-07-9130941, 725 pages)

————. "Sizing Up Software." *Scientific American* 1998; 279(6): 104–111.

————. *The Year 2000 Software Problem: Quantifying the Costs and Assessing the Consequences.* Reading, MA: Addison Wesley, 1998. (ISBN 0-201-30964-5, 303 pages)

Kan, Stephen H. *Metrics and Models in Software Quality Engineering.* Reading, MA: Addison Wesley Longman, 1994. (ISBN 0-201-63339-6, 344 pages)

Kemerer, C. F. "Reliability of Function Point Measurement: A Field Experiment." *Communications of the ACM* 1993; 36: 85–97.

Keys, Jessica. *Software Engineering Productivity Handbook.* New York: McGraw Hill, 1993. (ISBN 0-07-911366-4, 651 pages)

Marciniak, John J., ed. *Encyclopedia of Software Engineering.* New York: John Wiley & Sons, 1994. (ISBN 0-471-54002, in two volumes)

McCabe, Thomas J. "A Complexity Measure." *IEEE Transactions on Software Engineering* 1976; 308–320.

Melton, Austin. *Software Measurement.* London: Chapman & Hall, 1995. (ISBN 0412551802)

Mertes, Karen R. *Calibration of the CHECKPOINT Model to the Space and Missile Systems Center (SMC) Software Database (SWDB).* Thesis AFIT/GCA/LAS/96S-11. Wright Patterson AFB, OH: Air Force Institute of Technology, September 1996. (119 pages)

Mills, Harlan. *Software Productivity.* New York: Dorset House Publishing, 1988. (ISBN 0-932633-10-2, 288 pages)

Muller, Monika, and Alain Abram, eds. *Metrics in Software Evolution.* Munich: R. Oldenbourg Vertag GmbH, 1995. (ISBN 3-486-23589-3)

Multiple authors. *Rethinking the Software Process*. CD-ROM. Lawrence, KS: Miller Freeman, 1996. (This is a new CD-ROM book collection produced jointly by the book publisher Prentice Hall and the journal publisher Miller Freeman. This CD-ROM disk contains the full text and illustrations of five Prentice Hall books: *Assessment and Control of Software Risks* by Capers Jones, *Controlling Software Projects* by Tom DeMarco, *Function Point Analysis* by Brian Dreger, *Measures for Excellence* by Larry Putnam and Ware Myers, and *Object-Oriented Software Metrics* by Mark Lorenz and Jeff Kidd.)

Oman, Paul, and Shari Lawrence Pfleeger, eds. *Applying Software Metrics*. Los Alamitos, CA: IEEE Computer Society Press, 1996. (ISBN 0-8186-7645-0, 336 pages)

Park, Robert E. "Software Size Measurement: A Framework for Counting Source Statements." Technical Report CMU/SEI 92-TR-020, Pittsburgh, PA: Software Engineering Institute, June 1992.

Perlis, Alan J., Frederick G. Sayward, and Mary Shaw, eds. *Software Metrics*. Cambridge, MA: MIT Press, 1981. (ISBN 0-262-16083-8, 404 pages)

Perry, William E. *Data Processing Budgets: How to Develop and Use Budgets Effectively*. Englewood Cliffs, NJ: Prentice Hall, 1985. (ISBN 0-13-196874-2, 224 pages)

Putnam, Lawrence H. *Measures for Excellence: Reliable Software On Time, Within Budget*. Englewood Cliffs, NJ: Prentice Hall, 1992. (ISBN 0-13-567694-0, 336 pages)

Putnam, Lawrence H., and Ware Myers. *Industrial Strength Software: Effective Management Using Measurement*. Los Alamitos, CA: IEEE Computer Society Press, 1997. (ISBN 0-8186-7532-2, 320 pages)

Roetzheim, William J., and Reyna A. Beasley. *Software Project Cost & Schedule Estimating*. Upper Saddle River, NJ: Prentice Hall, 1998. (ISBN 0-13-682089-1)

Rubin, Howard. *Software Benchmark Studies for 1998*. Pound Ridge, NY: Howard Rubin Associates, 1998.

Shepperd, M. "A Critique of Cyclomatic Complexity as a Software Metric." *Software Engineering Journal* 1988;3:30–36.

Software Productivity Consortium. *The Software Measurement Guidebook*. Boston, MA: International Thomson Computer Press, 1995. (ISBN 1-850-32195-7, 308 pages)

Software Productivity Research. *Quality and Productivity of the SEI CMM*. Burlington, MA: Software Productivity Research, 1994.

St-Pierre, Denis, Marcela Maya, Alain Abran, and Jean-Marc Desharnais. *Full Function Points: Function Point Extensions for Real-Time Software, Concepts and Definitions*. TR 1997-03. Quebec: University of Quebec, Software Engineering Laboratory in Applied Metrics, March 1997. (18 pages)

Strassmann, Paul. *The Politics of Information Management: Policy Guidelines*. New Canaan, CT: The Information Economics Press, 1995. (ISBN 0-9620413-4-3, 523 pages)

————. *The Squandered Computer*. New Canaan, CT: The Information Economics Press, 1997. (ISBN 0-9620413-1-9, 426 pages)

Symons, Charles R. *Software Sizing and Estimating: Mk II FPA (Function Point Analysis)*. Chichester, UK: John Wiley & Sons, 1991. (ISBN 0 471-92985-9, 200 pages)

Weinberg, Gerald. *Quality Software Management. Vol. 2, First-Order Measurement*. New York: Dorset House Publishing, 1993. (ISBN 0-932633-24-2, 360 pages)

Whitmire, S. A. "3-D Function Points: Scientific and Real-Time Extensions to Function Points." Presented at the Proceedings of the 1992 Pacific Northwest Software Quality Conference. June 1, 1992.

Zuse, Horst. *Software Complexity: Measures and Methods*. Berlin: Walter de Gruyter, 1990. (ISBN 3-11-012226-X, 603 pages)

————. *A Framework of Software Measurement*. Berlin: Walter de Gruyter, 1997. (ISBN 3-110-155877)

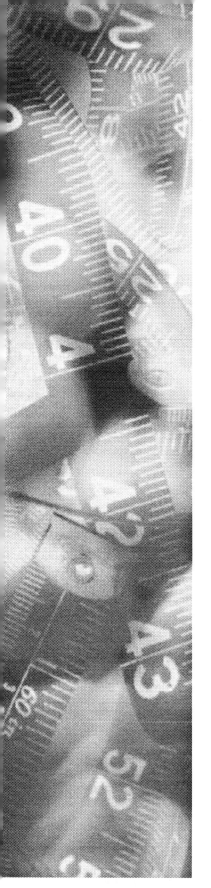

CHAPTER FOUR

Thirty-six Key Factors for Software Assessment and Benchmark Studies

In total, software projects are influenced by as many as 250 different factors that can affect schedule, cost, quality, and user satisfaction. (The Appendix lists many of these factors.) Individual projects are not affected by all 250 factors, but are usually affected by ten to 20 major issues. Some of the factors are associated with the project, some of the factors are technical, and others are cultural. However, in this book we focus on six sets of factors, each with six topics. These 36 items of data are important enough that they should be captured during all assessment and benchmark studies.

One of the current problems in the software industry is the fact that assessments and benchmarks are all performed by different consulting companies, and they all capture different kinds of information. Thus, it is very difficult to perform large-scale studies that consolidate data from multiple companies. For example, if the data collected by SPR, Howard Rubin Associates, and QSM could be consolidated, then more than 30,000 projects from more than 1,500 companies and government agencies could be included. However, because these three companies are competitors that collect different factors, such consolidation would not be easy, even if the organizations agreed to do it.

The 36 factors discussed in this chapter represent a nucleus of key data elements that should be included in all assessment and benchmark studies intended to be published in the general literature. There are six general categories of factors that should be collected, and each category contains six data types. The six major categories include

1. Classification factors
2. Project-specific factors
3. Technology factors
4. Sociological factors
5. Ergonomic factors
6. International factors

Thirty of the 36 factors occur for any software project within any country. The last six factors are significant for international projects that involve more than a single country, or for comparisons of productivity and costs between different countries.

The 36 factors are not all of the factors that influence the outcomes of software projects, but they are very important and should be included in all software assessment, baseline, and benchmark data collections. Some international benchmarking tools, such as SPR's CHECKPOINT (CHECKMARK in Japan and the United Kingdom) can capture all 36 factors, as can SPR's KnowledgePlan software cost-estimating tool.

Many of the commercial software cost-estimating tools such as COCOMO II, SLIM, PRICE-S, SEER, and SoftCost contain adjustments that are based on some of these 36 factors. The reason for this is that these are the key factors that actually determine the results of software projects in real life.

The following sections present the 36 factors that illustrate the kinds of things that can influence whether software projects will be successful or unsuccessful.

Software Classification Factors

Because quality and productivity results can vary widely based on the kind of software being studied, it is critical to record the specific nature of the software project. Six major forms of software include

1. Systems software (used to control physical devices)
2. Commercial software (leased or marketed to external clients)
3. Information systems software (software for business information)
4. Outsourced software (software developed under contract)
5. Military software (software adhering to DoD standards)
6. End user software (private software for personal use)

This taxonomy of major software types has been used for more than ten years for statistical purposes and has proved to be very useful. Each of these types has its own characteristic set of preferred tools and methods, unique activity patterns, and also tends to have different ranges for productivity and quality.

Project-Specific Factors

The characteristics of individual projects need to be recorded to ensure that comparisons are made between projects that have similar attributes. It would be folly to compare the productivity levels of small projects of 10 function points against major systems of 100,000 function points. Therefore, project characteristics must be recorded with care and precision:

1. Size of the application (function points, LOC, classes/methods, and so on)
2. Complexity of the application (cyclomatic, essential, and so on)
3. Constraints of the application (performance, schedule, security, and so on)
4. Nature of the project (enhancement, new, maintenance)
5. Class and type of the application (internal, external, civilian, military, and so on)
6. Scope of the application (program, system, major system, and so on)

Although it is obvious that these six factors influence software outcomes, factor 3 (constraints) is not often discussed in the software literature. The term *constraint* means that the software project is required by contract or executive decree to meet certain specific criteria. The most common constraints that we encounter are

- Fixed delivery dates
- Fixed-price contracts
- Staffing or team size limitations
- Performance or throughput constraints
- Storage or memory utilization constraints
- Reliability constraints

If any of these constraints are present, the risks of the project are increased significantly. If several or all of these constraints are present simultaneously, and the project is larger than 1,000 function points, it will be a very risky undertaking.

These six project-specific factors are used to give a very precise description of a software project for comparative purposes, and they are quite useful for comparisons during assessment and benchmark results.

Technology Factors

To determine "best practices," it is necessary to record the specific tools and methodologies utilized. This aspect of benchmarking is fairly complicated, due to the fact that new tools and methods are used at any time.

Because there are more than 1,500 software tools on the market, more than 500 programming languages in use, and at least 50 major varieties of development methodology, this aspect of benchmarking can be quite complex. The six technology factors are

1. Any formal methodology used (Merise, Jackson, Booch, Yourdon, and so on)
2. Project management and development tool suites used on the project
3. Defect prevention approaches used (JAD, Clean-room, Kaizen, QFD, total quality management, and so on)
4. Defect removal operations and tools used (design, code inspections, tests, and so on)
5. Programming languages selected and used
6. Volume of reusable materials available and used

My colleagues and I at SPR find one of the most challenging aspects of assessment and benchmark studies is to keep up with the rapid evolution of available software technologies. New tools are coming out every week, and often similar projects within the same company use very different tools and technology patterns.

Sociological Factors

Knowledge of tools, languages, and methods are not sufficient to determine best practices. Social and experience factors also need to be recorded to ensure that results are not simply because of imbalances in team experience levels, but are due to variations in the tools and methods used. Therefore, it is necessary to record the following sociological factors:

1. Experience level of the development team
2. Experience level of the project managers
3. Experience level of the clients
4. Organizational structures and specialists available for the project
5. Morale factors for the project team (overtime, stress, irrational decisions, and so on)
6. SEI or SPR capability level of development organization

As long as software is developed by human beings, sociological factors will be even more important than technology factors for software projects. Gathering information on sociological factors is a fairly sensitive issue. For example, in a number of European companies it is not permitted to ask questions about team capabilities, due either to national laws or to union regulations.

Ergonomic Factors

Although ergonomic factors are not as well understood as technology and sociological factors, they are surprisingly important for software projects. Indeed, studies such as those described by Tom DeMarco and Tim Lister in *Peopleware* (DeMarco and Lister 1987) noted that office space and noise levels impacted software productivity even more than tool suites. The six ergonomic factors are

1. Sizes of private office space available to team members
2. Interruptions and distraction levels of office space
3. Meeting space available for group activities such as inspections
4. Network and remote communications for virtual teams
5. Telecommuting support for work at home
6. Network and video conferencing facilities for client communications

As the twenty-first century begins, software development is moving toward the concept of virtual teams that communicate over the Internet rather than being housed in normal office facilities. This trend is in progress, but is likely to be the normal mode of software work within a few more years. Office ergonomics and communication methods will continue to be significant topics for software, as long as software remains a labor-intensive occupation. However, the advent of portable computers, the Internet, intranets, and groupware tools are transforming software development and maintenance in unexpected ways. Unlike the manufacture of physical products, everything connected with a software project can be transmitted electronically. This means that the physical location of the team is rapidly becoming a secondary issue.

In the near future, we may well see software projects developed by international teams located eight times zones apart. When the working day is finished in one location, the project will be moved electronically to the next location. Thus, three teams located eight time zones apart can work 24 hours a day, without any single team needing to work more than a single shift.

International development will raise some significant challenges for assessment and benchmark studies. Obviously, cost data in multiple currencies such as dollars and Euros will have to be supported. Less obviously, some countries have laws or policies that affect the kinds of data that can be collected.

International Factors

When international projects are considered, a significant new set of factors is added to the list that must be evaluated and addressed. The following are the six factors that influence the outcome of global and international software projects:

1. Local laws or union regulations that affect international software projects
2. Communication channels between clients and developers in different countries
3. Variations in compensation levels for the countries involved
4. Variations in public holidays and vacation periods in different countries
5. Variations in staff compensation levels in different countries
6. Variations in national work habits in different countries

Local practices within various countries are quite important for international studies. For example, comparing a Japanese project for which the team worked 48 hours a week versus a Canadian project for which the team worked 35 hours a week would favor the Japanese in terms of shorter schedules. However, the actual number of hours might be the same in both cases. It can be seen that recording the hours worked per week is a significant factor for international benchmark studies.

The set of international factors alone can affect productivity, schedules, and quality levels by significant amounts that can approach or exceed 50% between best-case and worst-case conditions. Therefore, it is important to understand how all of the factors that influence software projects interrelate.

A simple illustration of international ranges for one specific factor may be of interest. There are major national differences in terms of work hours per week, quantities of unpaid overtime, numbers of annual holidays, and annual vacation periods. In fact, it is very dangerous to perform international studies without taking international factors into account. Variations in work practices is a major differentiating factor for international software productivity and schedule results.

Table 4.1 makes a number of simplifying assumptions and does not deal with the specifics of sick time, lunch and coffee breaks, meetings, courses, and nonwork activities that might occur during business hours. This table is derived

Table 4.1   Number of Software Work Hours per Year in Ten Countries

Country	Work Days per Year	Work Hours per Day	Overtime per Day	Work Hours per Year	Percent of U.S. Results
Japan	260	9.00	2.5	2,990	139
China	260	9.00	1.5	2,730	127
India	245	8.50	2.0	2,573	120
Italy	230	9.00	1.0	2,300	107
United States	239	8.00	1.0	2,151	100
Brazil	234	8.00	1.0	2,106	98
United Kingdom	232	8.00	1.0	2,088	97
France	230	8.00	1.0	2,070	96
Germany	228	8.00	0.0	1,824	85
Russia	230	7.50	0.0	1,725	80
Average	238.8	8.30	1.1	2,245	104

from basic assumptions about national holidays and average annual vacation times. The table also ignores telecommuting, home offices, flex time, and a number of other factors that are important for detailed analyses. Table 4.1 is based on observations of the global software community. It should be recalled that software work is quite labor intensive, and software workers in many countries put in longer hours than workers in many other occupations.

Because there are significant local and industry differences within every country, the data in Table 4.1 should be used just as a starting point for more detailed exploration and analysis. Note that software as an occupation has more overtime associated with it than most other occupations. A rough analysis of work patterns indicates that medical residents, legal associates, and software practitioners tend to have the longest work weeks and the greatest number of overtime hours among major civilian occupations. Software is currently among the most labor-intensive commodities on the global market. Therefore, work practices and work effort applied to software exerts a major influence on productivity and schedule results. In every country, the top software personnel tend to work rather long hours, so Table 4.1 can be used only for very rough comparisons. The differences in national work patterns compounded with differences in burdened cost structures can lead to very significant international differences in software costs and schedules for the same size and kind of application.

All 36 of the factors presented are important, and each one can exert as much as a ± 20% impact on software schedules, costs, or quality when there are extreme variances between best- and worst-case situations.

If all or a majority of the 36 factors are at the worst-case end of the spectrum, any software project is a candidate for disaster. If all or a majority of the 36 factors are at the best-case end of the spectrum, the project might be moving toward setting a new record for productivity and quality. Between these two extremes, any combination of possible outcomes can occur.

Readings and References on Factor Analysis

The topic of what factors should be included in software assessments and benchmark studies is fragmented and somewhat contradictory. The books that discuss data collection are written by companies that gather data, but each company has its own views. The SEI has also contributed both books and monographs to the topic of software factor analysis.

Austin, Robert D. *Measuring and Managing Performance in Organizations*. New York: Dorset House Publishing, 1996. (ISBN 0-932633-36-6, 216 pages)

Bogan, Christopher E. and Michael J. English. *Benchmarking for Best Practices*. New York: McGraw Hill, 1994. (ISBN 0-07-006375-3, 312 pages)

Brooks, Frederick P. *The Mythical Man-Month*. Reading, MA: Addison-Wesley Longman, 1995. (ISBN 0-201-00650-2, 295 pages)

Brown, Norm, ed. *The Program Manager's Guide to Software Acquisition Best Practices*. Version 1.0. Washington, DC: U.S. Department of Defense, July 1995. (142 pages)

Caputo, Kim. *CMM Implementation Guide*. Reading, MA: Addison Wesley Longman, 1998. (ISBN 0-201-37938-4, 319 pages)

Carnegie Mellon University. *The Capability Maturity Model: Guidelines for Improving the Software Process*. Reading, MA: Addison Wesley Longman, 1995. (ISBN 0-201-54664-7, 441 pages)

Conte, S. D., H. E. Dunsmore, and V. Y. Shen. *Software Engineering Models and Metrics*. Menlo Park, CA: The Benjamin Cummings Publishing Company, 1986. (ISBN 0-8053-2162-4, 396 pages)

Curtis, Bill, William E. Hefley, and Sally Miller. *People Capability Maturity Model.* Pittsburgh, PA: Software Engineering Institute, Carnegie Mellon University, 1995.

DeMarco, Tom. *Controlling Software Projects.* New York: Yourdon Press, 1982. (ISBN 0-917072-32-4, 284 pages)

————. *Why Does Software Cost So Much?* New York: Dorset House Publishing, 1995. (ISBN 0-917072-32-4, 237 pages)

————. *The Deadline.* New York: Dorset House Publishing, 1997. (ISBN 0-932633-39-0)

DeMarco, Tom and Tim Lister. *Peopleware.* New York: Dorset House Publishing, 1987. (ISBN 0-932633-05-6, 188 pages)

Department of the Air Force. *Guidelines for Successful Acquisition and Management of Software Intensive Systems.* Vol. 1 and 2. Hill Air Force Base, UT: Software Technology Support Center, 1994.

Dreger, J. Brian. *Function Point Analysis.* Englewood Cliffs, NJ: Prentice Hall, 1989. (ISBN 0-13-332321-8, 185 pages)

El Emam, Khaled, and Nazim Madhavji, eds. *Elements of Software Process Assessment and Improvement.* Los Alamitos, CA: IEEE Computer Society Press, 1999. (ISBN 0-8185-8523-9, 384 pages)

Garmus, David, and David Herron. *Measuring the Software Process: A Practical Guide to Functional Measurement.* Englewood Cliffs, NJ: Prentice Hall, 1995. (ISBN 0-13-349002-5)

Grady, Robert B. *Practical Software Metrics for Project Management and Process Improvement.* Englewood Cliffs, NJ: Prentice Hall, 1992. (ISBN 0-13-720384-5, 270 pages)

————. *Successful Software Process Improvement.* Upper Saddle River, NJ: Prentice Hall, 1997. (ISBN 0-13-626623-1, 314 pages)

Grady, Robert B., and Deborah L. Caswell. *Software Metrics: Establishing a Company-Wide Program.* Englewood Cliffs, NJ: Prentice Hall, 1987. (ISBN 0-13-821844-7, 288 pages)

Humphrey, Watts S. *Managing the Software Process.* Reading, MA: Addison Wesley Longman, 1989. (ISBN 0-201-18095-2)

————. *Introduction to the Personal Software Process.* Reading, MA: Addison Wesley Longman, 1997.

————. *Managing Technical People.* Reading, MA: Addison Wesley Longman, 1997. (ISBN 0-201-54597-7, 326 pages)

IFPUG. *IFPUG Counting Practices Manual.* Release 4. Westerville, OH: International Function Point Users Group, April 1995. (83 pages)

Janulaitis, Victor M. *Information Systems, Communication and Data Processing Metrics HandiGuide.* Santa Monica, CA: Positive Support Review, 1993.

Jones, Capers. "Measuring Programming Quality and Productivity." *IBM Systems Journal* 1978; 17(1): 39–63.

———. *Programming Productivity: Issues for the Eighties.* Los Alamitos, CA: IEEE Computer Society Press, 1st ed., 1981; 2nd ed., 1986. (ISBN 0-8186-0681-9, IEEE Computer Society Catalog 681, 489 pages)

———. *Assessment and Control of Software Risks.* Englewood Cliffs, NJ: Prentice Hall, 1993. (ISBN 0-13-741406-4, 711 pages)

———. *Critical Problems in Software Measurement.* Carlsbad, CA: Information Systems Management Group, 1993. (ISBN 1-56909-000-9, 195 pages)

———. *Software Productivity and Quality Today: The Worldwide Perspective.* Carlsbad, CA: Information Systems Management Group, 1993. (ISBN -156909-001-7, 200 pages)

———. *Patterns of Software System Failure and Success.* Boston, MA: International Thomson Computer Press, December 1995. (ISBN 1-850-32804-8, 292 pages)

———. *Applied Software Measurement.* 2nd ed. New York: McGraw Hill, 1996. (ISBN 0-07-032826-9, 618 pages)

———. *Software Quality: Analysis and Guidelines for Success.* Boston, MA: International Thomson Computer Press, 1997. (ISBN 1-85032-876-6, 492 pages)

———. *Estimating Software Costs.* New York: McGraw Hill, 1998. (ISBN 0-07-9130941, 725 pages)

———. "Sizing Up Software." *Scientific American* 1998; 279(6): 104–111.

———. *The Year 2000 Software Problem: Quantifying the Costs and Assessing the Consequences.* Reading, MA: Addison Wesley, 1998. (ISBN 0-201-30964-5, 303 pages)

Kan, Stephen H. *Metrics and Models in Software Quality Engineering.* Reading, MA: Addison Wesley Longman, 1994. (ISBN 0-201-63339-6, 344 pages)

Kemerer, C. F. "Reliability of Function Point Measurement: A Field Experiment." *Communications of the ACM* 1993;36:85–97.

Marciniak, John J., ed. *Encyclopedia of Software Engineering.* New York: John Wiley & Sons, 1994. (ISBN 0-471-54002, in two volumes)

McCabe, Thomas J. "A Complexity Measure." *IEEE Transactions on Software Engineering* 1976: 308–320.

Melton, Austin. *Software Measurement.* London: Chapman & Hall, 1995. (ISBN 0-412-55180-2)

Mills, Harlan. *Software Productivity*. New York: Dorset House Publishing, 1988. (ISBN 0-932633-10-2, 288 pages)

Muller, Monika, and Alain Abram, eds. *Metrics in Software Evolution*. Munich: R. Oldenbourg Vertag GmbH, 1995. (ISBN 3-486-23589-3)

Multiple authors. *Rethinking the Software Process*. CD-ROM. Lawrence, KS: Miller Freeman, 1996. (This is a new CD-ROM book collection produced jointly by the book publisher Prentice Hall and the journal publisher Miller Freeman. This CD-ROM disk contains the full text and illustrations of five Prentice Hall books: *Assessment and Control of Software Risks* by Capers Jones, *Controlling Software Projects* by Tom DeMarco, *Function Point Analysis* by Brian Dreger, *Measures for Excellence* by Larry Putnam and Ware Myers, and *Object-Oriented Software Metrics* by Mark Lorenz and Jeff Kidd.)

Oman, Paul, and Shari Lawrence Pfleeger, eds. *Applying Software Metrics*. Los Alamitos, CA: IEEE Computer Society Press, 1996. (ISBN 0-8186-7645-0, 336 pages)

Park, Robert E., et al. *Software Cost and Schedule Estimating: A Process Improvement Initiative*. Technical report CMU/SEI 94-SR-03. Pittsburgh, PA: Software Engineering Institute, May 1994.

————. *Checklists and Criteria for Evaluating the Costs and Schedule Estimating Capabilities of Software Organizations*. Technical report CMU/SEI 95-SR-005. Pittsburgh, PA: Software Engineering Institute, January 1995.

Perlis, Alan J., Frederick G. Sayward, and Mary Shaw, eds. *Software Metrics*. Cambridge, MA: MIT Press, 1981. (ISBN 0-262-16083-8, 404 pages)

Putnam, Lawrence H. *Measures for Excellence: Reliable Software On Time, Within Budget*. Englewood Cliffs, NJ: Prentice Hall, 1992. (ISBN 0-13-567694-0, 336 pages)

Putnam, Lawrence H., and Ware Myers. *Industrial Strength Software: Effective Management Using Measurement*. Los Alamitos, CA: IEEE Computer Society Press, 1997. (ISBN 0-8186-7532-2, 320 pages)

Roetzheim, William J., and Reyna A. Beasley. *Software Project Cost & Schedule Estimating*. Upper Saddle River, NJ: Prentice Hall, 1998. (ISBN 0-13-682089-1)

Rubin, Howard. *Software Benchmark Studies for 1999*. Pound Ridge, NY: Howard Rubin Associates, 1999.

Shepperd, M. "A Critique of Cyclomatic Complexity as a Software Metric." *Software Engineering Journal* 1988;3:30–36.

Software Productivity Consortium. *The Software Measurement Guidebook*. Boston, MA: International Thomson Computer Press, 1995. (ISBN 1-850-32195-7, 308 pages)

Symons, Charles R. *Software Sizing and Estimating: Mk II FPA (Function Point Analysis)*. Chichester, UK: John Wiley & Sons, 1991. (ISBN 0 471-92985-9, 200 pages)

Weinberg, Gerald. *Quality Software Management. Vol. 2, First-Order Measurement*. New York: Dorset House Publishing, 1993. (ISBN 0-932633-24-2, 360 pages)

Zvegintzov, Nicholas. *Software Management Technology Reference Guide*. New York: Software Maintenance News, 1994. (ISBN 1-884521-01-0, 240 pages)

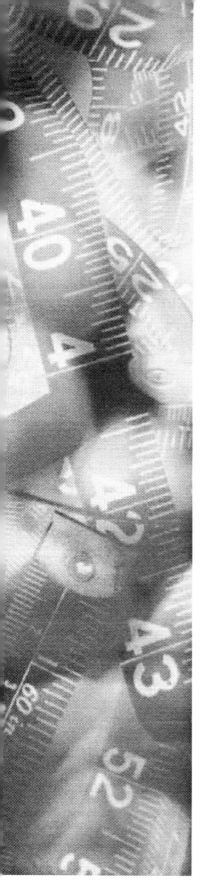

CHAPTER FIVE

Identifying Software Best and Worst Practices

Although software process assessments, software benchmarks, and software baseline studies can be performed separately and still be valuable, these three approaches complement one another. When software assessment data, software benchmark data, and software baseline data are joined together and analyzed, it is possible to show which tools and practices are associated with results that are better than industry averages, and which practices are associated with results that are worse than industry averages. Thus it is now possible to make reasonable assertions about best and worst practices using empirical data.

The phrase *best practices* is used in the software industry without a great deal of precision. In this book the concept of best practices is applied to methodologies and tools that yield productivity and quality results that are in roughly the top 5% of our client data, but other criteria are used as well.

For example, to be deemed a "best practice," it would be reasonable to require that the practice must have been observed in a minimum of ten companies and 50 software projects. Furthermore, the practice must be considered by those who used it to have been beneficial in all or most of the projects. If the practice is one that sometimes causes major problems or degrades performance, it should not be deemed a best practice other than for a specific context.

It is useful to consider an example outside of software. In medicine, for many years the best practice for treating bronchitis was the administration of an antibiotic such as penicillin. However, some patients are allergic to penicillin and may go into anaphylactic shock if this drug is used. Therefore, this therapy must be used with caution, and not ascribed to all patients, especially those who have a history of allergic reactions to antibiotics.

For software best practices, a similar degree of caution is indicated. Because a practice yields favorable results on large military projects does not necessarily indicate that it would be suitable for small projects such as Web applets.

Software productivity and quality levels approximate a normal bell-shaped curve when the number of companies and projects is large enough (Table 5.1).

The tool suites and methods that are found in companies within the highest 5% of quality and productivity levels are often acceptable candidates for the phrase *best practices*.

An interesting question arises. How would you classify a tool or methodology that occurs simultaneously in the top 5% and the bottom 5%? Obviously there are some methods and tools that are deployed widely across all levels of performance. The practical way to deal with this issue is to segregate tools and methods into three large classes: (1) tools and methods used across all levels of achievement, (2) tools and methods found primarily in the excellent end of the spectrum, and (3) tools and methods found primarily in the poor end of the spectrum.

Although this method is effective in a practical way, there are still some ambiguous situations. For example, the use of formal testing supported by written test plans is found in almost 100% of the organizations that achieve excellent software quality results. However, formal testing is also found in some organizations that are average in terms of quality, and even in a small number of organizations that are below average. This situation is fairly common, and leads to a useful but not perfect way of judging the effectiveness of tools and methods. If a

Table 5.1   Distribution of Software Productivity and Quality

Distribution	Definition
Top 5%	Excellent
Next 20%	Good or above average
Central 50%	Average
Next 20%	Below average
Bottom 5%	Poor

method is successful and leads to better than average results for 75% or more of the projects that use it, then the method is a candidate to be viewed as a best practice. Consider the implications of Table 5.2.

If we revisit the use of formal testing and written test plans, this technology is associated with approximately 90% of the projects that are better than average in terms of software quality and delivered bugs or defects. But for approximately 7% of projects using formal testing, quality levels are only average. Approximately 3% of projects using formal testing are below average in terms of quality compared with similar projects. With a new 90% success rate and only a 10% failure rate, it would be appropriate to say that testing can be placed in the best practice category.

When ISO 9000–9004 certification is examined, a very different pattern emerges. For example, ISO certification is found in approximately 30% of the companies with quality levels that are significantly better than average. However, these companies also tend to use formal software quality departments, formal design and code inspections, formal testing, and other sophisticated quality control approaches.

Approximately 50% of ISO-certified companies have software quality levels in the average range. Approximately 20% of ISO-certified companies have software quality levels in the below-average range. (These statements are derived from our clients who are also ISO certified.) Although ISO successes outnumber failures by approximately 10%, it cannot really be said that the ISO results are sufficiently good to consider ISO certification a best practice. In terms of actual

Table 5.2   Best Practices and Success Rates of Usage

Success Rate	Type of Practice
100% of cases	Best
> 90% of cases	Best
> 75% of cases	Good
> 50% of cases	Useful
< 50% of cases	Possibly hazardous
> 25% of cases	Hazardous
> 10% of cases	Harmful
0% of cases	Dangerous

software quality, ISO certification can be viewed as a neutral practice with no significant patterns of either success or failure.

There is one other form of analysis that is useful: examining the opposite ends of the spectrum of results. For example, all the software projects we have found that have topped 99% in cumulative defect removal efficiency levels have utilized formal code inspections. However, of the projects that are less than 75% in cumulative defect removal efficiency, which might be termed the *malpractice level,* none of these projects utilized formal code inspections.

By examining the opposite ends of the spectrum, it is fairly clear that formal code inspections are associated with very high levels of defect removal efficiency. Conversely, failure to use formal code inspections is associated with projects that have dangerously low levels of defect removal efficiency. Incidentally, a few projects used formal code inspections but were below average in terms of quality. These projects were usually enhancements to aging legacy applications. The inspections were used on the new code, but not on the residual base code in the legacy application. Thus, error-prone modules and other legacy problems escaped detection.

Our method of determining best practices is not perfect, but no tool or methodology has been found to be effective for 100% of the projects that used it. The situation with software tools and methods is somewhat analogous to the situations with medicines used for treating various illnesses. For example, penicillin used to be effective against bacterial pneumonia in approximately 75% of patients. However, some patients are allergic to penicillin and some strains of pneumonia are resistant to this antibiotic. In medicine, as with software, therapies are never 100% effective.

Another dimension to exploring best practices is to consider productivity and quality levels from a sample of projects. There will, of course, be an average for the overall sample, and there will be projects that are better or worse than average values.

Suppose we are concerned with defect removal efficiency levels. If we examine 100 projects that used formal code inspections and compare them with 100 similar projects that did not use formal code inspections, the results are interesting.

Defect removal efficiency is calculated by comparing the number of defects found before delivery with the total number found after a predetermined period, such as 90 days. Thus, if 95 bugs or errors were found during development of a software project and users found five bugs in the first three months of usage, the removal efficiency would be 95%.

The average defect removal efficiency of the 100 projects using formal code inspections is higher than 95%, and some projects top 99%. Almost none will be less than 90%. The average defect removal efficiency of projects not using code inspections is only near 80%. A few projects may top 90% without inspections, but many more will be less than 75%.

Because the use of formal code inspections yields an approximate 15% net increase in defect removal efficiency, it could be stated that if a client's goal is to improve software quality, then formal code inspections would be considered a best practice. Consider Table 5.3 as a possible guide for determining best practice status.

Of course, one dimension is not quite enough to determine a best practice. Sometimes a method or tool works well for one size of software project but is not optimal for some other size. Continuing with the example of formal code inspections, if quality is improved but schedules, costs, and productivity are degraded, then the method would have some serious drawbacks.

With formal code inspections, projects larger than 1,000 function points have higher productivity levels and shorter development schedules than similar projects that did not use inspections. For projects between 500 and 1,000 function points, schedules are about the same in the inspection and noninspection samples. Less than 500 function points, the noninspection samples have a slight edge in terms of schedules and productivity. Thus, for projects larger than 1,000 function points, formal code inspections would be squarely in the best-practice category because they benefit quality in a very significant way, and schedules do in a smaller but still positive direction.

Table 5.3 Ranges of Productivity and Quality Data

Productivity and Quality	Type of Practice
Better than average by > 15%	Excellent or best
Better than average by > 10%	Very good
Better than average by > 5%	Good
Average value of sample	Average
Worse than average by > 5%	Below average
Worse than average by > 10%	Needs improvement
Worse than average by > 15%	Hazardous

However, for a small and simple project less than 100 function points, formal code inspections would be an optional technology rather than a best practice. For such small projects, quality levels are often fairly high regardless of whether inspections are used. Small software projects are sometimes built by individual programmers. Thus, there may be no convenient colleagues available to hold code inspections.

When assessment, benchmark, and baseline data from the same organization is analyzed, it is also possible to show the measured effects of key topics such as moving up the five levels of the SEI CMM or achieving certification to the ISO 9000–9004 standards. Assessments, baselines, and benchmarks together can also demonstrate the benefits (or harm) of various software methodologies such as information engineering, JAD, RAD, OO methods, the Merise methodology, the Kaizan methodology, and many others.

Software process assessments by themselves are not sufficient to determine best and worst practices, because unless a practice causes some variation in quantitative results, it cannot be proved to be better or worse than alternative practices. Software benchmarks by themselves are also not sufficient to determine best and worst practices, because quantitative benchmarks also need to be joined with detailed information about the specific tools and methods used, in addition to information on the experience and capabilities of the software personnel involved, which are normally derived from assessments. Thus, the effectiveness of a tool used by an SEI CMM level 3 organization may differ strikingly from the use of the same tool in an SEI CMM level 1 organization. To determine best practices by statistical means, assessment, benchmark, and baseline information are all needed.

A combination of software process assessment information and software benchmark and baseline information opens the door to a very powerful mode of software analysis because this combination can be used to explore both ends of the spectrum: methods that yield results better than industry averages and methods that yield results worse than industry averages.

Factors That Influence Software Development Productivity

Table 5.4 shows a number of factors that exert a positive impact on software productivity and raise results to higher than average values.

The three most influential factors for elevating software productivity are the use of high-quality reusable materials, and the experience levels of both the managers and the technical staff in building similar kinds of applications.

Table 5.4   Impact on Productivity of Positive Adjustment Factors (sorted in order of maximum positive impact)

New Development Factors	Positive Range, %
Reuse of high-quality deliverables	350
High management experience	65
High staff experience	55
Effective methods/process	35
Effective management tools	30
Effective technical CASE tools	27
High-level programming languages	24
Quality estimating tools	19
Specialist occupations	18
Effective client participation	18
Formal cost/schedule estimates	17
Unpaid overtime	15
Use of formal inspections	15
Good office ergonomics	15
Quality measurement	14
Low project complexity	13
Quick response time	12
Moderate schedule pressure	11
Productivity measurements	10
Low requirements creep	9
Annual training of > 10 days	8
No geographic separation	8
High team morale	7
Hierarchical organization	5
Sum	800

CASE = computer-aided software engineering.

Let us now consider some of the factors that can reduce or degrade software productivity, and cause it to lag behind average values (Table 5.5).

Table 5.5   Impact on Productivity of Negative Adjustment Factors (sorted in order of maximum negative impact)

New Development Factors	Negative Range, %
Reuse of poor-quality deliverables	−300
Management inexperience	−90
Staff inexperience	−87
High requirements creep	−77
Inadequate technical CASE tools	−75
No use of inspections	−48
Inadequate management tools	−45
Ineffective methods/processes	−41
No quality estimation	−40
High project complexity	−35
Excessive schedule pressure	−30
Slow response time	−30
Crowded office space	−27
Low-level languages	−25
Geographic separation	−24
Informal cost/schedule estimates	−22
Generalist occupations	−15
No client participation	−13
No annual training	−12
No quality measurements	−10
Matrix organization	−8
No productivity measurements	−7
Poor team morale	−6
No unpaid overtime	0
Sum	−1,067

CASE = computer-aided software engineering.

What is most interesting about Table 5.5 is that the same factor—software reuse—that can exert the largest positive impact on improving software productivity can also exert the largest negative impact on reducing productivity. How is it possible for software reuse to exert such a large influence in both directions?

The critical difference between the positive and negative influences of software reuse can be expressed in one word: *quality*. The positive value of software reuse occurs when the reusable artifacts approach or achieve zero-defect levels. The negative value of software reuse, on the other hand, occurs if the reusable materials are filled with errors or bugs. Imagine the result of reusing a software module in 50 applications only to discover that it contains a number of high-severity errors that trigger massive recalls of every application!

Note that software reuse encompasses much more than just source code. An effective corporate reuse program includes at a minimum the following five reusable artifacts:

1. Reusable requirements
2. Reusable designs
3. Reusable source code
4. Reusable test materials
5. Reusable user documentation

To gain the optimum positive value from software reuse, each major software deliverable should include at least 75% reused material, which is certified and approaches a zero-defect level.

Another interesting aspect of Table 5.5 is that the cumulative results are much larger than those of Table 5.4. Essentially this means that it is far easier to make mistakes and degrade productivity than it is to get things right and improve productivity.

In general, there is often a lack of symmetry between positive influences and negative influences. For example, a good development process exerts a moderate positive influence on software productivity, but a really bad development process can exert a very severe negative impact on productivity.

Consider a topic unrelated to software for a moment: use of tobacco. Heavy use of tobacco products exerts a severe negative impact on human tissues and causes a number of medical problems. On the other hand, not using tobacco does not make a person healthy, it simply minimizes the risk of becoming unhealthy. Here, too, there is a lack of symmetry between positive and negative impact. Use of tobacco has a severe negative impact, but not using tobacco has no particular positive impact, as might regular exercise or a diet high in fiber.

Factors That Influence Software Maintenance Productivity

The word *maintenance* is highly ambiguous in the software domain. The common meaning for the term *maintenance* includes both defect repairs and also enhancements in response to new requirements. Although this definition is imperfect, it serves to show the positive and negative factors that influence the modification of existing software applications. Table 5.6 illustrates a number of factors that have been found to exert a beneficial, positive impact on the work of updating aging applications.

Because software reuse is not a factor in either defect repairs or adding features to existing applications, the overall positive impact on the maintenance domain is not as strong as that for new development projects. The top three factors that exert a positive influence are those associated with the use of full-time maintenance specialists, with having extensive experience in the application being updated, and with experience using tables for holding variables and constants rather than embedding them in the source code itself.

Let us now consider some of the factors that exert a negative impact on the work of updating or modifying existing software applications (Table 5.7). Note that the top-ranked factor that reduces maintenance productivity—the presence of error-prone modules—is very asymmetrical.

Error-prone modules were discovered in the 1960s when IBM began a methodical study of the factors that influenced software maintenance. It was discovered that errors or bugs in IBM software products such as the IMS database and the MVS operating system tended to "clump" in a very small number of modules that were extremely buggy indeed. In the case of the MVS, approximately 38% of customer-reported errors were found in only 4% of the modules. In the case of IMS, an even more extreme skew was noted. There were 300 zero-defect modules out of a total of 425, and 57% of all customer-reported errors were against only 31 modules.

Although IBM first discovered the existence of error-prone modules, they are remarkably common and have been found by dozens of companies and government agencies. Fortunately, error-prone modules are a completely curable problem, and the usage of formal design and code inspections has the effect of completely immunizing software projects against these troublesome entities.

Table 5.6   Impact on Maintenance Productivity of Positive Factors (sorted in order of maximum positive impact)

Maintenance Factors	Positive Range, %
Maintenance specialists	35
High staff experience	34
Table-driven variables and data	33
Low complexity of base code	32
Y2K search engines	30
Code-restructuring tools	29
Reengineering tools	27
High-level programming languages	25
Reverse-engineering tools	23
Complexity analysis tools	20
Defect tracking tools	20
Y2K specialists	20
Automated change control tools	18
Unpaid overtime	18
Quality measurements	16
Formal base code inspections	15
Regression test libraries	15
Excellent response time	12
Annual training of > 10 days	12
High management experience	12
HELP desk automation	12
No error-prone modules	10
On-line defect reporting	10
Productivity measurements	8
Excellent ease of use	7
User satisfaction measurements	5
High team morale	5
Sum	503

Table 5.7   Impact on Maintenance Productivity of Negative Factors (sorted in order of maximum negative impact)

Maintenance Factors	Negative Range, %
Error-prone modules	−50
Embedded variables and data	−45
Staff inexperience	−40
High complexity of base code	−30
No Y2K search engines	−28
Manual change control methods	−27
Low-level programming languages	−25
No defect tracking tools	−24
No Y2K specialists	−22
Poor ease of use	−18
No quality measurements	−18
No maintenance specialists	−18
Poor response time	−16
Management inexperience	−15
No base code inspections	−15
No regression test libraries	−15
No HELP desk automation	−15
No on-line defect reporting	−12
No annual training	−10
No code-restructuring tools	−10
No reengineering tools	−10
No reverse-engineering tools	−10
No complexity analysis tools	−10
No productivity measurements	−7
Poor team morale	−6
No user satisfaction measurements	−4
No unpaid overtime	0
Sum	−500

Patterns of Positive and Negative Factors

SPR collects quantitative and qualitative data on approximately 50 to 70 software projects every month, and has been doing so for almost 12 years. Software projects and software organizations tend to follow relatively normal bell-shaped curves. There are comparatively few projects and companies that are good in almost every aspect of software, and there are few that are really bad in almost every aspect of software.

Table 5.8 illustrates a typical pattern of responses on the part of our clients to a set of more than 100 questions that we use in our software process assessment studies.

Note that both best-in-class companies and worst-in-class companies are average in approximately 50% of all the topics we examine. However, the best-in-class organizations rank as good or excellent in roughly 45% of the topics, and only lag in approximately 5% of the topics. By contrast, the worst-in-class organizations lag in approximately 44% of all topics, and are only good or excellent in approximately 6% of the topics. This pattern of being average in many factors but good or bad in some is not unique to software. Similar patterns can be found in professional sports, in scientific discoveries, in artistic creation, in musical composition, and in many knowledge-based occupations.

The most common pattern that we encounter is projects and companies in which the technical work of building software in terms of design and coding is reasonably good, but project management factors and quality control factors are

Table 5.8   Patterns of Software Factors Noted During SPR Studies

Rating	Excellent, %	Good, %	Average, %	Marginal, %	Poor, %	Total, %
Best in class (top 5%)	15.00	30.00	50.00	4.00	1.00	100.00
Better than average	10.00	25.00	50.00	10.00	5.00	100.00
Average (central 50%)	5.00	15.00	50.00	20.00	10.00	100.00
Worse than average	3.00	12.00	50.00	23.00	12.00	100.00
Worst in class (bottom 5%)	1.00	5.00	50.00	29.00	15.00	100.00
Average	6.80	17.40	50.00	17.20	8.60	100.00

fairly weak. This combination of factors is a reasonable characterization of the information systems domain, which (numerically) is the most common form of software development.

A variant of information systems projects, those produced by outsource contractors, have a somewhat better chance of having good project management methods than do other forms of information systems development. However, not all outsource projects use good project management tools and methods.

For a variety of reasons, the systems software domain has a greater likelihood of having fairly good quality control as well as fairly good development skills. Here, too, project management is often the weak link. Quality control is better in the systems software domain because the hardware devices that the software controls (switching systems, computers, aircraft, and so on) need stringent quality control to function.

The military software domain, like the systems software domain, is often characterized by rather good development methods and fairly good quality control methods, but marginal or deficient project management methods.

The large commercial software vendors tend to have better than average software development methods and much better than average maintenance methods. Here, too, quality control and project management are the weaknesses noted most often in assessment and benchmark studies.

Among the organizations with productivity rates that are in the top 5% of our client results, there is a very strong tendency for most of these factors to be better than average:

- Project management tools and methods
- Quality control tools and methods
- Maintenance tools and methods
- Development tools and methods

Conversely, among the clients who bring up the rear in terms of productivity, there is a strong tendency for this pattern to be noted:

- Poor project management tools and methods
- Poor quality control tools and methods
- Poor maintenance tools and methods
- Adequate development tools and methods

On the whole, the software technical community of analysts and programmers seems to be better trained and equipped for their jobs than the software project management community.

Software productivity and best practices are very complex topics. There are many wrong ways to go about building and maintaining software, and only a few ways of getting it right. As a result, average productivity and quality levels for software projects are not particularly impressive. There is fairly extensive literature on methods that might improve software productivity, although empirical data is somewhat sparse. However, the factors that degrade and reduce software productivity are not explored or published very often.

Readings and References on Software Best and Worst Practices

Although there are many articles and a few books that discuss best practices, there is a tendency for the literature to exhibit "tunnel vision." The phrase *tunnel vision,* in this book, implies that a technology or tool that proved valuable for a few specific projects is assumed to be valuable for all software projects, regardless of their size, type, or whether they are new projects or maintenance projects.

Austin, Robert D. *Measuring and Managing Performance in Organizations.* New York: Dorset House Publishing, 1996. (ISBN 0-932633-36-6, 216 pages)

Boehm, Barry. *Software Engineering Economics.* Englewood Cliffs, NJ: Prentice Hall, 1981. (ISBN 0-13-822122-7, 900 pages)

Bogan, Christopher E., and Michael J. English. *Benchmarking for Best Practices.* New York: McGraw Hill, 1994. (ISBN 0-07-006375-3, 312 pages)

Jones, Capers. *Assessment and Control of Software Risks.* Englewood Cliffs, NJ: Prentice Hall, 1993. (ISBN 0-13-741406-4, 619 pages)

Jones, Capers. *Patterns of Software Systems Failure and Success.* Boston, MA: International Thomson Computer Press, 1995. (ISBN 1-850-32804-8, 292 pages)

Jones, Capers. *Applied Software Measurement. 2nd ed.* New York: McGraw Hill, 1996. (ISBN 0-07-032826-9, 618 pages)

Jones, Capers. *Software Quality: Analysis and Guidelines for Success.* Boston, MA: International Thomson Computer Press, 1997. (ISBN 1-85032-867-6, 492 pages)

Putnam, Lawrence H. *Measures for Excellence: Reliable Software On Time, Within Budget.* Englewood Cliffs, NJ: Prentice Hall, 1992. (ISBN 0-13-567694-0, 336 pages)

Putnam, Lawrence H., and Ware Myers. *Industrial Strength Software: Effective Management Using Measurement.* Los Alamitos, CA: IEEE Computer Society Press, 1997. (ISBN 0-8186-7532-2, 320 pages)

Rubin, Howard. *Software Benchmark Studies for 1999.* Pound Ridge, NY: Howard Rubin Associates, 1999.

CHAPTER SIX

Software Process Improvements

Once an assessment or benchmark study is completed, the patterns of strengths and weaknesses observed usually lead to a desire to improve software development processes. Because improvement programs are derived from problems noted, you can see that assessments and benchmarks are the usual starting point.

The SEI CMM provides some useful information on what technologies and practices are normally observed at each level of the CMM. However, data on what it might cost to reach a given level, and what kind of productivity and quality results can be achieved, is not easy to find. Many cities now have nonprofit SPIN groups. The recent national SPIN conference in Boston drew several thousand attendees and was a visible sign that process improvement is now a mainstream technology. Other signs are the frequent articles devoted to process improvement in the software journals. In Europe and abroad, process improvements are also expanding rapidly, as seen in the ESPRIT, SPICE, and Bootstrap programs in the European Union. However, despite the widespread interest in software process improvement, empirical data remains fairly sparse.

SPR agrees that the higher levels of the SEI CMM are suitable destinations for software organizations. However, SPR has also done substantial research in the corollary topics of how long it takes to reach a given level, how much must be spent, and what results will be found at each level.

Significant software process improvements do not occur in random patterns. When you generalize the patterns used by companies that have gone the farthest and are the best overall, you can see that the initial activity is an assessment and a baseline, followed by a six-stage improvement program:

- Stage 0: Software process assessment, baseline, and benchmark
- Stage 1: Focus on management technologies
- Stage 2: Focus on software processes and methodologies
- Stage 3: Focus on new tools and approaches
- Stage 4: Focus on infrastructure and specialization
- Stage 5: Focus on reusability
- Stage 6: Focus on industry leadership

These six general phases provide an overall framework or structure for software improvement strategies. However, each company is different, and therefore the specifics of each company's improvement strategy must be molded to match the company's culture and needs.

There are reasons why the sequence of improvement is in this particular order and cannot be changed easily. It is useful to discuss why the sequence is as it is. Stage 0 is primarily a diagnostic phase that identifies both strengths and weaknesses. The process improvement stages are therapeutic and are aimed at curing the weaknesses identified during stage 0.

Stage 1 concentrates on management issues, which are critical to all downstream activities. Software process improvement is a fairly expensive undertaking that can stretch out over three to five years. To justify the investment in software process improvement, managers must be able to calculate and defend the anticipated ROI in the tools and training that are needed. Unless the management community is at state-of-the-art levels in cost estimating, value analysis, and risk analysis, funding for process improvement may be denied. Thus, stage 1 in the SPR improvement cycle begins with upgrading the tools and abilities of the software management community as a necessary precursor to other changes.

Stage 2 of improvement programs involves the introduction of specific process methodologies. For example, formal design and code inspections and JAD are examples of process improvements that might be introduced during the second stage. Stage 2 improvements require training and cultural adjustments, but are not very expensive in terms of capital equipment or major investments. Usually, it is best to develop a solid ground of effective processes before embarking on the most costly improvements in later stages.

Stage 3 improvements may involve fairly costly tool suites and capital equipment, such as better workstations. Because tools support processes, rather than the other way around, one can see why process improvements precede changes in tool suites.

Stage 4 improvements deal with corporate "infrastructures." An example of such a change is the establishment of formal quality assurance departments, formal measurement departments, and testing and maintenance departments. Because infrastructure changes are both expensive and complex, they need to be deferred until the value of the previous kinds of changes has started to become obvious.

Stage 5 improvements are the most valuable in terms of improving quality and productivity, but they are also the most challenging. Stage 5 moves toward a full and formal software reusability program. However, reuse is a double-edge sword. If the reusable materials are of top quality, then reuse has the best positive ROI of any software technology. However, if the reusable materials are error prone and filled with defects, then the ROI of software reuse switches from positive to sharply negative.

Stage 6 is the final destination under the SPR improvement program. Stage 6 involves using software excellence for competitive purposes, such as winning a Baldrige Award and using this award to aid in gaining market shares. Organizations reaching stage 6 are ranked among the best organizations in the world for which to work. Therefore, organizations achieving this target should have no trouble in attracting and retaining capable personnel.

Annual Tactical and Strategic Software Improvement Plans

Because there are too many things to be done on the path to software excellence to trust to chance, it is desirable to construct formal software improvement plans. I suggest an annual software planning cycle with two key components:

1. A *tactical* plan that details the specific process improvements for the next 12 months
2. A *strategic* plan that outlines the general stages over a three- to five-year period

The tactical plan is the more specific of the two because it deals with the next 12 months in considerable detail. The strategic plan gives a longer range view and may cover as much as five years out. Tactical plans need to be created each year.

The strategic plan needs to be extended each year, but the basic structure can remain stable for several years.

Annual Software Progress Report

In addition to annual plans, I also strongly recommend that every company moving toward best-in-class status also produce an annual progress report of their accomplishments during the most recent calendar or fiscal year. The annual report should cover the same topics identified in the tactical improvement plan, and the combination of careful plans and annual progress reports may satisfy executive demands for proof of progress.

In the autumn of each calendar year (or the last quarter of each fiscal year), the software improvement team should begin to assemble the data for the annual progress report. This data also serves as the nucleus of the next-year tactical software improvement plan.

Both the annual progress report and the tactical improvement plan should be released in synchronization with other major corporate plans and reports. The tactical plan is usually published just before the beginning of the next calendar or fiscal year, and the annual progress report is published within a month of the end of the year.

It is an interesting observation that software staffs are usually one of the largest occupational groups in many companies, and software systems are one of the major business assets of a corporation. Therefore, it is reasonable and prudent to want to place software at the same level of planning and reporting rigor as other segments of business and corporate operations.

The Six Stages on the Path to Software Excellence

As already mentioned, there are six overall stages along the path to software excellence. The sequence of the stages is based on practical considerations. For example, software managers have to produce the cost justifications for any substantial investment, so they need to be fully apprised of the downstream implications of the latter stages. Furthermore, unless project management excellence is achieved first, it is unlikely that the latter stages will occur at all!

Let us examine each of the six improvement stages in turn and consider what goes on during each stage, and why the sequence is what it is.

Stage 0: Software Process Assessment, Baseline, and Benchmarks

The first stage, or stage 0, is numbered so that it is outside the set of six improvement phases. There is a practical reason for this. Neither an assessment nor a baseline nor benchmarks by themselves cause any tangible improvements. Some companies forget this important point and stop doing anything after their initial assessment and baseline. However, the basis of all software process improvement strategies begins with a formal process assessment and the establishment of a quantitative baseline of current productivity and quality levels.

- The *assessment* finds all the strengths and weaknesses associated with software.
- The *baseline* provides a firm quantitative basis for productivity, schedules, costs, quality, and user satisfaction to judge rate of improvement.
- The *benchmark* is a formal comparison of software methods and results against those of other organizations. External benchmarks are often performed in conjunction with consulting groups such as Gartner Group, Meta Group, Howard Rubin Associates, or SPR, who have large collections of software data from many companies and industries.

Assessments, benchmarks, and baselines are all useful. Assessments alone lack the quantification of initial quality and productivity levels needed to judge improvements later. A quantitative baseline is a necessary prerequisite for serious process improvements because the cost justification for the investments required usually has to be proved by comparing results against the initial baseline. A benchmark comparison against industry data serves as a strong impetus for improvement if the organization is below average in any significant metrics.

An external benchmark against other companies is a useful adjunct to software process improvements. Indeed, you will never be sure that you have achieved best-in-class status unless you actually compare your results against those of competing organizations in the same industry.

For example, consider the SPR observations of the quality ranges associated with the five levels of the SEI CMM. This data has a high margin of error, but as with many preliminary studies it is hoped that publishing data that may be incorrect will spur the software community to find better data and correct the errors in the future.

Note that the defect potentials shown here include these five categories of software defects that, in aggregate, form the *defect potentials* for software applications:

1. Requirements defects
2. Design defects
3. Code defects
4. User documentation defects
5. Bad fixes, or secondary defects

The SPR data on defect removal efficiency levels refers to the cumulative percentage of bugs or defects found prior to release compared with the defects reported by clients in the first year of usage. For example, if developers find 90 bugs and clients find 10 bugs, then the defect removal efficiency would be 90%.

CMM level 1 quality: The software defect potentials noted from several hundred projects in level 1 organizations run from approximately three defects to more than 15 defects per function point, but average 5.0 defects per function point. Defect removal efficiency runs from less than 70% to more than 95%, but only averages approximately 85%. Thus the average number of delivered defects for level 1 organizations is approximately 0.75 defects per function point.

CMM level 2 quality: The software defect potentials noted from approximately 50 projects in level 2 organizations run from approximately three defects to more than 12 defects per function point, but average 4.8 defects per function point. Defect removal efficiency runs from less than 70% to more than 96%, but averages approximately 87%. Thus the average number of delivered defects for level 2 organizations is approximately 0.6 defects per function point.

CMM level 3 quality: The software defect potentials noted from approximately 30 projects in level 3 organizations run from approximately 2.5 to more than nine defects per function point, but average 4.3 defects per function point. Defect removal efficiency runs from less than 75% to more than 97%, but averages approximately 89%. Thus the average number of delivered defects for level 3 organizations is approximately 0.47 defects per function point.

CMM level 4 quality: The software defect potentials noted from nine projects in level 4 organizations run from approximately 2.3 defects to more than six defects per function point, but average approximately 3.8 defects per function point. Defect removal efficiency runs from less than 80% to more than 99%, but averages approximately 94%. Thus, the average number of delivered defects for level 4 organizations is approximately 0.2 defects per function point.

CMM level 5 quality: The software defect potentials noted from four projects in a level 5 organization run from approximately two to five defects per function point but currently seem to average 3.5 defects per function point. Defect removal efficiency runs from less than 90% to more than 99%, but averages approximately 97%. Thus, the average number of delivered defects for a level 5 organization is approximately 0.1 defects per function point, although there is obviously an insufficient sample at this level.

To illustrate the overlap of quality among the five levels of the SEI CMM, Table 6.1 shows our minimum, average, and maximum numbers of delivered defects per function point for each of the five CMM levels. Note that the best results from level 1 are actually better than the worst results from levels 3 and 4, even though the average results improve as the CMM ladder is climbed.

There is increasing evidence from studies such as the ones carried out by SPR in 1994 for the Air Force that indicate that when organizations do move from CMM level 1 up to the higher levels, their productivity and quality levels tend to improve. However, there is quite a bit of overlap among the five CMM levels. After the assessment and benchmark studies are complete, the actual improvement stages follow.

Stage 1: Focus on Management Technologies

Because software project management is the weakest link in software, the first improvement stage concentrates on bringing managers up to speed in critical technologies such as planning, sizing, estimating, tracking, measurement, risk analysis, and value analysis. It is important to begin with managers because they are the ones who need to calculate the ROIs that occur later. They also have to collect the data to demonstrate progress, so it is folly to even begin unless managers are trained and equipped for their roles.

Table 6.1   Software-Delivered Defects at Each Level of the SEI CMM (defects expressed in terms of defects per function point)

SEI Level	Minimum	Average	Maximum
1	0.150	0.750	4.500
2	0.120	0.624	3.600
3	0.075	0.473	2.250
4	0.023	0.228	1.200
5	0.002	0.105	0.500

Table 6.2   Numbers and Sizes of Project Management Tools (size data expressed in terms of function point metrics)

Project Management	Lagging	Average	Leading
Project planning	1,000	1,250	3,000
Project cost estimating	–	–	3,000
Statistical analysis	–	–	3,000
Methodology management	–	750	3,000
Y2K analysis	–	–	2,000
Quality estimation	–	–	2,000
Assessment support	–	500	2,000
Project measurement	–	–	1,750
Portfolio analysis	–	–	1,500
Risk analysis	–	–	1,500
Resource tracking	300	750	1,500
Value analysis	–	350	1,250
Cost variance reporting	–	500	1,000
Personnel support	500	500	750
Milestone tracking	–	250	750
Budget support	–	250	750
Function point analysis	–	250	750
Backfiring: LOC to function points	–	–	750
Function point subtotal	1,800	5,350	30,250
No. of tools	3	10	18

Unless the software management community can perform ROI calculations and can understand software economics, none of the downstream improvements are likely to occur because senior corporate management usually will not fund fanciful activities that are not based solidly on empirical data. During stage 1, it is important that software managers learn the basics of software economic analysis and function point metrics. The older LOC metric is not suitable for performing quality studies, economic studies, or even for measuring software productivity.

One of the newer and more interesting uses of function point metrics is to quantify the volumes of tools used by lagging, average, and leading organizations. Table 6.2 shows the kinds of software project management tools available.

As you can see, there is more than a 20:1 difference between the lagging organizations and the leading organizations in terms of the volumes of software project management tools deployed and available.

Stage 2: Focus on Software Processes and Methodologies

The second stage concentrates on solid approaches for dealing with requirements, design, development, and quality control. Because tools support processes, the processes need to be selected before heavy investments occur.

Some of the processes deployed in this stage include JAD; formal design methods such as Warnier-Orr, Yourdon, Merise, Jackson, or others; formal design and code inspections; and formal change management procedures.

There are many software process possibilities. SPR has identified some 65 major "flavors" of methodologies or processes including but not limited to the DMR approach, information engineering, PRIDE, PRISM, Merise, METHOD/1, NAVIGATOR, RAD, SPICE, STRADIS, and a host of others.

Many aspects of software methodologies are consolidated into various methodology management tools, such as the Learmonth & Burchett Management Systems (LBMS) process engineering tool suite. This consolidation greatly eases the burden of using methodologies for actual development projects.

Because all vendor claims are glowing, and most lack solid quantified data, the choice of selecting a process or methodology is currently a very difficult one. This is why management must be brought up to speed before heavy investments are contemplated.

A study carried out within ITT on the effects of formal methods reached an interesting conclusion. The projects that used no formal methods at all lagged in terms of productivity, schedules, defect prevention, and defect removal efficiency levels. The projects that did use formal methods averaged approximately 30% better in their tangible results compared with similar projects of the same size. However, the specific formal method utilized seemed to have a comparatively minor impact. It was the formality and rigor that influenced the results. Thus Warnier-Orr, Yourdon, Jackson, and Merise all achieved more or less similar results, and all were superior to the projects that used casual, informal processes.

Stage 3: Focus on New Tools and Approaches

Once software methods and processes are pinned down, it is appropriate to acquire various improved tools and to explore advanced or new technologies. This is when integrated computer-aided software engineering (CASE) or I-CASE is acquired, together with other new or upgraded tools. It is also the time to explore difficult technologies with steep learning curves, such as client/server methods and the OO paradigm. Jumping prematurely into client/server projects, or moving too quickly toward OO analysis and design, usually means trouble because poorly trained practitioners are seldom successful.

As discussed, one of the most interesting new uses for function point metrics is to quantify the software tool capacities utilized in lagging, average, and leading companies. Table 6.3 illustrates this usage of function point metrics for quality assurance tools.

The methodology of using function points for correlating tool capacity with performance is still an experimental method, but the initial results are proving to be very interesting. For software quality assurance, testing, and for software project managers, the correlation between tool capacity and job performance is rather strong. Table 6.3 presents the major kinds of quality assurance tools and their approximate function point size totals.

The most striking and significant observation associated with Table 6.3 is that the lagging organizations have no quality assurance departments and no quality assurance tools.

Although quality assurance work is associated with best-in-class organizations, every company tests its software. Therefore, the ranges in numbers of tools and tool capacities is not as extreme for testing tools as for software quality assurance, but still indicate a large range, which can be viewed as both interesting and significant (Table 6.4).

This method of analysis leads to some interesting results. For example, some of the most significant differences in tool capacities between leading and lagging companies are in the domains of quality assurance tools, testing tools, and project management tools. As just shown, there is a 20:1 differential in terms of quality tools between laggards and leaders. (For project management tools, the results are also dramatic, with a near 20:1 differential in tool capacities for project managers between the leaders and the laggards.) However, average companies, leaders, and laggards are seldom very far apart in basic software development tools: The values run from approximately 30,000 function points to more than 50,000

Table 6.3   Numbers and Sizes of Software Quality Tools (size data expressed in terms of function point metrics)

Quality Assurance	Lagging	Average	Leading
Quality estimation	–	–	2,000
Data quality analysis	–	–	1,500
Code restructuring	–	1,000	1,250
QFD support	–	–	1,000
TQM support	–	–	1,000
Inspection support	–	–	1,000
Reliability estimation	–	–	1,000
Defect tracking	–	750	1,000
Complexity analysis	–	500	1,000
Function point subtotal	0	2,250	10,750
No. of tools	0	3	9

QFD = quality function deployment; TQM = total quality management.

Table 6.4   Numbers and Sizes of Software Testing Tools (size data expressed in terms of function point metrics)

Testing	Lagging	Average	Leading
Test case generation	–	–	1,500
Complexity analysis	–	500	1,500
Y2K test support	–	500	1,500
Data quality analysis	–	–	1,250
Defect tracking	500	750	1,000
Test library control	250	750	1,000
Performance monitors	–	750	1,000
Capture/playback	–	500	750
Test path coverage	100	200	350
Test case execution	–	200	350
Function point subtotal	850	4,150	10,200
No. of tools	3	8	10

function points for software engineering tool suites encompassing normal analysis, design, development, configuration control, and testing tools.

Stage 4: Focus on Infrastructure and Specialization

To reach the top plateau of software excellence, it is necessary to have a top-notch organization as well as excellent tools and methods. The infrastructure stage addresses issues of organization and specialization, and begins to move toward the establishment of specialized teams for handling testing, maintenance, integration, and configuration control. Formal quality assurance departments are also important. Policies on continuing education are important as well.

As of 1999, large enterprises can employ as many as 100 different kinds of software specialists. Better results are usually achieved with specialists than generalists in the following domains: testing, maintenance, measurement, quality assurance, technical writing, database administration, and planning and estimating.

The importance of this stage is illustrated by the success of Microsoft, whose overall software personnel rank among the best in the world. Without excellent personnel, even good to excellent processes can only achieve marginal results.

Stage 5: Focus on Reusability

Reusability has the best ROI of any technology, but effective reuse is not a game for amateurs. If your quality control is not top notch, then you will be reusing garbage, and your costs will go up instead of down.

Effective reuse includes much more than just code. In fact, an effective software reuse program includes at least 12 reusable components:

1. Reusable architecture
2. Reusable requirements
3. Reusable plans
4. Reusable estimates
5. Reusable designs and specifications
6. Reusable interfaces
7. Reusable data
8. Reusable screens or screen elements
9. Reusable source code
10. Reusable user documents
11. Reusable test plans
12. Reusable test cases

Efforts to reuse only source code do not have a particularly good ROI. Coding is only the fourth most expensive activity when building large software applications, and ranks *behind* the construction of paper documents, defect removal activities, and even behind meetings and communication for some systems. An effective reuse program needs to encompass all deliverables.

Moreover, successful software reuse demands state-of-the-art quality control that approaches (and even achieves) zero-defect levels. It is folly to contemplate software reuse prior to formalizing software quality, software measurement, and software management training.

Stage 6: Focus on Industry Leadership

Organizations that go all the way to the sixth stage are usually the leaders in their respective industries. These organizations are often in a position to acquire competitors, or to become outsourcers if they desire.

Industry leadership is a coveted goal that many companies strive to achieve, but very few really do. Among the attributes of industry leadership that are visible to outside consultants, the following stand out:

- Executives who understand and support software
- Software project managers of exceptional ability
- Software technical staff of exceptional ability
- More specialists than average organizations
- Better measurements than average organizations
- Better than average customer satisfaction levels
- Better than average staff morale levels
- Powerful project management tool suites
- Powerful software development tool suites
- Powerful quality assurance and testing tool suites
- Powerful geriatric tools for aging software
- Y2K repairs under control

Software excellence is a multifaceted domain. There is no single solution. For some companies, software excellence may always be beyond their grasp, due to failure of vision on the part of top executives or to inadequate funding to cure the accumulated deficiencies.

Let us now consider the costs, timing, and anticipated results of moving along the path of software excellence.

The Costs, Timing, and Value of Process Improvements

To be really accurate, companies need to create an individualized plan and budget for their improvement strategy. However, the following pages contain some general information based on the overall size of companies in terms of software personnel.

The cost data in Table 6.5 is expressed in terms of cost per capita, or the approximate costs for each employee. The cost elements include training, consulting fees, capital equipment, software licenses, and improvements in office conditions.

Our next topic is how long it takes to move through each stage of the process improvement sequence. As you can see, smaller companies move much more rapidly than larger corporations and government agencies.

Process improvement is, of necessity, a multiyear undertaking. Corporations and government agencies cannot move quickly even when everyone is moving in the same direction. When there is polarization of opinion or political opposition, progress can be very slow or nonexistent.

Our third topic is the value or ROI realized from software process improvement. Table 6.6 shows only the approximate improvements for schedules, costs, and quality (defined here as software defect levels). The results are expressed as

Table 6.5   Process Improvement Expenses per Capita

Stage	Meaning	Small, <100 staff	Medium, <1,000 staff	Large, <10,000 staff	Giant, >10,000 staff	Average
0	Assessment	$100	$125	$150	$250	$156
1	Management	$1,500	$2,500	$3,500	$5,000	$3,125
2	Process	$1,500	$2,500	$3,000	$4,500	$2,875
3	Tools	$3,000	$4,000	$5,000	$8,000	$5,000
4	Infrastructure	$1,000	$1,500	$3,000	$6,500	$3,000
5	Reuse	$500	$2,500	$4,500	$6,000	$3,375
6	Industry leadership	$1,500	$2,000	$3,000	$4,500	$2,750
Total expenses		$9,100	$15,125	$22,150	$34,750	$20,281

Table 6.6   Process Improvement Stages in Calendar Months

Stage	Meaning	Small, <100 staff	Medium, <1,000 staff	Large, <10,000 staff	Giant, >10,000 staff	Average
0	Assessment	2.00	2.00	3.00	4.00	2.75
1	Management	3.00	6.00	9.00	12.00	7.50
2	Process	4.00	6.00	9.00	15.00	8.50
3	Tools	4.00	6.00	9.00	12.00	7.75
4	Infrastructure	3.00	4.00	9.00	12.00	7.00
5	Reuse	4.00	6.00	12.00	16.00	9.50
6	Industry leadership	6.00	8.00	9.00	12.00	8.75
	Sum (worst case)	26.00	38.00	60.00	83.00	51.75
	Overlap (best case)	16.90	26.60	43.20	61.42	33.64

percent improvement compared with the initial baseline at the start of the improvement process. As you can see from this rough analysis, the maximum benefits do not occur until stage 5, when full software reusability programs are implemented. Because reusability has the best return and greatest results, it is frequently asked why it is not the first stage.

The reason that software reuse is offset to stage 5 is that a successful reusability program depends on mastery of software quality and a host of precursor software technologies, such as formal inspections and formal development processes. Unless software quality is at state-of-the-art levels, any attempt to reuse materials results in longer schedules and higher costs than you incur right now!

An interesting question is: What is the *smallest* amount of money that can be spent to achieve any tangible benefits whatsoever? What appears to be the cheapest improvement strategies for software within large corporations or government agencies are the methodological improvements that do not require capital investments in new tools. For example, JAD, usage of function point metrics, and the usage of inspections can be deployed with only training expenses. These three methods usually require a two-day training session for a nominal cost of $800 per person, plus any travel expenses. Because any one of these methods will produce tangible benefits, the minimum cost to make visible improvements is roughly $800 per person. However, the improvements in schedules, costs, and quality seldom exceed 10% for minimal investments.

For small, individual projects, even lower cost improvements are possible. Moving to a modern "visual" programming language and its associated environment can be done for less than $500, and will result in tangible productivity gains compared with older procedural languages and sparse environments.

A somewhat alarming corollary is: What is the largest amount that companies have spent without achieving any benefit or value at all? Several companies and government agencies have managed to spend in excess of $10,000 per capita without accruing tangible benefits.

Our second topic is how long it takes to move through each stage of the process improvement sequence. This topic is highly variable based on the size of the enterprise and the level of sophistication when first starting out on the process improvement path.

For example, a company that is near the bottom of the SEI capability scale (a very low level 1 ranking) can still achieve only a level 1 ranking after 12 to 18 months because organizations in this much distress can seldom do anything quickly. On the other hand, an organization that may be a level 1 on the SEI CMM but is near the level 2 boundary can move up to level 3 in the same 12- to 18-month period. Organizations that are energetic and active can even accelerate during their process improvement cycles. Table 6.6 shows some rough approximations of the time spans in calendar months to move through each stage of software process improvement.

As you can see, smaller companies can move much more rapidly than large corporations and government agencies.

Our next topic is the kind of value or ROI realized from software process improvement. From developing ROI models and analyzing client data, the approximate range of ROI for software improvement programs typically runs from approximately $3.00 to more than $30.00 for every dollar invested, with the returns measured over a 48-month period. Of course, not every technology returns its maximum ROI in every case. Table 6.7 shows only the approximate improvements for schedules, costs, and quality (defined here as software defect levels). The results are expressed as percent improvement compared with the initial baseline at the start of the improvement process.

Software assessments, benchmarks, and baselines are very powerful diagnostic tools, but they do not cure software problems. However, they do make prob-

Table 6.7   Improvements in Software Defect Levels, Productivity, and Schedules

Stage	Meaning	Defect Improvement, %	Productivity Improvement, %	Schedule Improvement, %
0	Assessment/baseline	–	–	–
1	Management	–10	–	–10
2	Methods/processes	–50	25	–15
3	New tools	–10	35	–15
4	Infrastructure	–5	10	–5
5	Reusability	–85	65	–50
6	Leadership	–5	5	–5
Approximate compound totals		–90	350	–70

lems visible so that effective therapy programs can be planned and implemented. Once an assessment, benchmark, and baseline has been performed, the next step is to use the results to plan a software improvement program, unless the studies indicate your organization is already at best-in-class levels, which does not happen very often.

Benchmark and baseline data is quite useful during the planning of software process improvements because the data allows tangible and meaningful targets to be set. Simplistic improvement targets such as "let's improve by ten to one" have no place in a serious software process improvement program. A realistic target such as "let's average more than 96% in defect removal efficiency" can be an important motivating factor.

During the course of planning an improvement program, it is important to select and deploy technologies that work while avoiding technologies that might be hazardous or inappropriate. Here, too, benchmark and baseline results can help in making rational technical decisions.

Once the improvement program begins, then annual assessments, benchmarks, and baseline studies can monitor progress toward corporate goals. Success in software derives from doing things right and avoiding errors of judgment that lower the odds of a successful project outcome. Assessments, benchmarks, and baselines are effective guides on the path to software process improvements.

The software literature often talks about best-in-class practices: however, it is surprisingly sparse on quantification or exact definitions of what the phrase best-in-class really means. The citations included here are not completely objective, nor do they quantify the exact results achieved at excellent organizations. However, in spite of some ambiguity these citations do at least indicate the practices that differentiate superior software organizations from average or lagging organizations.

Readings and References on Software Process Improvements

Abdel-Hamid, Tarek, and Stuart Madnick. *Software Project Dynamics*. Englewood Cliffs, NJ: Prentice Hall, 1993. (ISBN 013-8220409)

Austin, Robert D. *Measuring and Managing Performance in Organizations*. New York: Dorset House Publishing, 1996. (ISBN 0-932633-36-6, 216 pages)

Bogan, Christopher E., and Michael J. English. *Benchmarking for Best Practices*. New York: McGraw Hill, 1994. (ISBN 0-07-006375-3, 312 pages)

Briand, Loic, and Daniel Roy. *Meeting Deadlines in Hard Real-Time Systems*. Los Alamitos, CA: IEEE Computer Society Press, 1997. (ISBN 0-8186-7406-7, 300 pages)

Brooks, Frederick P. *The Mythical Man-Month*. Reading, MA: Addison-Wesley Longman, 1995. (ISBN 0-201-00650-2, 295 pages)

Brown, Norm, ed. *The Program Manager's Guide to Software Acquisition Best Practices*. Version 1.0. Washington, DC: U.S. Department of Defense, July 1995. (142 pages)

Caputo, Kim. *CMM Implementation Guide*. Reading, MA: Addison Wesley Longman, 1998. (ISBN 0-201-37938-4, 319 pages)

Carnegie Mellon University. *The Capability Maturity Model: Guidelines for Improving the Software Process*. Reading, MA: Addison Wesley Longman, 1995. (ISBN 0-201-54664-7, 441 pages)

Curtis, Bill, William E. Hefley, and Sally Miller. *People Capability Maturity Model*. Pittsburgh, PA: Software Engineering Institute, Carnegie Mellon University, 1995.

DeMarco, Tom. *Controlling Software Projects*. New York: Yourdon Press, 1982. (ISBN 0-917072-32-4, 284 pages)

————. *Why Does Software Cost So Much?* New York: Dorset House Publishing, 1995. (ISBN 0-932633-34-X, 1995, 237 pages)

————. *The Deadline*. New York: Dorset House Publishing, 1997. (ISBN 0-932633-39-0)

DeMarco, Tom, and Tim Lister. *Peopleware*. New York: Dorset House Publishing, 1987. (ISBN 0-932633-05-6, 188 pages)

Department of the Air Force. *Guidelines for Successful Acquisition and Management of Software Intensive Systems*. Vol. 1 and 2. Hill Air Force Base, UT: Software Technology Support Center, 1994.

El Emam, Khaled and Nazim Madhavji, eds. *Elements of Software Process Assessment and Improvement*. Los Alamitos, CA: IEEE Computer Society Press, 1999. (ISBN 0-8185-8523-9, 384 pages)

Grady, Robert B. *Successful Software Process Improvement*. Upper Saddle River, NJ: Prentice Hall, 1997. (ISBN 0-13-626623-1, 314 pages)

Humphrey, Watts S. *Managing the Software Process*. Reading, MA: Addison Wesley Longman, 1989. (ISBN 0-201-18095-2)

————. *Introduction to the Personal Software Process*. Reading, MA: Addison Wesley Longman, 1997. (ISBN 0201548097)

————. *Managing Technical People*. Reading, MA: Addison Wesley Longman, 1997. (ISBN 0-201-54597-7, 326 pages)

Jones, Capers. *Programming Productivity*. New York: McGraw Hill, 1986. (ISBN 0-07-032811-0, 280 pages)

————. *A Ten-Year Retrospective of the ITT Programming Technology Center*. Burlington, MA: Software Productivity Research, Burlington, 1988.

————. *Assessment and Control of Software Risks*. Englewood Cliffs, NJ: Prentice Hall, 1993. (ISBN 0-13-741406-4, 711 pages)

————. *Critical Problems in Software Measurement*. Carlsbad, CA: Information Systems Management Group, 1993. (ISBN 1-56909-000-9, 195 pages)

————. *Software Productivity and Quality Today: The Worldwide Perspective*. Carlsbad, CA: Information Systems Management Group, 1993. (ISBN 156909-001-7, 200 pages)

————. *New Directions in Software Management*. Carlsbad, CA: Information Systems Management Group, 1994. (ISBN 1-56909-009-2, 150 pages)

————. *Patterns of Software System Failure and Success*. Boston, MA: International Thomson Computer Press, December 1995. (ISBN 1-850-32804-8, 292 pages)

————. *Applied Software Measurement*. 2nd ed. New York: McGraw Hill, 1996. (ISBN 0-07-032826-9, 618 pages)

————. *Software Quality: Analysis and Guidelines for Success*. Boston, MA: International Thomson Computer Press, 1997. (ISBN 1-85032-876-6, 492 pages)

————. *Becoming Best in Class*. SPR technical report. Burlington, MA: Software Productivity Research, January 1998. (40 pages)

————. *Estimating Software Costs*. New York: McGraw Hill, 1998. (ISBN 0-07-9130941, 725 pages)

————. "Sizing Up Software." *Scientific American* 1998; 279(6):104–111.

————. *The Costs, Schedule, and Value of Software Process Improvement*. SPR technical report. Burlington, MA: Software Productivity Research, January 1998. (27 pages)

————. *The Year 2000 Software Problem: Quantifying the Costs and Assessing the Consequences*. Reading, MA: Addison Wesley, 1998. (ISBN 0-201-30964-5, 303 pages)

Kan, Stephen H. *Metrics and Models in Software Quality Engineering*. Reading, MA: Addison Wesley, 1994. (ISBN 0-201-63339-6, 344 pages)

Keys, Jessica. *Software Engineering Productivity Handbook*. New York: McGraw Hill, 1993. (ISBN 0-07-911366-4, 651 pages)

Love, Tom. *Object Lessons*. New York: SIGS Books, 1993. (ISBN 0-96274773-4, 266 pages)

Melton, Austin. *Software Measurement*. London: Chapman & Hall, 1995. (ISBN 1-85032-7178-7)

Mills, Harlan. *Software Productivity*. New York: Dorset House Publishing, 1988. (ISBN 0-932633-10-2, 288 pages)

Multiple authors. *Rethinking the Software Process*. CD-ROM. Lawrence, KS: Miller Freeman, 1996. (This is a new CD-ROM book collection produced jointly by the book publisher Prentice Hall and the journal publisher Miller Freeman. This CD-ROM disk contains the full text and illustrations of five Prentice Hall books: *Assessment and Control of Software Risks* by Capers Jones, *Controlling Software Projects* by Tom DeMarco, *Function Point Analysis* by Brian Dreger, *Measures for Excellence* by Larry Putnam and Ware Myers, and *Object-Oriented Software Metrics* by Mark Lorenz and Jeff Kidd.)

Park, Robert E., et al. *Software Cost and Schedule Estimating: A Process Improvement Initiative*. Technical report CMU/SEI 94-SR-03. Pittsburgh, PA: Software Engineering Institute, May 1994.

Pressman, Roger. *Software Engineering: A Practitioner's Approach*. New York: McGraw Hill, 1982.

Putnam, Lawrence H. *Measures for Excellence: Reliable Software On Time, Within Budget*. Englewood Cliffs, NJ: Prentice Hall, 1992. (ISBN 0-13-567694-0, 336 pages)

Putnam, Lawrence H., and Ware Myers. *Industrial Strength Software: Effective Management Using Measurement*. Los Alamitos, CA: IEEE Computer Society Press, 1997. (ISBN 0-8186-7532-2, 320 pages)

Roetzheim, William H., and Reyna A. Beasley. *Software Project Cost & Schedule Estimating*. Upper Saddle River, NJ: Prentice Hall, 1998. (ISBN 0-13-682089-1)

Rubin, Howard. *Software Benchmark Studies for 1998*. Pound Ridge, NY: Howard Rubin Associates, 1998.

Software Productivity Research. *Quality and Productivity of the SEI CMM*. Burlington, MA: Software Productivity Research, 1994.

Strassmann, Paul. *The Politics of Information Management: Policy Guidelines*. New Canaan, CT: The Information Economics Press, 1995. (ISBN 0-9620413-4-3, 523 pages)

————. *The Squandered Computer*. New Canaan, CT: The Information Economics Press, 1997. (ISBN 0-9620413-1-9, 426 pages)

Symons, Charles R. *Software Sizing and Estimating: Mk II FPA (Function Point Analysis)*. Chichester, UK: John Wiley & Sons, 1991. (ISBN 0 471-92985-9, 200 pages)

Thayer, Richard H., ed. *Software Engineering Project Management*. Los Alamitos, CA: IEEE Computer Society Press, 1988. (ISBN 0-8186-075107, 512 pages)

Weinberg, Gerald. *Quality Software Management. Vol. 2, First-Order Measurement*. New York: Dorset House Publishing, 1993. (ISBN 0-932633-24-2, 360 pages)

Wiegers, Karl A. *Creating a Software Engineering Culture*. New York: Dorset House Publishing, 1996. (ISBN 0-932633-33-1, 358 pages)

Zvegintzov, Nicholas. *Software Management Technology Reference Guide*. New York: Software Maintenance News, 1994. (ISBN 1-884521-01-0, 240 pages)

CHAPTER SEVEN

Benchmarks and Best Practices for MIS Software Projects

The phrase *management information systems* refers to the type of applications that enterprises produce in support of their own business and administrative operations: payroll systems, accounting systems, front- and back-office banking systems, insurance claims handling systems, airline reservation systems, electronic business, and the like. This term was first used circa 1963, when computers started their explosive growth as business tools. More recent terms for similar applications include the familiar *information technology* circa 1980. Now that companies are rushing to use the Internet and World Wide Web for business purposes, many of the more recent information applications have been aimed at electronic business, or *e-business*, as this domain has come to be called. However, more than half of the managers and personnel who provided the data for this chapter are older than 40 years of age and still use the term *MIS* for the bulk of applications in their corporate portfolios.

Traditionally, from the 1960s through the early 1990s, MIS applications ran on mainframes and minicomputers. Mainframes were dominant for large corporate applications in large companies. Smaller minicomputers and mid-range computers were dominant for divisional applications and for small companies. End users of MIS applications utilized dedicated "dumb" terminals connected to host computers. The advent of the PC triggered the development of new forms of MIS applications. Distributed client/server applications are a major subtype, and in turn can be divided into two-tier and three-tier client/ server subtypes.

The two-tier client/server application type uses PCs for *clients*, or the actual computers in the hands of users. The *server* provides support and actually executes some applications, such as shared database programs. Servers are often mainframes or minicomputers, although PC-based servers are very common too.

The three-tier form of client/server application uses a central host computer, usually a mainframe, for large databases. Smaller server computers are used to provide services to PC clients. The three-tier client/server model is somewhat more common in large companies because it offers better security for valuable or proprietary data. The three-tier client/server model also offers somewhat better performance when the numbers of users climbs higher than 100 knowledge workers.

As the century begins, notebook computers and small, hand-held *personal digital assistants* are also present in increasing numbers. (Indeed, this paragraph was first written on a Hewlett-Packard Jornada 680 palmtop while enroute to Seattle.) In addition, usage of networks, the Internet, and the World Wide Web have become daily tools of corporate and government knowledge workers. Supporting Internet and Web-based users are a host of very recent and very small applications termed *Web applets*, with the phrase *applet* used as a diminutive term for Web applications that are usually less than 100 function points, often written in the JAVA programming language.

Thus the nature of MIS is expanding in several directions. There are major lateral expansions to deal with networks and users scattered, literally, all over the world. There are vertical expansions in both directions. Many small applets are being constructed for Web use. At the other end of the spectrum, massive ERP applications are attempting to integrate all corporate data and much of corporate information processing. The MIS domain is evolving rapidly as the twentieth century ends, and no final destination is in sight.

Another expansion has to do with moving from "information" to "knowledge." Information is viewed as being more or less equivalent to ore, which might require extensive processing to yield a valuable mineral. Using this analogy, which is not perfect, information stored in corporate databases and data warehouses can be refined to create a more valuable end product or knowledge. Knowledge, in this analogy, is a combination of information and business rules associated with major business or technical issues.

MIS Applications and Corporate Databases

The nature of MIS implies that they are often linked to corporate databases, and one of their main purposes is the extraction, consolidation, and manipulation of information from databases. Although MIS projects are often developed using the COBOL programming language, data extraction and manipulation is usually performed with specialized languages such as the Structured Query Language (SQL) or Query by Example (QBE).

The history of MIS applications and their relationship to data is interesting. Most corporations are somewhat "feudal" in their organizational structures. That is, various business units such as manufacturing, marketing, sales, finance, engineering, administration, and human resources have each funded MIS applications that meet their specific needs. However, because these various business units may be somewhat competitive, the separate MIS applications they build do not always communicate or share data easily. From the vantage point of corporate executives seeking overall information about the entire business, it has been hard to extract consolidated data from these separate business unit applications.

To deal with the problem of incompatible databases and incompatible MIS applications among business units, a number of recent technologies have become popular in the MIS domain starting in the 1990s. Companies are beginning to build *data repositories* or *data warehouses* or *data marts* to consolidate information from multiple business units. Technologies such as *data mining* are now available to extract useful information from incompatible business unit databases, with moderate success.

Recent attempts in the MIS domain to move beyond the concept of information and toward the concept of *knowledge* have not been fully successful. Knowledge in this context is extracting and analyzing enough useful information from disparate corporate databases to yield insights into important business topics. The data is then merged with insights from various domain experts employed by the enterprise.

This technology of going beyond information to knowledge is still experimental and unproved as this book is written, but with interesting potential. A few pioneering companies are creating positions such as chief knowledge officer.

Knowledge management research is an extension of older MIS studies and applications aimed at *decision support*. Decision support applications were expert systems aimed at providing a measure of guidance to executives in key business decisions. An example of a typical decision would be whether to invest in a new product line.

Lack of Data Metrics

Because of the close coupling of MIS applications with large databases, the MIS domain has long been troubled by data errors as well as errors in software applications. Unfortunately, the literature on data quality remains sparse, and quantitative information on data quality is essentially nonexistent. The reason for this is due to a curious gap in measurement technology. Unlike software, for which metrics such as function points and LOC can be used to show average values and ranges, there are no units of measure for data.

Because of the lack of a useful *data point* size metric, there are no published studies on the volumes of data owned by corporations, the cost of gathering data, the numbers of errors in the data, the cost of fixing data errors, and the cost of retiring obsolete and unused data. Thus, a major corporate asset—data—is currently outside the scope of economic analysis. It appears that companies own more data than they do software, but the volumes of corporate data have never been quantified or measured.

Data *quality* is also difficult to explore due to the lack of a data size metric. It is suspected by data quality researchers, including myself, that data errors are more common and at least as serious as software errors. Here, too, there are no solid empirical studies due to the lack of data metrics.

Although several books have been published about data quality, and MIT's Sloan School has a research program in this topic, the lack of metrics for normalizing data volumes and data defect levels makes this literature somewhat subjective and anecdotal. Essentially, statistical and economic studies of data quality are not possible until the development of a data point metric.

The same lack of metrics that has long been a weakness of the database world remains a weakness in the more recent domains of information management and knowledge management. Due to the lack of a standard size metric for data, information, or knowledge, the entire domain has no solid basis for economic research, no quality benchmarks, and no studies on topics such as ROI in knowledge acquisition.

There is some research underway by the author to create a data point metric based on the structure of the function point metric (Jones 1999a), but this research is experimental and not yet proved to be effective.

MIS and Enterprise Resource Planning

Another interesting trend in the MIS domain has been the growth of ERP applications. In general, ERP applications are commercial packages rather than in-house software. Indeed, ERP applications are intended to replace many incompatible legacy MIS applications. Some of the ERP vendors include SAP, Oracle, Baan, JD Edwards, and Peoplesoft.

The rationale behind the ERP market is the hypothesis that disparate business unit software applications and data can never be fully integrated, or at least not done so economically. The ERP concept is that rather than attempting costly and perhaps futile integration of dozens of aging and incompatible MIS applications and their equally incompatible data, it is more efficient to deploy an integrated ERP application that supports all business units and corporate executives. Thus ERP applications such as SAP, Oracle, and Baan are aimed at the level of entire corporations, rather than at smaller divisions or business units.

Of course the ERP applications do not support every function, so custom applications are still needed. However, these can be developed in the ERP environment, and hence can share common resources. Some of these new applications in an ERP environment are created using special programming languages, such as SAP's ABAP/4 programming language.

A full-scale ERP deployment for a large company can top 250,000 function points. Over time, an additional set of customized ERP applications can double that size to 500,000 function points. ERP applications support the classic suite of MIS functions for business units, such as manufacturing, purchasing, human resources, sales, and marketing. However, in an ERP context, the data is designed to be compatible across all business units.

Acquiring and deploying an ERP package is a major project in its own right. ERP deployment often takes more than 24 calendar months, and requires perhaps 50 outside consultants and substantial conversion from legacy applications and databases. The ERP decision is not without risk, and some ERP deployments have been unsuccessful. One ERP acquisition has even been cited as a partial cause of a corporate bankruptcy.

MIS Applications, the Euro, and the Year 2000

From 1995 through the end of the century, the MIS domain has had to deal with the two largest software projects in human history: the new unified European currency or Euro, and the even larger Y2K problem.

In the countries of the European monetary union, approximately 25% of our clients' MIS personnel worked on the Euro during calendar years 1996, 1997, and 1998 in preparation for the initial rollout of the Euro in January 1999. Unfortunately, the timing of the Euro in 1999 caused these two massive projects to compete head-on for scarce software resources. As a result, Western Europe lagged in Y2K repairs.

Our clients in the United States deployed approximately 25% of their MIS personnel on Y2K repairs starting in 1996 or 1997. However, because Y2K repairs have not been 100% effective, many prudent companies created contingency plans. Substantial "second-wave" Y2K repair work occurred during 1999 because many fiscal years changed before calendar year 2000. Many large companies had software personnel on 24-hour readiness as the century ended. Some created special Y2K command centers to coordinate both their own repairs and to offer assistance to clients, suppliers, and some government agencies.

The overall impact of the Y2K problem did not stop in January 2000. Repairs and recovery operations continue through the spring and summer of 2000. Litigation and long-range damages will continue to amass for at least another five years.

MIS Technologies

A number of interesting technologies have been developed in the MIS domain. Because data and software are so closely coupled for MIS applications, a number of these technologies overlap both database development and software development.

One of the more popular MIS development approaches is termed *information engineering*. There are several specific commercial variations in the information engineering market, such as the methods of Texas Instruments and James Martin Associates. However, all information engineering approaches are aimed at the design and development of database applications and include data design principles as well as software design principles.

There are also a number of software design methods aimed primarily at MIS applications. Among these are the Warnier-Orr approach, the Michael Jackson approach, and the James Martin approach. I use the phrase *data analytic* to describe these MIS design methods. This is because these methods tend to focus on the flow of data and information through software applications, and include database design as a fundamental element of software design.

The project management aspects of MIS applications are supported by a number of software cost-estimating tools aimed at MIS applications. One of the earliest of these MIS estimating tools was Estimacs, designed by Dr. Howard Rubin in the 1970s. Other more recent estimating tools with MIS support include (in alphabetic order) Adaptive Estimating Model, Bridge Modeler, CHECKPOINT, COCOMO II, Cost Expert, KnowledgePlan, SEER, SLIM, and ValPro.

In addition to stand-alone estimating tools, there are also some embedded estimating tools that are part of larger MIS development tool suites. For example the Texas Instruments Information Engineering Facility contains an embedded tool that can create function point size estimates, and then produce software cost and schedule estimates.

Because function point metrics are the most widely used metric in the MIS domain, there are at least a half dozen function point counting tools marketed to MIS companies. Here, too, both stand-alone and embedded tools are available, such as Function Point Workbench—a stand-alone tool. The Bachman Analyst design tool offered an embedded function point module that could derive function point totals from software designs.

Because MIS applications have often been funded by specific client organizations to solve specific problems, the requirements for MIS applications are often derived from a small number of users. This is in contrast to the requirements for many systems software applications such as Windows 98, which is intended to support millions of clients.

Because many MIS requirements are developed for specific purposes, the requirements-gathering and analysis methods for MIS applications are quite important. The most popular and successful method among our clients for ascertaining requirements is JAD. This method was developed in the 1970s at IBMs' software development lab in Toronto, Canada. The JAD approach features joint requirements development by teams representing both the software users and the software development organization. The requirements planning sessions are often held off-site to ensure that the work proceeds without interruption. Trained JAD facilitators moderate the JAD sessions to ensure that the requirements include all relevant factors.

The JAD approach has been quite successful among our clients. One of the virtues of the JAD approach is a significant reduction in "creeping requirements," which are normally a major problem for MIS applications. After JAD requirements are gathered and finalized, the rate of monthly change is less than 0.5%

per month. The older informal methods for gathering MIS requirements tended to experience changes that approximated 2% per month during the design and coding phases. (Requirements creep can be measured directly and quite accurately by counting the function points in the initial requirements and comparing this count to the volume of function points when the application is finished and delivered.)

For many years, COBOL was the dominant language used for information systems, although PL/I, Assembly, FORTRAN, RPG, and APL showed up occasionally. In Europe, PL/I was a popular language for information systems, although it was not so popular in the United States. In recent years the JAVA programming language and Visual Basic have joined the family of languages commonly used for information systems programming.

For the database portion of information systems, languages such as SQL and specialized database languages were predominant. From the 1980s onward, a host of new languages, and even new kinds of languages such as program and application generators, swept through the information systems domain.

As of 2000, a total of more than 200 programming languages are now found in the information systems domain, including C and C++, JAVA, Powersoft, RPG, Telon, Pacbase, Visual Basic, Magec, Realizer, and countless more. This diversity of programming languages is actually making hiring suitable programming personnel difficult, and it is making software maintenance a nightmare.

Although hundreds of programming languages are found in the MIS domain, the COBOL language remains the cornerstone of MIS development. (There are several COBOL variants in use, but all share a basic syntax and common structures.) In the United States there are at least 600,000 COBOL programmers—making COBOL the most widely utilized programming language of all. Of course, because a program uses COBOL does not preclude the programmer from using other languages such as JAVA or Visual Basic. However, due to the large numbers of legacy applications written in COBOL during the past 20 years, COBOL is still a major presence in the information systems world.

COBOL has stood the test of time, and will remain an effective language even in the twenty-first century. Because COBOL is so popular, there are more programming tools available for COBOL than for any other language. This is true of both development and maintenance tools. There are also substantial volumes of reusable COBOL code available, in both commercial and proprietary forms.

Because COBOL is the most widely deployed business programming language, it was among the most widely affected by the dreaded Y2K problem.

However, COBOL was among the first programming languages with automated Y2K search and repair tools available. COBOL running on IBM mainframe computers also has a unique Y2K solution in the form of a dynamic object-code Y2K repair method that intercepts and corrects dates in executable code.

Although COBOL has been chided as not being a "modern" language, it has continued to evolve, and even boasts an OO form. Whether standard COBOL is totally modern is not as important as the ready availability of experienced COBOL programmers, who are present in larger numbers in businesses than programmers of any other language. Thus, even though there is a widespread shortage of software and programming personnel, COBOL skills are still easier to find than other programming languages.

A number of tool and methodology vendors have also specialized or concentrated on the MIS domain: Platinum, Sterling, Computer Associates, Oracle, Intersolv, LBMS, KnowledgeWare, SQA, James Martin, Texas Instruments, and many more. Essentially all of the vendors that specialize in topics such as RAD, information engineering, client/server technologies, and database technologies are aiming at the MIS world. There are also MIS specialists in the consulting business, just as there are specialized consulting companies in the systems and military software domains.

In companies that employ both MIS and systems software personnel, such as IBM or AT&T, it is interesting that these two domains are quite separate and seldom share technologies, office space, computers, or other facilities. Normally the MIS organizations report to a CIO, who may in turn report to the chief financial officer. The systems software organizations report to one or more vice presidents of engineering, and are often located in large laboratories in which research and development take place. These labs include electrical and mechanical engineers, and support hardware development as well as software development.

It is unfortunate that the MIS domain does not use more of the technologies developed for systems software, such as formal design and code inspections. As it happens, the MIS domain does not often excel in large software projects. For projects more than 10,000 function points, schedule delays, cost overruns, and outright cancellations of projects have outnumbered successes by a considerable margin. As a result, the top executives of many companies are questioning whether outsourcing might be a better long-range solution.

The primary reasons why large MIS projects fail are poor quality control and inadequate project management tools and methods. Compared with the systems software domain, very few MIS projects utilize formal design and code inspections or have trained software quality assurance personnel, test specialists, and quality measurements.

As a result of skimping on quality during the early phases, large MIS projects give a false appearance of being more or less under control and on schedule until testing begins. Then it is discovered that the project has so many design and coding errors that it cannot be released without months of testing and extensive repairs. Often the defects are so severe and so numerous that the application cannot be fully repaired, and is cancelled instead. If the MIS project managers had performed careful schedule, cost, and quality estimates, and used appropriate quality control techniques, many MIS disasters may have been successes instead of failures.

The combination of poor results on large software projects and the ever-growing backlog of MIS applications has created an interesting industry, called *outsourcing*, which is discussed in the next chapter of this book. The information systems community's ever-growing need for custom software coupled with significant MIS problems has created the largest outsourcing and contract software organizations in the world. Enterprises such as Andersen Consulting, Computer Sciences Corporation (CSC), EDS, Perot Systems, Keane Associates, Unisys, COMPAQ (formerly DEC), and IBM's outsourcing subsidiary employ many thousands of information systems software personnel and support hundreds of client organizations, as discussed in the next chapter.

Diverse Origins of Information Systems and Systems Software

There are deeper reasons beneath the surface for poor management information systems quality. The systems software domain emerged from older forms of engineering such as electrical engineering and mechanical engineering. In the engineering world, the need for quality control has been understood for quite a long time, even if quality control is not always achieved. In fact, substantial testing and quality control groups have been part of the telecommunications industry since the days when switching systems were electromechanical and did not use computers at all. The same is true for aircraft and automobile manufacturing.

Systems software is typically built to control devices that may be marketed in huge volumes, such as automobiles, aircraft, and computers. If these high-volume devices fail, the warranty repairs could be horrendous to say nothing of potential litigation or loss of market shares. Therefore, quality control is a normal aspect of business, and this concept is true of systems software and hardware.

The information systems domain evolved from a different background. For example, in the days before computers, most banks, insurance companies, accounting companies, state governments, and other service-related industries did not have quality assurance or quality control groups, as did manufacturing companies. They often made mistakes and errors, but because of the nature of the work, the mistakes were viewed as exceptions due to individual human error.

Thus the information systems community tends to build software as custom, unique artifacts, rather than as high-volume commercial products. Bugs and errors were expected in MIS projects. This was viewed as no different from the mistakes that sometimes occurred during the previous manual operations the software was replacing or augmenting.

The difference in the origins of information systems software and systems software is strikingly visible in companies that create both kinds, such as AT&T and IBM. Within IBM, for example, the systems software aimed at the outside world was developed using state-of-the-art review, inspection, and testing technologies supported by one of the most sophisticated quality assurance groups in all industry. The internal information systems that IBM created for their own use seldom utilized inspections, and indeed did not even have quality assurance personnel assigned to the project.

The differences in origin between systems software and information systems eventually led to a kind of mutual distrust. The systems software community regarded the information systems community as second tier, and seldom used tools, languages, or methods that were aimed at information systems. The same situation was true in reverse, and the information systems community did not move readily toward technologies that were common in the systems software world.

This sociological pattern is the probable explanation for why approaches such as function points, which were first applied to information systems, have lagged in the systems software domain. Conversely, approaches such as formal design and code inspections that originated for systems software have not caught on in the information systems domain.

As far back as the 1960s, the business software world and the technical software world went about their work in different ways. The MIS community adopted COBOL as the major language, whereas the systems software world continued with Assembly or moved toward C, C++, and the OO paradigm, such as Objective C.

As the twentieth century comes to an end, the dividing line between systems software and information systems is no longer clear. For example, information systems concerned with automatic teller machines for banks also control physical devices. Many systems in both domains now include communications capabilities and operate on networks. Also, both the systems software and information systems domains are developing applications that are ten to 100 times larger than the software typically developed in the 1970s and 1980s.

These trends are beginning to forge a new bond between the previous disparate worlds of systems software and information systems. The leaders of the MIS community are beginning to adopt inspections, formal testing, and quality assurance. The systems software community is beginning to explore function points, sizing tools, cost-estimating tools, and other project management aids that were long used for information systems.

The information systems community is literally whirling with explosions of new concepts and new tools: Client/server applications are expanding across the information systems community, and business process reengineering is a factor in perhaps a third of the large organizations that produce MIS software, and it introduces major modifications in development processes and staffing levels.

The best information systems producers are getting better, but the great majority may not really be able to absorb so much change so fast. This explains why outsourcing is on such a fast growth track, as discussed in the next chapter.

In the systems software domain, the software is part of the main commercial products that companies sell. In the information systems domain, the software typically does not bring in direct revenues. Rather, the software affects operating costs and, if developed well, can lower expenses.

There is a significant business need to become very good or *best in class* in the kind of software that controls a company's main business offerings and commercial products such as computers, switching systems, aircraft flight control systems, and the like. This is why companies such as AT&T, Hewlett-Packard, DEC, and other hardware manufacturers employ so many systems software personnel and expend so much money for assessments, process improvements, and best-in-class drives.

For information systems in many service industries such as banking and insurance, there is significant debate at board room levels on whether software should continue to be developed by full-time employees, turned over to outside contractors or outsource vendors, or whether commercial software packages might not substitute for custom development. In many financial and service companies, software and data-processing personnel can exceed 15% of total corporate employment, and the associated expenses can exceed 18% of annual budgets. This is quite a major expense level for activities that are not associated with bringing in direct revenues or profitability.

If an enterprise is currently good or excellent in information systems development and maintenance, then it would be advantageous to continue with in-house development. On the other hand, if an enterprise lags behind all major competitors in software practices, the investment required to achieve a parity, and the time required, may both be excessive. In this case, outsourcing might be a more cost-effective alternative. For many enterprises, the situation is ambiguous. They may be neither very good nor very bad. In this case, a decision on whether to invest in software process improvements or to outsource needs additional research.

The well-known CMM, developed by the SEI, is not widely used among the MIS community. Among our MIS clients between 1995 and 2000, less than 15% had any active involvement with the SEI CMM approach.

Part of the reason for the lack of penetration of the SEI CMM among the MIS domain has to do with the fact that the SEI was originally funded by the DoD. However, in recent years, the SEI has attempted to broaden the range of applicability of the CMM. Although the CMM is not yet widely deployed among MIS organizations, the latest versions of the CMM are now suitable for adoption by the MIS community.

Another software technology topic with very low penetration among the MIS community is that of certification to the ISO 9000–9004 quality standards. The primary users of these standards are commercial, systems, and military vendors who wish to market products within the European economic union. Because, by definition, MIS projects are internal applications that are not marketed, they have no urgent business reason for adopting the ISO standards.

Although it is true that MIS quality is not very good, there is no empirical data available that indicates that ISO certification improves software quality in any tangible way. Our quality benchmarks between companies that are ISO compliant and those that are not reveals little difference in defect potentials or defect removal efficiency levels. There are much less expensive and more effective approaches to software quality improvement than ISO certification, so the MIS community should not be faulted for lack of ISO certification.

Let us now consider the overall demographics of MIS applications and MIS personnel working in the United States.

MIS Demographics

The MIS domain has not been as diverse as the systems software domain in terms of specialization. For example comparatively few MIS shops have established software quality assurance departments with software quality assurance specialists. Neither do many MIS organizations employ testing and maintenance specialists. Indeed, quite a few MIS organizations are built on the "generalist" principle; that is, the general programming population handles requirements, design, coding, integration, testing, and maintenance after the applications go into production. The job title of programmer/analyst is often used for these generalist personnel who perform many diverse kinds of software work. The most common specialists noted in our MIS assessments and benchmark studies include systems analysis, database administration, and function point analysis.

One unexpected benefit of the Y2K problem has been the fact that companies now know how much software they own. Prior to the Y2K problem, most corporations did not have accurate records of the software applications in their portfolios. As a result of the Y2K problem, major companies know the size and status of every software application in their inventory, including MIS projects, commercial packages, and systems and embedded applications.

Due to the Y2K problem, MIS portfolios have been undergoing intense scrutiny and massive amounts of updates. Many applications were also retired and replaced either by commercial packages or by newer Y2K-compliant applications.

Because most of our clients do not keep very good records of projects less than 100 function points, Table 7.1 lacks information on very small projects in the 1- and 10-function point size ranges. Often these very small "projects" are carried out informally without any kind of cost estimates, budgets, or much in the way of measurement data. The reason is that projects less than 10 function points run from less than one day to less than one week of effort, and often involve only one technical staff member. Sometimes an MIS programmer might work on two or three such small projects during the same day.

Because of the Euro and Y2K problems, an unusually large number of applications were withdrawn or modified in 1999, as indicated by Table 7.1. Incidentally, this table has a high margin of error and is merely a national extrapolation using data from our client base.

The combined resource drain of the Euro and Y2K problems has created a major backlog of applications in the MIS domain. Also, this backlog is occurring

Table 7.1   U.S. MIS Projects circa 1999

Size, function points	No. of Legacy Applications	No. Withdrawn in 1999	No. Under Development	No. Completed in 1999	No. Updated in 1999
100	1,450,000	225,000	174,000	200,000	1,000,000
1,000	750,000	90,000	75,000	18,000	500,000
10,000	65,000	9,000	9,750	2,000	50,000
100,000	150	20	10	3	100
Total	2,265,150	324,020	258,760	220,003	1,550,100

Table 7.2   Estimated U.S. MIS Software Population circa 2000

Software Occupation Groups	No. Employed	MIS Software	Percent of Total
Programmer/analyst	400,000	260,000	65.00
Programmer, maintenance	350,000	122,500	35.00
Programmer, development	275,000	110,000	40.00
Project manager, first level	225,000	78,750	35.00
Software engineer, systems	200,000	2,000	1.00
Testing specialist	125,000	12,500	10.00
Systems analyst	100,000	62,500	62.50
Software engineer, real-time	75,000	750	1.00
Software technical writer	75,000	7,500	10.00
Software engineer, embedded	70,000	700	1.00
Data administration specialist	50,000	25,000	50.00
Project manager, second level	35,000	12,250	35.00
Software quality assurance specialist	25,000	1,875	7.50
Configuration control specialist	15,000	3,000	20.00
Performance specialist	7,500	188	2.50
Project manager, third level	5,000	1,500	30.00
Software architect	1,500	150	10.00
Subtotal	2,034,000	701,163	34.47
Support Occupations			
Software sales specialist	105,000	0	0.00
Customer support specialist	80,000	16,000	20.00
Systems administration	50,000	18,000	36.00
Software management consultant	45,000	9,000	20.00
Software education specialist	30,000	3,000	10.00
Software librarian	15,000	3,000	20.00
Process auditor/assessor	7,500	1,125	15.00
Process improvement specialist	5,000	500	10.00
Measurement specialist	3,500	1,750	50.00

Support Occupations	No. Employed	MIS Software	Percent of Total
Software marketing specialist	3,000	0	0.00
Cost-estimating specialist	2,000	200	10.00
Human factors specialist	1,000	100	10.00
Certified function point counter	500	275	55.00
Subtotal	322,000	52,950	16.44
Total	2,356,000	754,113	32.01

at a time when there is already an existing software personnel shortage. As this book is written at the end of 1999 and early 2000, the MIS domain is lagging far behind in meeting the demands for new and updated applications. The typical backlog among Fortune 500 companies in our client set is now approximately 100,000 function points apportioned among several new applications and scores of major enhancements. Most of our major clients have openings for 50 to more than 100 new software personnel in their MIS groups.

This shortage of MIS personnel has raised a major issue, and employment opportunities for older software workers who are older than 50 years of age. Because younger, entry-level personnel have lower salaries than more experienced personnel, some companies seem to give hiring preferences to young employees rather than mature employees. This issue is outside the scope of this book, but it is a major topic of controversy.

Incidentally, there are a number of topics that are omitted deliberately from software assessments and benchmark studies because of legal or ethical considerations. Some of these omitted topics include age of employees, gender of employees, ethnic origin of employees, religious preference of employees, sexual orientation of employees, political preference of employees, and employee membership in trade unions.

The MIS domain is, numerically, the largest overall employer of software personnel in the United States, as seen in Table 7.2.

Every industry listed in the Department of Commerce SIC codes produces MIS. Some of the major producers of MIS applications include airlines, banks, brokerage houses, insurance companies, manufacturing companies, wholesale and retail outlets, and telecommunication companies. However, the SIC codes with the largest concentration of MIS employees include those listed in Table 7.3.

The telecommunications industry is a major employer of both systems software personnel and MIS personnel. The telecommunications manufacturing companies employ very large numbers of systems software personnel, whereas the telecommunications operating companies such as Bell South, Bell Atlantic, and Pacific Bell employ very large numbers of MIS personnel, often more than 5,000 in the larger locations.

The financial and insurance sectors are the largest overall employers of MIS personnel throughout the industrialized world. Large banks and insurance companies often have MIS staffs that top 5,000 personnel. Mergers and acquisitions in the telecommunications domain make demographics a fluid and variable matter that changes from month to month.

Government agencies also produce information systems, such as the various kinds of taxation software produced at local, state, and national levels. Child care applications, law enforcement applications, social security benefit tracking systems, and driver's license and vehicle registration systems are additional examples.

The domain of MIS constitutes a very broad range of application sizes and types. At the upper end are massive ERP systems of more than 250,000 function points, if all features are deployed in a large company. Major corporations also build some large mainframe systems in excess of 50,000 function points at the upper end of the spectrum, and small PC applications or Web applets of less than 100 function points at the low end of the spectrum.

The information systems community in the United States has been far and away the largest employer of professional software personnel: Approximately 750,000 personnel out of an approximate U.S. total of 2,350,000 work in the domain of information systems. More than 25,000 U.S. organizations employ

Table 7.3   SIC Codes with the Largest Concentration of MIS Employees

SIC Code	Industry
48	Communications (telephone operating companies)
60	Depository Institutions (banking)
61	Security and Commodity Brokers
62	Insurance Carriers
91	Executive, Legislative, and General Government

information systems personnel. However, the bulk of MIS employment is noted within large corporations, such as the Fortune 500 set. The average MIS employment among Fortune 500 companies is close to 1,000 MIS personnel. Of course, many Fortune 500 companies also employ systems software personnel, use contract personnel, and have many ancillary occupations as well.

The high employment of information systems personnel is also true for every industrialized country in Western Europe, South America, and the Pacific Rim. The global information systems community is the largest in every industrialized country. There are some significant exceptions to this rule. In China and Russia, military software and systems software dominate. Both countries develop MIS applications, of course, but to date have used computers more for military than for civilian purposes. SPR estimates that the worldwide total of information systems personnel outside the United States is approximately 8,000,000, making this subindustry the largest employer of software personnel overall.

The major employers of information systems software personnel are the industries that were early adopters of mainframe computers: banks, insurance companies, manufacturing companies, government agencies, and the like. Insurance, for example, has at least a dozen major companies that employ many thousands of software personnel: Aetna Insurance, Travelers Insurance, CIGNA, Hartford Insurance, Sun Life Insurance, and so forth. (The city of Hartford, Connecticut, is a major hub of insurance companies. More than 25,000 MIS personnel work in the Hartford area in insurance alone.)

Of course, corporations that are better known for other kinds of software also produce information systems in large volume: AT&T, IBM, and Boeing Computer Services are also information systems producers. In addition, the DoD and the military services produce huge volumes of information systems.

MIS Benchmarks

To begin our discussion of MIS benchmarks, Figure 7.1 illustrates overall trends in the MIS domain. The most notable feature of the MIS productivity data is that MIS projects less than 1,000 function points are often quite productive. However, at more than 10,000 function points, MIS projects lag behind systems software and outsource results.

Many of the MIS tools and development practices are optimized for small projects. The lack of real rigor in software quality methods leads to serious trouble for large systems in the MIS domain. Not only is productivity often low, but cancelled projects and outright failures are common.

With all types of software, small maintenance and enhancement projects and small development projects have very different productivity levels. Small maintenance projects require regression testing of the entire application plus recompilation of much of the application. The difficulty of adding small updates to large systems safely is the general reason for the lower productivity levels of small maintenance projects.

Figure 7.1 illustrates an important aspect of the MIS domain. Small projects at or less than 1,000 function points are quite productive, but the MIS domain is visibly unsuccessful at the larger size ranges of 10,000 and 100,000 function points.

Repeated MIS failures in attempts to develop large applications have triggered two significant new businesses in recent years: the outsourcing subindustry and the ERP class of products. Both of these new business sectors have grown as a direct response to the MIS failures on large applications in excess of 10,000 function points.

Because MIS applications are very common and are created by hundreds of our clients, they tend to have the greatest ranges in terms of productivity and quality levels. The differences between the worst, average, and the best results are

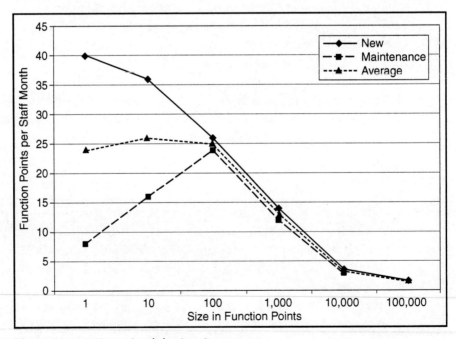

Figure 7.1   MIS productivity levels

sometimes surprisingly broad. Table 7.4 illustrates approximate average values derived from roughly 1,000 projects examined between 1995 and 1999.

Although the overall results of Table 7.4 are interesting, it is always useful to get below the level of gross averages and consider the activities that are commonly used in building MIS applications. Table 7.5 illustrates a typical activity pattern for an MIS application of 10,000 function points. This is a size at which MIS projects are seldom successful. In fact, it is the repeated failure of MIS

Table 7.4   Overall MIS Software Benchmarks

Benchmark	Value
No. of new projects from 1995 through 1999	505
No. of enhancement projects from 1995 through 1999	560
Total no. of projects from 1995 through 1999	1,065
Average new project size, function points	950
Maximum new project size, function points	35,000
Average enhancement size, function points	85
Maximum enhancement size, function points	2,900
Average new development assignment scope, function points	175
Maximum development assignment scope, function points	480
Average maintenance assignment scope, function points	950
Maximum maintenance assignment scope, function points	4,900
Average productivity, function points per staff month	9.6
Maximum productivity, function points per staff month	63.5
Average productivity, work hours per function point	13.75

continued

Table 7.4 *continued*

Benchmark	Value
Maximum productivity, work hours per function point	2.08
Average effort, staff months	9,120
Maximum effort, staff months	168,000
Average new project staff size	5
Maximum new project staff size	286
Average new project schedule, calendar months	15.53
Maximum new project schedule, calendar months	63.00
Average monthly compensation, burdened	$9,800
Maximum monthly compensation, burdened	$23,500
Average cost per function point	$1,020.83
Maximum cost per function point	$7,800.00
Average defect potential per function point	4.8
Maximum defect potential per function point	9.2
Average defect removal efficiency	84.70%
Maximum defect removal efficiency	96.50%
Average monthly rate of requirements creep	1.20%
Maximum monthly rate of requirements creep	5.10%

projects in the 10,000-function point range that has fueled the rapid expansion of outsourcing.

Note that MIS projects are often developed using a "generalist" philosophy; that is, the general population of programmers or programmer/analysts handles requirements, design, coding, testing, and quality assurance (if any). Often, the only specialists used on MIS projects are technical writers, because writing is such a rare human talent. Database administrators may also be used for MIS projects if the project accesses corporate data. The generalist approach for MIS projects is in sharp contrast to systems software projects, for which specialists usually perform tasks such as testing, integration, and quality assurance.

In Table 7.5 the Assignment Scope ("A-Scope") column is the amount of work normally assigned to one staff member. The Production Rate ("P-Rate") column reflects the amount of work normally accomplished in a standard time period, which in this case is a work month. The other columns are fairly self-explanatory and show the staffing level, number of staff months of effort, number of calendar months, activity-level costs, and the overall percentage of cost that each activity contributes to the entire project.

It should be noted that although function points can be used to show monthly productivity, applications are not built a few function points at a time. A useful analogy is "cost per square foot" for home construction. Although cost per square foot is a useful metric, homes are not built a few square feet at a time. In both cases, the data is derived by arithmetic means after construction is finished.

MIS applications use only a dozen or so of the 25 standard activities that we measure. Many of the more specialized activities, such as design and code inspections, quality assurance, and formal integration, are more or less bypassed on MIS applications. The client/server subtype is often even less formal than conventional monolithic applications.

MIS informality, use of generalists rather than specialists, and lack of both quality assurance roles and lack of inspections explain the frequent MIS failures for projects larger than 10,000 function points. These same factors explain the fairly high productivity levels for smaller projects. A capable team can do well on small projects without much in the way of formal processes and formal quality control. However, large systems require much more formal development practices and much more formal quality control to succeed.

When MIS activity costs are aggregated, you can see that the MIS tendency to bypass design inspections leads to very considerable testing costs. If bugs or defects are not removed early, then they cannot be removed at a low cost. In our 10,000-function point case study, defect removal costs topped 50% of total expenses (Table 7.6).

Although coding costs are somewhat greater than production of paper documents for large MIS applications, the fact that defect removal and paperwork comprise more than 80% of the total costs explains why LOC is a poor metric for economic studies. Much of the effort on large MIS projects cannot be explored using LOC metrics.

Table 7.5   MIS Software Activities and Rates for 10,000 Function Points

Parameter	Value
Application size	10,000 function points
Application size	1,050,000 LOC
Source language	COBOL
Work hours per month	132
Monthly compensation	$9,800

Activities Performed	A-Scope, function points	P-Rate, function points	Staff	Effort, months	Schedule, months	Cost	Percent
01 Requirements	400	90	25	111.11	4.44	$1,088,889	3.66
02 Initial design	200	100	50	100.00	2.00	$980,000	3.29
03 Detail design	200	75	50	133.33	2.67	$1,306,667	4.39
04 Coding	150	18	67	555.56	8.33	$5,444,444	18.29
05 Reuse acquisition	2,000	1,000	5	10.00	2.00	$98,000	0.33
06 Configuration management	1,500	250	7	40.00	6.00	$392,000	1.32
07 Documentation	1,000	75	10	133.33	13.33	$1,306,667	4.39
08 Unit testing	150	20	67	500.00	7.50	$4,900,000	16.46

Activities Performed	A-Scope, function points	P-Rate, function points	Staff	Effort, months	Schedule, months	Cost	Percent
09 Function testing	150	23	67	434.78	6.52	$4,260,870	14.32
10 System testing	150	25	67	400.00	6.00	$3,920,000	13.17
11 Acceptance testing	400	35	25	285.71	11.43	$2,800,000	9.41
12 Project management	1,000	30	10	333.33	33.33	$3,266,667	10.98
Totals/averages	180[1]	3.29[1]	56[1]	3,037.16[2]	54.67[1]	$29,764,203[2]	100.00[2]

Cost per function point, $2,976; cost per LOC, $28.35.
[1]Average
[2]Total

Table 7.6   Major Cost Drivers for Information Systems

MIS Application Cost Drivers	Staff Months	Percent
Defect removal	1,620.50	53.36
Paper documents	477.78	15.73
Code related	688.89	22.68

Although averages are interesting, the most common request from our clients is for best-in-class data derived from the top 5% of the projects we have examined. For best-in-class data to be meaningful, it has to be shown for specific size plateaus. Because MIS applications greater than 10,000 function points are rarely successful, it is appropriate to show the size plateaus of 100, 1,000, and 10,000 function points for best-in-class MIS results.

Note that the cost information in Table 7.7 uses average values of $9,800 per staff month as a constant value. This is to emphasize the technological differences that affect productivity. Comparing cost per function point for a large company in an urban area with high labor rates such as New York against a small company in a rural area with low labor rates will obviously favor the small company.

As mentioned several times, MIS applications less than 1,000 function points are frequently successful, but as the size increases, failures increase dramatically. In addition, the probability of major schedule slippage rises in direct proportion to application size in the MIS domain.

A topic of continuing interest is the relative success of MIS projects in meeting their planned schedules (Table 7.8). As discussed previously, the MIS domain does well for small projects less than 1,000 function points, but has major problems completing large systems in the 1,000-function point and 100,000-function point size ranges on time. In fact, the MIS domain has major problems completing large systems at all.

The considerable number of cancellations, delays, and overruns in projects larger than 10,000 function points is a key reason why so many corporations are debating the merits of outsourcing. Corporations face an important binary choice: either invest substantially in process improvement, or turn over large application development projects to outsource vendors. Of course, outsource projects may run late too, but the performance of the outsource domain is better than the MIS domain for applications larger than 10,000 function points.

Table 7.7   Average and Best-in-Class Results for MIS Software

Key Software Topics	100 Function Points	1,000 Function Points	10,000 Function Points
Average staff size	1	7	67
Best-in-class staff size	1	4	44
Average schedule, months	5.75	15.85	43.65
Best-in-class schedule, months	3.98	10.47	33.11
Average function points per staff month	27.80	9.46	3.44
Best-in-class function points per staff month	40.19	23.87	6.79
Average work hours per function point	4.75	13.95	38.41
Best-in-class work hours per function point	3.28	5.53	19.43
Average LOC per staff month in COBOL	2,920	994	361
Best-in-class LOC per staff month in COBOL	4,220	2,507	713
Average effort, staff months	4	106	2,910
Best-in-class effort, staff months	2	42	1,472
Average cost per function point	$352.46	$1,035.46	$2,851.90
Best-in-class cost per function point	$243.84	$410.47	$1,442.26
Average defects per function point	3.00	4.90	5.90
Best-in-class defects per function point	1.25	3.30	4.50
Average defect removal efficiency	95.00%	88.00%	82.00%
Best-in-class defect removal efficiency	98.00%	98.00%	94.00%
Average delivered defects per function point	0.150	0.588	1.062
Best-in-class delivered defects per function point	0.025	0.066	0.270
Average no. of delivered defects	15	588	10,620
Best-in-class no. of delivered defects	3	66	2,700
Average no. of high-severity defects	2	88	1,593
Best-in-class no. of high-severity defects	0	8	324

Table 7.8   MIS Software Schedule Adherence circa 1999

Size, function points	Early Projects, %	On-Time Projects, %	Late Projects, %	Cancelled Projects, %	Total Projects, %
1	6.00	92.00	1.00	1.00	100.00
10	8.00	89.00	2.00	1.00	100.00
100	7.00	80.00	8.00	5.00	100.00
1,000	6.00	60.00	17.00	17.00	100.00
10,000	3.00	23.00	35.00	39.00	100.00
100,000	1.00	15.00	36.00	48.00	100.00
Average	5.17	59.83	16.50	18.50	100.00

MIS Software Successes and Failures

Table 7.9 presents the major success and failure factors associated with MIS. Successful MIS projects add positive value to the corporations that fund them. Unsuccessful MIS projects waste money and resources, and may even degrade both competitive abilities and staff morale.

The information systems community was among the first to make large-scale usage of mainframe computers, and is also leading in recent migration to client/server applications. In fact, the information systems community deploys and utilizes more mainframes, minicomputers, and PCs than any other. Only in the case of technical workstations and specialized computer-aided design systems does the information systems world take a back seat.

An important aspect of the success and failure criteria for information systems is that the majority of such systems are commissioned by clients or users from within the enterprise. In general, information systems are derived from the operational needs of enterprise executives, managers, and knowledge workers. Information systems software is created to benefit these users in terms of giving them new capabilities, reducing the chances of error, speeding up performance, or creating some other advantageous condition. An implied criterion of information systems is that they return some kind of positive value to the enterprise to defray the expense of building and operating the system. This criterion is not always met. However, a very common practice among our clients for funding MIS applications is to insist on a positive ROI within a fixed time period, such as three years.

Table 7.9   MIS Success and Failure Factors

Information Systems Success Factors	Information Systems Failure Factors
Provides new business capability	Degrades a current business capability
Returns a tangible and positive value	Returns a negative value
Improves operating speed	Degrades operating speed
Reduces operating costs	Increases operating costs
Enhances competitive abilities	Degrades competitive abilities
Improves employee morale	Reduces employee morale
Satisfies all user requirements	Fails to meet significant user requirements
Achieves high levels of user satisfaction	Achieves poor levels of user satisfaction
Schedules predictable within 5%	Schedules are out of control
Costs predictable within 5%	Costs are out of control
User requirements stable to within 5%	Requirements creep out of control
Application is Y2K compliant	Application contains Y2K errors

The topic of ROI in the MIS community has triggered some very heated controversy in recent years. There is a topic of debate in the MIS domain called *the productivity paradox.* Some researchers have asserted that although MIS applications are intended to increase business productivity, in fact there has been no measurable increase in business performance that can be traced directly to the use of computers and MIS applications.

Other researchers challenge the validity of the data supporting the productivity paradox, and cite many corporations in which computers and MIS applications do seem to create productivity gains.

Although the topic is controversial, it is generating some useful insights into the roles of computers and data processing in modern business. One prominent author examining the value of MIS applications is Paul Strassmann, the former

CIO of the DoD. His books such as *The Squandered Computer* (Strassmann 1997) and *The Politics of Information Management* (Strassmann 1995) cover some very important issues in the role of computers and applications within major corporations.

Curiously, the MIS community has not followed the examples set by the systems software and military software domains in creating large research laboratories for improved software tools, methods, and practices that affect information systems, database development methods, and the like.

There is nothing in the MIS world that has the stature and research power of Bell Labs, IBM's Research Division, or the Mitre Corporation. Some corporations such as IBM and AT&T, which fund systems software research, also fund MIS research. However, the only really notable large MIS research labs are those within the major outsource corporations such as Andersen, ISSC, and EDS.

There are some commercial research companies that serve the MIS domain, such as the Gartner Group, the Meta Group, Auerbach, IDC, and quite a few others. However, these groups focus primarily on surveys and statistical studies. They do not do intensive experimental research of the type that is performed at a Bell Labs or an IBM research division.

What is termed *research* in the MIS domain consists primarily of large-scale surveys within the MIS community of topics such as how much is spent, what tools have the largest market shares, and peripheral information of this type. Controlled experiments during which specific tools or methods are evaluated and measured are very rare in the information systems domain.

Some companies may evaluate various tool classes and methodologies such as JAD or RAD, but the evaluations are often based on user surveys or very short-term examinations. Also, the data from such studies is marketed for recurring fees, and comparatively little is passed to the larger information systems companies who are not subscribers to the service.

There are also management consulting companies such as McKinsey, Andersen, Deloitte and Touche, KPMG Peat Marwick, SPR, and others that perform research on selected topics in response to requests from clients. However, these studies are often proprietary and the data may only be made available to the sponsors and direct participants.

Because of the huge volume of aging mainframe software in the information systems world, an area of MIS technical leadership has been that of "geriatric" technologies associated with aging legacy systems: complexity analysis, code restructuring, reverse engineering, reengineering, and the like. In general, the

MIS domain is fairly successful in maintenance and enhancement technologies. However, as the volume of maintenance work expanded in the 1980s and 1990s, maintenance and enhancement projects became the most numerous applications. As a result, many companies have outsourced routine maintenance projects while keeping new development in-house.

A domain in which the information systems community is clearly the major player is the adoption of the function point metric for productivity and quality studies. IFPUG is now the largest measurement association in approximately 25 countries, including the United States. Roughly two thirds of the IFPUG member organizations are in the MIS business.

There are now approximately 60 commercial software cost-estimating tools sold in the United States that support function points, and many vendors have added function point support to their tools also: Texas Instruments, Bachman, Visible Systems, Amdahl, Unisys, and so forth.

Unfortunately, the MIS community has lagged behind the systems, military, and commercial domains in quality control approaches. The MIS community also lags behind the systems and military domains in approaches for building large systems in excess of 10,000 function points. (The commercial software world is not very good at the high end either.)

As of 1999, the information systems community tends to have one of the worst track records of any industry segment in terms of the relative proportions of failures and successes. For large systems of 10,000 function points or more, there will be at least one failure for every successful project. For even larger attempts, say at the 20,000- to 50,000-function point domain, the information systems community fails far more often than it succeeds. This is one of the reasons why so many large MIS producers are considering the prospects of outsourcing.

These high-end large-system failures are due to a number of interrelated factors:

1. The MIS community lags in software specialization and tends to jump in to developing large systems using generalists with limited experience.
2. The information systems world has a notable volume of creeping user requirements, which are endemic and serious within the information systems domain, where they rank second to military software in terms of volume.
3. Excessive schedule pressure is often present, coupled with a very naive lack of understanding of key issues.

4. Quality control is a critical component of schedule control, and the information system domain lags in formal quality assurance, inspections, defect tracking, testing specialization, and many other quality-related concepts.

There are exceptions of course. Some MIS companies do use inspections, do have formal quality assurance practices, and do track defects. However, the MIS world, on the whole, is not very sophisticated in software quality assurance.

For smaller software projects less than 1,000 function points, the information systems community succeeds rather well, and indeed has the shortest schedules and lowest costs of almost any software domain. For really large systems (>10,000 function points), delays and disasters are much more common for information systems than for systems software.

MIS Success Factors

The information systems domain has some bright spots and outstanding successes as well as some problem areas. The major success areas for information systems include the following:

- MIS producers have the highest rates of function point usage.
- MIS producers have the best productivity measurement systems.
- MIS producers have the best sizing tools, based on function points.
- MIS producers have the most sophisticated requirements-gathering methods.
- MIS producers are the most effective in building database applications.
- MIS producers have the highest productivity for projects less than 1,000 function points.
- MIS producers have the shortest schedules for projects less than 1,000 function points.
- MIS producers have the highest usage of geriatric tools for aging software.
- MIS producers have the best and most plentiful geriatric tools.

As a general rule, the information systems community tends to lead in factors in which software and users come together; in other words, user interface design, ease of use, requirements gathering, database construction, and the like.

MIS Failure Factors

Among the factors in which the information systems community lags behind other software domains are the following:

- MIS producers are among the worst in use of pretest inspections.
- MIS producers are among the worst in quality control of any kind.
- MIS producers are among the worst in test planning.
- MIS producers are among the worst in test case development.
- MIS producers lag in software quality measurements.
- MIS producers lag in software defect tracking.
- MIS producers lag in project milestone tracking.
- MIS systems producers lag in project cost tracking.
- MIS systems have the highest creep in user requirements.
- MIS producers have the highest incidence of "silver bullet" syndrome.
- MIS projects of more than 10,000 function points fail more often than they succeed.

The MIS community lags in the important topic of software quality control. In turn, this impacts the ability to plan, develop, and execute large new systems in a timely and cost-effective manner. For most of the major failures of large information systems, the problems do not become visible until testing starts, when it becomes evident that the products have so many bugs that they cannot work.

Best Technical Practices for MIS Software

The MIS software domain is among the most sophisticated of any software domain in two topics: requirements analysis and database design. The MIS domain is also quite sophisticated in geriatric technologies for aging legacy applications. However the MIS domain lags in terms of quality control and use of specialists.

Because best practice data comes from assessment and benchmark studies, this section is based on the same set of ten key factors that are examined during SPR assessments and benchmarks:

1. Project management methods such as estimating
2. Requirements-gathering and analysis methods
3. Design and specification methods
4. Coding methods
5. Reusability methods
6. Change control methods
7. User documentation methods
8. Pretest defect removal methods such as inspections

9. Testing methods and tools
10. Maintenance methods and tools

To be cited among the "best practices for MIS software," the approaches have been used on at least 50 successful projects in ten companies. In the eyes of the project managers and technical personnel, the practices must have contributed to a successful outcome. The practices must not have been cited as contributing to failures, cost overruns, or major schedule slips. These are practices that add positive value.

Best Project Management Practices for MIS Software

In every domain, project management is a key technology. This is one of the critical factors that differentiates successful projects from failures and disasters. Excellence in project management is associated with 100% of successful projects for projects larger than 1,000 function points. Inadequate estimates, careless planning, and inadequate tracking are associated with 100% of project failures, although other factors contribute to failures too.

Major MIS software producers such as Hartford Insurance, Pacific Bell, and Fidelity Systems have been pioneers in several aspects of software project management. These organizations have created excellent measurement programs for productivity, and utilize the data to refine estimates for new projects.

Function Point Analysis

It is a best practice in the MIS domain for all productivity and quality studies and benchmarks to be based on function point analysis. In the United States, use of the function point, as defined by IFPUG, is a best practice. (This is the only function point metric with substantial, published benchmark data available.) Other function point variants such as 3D function points or full function points lack enough empirical data to be deemed a best practice. LOC metrics can be used, but are hazardous for cross-language comparisons and are not a best practice. I believe that LOC metrics alone can be deemed professional malpractice in situations in which multiple programming languages are used.

Productivity Measures

It is a best practice in the MIS domain to have a formal software measurement program that measures productivity for all projects above a cutoff point of perhaps 50 function points in size. (The cutoff point varies from 10 to 100 function points among our clients.) It is a best practice to have an in-house measurement group rather than depending on external consultants, except for benchmarks against other companies, for which external consultants are usually necessary. The measurement program captures data on size, staffing, schedules, and effort. Although function point metrics are the best practice for normalization, LOC data is collected too, as a supplemental metric.

Annual Assessments and Benchmarks

A best practice in the MIS domain is to have process assessments on an annual basis, and external benchmark studies every year as well. It is also a best practice to continue productivity measurements in the intervening periods. Although usage of the SEI assessment method is a best practice in the systems and military domains, not enough MIS organizations utilize this method for it to be viewed as a best practice in the MIS domain. Assessments and benchmarks in the MIS domain are more likely to use some of the consulting groups that serve the MIS community, such as Howard Rubin Associates, Meta Group, Quality and Productivity Consulting Group, or SPR.

Project Management Training

It is a best practice for MIS software project managers to be trained in software sizing, cost estimating, quality estimating, milestone tracking, and cost tracking. All project managers should be able to create accurate plans and estimates for projects at least 1,000 function points in size. Entry-level training on promotion to project manager is a definite best practice among large MIS companies. Setting aside five to ten days a year for project management training is also a best practice, but is only about half as common as entry-level training. Note that although it is a best practice for MIS project managers to know how to use function point metrics, it is not necessary for them to know how to count function points. This task is so complex that it can only be entrusted to certified function point counting personnel.

Project Management Tools

It is a best practice for MIS project managers to have available a suite of project management tools including sizing, cost and resource estimating, standard project management for critical path analysis, cost tracking, and milestone tracking capabilities. In some very large companies, estimating specialists are also available to assist project managers, as are certified function point counting personnel.

Personnel Management Tools

It is a best practice among larger MIS companies in the United States to utilize automated tools for appraisals and job objective planning. Personnel-related automated tools are not a best practice in parts of Europe, where they may be prohibited by national laws or union regulations. Automated personnel tools are not encountered often in small MIS shops with less than 50 total software personnel.

Activity-Based Cost Estimates

All MIS software cost estimates for projects larger than 1,000 function points should be at the activity or task levels. Project-level or phase-level estimates are inadequate for large projects in every domain. Estimation for small one-person projects can be at the project level. This practice is unsafe for projects larger than 100 function points, and it is a hazardous practice for projects larger than 1,000 function points. Software cost estimates more than 1,000 function points should be prepared professionally using state-of-the-art estimating tools and empirical data. Informal estimates and rules of thumb are hazardous and unprofessional higher than 1,000 function points, although they are acceptable less than 100 function points.

Empirical Productivity Data

All MIS software project managers should know the ranges of quality and productivity levels derived from empirical studies for the kinds of software for which they are responsible. In particular, MIS project managers should know productivity and quality levels for client/server and database software projects. Otherwise, it is difficult for managers to defend accurate estimates against arbitrary overrides by clients and senior executives.

ERP Data

All MIS software project managers should be trained in the basic operations and deployment strategies of ERP applications. As the century ends, ERP applications are deployed in approximately 20% of our MIS client organizations, and the number will continue to grow in the next century.

Client/Server Planning Data

Because of the widespread deployment of both two-tier and three-tier client/server applications in the MIS domain, it is a best practice for MIS project managers to be trained in the estimating and development methods that work best for such projects. Client/server projects are much more troublesome than monolithic projects and require specialized estimating approaches. Without adequate training, the probabilities of overruns and high maintenance costs are extreme.

Milestone Tracking

All MIS software projects more than 1,000 function points in size should use formal milestone tracking. This is a best practice that can minimize unpleasant problems such as major schedule delays, or can at least provide early warnings. Major milestones include completion of requirements, external specifications, internal specifications, inspection plans, design inspections, code inspections, test plans, all forms of testing, risk analysis plans, performance analysis plans, user documentation, and installation.

Best Requirements-Gathering and Analysis Practices for MIS Software

Requirements gathering and analysis in the MIS software domain are major technologies and are often more sophisticated than in many other domains. This is because the requirements for MIS projects usually come from specific users, who may even be the funding source of the projects to be developed. Although powerful requirements analysis technologies exist for MIS projects, requirements creep remains an endemic problem in MIS and all other software domains. Some of the best practices for requirements gathering and analysis in the MIS software domain include those presented in the following subsections.

Joint Application Design

The usage of JAD is a definite best practice among MIS groups. Indeed, the JAD method of gathering and analyzing requirements has been noted among more than 70% of our client's projects in excess of 100 function points. With the JAD approach, the requirements for an application are the joint responsibility of representatives from the client or user community and from the development organization. A key feature of the JAD approach is the use of a trained JAD facilitator. This facilitator can be either an in-house employee or an outside consultant. The JAD sessions are planned events, often held at outside facilities to prevent interruptions. The JAD team works out the requirements as a full-time job for a preplanned time period ranging from a few days to more than a month for large systems (>10,000 function points). A key benefit of the JAD approach is more stable requirements with a rate of change that is usually only a fraction of 1% per month, rather than the 1% to 3% noted more commonly for traditional requirements. The JAD approach originated in IBM's Toronto lab and has now spread throughout the world. This is an interesting example of a global software technology first developed in Canada.

Prototypes of Key Features

It is a best practice for MIS applications between 100 and 1,000 function points to create working prototypes of key features. Prototypes less than 100 function points may not be needed. Greater than 1,000 function points in size, the prototypes become significant projects in their own right and need more formality than prototypes for mid-size applications. For massive applications of 50,000+ function points, prototypes are not always effective because the applications have far too many features to "prototype" even the key ones. Prototypes are usually approximately 10% of the size of the final application. Of the three common forms of prototypes—disposable, time-box, and evolutionary—only the first two are best practices. Evolutionary prototypes are dangerous because prototypes are usually poorly structured and lack safe programming practices.

Requirements Inspections

For MIS applications, inspections of requirements are a best practice. However, this technology is used sparsely and we usually encounter requirements inspections only in large companies that also build systems software. The inspection team for MIS software requirements includes client representatives and also project technical personnel. Inspections and JAD are complementary, with the inspection stage following the JAD approach.

Requirements Notations

MIS software requirements often utilize notations that include database design concepts such as Warnier-Orr diagrams, Jackson diagrams, and the various forms of information engineering. This class of notation is a best practice, although the specific notation varies based on the needs of the project.

Function Point Size

A best practice for MIS software projects is to calculate initial function point size estimates from the requirements themselves. Once function point totals are known, they provide a useful baseline for measuring the rate of requirements creep. The MIS software domain can be volatile in terms of requirements stability, unless JAD sessions, prototypes, and inspections are utilized. In some cases, additions to requirements can top 2% per calendar month during the design and coding phases. *Requirements churn*, which does not add new features or change function point totals, is also common in the MIS domain. This phrase refers to things such as changing the placement of data items on a screen based on user preferences. Function point totals are also used for sizing various deliverables and are a key input to software cost and quality estimates.

Requirements Change Control

Even in the best of cases MIS requirements change during development. In the worst of cases, requirements changes can be so extreme that they jeopardize the prospect of completing the project. Therefore, it is a best practice to utilize formal change control methods for all MIS projects larger than 500 function points. Some of the methods noted among our clients include

- A formal change control board
- Formal change control requests
- Automated change control tools
- Use of JAD sessions for major changes
- Use of requirements inspections for major changes
- Function point sizing and estimating for all changes larger than 15 function points (which is the minimum size for function point counts)
- Application feature planning for several years in the future with a planned evolution of total functionality

Best Design and Specification Practices for MIS Software

The MIS software domain is very diverse in software specification approaches. The most common methods among our clients tend to utilize some of the data analytic specification methods such as Warnier-Orr diagrams or information engineering. However, more than 25 flavors of software specification methods have been noted among our clients. A number of the more sophisticated clients have developed their own proprietary specification methods. These are often hybrid approaches that use portions of several well-known industry design techniques. Because of the criteria of needing 50 projects in ten companies, it is hard to pin down a specific software design approach as being a "best practice." However, several of the data analytic approaches seem relatively successful in the MIS domain.

Specification Segmentation

Because the specifications for MIS software projects often deal with database design, a best practice is to segment the specifications of applications larger than

1,000 function points into a multivolume set, with each volume containing the details of a specific topic. A typical example includes requirements specifications, external design specifications, internal or logical design specifications, and database specifications. Each specification volume would be under formal change control, and would go through multiple iterations.

Prototypes

A best practice for MIS software projects is the creation of prototypes for key features. The two most common forms of prototype uses for MIS software are disposable prototypes and time-box prototypes. A time-box prototype has a chronological limit, and must be completed within a specific period, such as one calendar month. A disposable prototype is used to demonstrate feasibility, and is then discarded. Often the disposable prototypes are constructed using programming languages different from the final application. The use of evolutionary prototypes is not a best practice because the lack of structure in prototypes makes them unsuited for applications with high-quality and reliability targets. Normally MIS software prototypes amount to approximately 10% of the functionality of the finished application. The prototypes concentrate on key usability and user interface issues.

Design Inspections

A best practice for MIS software projects of all sizes, and for enhancements as well as new projects, is the use of formal design inspections on all specification documents. Although this is a best practice, the use of inspections is only found among less than 25% of our MIS clients. MIS software designs contain more than 1.25 defects per function point, on average. MIS design defects are often higher in severity than coding defects. Formal design inspections are very effective in defect removal, and average more than 65% efficiency in finding and removing design errors.

Inspections also serve as a defect prevention approach as well because participants will avoid problems in their own work that are pointed out during the inspection sessions. Although design inspections are a best practice, they are used sparsely for MIS applications. We have noted their use in less than 15% of MIS software applications. Formal design inspections are encountered primarily among companies that build large applications (>1,000 function points).

Best Coding Practices for MIS Software

The MIS software domain lagged behind the systems software domain in the use of formal programming structure techniques during the 1970s. This is probably because some of the pioneers of structured programming such as Edgar Dijkstra and Dr. Harlan Mills worked in the systems software domain. However, once structured programming caught on, it became a standard best practice for MIS projects throughout the 1970s and 1980s. Unfortunately, the advent of client/ server projects in the 1990s caused a serious backslide in the use of structured programming techniques. In addition, RAD degraded both specification and coding practices within the MIS domain.

Structured Programming

A definite best practice within the MIS domain is that of using formal program structure techniques that optimize binding and coupling, and minimize control flow complexity. Some of the structuring techniques pioneered by Wayne Stevens and Glenford Myers still stand out as being effective even after more than 25 years of usage.

Comment Density and Style

It is a best practice for all domains to utilize both module prologs and comments to explain key features and algorithms of programs. Studies performed within IBM found that comments approximately every ten statements was the density in which clarity seemed to peak. Fewer comments made it hard to understand the code. Surprisingly, too many comments also reduced code legibility. When the underlying code is changed, the comments should also be changed to reflect the new features or modifications.

Mnemonic Labels

It is a best practice to use labels for variables and branch instructions that are clear and easy to remember if possible. Abstract labels such as "routine2" may make it hard for new programmers to understand logic flow. It is a bad practice to use labels that have quirky or private meanings, such as using the names of relatives or movie stars.

Code Inspections

It is a best practice to use formal code inspections for all MIS projects that are important to the enterprise. In general, all applications or updates larger than

1,000 function points should receive code inspections. Not only should formal code inspections be used, but the inspections should include 100% of the modules of "mission-critical" MIS applications, as opposed to partial or subset inspections. Formal code inspections have the highest defect removal efficiency level of any known removal activity and are approximately twice as efficient as most forms of testing. Formal code inspections average 65% in defect removal efficiency, and have approached 90% in some trials. There is no better method for ensuring high quality and reliability levels. Unfortunately, although this is a best practice, code inspections are only noted in less than 25% of our MIS clients.

COBOL Complexity Reduction

A best practice often encountered within the MIS software domain is the use of automated complexity reduction tools, especially for COBOL applications. Because high levels of code complexity, as measured with the common metrics of cyclomatic and essential complexity, are known to degrade quality and lower the efficiency of defect removal operations, software that has high reliability criteria should use automated methods of complexity analysis and reduction. There are more tools in the class available for the COBOL programming language than for any other.

Error-Prone Module Elimination

A best coding practice within the MIS domain and all other domains for legacy applications concerns seeking out and eliminating error-prone modules. In the 1960s, IBM discovered that coding errors or bugs in large systems were not distributed randomly. They tended to clump in a small number of modules, and were assigned the title *error-prone modules*. Once discovered, it became imperative to remove or repair these troublesome entities. The method for dealing with error-prone modules is to give them a formal inspection, and then either restructure them, repair them, or redevelop them based on the recommendation of the inspection team.

Module-Level Defect Tracking

A best practice in the MIS domain is that of defect tracking methods and tools that are granular enough to identify error-prone modules. This practice is encountered primarily in large companies that also develop systems software. Defects are tracked by severity level and origin, and in particular are tracked down to the level of specific modules.

Programming Languages

Although the choice and use of a programming language is not a best practice by itself, it is significant that the MIS domain has actually developed a number of programming languages aimed at business software. Among the languages developed specifically for MIS are ABAP/4, COBOL, Forte, Realizer, Magec, SQL, and QBE. Languages that may be used for both MIS applications and other types of software include JAVA, PL/I, Visual Basic, and Pascal. The COBOL programming language remains the most common language used for MIS applications due to its presence in millions of legacy applications. Because COBOL is used on both successful projects and failures, use of COBOL is not really a best practice. However, COBOL is supported by more tools and has more programmers than any other language, so use of COBOL is a very good practice even if it is not quite a best practice.

Best Reusability Practices for MIS Software

Software reuse is a key technology that can benefit costs, schedules, and quality simultaneously. However, effective reuse programs are rare. Reuse is a fairly recent phenomenon, because our assessment and benchmark studies between 1985 and 1990 did not turn up any significant volume of reuse other than normal COBOL copybooks.

A full software reusability program in the MIS domain encompasses from six to more than ten software artifacts, including

1. Reusable requirements
2. Reusable external specifications
3. Reusable architecture and internal specifications
4. Reusable database designs and data structures
5. Reusable project plans and estimates
6. Reusable source code
7. Reusable quality and test plans
8. Reusable test cases
9. Reusable user documentation
10. Reusable HELP text

In general, the MIS software domain has concentrated on two aspects of reuse:

1. Reusable database designs and data structures
2. Reusable source code

Unfortunately the MIS software domain has not achieved a leadership position with other reusable artifacts, such as test materials.

Reusable Database Designs

Because of the strong coupling between corporate databases and MIS applications, the MIS domain has been fairly good in developing data structures that are reusable throughout an entire corporation. This is not always true, but it is a definite best practice in the MIS domain.

Reusable Source Code Libraries

It is a best practice in the MIS domain to establish formal libraries of reusable source code in common programming languages such as COBOL. To be effective, these libraries need to be at or near zero-defect status. This means that the library needs formal entry procedures that include inspections and thorough testing of candidate modules.

Some interesting reusability practices have not yet been utilized by enough of our clients to determine whether they will become best practices. The most significant practice is "component-based development." As this book is written, few of our clients use component-based development, few components are actually available, and the results of component development are ambiguous. In fact, failures and problems from using components actually outnumber successes.

Reusability based on the OO paradigm is fairly common among the MIS community, although not as common as among the systems software domain. Although some very successful OO projects have been noted, the learning curves of both OO design and OO programming are very steep. The OO paradigm is so difficult to master that it is abandoned about half the time when first starting out. This makes it difficult to assign OO projects to "best practice" status.

Best Change Control Practices for MIS Software

Change control is a complex and demanding technical challenge for any kind of software project. Best practices in change control for systems software include the items described in the following subsections.

Change Control Boards

For all projects larger than 5,000 function points, it is a best practice to utilize a formal change control board. This board is usually comprised of three to perhaps seven people. The board includes representatives from the application client and also the development team. The purpose of the change control board is to review suggested changes, prioritize them, and assign them to a specific release.

Automated Change Control

The MIS software artifacts that are subject to change include requirements, external specifications, internal specifications, database specifications, all test plans, and all user documentation and training materials. Because of the wide variety of changing artifacts, it is a best practice to have fully automated change control systems that can handle all major deliverables. The change control package should facilitate identifying links between artifacts, such as determining what code needs to be changed in response to a requirements or design change. Automated change control tools that support only source code are not adequate for projects larger than 100 function points.

Function Point Metrics for Changes

It is a common best practice in the MIS domain to estimate and measure the function point totals of all changes to software projects larger than 15 function points in size. Changes to software can comprise several kinds of modification. The most common form of change is adding a new feature. This is called *scope creep* or *requirements creep*. Less common but still a daily event is the removal of a feature, or at least its deferral to a later release because it cannot be finished in time for the current release. A more ambiguous form of change is termed *requirements churn*. This complex topic deals with modifying features in such a way that the function point totals do not increase or decrease. An example of requirements churn is changing the placement of data on an input screen, without adding any new kinds of input.

Best User Documentation Practices for MIS Software

The development and production of user manuals, tutorial materials, HELP screens, and "wizards" is a weak link in the software industry. Complaints about poor documents are just as common as complaints about poor software quality, and have as much justification.

Technical Writers

A best practice encountered mainly among large corporations is the use of professional writers for the production of user manuals and tutorial materials. These technical writers are often contractors rather than permanent employees, although major corporations do employ technical writers. Technical writing is a fairly rare skill. Professional writers create better manuals and tutorials than untrained personnel.

Document Models

A best practice for technical writing is to copy the format and outlines of manuals and tutorial materials deemed "excellent" by readers or by trial and error. Many technical writers do this spontaneously. This practice is encountered primarily in large companies with software staffs in excess of 1,000 personnel, who also employ technical writers as contractors or full-time personnel.

Document Testing

A best practice for all domains is testing documentation concurrently with software testing. This means that at least drafts of the major user manuals and HELP text must be completed in time to use the drafts during software testing.

Reader Suggestions

A fairly minor best practice for MIS software is to supply reader comment forms for correcting errors and pointing out problems as part of every published document. On-line reader comments sent in via the Internet or Web are also encompassed under this best practice.

Hypertext Links

A best practice for all user manuals is to include a detailed index with cross-references. Hypertext links for on-line documents are also included under this best practice.

Working Examples

A very common best practice found for all kinds of software is the utilization of actual examples of key features. The examples take a user step by step through the process of invoking a function, using it, and then turning it off or moving to something else when finished.

Best Quality Control and Pretest Defect Removal Practices for MIS Software

The MIS domain has not been a stellar performer in software quality for a variety of reasons. These include lack of funds for formal quality assurance departments, depending on developers for testing rather than on test specialists, and underutilizing effective methods such as formal design and code inspections.

Fortunately, some MIS departments are exceptions and do utilize state-of-the-art quality methods. Note that in the MIS domain, defect prevention is critical as well, with requirements defects being the most critical. The MIS domain has done fairly well in terms of defect prevention, and has pioneered the usage of JAD, which is quite effective in minimizing requirements defects.

Joint Application Design

Because application design is most effective when requirements are firm, it is a best practice for MIS projects to utilize JAD sessions for both requirements analysis and for external design of application usability features.

Requirements Inspections

Because software requirements are critical to MIS applications, formal inspections of requirements is a useful best practice. Unfortunately, it is a best practice that is not as widely utilized as it should be.

Design and Code Inspections

An effective best practice for MIS software quality is the usage of formal design and code inspections. Formal inspections average more than 65% in defect removal efficiency, making them approximately twice as effective as any normal form of testing. Furthermore, inspections also raise testing efficiency and work as a defect prevention method. Although this is a best practice, inspections have been noted in less than one fourth of our MIS clients.

Error-Prone Module Elimination

An important best practice in the MIS software domain is preventing and removing error-prone modules. Complexity analysis tools, code-restructuring tools, module-level defect tracking, formal inspections followed by either repairs or redevelopment, plus assigning numeric quality targets to executives can stamp out error-prone modules and prevent their reoccurrence.

Quality Measurements

A best practice that originated in the systems software domain and moved to the MIS domain in the 1980s is that of formal quality measurements and defect-tracking measurements. Factors measured include defect volumes, defect severity levels, defect origins, defect removal methods, and complexity of the application and its modules. A key metric is defect removal efficiency—the percentage of defects found before delivery. Although U.S. averages for MIS projects are less than 85%, best-in-class results top 96%.

Quality Estimation Tools

A best practice pioneered by the systems software domain and now used by the MIS domain is utilizing quality and defect estimation tools to predict the probable number of bugs that might be encountered, and the set of defect prevention and removal operations to be used. Quality estimation tools can predict the numbers of bugs or errors in requirements, specifications, source code, user documents, and bad fixes or secondary defects. The tools can also predict the specific defect removal efficiency of each review, inspection, or test stage. The final predictions are the numbers of latent defects remaining at delivery, and how many of those will be found by customers.

Risk Analysis

A best practice in the MIS software domain is the production of a formal risk analysis for the project at or near the completion of the requirements phase. A formal risk analysis considers technical risks, financial risks, and schedule risks. The risk analysis plan identifies key risks and includes proposed remedies and methods to prevent or reduce the risks.

Because of the heavy usage of databases in the MIS domain, it would be nice to report that exploration of data quality is an MIS best practice. Unfortunately, taking effective actions to improve data quality has not been encountered often enough among our clients to include it in our set of best practices. The lack of data quality as a best practice is also true of information and knowledge, both of which have little or no empirical data available relative to quality.

Best Testing Practices and Tools for MIS Software

The MIS software domain has not been a leader in software testing. Testing in the MIS domain is usually assigned to development personnel rather than to test specialists. Although developers can be competent in performing unit tests of their own work, higher level testing and specialized testing for topics such as performance and data integrity require knowledge that development personnel often lack.

Automated Test Tools

A best practice that is frequently encountered in the MIS software domain is the usage of automated test library tools. Because major corporations have thousands of regression test cases, it is desirable to utilize automated tools for keeping track of these test cases, weeding out redundant tests, and linking tests to applications as needed.

Test Coverage Analysis

A best practice in analyzing the thoroughness of testing is to monitor the number of paths through software that are actually tested. A variety of commercial test monitors are available that can perform this function. Indeed, the overall best practice is to measure the percentage of all code actually tested. In applications with high cyclomatic and essential complexity, there are so many possible paths through the application that 100% testing is essentially impossible. It is a corollary best practice to redevelop or to simplify the complexity of applications that are so complex that complete testing is impossible. A variety of testing tools found in the systems software domain, such as test case generators, are not often encountered in the MIS domain.

Best Maintenance and Enhancement Practices for MIS Software

The MIS software domain is often quite good in the maintenance and enhancement of legacy applications. In general parlance the word *maintenance* can apply to any form of update on deployed software: repairs, new features, cosmetic improvements, mandatory or regulated changes, whatever. Although it is a common practice to use the term *maintenance* for a multitude of activities, it is far from being a best practice. Some of the best practices for maintenance and enhancement work in the systems software domain include the topics described in the following subsections.

Portfolio Analysis

Although the Y2K problem has made portfolio analysis a common activity, some MIS shops have been studying their software portfolios for more than 20 years. A *portfolio* is the total number of applications owned by a corporation. Portfolio analysis includes counting the applications, examining their status in terms of defect levels, and assigning them to various levels of importance to the corporation. The top level of importance is often termed *mission critical*. Software is an important corporate asset and it is a definite best practice for MIS groups to know exactly how much they own and its state of health.

Geriatric Care for Legacy Applications

The term *geriatric care* refers to a whole set of activities that can stretch the useful lives of legacy applications. Some of these geriatric activities include complexity analysis, applying standard naming conventions to variables and data items, improving comments, restructuring code, and removing error-prone modules. Many MIS applications are written in COBOL. There are more geriatric tools available for COBOL applications than for all other languages put together. In addition, formal inspection of mission-critical applications is a useful technique, but one not often encountered to include with more common best practices.

Because maintenance and enhancements of legacy applications are now the most common forms of software work in the MIS domain, a variety of maintenance tools and methods are being utilized. The data on these tools and methods is variable, with a mixture of both successes and failures.

Because the concept of a best practice demands almost 100% success and very few failures, these interesting maintenance topics are not currently included in the set of best practices. Some of the MIS maintenance approaches include replacement of custom software with commercial packages, domestic maintenance outsourcing, offshore maintenance outsourcing, and deployment of ERP packages.

Best Personnel Practices for MIS Software

As a class, the MIS software domain has been fairly benign in employee matters. Fairly good compensation and benefits programs have long been the norm. These have even gotten better under the impact of the software labor shortage. In this section we examine the personnel areas within the MIS software domain. There are ten key practices for personnel issues that are examined during assessment and benchmark studies, as discussed earlier:

1. Staff hiring practices
2. Staff training and education
3. Management training and education
4. Specialists and occupation groups
5. Compensation levels
6. Office ergonomics
7. Organizational structures
8. Morale surveys and results

9. Work patterns and overtime
10. Staff turnover rates

As in the previous section on best technical practices, best personnel practices must have been observed within at least ten companies to be included as best practices. However, the criterion of being noted on at least 50 projects is waived for personnel practices. The reason for this is because personnel practices are normally corporatewide. In other words, a practice such as "compensation level" is set by corporate guidelines and is not set by the project manager for a specific project. True, project managers have some latitude in compensation based on appraisals and bonus policies, but these must be within the overall corporate salary and compensation guidelines.

Best Staff Hiring Practices for MIS Software

University training in software engineering or computer science in the United States has not been extremely effective. In most cases graduating students cannot immediately go to work as programmers without some in-house training and mentoring. Surprisingly, first-year appraisals of new programmers indicate that students graduating with other majors are just as effective. Thus math majors and even music majors can do well as programmers.

A fundamental weakness of academia is a very marginal emphasis on software quality control, and a lack of courses in topics such as design and code inspections. Other academic weaknesses include lack of training in function point analysis and project management, lack of training in database design, and lack of training in geriatric technologies for legacy applications. All of these are important topics within the MIS domain. As a result of the limited value of academic preparation for serious software work, major MIS employers usually supplement academic deficiencies with fairly extensive in-house training for new hires.

Hiring Experienced Personnel

Due to common academic deficiencies, it is a best practice in the MIS software domain to hire technical personnel with at least three years to five years of prior experience in software development and maintenance. Often special criteria, such as a familiarity with SQL, are included in hiring programs. Experienced personnel are in great demand throughout the software world, and the MIS domain is no exception.

Signing Bonuses and Benefits

In recent years, since about 1995, the shortage of software personnel has led to unusual approaches such as offering signing bonuses. Other benefits programs have also had to be strengthened so that now the MIS domain is quite generous with benefits packages such as full medical and dental plans, and vacations. Flexible work hours and even telecommuting are now common. Unless benefits are competitive, loss of employees will occur.

The lack of personnel and the high labor costs for software staff is motivating many companies to consider outsourcing, both domestic and international. Some companies are also experimenting with *insourcing* or bringing in foreign workers to complete software projects here in the United States. Some other unusual approaches include hiring retired employees for special assignments, such as Y2K repairs. There is not enough data available to judge whether such practices can be deemed best practices.

Best Staff Training and Education Practices for MIS Software

Because of the marginal performance of U.S. universities in graduating effective software personnel to work in the MIS domain, the major employers of MIS personnel compensate by means of in-house curricula for key software topics.

Annual Staff Training Targets

It is a best practice for MIS employers to set targets for the number of days each calendar year that will be set aside for training of technical personnel. Among our MIS software clients, the most common target is ten days a year. However, due to the personnel shortage and to special emergency projects such as the Euro and Y2K, we have noted that these training targets were often suspended or bypassed in calendar years 1998 and 1999.

External Seminars and Conferences

It is a best practice for MIS employers to fund travel and tuition expenses for external conferences and seminars, such as the annual conferences offered by the Quality Assurance Institute (QAI). Among our clients, one external event per year has been common, but two or three external events also occur. The influence of the Euro in 1998 and the Y2K problem in 1999 have reduced attendance to many external conferences.

MIS Software Curriculum

Among the courses we have observed among our MIS clients, those dealing with JAD are the most common and are an educational best practice. Indeed, every MIS software professional should be well trained in the techniques of JAD because they are the most effective known ways of stabilizing software requirements. Other courses that can be viewed as best practices for MIS software staff include software inspections, software design and specification based on data analytic methods, data warehousing, software reusability techniques, structured programming techniques, change management and configuration control, MIS testing methods, productivity and quality measurements, function point analysis, and software maintenance techniques. These are courses noted most commonly as part of the in-house curricula of major MIS software producers.

There are a number of useful courses taught by vendors. Although these courses may be necessary to master the vendor's tools, there is insufficient data to place such courses in the best-practice category. For example, companies deploying the SAP ERP package no doubt train their programming staff in SAP's ABAP/4 programming language.

There are many courses available on interesting and important topics, but unless these topics have demonstrated empirical results in improving quality, productivity, or schedules, there is no justification for viewing them as best practices. This category includes courses in most programming languages and courses in various specific vendor tools. Courses in the unified Modeling Language (UML) are also in this category because UML has not yet proved to be effective under field conditions on actual projects.

Best Management Training and Education Practices for MIS Software

Software project management is even more poorly served by universities than software engineering. In fact, very few universities in the world offer courses in some of the more important software management topics such as function point analysis, software cost estimating, and software risk and value analysis. The MIS software domain has compensated for this academic gap reasonably well, although cost and schedule estimating remain chronic weaknesses in the MIS world.

Annual Management Training Targets

It is a best practice for MIS software to set targets for the number of days each calendar year that will be set aside for training of project management personnel.

Among our MIS clients, the most common target for managers is five days a year. This target is normally the minimum number of days, and we have noted that ten days of training are slated fairly often. However, due to the impact of the Euro in calendar year 1998 and the Y2K problem in calendar year 1999, training targets have been suspended temporarily in many companies.

External Management Seminars and Conferences

It is a best practice for MIS clients to fund travel and tuition expenses for external conferences and seminars for managers, such as the annual conferences offered by IFPUG, QAI, or various events on software project management and metrics. Among our clients, two external events per manager per year is most common, but three or four external events also occur. There are a number of specialized project management conferences that are also popular, such as those offered by the Project Management Institute (PMI) or by project management vendors such as Artemis.

Software Management Curriculum

It is a best practice for MIS software managers to understand both estimation and measurement. Therefore, courses on software cost estimation, function points, and software metrics are often noted among our clients. Other management courses noted among our clients that are included in the best-practice set are Y2K contingency plans, data warehousing, principles of software reuse, software quality estimating, software quality metrics and cost of quality, principles of the SEI CMM, and risk and value analysis. For European and multinational companies, courses in the Euro are part of the best practice too.

There are a number of rapidly emerging technologies that may become best educational practices in the near future, but have not yet been encountered among at least ten clients. The most notable are courses in e-business and Web-based management practices. Although these topics are important, the technology is changing so rapidly and the results are so ambiguous that it is difficult to create an effective course. Another emerging topic that may become a best practice, but is not one yet, is courses on component-based development.

The entire business world is in "revolution mode" as this book is written. We are trying to absorb the implications of the Internet and the World Wide Web. The Web is exploding in use and triggering major new corporations such as Amazon, with business models that are very unusual compared with traditional corporations. These changes are actually moving faster than the educational process can keep up. It will be several more years before the implications of the Web and the Internet can be fully grasped and converted into training curricula.

Best Practices for Specialization in the MIS Software Domain

The MIS software domain has generally pursued a policy of "generalists" rather than a policy of "specialists." MIS technical personnel include a majority of generalists, with titles such as programmer/analyst. However, as the twentieth century ends, the MIS software domain is beginning to expand in terms of specialization. New positions such as Web master and certified function point counter are occurring in increasing numbers.

Software Specialization

There are four key MIS areas in which specialization counts as a best practice, because the results are so much better than when the work is performed by generalists who lack specific training: software systems analysis, software database administration, function point analysis by certified function point counters, and software maintenance in the sense of defect repairs. An additional specialty, JAD facilitation, is often encountered, but the facilitators are usually external consultants. JAD facilitation also counts as a best practice. The MIS domain would do well to use additional specialists such as software quality assurance and testing specialists. However, although such specialists are encountered, they are not encountered often enough to join the best-practice set.

Best Compensation and Salary Practices for MIS Software

Due to the software personnel shortage, compensation levels for all domains have been increasing since about 1995. In the United States, banking is the industry that pays MIS software personnel and software managers the highest salary levels. In general, compensation levels for large companies in urban areas are higher than compensation levels for small companies in rural areas.

An interesting topic in which SPR has comparatively little data involves startup companies that offer equity as an inducement to both managers and technical personnel. As a rule, startup companies are not funded sufficiently to commission assessments and benchmarks. Also, startups are often building their very first applications so they have no historical data to analyze.

Compensation Benchmarks

It is a best practice among the MIS domain to perform annual compensation benchmark studies for both technical and managerial personnel. These benchmarks are normally "blind" studies for which various companies contribute compensation data that is analyzed statistically by a neutral external benchmark company. Each contributing company receives a report on how their compensation packages compare with the group, but the specifics of each company in the group are not included due to both competitive and antitrust reasons.

Compensation Levels

For large companies employing more than 1,000 software personnel, it is a best practice to be in the upper quartile of overall compensation including salaries, bonuses, equity, and medical and dental benefits. Otherwise the corporation will face a "brain drain" due to the software personnel shortage. In large corporations, compensation, quality, productivity, and schedules are more or less correlated. However for small companies with less than 100 software personnel, and especially for startups with less than 25 software personnel, immediate compensation is less significant and long-range topics such as equity are more significant.

Best Practices in Office Ergonomics for MIS Software

The topic of office ergonomics is surprisingly important. Studies by Tom DeMarco and Tim Lister, published in *Peopleware* (DeMarco and Lister 1987), confirmed findings that office space benefits MIS software productivity in a very significant fashion.

In our own assessment and benchmark studies, there are several interesting phenomena that often stand out among clients that have better than average software performance levels. One of the most visible, which can be noted almost as soon as a consultant enters the building, is the use of private, noise-free office space for software technical workers.

During a typical working day, a programmer or analyst needs quiet and solitude for approximately five hours, and needs to have discussions or meetings for only approximately one hour a day. Roughly two hours are spent on phone calls, using the Internet, or miscellaneous work. From this distribution of effort, it can be seen that private office space is optimal for the major portion of a day's work.

An informal study that I carried out at IBM San Jose prior to the opening of the Santa Teresa office noted that the mean time to interruption in a three-person cubicle was roughly 11 minutes. The mean time to interruption in a two-person cubicle was roughly 15 minutes.

The topics of telecommuting and working at home are of increasing interest. Some states such as New Jersey are offering tax incentives to initiatives that reduce daily commuting volumes, and tax penalties in the other direction. Unfortunately, we have not encountered telecommuting often enough in our studies to know whether or not it should be included in the best-practice category.

Private Office Space

It is a best practice to provide private, noise-free office space for software technical staff members such as systems analysts, programmers, and programmer/analysts. An area of at least 80 square feet is optimal. This best practice is only encountered within fairly sophisticated companies, but the results support the hypothesis that private office space is optimal for both software development and maintenance.

Networks and E-mail

It is a best practice to link all technical employees within a corporation by means of a network that supports e-mail, file transfer, and on-line inspection of key work products.

Meeting Rooms

Because group activities such as design and code inspections and team meetings are common for software projects, it is a best practice to provide small meeting rooms that can hold as many as ten people. Because usage is intermittent, one such meeting room should be able to support roughly 30 total staff members.

Best Practices in Organizational Structures for MIS Software

For historical reasons outside the scope of this book, the *span of control* or number of employees reporting to one manager is generally eight staff members. This has been true for more than 100 years, and is true for all forms of office work, not just for software. However, the range observed in span of control is quite broad. We have encountered departments with as few as two employees reporting to one manager, and one department in which 30 employees reported to one manager on a temporary basis.

It is a common belief in the software world that small teams are more productive than large departments. However, this belief probably confuses two issues. Small projects are more productive than large projects, and small projects usually have small-team organizations.

Some MIS software projects are very large (>10,000 function points) and have staffing levels that can rise to more than 100 personnel overall. For large projects with more than 50 staff members, small teams are actually not as productive as larger departments with ten to 12 people reporting to one manager.

The reason for this somewhat surprising finding seems to be that good managers are a fairly scarce commodity. If a company has a low span of control, then it will have a large management population. Because bad management is a common reason for project failure, it can be seen that having fewer but better managers may lead to overall improvements in both performance and productivity.

In general, software productivity levels decline as the number of workers increases. Here, too, this is a general finding from many industries, and not just a finding for software projects. However, there is a curious phenomenon within the software domain that was first noted in the 1970s. Productivity levels for software projects tend to decline as the number of managers goes up, rather than as the number of technical staff members goes up. The implications of this finding are that for large applications (>10,000 function points), small teams with four to eight workers are not as productive as larger departments with ten to 12 employees. As the management count goes up, coordination and cooperation between departments becomes difficult due to normal corporate politics.

Optimal Department Size

For large MIS software projects (>10,000 function points), it is a best practice to have more than ten employees reporting to one manager. Although this is controversial, this is the size at which productivity is highest. Smaller spans of control put too many people in management and raise the difficulty of coordinating between departments. Furthermore, a ten-plus staffing complement can handle a fairly large component whereas smaller departments might have to segment the work artificially. In addition, a larger span of control allows backup in case of illness and encourages mentoring of new team members. It is also easier to handle peer reviews and formal inspections.

Optimal Organizational Structures

For large MIS software projects (>10,000 function points), a hierarchical organizational structure is a best practice, as opposed to a matrix organizational structure. The hierarchical organization is similar to a military chain of command, in that each manager reports directly to a higher level manager, up to the level of the senior manager, who is responsible for the entire system. The matrix structure tends to raise the management head count for larger projects. Because software productivity declines as the management count goes up, this form of organization can be hazardous for software. (SPR lacks data on the effectiveness of the matrix organization for hardware or other kinds of projects besides software. I have no opinion on the effectiveness of the matrix organization outside the software domain.)

Virtual Organizations

For MIS software projects involving multiple cities and countries, it is a best practice to support broad-band communication channels so that e-mail, file transfer, and on-line inspection are all possible. Video conferencing among locations is also a best practice for projects that are dispersed geographically. Prior to the availability of the Internet and corporate intranets, projects developed over several geographic regions exhibited sharp productivity declines. In the 1970s, each time a different city was added to the same project, productivity declined by approximately 5%. Since 1995, virtual teams that are dispersed geographically are just as productive as single-site teams, if communication channels are effective.

Best Practices for Employee Morale in MIS Software

It should not be a surprise that employees who are satisfied with their jobs and their place of employment are more productive and develop higher quality deliverables than employees who are dissatisfied. Productivity data also favors organizations with high levels of morale.

Interestingly, one of the critical factors affecting employee morale is the ability of the project manager to whom the technical workers report. Companies that recognize the significance of this finding are very careful about who gets promoted to management, and are careful to weed out managers whose personalities are not suited for this very critical responsibility.

Morale and Opinion Surveys

It is a best practice for all software organizations to perform morale or opinion surveys of all employees, including administrative workers, technical staff members, and project managers. The normal frequency of morale surveys is once a year. Some of our clients conduct two surveys a year. In special situations, such as after a major downsizing, merger, or cancellation of a major project, additional special morale surveys may be needed.

Follow-up to Morale Surveys

It is a best practice to have immediate and formal follow-ups after morale surveys are taken. Asking questions about morale but taking no actions based on the responses degrades rather than improves morale. Normally, after a morale survey occurs the results are analyzed statistically within a week, and departmental group meetings are held to discuss the results within two weeks. Within a month, executives and top managers will have formulated a plan to deal with any serious morale issues that are encountered. Normally, within approximately six weeks, there will be an overall meeting or series of departmental meetings to discuss these action plans.

Open-Door Policy

It is a best practice to have a formal "open-door" policy within large corporations in the MIS software domain. The phrase *open door* means that any employee who feels that they have been treated unfairly by their manager, or by any other employee, can appeal to any higher level manager and request an investigation. (The appeal could also be made to the human resource department, but an appeal within the chain of command is usually more effective.) To work, the open-door policy must offer a firm promise that there will be no reprisals. That is, if an employee makes a specific complaint about his or her first-line manager, there must be a guarantee that he or she will not experience any reduction in appraisals or compensation as a result. Usually this means that as a result of an open-door appeal, the employee initiating the request is transferred to some other department.

Job Transfer Requests

It is a best practice within large corporations to have a job transfer request system that allows employees to request internal transfers to other cities, or to request a job change to another kind of position. Of course, the employees must have the relevant background and technical skills to perform well in the new situation. Some companies post internal job openings or make this information widely available. In other companies, job information is informal.

Merit Appraisals

In the United States it is a best practice to have annual performance appraisals for both technical staff members and project managers. During the first year of employment in a company there may be two or more performance appraisals. It is a best practice for employees and managers to agree jointly to performance goals or targets. Note that in some European countries, performance appraisals are forbidden by either national law or union regulations.

Awards and Recognition

It is a best practice to reward outstanding accomplishments. Many companies have a spectrum of awards ranging from local "dinner-for-two" awards, which are given at the discretion of a supervisor, up through major $100,000 awards for some breakthrough that had significant corporate value. Overall, numerous small awards tend to benefit morale more widely than a few very large awards. Although large awards can benefit morale, the odds of receiving one are low. Small awards, on the other hand, can be given to 5% and 10% of the corporate technical staff in the course of a year.

Due to the major shortage of software personnel in the United States and Europe, morale and personnel issues are now extremely important. There are many more topics under this heading that cannot be discussed using assessment and benchmark data because assessments and benchmarks do not cover every personnel topic. For example, stock option plans and equity may have an affect on employee morale and attrition rates, but we have not been tasked with examining this issue.

Another very strong morale factor is that of the medical and dental plans offered by employers. Here, too, we have not been commissioned to study this factor. Indeed, if we attempted to study this factor we would probably be asked to stop because human resource organizations regard this kind of information as sensitive.

Best Work Patterns and Overtime Utilization Practices for MIS Software

It was first noted more than 30 years ago that software development and maintenance tends to attract personnel who are fairly intense in their work practices. Within companies such as Morgan Stanley, IBM, Microsoft, and Pacific Bell, 50-hour weeks are the norm rather than the exception for software employees. Furthermore, because software personnel are usually salaried workers rather than hourly workers, they are considered "exempt" in the sense that software personnel do not automatically receive overtime pay.

Many corporate time and cost tracking systems exclude unpaid overtime, and it is difficult to gather reliable information on this topic. This is a chronic problem for MIS projects because MIS organizations are sometimes overhead groups that do not charge in-house clients for their services. If the MIS organization runs as a cost center or (rarely) a profit center, then unpaid overtime is more likely to be recorded. The SPR assessment approach includes questions and interviews about unpaid overtime, but our data is based on reconstruction from the memories of the participants and therefore may have a large margin of error.

Compensatory Time

It is a best practice for MIS software personnel to be allowed to take compensatory time during slack periods in return for contributing unpaid overtime during rushed periods.

The issue of unpaid overtime is often encountered during benchmark studies. This topic deserves greater coverage in the software literature because it has a tangible impact on productivity rates.

On the whole, the industrialized countries of Western Europe, such as France and Germany, have many more vacation days each year than the United States or Japan. Public holidays vary widely from country to country. This issue is very important for international benchmark analysis.

Best Practices for Minimizing MIS Staff Turnover Rates

Due to the shortage of software personnel in the United States and Europe, software producers are very concerned about losing key personnel. They are also concerned about the high costs of recruiting new personnel.

If a company is in financial distress and is downsizing, there are no effective techniques for keeping key personnel. Furthermore, both software productivity and quality levels suffer during periods of downsizing. However, if a company is growing rapidly and recruiting actively, it is very useful to pay serious attention to the factors that affect both attracting new hires and minimizing the attrition of existing personnel.

Reducing Voluntary Attrition

To minimize the attrition of key personnel, the set of best practices includes being in the top 50% in terms of compensation and benefits, weeding out less capable managers, and having proactive morale and opinion surveys to identify problems before they grow to a significant magnitude. A very complex issue is also important: Because "bad management" is the most common reason cited in exit interviews when technical workers quit, it is very important to weed out managers whose personalities are unsuited to management tasks. Thus, very careful management appraisals are a best practice.

Finding New Personnel

Obviously, large companies utilize multiple methods for finding new employees: advertisements, recruiters, and the World Wide Web. However, it is also a best practice to offer incentives or rewards if employees can bring in suitable candidates. The reason for this is because the software community is fairly good at spreading the word regarding interesting opportunities.

Contract Employees

It has been a best practice to utilize contract personnel for a percentage of MIS software technical work. The reason for this is because contractors can be brought in fairly quickly, and have relevant experience suitable to the projects in need of support. Additionally, when the projects are completed, the contract personnel can be released as quickly as they are brought onboard. However, a number of recent court actions involving contract personnel are raising new issues that we have not yet encountered in our benchmark and assessment studies. For example, stock options and other benefits may be assigned to contractors as well as to full-time employees. As a result, the contracting situation circa 1999 is somewhat ambiguous, even though past results have been favorable.

Personnel issues are outside the normal scope of assessment and benchmark studies. However we have been commissioned to explore some aspects of personnel topics, such as the number of specialists employed and the optimal methods for keeping their skills up to date.

Summary and Conclusions on MIS Software

MIS are key business tools. MIS applications in the 1990s handle most of the operational functions of both corporations and government agencies, such as payroll, accounting, inventory management, purchasing, marketing and sales data, customer information, and the like. More importantly, MIS applications are the bridge between executives and the huge masses of data now stored in corporate databases and repositories. Without MIS applications, the data would be unavailable and probably useless for day-to-day decision making.

In the near future, MIS applications will also be the bridge between executives and the knowledge needed to run a modern company. The word *knowledge* implies more than just raw data, and includes the concepts of filtering, business rules, and competitive information.

However, building software is not the primary goal of most of the companies that utilize MIS applications. Many companies are asking hard questions such as whether outsourcing or commercial software packages might not be more cost-effective than continuing with MIS development and maintenance.

Because MIS applications in large companies have often developed in a piecemeal fashion for individual business units, it has not been easy to integrate corporate-level data from incompatible divisional applications and databases. These incompatibilities have triggered an interesting new product market termed *enterprise resource planning*. ERP packages are intended to consolidate information from various divisional software applications and databases into overall corporate results. Deployment of an ERP package is a major corporate event, and is not always successful.

In recent years, the MIS domain has been undergoing very rapid changes. The impact of the Internet and the World Wide Web is a critical stage in business evolution. MIS applications are now being required to support e-business, as well as traditional business operations. As e-business explodes onto the scene, many new kinds of applications are being rushed to completion in support of the World Wide Web and the Internet.

The MIS domain has been impacted heavily by two of the largest "mass updates" in human history—the Euro and the Y2K problems. The Euro became operational in the European monetary union in January 1999; the Y2K problems began to occur when fiscal years changed from 1999 to 2000.

Additional bursts of Y2K problems occurred during the first week of January, and again at the close of business at the first month and first quarter of 2000. The MIS domain performed fairly well in achieving readiness for the Euro, although at great cost. Whether the MIS domain has done as well in Y2K preparation is uncertain as this book is written, but early evidence indicates fewer Y2K problems than expected.

In the past, the MIS community has not performed well on large applications in the 10,000-function point range. The repeated failures and overruns for large MIS applications is motivating a number of companies to migrate to outsource contractors.

The MIS domain has strong technologies available for requirements analysis at the beginning of software projects, and for geriatric care of aging legacy applications. The MIS domain also excels at design and development of database applications. Although MIS productivity is quite good for small applications, it lags severely at the large end of the size spectrum. The main reason appears to be poor quality control. The MIS domain has also had a problem with steep learning curves for several new technologies such as client/server applications and the OO paradigm. Both of these technologies have demonstrated significant startup problems.

The MIS deficiencies we note most in our assessments and benchmarks include poor quality control, lack of specialization, and a tendency to believe in "silver bullets," or the hazardous assumption that a new fad will make significant gains in software performance.

Without MIS applications, modern business and government could scarcely operate, but the value of MIS applications has come at considerable costs. Cancelled projects and schedule and cost overruns are endemic.

As this book is written, the MIS community now tops 15% of total employment within a number of businesses such as financial institutions and insurance companies. These businesses need the power of MIS applications, but whether they need hundreds of MIS personnel is an open question.

After the Y2K problem is past, many companies will be well positioned to explore their MIS needs for the next 25 years. The Y2K problem has at least caused companies to create extensive inventories of all software assets, and to explore development and maintenance costs. The future role of MIS applications is uncertain, but should be clarified within the first five years of this century.

Readings and References for MIS Software

The literature on MIS is fairly extensive. Well over 100 books and thousands of articles are available. There are also entire journals that specialize in topics of interest to the MIS community, such as the journal *CIO* or the weekly newpaper *ComputerWorld*.

Because the MIS community was an early adopter of function point metrics, many of the articles on this topic are aimed at MIS projects. In addition, there are many technologies that are aimed specifically at MIS projects, and these are documented in books and articles on client/server applications, ERP, JAD, information engineering, and many geriatric technologies such as code-restructuring tools.

Much of the literature on database topics, data warehousing, and data mining is also slanted toward the MIS community. This is because MIS applications are the primary software packages that deal with data. Some of the books on the emerging topic of knowledge management are also aimed at the MIS community.

Abran, A., and P. N. Robillard. "Function Point Analysis. An Empirical Study of Its Measurement Processes." *IEEE Transactions on Software Engineering* 1996; 22(12):895–909.

Andrews, Dorine C., and Susan K. Stalick. *Business Reengineering: The Survival Guide.* Englewood Cliffs, NJ: Prentice Hall, 1994. (ISBN 0-13-014853-9, 300 pages)

Applehans, Wayne. Alden Globe, and Greg Laugero. *Managing Knowledge: A Practical Web-Based Approach.* Reading, MA: Addison-Wesley, 1999. (ISBN 0-201-43315-X, 115 pages)

Austin, Robert D. *Measuring and Managing Performance in Organizations.* New York: Dorset House Publishing, 1996. (ISBN 0-932633-36-6, 216 pages)

Boar, Bernard H. *Application Prototyping.* New York: John Wiley & Sons, 1984. (ISBN 0-471-89317-X, 210 pages)

Bogan, Christopher E., and Michael J. English. *Benchmarking for Best Practices.* New York: McGraw Hill, 1994. (ISBN 0-07-006375-3, 312 pages)

Brooks, Frederick P. *The Mythical Man-Month.* Reading, MA: Addison Wesley Longman, 1995. (ISBN 0-201-00650-2, 295 pages)

Carmel, Erran. *Global Software Teams: Collaborating across Borders and Time Zones.* Upper Saddle River, NJ: Prentice Hall, 1999. (ISBN 0-13-924218-X, 269 pages)

Carnegie Mellon University. *The Capability Maturity Model: Guidelines for Improving the Software Process.* Reading, MA: Addison Wesley Longman, 1995. (ISBN 0-201-54664-7, 439 pages)

Charette, Robert N. *Application Strategies for Risk Analysis.* New York: McGraw Hill, 1990. (ISBN 0-07-010888-9, 570 pages)

Curtis, Bill, William E. Hefley, and Sally Miller. *People Capability Maturity Model.* Pittsburgh, PA: Software Engineering Institute, Carnegie Mellon University, 1995.

Davis, Alan M., and Marilyn D. Weidner. *Software Requirements.* Englewood Cliffs, NJ: Prentice Hall, 1993. (ISBN 0-13-805763-X, 521 pages)

DeMarco, Tom. *Controlling Software Projects.* New York: Yourdon Press, 1982. (ISBN 0-917072-32-4, 284 pages)

———. *Why Does Software Cost So Much?* New York: Dorset House Publishing, 1995. (ISBN 0-932633-34-X, 237 pages)

———. *The Deadline.* New York: Dorset House Publishing, 1997. (ISBN 0-932633-39-0)

DeMarco, Tom, and Tim Lister. *Peopleware*. New York: Dorset House Publishing, 1987. (ISBN 0-932633-05-6, 188 pages)

Dreger, J. Brian. *Function Point Analysis*. Englewood Cliffs, NJ: Prentice Hall, 1989. (ISBN 0-13-332321-8, 185 pages)

Garmus, David, and David Herron. *Measuring the Software Process: A Practical Guide to Functional Measurement*. Englewood Cliffs, NJ: Prentice Hall, 1995. (ISBN 0-13-349-002-5)

Gilb, Tom, and Dorothy Graham. *Software Inspections*. Reading, MA: Addison Wesley Longman, 1993. (ISBN 0-201631814, 471 pages)

Glass, Robert L. *Software Runaways: Lessons Learned from Massive Project Failures*. Upper Saddle River, NJ: Prentice Hall, 1997. (ISBN 0-13-673443-X, 259 pages)

Hansen, Kirk. *Data Structured Program Design*. Topeka, KS: Ken Orr & Associates, 1983. (ISBN 0-9605884-2-6, 414 pages)

Howard, Alan, ed. *Software Metrics and Project Management Tools*. Phoenix, AZ: Applied Computer Research, 1997. (30 pages)

IFPUG. *IFPUG Counting Practices Manual*. Release 4.1. Westerville, OH: International Function Point Users Group, April 1999. (93 pages)

Inmon, W. H. *Developing Client/Server Applications in an Architected Environment*. Boston, MA: QED Technical Publishing Group, 1991. (ISBN 0-89435-389-6, 199 pages)

Jones, Capers. *Assessment and Control of Software Risks*. Englewood Cliffs, NJ: Prentice Hall, 1993. (ISBN 0-13-741406-4, 711 pages)

———. *Applied Software Measurement*. 2nd ed. New York: McGraw Hill, 1996. (ISBN 0-07-032826-9, 618 pages)

———. *Software Quality: Analysis and Guidelines for Success*. Boston, MA: International Thomson Computer Press, 1997. (ISBN 1-85032-876-6, 492 pages)

———. *Estimating Software Costs*. New York: McGraw Hill, 1998. (ISBN 0-07-9130941, 725 pages)

———. "Sizing Up Software." *Scientific American* 1998; 279(6):104–111.

———. *The Year 2000 Software Problem: Quantifying the Costs and Assessing the Consequences*. Reading, MA: Addison Wesley Longman, 1998. (ISBN 0-201-30964-5, 303 pages)

———. *Function Points, Data Points, Service Points, and Value Points*. Burlington, MA: Software Productivity Research, June 1999a. (40 pages)

———. *Table of Programming Languages and Levels*. Burlington, MA: Software Productivity Research, March 1999b. (ten versions from 1985 through July 1999; 77 pages for Version 10)

Kalakota, Ravi, and Marcia Robinson. *e-Business: Roadmap for Success*. Reading, MA: Addison-Wesley, 1999. (ISBN 0-201-60480-9, 378 pages)

Kan, Stephen H. *Metrics and Models in Software Quality Engineering*. Reading, MA: Addison Wesley Longman, 1994. (ISBN 0-201-63339-6, 344 pages)

Kelly, Sean. *Data Warehousing: The Route to Mass Customization*. New York: John Wiley & Sons, 1996. (ISBN 0-471-96328-3, 200 pages)

Kemerer, Chris F. "An Empirical Validation of Software Cost Estimation Models." *Communications of the ACM* 1987; 30: 416–429.

———. "Reliability of Function Point Measurement: A Field Experiment." *Communications of the ACM* 1993; 36: 85–97.

Lacity, Mary C., and Rudy Hirschheim. *Information Systems Outsourcing*. New York: John Wiley & Sons, 1993. (ISBN 0-471938823, 273 pages)

Lozinsky, Sergio. *Enterprise-Wide Software Solutions*. Reading, MA: Addison Wesley Longman, 1998. (ISBN 020130971-8, 190 pages)

McCabe, Thomas J. "A Complexity Measure." *IEEE Transactions on Software Engineering* 1976; 308–320.

McMenamin, Stephen M., and John F. Palmer. *Essential Systems Analysis*. New York: Yourdon Press, 1984. (ISBN 0-91702-30-8, 392 pages)

Melton, Austin. *Software Measurement*. London: Chapman & Hall, 1995. (ISBN 0-412-55180-2)

Orr, Ken. *Structured Requirements Definition*. Topeka, KS: Ken Orr & Associates, 1981. (ISBN 0-9605884-0-X, 235 pages)

Perry, William E. *Data Processing Budgets*. Englewood Cliffs, NJ: Prentice Hall, 1985. (ISBN 0-13-196874-2, 224 pages)

———. *Handbook of Diagnosing and Solving Computer Problems*. Blue Ridge Summit, PA: TAB Books, 1989. (ISBN 0-8306-9233-9, 255 pages)

———. *Effective Methods for Software Testing*. Los Alamitos, CA: IEEE Computer Society Press, 1995. (ISBN 0 471 06097-6, 556 pages)

Putnam, Lawrence H. *Measures for Excellence: Reliable Software On Time, Within Budget*. Englewood Cliffs, NJ: Prentice Hall, 1992. (ISBN 0-13-567694-0, 336 pages)

Putnam, Lawrence H., and Ware Myers. *Industrial Strength Software: Effective Management Using Measurement*. Los Alamitos, CA: IEEE Computer Society Press, 1997. (ISBN 0-8186-7532-2, 320 pages)

Rubin, Howard. *Software Benchmark Studies for 1999*. Pound Ridge, NY: Howard Rubin Associates, 1999.

Strassmann, Paul. *The Politics of Information Management*. New Canaan, CT: The Information Economics Press, 1995. (ISBN 0-9620413-4-3, 523 pages)

———. *The Squandered Computer*. New Canaan, CT: The Information Economics Press, 1997. (ISBN 0-9620413-1-9, 426 pages)

Symons, Charles R. *Software Sizing and Estimating: Mk II FPA (Function Point Analysis)*. Chichester, UK: John Wiley & Sons, 1991. (ISBN 0 471-92985-9, 200 pages)

Weinberg, Gerald, and Daniel Friedman. *Handbook of Walkthroughs, Inspections, and Technical Reviews*. New York: Dorset House Publishing, 1990. (450 pages)

Wheeler, David A., Bill Brylcznski, and Reginald Meeson. *Software Inspection: An Industry Best Practice*. Los Alamitos, CA: IEEE Computer Society Press, 1996. (ISBN 0-8186-7430-0, 325 pages)

Yourdon, Edward. *Death March: The Complete Software Developer's Guide to Surviving "Mission Impossible" Projects*. Upper Saddle River, NJ: Prentice Hall, 1997. (ISBN 0-13-748310-4, 218 pages)

Zvegintzov, Nicholas. *Software Management Technology Reference Guide*. Release 4.2. New York: Software Maintenance News, 1994. (ISBN 1-884521-01-0, 240 pages)

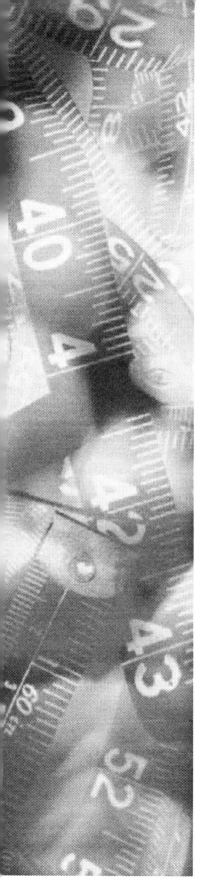

CHAPTER EIGHT

Benchmarks and Best Practices for Outsourced Software

The phrase *outsourced software* refers to software projects that are built under contract by an external company for a client organization. In recent years, since about 1990, the outsourcing industry has grown fairly rapidly. Our demographic data indicates that the total U.S. population of software contract and outsource personnel is now approximately 250,000 people or just more than 10% of the total U.S. software employment near the end of 1999.

A series of recent court actions involving contract employees at Microsoft has sent waves of alarm through the contract and outsource industry. Although the situation is still in flux as this book is written, preliminary court rulings have awarded a class of Microsoft contract employees some of the benefits formerly reserved for full-time employees. This decision raised the unusual issue that even though the contract employees worked for an external agency, they could be considered Microsoft employees too, because of the nature of the work and supervision they received on site at Microsoft's offices. The concept of *dual employment* is interesting, and seems to be based on how the Internal Revenue Service defines employment for tax purposes.

The situation with the Microsoft contract personnel is still fluid, and the final outcome is not known as this book is written. However, if some contractors do receive full-time benefits, this might cause future reductions in the usage of contract employees in the United States. The impact on outsourcing is ambiguous at present. The weight of recent legal decisions may be moving toward a possible reduction in the use of U.S. contract software personnel in the future.

This same ruling may lead to an increase in the use of offshore outsourcing organizations, because U.S. legal decisions on the status of contract workers presumably do not apply to contract employees in countries such as India and Russia.

Due to the shortage of software personnel and the backlog of applications caused by the Euro and Y2K problems, there is currently a significant demand for additional software workers. This demand could probably best be met via contracts and outsource agreements, assuming that the recent legal situation in the United States does not reduce the opportunities for contract software work.

The U.S. MIS community has not been a stellar performer in building in-house software applications. The rates of MIS cancellations, delays, and overruns on large applications is high enough to cause many chief executive officers (CEOs) to consider outsourcing as a way of bringing software under control.

Although every major corporation uses MIS applications in large volumes, the development of these applications is outside the main business direction of at least 300 of the Fortune 500 companies. Here, too, there are some significant business reasons for exploring outsourcing as an alternative to in-house development. Some of the major U.S. outsource vendors from whom we have gathered data include (in alphabetic order) American Management Systems (AMS), Andersen Consulting, Compaq, CSC, EDS, IBM, Keane Associates, Litton, Lockheed, Perot Systems, and Unisys.

We have encountered a number of different kinds of outsource contracts during our assessment and benchmark studies. Some of the many varieties of contract include the following:

- Large-scale corporate agreements under which the outsource contractor takes over employment of most or all of the software personnel who work for the client. These large-scale agreements usually mean that the clients have decided to concentrate on their core business and regard software as outside their main area of business skills. These agreements usually include both new development and maintenance work.
- Partial contracts under which the outsource vendor agrees to take over either maintenance work or new development work, but not both. Maintenance outsource contracts occur more than twice as often as development con-

tracts among our clients. These partial agreements may or may not involve absorption of employees by the outsource contractor.

- International outsource agreements under which development and maintenance work is performed abroad, usually in countries with fairly low labor rates such as the Czech Republic, India, Ireland, Russia, or the Ukraine. The work is performed by citizens of other countries, so U.S. employees do not become employees of the outsource vendor under such agreements.

- International outsource agreements that have come to be termed *insourcing.* Under these contracts, outsource personnel are brought to the United States under temporary work permits and work at the client's sites in the United States.

- Narrow-focus contracts for the development or maintenance of a single application or system. These narrow-focus agreements are usually for specialized applications for which special skills are needed. Examples of such specialized applications include banking applications, telephone switching applications, and child support applications for state governments. Not only are these applications specialized, but they are often rather large. A majority of the projects of this type that we have been commissioned to examine are more than 10,000 function points. This size would be more than 1,000,000 source code statements in the COBOL programming language.

- Specialized contracts for specific tasks, such as Y2K repairs or updates to applications to allow them to support the Euro. These specialized contracts can range from a single application to an entire corporate portfolio.

We have also encountered contract types that are outside the range of our standard benchmark and baseline analysis. For example, for military projects we often encounter contracts that include hardware, microcode, software, and support services concurrently. Because we gather data only on software projects, the other aspects of these large agreements are outside the scope of our analysis.

We have also encountered a variety of contracts that are not normally termed "outsource" contracts but are just a normal part of doing business. Many of our clients utilize contract personnel when extra technical staff are needed for a limited time period. This is done for load balancing between slack times and times of peak development activity. For example, a mixture of 90% in-house personnel and 10% contract personnel is a very common ratio. However, we have seen projects with a 50/50 split between contractor personnel and in-house personnel. We have even seen some projects for which contract personnel outnumber in-house personnel.

This kind of use of contract personnel to augment in-house personnel is now facing reevaluation in the United States based on the final outcome of the Microsoft contractor lawsuits. If some or all contractors become eligible for company benefits, then usage of contractors will be a much more complex arrangement than in the past.

We also encounter projects for which multiple contractors may be employed. For example, a prime contractor for a major software project may utilize one or more subcontractors.

This chapter deals with civilian contracts and civilian outsourcing primarily in the information systems domain. The military world has unique standards and procurement practices, and even a body of special contract law that does not apply to the civilian sector (although parts of it may show up in civilian contracts with the U.S. federal government). Some of these special situations are discussed in Chapter 11.

The systems software domain also has some extensive contract and outsource experiences, and indeed is more likely to go abroad for outsourcing than any other domain. Systems software outsourcing often requires special skills, such as telecommunication engineering. Therefore, systems software outsource agreements are usually for specific projects rather than for wide-scale development and maintenance of hundreds of applications. In the United States, the large outsource vendors such as Andersen, ISSC, EDS, and Keane tend to concentrate on the MIS market.

Contract software and outsourced software are alike in that the work is performed by personnel who are not employees of the client organization, using terms and conditions that are mutually agreed to and covered by contractual obligations. Contract software and outsourced software differ in the overall scope of the arrangement. Contracts are usually for specific individual projects, whereas an outsource arrangement might encompass hundreds or even thousands of projects under one general contractual umbrella.

Up through calendar year 1999, the software outsourcing community has grown rather rapidly. The diversity of organizations within the outsource and contract community runs from a host of one-person individual contractors up to the size of EDS, with perhaps 100,000 software professionals worldwide, and approximately half associated with U.S. projects. As an example of how rapidly outsourcing has grown, when I was part of an ITT team evaluating the possibility of purchasing of EDS circa 1982, their software population was only roughly 25,000, as opposed to today's number of approximately 100,000.

The Growth of International Outsourcing

Outsourcing has grown very rapidly abroad in the 1990s. In the days of mainframe computers circa 1960 to 1990, there were some substantial and costly entry barriers to software contracting and outsourcing. Mainframe programming requires expensive mainframe computers, special buildings with chilled water-cooling systems and air-conditioning, and other capital items. These conditions favor the industrialized nations and made it hard for emerging countries to compete in the software domain.

As the twenty-first century begins, PCs, workstations, and portable computers are now the dominant tools of software development. None of these require much electricity or have any special cooling requirements. In fact, the use of portable computers with battery packs makes even a reliable source of electricity an optional matter.

Software development today is an environmentally friendly industry that does not cause much pollution or environmental damage. Furthermore, software is one of the very few industries in which all of the major deliverable items can be transmitted electronically to any destination in the world. The software industry does not require either the time delays or the costs of shipping physical products from country to country, as do manufacturing industries. The bulk of all software deliverables can be shipped electronically and rapidly.

The only exception to this rule are the final magnetic tapes, CD-ROMs, or DVD disks that are normally used for final distribution of software to consumers. However, it is possible to download software and produce CD-ROMs or DVDs locally in every major country. Even the final deliverables of software projects may eventually be produced on the spot.

Because software projects are subject to frequent changes in user requirements during the development cycle, daily contact between clients and development personnel has been a standard practice in the software world. The need for frequent contact between clients and contractors made long-distance outsourcing very difficult during the 1980s; however, the Internet has changed the situation dramatically. The rapid expansion of the Internet and the World Wide Web has greatly eased the difficulties of international communications among geographically dispersed team members and between developers and clients.

Prior to the widespread deployment of the Internet, intranets, and the World Wide Web, international projects involving multiple cities had significantly lower productivity and quality levels than similar applications developed at one physical site. During the 1970s our rule of thumb was that each time a new city or geographic location became part of a large software project, productivity declined by approximately 5% compared with single-site projects. If the city was in a different country, productivity declined by roughly 10%. If the project involved prime contractors and subcontractors, each subcontract reduced productivity by approximately 2.5% compared with a single corporation.

However, the power of the Internet and the Web appear to be sufficient so that international applications, when the teams are in full network communication, are just as productive as single-site projects. Indeed, some of the recent projects examined circa 1999 are slightly more productive across multiple cities than single-site work. This appears to be due to the fact that top specialists are dispersed geographically.

Some major outsource vendors are experimenting with the possibility of having three major software "factories" located eight time zones apart. At the end of the first shift, the day's work would transfer to the next factory just starting their first shift. This would enable 24-hour-a-day development and would shorten significantly the schedules needed to complete large applications.

Because daily transfer of software artifacts is difficult and troublesome, these efforts to move toward around-the-world, around-the-clock development are very experimental and not yet standard practices. However, the fact that it is at least possible to envision software being developed in a 24-hour-7-days-a-week style (cited as *24*7* in some journal articles) shows that the research is at least worth pursuing.

SPR estimates that the non-U.S. total of outsource contractors is currently at approximately 450,000 contractors, and is growing rapidly. For outsourcing contracts with U.S. companies, India and Russia are the two countries that tend to dominate. However, more than 25 countries have been gearing up to attract outsourcing business. In fact, countries such as India, China, Russia, and the Ukraine have an available surplus of software personnel that, in aggregate, could top 1,000,000 software workers. Therefore, these countries and many developing nations would love to enter into outsource agreements.

For domestic outsource arrangements, a frequent pattern is that the outsourcing vendor acquires the existing staff, who may not even move from their current offices. Under many outsource agreements, the personnel involved change companies and become employees of the outsource vendor. For international outsourcing, a different pattern is needed. Usually the outsource personnel are local residents in the country acquiring the contract. They remain employees of the outsource vendor. The recent U.S. court rulings involving benefits offered to contract employees may not be relevant to international outsource agreements.

The volume of domestic outsourcing agreements between large information systems clients and outsource contractors is quite significant. Currently, SPR estimates that approximately 15% of all information systems software in the United States is produced under contract or outsource agreements. This volume has increased from less than 5% circa 1989. The impact of recent court decisions on the benefits that accrue to contract employees may slow the growth of U.S. software contract work in the future.

Contracts with software outsourcers located abroad, such as in the Ukraine or in India, would presumably follow local laws and regulations, and contract personnel would not be assigned the same benefits as full-time employees. Thus, the recent U.S. court decisions may favor offshore outsourcers at the expense of U.S. outsourcers.

As of 2000, the total volume of MIS software from the United States being outsourced internationally seems to be less than 2% of total MIS applications, based on preliminary data collected during assessments performed by SPR. Should the percent of offshore contract work rise significantly in the future, then the United States and other industrialized countries might face significant layoffs among MIS software personnel. In fact, the domestic U.S. outsource companies could also face significant problems too, unless they establish international subsidiaries.

The United States is not the only country that is exploring international software outsource arrangements. Most countries with high labor costs, such as Japan, Sweden, the United Kingdom, and Germany, are also interested in software development or maintenance in countries with lower labor costs.

As a general rule, any industries in any country in which the average cost of software development exceeds approximately $1,000 per function point are likely to be considering international outsourcing arrangements with countries in which the average cost of building a function point is less than $300. Expressed another way, executives in countries in which the fully burdened labor costs for software personnel top $100,000 per year are interested in the possibility of outsource agreements in countries in which the burdened labor costs are less than $30,000 per year.

These rules of thumb mean that most of Europe, Canada, Japan, and the United Kingdom, whose average costs are more than $1,000 per function point, are exploring potential arrangements with India, China, Russia, the Ukraine, Chile, Peru, the Philippines, Indonesia, and other countries in which the average costs are less than $300 per function point.

Cost is not the only factor for outsourcing, of course. The countries that are most likely to become the key software outsourcing centers of the twenty-first century are those with the following 15 key factors:

1. Low labor costs
2. Good voice communication channels
3. Good Internet access
4. Good educational facilities
5. Good transportation systems
6. Low crime rates
7. Low threat of war or insurrection
8. State-of-the-art computing equipment
9. State-of-the-art software tools
10. Government support of the software industry
11. Favorable tax structures
12. Favorable laws protecting intellectual property
13. Favorable human rights climate
14. Effective outsource marketing and sales channels
15. A surplus of qualified software personnel

It is interesting that the countries that have industrialized rapidly and become major economic powers since World War II (for example, Germany, Japan, South Korea, and Taiwan) have also increased their labor costs and the cost of living to a rough parity with the United States.

As of 1999, software is the most "transportable" high-technology occupation. A medical doctor, attorney, or an electrical engineer cannot just set up shop and start practicing in another country because of licensing requirements. There are no such barriers for software. Any good programmer who can get a work permit or permanent visa can go to work almost immediately.

Furthermore, thanks to the Internet and the fact that software can be transported rapidly, software is well on its way to becoming the first truly global business. Software developers thousands of miles apart can collaborate with each other almost as easily as if they were in the same room.

Choosing Outsourcing or In-house Development

Because software development is outside the primary business direction of at least 300 of the Fortune 500 companies, many are considering outsourcing as an alternative to costly in-house software organizations. Given the rather unfavorable ratio of successes to failures among in-house MIS departments, this factor is another reason for considering outsourcing.

A recent book by the well-known software economist Paul Strassmann examines the entire question of software economics. This new book is entitled *Information Productivity: Assessing the Information Management Costs of US Industrial Corporations* (Strassmann 1999). His conclusions are thought provoking and are likely to be controversial. In essence, he doubts that MIS applications have aided U.S. industrial productivity. Among his provocative observations is one that profitable and successful companies seem to spend less on information technology than unprofitable and unsuccessful ones of the same general size and within the same industry sector. Strassmann's book is among the most penetrating treatments of information costs and value yet published, and the data is entirely derived from actual companies, many of which are used as illustrative examples.

An alternative strategy available to the domestic U.S. outsource community in the face of global competition is to achieve such high productivity levels that the difference in labor costs between the United States and countries abroad are inconsequential.

The large outsourcing vendors such as Andersen, EDS, and IBM are already somewhat more productive than the clients they serve. This is especially true for major applications in the 10,000-function point range. This productivity advantage can be measured using "function points per staff month" or "work hours per function point." However, due to the fairly high costs of labor and burden rates in the outsource domain, the metric "cost per function point" is only marginally better for outsource projects. Indeed, for some kinds of specialized work, such as Y2K repairs, in-house costs may be substantially lower than outsourced costs. (Furthermore, the fact that costs are collected in almost random fashions by companies and government agencies means that there is a chronic shortage of accurate software cost data.)

In theory the major outsource vendors are in a position to become among the most efficient software developers in the world in terms of the amount of human effort required to build software applications. There are six reasons why large outsource vendors are in favorable positions.

1. They are large enough to establish international software factories eight hours apart and thus support 24-hour-a-day development cycles, at least in theory.
2. They are large enough to establish laboratories or solution centers in many countries in which state-of-the-art tools and technologies can be made available on behalf of the clients.
3. They create large volumes of reusable materials within specific industries such as banking, insurance, health care, and the like.
4. They foster a rather intense work ethic among their software employees in an industry in which an intense work ethic is quite common.
5. They have fairly high personnel and recruiting standards, and attract top candidates.
6. They have better than average training and educational facilities for their technical and managerial employees.

The future of outsourcing, in principle, can be very bright. There is a growing demand for software. Many potential clients are evaluating the outsourcing option due to fairly marginal performance by in-house MIS groups. The outsource combination of technical sophistication and an intense work ethic can compensate for the fairly high billable rates that outsource vendors often charge.

All modern companies use computers and software in significant amounts, and will use even more in the future. Efficiency in computer and software acquisition, deployment, and usage is an important competitive aspect of modern business and government operations. Inefficiency in computer and software acquisition, deployment, maintenance, and usage is a major contributor to business failure, loss of market shares, and delayed time-to-market for new products.

Software development and maintenance are expensive operations and have grown to become major cost components of corporate budgets. It is not uncommon for software personnel to exceed 12% of total corporate employment, and for the software and computing budgets to exceed 15% of annual corporate expenditures. Using the function point metric as the basis of comparison, most large companies now own more than 500,000 function points as the total volume of software in their mainframe portfolios, and some very large companies such as AT&T and IBM own well over 1,000,000 function points.

As an example of the more or less unplanned growth of software and software personnel in modern business, some of the larger banks and insurance companies now have software staffs that number in the thousands. In fact, software and computing technical personnel may comprise the largest single occupational group within many companies whose core business is far removed from software.

As business process reengineering becomes more widespread, the executives of many large corporations are asking a fundamental question: Should software be part of our core business or not? This is not a simple question to answer, and the exploration of some of the possibilities is the purpose of this section. You probably want to make software a key component of your core business operation under the following conditions:

- You sell products that depend on your own proprietary software.
- Your software is currently giving your company a significant competitive advantage.
- Your company's software development and maintenance effectiveness is far better than your competitors.

Some of the initial considerations for dealing with the topic of whether software should be an integral part of corporate operations or perhaps outsourced include the following 20 points.

1. Are you gaining significant competitive advantage from your current software?
2. Does your current software contain trade secrets or valuable proprietary data?
3. Are your company's products dependent on your proprietary software?
4. How much does your current software benefit the following business functions:
   - Corporate management
   - Finance
   - Manufacturing and distribution
   - Sales and marketing
   - Customer support
   - Human resources
5. How much software does your company currently own?
6. How much new software will your company need in the next five years?
7. How much of your software is in the form of aging legacy systems?
8. How many of your aging legacy systems were Y2K compliant?
9. How many of your aging legacy systems were Euro currency compliant?

10. Is your software development productivity rate better than your competitors?
11. Is your software maintenance more efficient than your competitors?
12. Is your time-to-market for software-related products better than your competitors?
13. Is your software quality better than your competitors?
14. Are you able to utilize substantial volumes of reusable artifacts?
15. How many software employees are currently on board?
16. How many software employees will be hired during the next five years?
17. How many users of software are there in your company?
18. How many users of software will there be in five years?
19. Are you considering enterprise software packages such as SAP or Oracle?
20. Are you finding it hard to hire new staff due to the personnel shortage?

The patterns of answers can vary widely from company to company, but will fall within a spectrum of possibilities: If your company is a software top gun and a notable leader in your industry, then you probably would not consider outsourcing at all. This very favorable condition only applies to approximately 5% of U.S. companies, so it is a rare condition indeed. At the opposite extreme, if your company trails all major competitors in software topics, then outsourcing should be on the critical path for immediate action. This condition of being a true laggard, or so close to being one that it barely matters, occurs in approximately 10% of U.S. companies. However, at least half of these companies have already become clients of outsource companies due to the problems they experienced with in-house failures.

There are two other situations in which the pros and cons of outsourcing are more ambiguous.

1. Your software operations are average within your industry and are neither better nor worse than your competitors in most respects. In this case, outsourcing may perhaps offer you some cost reductions, or at least a more predictable software budget in the future, if you select the right outsourcing partner. This situation occurs for approximately 35% of U.S. companies. Companies in this zone can either invest in software process improvements or can move toward outsourcing. The best choice depends on specific corporate factors that are too complex for generalized discussion.
2. A second ambiguous outsourcing situation is the following: You don't have the vaguest idea about whether your software operations are better or worse

than your competitors due to a chronic lack of data about software in your industry or in your company. This ambiguous situation is the case for approximately 50% of U.S. companies. The executives and officers do not have a clue as to whether their software operations are better or worse than industry norms.

In this latter situation, ignorance is dangerous. If you don't know, in a quantitative way, whether your software operations are good, bad, or indifferent, then you can be very sure that your company is not a top gun and is probably no better than average in overall software performance. It may be much worse, of course. This harsh statement is because all of the really good, top-notch software groups have quality and productivity measurement programs in place, and also perform benchmarks, so they know how good they are.

Assume, for example, that you are a CIO or senior software executive and can't answer the 20 questions presented earlier in this chapter, or can only answer a few of them. This should tell you that software is probably not under full management control within your company, and that your company's CEO or board of directors may very well be considering outsource possibilities.

If you don't know your quality levels, productivity levels, the amount of software your company owns, or who is using the software, then you clearly are working in the dark in an important business function that needs executive understanding and attention. In this case, outsourcing might be a useful option. Your executives do not have enough control of the software function to deal with it as your company does with its core business operations.

If you don't have the vaguest notion of your current software ownership, software productivity rates, software usage volumes, and other quantitative factors, you or your outsource negotiators will be at a disadvantage when you discuss an outsource contract, and this may lower the probability of a successful outcome. Several lawsuits have occurred because outsource agreements required that the outsource vendors improve productivity levels after the agreement started. Several lawsuits were caused primarily by the fact that the baseline productivity levels before the outsource contracts started could not be determined with enough accuracy to evaluate whether the outsource contractor had made the improvements written into the contracts.

Because corporate software cost and resource tracking systems usually "leak," and omit an average of approximately 35% of the actual effort and costs for software projects, using standard corporate tracking data as the baseline for comparison places the outsource vendor at an unfair disadvantage. The client's real productivity is somewhere between 30% and 50% worse than they believe it to be. (The most common omissions from corporate cost tracking systems include work before the tracking system is initialized with project data, unpaid overtime, project management effort, administrative and secretarial support, work of specialists [such as database administrators], and technical work performed by clients [such as acceptance testing].)

A worst-case scenario would be an outsource contract for which neither the client nor the outsource vendor had any quantitative baseline data on software productivity, quality, or schedule adherence. In this case, neither side of the outsource arrangement may be particularly capable. You certainly do not want to go to the trouble of setting up an outsource contract with a company no better than your own in dealing with critical software issues.

If you have determined that outsourcing is at least a potential option for your company, then you need to evaluate possible outsourcing partners. You may choose to evaluate the potential outsource partners with your own staff, or you can choose one or more of the external management consulting companies that specialize in this area.

A fundamental decision in outsourcing in the 1990s is to decide whether a domestic or an international outsource partner is preferred. The international outsource companies from countries such as India, Indonesia, or Russia can sometimes offer attractive short-term cost reductions. However, communication with international outsource partners is more complex than with domestic partners, and there are other issues that should be evaluated as well.

If you are considering an international outsource partner, some of the factors to include in your evaluation are

- The expertise of the candidate partner for the kinds of software your company utilizes
- The availability of satellite, Internet, or reliable broad-band communication between your office sites and the outsource location
- The local copyright, patent, and intellectual property protection regulations in the country of the outsource vendor
- The probability of political upheavals, or factors that might interfere with transnational information flow
- The basic stability and economic soundness of the outsource vendor, and what might occur should the vendor encounter a severe financial downturn

Domestic outsource companies can usually offer some level of cost reduction or cost stabilization, and also fairly convenient communication arrangements. Also, one sensitive aspect of outsourcing is the future employment of your current software personnel. The domestic outsource companies may offer an arrangement so that some or all of your personnel become their employees.

One notable aspect of outsourcing is the fact that outsource vendors who specialize in particular industries such as banking, insurance, and telecommunications may have substantial quantities of reusable material available. Because reuse is the technology that gives the best overall efficiency for software, the reuse factor is one of the key reasons why some outsource vendors may be able to offer cost savings. There are ten software artifacts for which reuse is valuable, and some of the outsource vendors may have reusable material from many of these ten categories: reusable architecture, plans, estimates, requirements, design, source code, data, human interfaces, user documentation, and test materials.

Some of the general topics to consider when evaluating potential outsource partners that are either domestic or international include the following:

- The expertise of the outsource vendor within your industry, and for the kinds of software your company utilizes. If the outsource vendor serves your direct competitors, be sure that adequate confidentiality can be ensured.
- The satisfaction levels of current clients who use the outsource vendor's services. You may wish to contact several clients and find out their first-hand experiences. It is particularly useful to speak with clients who have had outsource contracts in place for more than two or three years, and hence can talk about long-term satisfaction.
- Whether any active or recent litigation exists between the outsource company and current or past clients. Although active litigation may not be a showstopper in dealing with an outsource vendor, it is certainly a factor you will want to find out more about if the situation exists.
- How the vendor's own software performance compares against industry norms in terms of productivity, quality, reuse, and other quantitative factors. For this kind of analysis, the function point metric is now the most widely used in the world, and is superior to any alternative metrics. If outsource vendors have no data on their own quality or productivity, be cautious. They may not be very sophisticated.
- The kinds of project management tools the vendor utilizes. Project management is a weak link in the software industry, and the leaders tend to utilize a

suite of software project management tools including cost estimation tools, quality estimation tools, software planning tools, software tracking tools, and several others. If your candidate outsource vendor has no quantitative estimating or measurement capabilities, it is unlikely that their performance will be much better than your own.

- The kinds of quality assurance and quality control methods the vendor uses. Because poor software quality is a critical factor in litigation, overruns, and cancelled projects, only companies with sophisticated software quality methods are likely to be effective in the long run.

Bear in mind that an outsource contract is a major business decision that will affect your company's future for many years. In a sense, an outsource agreement is like a marriage contract. If you enter into an agreement with the wrong partner, it is not easy to correct the situation afterward. An outsource "divorce" is likely to be expensive and time-consuming.

Some of the software your company owns may have such a significant competitive value that you do not want to outsource it, or even to let any other company know of its existence. One of the basic preparatory steps before initiating an outsource arrangement is to survey your major current systems and arrange security or protection for valuable software assets with high competitive value. This survey has multiple benefits for your company, and you may want to undertake such a survey even if you are not considering outsource arrangements. The survey of current and planned software assets should deal with the following six important topics:

1. Identification of systems and programs that have high competitive value or utilize proprietary or trade secret algorithms. These systems may well be excluded from more general outsource arrangements. If they are to be included in an outsource contract, then special safeguards for confidential factors should be negotiated. Note also that preservation of proprietary or competitive software and data is very delicate when international outsource contracts are utilized. Be sure that local patent, copyright, and intellectual property laws are sufficient to safeguard your sensitive materials. You may need attorneys in several countries.

2. Analysis of the databases and files utilized by your software applications, and the development of a strategy for preserving confidential data under the outsource arrangement. If your databases contain valuable and proprietary information on topics such as trade secrets, competitors, specific customers,

employee appraisals, pending or active litigation, and the like, you need to ensure that this data is carefully protected under any outsource arrangement.

3. Quantification of the number of users of your key system, and their current levels of satisfaction and dissatisfaction with key applications. In particular, you will want to identify any urgent enhancements that may need to be passed on to an outsource vendor.

4. Quantification of the size of the portion of your current portfolio that is to be included in the outsource contract. Normally this quantification is based on the function point metric and includes the size, in function points, of all current systems and applications for which the outsource vendor will assume maintenance responsibility.

5. Analysis of the plans and estimates for future or partly completed software projects that are to be included in the outsource arrangement and hence to be developed by the outsource vendor. You need to understand your own productivity and quality rates, and then compare your anticipated results against those to which the outsource vendor will commit. Here, too, usage of the function point metric is the most common and the best choice for outsourcing contracts.

6. Quantification of your current or baseline quality and productivity levels. If you intend to ask the outsource vendor to improve on productivity and quality, you need to know your current levels. If you do not know your current levels, you may well find yourself in future litigation. This is a job for baseline and benchmark specialists, and is not one a company can handle easily by itself, unless it already has a sophisticated measurement program in place. However, most companies that are considering outsourcing don't measure productivity or quality. This is one of the reasons why outsourcing is being considered.

These topics are only the tip of the iceberg. Consulting companies that evaluate proprietary applications and data such as SEI or SPR may deal with more than 100 factors for critical applications and data repositories.

Minimizing the Risks of Disputes between Outsource Contractors and Their Clients

As of 2000 there is no overall census of how long typical outsource agreements last, how many are mutually satisfactory, how many are terminated, and how many end up in court. The longest running outsource agreements we have observed are approaching ten years in 2000.

Approximately half of our assessment and benchmark studies in the outsource domain are commissioned just before or during the initial year of an outsource agreement. These studies are for the purpose of creating the initial baseline against which future performance is measured for contractual purposes. We also do annual follow-up studies, although the initial baseline is a much more complex measurement task than the follow-up studies. From informal observations among SPR's clients, the approximate results resemble those presented in Table 8.1 after 24 months of the agreement.

When litigation does occur between outsource clients and vendors, three chronic problems have been observed:

1. The client charges that the vendor failed to meet the terms of the contract with regard to cost, quality, achieving contractual productivity gains, or delivery of applications in satisfactory working condition.
2. The vendor charges that the client expanded the scope of the contract unilaterally in terms of adding requirements or activities to those agreed to earlier. The vendor may also charge that the client did not provide timely feedback to materials that were delivered.
3. In cases where the outsource vendor has a contractual obligation to improve productivity or quality each year after the contract starts, the most frequent cause of litigation is ambiguity in the baseline against which the improvements should be measured. Because poor measurement practices are endemic in the software world, it is not surprising that baselines may exaggerate performance. All outsource agreements of this type should include a clause to validate the baseline before using it to judge contractual obligations.

Table 8.1   Outsource Results after 24 Months

Result	Percent
Generally satisfactory to both parties	70
Some dissatisfaction by client or vendor	15
Dissolution of agreement planned	10
Litigation between client and vendor probable	4
Litigation between client and vendor in progress	1

Once the problems begin to occur, the relationship between the clients and vendors usually spirals downhill until a dissolution of the agreement occurs, or litigation.

On the whole, outsource agreements work best if the client has a realistic expectation of what is likely to occur. Outsource agreements are likely to fail if the client expects miraculous improvements in productivity, major reductions in schedules, or some other tremendous improvement. Of course, the vendors should not promise miraculous improvements to get the business.

The outsource vendor also has a responsibility to deliver what is promised. In several court cases the outsource vendors have promised to utilize state-of-the-art technologies and provide experienced teams of personnel. From time to time, the outsource vendors had to substitute new and inexperienced personnel who did not use state-of-the-art technologies. These situations are likely to cause litigation.

The best outsource arrangements offer stability to both parties. For the client in particular, a good outsource agreement can relieve the company of a large software organization that was not part of their core business operations. Furthermore, if the software organization was not a best-in-class group, then the outsource arrangement can also offer tangible but not enormous improvements in schedules, costs, quality, and maintenance.

A significant factor in whether the agreement will be satisfactory or unpleasant resides in the outsource contract itself. A new form of outsource agreement based on function points is starting, gradually, to replace the older and more ambiguous agreements simply based on providing certain numbers of personnel or agreed-to quantities of effort.

A function point outsource agreement for new development would include a mutually agreed-to volume of function points delivered each year, for an agreed-to cost per function point. For example, the vendor might agree to develop and deliver 20,000 function points per year at a cost of $500 per function point, or $10,000,000 per year in total. This form of agreement has the advantage that it can be adjusted for creeping requirements, which are a common source of antagonism between outsource vendors and their clients. As an example, if the client needs an additional 3,000 function points over and above the agreed-to 20,000 function points, the extra quantity might be supplied, but at a cost of $600 per function point, or $1,800,000.

For maintenance agreements, the contract should include an explicit size of the portfolio being maintained. For example, suppose the client's portfolio of aging legacy applications totals 250,000 function points. The agreement might state that these legacy applications would be kept operational and have bugs repaired for an annual cost of $50 per function point, or $25,000,000.

Although the use of function points in outsource contracts is common, this method is not a panacea. Success in deploying function points in contracts is not easy. First, function point counts should be done by certified counting personnel. To ensure impartiality, function point counts may be done by an external group not employed by either the client or the outsource vendor. Second, function points themselves have some troublesome aspects. Function points are difficult to utilize on small enhancement and maintenance projects less than 50 function points in size. Because any large company may perform 20,000 function points worth of small updates each year, this is a difficult area. Third, there are many kinds of software activities that are outside the scope of successful measurement by function points. For example, if customer service or staffing telephone "hotlines" are included in the contract, the resources used for these tasks are determined more by the number of clients than by the sizes of the applications being serviced. Fourth, if the contract includes database or data warehouse construction, the lack of any kind of a data point metric means that the volumes of the databases and data quality cannot be measured directly using function points. Fifth, if the contract includes deploying commercial off-the-shelf software or installing and tuning ERP applications such as SAP, the function point totals of the commercial packages may not be available from the vendors.

On the whole, function points work well for developing new applications of a substantial nature, but are tricky for other kinds of work such as small enhancements, service work, and small maintenance projects.

Another frequent claim in software litigation involves poor quality. It is possible to include explicit quality requirements in the contract. The current U.S. average for in-house MIS projects is to have a total volume of defects that approximates 5.0 defects per function point. Various reviews and testing operations remove approximately 85% of these defects prior to delivery, so the volume of latent defects still in the software is roughly 0.75 defects per function point at delivery.

It is possible to include a clause in an outsource agreement that requires the vendor to achieve a value such as more than 95% defect removal efficiency. This is calculated by comparing the total number of defects found by the vendor during development with the number found by the client during the first 90 days of software application use. For example, if the vendor found 950 software defects and the client found 50 defects in the first 90 days of usage, then the vendor achieved a removal rate of 95%.

These simplistic examples illustrate that function point metrics and defect removal metrics can minimize the ambiguity of software contracts and outsource agreements. From working as an expert witness in a dozen software contract cases, ambiguity in the contract is a very common problem.

As a general but not universal rule, the performance of outsource vendors is significantly better than the average performance of the clients they serve. If this were not the case, the outsource business would wither and die.

As we move into the new century, an increasing number of large companies is seeking ways to reduce their expenses and reengineer their business processes. Exploration of software outsourcing is an important topic under the general heading of business process reengineering. Although large companies utilize enormous volumes of software, building and maintaining that software may not be part of the company's core business strategy.

Outsourcing is an important business consideration. Selection of a suitable outsource partner is also an important business consideration. Both topics deserve thoughtful analysis and careful preparatory work. The ultimate goal of outsourcing is for the client to receive enhanced benefits and advantages from software. The main advantage offered by the top outsource vendors is high levels of expertise coupled with larger volumes of reusable material, and hence more efficient development and maintenance.

As the World Wide Web and Internet become more common as daily business tools, it should be possible for outsource vendors to have virtual development factories located eight time zones apart. Thus, at the end of the first shift of work in the United States, the project could be transferred to an Asian lab, which in turn would transfer the work to a European lab. The next morning, the U.S. lab would take over again at the start of the U.S. business day. Developing software around the clock would be a major breakthrough in reducing the lengthy multiyear schedules now common on projects larger than 10,000 function points. The outsource domain is much better positioned than most companies to pioneer this approach.

Outsourcing Technologies

The larger outsource vendors such as Andersen, EDS, IBM and the like have rather active technology research programs underway. The large outsource vendors also have their own "best-practice" guides and substantial training curricula available for both their own employees and for their clients. However, when working under contract, the outsourcing community may be constrained to use specific technologies mandated by clients and stated in the outsource contracts. Not every contract includes requirements that the vendor use specific tools, programming languages, or methodologies, but many contracts do.

The major outsource vendors such as Andersen and EDS are fairly sophisticated in their utilization of software tools and methods. In addition, the major outsource vendors often have very effective in-house training programs for software personnel, and especially for new hires. It is a normal practice for new employees of outsource vendors to be put through a very intensive training program for six weeks to ten weeks. Indeed, completing this training program successfully is a condition of achieving permanent employment.

The intensive training of new hires also serves another purpose. It tends to foster a very intense work ethic among outsource employees. One of the reasons why outsource projects appear to be much more productive than similar in-house projects is because of the amount of unpaid overtime that the outsource employees typically work. Indeed, one outsource vendor actually has a television commercial showing the employees thinking about client problems while doing other activities such as playing sports and traveling.

In the MIS domain, the large outsource vendors often have interesting software research programs. These programs can lead to internal standards for best practices that may be beneficial to clients. In fact the software standards and best-practice manuals developed by major software outsource vendors are often much more sophisticated than university software engineering curricula.

The larger outsource vendors have long been active in running data centers. In fact, some outsourcers such as EDS had contracts for managing client data centers long before they entered the software development outsource market. This long experience with running computer centers implies very efficient hardware management, often with better service levels and lower costs of ownership than clients might be able to achieve on their own.

The most notable software technologies at which outsource vendors are usually much better than their clients are in the areas of software reusability and software maintenance activities. Because outsource vendors have vertical practices within specific industries such as banking, insurance, pharmaceuticals, hospital administration, and state government operations, they are in a very good position to develop libraries of reusable components for these industries. Indeed, the outsource domain has developed entire reusable applications for specific purposes such as insurance claims handling or child care administration.

Because contracts for maintenance of legacy applications are so common, the outsource domain has developed fairly successful practices for handling updates to aging legacy applications. Some of these practices include

- Automated complexity analysis of modules (cyclomatic and essential complexity)
- Automated complexity reduction of modules with high complexity levels
- Automated change control tools
- Standardized naming conventions
- Improved comment density and code readability
- Use of formal inspections on legacy applications
- Dead code removal in legacy applications
- Error-prone module removal in legacy applications

In some of the maintenance studies we have benchmarked, the outsource domain was approximately 50% more productive than the client when measured using several key maintenance indicators:

- Assignment scopes for outsource maintenance topped 1,500 function points versus approximately 800 function points for in-house maintenance.
- Monthly defect repairs topped 12 to 15 defects fixed per month for outsource maintenance versus eight to nine for in-house maintenance.

On the whole, maintenance in the form of defect repairs and minor updates (in other words, those taking less than five staff days) are much more efficient in the hands of specialists, such as maintenance outsourcers, than in the hands of the general programming population.

Over and above fixing errors, customer support is also a technology that is frequently turned over to outsource vendors. The phrase *customer support* is very broad and can include telephone support, e-mail support, and operating the maintenance portions of corporate Web sites. Among SPR's benchmark studies, outsourcing customer support is one of the more common forms of a maintenance agreement. Even major commercial software houses such as Microsoft and Computer Associates outsource some of their customer support work.

The staffing requirements for customer support are based on three key metrics: the number of customers, the number of defects or bugs in the application, and the ease of use of the application.

A chronic problem for the software industry has been releasing software applications that have so many bugs and are so hard to use that customer support groups are swamped and overloaded. There is no economic method for supporting large numbers of clients who are trying to use buggy software with a steep learning curve.

For software that is low in defects (<0.2 defects per function point at deployment), one customer support telephone operator can deal with more than 100 users, but for software with poor quality (>0.8 defects per function point) one customer support staff member will be swamped with only 50 users.

Incidentally, customer support groups are an important source of information for commercial software vendors and for outsource vendors as well. Incoming phone calls and e-mails can provide very useful insight into both customer satisfaction issues and major quality problems such as error-prone modules. Thus, data from customer support groups should be studied carefully by project managers and development and maintenance personnel.

Because requirements are so often troublesome for software projects, the outsource community is often at the leading edge in terms of requirements gathering and requirements analysis. For example, outsource projects often use JAD for gathering user requirements. In addition, prototypes and requirements inspections are found more often on outsource projects than on in-house projects.

In the important area of quality control, the outsource community is generally better than the MIS community, but not as good as the systems software community. Outsource companies are more likely to use techniques such as formal inspections than the MIS domain. However, establishing formal software quality assurance departments is still comparatively rare among both MIS and outsource groups.

In terms of software project management, the outsource domain is fairly sophisticated compared with the MIS domain and even compared with the systems software domain. Many project managers employed by major outsource vendors have a lot of experience and are well versed in the use of standard project management and software cost-estimating tools.

Two fairly recent technology issues have affected outsource technologies in recent years: the Y2K problem and the expansion of ERP applications. Although many outsource vendors have done significant business in Y2K repairs, others have not done well, and some have even failed and gone out of business. The mixed results of Y2K outsourcing can be traced to several factors. One of the factors is interesting from a sociological viewpoint. Because the outsource community is somewhat more sophisticated than the MIS community, the outsource vendors began to market Y2K services before the MIS community was fully awake to the seriousness of the Y2K problem. Starting around 1995, hundreds of Y2K vendors started to market their services. Unfortunately, the main MIS repair efforts for Y2K problems did not peak until 1998 or even 1999. Thus the Y2K business started later than expected. Furthermore, with hundreds of vendors offering services that appeared to be virtually identical, Y2K repair companies that were marginally funded had trouble with cash flow and some went out of business, or at least out of the Y2K business.

A secondary problem with the Y2K market can be traced to the pricing structures that some Y2K vendors utilized initially. Many vendors attempted to price their Y2K repairs based on a cost-per-LOC basis, using rates of at least $1.00 per source line. Unfortunately, the most common Y2K use of the LOC metric was a simple count of physical lines. Thus the cost structure could include comments, blank lines, and dead code. The more sophisticated potential clients realized that they could do the repairs in-house for approximately 50% less than the vendor might charge because a simple count of physical lines led to overcharges. The use of physical LOC as the basis for contractual repair work is a decided "worst practice."

For several years the ERP market was a great success for outsource vendors. Deploying a full-scale ERP package in a major corporation could take more than 24 calendar months and require perhaps 50 highly trained consultants. Indeed, contract work dealing with installing and tuning ERP packages was probably at least as profitable as the sale of the ERP packages themselves. A number of outsource vendors established interesting and profitable markets in the ERP domain, supporting the deployment of products from SAP, Oracle, Baan, Peoplesoft, and JD Edwards.

The Y2K problem and ERP deployment are related markets. Some corporations hoped that deploying an ERP package would solve some of their Y2K problems by eliminating a variety of legacy applications, which would not be needed after the ERP package was installed. This was a reasonable strategy from 1995 through late 1997. By the end of 1997, the two-year installation cycle for major ERP packages was pushing too close to the Y2K date for the strategy to remain viable. Indeed, due to many fiscal years starting before the calendar year, the last time for successful ERP deployment was sometime in early 1998, if full deployment before the end of the century was the goal.

By 1998 and early 1999, the market for new ERP installations shrank significantly as potential clients realized that it was too late to gain any Y2K benefits. Indeed, acquisitions of many software packages and in-house development were suspended temporarily as companies mounted a final effort to achieve Y2K compliance.

The ERP and Y2K phenomena illustrate an interesting aspect of the outsource domain. In general, the major outsource vendors tend to stay at the leading edge in terms of software technologies. As this book is written, the next major wave of technologies affecting software is rapidly approaching. The next wave is that of *e-business,* as it is called in the trade press. The e-business phenomenon deals with using the Internet and the World Wide Web to market products, to take orders, and to handle payments for consumer goods.

The major outsource vendors are gearing up to offer extensive services to clients for migrating into the e-business domain. However, as this book is written the e-business world is still in its infancy, although billions of dollars are already being spent via the World Wide Web. One can anticipate that e-business will also affect outsource vendors themselves. A substantial amount of software development can now be performed by teams that communicate electronically rather than face to face. Thus, virtual departments and even virtual companies can operate with little or no face-to-face contact among the workers involved.

Outsource Demographics

The large outsource vendors are almost as diverse as the systems software domain in terms of specialization. For example, major outsource vendors employ a number of specialists in areas such as cost and schedule estimating, software quality assurance, testing, technical writing, database administration, and function point analysis. Other kinds of specialists observed within large outsource vendors have generic job titles such as "systems analyst," but are well trained in certain technical activities such as facilitating JAD sessions, moderating design and code inspections, performing assessments based on the SEI model, and developing process improvement plans.

There are a number of specialist areas in which practitioners can support several projects at the same time because their skills may only be needed at specific times. The large outsource vendors may employ specialized personnel in technical areas such as performance analysis and tuning of applications with timing constraints, security and encryption of confidential data, networks and communications, and dealing with ERP applications. An exploding recent area of specialization involves e-business and Web-based applications.

A unique form of specialization found almost exclusively within the outsource community is that of vertical specialization within the industries that the outsource vendors serve. The large outsource vendors will have specialists in a number of specific industry software topics, such as banking, insurance, health care, municipal and state governments, defense, manufacturing, wholesale and retail, and so forth.

This aspect of the outsource business has been fruitful in developing reusable applications that support multiple clients in the same industry. As a result of both vertical specialization and extensive quantities of reusable artifacts, the outsource vendors are often much more productive than the clients they serve. (I first began to study outsource projects when several banking applications were found to be more than twice as productive as financial industry averages. These applications had been produced by an outsource vendor who specialized in financial applications. The applications contained more than 50% reusable material by volume.)

Two forms of specialization stand out as being very effective and more productive than generalists for the same activities: testing specialists and maintenance specialists. The outsource vendors are much more likely than their MIS clients to use specialists for these two key areas.

Since about 1995, two new forms of specialization exploded across the outsource domain: work on modifying software to support the Euro, and making Y2K repairs. During calendar years 1997 through 1999, all of the major outsource vendors were supporting their main clients for Euro and Y2K work.

Incidentally, one of the chronic problems of the outsourcing business has been ambiguity in the contracts. Outsource agreements drafted before 1996 seldom included explicit responsibilities for making Y2K repairs. Thus, for a significant number of maintenance outsource agreements, there have been disputes between the clients and the vendors in terms of who will fund the Y2K work.

One benefit of the Y2K problem has been the fact that companies now know how much software they own. Prior to the Y2K problem, most corporations did not have accurate records of the software applications in their portfolios. As a result of the Y2K problem, major companies know the size and status of every software application in their inventory, including MIS projects, commercial packages, and also systems and embedded applications. Due to the Y2K problem, the corporate portfolios have been undergoing intense scrutiny and massive amounts of updates. Many applications were also retired and replaced either by commercial packages or by newer Y2K-compliant applications.

The combined resource drain of the Euro and Y2K problems has created a major backlog of applications in every software domain. This backlog is occurring at a time when there is already an existing software personnel shortage. In general the Euro and the Y2K problems have led to more business in the outsource domain. However, not every outsource vendor has profited from Y2K work because so many companies entered this market at roughly the same time.

As this book is written, at the end of 1999 and early 2000, all U.S. software domains are lagging in meeting the demands for new and updated applications. The typical backlog among Fortune 500 companies in our client set is now approximately 100,000 function points apportioned among several new applications and scores of major enhancements. As a result, the outsource business has been growing, although outsource vendors themselves have personnel shortages too. Table 8.2 presents my estimate of the numbers of software personnel employed by outsource vendors in the United States at the end of the twentieth century.

As you can see from Table 8.2, the total U.S. employment by outsource companies is just more than 10% of the total software population. However, the outsource domain tends to support the MIS community to a larger degree than the systems, military, and commercial communities. Table 8.3 illustrates my view of the distribution of outsource personnel by software class, based on observations among our clients in these classes during 1998 and 1999.

Table 8.2   Estimated U.S. Outsource Software Population circa 1999

Software Occupation Groups	No. Employed	Outsource Software	Percent of Total
Programmer/analyst	400,000	44,000	11.00
Programmer, maintenance	350,000	45,500	13.00
Programmer, development	275,000	27,500	10.00
Project manager, first level	225,000	22,500	10.00
Software engineer, systems	200,000	6,000	3.00
Testing specialist	125,000	12,500	10.00

continued

Table 8.2 *continued*

Software Occupation Groups	No. Employed	Outsource Software	Percent of Total
Systems analyst	100,000	12,500	12.50
Software engineer, real-time	75,000	3,000	4.00
Software technical writer	75,000	7,500	10.00
Software engineer, embedded	70,000	2,800	4.00
Data administration specialist	50,000	6,250	12.50
Project manager, second level	35,000	3,500	10.00
Software quality assurance specialist	25,000	2,250	9.00
Configuration control specialist	15,000	1,875	12.50
Performance specialist	7,500	750	10.00
Project manager, third level	5,000	500	10.00
Software architect	1,500	225	15.00
Subtotal	2,034,000	199,150	9.79
Support Occupations			
Software sales specialist	105,000	15,750	15.00
Customer support specialist	80,000	9,600	12.00
Systems administration	50,000	5,000	10.00
Software management consultant	45,000	15,750	35.00
Software education specialist	30,000	3,000	10.00
Software librarian	15,000	1,500	10.00
Process auditor/assessor	7,500	750	10.00
Process improvement specialist	5,000	500	10.00
Measurement specialist	3,500	350	10.00
Software marketing specialist	3,000	450	15.00
Cost-estimating specialist	2,000	250	12.50
Human factors specialist	1,000	100	10.00
Certified function point counter	500	50	10.00
Subtotal	322,000	53,050	16.48
Total	2,356,000	252,200	10.70

Table 8.3   Estimated Distribution of U.S. Outsource Personnel by Software Class

Software Class	Technical Personnel	Support Personnel	Total Personnel	Percent
MIS outsource staff	85,635	22,812	108,446	43.00
Commercial outsource staff	49,788	13,263	63,050	25.00
Military outsource staff	39,830	10,610	50,440	20.00
Systems outsource staff	23,898	6,366	30,264	12.00
Total	199,150	53,050	252,200	100.00

If Table 8.3 had been produced ten years ago, the results would be quite different. In the 1980s MIS outsourcing would still be number one, but military outsourcing would be in second place, with almost a third of the total. The decline of military budgets and procurement contracts was taking place at about the same time that the U.S. commercial software market was expanding rapidly.

Every industry listed in the Department of Commerce SIC codes uses contract personnel to a greater or lesser degree. Some of the major employers of outsource personnel include banks, brokerage houses, insurance companies, manufacturing companies, wholesale and retail outlets, and telecommunication companies. However, the SIC codes with the largest concentration of outsource employees include those presented on Table 8.4

In general, the employment of contract and outsource personnel mirrors the employment of other software personnel. The financial and insurance sectors are the largest overall employers of MIS personnel throughout the industrialized world, and are the largest users of contract and outsource personnel. Large banks and insurance companies often have MIS staffs that top 5,000 personnel. These industries are currently also major employers of outsource personnel, and many are planning additional outsource agreements after the Y2K problem is settled.

Government agencies also utilize outsource vendors in large numbers. Government applications include hundreds of information systems, such as the various kinds of taxation software produced at local, state, and national levels. Child care applications, law enforcement applications, social security benefit tracking systems, and driver's license and vehicle registration systems are additional examples.

Table 8.4   SIC Code Industries that Support Outsourcing

SIC Code	Industry
13	Oil and gas extraction
27	Printing and publishing
28	Chemicals and allied products
29	Petroleum refining and related industries
33	Primary metal industries
35	Industrial and commercial machinery
37	Transportation equipment
40	Railroad transportation
45	Air transportation
48	Communications (telephone operating companies)
49	Electricity, gas, and sanitary services
50	Wholesale trade (durable goods)
53	Retail trade (general merchandise stores)
60	Depository institutions (banking)
62	Security and commodity brokers
63	Insurance carriers
70	Hotels
73	Business services
91	Executive, legislative, and general government

Software is a curious industry, almost unique in human history. It is currently the most labor intensive of any commercial product. Software has also been the most resistant to automated development methods. Even reusable components have been difficult to utilize. As a result, hundreds of major corporations now employ many thousands of software personnel, even though their main business activities have little or nothing to do with software, other than using it.

The unusually difficult attributes of software have created the outsourcing industry, and are fueling its continued growth. Because software is outside the main thrust of many businesses, and is notoriously hard to control, many corporate executives would like to turn software over to outsource vendors.

As the twentieth century was ending, many countries outside the United States recognized that outsourcing might become a major industry for developing nations. The twenty-first century may well witness the globalization of software. Of all commercial products, software is the most amenable to international development because software can be distributed rapidly to any location in the world.

The United States is the current world technical leader in outsourcing. The major U.S. outsource vendors such as Andersen, EDS, and IBM tend to be the largest outsource vendors in many countries. However, software is extremely labor intensive and requires smart and well-trained personnel. Many countries have a surplus of intelligent, well-trained personnel, coupled with labor and overhead costs significantly below U.S. averages.

Because software is a "green" industry (in other words, does not pollute the environment), it is a very attractive industry for any developing country. Software is also unique in that all of the major deliverables can be transmitted rapidly via the Internet. Thus, software outsourcing is one of the most attractive industries that a developing nation could possibly cultivate. Several developing nations, such as India, the Ukraine, and Russia, have already targeted software outsourcing as key industries at the national level. Many other developing nations would love to become outsource partners, and are actively encouraging local software vendors to enter the global outsource domain.

Outsource Benchmarks

The assessment and benchmark studies we have carried out in the outsource domain fall into three broad categories: benchmarks commissioned by outsource clients to validate contractual obligations, benchmarks commissioned by outsource vendors themselves to ascertain their performance levels against industry data, and benchmarks performed as a by-product of litigation, while working as expert witnesses in breach-of-contract, taxation, or Y2K lawsuits.

Figure 8.1 illustrates overall trends in the outsource domain. The most notable feature of our outsource productivity data is that outsource vendors often outperform the MIS domain, and especially so for projects larger than 1,000 function points. Our analysis of the reasons why outsource productivity levels are often higher than the productivity levels of their clients can be narrowed down to four critical factors.

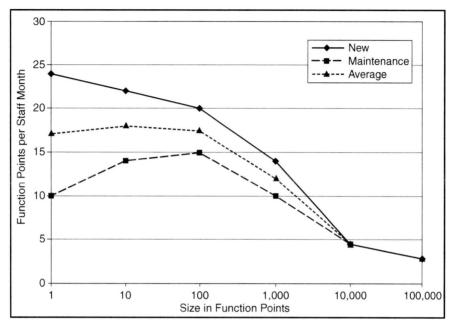

Figure 8.1   Outsource software productivity levels

1. The outsource work ethic is intense and includes substantial unpaid over-time.
2. Outsource personnel are often well trained and very experienced.
3. The outsource domain has substantial volumes of reusable artifacts available.
4. The outsource domain tends to utilize technologies that minimize requirements creep.

Not every outsourced project is more productive than every client project, but for projects that are fairly large and important, say those in the range of 1,000 function points to 10,000 function points, the outsource domain is usually more successful than the MIS domain. Larger than 10,000 function points, the systems software domain is ahead of all others, but the outsource domain is still better than the MIS domain.

With all types of software, small maintenance and enhancement projects and small development projects have very different productivity levels. Small maintenance projects require regression testing of the entire application plus recompilation of much of the application. The difficulty of adding small updates to large applications is the general reason for the lower productivity levels of small maintenance projects.

Figure 8.1 also illustrates overall outsource productivity trends. Small projects ($\leq$ 1,000 function points) are quite productive, but productivity declines for the larger size ranges of 10,000 and 100,000 function points.

Part of the reason for the growth of the outsource business has been repeated failures by the MIS domain in attempts to develop large applications of 10,000 function points or more. These failures have been a motivation to both the growth of outsourcing and the growth of the ERP class of products. Both of these new business sectors have grown as a direct response to the frequent MIS failures on large applications in excess of 10,000 function points.

Interestingly, the systems software domain has the best track record of any domain with applications in the 10,000 function point and higher levels. Systems software is more successful, and has higher productivity and quality levels than even the outsource domain in projects larger than 10,000 function points. Therefore, the motivation for using outsource vendors for systems software is quite different from the MIS motivation. The systems software domain tends to utilize external vendors for specific projects, or because of temporary in-house resource limitations. Very seldom do blanket or inclusive outsource agreements occur in the systems software arena. This is because the major systems software producers have staffs and technologies that are at least equal to the major outsource vendors, so in-house failure is not a factor leading to outsource decisions in the systems software domain, as it is in the MIS domain.

Because outsource applications are now common, they tend to have broad ranges in terms of productivity levels and quality levels. The differences between the worst, average, and best results are often quite broad. Table 8.5 illustrates approximate average values derived from roughly 970 outsource projects examined between 1995 and 1999.

Although the gross results shown in Table 8.5 are interesting, they are not sufficient to understand what really goes on in a major outsource project.

Table 8.6 gets below the level of gross averages and considers the activities that are commonly used in building major outsource applications. The table illustrates a typical activity pattern for an outsourced application of 10,000

Table 8.5   Overall Outsource Software Benchmarks

Benchmark	Value
No. of new projects from 1995 through 1999	415
No. of enhancement projects from 1995 through 1999	455
Total no. of projects from 1995 through 1999	970
Average new project size, function points	2,750
Maximum new project size, function points	35,000
Average enhancement size, function points	145
Maximum enhancement size, function points	1,650
Average new development assignment scope, function points	165
Maximum development assignment scope, function points	420
Average maintenance assignment scope, function points	1,200
Maximum maintenance assignment scope, function points	4,650
Average productivity, function points per staff month	7.8
Maximum productivity, function points per staff month	42.7
Average productivity, work hours per function point	16.92
Maximum productivity, work hours per function point	3.09
Average effort, staff months	21,450
Maximum effort, staff months	136,500
Average new project staff size	17
Maximum new project staff size	303
Average new project schedule, calendar months	20.27
Maximum new project schedule, calendar months	63.00
Average monthly compensation, burdened	$14,000
Maximum monthly compensation, burdened	$22,000
Average cost per function point	$1,794.87
Maximum cost per function point	$7,800.00
Average defect potential per function point	5.2
Maximum defect potential per function point	7.8
Average defect removal efficiency	94.00%
Maximum defect removal efficiency	99.70%
Average monthly rate of requirements creep	1.10%
Maximum monthly rate of requirements creep	3.40%

Table 8.6   Outsource Software Activities and Rates for 10,000 Function Points

Parameter	Value
Application size	10,000 function points
Application size	1,050,000 LOC
Source language	COBOL
Work hours per month	132
Monthly compensation	$14,000

Activities Performed	Assignment Scope, function points	Production Rate, function points	Staff	Effort, months	Schedule, months	Cost	Percent
01 Requirements	500	85	20	118	5.88	$1,647,059	5.33
02 Prototyping	2,000	125	5	80	16.00	$1,120,000	3.63
03 Architecture	2,500	300	4	33	8.33	$466,667	1.51
04 Initial design	250	75	40	133	3.33	$1,866,667	6.05
05 Detail design	175	60	57	167	2.92	$2,333,333	7.56
06 Design reviews	175	125	57	80	1.40	$1,120,000	3.63
07 Coding	115	25	87	400	4.60	$5,600,000	18.14
08 Reuse acquisition	2,000	1,000	5	10	2.00	$140,000	0.45
09 Code inspections	115	100	87	100	1.15	$1,400,000	4.53
10 Configuration management	1,500	500	7	20	3.00	$280,000	0.91

Activities Performed	Assignment Scope, function points	Production Rate, function points	Staff	Effort, months	Schedule, months	Cost	Percent
11 Formal integration	2,000	500	5	20	4.00	$280,000	0.91
12 Documentation	1,000	75	10	133	13.33	$1,866,667	6.05
13 Unit testing	125	45	80	222	2.78	$3,111,111	10.08
14 Function testing	150	60	67	167	2.50	$2,333,333	7.56
15 Integration testing	150	75	67	133	2.00	$1,866,667	6.05
16 System testing	200	100	50	100	2.00	$1,400,000	4.53
17 Acceptance testing	300	150	33	67	2.00	$933,333	3.02
18 Project management	1,200	45	8	222	26.67	$3,111,111	10.08
Totals/averages	166, avg.	4.53, avg.	60, avg.	2,205, total	36.57, avg.	$30,875,948, total	100.00, total

Cost per function points, $3,088; Cost per LOC, $29.41.

function points, which is a size that is often troublesome for MIS projects. This size is troublesome for all domains, but the outsource domain is somewhat more successful than the MIS domain, although not as successful as the systems software domain. In fact, 10,000 function points is a size at which MIS projects fail more often than they succeed.

In Table 8.6 the Assignment Scope column is the amount of work normally assigned to one staff member. The Production Rate column reflects the amount of work normally accomplished in a standard time period, which in this case is a work month. The other columns are self-explanatory and show the staffing level, number of staff months of effort, number of calendar months, activity-level costs, and the overall percentage of cost that each activity contributes to the entire project.

Function point metrics can be used to show monthly productivity, but applications are not built a few function points at a time. A useful analogy is "cost per square foot" for home construction. Although cost per square foot is a useful metric, homes are not built a few square feet at a time. In both cases, the data is derived by arithmetic means after construction is finished.

Outsourced applications of 10,000 function points use fewer activities than systems software or military software projects of 10,000 function points. However, the overall results are fairly close between the outsource domain and the systems software domain.

Table 8.6 assumes little or no reusability. If this same project had been developed with a 50% volume of reusable requirements, specifications, source code, user documents, and test cases, then its productivity level would have approached 10 function points per staff month, or just about twice the value shown in the table.

Table 8.6 assumes a capable team and formal development processes. Quality control does not include a formal software quality assurance department. However, quality control does assume formal design and code inspections, and a full gamut of test activities, with all tests after unit test being carried out by testing specialists. To be completed successfully, large systems require formal development practices and excellent quality control.

When outsource costs for this 10,000-function point project are aggregated, you can see that three major categories of expense are weighted toward the costs of defect removal (Table 8.7). This is a normal situation for 10,000-function point applications.

For large systems in the 10,000-function point range, defect removal is the

Table 8.7   Major Outsource Software Cost Drivers

Outsource Software Cost Drivers	Staff Months	Percent
Defect removal	869	39.40
Paper documents	584	26.49
Code related	530	24.03

major cost driver. Paperwork is in second place, and code-related activities are in third place. This explains why LOC is a poor metric for economic studies. More than two thirds of the effort on large outsource projects cannot be explored using LOC metrics.

Although averages are interesting, the most common request from our clients is for best-in-class data derived from the top 5% of the projects that we have examined. For best-in-class data to be meaningful, it has to be shown for specific size plateaus. It is useful to show the size plateaus of 100, 1,000, and 10,000 function points for best-in-class outsource results. Less than 100 function points, individual human variances are too large for statistics to be meaningful. There are not enough projects at the 100,000-function point size range to gather useful statistics.

Note that the cost information in Table 8.8 uses average values of $14,000 per staff month as a constant value. This assumes fully burdened costs, with a

Table 8.8   Average and Best-in-Class Results for Outsource Software

Key Software Topics	100 Function Points	1,000 Function Points	10,000 Function Points
Average staff size	1	6	57
Best-in-class staff size	1	3	48
Average schedule, months	5.25	13.80	36.31
Best-in-class schedule, months	3.98	9.77	27.54
Average function points per staff month	30.49	12.68	4.82
Best-in-class function points per staff month	40.19	30.70	7.62

continued

Table 8.8   *continued*

Key Software Topics	100 Function Points	1,000 Function Points	10,000 Function Points
Average work hours per function point	4.33	10.41	27.39
Best-in-class work hours per function point	3.28	4.30	17.31
Average LOC per staff month in COBOL	3,201	1,331	506
Best-in-class LOC per staff month in COBOL	4,220	3,223	801
Average effort, staff months	3	79	2,075
Best-in-class effort, staff months	2	33	1,312
Average cost per function point	$459.21	$1,104.31	$2,904.62
Best-in-class cost per function point	$348.34	$456.04	$1,836.15
Average defects per function point	3.00	4.80	5.60
Best-in-class defects per function point	1.25	3.20	4.30
Average defect removal efficiency	97.00%	95.00%	93.00%
Best-in-class defect removal efficiency	99.00%	99.00%	96.00%
Average delivered defects per function point	0.090	0.240	0.392
Best-in-class delivered defects per function point	0.013	0.032	0.172
Average no. of delivered defects	9	240	3,920
Best-in-class no. of delivered defects	1	32	1,720
Average no. of high-severity defects	1	36	588
Best-in-class no. of high-severity defects	0	4	206

burden rate of approximately 100%. This constant value is to highlight the technological differences that affect productivity. Comparing cost per function point for a large outsource project in an urban area with high labor rates, such as New York, against a small project in a rural area with low labor rates will obviously favor the small rural project.

As mentioned several times, outsource applications less than 10,000 function points are frequently successful, but as the size gets larger failures and delays

Table 8.9   Outsource Software Schedule Adherence circa 1999

Size, function points	Early Projects, %	On-Time Projects, %	Late Projects, %	Cancelled Projects, %	Total Projects, %
1	5.00	93.00	1.00	1.00	100.00
10	8.00	90.00	1.00	1.00	100.00
100	7.00	85.00	6.00	2.00	100.00
1,000	8.00	67.00	15.00	10.00	100.00
10,000	1.00	38.00	34.00	27.00	100.00
100,000	1.00	26.00	40.00	33.00	100.00
Average	5.00	66.50	16.17	12.33	100.00

increase significantly. A topic of continuing interest is the relative success of outsource projects in meeting their planned schedules (Table 8.9).

On the whole, schedule adherence for projects larger than 1,000 function points is better in the outsource domain than in the MIS domain, although not quite as good as in the systems software domain. The considerable number of MIS application cancellations, delays, and overruns for projects larger than 10,000 function points is a key reason why so many corporations are evaluating the merits of outsourcing.

Many corporations face an important binary choice: either invest substantially in process improvement or turn over large application development projects to outsource vendors. Of course outsource projects may run late too, but performance in the outsource domain is better than the MIS domain for applications larger than 1,000 function points, and is much better for applications larger than 10,000 function points.

Outsourcing Successes and Failures

The word *failure* in a software context can have several meanings, and all of them are unpleasant. The most common meaning of the word *failure* is for projects that are cancelled prior to completion due to excessive cost or schedule overruns. A secondary definition of failure implies projects that were eventually delivered and deployed, but proved to be unusable for their intended purposes. A tertiary definition of failure implies software projects that overran their budgets and schedules by such large amounts that the ROI for the project will be negative for its entire useful life expectancy.

For large software applications (≥10,000 function points), failures tend to outnumber successes as a whole, and for MIS projects in particular. Failures are common for large outsource projects too, but the outsource vendors have a better chance of completing large projects than the clients they serve.

Although in-house software projects fail far more often than outsource projects, in-house software failures do not end up in court. When failures occur for major outsource projects, there is a very strong probability that litigation will occur. Table 8.10 presents the major success and failure factors for contract and outsourced software.

Table 8.10   Outsource Software Success and Failure Factors

Outsource Software Success Factors	Outsource Software Failure Factors
Contract concluded without litigation	Contract concluded with litigation
Software operational when delivered	Software is not operational at contract end
User requirements stable to within 5%	Requirements creep out of control
Project delivers 100% of requirements	Project omits more than 20% of requirements
Software costs lower than in-house norms	Contract costs higher than non-contract
Costs predictable within 5%	Costs overrun by more than 20%
Schedules better than in-house norms	Schedules longer than in-house norms
Schedules predictable within 1%	Schedules missed by more than 20%
Software maintainable after delivery	Software essentially unmaintainable
Contract benefits both parties	Contract harmful to one or both sides
Contract is explicit on Y2K repairs	Contract is ambiguous on Y2K repairs

Because outsource failure is likely to be accompanied by breach-of-contract litigation, it is important for the outsource domain to use technologies and practices that optimize the chances of success. In general, successful software projects utilize excellent project management approaches and top-notch quality control approaches.

My colleagues and I are often called on to be expert witnesses in software breach-of-contract cases. Table 8.11 illustrates some of the major differences noted between successful software projects and those that show up in litigation.

Success or failure of an application in the 10,000-function point range is not a matter of chance. A comparison of the use of certain key technologies in the context of applications that are the subject of contested litigation with those same technologies observed in the context of successful applications is instructive.

Note that the patterns of technology deployment in successful applications indicate more rigor than in those technologies deployed in applications undergoing some form of litigation.

It is important to understand why quality control differentiates successful projects from those that end up in litigation. For major applications in the 10,000-function point class, the primary cost and schedule drivers are

- Finding and fixing defects
- Producing paper documents such as specifications
- Communications among teams and with clients
- Coding
- Change control
- Project management

Because finding and fixing defects is the most expensive and time-consuming aspect of large-system development, it is not possible to achieve short development schedules for projects with large numbers of bugs or defects. Such projects may enter testing early, but they do not complete testing early, if at all.

The most common point at which project failures first become clearly apparent to clients and senior executives is when the applications are being tested and are found to be so buggy that testing cannot be completed as planned. At this point, it is too late to bring the project back under control in terms of scheduled completion. Indeed, it may be necessary to suspend testing and perform detailed inspections to complete the project.

Successful outsource software projects, by contrast, are much more sophisticated in software quality topics than those undergoing litigation. The applications

Table 8.11   Differences between Successful Outsource Projects and Those Involved in Breach-of-Contract Litigation

Technologies	Successful Applications	Applications in Litigation
Defect prevention		
JAD	Used	Not used
Prototypes	Used	Not used
Defect tracking	Used	Used late
Change management	Formal	Informal
Complexity analysis	Used	Used late
Defect estimation	Used	Not used
Defect removal metrics	Used	Not used
Pretest defect removal		
Design inspections	Used	Rushed or omitted
Code inspections	Used	Rushed or omitted
Testing		
Subroutine test	Used	Used
Unit test	Used	Used
New function test	Used	Rushed or omitted
Regression test	Used	Rushed or omitted
Integration test	Used	Used
System test	Used	Rushed or omitted
Performance test	Used	Rushed or omitted
Capacity test	Used	Rushed or omitted
Acceptance test	Used	Application failed
Specialization		
Software quality assurance	Used	Informal
Software testing specialists	Used	Not used

with sophisticated quality control activities tend to flush out errors early, and hence they are not delayed in testing. Both defect prevention methods and defect removal methods are usually much better on successful projects than those undergoing litigation.

Project management is also a differentiating factor between outsource projects that are completed successfully and those that end up in court. Successful outsource projects in the 10,000-function point domain utilize the following set of project management approaches:

- Formal sizing of major deliverables using automated tools
- Formal software cost estimates using automated tools
- Formal schedule plans using automated tools
- Formal defect and quality estimates using automated tools
- Estimates of requirements creep using automated tools
- Milestone tracking using automated tools
- Cost tracking using automated tools

Manual estimates and informal project management can sometimes be successful for small applications less than 1,000 function points. However, informality and casual project management have no place on software projects that are in the 10,000-function point range.

Outsourcing and Contract Software Success Factors

The following is a list of the general technology areas in which outsource contractors and software contractors tend to exceed the average performance levels of other kinds of software, including some in-house development efforts:

- Outsource contractors lead in effective reuse of software components.
- Outsource contractors lead in breadth of experience for many industries.
- Outsource contractors are among the best in adopting function points for contracts.
- Outsource contractors are among the best in using software estimating tools.
- Outsource contractors are among the best in using project planning tools.
- Outsource contractors are among the best in staff training.
- Outsource contractors are among the best in software technology research.
- Outsource contractors are among the best in data center efficiency.
- Outsource contractors are among the best in geriatric methods for aging software.

- Large outsourced or contracted systems with more than 10,000 function points are usually more productive than similar in-house software applications.

When outsource vendors specialize in particular industries, such as health care, banking, or insurance, they tend to accumulate substantial volumes of reusable materials that benefit software applications within those industries. Not only that, but the software personnel who work for the outsource vendor might have worked on similar applications in a dozen or more companies within the industry being served. This broad experience and the high volume of reusable material are what give outsourcing companies a competitive advantage.

Outsourcing and Contract Software Failure Factors

On the downside of the outsourcing and contract software domain are the following chronic problems:

- Litigation between contractors and clients is troubling and costly to both sides.
- Creeping user requirements remain troublesome to both sides.
- Outsource vendors may use massive amounts of unpaid overtime.
- Tool suites for international outsource vendors may be sparse in some countries.
- Quality levels of outsource software may be deficient unless the contract includes specific quality performance levels.
- Maintenance contracts may be ambiguous about Y2K repairs due to the failure to identify explicitly Y2K responsibilities in contracts written prior to 1996.

In general, outsource vendors outperform their clients in terms of both quality and productivity. But it should not be forgotten that software development is still a fairly primitive and labor-intensive kind of work. Therefore, some failures can occur on outsource projects, as they do on all other kinds of software.

Best Technical Practices for Outsourced Software

Because of rather good training and hiring practices, the outsource software domain is often quite sophisticated in many software technologies. Several technologies in which the outsource domain often excels include software reuse, requirements analysis, and geriatric care for aging legacy applications. Other topics in which the outsource domain often performs well include change control and database application design. The outsource community has also developed some specialized skills, such as installation and deployment tuning of ERP applications.

As the new century begins, the outsource community is gearing up to move into the e-business domain. However, although e-business is on an explosive growth path, the final destination of e-business is uncertain as this book is written. No doubt e-business will change the structure and business practices of millions of companies, and will affect billions of consumers. However, whether e-business replaces traditional methods or augments them is not yet clear.

Because best-practice data comes from assessment and benchmark studies, this section is based on the standard set of ten key factors that are examined during SPR assessments and benchmarks:

1. Project management methods such as estimating
2. Requirements-gathering and analysis methods
3. Design and specification methods
4. Coding methods
5. Reusability methods
6. Change control methods
7. User documentation methods
8. Pretest defect removal methods such as inspections
9. Testing methods and tools
10. Maintenance methods and tools

To be cited among the best practices for outsource software, the approaches have to have been used on at least 50 successful projects within ten companies. In the opinions of the project managers and technical personnel, the practices must have contributed to a successful outcome. The practices must not have been cited as contributing to failures, cost overruns, or major schedule slips. Best practices add positive value.

A final caveat for outsource best practices is that the technologies discussed must have been used on projects for external clients. Outsource vendors create a great deal of software for their own internal purposes, as do all large corporations. However, this section discusses the best practices noted when outsource vendors are working on behalf of their clients.

Best Project Management Practices for Outsourced Software

In every software domain, project management is a key technology. Project management is one of the critical factors that differentiates successful projects from failures and outsource contracts in litigation. Excellence in project management is associated with 100% of successful projects for projects larger than 1,000 function points. Inadequate estimates, careless planning, and inadequate tracking are associated with 100% of project failures, although other factors contribute to failures too.

Major outsource vendors such as Andersen, EDS, and IBM have been fairly effective in many aspects of software project management. These companies have created excellent measurement programs for productivity and they utilize the data to refine estimates for new projects.

Function Points and Outsource Contracts

It is a best practice in the outsource domain for all contracts that include productivity and quality clauses to be based at least in part on function point analysis. In the United States, use of the form of function points defined by IFPUG is a best practice. (This is the only function point metric with substantial published data available.) Other function point variants such as 3D function points or full function points lack enough empirical data for their use to be deemed a best practice. LOC metrics can be used in contracts, but are hazardous for cross-language comparisons and are not a best practice. I consider LOC metrics alone to be professional malpractice in situations in which multiple programming languages are used.

Validated Benchmarks

Because standard corporate cost and resource tracking systems are known to "leak," or omit approximately 35% of actual effort on average, it is a best practice for outsource agreements to include a clause requiring that any precontract benchmarks, against which improvements will be measured, should be validated independently. Topics that should be validated include application size in terms of both function points and LOC, staffing levels, development effort, development schedules, and quality in terms of defect potentials and defect removal efficiency. For maintenance projects, factors needing independent validation include maintenance assignment scopes and defect repairs per time period. User satisfaction and aging of reported defects should also be validated if these factors are written in the outsource contract. For customer support, number of clients or customers served per staff member is also a topic that should be validated.

Managing Virtual Teams

It is a best practice for outsource project managers to be trained in managing teams of technical workers who are dispersed geographically in multiple cities and countries. Virtual teams are fairly common among the major outsource vendors.

Activity-Level Benchmarks

Because gross benchmarks at the project level cannot be validated easily in terms of identifying "leakage," or missing effort, it is a best practice to utilize activity-level benchmarks. The specific activities that should be validated include requirements gathering and analysis, internal and external design, code development, design and code inspections, change control and configuration management, all forms of testing and quality control, and document development and development of tutorial materials.

Productivity Measures

It is a best practice in the outsource domain to have a formal software measurement program that measures activity-level development productivity for all projects above a cutoff point of perhaps 100 function points in size. (The cutoff point varies from 50 to 150 function points among outsource vendors.) The measurement program captures data on size, staffing, schedules, and effort. Although function point metrics are the best practice for normalization, LOC data is collected too. For maintenance projects, information on staff assignment scopes and defect repair rates are important as well. Normally measurement data is reported quarterly and is then put into a major annual report to satisfy contract terms.

Annual Assessments and Benchmarks

A best practice in the outsource domain is to have process assessments and external benchmark studies every year on work for all major clients. Indeed, this may be a requirement of the outsource contract itself. If there is a contractual obligation for annual assessments and benchmarks, then the data should be gathered by a neutral, independent organization to ensure its validity. The annual assessments and benchmarks serve the purpose of ensuring that the outsource contractor is meeting the terms of the agreement if the agreement includes productivity and quality improvement criteria.

Project Management Training

All outsource software project managers should be trained in software sizing, cost estimating, quality estimating, milestone tracking, and cost tracking. All project managers should be able to create accurate plans and estimates for projects at least 1,000 function points in size. Entry-level training on promotion to project manager is a definite best practice among large outsource companies. Setting aside five to ten days a year for project management training is also a best practice. New and special topics such as ERP project management and managing virtual teams should be taught.

Project Management Tools

Outsource project managers should be trained in and have available a suite of project management tools that includes sizing using both function points and LOC metrics, cost and resource estimating, schedule estimating, standard project management for critical path analysis, cost tracking, and milestone tracking capabilities. Our observations indicate that a total volume of more than 15,000 function points of project management tools should be available to outsource project managers.

Personnel Management Tools

It is a best practice among large outsource companies in the United States to utilize automated tools for appraisals and job objective planning. Personnel-related automated tools are not a best practice in parts of Europe, where they may be prohibited by national laws or union regulations.

Activity-Based Cost Estimates

All outsource software cost estimates for projects more than 1,000 function points should be at the activity or task levels. Project-level or phase-level estimates are inadequate for large projects in every domain. Estimation for small one-person projects can be at the project level. This practice is unsafe for projects larger than 100 function points, and is a hazardous practice.

Empirical Productivity Data

All outsource software project managers should know the ranges of quality and productivity levels derived from empirical studies for the kinds of software for which they are responsible. In particular, outsource project managers should know productivity and quality levels for ERP deployment, virtual teams, and client/server and database software projects. Outsource project management needs solid data for projects larger than 1,000 function points; otherwise, it is difficult for project managers to defend their estimates against arbitrary overrides by clients and senior executives.

Enterprise Resource Planning Data

All outsource software project managers should be trained in the basic operations and deployment strategies of ERP applications. As the century ends, ERP applications are deployed in approximately 20% of our MIS client organizations and the number will continue to grow. Outsource companies are involved heavily in ERP deployment, and therefore outsource project managers should be very knowledgeable about this topic.

Client/Server Planning Data

Because of the widespread deployment of both two-tier and three-tier client/server applications among outsource clients in the MIS domain, it is a best practice for outsource project managers to be trained in the estimating and development methods that work best for such projects. Client/server projects are much more troublesome than monolithic projects, and they require specialized estimating approaches. Without adequate training, the probabilities of overruns and high maintenance costs are extreme.

Milestone Tracking

All outsourced software projects larger than 1,000 function points should use formal milestone tracking. This is a best practice that can minimize unpleasant problems such as major schedule delays, and can provide an early warning. Major milestones include completion of requirements, external specifications, internal specifications, inspection plans, design inspections, code inspections, test plans, all forms of testing, risk analysis plans, performance analysis plans, user documentation, and installation.

Best Requirements-Gathering and Analysis Practices for Outsourced Software

Requirements gathering and analysis are critical tasks under outsource agreements. As a result, outsource vendors are often more sophisticated than many other domains. This is because the requirements for outsource projects usually come from specific clients who are also the funding source for the projects to be developed. Although powerful requirements analysis technologies exist for outsourced projects, requirements "creep" and "churn" remain endemic problems, and are cited frequently in breach-of-contract litigation. Some of the best practices for requirements gathering and analysis in the outsource domain include those presented in the following subsections.

Joint Application Design

The usage of JAD is a standard best practice for large outsource projects. Using JAD, the requirements for an application are the joint responsibility of representatives from the client or user community and from the development organization. A key feature of the JAD approach is the use of a trained JAD facilitator. (Most large outsource companies have JAD facilitators available.) The JAD team works on the application requirements as a full-time job for a preplanned time period ranging from a few days to more than a month. A key benefit of the JAD approach is more stable requirements with a rate of change that is usually only a fraction of 1% per month, rather than the 1% to 3% noted more commonly for traditional requirements.

Requirements Tracing

It is a best practice for outsource projects to utilize a concept called *requirements tracing*. This concept means that every major feature in a delivered software application can be traced back to a specific user requirement. Requirements tracing is mandatory for military software contracts, and may also be a feature of civilian software contracts and outsource agreements. However, although requirements tracing is a best practice, it is not a common best practice. We have noted requirements tracing in less than 25% of the outsource applications that we have studied during our assessment and benchmark studies.

Prototypes of Key Features

It is a best practice for many outsource applications between 500 function points and 10,000 function points to create working prototypes of key features. Prototypes smaller than 500 function points may not be needed. Larger than 10,000 function points in size, the prototypes become significant projects in their own right and need more formality than prototypes for mid-size applications. Prototypes are usually approximately 10% of the size of the final application but can vary with specific applications. Of the three common forms of prototypes—disposable, time-box, and evolutionary—only the disposable and time-box forms are best practices. Evolutionary prototypes are dangerous, because prototypes are usually poorly structured and lack safe programming practices.

Requirements Inspections

For outsource applications larger than 1,000 function points, inspections of requirements are a best practice. The requirements inspection technology is used sparsely and we don't encounter requirements inspections as often as this method should be used. The inspection team for outsourced software requirements includes both client representatives and project technical personnel. Inspections and JAD are complementary, with the inspection stage following the JAD approach.

Function Point Size

A best practice for outsource software projects is to calculate initial function point size estimates from the requirements themselves. Once function point totals are known, they provide a useful baseline for measuring the rate of requirements creep. The outsource domain, like the MIS software domain, can be volatile in terms of requirements stability, unless JAD sessions, prototypes, and inspections are utilized. In some cases, additions to requirements can top 2% per calendar month during the design and coding phases. Requirements churn, which does not add new features or change function point totals, is also common in the outsource domain. The phrase *requirements churn* refers to things such as changing the placement of data items on a screen based on user preferences. Function point totals are also used for sizing various deliverables, and they are a key input to software cost and quality estimates.

Requirements Change Control

Even in the best of cases outsource project requirements will change during development. In the worst of cases, the requirements changes can be so extreme as to jeopardize the prospects of completing the project. Therefore, it is a best practice to utilize formal change control methods for all outsource projects larger than 1,000 function points. Some of the change control methods noted among our clients include

- A formal change control board
- Formal change control requests
- Automated change control tools

- Use of JAD sessions for major changes
- Use of requirements inspections for major changes
- Function point sizing and estimating for all changes larger than 15 function points (which is the minimum size for function point counts)
- Application feature planning for several years in the future with a planned evolution of total functionality
- Formal cost estimates for enhancements larger than 50 function points in size

Best Design and Specification Practices for Outsourced Software

The outsource domain and the related MIS software domain are very diverse in software specification approaches. The most common methods among our outsource clients tend to utilize some of the "data analytic" specification methods such as Warnier-Orr diagrams or information engineering. However, more than 35 flavors of software specification methods have been noted among outsource clients, including some proprietary methods. A number of the more sophisticated outsource vendors have developed their own proprietary specification methods. These are often hybrid approaches that use portions of several well-known industry design techniques. In some engagements, outsource vendors are obligated contractually to utilize design approaches already in use by the clients with whom they are working.

Specification Segmentation

Because the specifications for large outsource software projects often deal with database design, a best practice is to segment the specifications into a multivolume set, with each volume containing the details of a specific topic. A typical example includes requirements specifications, external design specifications, internal or logical design specifications, and database specifications. Each specification is under formal change control, and goes through multiple iterations. This is a best practice for applications larger than 1,000 function points. For smaller applications and enhancements, subsets and partial specifications are the norm.

Prototypes

A best practice for outsource software projects is the creation of prototypes for key features. The two forms of prototypes considered best practices for outsource software are disposable prototypes and time-box prototypes. A time-box prototype has a chronological limit, and must be completed within a specific period, such as one calendar month. A disposable prototype is used to demonstrate feasibility, and is then discarded. Often, the disposable prototypes are constructed using programming languages different from the final application. The use of evolutionary prototypes is not a best practice because the lack of structure in prototypes makes them unsuited for applications with high quality and reliability targets. Normally, outsource software prototypes amount to approximately 10% of the functionality of the finished application. The prototypes concentrate on key usability and user interface issues.

Design Inspections

A best practice for outsource software projects of all sizes, and for enhancements as well as new projects, is the use of formal design inspections on all specification documents. Although this is a best practice, the use of inspections is only found among less than 50% of our outsource clients. Both outsource and MIS software designs contain more than 1.25 defects per function point, on average. Design defects are often higher in severity than coding defects. A majority of severity 2 defects originate in designs and specifications. Formal design inspections are very effective in defect removal, and average more than 65% efficiency in finding and removing design errors. Inspections also serve as a defect prevention approach because participants will avoid problems in their own work that are pointed out during the inspection sessions.

Reusable Designs

Because many outsource vendors serve numerous companies within vertical industries such as banking and insurance, it is a best practice in the outsource domain to reuse portions of specifications from project to project, assuming the projects are near replicas of each other. Reuse of design segments is a best practice for banking, insurance, wholesale, retail, and government applications.

Best Coding Practices for Outsourced Software

The outsource software domain includes courses in structured programming techniques as part of the standard curricula for new programming personnel. As a result, use of structured programming among outsource projects was both common and usually well done for mainframe applications. Unfortunately, the advent of client/server projects in the 1990s caused a serious backslide in the use of structured programming techniques. Client/server projects are often developed in a "quick-and-dirty" fashion for both MIS and outsource projects. As a result, client/server projects are proving to be more troublesome than anticipated.

Structured Programming

A definite best practice within the outsource domain is that of using formal program structure techniques that optimize binding and coupling, and minimize control flow complexity. Most of the major outsource vendors such as Andersen, CSC, EDS, and IBM include training in formal program structuring techniques as a mandatory course for all new programming personnel.

Comment Density and Style

It is a best practice for all domains to utilize both module prologs and comments to explain key features and algorithms of programs. Studies performed within IBM found that comments roughly every ten statements was the density at which clarity seemed to peak. Fewer comments made it hard to understand the code. Surprisingly, too many comments also reduced code legibility.

Mnemonic Labels

It is a best practice to use labels for variables and branch instructions that are clear and easy to remember, if possible. Abstract labels such as "routine2" may make it hard for new programmers to understand logic flow. It is a bad practice to use labels that have quirky or private meanings, such as using the names of relatives or movie stars.

Code Inspections

It is a best practice to use formal code inspections for all outsource projects that are important to the client or the enterprise. Not only should formal code inspections be used, but the inspections should include 100% of the modules of mission-critical applications, as opposed to partial or subset inspections. Formal code inspections have the highest defect removal efficiency level of any known removal activity, and are approximately twice as efficient as most forms of testing. Formal code inspections average 65% in defect removal efficiency, and have approached 90% in some trials. There is no better method for ensuring high quality and reliability levels. Although this is a best practice, code inspections were noted in less than 50% of outsource projects between 1995 and 1999, which is a reduction from older studies. The relatively careless practices associated with client/server projects and RAD have triggered this unfortunate reduction in usage.

COBOL Complexity Reduction

A best practice often encountered within the outsource and MIS software domains is the use of automated complexity reduction tools, especially for

COBOL applications. Because high levels of code complexity as measured with the common metrics of cyclomatic and essential complexity are known to degrade quality and lower the efficiency of defect removal operations, software that has high reliability criteria should use automated methods of complexity analysis and reduction. There are more tools in the class available for the COBOL programming language than for any other language.

Error-Prone Module Elimination

A best coding practice within both the outsource and MIS domains for legacy applications concerns seeking out and eliminating error-prone modules. In the 1960s, IBM discovered that coding errors, or bugs, in large systems were not distributed randomly. They tended to clump in a small number of modules and were assigned the title of *error-prone modules*. The standard method for dealing with error-prone modules is to give them a formal inspection, and then either restructure them, repair them, or redevelop them based on the recommendation of the inspection team.

Module-Level Defect Tracking

A best practice in the outsource domain is that of defect tracking methods and tools that are granular enough to identify error-prone modules. This practice is encountered primarily in large companies that also develop large software applications (>10,000 function points). Defects are tracked by severity level, origin, and, in particular, are tracked down to the level of specific modules. Supplemental data includes aging of defects or the length of time needed to repair them. Effort and costs for repair are also recorded, as is information on duplicate defects.

Best Reusability Practices for Outsourced Software

Software reuse is a key technology and one in which the outsource domain is an industry leader. Because outsource vendors often serve many clients within specific industries such as banking, insurance, and manufacturing, they are in a good position to develop reusable applications or components within those industries.

Software reuse is one of the few technologies that can benefit costs, schedules, and quality simultaneously. The outsource community has been able to reuse entire applications and components of specific features from larger applications. However, effective reuse programs are still rare and are not always as effective as theory predicts. For success, reusable material should be at or near the zero-defect level. Reusing materials with high defect levels is not economical.

A complete software reusability program in the outsource domain encompasses ten software artifacts including

1. Reusable requirements
2. Reusable external specifications
3. Reusable architecture and internal specifications
4. Reusable database designs and data structures
5. Reusable project plans and estimates
6. Reusable source code
7. Reusable quality and test plans
8. Reusable test cases
9. Reusable user documentation
10. Reusable HELP text

Reusing only source code is useful, but not sufficient. In the outsource domain, the most effective reuse programs are those that encompass reusable requirements, reusable architecture and specifications, reusable database designs, reusable source code, reusable documentation, and reusable test materials.

The volume of reusable materials noted have ranged from token amounts of less than 10% to really significant usage that tops 50%. The theoretical maximal volume of reusable material within the same industry, such as finance or insurance, can approach 90%. However, we have not yet noted volumes of reusable material that top 75% when applications are developed for different clients.

Reusable Proposals

Because outsource vendors serve multiple clients within the same industry, it is a best practice to modify proposals for certain kinds of software applications so that they can be reused. Proposal reuse is noted most often in vertical industry situations in which the outsource vendors serve multiple clients. Industries in which reusable proposals are common include banking, insurance, manufacturing, pharmaceuticals, wholesale, retail, and state and local governments.

Reusable Requirements

Although the requirements for outsource applications are normally developed by the clients, once an outsource agreement is underway the outsource vendors can utilize standard requirements derived from similar applications within the same industry. This is a delicate issue because each client will have nondisclosure agreements with the outsource vendor. However, because all banks and all insurance companies use software for very similar purposes, once an outsource vendor has worked with several clients in the same industry, the major features of key applications become well-known. Thus, outsource vendors with a substantial presence in vertical markets are able to create "generic" requirements for common applications that can greatly facilitate the requirements-gathering and analysis phases. Indeed, these generic requirements are also effective in reducing requirements creep because they are derived from applications that are already finished.

Reusable Source Code Libraries

Software reuse in the outsource domain occurs in multiple levels. At the top level are entire applications that are more or less reusable within a specific industry. A lower level of reuse consists of individual features or components. Components are not complete applications, but rather are portions of applications that accomplish specific functions. It is a best practice in the outsource domain to establish formal libraries of reusable source code in common programming languages such as COBOL, JAVA, Visual Basic, and the like. To be effective, these libraries need to be at or near zero-defect status. This means that the library needs formal entry procedures that include inspections and thorough testing of candidate modules.

Reusability based on the OO paradigm is fairly common among both the outsource and the MIS communities, although not as common as among the systems software domain. Although some very successful OO projects have been noted, the learning curves of both OO design and OO programming are very steep. The OO paradigm is so difficult to master that it is abandoned roughly half the time when first starting out. This makes it difficult to assign OO projects to best-practice status.

Reusable Test Materials

A best practice that is more common in the outsource domain than any other is to test plans and test cases. What makes this form of reuse common amoung major outsource vendors is the fact that they serve many companies within the same industry. As a result, outsource vendors are able to develop generic applications for key industries such as banks, insurance companies, and state governments. Not only are the specifications and code reusable for such applications, but a substantial portion of the test cases are reusable too.

Reusable User Documentation

As a by-product of building generic applications that can be used by multiple companies within an industry, the outsource community is able to reuse substantial portions of user training documents, reference documents, and HELP text. Both paper documents and screens are included in the class of reusable documentation.

In general, the outsource community has been more sophisticated in achieving practical levels of software reuse than any other domain.

Best Change Control Practices for Outsourced Software

Change control is a topic in which the larger outsource vendors are often quite expert. For the software industry as a whole, change control is a complex and demanding technical challenge for any kind of software project. During initial software development cycles, changing requirements average between 1% and 3% a month during the design and coding phases. Once an application has been deployed, new features and modifications average approximately 7% per year for many years in a row. That is, new and changed features will approximate 7% of the number of function points in the basic applications. Best practices in change control for systems software include those presented in the following subsections.

Change Estimation and Costing in Contracts

Because changing requirements are a frequent source of dispute and are often cited in breach-of-contract cases, it is a best practice to include specific clauses for change control in outsource agreements. The form of the clauses varies with the specific needs of the client, but are often based on predicted volumes of changes. Because software requirements changes have been measured in the past, it is now possible to predict the rate of change in the future. A sliding scale of costs for changing requirements is also a best practice. That is, a contract will agree to a fixed price for the initial set of agreed requirements. However, new requirements added later will be included at a higher price. Cost per function point is often utilized for change pricing, and can be considered a best practice for this purpose.

Function Point Metrics for Changes

It is a best practice in the outsource domain to estimate and measure the function point totals of all changes to software projects larger than 15 function points. Changes to software can comprise several kinds of modification. The most common form of change is adding a new feature. This is called *scope creep* or *requirements creep*. Less common, but still a daily event, is the removal of a feature, or at least its deferral to a later release because it cannot be finished in time for the current release. A more ambiguous form of change is termed *requirements churn*. This complex topic deals with modifying features in such a way that the function point totals do not increase or decrease. An example of requirements churn is changing the placement of data on an input screen without adding any new kinds of input.

Change Control Boards

For all outsource software projects larger than 5,000 function points, it is a best practice to utilize a formal change control board. This board is normally composed of three to perhaps seven personnel. The panel includes representatives from the application client and the development team. The purpose of the change control board is to review suggested changes, prioritize them, and assign them to a specific release. Applications larger than 5,000 function points tend to evolve rapidly during their initial development cycles. Changes have been noted that exceed 2% per month, using the function point totals derived from initial requirements as the baselines.

Automated Change Control

The outsource software artifacts that are subject to formal change control include requirements, external specifications, internal specifications, database specifications, all test plans, and all user documentation and training materials. Because of the wide variety of changing artifacts, it is a best practice to have fully automated change control systems that can handle all major deliverables. The change control package should facilitate identifying links between artifacts, such as determining what code needs to be changed in response to a requirements or design change. Automated change control tools that support only source code are not adequate for projects larger than 100 function points.

Best User Documentation Practices for Outsourced Software

The development and production of user manuals, tutorial materials, HELP screens, and "wizards" is a weak link in the entire software industry. Complaints about poor documents are just as common as complaints about poor software quality, and have as much justification. However, the outsource community is slightly better than average in the production of user manuals and tutorial materials.

Outsource vendors are likely to have at least a few professional technical writers and editors available for major applications. Also, from working within specific industries such as banks and insurance companies, outsource vendors have useful amounts of "reusable" documentation available.

Technical Writers and Editors

A best practice encountered mainly among large outsource vendors is the use of professional writers and editors for the production of user manuals and tutorial materials. Technical writing is a fairly rare skill. Therefore, professional writers create better manuals and tutorials than untrained personnel. Some companies also use graphics specialists for illustrations, but we have not encountered this enough to include it in the best-practice set.

Document Inspections

Formal inspections of user manuals and on-line text is very efficient and effective. This technique is encountered mainly among large outsource vendors and is just over the dividing line in frequency of use to be included as a best practice. The practice of document inspections is very useful, but frequency of use remains sparse.

Document Models

A best practice for technical writing in the outsource domain is to copy the formats and outlines of manuals and tutorial materials deemed "excellent" by readers or by trial-and-error methods. The outsource domain is able to reuse documents due to the fact that major vendors often serve multiple clients within the same industry. Therefore, outsource vendors are likely to produce similar user's guides and reference materials for similar applications.

Reusable Documentation

Although manuals such as user's guides can be reused casually as models for similar applications, the outsource domain is able to go beyond this and actually reuse text and illustrations. This situation occurs most often for vertical industries such as banking and insurance for whom an outsource vendor has many clients that utilize very similar applications. Note that for reusable documentation to be legal, the vendor must own the copyright of the material being reused.

Document Testing

A best practice for all domains is testing documentation concurrently with software testing. This means that at least drafts of the major user manuals and HELP text must be completed in time to use the drafts during software testing. For out-source projects, document testing can be started during system testing and can be continued during user acceptance testing.

Hypertext Links

A best practice for all user manuals is to include a detailed index with cross-references. Hypertext links for on-line documents would also be included under this best practice.

Working Examples

A very common best practice found for all kinds of software is the utilization of actual examples of key features. The examples take a user step by step through the process of invoking a function, using it, and then turning it off or moving to something else when finished.

Best Quality Control and Pretest Defect Removal Practices for Outsourced Software

The outsource domain has been better than average in software quality, but not as good as the systems software domain. In general, outsource vendors have bet-ter defect prevention and defect removal methods than the clients they serve. However, the outsource domain is not as sophisticated as the systems software domain in overall software quality control.

The outsource community is somewhat more likely to use software quality assurance departments than the MIS community, and much more likely to use testing specialists. However, defect estimation, defect tracking, and defect pre-vention are not yet up to the levels of the systems software domain.

Fortunately, some major outsource vendors do utilize state-of-the art quality methods. More would probably do so, except for the difficulty of convincing clients that quality is on the critical path to achieving short schedules and low costs. The following subsections present some of the software quality approaches noted in the outsource domain.

Joint Application Design

Because application design is most effective when requirements are firm, it is a best practice for both outsource and MIS projects to utilize JAD sessions for both requirements analysis and for external design of application usability features. The JAD approach uses joint teams of clients and developers, supported by a trained facilitator. The JAD approach can minimize requirements creep, which is often a serious problem for software projects.

Requirements Inspections

Because software requirements are critical to many applications, formal inspections of requirements is a useful best practice. Unfortunately, it is a best practice that is not as widely utilized as it should be, although it is more likely to be noted among outsourced projects than MIS projects. Software requirements are carried out jointly by clients and developers. The inspection sessions use a moderator, recorder, and in general follow the normal protocols of other kinds of inspections. Because requirements defects are difficult to remove once they pass downstream to design and code, requirements inspections are a key activity for outsource projects.

Design and Code Inspections

An effective best practice for both outsource and MIS software projects is the usage of formal design and code inspections. Formal inspections average more than 65% in defect removal efficiency, making them approximately twice as effective as any normal form of testing. Furthermore, inspections also raise testing efficiency and work as a defect prevention method. Although this is a best practice, design and code inspections have been noted in less than one fourth of our MIS clients but in approximately half of our outsource clients.

Error-Prone Module Elimination

An important best practice in both the outsource and the MIS software domains (and in all other domains) is preventing and removing error-prone modules. As a rule of thumb, less than 5% of the modules in large software applications will contain approximately 50% of all bugs or defects. Complexity analysis tools, code restructuring tools, module-level defect tracking, formal inspections followed by either repairs or redevelopment, plus assigning numeric quality targets to executives can stamp out error-prone modules and prevent their recurrence.

Quality Measurements

A best practice that originated in the systems software domain and moved to the outsource and MIS domains in the 1980s is that of formal quality measurements and defect tracking measurements. Factors measured include defect volumes, defect severity levels, defect origins, defect removal methods, and complexity of the application and its modules. A key metric is *defect removal efficiency*. This is the percentage of defects found before delivery. Although U.S. averages for MIS projects are less than 85%, best-in-class results top 96%. Averages for outsource projects are higher than for MIS projects—90% is the approximate average. The top outsource projects have exceeded 98% in cumulative defect removal efficiency, although this is rare indeed. It is a best practice to begin defect tracking and quality measures during requirements. Once the measures are started, they continue throughout the life of the application. Data collected shows defect volumes, severity levels, and points of origin. Additional data shows defect removal effort, defect removal efficiency levels, and bad-fix injection rates.

Quality Estimation Tools

A best practice pioneered by the systems software domain and now widely used by the outsource domain is that of quality and defect estimation tools to predict the probable number of bugs that might be encountered, and the set of defect prevention and removal operations to be used. Quality estimation tools can predict the numbers of bugs or errors in requirements, specifications, source code, user documents, and bad fixes or secondary defects. The tools can also predict the specific defect removal efficiency of each review, inspection, or test stage. The final predictions are the numbers of latent defects remaining at delivery, and how many defects will be found by customers.

Risk Analysis

A best practice in the outsource software domain is the production of a formal risk analysis for the project at or near the completion of the requirements phase. A formal risk analysis considers technical risks, financial risks, and schedule risks. Although risk analysis is a best practice, it is not yet a common practice. We have noted formal risk analyses on less than 30% of the outsource projects that we have examined during our benchmark and assessment studies. Most of the formal risk assessments have been for projects in the 10,000-plus-function point size range. Actually, because more than half of such large projects run late, exceed their budgets, or are terminated without completion, formal risk analysis should be mandatory.

Best Testing Practices and Tools for Outsourced Software

The outsource software domain has been fairly good in software testing, although not yet up to the level of the systems software domain. Testing in the outsource domain is often assigned to development personnel rather than to test specialists. Although developers can be competent in performing unit tests of their own work, higher level testing and specialized testing for topics such as performance and data integrity require knowledge that general development personnel often lack. However, the outsource community is more likely to utilize testing specialists than the MIS community and the commercial software community.

Test Training

It is a common best practice among large outsource vendors to include formal courses in testing and test case development as a standard part of the curriculum for new programming employees. Testing is not a "natural" skill, and unless training is received in test case design, test library control, and test coverage analysis, the effectiveness of testing may be much lower than when performed by trained personnel.

Automated Test Library Tools

A best practice that is encountered frequently in the outsource software domain is the usage of automated test library tools. Because major corporations have thousands of regression test cases, it is desirable to utilize automated tools for keeping track of these test cases, weeding out redundant tests, and linking tests to applications as needed.

Test Coverage Analysis

A best practice in analyzing the thoroughness of testing is to monitor the number of paths through software that are actually tested. This is a common best practice encountered in all domains, including outsourcing. A variety of commercial test monitors are available that can perform this function. Indeed, the overall best practice is to measure the percentage of all code actually tested. In applications with high cyclomatic and essential complexity, there are so many possible paths through the application that 100% testing is essentially impossible. It is a corollary best practice to redevelop or to simplify the complexity of applications that are so complex that complete testing is impossible.

Test Stages Utilized

The number of forms of testing varies with the size and nature of software applications. Several common kinds of testing are encountered often enough to be classed as best practices for outsource projects. These common forms of testing include unit testing of individual modules, function testing of related modules, regression testing to ensure that changes do not damage existing features, integration testing of the entire application, system testing of the application and the production hardware environment, and customer acceptance testing. For those applications that have stringent performance criteria, performance testing and load testing is also classified as a best practice. Specialized forms of testing may also be a best practice when the situation merits. Examples of specialized testing in recent years includes testing for Y2K compliance, and testing to ensure that the Euro has been added correctly to software applications.

Best Maintenance and Enhancement Practices for Outsourced Software

The outsource software domain is often quite good in maintenance and enhancement of legacy applications. Outsource vendors are often much better at software maintenance than the clients they serve. Indeed, maintenance contracts are a very common and profitable form of outsource work.

In general parlance, the word *maintenance* can apply to any form of update on deployed software: repairs, new features, cosmetic improvements, mandatory or regulated changes, whatever. Although it is a common practice to use the word *maintenance* for a multitude of activities, that is far from being a best practice. Some of the best practices for maintenance and enhancement work in the outsource software domain include those presented in the following subsections.

Maintenance Specialists

In every human activity, specialists can outperform generalists—and software maintenance is no exception. It is a best practice among the outsource community to utilize full-time, trained maintenance personnel for defect repairs. Indeed, many outsource contracts are written for this very purpose. Our benchmark studies have noted that maintenance specialists are approximately twice as productive as generalists in terms of maintenance assignment scopes and monthly defect repair rates. Outsource maintenance personnel can assume responsibility for approximately 3,000 function points of software, which is more than twice the industry average. Monthly defect repairs among the outsource domain average approximately 12 defects per month, and some months can top 20 defects. By contast, MIS norms would be only roughly eight defects per month on average.

Portfolio Analysis

A software *portfolio* is the total number of applications owned by a corporation. Portfolio analysis includes counting the applications, examining their status in terms of defect levels, and assigning them to various levels of importance to the corporation. The top level of importance is often termed *mission critical*. Software is an important corporate asset, and it is a definite best practice at the start of an outsource agreement to know exactly how much software is owned by the corporation, and hence will be included in the outsource agreement.

Geriatric Care for Legacy Applications

The term *geriatric care* refers to a whole set of activities that can stretch the useful lives of legacy applications. Some of these geriatric activities include complexity analysis, applying standard naming conventions to variables and data items, improving comments, restructuring code, and removing error-prone modules. Many applications in the outsource domain are written in COBOL. There are more geriatric tools available for COBOL applications than for all other languages put together. In addition, formal inspections of mission-critical applications is a useful technique. As a rule, the outsource domain is much better than MIS clients in all aspects of geriatric care for legacy applications.

Maintenance of Reusable Materials

A specialized form of maintenance found primarily in the systems, outsource, and commercial domains is maintenance of libraries of reusable artifacts. When reusable objects are placed in several or scores of applications, it is necessary to keep records of who is using what, in case defects are noted that could trigger a recall.

Best Personnel Practices for Outsourced Software

As a class, the outsource software domain has been unusually sophisticated in employee matters. Very good selection and training programs for new hires are the norm among the major outsource vendors. Once employed, fairly good compensation and benefits programs have long been the norm. However, the downside of outsource employment has been an intense work ethic for which 50-hour weeks are far more common than 40-hour weeks. It should be noted that these intense work periods are not mandated by the outsource vendors. They seem to occur spontaneously because software in general and outsourcing in particular attracts individuals with a knack for technical work and with what seems to be more energy than may be found in less demanding kinds of office work.

In this section we examine the personnel areas within the outsource software domain. As with all other domains, there are ten key practices for personnel issues that are examined during assessment and benchmark studies:

1. Staff hiring practices
2. Staff training and education
3. Management training and education
4. Specialists and occupational groups
5. Compensation levels
6. Office ergonomics
7. Organizational structures
8. Morale surveys and results
9. Work patterns and overtime
10. Staff turnover rates

As in the previous section on best technical practices, best personnel practices must have been observed within at least ten companies to be included as best practices. However, the criterion of being noted on at least 50 projects is waived for personnel practices. The reason for this is because personnel practices are normally corporatewide.

Best Staff Hiring Practices for Outsourced Software

As mentioned previously, university training in software engineering or computer science in the United States has not been extremely effective in graduating students who can immediately go to work as programmers without some in-house training and mentoring. The outsource community was among the first industries to recognize academic deficiencies. As a result, a standard practice among outsource vendors includes a very intense six- to ten-week training program for new hires. These programs are effective enough so that they raise the market value of graduates, leading one outsource vendor to require that employees pay back the costs of the training if they leave the company in less than 36 months.

A chronic weakness of academic software education is a very marginal emphasis on software quality control, and a lack of courses in topics such as design and code inspections. Other academic weaknesses include lack of training in function point analysis and project management, lack of training in database design, and lack of training in geriatric technologies for legacy applications. All of these are important topics within the outsource domain.

Absorbing Personnel from Clients

In a significant percentage of domestic outsource contracts, the employees from the client organization become employees of the outsource vendor. This is sometimes a stressful experience because it may involve changes in pension and benefit plans. However, the outsource community has generally done a creditable job in handling the situation of reluctant new hires. The best-practice aspects of acquiring personnel from client organizations includes the significant training and mentoring that the outsource vendors provide in the first year following a changeover. Employees who stay with the organization through the first year often receive enough training and new skills to raise their market values.

Criteria for Continued Employment of New Hires

The outsource community makes its money by providing capable and well-trained employees. Thus, excellent personnel are the primary asset of the outsource vendors. To ensure that personnel excellence is maintained, a best practice among the major outsource vendors is to require successful completion of a rigorous training program in the first six months as a condition of long-term employment. These training programs are somewhat equivalent to "boot camps" used by the military services for training recruits. The hours are long and the assignments are tough, and dropouts are common. However, successful graduates are justifiably proud of their accomplishments and are able to commence work as productive team members.

Best Staff Training and Education Practices for Outsourced Software

Because of the marginal performance of U.S. universities in graduating effective software personnel to work in the software and outsource domain, the major outsource vendors compensate by means of in-house curricula for key software topics.

Annual Staff Training Targets

It is a best practice for major outsource vendors to set targets for the number of days each calendar year that will be set aside for training of technical personnel. Among our outsource software clients, the most common target is ten days a year, with 15 days being almost as common. However, due to the software personnel shortage and to the emergency aspect of the Y2K problem, we have noted that these training targets have sometimes been suspended or bypassed in calendar years 1998 and 1999.

External Seminars and Conferences

It is a best practice for outsource vendors to fund travel and tuition expenses for external conferences and seminars, such as the annual conferences offered by the QAI or the SEI. Among our outsource clients, two external events per year have been common. Incidentally, the major outsource vendors also host internal technical conferences and symposia for their own technical personnel too. The Y2K problem reduced conference attendance in 1999.

Outsource Software Curriculum

Among the courses we have observed among our outsource clients, those dealing with JAD are the most common and are an educational best practice. Indeed, every outsource software professional should be well trained in the techniques of JAD because they are the most effective known ways of stabilizing software requirements. Other courses that can be viewed as best practices for outsource software staff include software design and code inspections, function point analysis, software design and specification techniques, software reusability techniques, structured programming techniques, change management and configuration control, testing methods, productivity and quality measurements, software cost and schedule estimating, and software maintenance techniques.

There are a number of useful courses taught by vendors. Although these courses may be necessary to master the vendor's tools, there is insufficient data to place such courses in the best-practice category. For example companies deploying the SAP ERP package will no doubt train their programming staff in SAP's ABAP/4 programming language.

Best Management Training and Education Practices for Outsourced Software

Software project management curricula are even worse at universities than software engineering. In fact, very few universities in the world offer courses in some of the more important software management topics such as function point analysis, software cost estimating, and software risk and value analysis. The outsource software domain has compensated for this academic gap reasonably well by means of internal classes.

Annual Management Training Targets

It is a best practice for outsource vendors to set targets for the number of days each calendar year that will be set aside for training of project management personnel. Among our outsource clients, five days a year is a common target, but we have noted ten days to occur fairly often. However, due to the impact of the Y2K problem in calendar year 1999, training targets were suspended temporarily in some companies.

External Management Seminars and Conferences

It is a best practice for outsource vendors to fund travel and tuition expenses for external conferences and seminars for managers, such as the annual conferences offered by IFPUG or the PMI. Among our clients, two external events per manager per year are common, but three or four external events also occur. Major outsource vendors also host internal seminars and conferences, often with very interesting lineups of speakers and topics.

Software Management Curriculum

It is a best practice for outsource project managers to understand both estimation and measurement. Therefore, courses on software cost estimation, function point analysis, and software metrics are often noted among our outsource clients. Other management courses noted among our clients that are included in the best practice set are contingency plans, data warehousing, principles of software reuse, software quality estimating, software quality metrics and cost of quality, principles of the SEI CMM, and risk and value analysis.

There are a number of emerging technologies that may become best educational practices in the near future, but have not yet been encountered among at least ten clients. The most notable here would be courses in e-business and Web-based management practices. Although these topics are important, the technology is changing so rapidly and the results are so ambiguous that it is difficult to create an effective course. Another emerging topic that may become a best practice, but is not there yet, is component-based development.

The entire business world, including the outsource domain, is trying to absorb the implications of the Internet and the World Wide Web. The web is exploding in use and triggering major new practices such as "virtual teams," which are dispersed geographically. These changes are moving faster than the educational process can keep up. It will be several more years before the implications of the Web and the Internet can be fully grasped and converted into effective curricula for outsource project managers.

Best Practices for Specialization in the Outsource Software Domain

The outsource domain has been intermediate between the MIS domain and the systems software domain in its use of specialists. The outsource community has more specialists than the MIS community, but not as many as the systems software community.

Software Specialization

There are six key areas in which specialization counts as a best practice in the outsource domain because the results are so much better than when the work is performed by generalists: software testing for all software test stages after unit test software quality assurance, software database administration, function point analysis by certified function point counters, software technical writing, and software maintenance in the sense of defect repairs.

Other specialties are not full-time occupations, but can be useful and valuable. For example, the roles of facilitating JAD or moderating formal inspections are normally assigned to trained specialists, but these specialties are not full-time occupations. They are performed as needed by personnel such as systems analysts or software engineering personnel. In these two cases, use of specialists is common enough to count as best practices.

Outsource vendors also utilize specialists in project management roles, such as cost estimating and project planning. Here, too, the work is not normally a full-time occupation. However, utilization of cost-estimating specialists on projects larger than 1,000 function points is a best practice. With less than 1,000 function points, project managers normally handle estimates themselves.

In addition to these job specialties, the major outsource vendors also employ other specialized occupations and professions such as corporate attorneys, accountants, and human resources specialists. However, these business specialties are not usually associated with software development work and are outside the scope of our normal study.

Best Compensation and Salary Practices for Outsourced Software

Due to the software personnel shortage, compensation levels for all domains have been increasing since about 1995. In the United States, the outsource community has been competitive with other industries in compensation and benefits packages. However as this book is written, a number of contract personnel working at Microsoft have received a favorable court ruling that assigned to them some of the benefits Microsoft offered only to full-time employees. If this ruling is not overturned by appeals, then it will have a significant impact on future benefits programs in the outsource community.

In the outsource domain, as in other industries, compensation levels for large companies in urban areas are higher than compensation levels for small companies in rural areas.

Compensation Benchmarks

It is a best practice among the outsource domain to perform annual compensation benchmark studies for both technical and managerial personnel. These benchmarks are normally "blind" studies during which various companies contribute compensation data that is analyzed statistically by a neutral external benchmark company. Each contributing company receives a report on how their compensation packages compare with the group, but the specifics of each company in the group is not included due to both competitive and antitrust reasons.

Compensation Levels

For large outsource companies employing more than 10,000 software personnel it is a best practice to be in the upper quartile of overall compensation including salaries, bonuses, equity, and medical and dental benefits. Otherwise, the corporation will face a "brain drain" due to the software personnel shortage. In large corporations, compensation, quality, productivity, and schedules are more or less correlated.

There are many aspects of compensation, such as equity, that are outside the scope of software assessments, benchmarks, and baselines. These topics may be covered in general business benchmarks, however. Nonfinancial employment benefits such as medical and dental plans, company automobiles, and child care are also outside the scope of our normal study.

Best Practices in Office Ergonomics for Outsourced Software

The topic of office ergonomics is surprisingly important. However, because a majority of outsource work is performed on client sites, the outsource community has only a limited ability to determine office ergonomics.

Studies by Tom DeMarco and Tim Lister, published in *Peopleware* (Demarco and Lister 1987), confirmed findings that office space benefits systems software productivity in a very significant fashion. During a typical working day, a programmer or analyst needs quiet and solitude for approximately six hours to perform technical work such as programming. Technical outsource personnel need to have discussions or meetings for only about 1.5 hours a day. Roughly two hours are spent on phone calls, using the Internet, or miscellaneous work. Note that a typical "outsource day" is 9.5 hours rather than the more traditional eight hours. From this distribution of effort, it can be seen that private office space is optimal for the major portion of a day's work.

Private Office Space

It is a best practice, but a rare one, to provide private, noise-free office space for software technical staff members such as systems analysts, programmers, and programmer/analysts. An area of at least 80 square feet is optimal. This best practice is encountered only within fairly sophisticated (and profitable) companies, but the results support the hypothesis that private office space is optimal for both software development and maintenance.

Networks and E-mail

It is a best practice to link all technical employees within a corporation by means of a network that supports e-mail, file transfer, and on-line inspection of key work products. In general, the outsource community is fairly sophisticated in interemployee communication. Some outsource companies also pay for home communication facilities, cellular phones, and other communication methods used outside of offices.

Meeting Rooms

Because group activities such as design and code inspections and team meetings are common for software projects, it is a best practice to provide small meeting rooms that can hold ten people. Because usage is intermittent, one such meeting room should be able to support roughly 30 total staff members. This topic is ambiguous in an outsource context. The reason is that much of the work of the outsource community takes place in the office buildings of the clients. Therefore, the outsource vendors have little or no direct control over the space provided.

Best Practices in Organizational Structures for Outsourced Software

For reasons outside the scope of this book, the *span of control* or number of employees reporting to one manager is generally about eight staff members. This has been true for all forms of office work and not just for software. However, the ranges observed in the span of control are quite broad. We have encountered departments with as few as two software employees reporting to one manager, and one department in which 30 employees reported to one manager on a temporary basis.

It is a common belief in the software world that small teams are more productive than large departments. However, this belief confuses two issues. Small *projects* are more productive than large projects, and small projects usually have small-team organizations.

Major outsource software projects are large (>10,000 function points) and have staffing levels that can rise higher than 100 personnel overall. For large projects with more than 50 staff members, small teams of four or five personnel are not as productive as larger departments with 10 to 12 people reporting to one manager. This observation seems true in the outsource domain, as well as in the domains of systems and MIS software projects.

The reason for this finding seems to be that good managers are a scarce commodity. If a company has a low span of control, then it will have a large management population. Because bad management is a common reason for project failures, it can be seen than having fewer but better managers may lead to overall improvements in both performance and productivity.

In general, productivity levels decline as the number of workers increases. Here, too, this is a general finding from many industries, and not just a finding for software projects. However, there is a curious phenomenon within the software domain that was first noted in the 1970s. Productivity levels for software projects tend to decline as the number of managers goes up, rather than as the number of technical staff members goes up. The implications of this finding are that for large applications (>10,000 function points), small teams with four to eight workers are not as productive as larger departments with ten to 12 employees. As the management count goes up, coordination and cooperation between departments becomes difficult due to normal corporate politics.

Optimal Department Size

For large outsource software projects (>10,000 function points) it is a best practice to have between eight and 12 employees reporting to one manager. This is admittedly controversial. Smaller spans of control put too many people in management and raise the odds that some managers will be unqualified. Small departments also increase the difficulty of coordination between departments and raise the odds of political disputes. Furthermore, a staffing complement of perhaps ten software workers can handle a large software component of more than 1,000 function points. Smaller departments might have to segment an application artificially. In addition, a larger span of control allows backup in case of illness, and encourages mentoring of new team members. It is also easier to handle peer reviews and formal inspections.

Optimal Organizational Structures

For outsource software projects larger than 10,000 function points a hierarchical organizational structure is a best practice as opposed to a matrix organizational structure. The hierarchical organization is similar to a military chain of command in that each manager reports directly to a higher level manager, up to the level of the senior manager responsible for the entire system. The matrix structure tends to raise the management head count for larger projects. Because software productivity declines as the management count goes up, this structure can be hazardous for software.

Virtual Organizations

For distributed outsource software projects involving multiple cities and countries, it is a best practice to support broad-band communication channels so that e-mail, file transfer, and on-line inspection are all possible. Video conferencing among locations is also a best practice for projects that are dispersed geographically. Prior to the availability of the Internet and corporate intranets, projects developed over several geographic regions exhibited sharp productivity declines. In the 1970s, each time a different city was added to the same project, productivity declined by approximately 5%. Since about 1995, virtual teams that are dispersed geographically are just as productive as single-site teams, if communication channels are effective.

Best Practices for Employee Morale among Outsource Vendors

Outsource employees who are satisfied with their jobs and their places of employment are more productive and develop higher quality deliverables than employees who are dissatisfied. Both productivity and quality data favor organizations with high levels of morale.

Interestingly, one of the critical factors affecting outsource employee morale is the ability of the project managers to whom the technical workers report. Outsource vendors that recognize the significance of this finding are very careful about who gets promoted to management, and are careful to weed out managers whose personalities are not suited for this very critical responsibility.

Morale and Opinion Surveys

It is a best practice for all software organizations, including outsource vendors, to perform morale or opinion surveys of all employees, including administrative workers, technical staff members, and project managers. The normal frequency of morale surveys is once a year. After a major perturbation such as mass transfer of personnel from a client to an outsource vendor, two surveys in the first year is normal.

Follow-up to Morale Surveys

It is always a best practice to have rapid follow-up after a morale survey is taken. Asking questions about morale but taking no action based on the responses degrades rather than improves morale. Normally after a morale survey occurs the results are analyzed statistically within a week, and departmental group meetings are held to discuss the results within two weeks. Within a month, executives and top managers should have formulated a plan to deal with any serious morale issues that were encountered. Normally, within approximately six weeks there is an overall meeting or series of departmental meetings to discuss the action plans.

Job Transfer Requests

It is a best practice within large outsource corporations to have a job transfer request system that allows employees to request internal transfers to other cities, or to request a job change to another kind of position. Of course, the employees must have the relevant backgrounds and technical skills to perform well in the new situation.

Merit Appraisals

In the United States it is a best practice to have annual performance appraisals for both technical staff members and project managers. During the first year of employment in a company, there may be two or more performance appraisals. It is a best practice for employees and managers to agree jointly to performance goals or targets. Note that in some European countries, performance appraisals are forbidden by either national law or union regulations.

Awards and Recognition

It is a best practice to reward outstanding accomplishments. Many companies have a spectrum of awards ranging from local dinner-for-two awards, which are given at the discretion of a supervisor, up to major $100,000 awards for breakthroughs that have significant corporate value. Overall, numerous small awards tend to benefit morale more widely than a few very large awards. Although large awards can benefit morale, the odds of receiving one are low. Small awards, on the other hand, can be given to 5% to 10% of the outsource vendor's technical staff during the course of a year.

Due to the major shortage of software personnel in the United States, morale and personnel issues are now extremely important. There are many more topics under this heading than can be discussed using assessment and benchmark data because assessments and benchmarks do not cover every personnel topic. For example, stock option plans and equity may have an affect on employee morale and attrition rates, but we have not been tasked with examining these issues.

Another very strong morale factor is that of the medical and dental plans offered by employers. Here, too, we have not been commissioned to study this factor. Indeed, if we attempted to study this factor we would probably be asked to stop because human resource organizations regard this kind of information as sensitive.

Best Work Patterns and Overtime Utilization for Outsourced Software

The software industry in general is populated by employees with fairly strong work ethics. The outsource domain is at the far end of this spectrum, and seems to have a very intense work ethic and the longest work days of many other large groups of employees. The average work day among technical employees in the outsource domain approximates 9.5 hours. Work on weekends is also common (although not often measured). These intense work habits are not mandated by the outsource companies, but seem to reflect the spontaneous urges of the kinds of workers who are attracted to the outsource domain.

It was first noted more than 30 years ago that software development and maintenance tends to attract personnel who are fairly intense in their work practices. Within companies such as Andersen, EDS, IBM, Keane, Lockheed, and Unisys, 50-hour weeks are the norm rather than the exception for software employees. Sixty-hour weeks are not uncommon during critical periods, such as the testing phase of major applications. Although the work ethic of all software domains appears to be higher than average, the outsource community gives the appearance of being staffed by very dedicated workers indeed.

Because U.S. outsource software personnel are usually salaried workers rather than hourly workers, they are considered "exempt" in the sense that software personnel do not automatically receive overtime pay. Many corporate time and cost tracking systems exclude unpaid overtime. Therefore it is difficult to gather reliable information on this topic. (We ask employees to reconstruct overtime patterns during assessment and benchmark interview sessions.)

Compensatory Time

It is a best practice for outsource software personnel to be allowed to take compensatory time during slack periods in return for contributing unpaid overtime during rushed periods.

Note that the topic of unpaid overtime deserves greater coverage in the software literature than it has received because unpaid overtime has a major and tangible impact on productivity rates. On the whole, the industrialized countries of Western Europe, such as France and Germany, have many more vacation days each year than the United States or Japan. Public holidays vary widely from country to country. This issue is very important for international benchmark analysis.

Best Practices for Minimizing Outsource Staff Turnover Rates

Due to the shortage of software personnel in the United States and Europe, outsource vendors, like all other software employers, are very concerned about losing key personnel. They are also concerned about the high costs of recruiting new personnel.

Reducing Voluntary Attrition

To minimize the attrition of key outsource personnel, the set of best practices includes being in the top 25% in terms of compensation and benefits, weeding out less capable managers, and having proactive morale and opinion surveys to identify problems before they grow to a significant magnitude. A very complex issue is very important: Because bad management is the most common reason cited in exit interviews when technical workers quit, it is critical to weed out managers whose personalities are unsuited to management tasks. Thus, very careful management appraisals are a best practice among outsource vendors, and indeed among all software employers.

Finding New Personnel

Obviously, large outsource vendors utilize multiple methods for finding new employees: advertisements, recruiters, and the World Wide Web. However it is a best practice to offer incentives or rewards if employees can bring in suitable candidates. The reason for this is that the software community is fairly good at spreading the word about interesting opportunities. The outsource community is unique in that an aspect of many contracts includes the mass transfer of client personnel to the outsource vendor, sometimes under stressful conditions.

Personnel issues are outside the normal scope of assessment and benchmark studies. But we have been commissioned to explore some aspects of personnel topics, such as the number of specialists employed and the optimal methods for keeping their skills up to date.

Summary and Conclusions on Outsourced Software

The outsource community has been a fast-growing and successful subindustry within the larger community of software employers. In general, software development has been considered a craft rather than a profession. As a craft, success depends on a nucleus of very-well trained and very hard-working technical personnel. The outsource domain has accomplished both sides of this equation. Outsource personnel are usually better trained than the software personnel of the clients they serve. In addition, the work ethic noted among the outsource community is more intense than any other segment.

At a technical level, the outsource community is also fairly sophisticated in the usage of software engineering tools and in the adoption of best practices. No domain is perfect, of course, and there are failures among outsource projects as there are among all software domains.

Because the major outsource vendors have served key industries such as banking and insurance, the outsource community is more sophisticated in the important technology of software reuse than any other, although much improvement is still possible.

The larger outsource vendors are pioneering the concept of "virtual teams," in which software personnel are dispersed geographically, but utilize the power of the Internet, intranets, and the World Wide Web to communicate on a daily basis. The outsource community is also on the verge of pioneering an important topic that promises to reduce software development schedules by more than 60%: establishing a series of software factories located eight time zones apart, so that projects move from factory to factory and thus are under development 24 hours a day.

Software in the 1990s handles most of the operational functions of both corporations and government agencies, such as payroll, accounting, inventory management, purchasing, marketing and sales data, customer information, and the like. However, building software is not the primary business goal of most companies. Most companies do not build large software applications well, and failures outnumber successes. Therefore, many companies are asking hard questions, such as whether outsourcing might not be more cost-effective than continuing with in-house software development and maintenance.

As this book is written, contract and outsource software development in the United States is awaiting the final word on recent court decisions awarding some contract employees at Microsoft benefits given normally only to full-time personnel. This situation is currently ambiguous, but one potential outcome would be to reduce the competitiveness of U.S. software outsource vendors and increase the competitiveness of international software outsource vendors.

Readings and References for Outsourced Software

The MIS community and the outsource community overlap sufficiently so that many of the same books and journals are of mutual interest. The outsource community is often involved in database applications, client/server applications, data warehousing, and ERP applications, as is the MIS community. Many of the technologies that are common for MIS projects are also common for outsourced projects—for example, the use of JAD, information engineering, and function point analysis. The outsource community is also very sophisticated in geriatric technologies for legacy applications such as complexity analysis and code restructuring. Obviously the outsource community has been very active in refurbishing projects for their clients to deal with the Euro and Y2K. The outsource community is somewhat more advanced than the MIS domain in quality control, testing, and software reusability principles and practices.

Abran, A., and P. N. Robillard. "Function Point Analysis. An Empirical Study of Its Measurement Processes." *IEEE Transactions on Software Engineering* 1996; 22(12): 895–909.

Andrews, Dorine C., and Susan K. Stalick. *Business Reengineering: The Survival Guide*. Englewood Cliffs, NJ: Prentice Hall, 1994. (ISBN 0-13-014853-9, 300 pages)

Applehans, Wayne, Alden Globe, and Greg Laugero. *Managing Knowledge: A Practical Web-Based Approach*. Reading, MA: Addison-Wesley, 1999. (ISBN 0-201-43315-X, 115 pages)

Austin, Robert D. *Measuring and Managing Performance in Organizations*. New York: Dorset House Publishing, 1996. (ISBN 0-932633-36-6, 216 pages)

Boar, Bernard H. *Application Prototyping*. New York: John Wiley & Sons, 1984. (ISBN 0-471-89317-X, 210 pages)

Bogan, Christopher E., and Michael J. English. *Benchmarking for Best Practices*. New York: McGraw Hill, 1994. (ISBN 0-07-006375-3, 312 pages)

Brooks, Frederick P. *The Mythical Man-Month*. Reading, MA: Addison Wesley Longman, 1995. (ISBN 0-201-00650-2, 295 pages)

Carmel, Erran. *Global Software Teams: Collaborating across Borders and Time Zones*. Upper Saddle River, NJ: Prentice Hall, 1999. (ISBN 0-13-924218-X, 269 pages)

Carnegie Mellon University. *The Capability Maturity Model: Guidelines for Improving the Software Process*. Reading, MA: Addison Wesley Longman, 1995. (ISBN 0-201-54664-7, 439 pages)

Charette, Robert N. *Application Strategies for Risk Analysis*. New York: McGraw Hill, 1990. (ISBN 0-07-010888-9, 570 pages)

Curtis, Bill, William E. Hefley, and Sally Miller. *People Capability Maturity Model*. Pittsburgh, PA: Software Engineering Institute, Carnegie Mellon University, 1995.

Davis, Alan M., and Marilyn D. Weidner. *Software Requirements*. Englewood Cliffs, NJ: Prentice Hall, 1993. (ISBN 0-13-805763-X, 521 pages)

DeMarco, Tom. *Controlling Software Projects*. New York: Yourdon Press, 1982. (ISBN 0-91702-32-4, 284 pages)

———. *Why Does Software Cost So Much?* New York: Dorset House Publishing, 1995. (ISBN 0-932633-34-X, 237 pages)

———. *The Deadline*. New York: Dorset House Publishing, 1997. (ISBN 0-932633-39-0)

DeMarco, Tom, and Tim Lister. *Peopleware*. New York: Dorset House Publishing, 1987. (ISBN 0-932633-05-6, 188 pages)

Dreger, J. Brian. *Function Point Analysis*. Englewood Cliffs, NJ: Prentice Hall, 1989. (ISBN 0-13-332321-8, 185 pages)

Garmus, David, and David Herron. *Measuring the Software Process: A Practical Guide to Functional Measurement.* Englewood Cliffs, NJ: Prentice Hall, 1995. (ISBN 0-13-349002-5)

Gilb, Tom, and Dorothy Graham. *Software Inspections.* Reading, MA: Addison Wesley Longman, 1993. (ISBN 0-201631814, 471 pages)

Glass, Robert L. *Software Runaways: Lessons Learned from Massive Project Failures.* Upper Saddle River, NJ: Prentice Hall, 1997. (ISBN 0-13-673443-X, 259 pages)

Hansen, Kirk. *Data Structured Program Design.* Topeka, KS: Ken Orr & Associates, 1983. (ISBN 0-9605884-2-6, 414 pages)

Howard, Alan, ed. *Software Metrics and Project Management Tools.* Phoenix, AZ: Applied Computer Research, 1997. (30 pages)

Humphrey, Watts S. *Managing the Software Process.* Reading, MA: Addison Wesley Longman, 1989. (ISBN 0-201-18095-2)

——. *Introduction to the Personal Software Process.* Reading, MA: Addison Wesley Longman, 1997. (ISBN 0201548097)

——. *Managing Technical People.* Reading, MA: Addison Wesley Longman, 1997. (ISBN 0-201-54597-7, 326 pages)

IFPUG. *IFPUG Counting Practices Manual.* Release 4.1. Westerville, OH: International Function Point Users Group, April 1999. (93 pages)

Inmon, W. H. *Developing Client/Server Applications in an Architected Environment.* Boston, MA: QED Technical Publishing Group, 1991. (ISBN 0-89435-389-6, 199 pages)

Jones, Capers. *Assessment and Control of Software Risks.* Englewood Cliffs, NJ: Prentice Hall, 1993. (ISBN 0-13-741406-4, 711 pages)

——. *Applied Software Measurement.* 2nd ed. New York: McGraw Hill, 1996. (ISBN 0-07-032826-9, 618 pages)

——. *Software Quality: Analysis and Guidelines for Success.* Boston, MA: International Thomson Computer Press, 1997. (ISBN 1-85032-876-6, 492 pages)

——. *Estimating Software Costs.* New York: McGraw Hill, 1998. (ISBN 0-07-9130941, 725 pages)

——. "Sizing Up Software." *Scientific American* 1998; 279(6): 104–111.

——. *The Year 2000 Software Problem: Quantifying the Costs and Assessing the Consequences.* Reading, MA: Addison-Wesley, 1998. (ISBN 0-201-30964-5, 303 pages)

——. *Table of Programming Languages and Levels.* Burlington, MA: Software Productivity Research, March 1999. (ten versions from 1985 through July 1999; 77 pages for Version 10)

Kalakota, Ravi, and Marcia Robinson. *e-Business: Roadmap for Success*. Reading, MA: Addison Wesley, 1999. (ISBN 0-201-60480-9, 378 pages)

Kan, Stephen H. *Metrics and Models in Software Quality Engineering*. Reading, MA: Addison Wesley Longman, 1994. (ISBN 0-201-63339-6, 344 pages)

Kelly, Sean. *Data Warehousing: The Route to Mass Customization*. New York: John Wiley & Sons, 1996. (ISBN 0-471-96328-3, 200 pages)

Kemerer, Chris F. "An Empirical Validation of Software Cost Estimation Models." *Communications of the ACM* 1987; 30: 416–429.

———. "Reliability of Function Point Measurement: A Field Experiment." *Communications of the ACM* 1994; 36: 85–97.

Lacity, Mary C., and Rudy Hirschheim. *Information Systems Outsourcing*. New York: John Wiley & Sons, 1993. (ISBN 0-471-938823, 273 pages)

Lozinsky, Sergio. *Enterprise-Wide Software Solutions*. Reading, MA: Addison Wesley Longman, 1998. (ISBN 0-201-30971-8, 190 pages)

McCabe, Thomas J. "A Complexity Measure." *IEEE Transactions on Software Engineering* 1976: 308–320.

McMenamin, Stephen M., and John F. Palmer. *Essential Systems Analysis*. New York: Yourdon Press, 1984. (ISBN 0-91702-30-8, 392 pages)

Melton, Austin. *Software Measurement*. London: Chapman & Hall, 1995. (ISBN 0-412-55180-2)

Orr, Ken. *Structured Requirements Definition*. Topeka, KS: Ken Orr & Associates, 1981. (ISBN 0-9605884-0-X, 235 pages)

Perry, William E. *Data Processing Budgets*. Englewood Cliffs, NJ: Prentice Hall, 1985. (ISBN 0-13-196874-2, 224 pages)

———. *Handbook of Diagnosing and Solving Computer Problems*. Blue Ridge Summit, PA: TAB Books, 1989. (ISBN 0-8306-9233-9, 255 pages)

———. *Effective Methods for Software Testing*. Los Alamitos, CA: IEEE Computer Society Press, 1995. (ISBN 0-471-06097-6, 556 pages)

Putnam, Lawrence H. *Measures for Excellence: Reliable Software On Time, Within Budget*. Englewood Cliffs, NJ: Prentice Hall, 1992. (ISBN 0-13-567694-0, 336 pages)

Putnam, Lawrence H., and Ware Myers. *Industrial Strength Software: Effective Management Using Measurement*. Los Alamitos, CA: IEEE Computer Society Press, 1997. (ISBN 0-8186-7532-2, 320 pages)

Rubin, Howard. *Software Benchmark Studies for 1999*. Pound Ridge, NY: Howard Rubin Associates, 1999.

Strassmann, Paul. *The Politics of Information Management*. New Canaan, CT: The Information Economics Press, 1995. (ISBN 0-9620413-4-3, 523 pages)

————. *The Squandered Computer*. New Canaan, CT: The Information Economics Press, 1997. (ISBN 0-9620413-1-9, 426 pages)

————. *Information Productivity: Assessing the Information Management Costs of US Industrial Corporations*. New Canaan, CT: The Information Economics Press, 1999. (ISBN 0-9620413-8-6, 157 pages)

Symons, Charles R. *Software Sizing and Estimating: Mk II FPA (Function Point Analysis)*. Chichester, UK: John Wiley & Sons, 1991. (ISBN 0-471-92985-9, 200 pages)

Weinberg, Gerald, and Daniel Friedman. *Handbook of Walkthroughs, Inspections, and Technical Reviews*. New York: Dorset House Publishing, 1990. (ISBN 0-9326833-19-6, 450 pages)

Wheeler, David A., Bill Brylcznski, and Reginald Meeson. *Software Inspection: An Industry Best Practice*. Los Alamitos, CA: IEEE Computer Society Press, 1996. (ISBN 0-8186-7430-0, 325 pages)

Yourdon, Edward. *Death March: The Complete Software Developer's Guide to Surviving "Mission Impossible" Projects*. Upper Saddle River, NJ: Prentice Hall, 1997. (ISBN 0-13-748310-4, 218 pages)

Zvegintzov, Nicholas. *Software Management Technology Reference Guide*. Release 4.2. New York: Software Maintenance News, 1994. (ISBN 1-884521-01-0, 240 pages)

CHAPTER NINE

Benchmarks and Best Practices for Systems Software

The type of application defined as *systems software* is software that controls a physical device such as a computer or a telephone switching system. Within this primary type can also be found the subtype of *embedded software*. Embedded software also controls a physical device and is located inside the device, such as an automotive fuel injection system or an aircraft navigational device. Although systems software and embedded software serve the same purposes, they differ in several attributes. Ordinary systems software runs on general-purpose computers and can be updated if needed. Embedded software often runs on specialized computers. Moreover, embedded software is often stored in read-only memory (ROM) and cannot be modified easily. The entire chip containing the embedded software may need to be replaced.

The fact that embedded software is inaccessible and cannot be modified without replacing a chip made embedded software very troublesome for Y2K repairs. Many embedded devices are located in hard-to-reach spots, such as offshore oil rigs, and thus are not easy to find and repair. Also, some of the manufacturers of embedded devices have changed product lines or even gone out of business. Therefore, even when embedded devices are located, replacement of chips with Y2K problems was not easy.

Systems software in all forms is characterized by a need for very high levels of quality and reliability. If a company sells a large and complex physical device such as a telephone switching system, the need for very high quality levels in the controlling software is an obvious necessity. Without excellent software quality, the product might fail and damage the product's sales potentials.

The need for high quality and reliability is also true for embedded software, although it is not achieved quite as often for this subtype. Embedded software controls an astonishing variety of physical devices, including automobile engines, aircraft avionics, digital cameras, medical instruments, machine tools, weapons systems, and even some home appliances.

Systems software originated early in the computer era to control digital computers and attached devices such as card readers, paper tapes, and magnetic tapes. When random-access storage was introduced in the late 1950s, systems software became more complex.

The archetype of systems software was operating systems such as CP/M, DOS, OS/2, MVS, Windows 3.1, Windows 95 and 98, Windows NT, UNIX, and the LINUX variant. All of these operating systems control computer hardware and illustrate what is meant by the phrase *systems software*. Other examples of systems software include telephone switching systems such as AT&T's 5ESS central office switching systems, smaller private branch exchange switches, local area network controllers, and the like.

Within the subtype of embedded software can be found software that controls automobile fuel injection systems, civilian aircraft flight control software, medical instrument software, and even the software embedded in home appliances such as microwaves and clothes dryers.

Systems software originated early in the computer era. From roughly 1950 until about 1990, the line of demarcation between systems software and other types was fairly clear. Systems software controlled computer hardware and provided a platform on which application software operated. In recent years, the line between systems software and other types has blurred. Starting with the many generations of Microsoft's Windows operating system, the role of systems software has expanded to include a host of utilities and supplemental functions. In addition, a form of software termed *middleware* has come into being that operates between the layer of traditional systems software and the applications themselves. Middleware also shares some of the attributes of systems software in terms of development methods and results.

Systems Software Demographics

Since 1985 roughly one third of the projects examined by SPR have been of the systems software type, or approximately 3,400 projects out of 9,100. *Applied Software Measurement* (Jones 1996) contains systems software benchmark data through calendar year 1996. Although there is some overlap, the benchmarks in the book you are now reading are derived from the more recent systems software projects examined from 1995 through 1999.

Some of the corporations producing systems software whose systems software data has been included in the current benchmarks include (in alphabetical order) AT&T, Bellcore, Bell Northern Research, Bell Sygma, Bendix, Cincinnati Bell, Compaq (formerly DEC), Ford Motors, General Electric, General Motors, GTE, Hewlett-Packard, IBM, Lucent, MCI, Microsoft, Motorola, NCR, Nippon Telegraph, Pacific Bell, Siemens-Nixdorf, TRW, and Unisys. This more recent data is also normalized using Version 4.0 and Version 4.1 of the function point counting rules published by IFPUG. *Applied Software Measurement* (Jones 1996) utilized Version 3.4 of the IFPUG counting rules. Because Version 4.0 rules reduced the weight of error messages, there is a reduction of perhaps 15% in the function point totals counted with the newer rules for some applications. However, this reduction only applies to software with a significant volume of error messages. In a random mix of projects, the differences between Version 3.4 and 4.0 rules would be perhaps 10%. The newer 4.1 IFPUG counting rules released in May 1999 (IFPUG 1999) add some refinements in the explanations of the rules but do not change the counts compared with the 4.0 rules.

I estimate that there are approximately 2,000,000 systems software applications in existence in the United States at the start of 2000. Roughly 1,500,000 are conventional systems software and approximately 500,000 are embedded applications. I am speaking of unique master copies of applications. Some of these applications have millions of copies, such as the many millions of copies of Windows CE embedded in hand-held and palmtop computing devices. I estimate that before the Y2K crisis in the United States, roughly 10,000 new systems software applications were developed each year, and approximately 3,000 to 4,000 new embedded applications were developed annually.

Due to the massive repair and replacement activities associated with the Y2K problem, the years 1998 and 1999 witnessed an unprecedented number of replacements and updates to systems and embedded applications that were not Y2K compliant. Table 9.1 illustrates my view of the total volume of systems and

Table 9.1   U.S. Systems and Embedded Software Projects circa 1999

Size, function points	No. of Legacy Applications	No. Withdrawn in 1999	No. Under Develop-ment	No. Completed in 1999	No. Updated in 1999
100	850,000	297,500	85,000	170,000	467,500
1,000	450,000	67,500	40,500	16,875	270,000
10,000	95,000	7,600	2,375	1,900	57,000
100,000	250	10	13	4	150
Total	1,395,250	372,610	127,888	188,779	794,650

embedded software applications circa 1999. Note that Table 9.1 only includes projects and software that range from 100 to 100,000 function points. Normally our clients do not keep accurate records of the numbers of projects less than 100 function points because many of these projects are minor updates that are carried out informally.

The unusually large number of withdrawals and updates in 1999 is due entirely to the massive efforts associated with Y2K repairs. It should be noted that systems and embedded applications are both troubled by Y2K date problems. Often these applications control critical devices such as water purification plants, electric power generators, and medical equipment. For additional information on systems and embedded Y2K problems, refer to *The Year 2000 Software Problem: Quantifying the Costs and Assessing the Consequences* (Jones 1998).

Embedded devices have been on an explosive growth path since about 1995. It can be predicted that by early in the new century almost every business traveler will be equipped with a cellular phone, notebook computer, palmtop organizer, and paging device. Of course, some of these features will blend together into hybrid multifunctional devices. Indeed, due to *convergence,* the dividing lines between palmtop computers, cellular phones, pagers, and global positioning systems is blurring as more and more features come together in the same device. In today's world any complicated machine can be controlled by embedded computers. This includes manufacturing equipment, medical devices, oil and chemical refining equipment, water purification systems, and many household devices.

The systems software domain contains some very large applications. For example IBM's MVS operating system has grown to more than 100,000 function points, or more than 20,000,000 source code statements. Microsoft's Windows NT, 95, and 98 operating systems are not far behind. Even the comparatively small UNIX operating system tops 50,000 function points, or 6,000,000 source code statements, in some incarnations.

By contrast, embedded applications are usually rather small. Most are less than 1,000 function points, or less than 125,000 source code statements in a procedural language such as C. Indeed, some applications embedded in Windows CE devices are less than 250 function points because they are intended to be stored in limited amounts of ROM.

On the whole, the set of applications termed *middleware* is also fairly small, and most of these applications are less than 1,000 function points as well.

Based on demographic studies among SPR's clients extrapolated to national levels, the systems software domain in the United States contains approximately 650,000 professional software personnel and managers, or roughly 28% of the approximate total of 2,350,000 U.S. software personnel. Table 9.2 shows the estimated percentage of total U.S. software personnel working in the domain of systems software, including the embedded software subtype.

The systems software domain employs specialists in significant numbers, as can be seen from Table 9.2. The data in Table 9.2 is derived in part from an SPR study funded by AT&T in 1995. This study examined the software demographic

Table 9.2   Estimated U.S. Systems Software Population circa 2000

Software Occupational Groups	No. Employed	Systems Software	Percent of Total
Programmer/analyst	400,000	20,000	5.00
Programmer, maintenance	350,000	87,500	25.00
Programmer, development	275,000	41,250	15.00
Project manager, first level	225,000	56,250	25.00
Software engineer, systems	200,000	130,000	65.00
Testing specialist	125,000	62,500	50.00
Systems analyst	100,000	10,000	10.00
Software engineer, real-time	75,000	52,500	70.00
Software technical writer	75,000	37,500	50.00

continued

Table 9.2   *continued*

Software Occupational Groups	No. Employed	Systems Software	Percent of Total
Software engineer, embedded	70,000	45,500	65.00
Data administration specialist	50,000	2,500	5.00
Project manager, second level	35,000	8,750	25.00
Software quality assurance specialist	25,000	12,500	50.00
Configuration control specialist	15,000	4,725	31.50
Performance specialists	7,500	3,750	50.00
Project manager, third level	5,000	1,250	25.00
Software architect	1,500	750	50.00
Subtotal	2,034,000	577,225	28.38

Software Occupational

	No. Employed	Systems Software	Percent of Total
Software sales specialist	105,000	26,250	25.00
Customer support specialist	80,000	16,000	20.00
Systems administration	50,000	12,500	25.00
Software management consultant	45,000	6,750	15.00
Software education specialist	30,000	9,000	30.00
Software librarian	15,000	4,500	30.00
Process auditor/assessor	7,500	2,625	35.00
Process improvement specialist	5,000	2,000	40.00
Measurement specialist	3,500	875	25.00
Software marketing specialist	3,000	750	25.00
Cost-estimating specialist	2,000	600	30.00
Human factors specialist	1,000	350	35.00
Certified function point counter	500	75	15.00
Subtotal	322,000	82,275	25.55
Total	2,356,000	659,500	27.99

and specialization patterns of a number of major organizations including AT&T, the U.S. Air Force, IBM, Texas Instruments, and several other similar enterprises. SPR is continuing this long-range exploration because new occupations are appearing in the software world.

The number of U.S. companies that produce systems software totals more than 2,500 and includes some of the largest employers of software personnel in the world. For example, both AT&T and IBM have more than 25,000 software personnel, and roughly half are in the systems software domain. Many other companies have 10,000 or more software personnel, such as Motorola, Raytheon, and Hewlett-Packard, with approximately 50% or more of these populations working on systems software or subtypes such as embedded software.

Other examples of systems software producers include automotive manufacturers such as Ford, Chrysler, and General Motors; aircraft manufacturers such as Boeing; and a host of well-known computer and telecommunication companies such as Lucent, Sun, Unisys, GTE, and the like. Pure software companies such as Microsoft also produce systems software, although Microsoft is also discussed under the topic of commercial software in this book.

Abroad, the countries that produce systems software in the largest volumes include Germany, Japan, France, the United Kingdom, Russia, China, India, Brazil, Argentina, Mexico, Taiwan, and South Korea. However, systems software is produced in every industrialized country. Some countries that are small in total population are quite significant in the volumes of system software created: Canada, Sweden, the Netherlands, and Norway, are examples. The non-U.S. total of systems software personnel is approximately 1,500,000. Overseas, examples of major systems software producers include Alcatel, Fiat, Nippon Telegraph, Siemens-Nixdorf, LM Ericsson, Philips, Hitachi, Toyota, Tata, and Hyundai.

Some of the industries and SIC codes that produce the greatest amount of systems software include those listed on Table 9.3.

These industries often produce customized systems and embedded applications for use in their marketed hardware products and services. Almost every industry uses systems software, but the ones shown on Table 9.3 tend to create systems and embedded software in significant volumes.

Because of the great importance of systems software to high-technology products and to manufacturing processes, the systems software domain has established a number of leading-edge research laboratories. In fact, there are probably more software research labs and software researchers in the systems software domain than in all of the universities of the world put together. Many of

Table 9.3   Systems Software Producers by SIC Code and Industry

SIC Code	Industry
2911	Petroleum refining
3511	Turbines and turbine generators
3559	Industrial machinery
3561	Pumps and pumping equipment
3571	Electronic computers
3579	Office machines
3661	Telephone and telegraph apparatus
3663	Radio and TV communication equipment
3674	Semiconductors and related devices
3711	Motor vehicles and automobile bodies
3724	Aircraft engines and engine parts
3761	Guided missiles and space equipment
3841	Surgical and medical equipment

these research labs explore much more than software, of course. But very capable studies on software topics are taking place as well. Examples of such leading and advanced research facilities include the numerous labs of IBM's research and product divisions, Bell Labs, Alcatel, Philips, Siemens-Nixdorf, Xerox, and Hitachi's software research laboratories. Microsoft has also created a major software laboratory. Indeed, the Microsoft research lab has become so prominent that some universities fear a "brain drain" to the Microsoft facility, which is better equipped and has better compensation levels than universities.

The systems software domain is also very strong in on-the-job training and formal education. In fact, the faculty of major corporations such as IBM, AT&T, Lucent, or Siemens-Nixdorf rival a major university in numbers of instructors. From examining some of the curricula within these large corporations, at least some of the courses, such as those dealing with quality and management issues, appear to be superior to most university courses at both the undergraduate and graduate levels.

The systems software domain in Europe has been particularly active in software research into improved methods. Indeed, the number and variety of systems software practices and approaches in Europe probably exceeds any other geographic area. Some examples of European software initiatives include APPRAISAL, Bootstrap, ESPRIT, Merise, and SPICE.

Japan and South Korea have also been active in systems software research programs, and both Russia and China are active as well. India is also beginning to take energetic steps in the systems software domain, and indeed has more companies at or above SEI CMM level 3 than any country besides the United States. For example, the Motorola software lab in India is one of the few in the world rated a level 5 on the SEI CMM scale.

The major programming languages used for systems software production are Assembly, C, C++, Objective C, and other C variants. JAVA is a recent addition to the systems and embedded community, but is growing rapidly in usage and diversity of applications. Ada83 and Ada95 are often used in Europe for systems software as was Algol. Other programming languages utilized include Smalltalk, FORTRAN, Forth, CHILL, CORAL, and perhaps 30 others. The systems software community is actively pursuing reusability, and hence is moving rapidly toward OO technologies.

Systems software is often built for custom hardware platforms and may use custom or proprietary operating systems. Systems software also tends to utilize the UNIX operating system to a higher degree than other software classes.

The embedded software subtype uses a variety of platforms and operating systems, including Windows CE, the Palm Pilot operating system, the Psion operating system, and a variety of custom operating systems inside specific devices such as military equipment, telephone equipment, manufacturing robots, and the like.

The systems software domain is also the main user of high-end development workstations. As a result of the special needs of systems software, the vendors serving this community are often quite distinct from those serving the information systems domain or the military domain.

Systems Software Benchmarks

To provide a context for further discussion, Figure 9.1 illustrates a broad overview of the productivity levels in the systems software domain. The main point to be derived from Figure 9.1 is the fact that small-project productivity levels vary significantly between new projects and maintenance projects. Of course, Figure 9.1 oversimplifies the situation and merely provides a general graphical illustration of trends. The reason why new projects are so much more productive than maintenance projects less than 10 function points is due to the fact that maintenance requires regression testing and recompilation of the entire application.

As can be seen from Figure 9.1 there is an interesting node point at approximately 100 function points. This happens to be the size range at which new development projects and enhancement and maintenance projects come together in terms of net productivity rates. Smaller maintenance and enhancement projects have reduced productivity levels due to the overhead associated with regression testing and recompilation of the base application.

Because of the urgent need for high quality and reliability coupled with rather sophisticated software quality assurance groups, it is not surprising that the systems software domain has the highest levels of defect removal of any type of software SPR has studied. More systems software projects top 95% in defect removal efficiency than any other type. Indeed, more systems software projects measure defect removal than any other type.

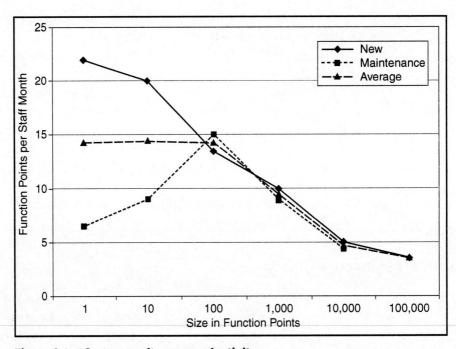

Figure 9.1   Systems software productivity

There are more software quality assurance departments associated with systems software than with all other types of software put together. Even though systems software employs only approximately 28% of the total U.S. software work force, roughly 50% of the U.S. software quality personnel work in the systems software domain.

From a historical point of view, it is interesting to consider why quality control in the systems software domain is usually more sophisticated than other kinds of software, such as information systems and commercial software. The main reason for this phenomenon is because systems software controls complicated physical devices that don't work unless the software is of extremely high quality and reliability.

Some physical devices such as telephone switching systems have existed in electromechanical versions long before software was applied to telephone switching. The manufacturers had long recognized a need for very high quality and reliability, and therefore have had state-of-the-art quality assurance departments for more than 50 years. When software began to take over the control of such physical devices, the existing quality assurance groups expanded their roles to cover software as well as engineered components. The important aspect of the situation is that a culture of quality already existed in the systems domain, as did substantial organizations of quality specialists.

By contrast, the information systems community derived from the application of software to administrative, financial, and accounting tasks. The organizations that performed these tasks prior to the computer era usually had no special quality assurance departments other than auditors. The role of auditing was to ensure correct numerical results, and not to monitor the process by which these results were achieved. Hardware reliability, a major aspect of systems software, was never really a consideration in the information systems domain. Even at the end of the twentieth century, formal quality assurance departments are comparatively rare in the information systems domain. Less than 25% of information systems departments among our clients have formal software quality assurance teams associated with them. By comparison, more than 75% of the systems and embedded software departments have formal quality assurance support.

Also, in the MIS domain many of the departments called "quality assurance" are actually test groups. Within the systems software domain, on the other hand, the software quality assurance departments are not the primary test groups. The functions of this group in the systems software domain are much broader than testing and include moderating inspections, teaching, quality estimation, and quality measurement.

Indeed, some of the companies in the systems software domain even fund software quality assurance laboratories or research groups. These groups are normally free from day-to-day quality assurance work on actual projects. Although quality research groups are few in number in the United States, they have been unusually effective in advancing the state of the art of quality control. Many of the most effective software quality techniques of the past 50 years have derived from the quality research labs of companies such as AT&T, IBM, and Motorola. Quality estimation tools, formal inspections, quality measurement approaches, and many other techniques derive from such quality research organizations.

The importance of quality control and formal processes within the systems software domain explains two interesting phenomena:

1. Compared with other types of software, many more systems software producers can be found at or higher than level 3 on the SEI CMM than any other form other than defense contractors.
2. Compared with other types of software, many more systems software producers have been certified under ISO 9000–9004 standards than any other type.

In addition, a number of fairly sophisticated software quality approaches are quite common in the systems software domain, although they are somewhat rare in other domains. Some of these software quality approaches include

- Funding software quality research programs
- Use of formal design and code inspections
- Use of quality estimation tools
- Use of quality and defect removal targets for key projects
- Use of QFD
- Use of "six-sigma" quality targets
- Use of the "clean room" technique developed by IBM
- Use of the "orthogonal" defect classification developed by IBM
- Use of complexity analysis tools
- Use of automated defect tracking systems
- Use of test library automation support
- Use of automated change control tools

- Use of trained testing specialists
- Use of formal regression test suites
- Use of full life cycle quality measurements

The overall results of the systems software quality approaches have been generally successful. Defect removal efficiency levels in the systems software domain is almost 10% higher than U.S. averages. More systems software projects exceed 95% in cumulative defect removal than any other type. Indeed, only systems software and military software have approached or exceeded 99% in cumulative defect removal efficiency levels.

Although many systems software producers have been certified to conform to ISO quality standards such as ISO 9001, some systems software producers such as Motorola have even criticized the ISO quality standards as being a step backward from their own six-sigma quality program. In fact, there is little or no empirical evidence that ISO certification has any tangible benefits in terms of systems software quality levels.

Net productivity levels in the systems software domain have been lower than all other types except military software except for very large systems, for which the systems domain is higher than average. The reason for this is because the systems software domain creates very complete and hence very large specification sets. The volume of systems specifications tends to slow down productivity for applications less than 1,000 function points, which numerically comprise more than 75% of all systems software projects.

On the other hand, for applications in the 10,000-function point and 100,000-function point domains, systems software is higher than average. Indeed, for the top size plateau of 100,000 function points, systems software is the overall leader. It can be said that the strong emphasis in the systems software domain on rigorous processes, complete specifications, and formal quality assurance controls produce optimal results in projects more than 10,000 function points. At the low end of the size spectrum (<1,000 function points), the rigor of systems software development practices tends to lead to somewhat lower productivity than most other forms of software.

Small applications can sometimes be built using casual processes and little rigor, if the developers themselves are reasonably competent. However, for large systems, a great deal of rigor and formality is necessary to complete the application at all, and even more if the application is to achieve very high levels of operational reliability.

Within all size plateaus, actual coding or programming productivity in the systems domain is often higher than other types, due in part to significant volumes of reusable code. However, coding is less than 20% of the total effort devoted to systems software, whereas production of paper documents tops 25%.

Let us now consider some overall benchmark results from the systems software domain concentrating on more recent studies circa 1995 through 1999. Table 9.4 merely summarizes some of the interesting data points from the SPR studies of systems software.

Although overall benchmarks are interesting, they do not really provide enough information to understand the nature of the work involved. Let us now examine a more detailed activity-level benchmark. To do this, we need to select a specific size application. Because the class of 10,000-function point applications is both common and important within the systems software domain, let us look at the typical activity patterns for that size of project.

The next benchmark of interest is to show the activities associated with a typical systems software project of 10,000 function points (Table 9.5). Assuming that the C programming language is used, this would be approximately 1,250,000 C statements in size. The C programming language requires roughly 125 statements per function point.

In Table 9.5 the Assignment Scope column refers to the number of function points normally assigned to one staff member. The Production Rate column refers to the volume of function points that can be completed in a standard time period. Assignment scopes and production rates are key metrics that can be derived from benchmark studies. The importance of these metrics is that they are fundamental metrics for software cost estimating. The standard time period in Table 9.5 is the "staff month," which contains approximately 22 working days. Each working day is assumed to be of a nominal eight hours in duration, but only six hours a day are devoted to productive work. This totals 132 effective work hours per month. These assumptions are nominal or default values.

As you can see from Table 9.5, systems software utilizes a rather complete set of activities, with a significant concentration of resources on quality-related topics such as formal inspections, testing, and quality assurance work. In terms of quality-related activities, Table 9.5 includes formal quality assurance teams, design inspections, code inspections, and six discrete forms of testing. It is not uncommon for systems software to utilize between six and ten discrete forms of testing for major projects. This is more than any other type of software other than military applications.

Table 9.4 Overall Systems Software Benchmarks

Benchmark	Value
No. of new projects from 1995 through 1999	345
No. of enhancement projects from 1995 through 1999	575
Total no. of projects from 1995 through 1999	920
Average new project size, function points	2,400
Maximum new project size, function points	97,000
Average enhancement size, function points	95
Maximum enhancement size, function points	2,350
Average new development assignment scope, function points	145
Maximum development assignment scope, function points	315
Average maintenance assignment scope, function points	725
Maximum maintenance assignment scope, function points	4,275
Average productivity, function points per staff month	5.8
Maximum productivity, function points per staff month	31.5
Average productivity, work hours per function point	22.76
Maximum productivity, work hours per function point	4.19
Average effort, staff months	13,920
Maximum effort, staff months	281,300
Average new project staff size	17
Maximum new project staff size	956
Average new project schedule, calendar months	22.49
Maximum new project schedule, calendar months	78.00
Average monthly compensation, burdened	$14,000
Maximum monthly compensation, burdened	$21,000
Average cost per function point	$2,413.79
Maximum cost per function point	$7,800.00
Average defect potential per function point	5.4
Maximum defect potential per function point	8.5
Average defect removal efficiency	93.50%
Maximum defect removal efficiency	99.60%
Average monthly rate of requirements creep	2.00%
Maximum monthly rate of requirements creep	4.60%

Table 9.5 Systems Software Activities and Rates for 10,000 Function Points

Parameter	Value
Application size	10,000 function points
Application size	1,250,000 LOC
Source language	C
Work hours per month	132
Monthly compensation	$14,000

Activities Performed	Assignment Scope, function points	Production Rate, function points	Staff	Effort, months	Schedule, months	Cost	Percent
01 Requirements	400	125	25	80	3.20	$1,120,000	4.00
02 Prototyping	1,000	100	10	100	10.00	$1,400,000	5.00
03 Architecture	1,500	300	7	33	5.00	$466,667	1.67
04 Initial design	250	100	40	100	2.50	$1,400,000	5.00
05 Detail design	175	75	57	133	2.33	$1,866,667	6.66
06 Design reviews	175	125	57	80	1.40	$1,120,000	4.00
07 Coding	125	30	80	333	4.17	$4,666,667	16.65
08 Reuse acquisition	2,000	1,000	5	10	2.00	$140,000	0.50
09 Code inspections	115	90	87	111	1.28	$1,555,556	5.55
10 Configuration management	1,500	750	7	13	2.00	$186,667	0.67

11 Formal integration	2,000	500	5	20	4.00	$280,000	1.0
12 Documentation	1,000	75	10	133	13.33	$1,866,667	6.66
13 Unit testing	125	60	80	167	2.08	$2,333,333	8.33
14 Function testing	150	75	67	133	2.00	$1,866,667	6.66
15 Integration testing	150	95	67	105	1.58	$1,473,684	5.26
16 System testing	200	125	50	80	1.60	$1,120,000	4.00
17 Field testing	250	250	40	40	1.00	$560,000	2.00
18 Acceptance testing	300	250	33	40	1.20	$560,000	2.00
19 Quality assurance	1,250	150	8	67	8.33	$933,333	3.33
20 Project management	1,200	45	8	222	26.67	$3,111,111	11.10
Totals/averages	171[1]	5.00[1]	59[1]	2,002[2]	34.18[1]	$28,027,018[2]	100.00[2]

Cost per function point, $2,803; Cost per LOC, $22.42.
[1]Average
[2]Total

The detailed list of activities in Table 9.5 is useful when considering only summary or project-level data. Without knowing how many different kinds of work are involved in systems software, it would be difficult to understand why productivity levels for smaller projects are somewhat less than other types of software, other than military software of course.

When various activities from Table 9.5 are aggregated, it is interesting to note that the sum of the work devoted to defect removal is by far the largest cost driver of systems software, followed by the production of paper documents. Code-related work in the form of prototypes and product programming is only the third largest cost element (Table 9.6).

Because our clients are extremely interested in "best in class," Table 9.7 contrasts average values with best-in-class results for a number of key metric areas in the productivity and quality domains. However, a few words of explanation are needed to interpret the table. First, systems software projects range from less than 100 function points to more than 100,000 function points. Therefore it is necessary to display the sizes in order for the data to be relevant. In Table 9.7, three important size categories are used: 1,000, 10,000, and 100,000 function points. For smaller projects (<1,000 function points), individual human variance becomes a major factor, so the results are statistically uncertain. Also, the enormous differences between new projects and maintenance projects at the low end really require separate data points. Second, in Table 9.7 "function point" refers to function points counted using Version 4.1 of the IFPUG counting rules. The LOC metric actually refers to logical statements, rather than to physical lines. This is so that I am consistent with my previous books and with the best practice for code counting. Third, for the cost items shown in Table 9.7, a constant burdened compensation rate of $14,000 per staff month is assumed. The reason for using a constant value is because the actual difference in monthly compensation is a complex topic. As pointed out earlier, compensation varies by industry, size of company, geographic region, and occupational group. When a productivity

Table 9.6   Major Systems Software Cost Drivers

Systems Software Cost Drivers	Staff Months	Percent
Defect removal	876	43.78
Paper documents	480	23.98
Code related	477	23.81

database such as ours includes information from low-cost countries such as India and high-cost countries such as Switzerland, simply comparing costs in a table could be misleading. The purpose of Table 9.7 is to show how technologies

Table 9.7   Average and Best-in-Class Results for Systems Software

Key Software Topics	1,000 Function Points	10,000 Function Points	100,000 Function Points
Average staff size	6	67	690
Best-in-class staff size	4	45	500
Average schedule, months	15.85	36.31	70.79
Best-in-class schedule, months	11.22	25.12	56.23
Average function points per staff month	10.10	4.13	2.05
Best-in-class function points per staff month	22.28	8.76	3.56
Average work hours per function point	13.08	31.95	64.45
Best-in-class work hours per function point	5.92	15.07	37.11
Average LOC per staff month in C	1,262	516	256
Best-in-class LOC per staff month in C	2,785	1,095	445
Average effort, staff months	99	2,421	48,824
Best-in-class effort, staff months	45	1,142	28,117
Average cost per function point	$1,386.78	$3,388.73	$6,835.34
Best-in-class cost per function point	$628.33	$1,598.47	$3,936.39
Average defects per function point	5.00	5.50	6.60
Best-in-class defects per function point	2.50	4.00	5.00
Average defect removal efficiency	95.00%	92.00%	89.00%
Best-in-class defect removal efficiency	99.50%	98.00%	97.00%
Average delivered defects per function point	0.250	0.440	0.726

continued

Table 9.7 *continued*

Key Software Topics	1,000 Function Points	10,000 Function Points	100,000 Function Points
Best-in-class delivered defects per function point	0.013	0.080	0.150
Average no. of delivered defects	250	4,400	72,600
Best-in-class no. of delivered defects	13	800	15,000
Average no. of high-severity defects	38	660	10,890
Best-in-class no. of high-severity defects	2	96	1,800

and application size affect the results. Therefore, monthly compensation rates are held constant so that other factors become clearly visible.

As you can see from the results in this section, the systems software domain is quite effective in software quality control. It has very respectable productivity rates for large systems (>10,000 function points) but lags at the low end.

For applications in the 100,000-function point plateau, the systems software domain is as good as it gets—with the best success rates, lowest failure rates, and highest overall quality and productivity levels. However, for smaller applications (<1,000 function points) the process rigor and specification volumes noted in the systems software domain reduce productivity rates somewhat.

The next benchmark of interest is how well systems software meets its anticipated schedules. Table 9.8 includes four columns of relevant data: projects that are early, projects that are on time relative to their formal schedules, projects that are late, and projects that are cancelled and never finished at all. The systems software domain has the best on-time completion of 100,000-function point projects, although this is not saying very much because failures and delays outnumber successes at the large end of the size spectrum.

Much of the work in the systems software domain has centered around the development of very large systems between 10,000 and 100,000 function points in size. There are thousands of ways of failing when building large systems, and only a few ways to succeed. In general, the systems software domain succeeds better than any other, but the construction of large software applications is a high-risk activity at best. Every major company has experienced failures in the large

Table 9.8   Systems Software Schedule Adherence circa 1999

Size, function points	Early Projects, %	On-time Projects, %	Late Projects, %	Cancelled Projects, %	Total Projects, %
1	6.00	90.00	3.00	1.00	100.00
10	8.00	85.00	5.00	2.00	100.00
100	10.00	78.00	8.00	4.00	100.00
1,000	5.00	68.00	17.00	10.00	100.00
10,000	3.00	40.00	32.00	25.00	100.00
100,000	1.00	35.00	34.00	30.00	100.00
Average	5.50%	66.00%	16.50%	12.00%	100.00

system domain. To optimize the probability of success for building large applications, project management, process rigor, and quality control must be at state-of-the-art levels. Any deficiencies in these three fundamental disciplines can lead to delays or outright failure.

Systems Software Successes and Failures

The systems software domain has a better ratio of successful projects to failures, cancellations, and severe overruns than any other type of software. However, when software projects climb above 10,000 function points, and especially when they climb above 100,000 function points, failures still outnumber successes, even for systems software. In general, the systems software domain produces more large applications (>10,000 function points) than other types, and has a better success record.

Table 9.9 provides an overview of the factors that are associated with successful systems software projects, and also the factors that are associated with failed or delayed projects.

Systems software is very high in algorithmic complexity and, because of timing and memory constraints, there is a need for "tight" code. Indeed, high-performance under real-time conditions is one of the driving forces of the systems software world.

Table 9.9   Systems Software Success and Failure Factors

Systems Software Success Factors	Systems Software Failure Factors
Highly reliable with excellent quality	Very unreliable with poor quality
Excellent high-speed performance	Slower than needed performance levels
Competitive feature set	Noncompetitive feature set
Meets or beats storage targets	Too large for available storage
Schedules predictable within 5%	Schedules out of control
Costs predictable within 5%	Costs out of control
Requirements stable within 5%	Requirements out of control
Conforms to major industry standards	Violates one or more industry standards
Upward compatible with prior versions	Significant incompatibilities
Plug-and-play with other components	Arcane connections and interfaces
Fully Y2K compliant	Contains latent Y2K errors

Because systems software controls physical devices such as aircraft, computers, and medical apparatus, the success and failure criteria include some quality and reliability factors that are not always present with other kinds of software. Systems software demands very high levels of reliability, and it may demand seven-day-per-week, 24-hour-per-day operation with no shutdowns.

The need to achieve high quality and high-speed performance simultaneously has caused the systems software community, as a class, to pay very close attention to quality control and to expend substantial efforts in topics such as architecture, design, and performance modeling. As it happens, close attention to quality and also care in architecture and design prior to coding tend to maximize the probability of a successful completion. On the whole, the systems software community has the best and most favorable ratio of successes to failures, and certainly the best results for large systems more than 10,000 function points in size.

The systems software successes can be attributed primarily to the strong emphasis on software quality control. Another important factor that contributes to the favorable success ratio is the fact that creeping user requirements are not as likely to occur for systems software as for other kinds of software applications. This is because many of the requirements for systems software derive from marketing and competitive analysis, rather than from the inputs of specific customers. However, from time to time requirements changes can be abrupt and major. For example, if a systems software company discovers that a competitor is about to introduce major new features, it is probable that these same features will be rushed into production as quickly as possible, even if they cause some disruption and quite a bit of overtime.

As a class, the systems software community is often equipped with the most complete set of tool suites and the most powerful development tool sets. A well-equipped software engineering group in the systems software world can have in excess of 75,000 function points of tool capacity per software engineer, which is higher than most other domains. Powerful workstations, very good development and maintenance tools, and excellent communication among development teams are common attributes noted within the systems software domain.

The fact that creeping user requirements are often comparatively benign in the systems software domain is a partial explanation for why systems software is among the most likely domains to become a major target for international outsourcing. In fact, systems software is also one of the major domains for domestic outsource contracts too, as companies such as Microsoft recognize that software demands are greater than their ability to supply software without massive expansion of personnel.

Systems Software Success Factors

From hundreds of SPR assessments and benchmark studies carried out from 1985 through early 2000, the systems software domain is among the most sophisticated of any domain in terms of software engineering tools and practices. The larger systems software companies rank among the best of all domains in a number of key software attributes. The systems software domain stands out from other classes and types of software in handling the following attributes very well indeed.

- Systems software has the best quality measurement approaches.
- Systems software has the best quality control approaches.
- Systems software has the best quality prediction tools.
- Systems software has more companies at high SEI CMM levels.
- Systems software has more ISO 9000–9004-certified companies.

- Systems software has the most complete development tool suites.
- Systems software has among the best milestone tracking systems.
- Systems software has among the best cost tracking systems.
- Systems software has more "project offices" than other types of software.
- Systems software leads in complexity analysis and reduction.
- Systems software leads in performance modeling and simulation technologies.
- Systems software has the most widespread use of formal inspections.
- Systems software has the best software process improvement strategies.
- Systems software has the most extensive reusability programs.
- Systems software has the best configuration control approaches.
- Systems software has the best complexity analysis approaches.
- Systems software leads in adopting OO approaches.
- Systems software has the best track record for systems larger than 10,000 function points.
- Systems software has the largest and most sophisticated research laboratories.
- Systems software has the best in-house training and education capabilities.
- Systems software has the best libraries and information-gathering approaches.
- Systems software has the most complete sets of software specialists.
- Systems software has the best benefit and compensation plans for staff members.

Because much of the work of the systems software domain is concerned with very large systems with high performance and reliability criteria, the systems software domain has evolved approaches that are very successful at the large end of the spectrum. The overall track record for successful completions of applications between 10,000 function points and 100,000 function points is much better for systems software than any other domain.

Systems Software Failure Factors

The downside of the systems software domain is that it is not as innovative in project management and cost estimating as some of the other areas.

- Systems software lags in the adoption of functional metrics.
- Systems software uses LOC metrics without understanding the problems.
- Systems software lags in the usage of automated cost-estimating tools.
- Systems software lags in the usage of productivity measurements.

- Systems software ranks second to the military in the production of huge volumes of paperwork.
- Systems software is sometimes troubled by layoffs and downsizings.

Several curious sociological phenomena have been noted within the systems software domain. Because function point metrics were first applied to information systems in the 1970s, the systems software domain tended to assume that function point metrics would not work on systems projects. This meant that it was difficult to get systems software projects to use function points in the 1980s because the systems domain is somewhat elitist and does not readily embrace technologies from the information systems domain.

In 1986, a variant of the function point metric called *feature points* was developed specifically to solve this sociological problem. The feature point metric added one new parameter derived from the systems software domain: a count of the algorithms that were in the application. The feature point metric also reduced the weights assigned to logical files. Feature points were first applied to telephone switching systems, and were then used for other forms of systems and embedded software.

Because feature point metrics were aimed at a sociological problem, this metric tried to conform to the numerical results of standard function points. The feature point modifications did not change the final counts for most projects. Function points and feature point totals were essentially the same for more than 90% of all projects. Only for outliers with very large numbers of algorithms, or very large numbers of logical files, would there be a difference in results between function points and feature points. Even then, the difference would usually be only 10% or so.

The feature point metric was developed in cooperation with Allan Albrecht, the inventor of function points. Indeed, the training course on function point metrics Albrecht developed for SPR in 1986 included both function points and feature points.

When productivity of systems software projects is measured using either function point or feature point metrics, the technical difficulty of systems software and the very full set of activities performed leads to rather low productivity levels. Smaller systems software projects (<1,000 function points), which are of course the most common, lag behind other domains in productivity levels except for military software, which lags behind all types. This situation has caused some metrics researchers who work in the systems software domain to criticize the use of standard function point metrics, such as the current Version 4.1 published by IFPUG.

Several recent function point variations have been developed for use with systems software projects such as Boeing 3D function points, object points, and full function points. The impetus for these metrics is to give larger function point totals to systems software projects and OO projects, and hence raise their apparent productivity levels compared with information systems. These functional metric variants typically generate much larger totals for systems software projects than standard IFPUG function points. As a result, these variants of standard function points cannot be compared directly with results published using standard IFPUG function points. Some of these variant metrics are interesting, but they tend to focus attention on the wrong problem. What is important, is to understand why systems software productivity is lower than other types of software projects (except military software). This is due to the large volumes of specifications and the extensive set of activities that are carried out.

Developing alternative function point metrics that give an artificial boost to systems software productivity due to modifications of the counting rules is not a positive step that will lead to process improvements. In fact, the alternatives are lowering the credibility of function point metrics and not adding any new insights or data to the software productivity literature, in terms of generating empirical data of productivity and quality levels. Many of the variants have so few users that the volume of published data using the variant metrics is close to zero.

Unfortunately, so many of these minor function point variants have popped up that data expressed in terms of function points is now ambiguous as the century begins. It is necessary to know which specific kind of function point is being used. Even worse, most of the variants of standard function points have no published conversion rules. The developers seem to think that their responsibility ends with the creation of a new metric variant, and someone else should carry out studies to develop conversion rules.

Due to the lack of conversion rules between function point variants and standard IFPUG function points, it is very difficult to pool or consolidate benchmark studies that use standard IFPUG function points with studies based on some of the minor variants such as Mark II function points, Boeing 3D function points, full function points, and object points. This does not happen often, of course, because the total volume of data in these minor variants is currently less than 5% of the volume of data published using standard IFPUG function points.

As this book is written, more than 125,000 projects have been measured using standard function points. There is no exact count of the projects measured using the minor variants, but the total is probably less than 5,000—even when all the variants are added together. Even so, it would be helpful if the developers of these alternative metrics had developed conversion rules between their variations and standard IFPUG function points. For that matter, there are no conversion rules between the variations either. For example, if the same project is measured using Mark II function points, full function points, and Boeing 3D function points, what would the results be? As this book is written, no such studies have been performed.

It should not be forgotten that Albrecht, the inventor of function point metrics, is an electrical engineer by training and background. The original function point metric developed in the 1970s was always planned as a general metric that could support systems software, information systems, and military projects.

In theory, the systems software domain should be a world leader in software reusability. However, the outsourcing community and even the commercial software world have been significantly ahead of the systems domain in day-to-day reuse between about 1985 and 1995, based on SPR assessments and benchmark studies during that time period.

Even the military world, which is often conservative, is doing excellent research on reusability. On the other hand, since about 1995, the systems software world has had a number of large and well-funded research programs underway aimed at achieving world leadership in software reuse. Every major systems company in the size range of AT&T, Siemens, Nippon Telegraph, or IBM is now exploring software reuse in a number of well-staffed research programs.

Because many systems software projects are highly complex and have severe timing constraints, the development cycles for systems software are not particularly fast. However, the systems software community has long recognized this problem and has introduced some reasonably effective approaches to minimize the consequences. One of the notable approaches is the concept of fixed release intervals at 12- or 18-month periods for bringing out major new features.

The larger systems software applications, such as AT&T's 5ESS switching system, Alcatel's System 12, or IBM's MVS operating system operate on fixed release cycles, and new capabilities are slotted into specific releases. Because the release intervals are well-known and firm, all managers tend to know how to size and schedule features to meet the constraints.

On the whole, the large systems software companies are very capable in the production of large real-time software systems. They are much better than average for systems in excess of 10,000 function points. Only the civilian systems software domain and the military software domain have attempted successfully to implement systems in the 100,000-function point range. Of course both systems and military projects do fail at the large end of the spectrum, but they succeed more than information systems or commercial software applications. The outsource community is also fairly capable at the large end of the spectrum for similar reasons, such as using formal quality control approaches.

Because systems software is often associated with advanced technologies in other domains such as electrical engineering or telecommunications, the systems software domain has benefited from some of the research tools long available to electrical engineers and telecommunication engineers: good libraries, good reference sources, and well-funded research and development laboratories.

Best Technical Practices for Systems Software

The systems software domain is the most sophisticated of any kind of software production in all forms of software quality control, including use of formal inspections, all types of testing, and measurement of defect levels. Because best-practice information derives from assessment and benchmark studies, this section is organized using the same set of ten key factors that are examined during SPR assessments and benchmarks.

1. Project management methods such as estimating
2. Requirements-gathering and analysis methods
3. Design and specification methods
4. Coding methods
5. Reusability methods
6. Change control methods
7. User documentation methods
8. Pretest defect removal methods such as inspections
9. Testing methods and tools
10. Maintenance methods and tools

To be cited, the sets of practices termed *best practices for systems software* have been used within at least 50 successful projects within ten companies. In the opinions of the project managers and technical personnel, the practices need to have contributed to a successful outcome. Furthermore, to be included in the set of best practices, the practices must not have been cited as contributing to failures, overruns, or litigation for breach of contract. In other words, these are practices that add positive value.

Best Project Management Practices for Systems Software

Project management is a key technology for every domain, and one of the critical factors that differentiates successful projects from failures and disasters. Excellence in project management is associated with almost 100% of successful projects for projects larger than 1,000 function points. Inadequate estimates, careless planning, and inadequate tracking are associated with very close to 100% of project failures.

Major systems software producers such as IBM, AT&T, Lucent, and Motorola have been pioneers in several aspects of software project management. For controlling larger projects in the systems software domain, it is common to utilize a formal *project office* that provides support to project managers in terms of schedule planning, cost estimating, and milestone tracking. The set of systems software best practices in project management include those presented in the following subsections.

Process Improvement Programs

Because both assessments and benchmarks are diagnostic studies rather than therapies, it is appropriate to follow such studies with planned process improvement programs that can eliminate or minimize the problems that were noted. It is a best practice in the systems software domain to implement process improvement programs following assessments and benchmark studies.

Annual Assessments and Benchmarks

An assessment or benchmark study is like a snapshot at a moment in time. Once a company undertakes process improvement work, it is useful to have follow-on assessments and external benchmarks. A best practice in the systems software domain is to have process assessments on an annual basis, and external benchmark studies approximately every two years. It is also a best practice to have formal productivity and quality measurements in the intervening periods. Quality data should be summarized and published monthly. Productivity data needs to be reported annually.

Project Offices

For systems software applications larger than 10,000 function points, a formal *project office* should be established for overall schedule planning, cost estimating, cost tracking, and milestone tracking. The staff of the project office should be well equipped with planning tools, cost-estimating tools, and quality-estimating tools. The staff should be experienced in the principles of large-project management. (Less than 1,000 function points, project offices are seldom encountered and are not a best practice. Their value rises with the size of the application.)

Estimating Specialists

For applications larger than 10,000 function points, the use of trained software cost-estimating specialists is a best practice. Less than 10,000 function points, cost estimates prepared by project managers is the norm. These estimating specialists are normally equipped with at least two software cost-estimating tools. Some of the cost-estimating tools encountered in the systems software domain include CHECKPOINT, COCOMO II, KnowledgePlan, Price-S, SEER, and SLIM, all of which support systems software estimation.

Project Management Training

All systems software project managers should be trained in software sizing, cost estimating, quality estimating, milestone tracking, and cost tracking. All project managers should be able to create accurate plans and estimates for projects at least 1,000 function points in size. Entry-level training on promotion to project manager is a definite best practice. Setting aside five to ten days a year for project management training is a somewhat best practice. The in-house curricula for management training in the larger companies of the systems software domain compares very favorably with all other types of software, and with university training as well. However, management training for software project managers is not as sophisticated as technical training for software engineers, in general.

Project Management Tool Suites

All systems software project managers should be trained in and have available a suite of project management tools, including sizing of key deliverables, cost and resource estimating, quality estimating, standard project management for critical path analysis, cost tracking, and milestone tracking capabilities. Tools supporting process assessments are also a best practice, as are tools for risk and value analysis. Project managers in leading companies use at least 20,000 function points of project management tools.

Personnel Management Tool Suites

Personnel management tools for appraisals, skills inventories, and job planning support are also a best practice for systems software in the United States, but not in Europe, where they may be prohibited.

Activity-Based Cost Estimates

All systems software cost estimates for projects larger than 1,000 function points should be at the activity or task levels. Project-level or phase-level estimates are inadequate for large projects. Estimation for small projects can be at the phase level, but for large projects this is an unsafe and hazardous practice.

Function Point Analysis

All systems software project managers should be trained in the basics of function point analysis. Managers do not need to be certified function point counters, however. All productivity and quality studies, and benchmarks, should include function point analysis. LOC metrics are hazardous for cross-language comparisons. It is actually a best practice to utilize both function point metrics and LOC for benchmark studies. LOC metrics alone are inaccurate enough to be deemed professional malpractice in situations in which multiple programming languages are used. Function point metrics alone are suitable for benchmarks, but collecting both function point and LOC metrics can demonstrate why LOC metrics are hazardous. Unless LOC metrics are collected too, it may be difficult to explain why they are hazardous. However, the combined use of function points and LOC metrics for similar projects developed using different programming languages can demonstrate why LOC metrics are dangerous for economic analysis.

Empirical Data

All systems software project managers should know the ranges of quality and productivity levels derived from empirical studies for the kinds of software for which they are responsible. In particular, project managers should know defect removal efficiency levels and productivity levels for systems software projects. Otherwise, it is difficult for managers to defend accurate estimates against arbitrary overrides by clients and senior executives.

Capability Maturity Model

A frequent best practice in the systems software domain is the utilization of the CMM published by the SEI. Not only is the CMM widely used within the systems software domain, but approximately 35% of our systems software clients have been at level 3 or higher in the sites or programming labs that have commissioned our benchmark studies. The systems software domain has more companies at the higher CMM levels than any other type, although military software is roughly equal. This is true abroad as well as in the United States. Of course, there is probably a bias in our data because companies at the higher CMM levels are much more likely to commission benchmark studies than those at CMM level 1. The adoption of the SEI CMM by the civilian systems software domain is a fairly recent phenomenon, which has been accelerating since about 1995. This trend can be expected to expand.

Milestone Tracking

All systems software projects larger than 100 function points should use formal milestone tracking. This is a best practice that can minimize the odds of unpleasant problems such as major schedule delays, or can at least provide an early warning. Major milestones include completion of requirements, external specifications, internal specifications, inspection plans, design inspections, code inspections, test plans, all forms of testing, risk analysis plans, performance analysis plans, user documentation, and installation.

Activity Cost Tracking

All systems software projects larger than 100 function points should use formal cost tracking at the activity level. Normalized costs such as "cost per function point" are also a best practice. Costs based on LOC are optional, but are not a best practice. Indeed, if LOC metrics are the only productivity measure, it constitutes professional malpractice. Use of both LOC metrics and function points together are also a best practice.

Project Postmortems

A best practice often encountered for systems software but applicable to any type is that of a postmortem at the end of the project. The purpose of this meeting of the software team is to analyze the processes used and point out areas of strength and weakness. In recent years this practice has often been replaced by a formal assessment and benchmark analysis at the end of the project, which serves the same purpose but gathers additional data.

Because of the caveat that best practices need to have been observed in at least ten companies and 50 projects, some very interesting practices are not deployed often enough to be included at present. For example the earned-value cost tracking approach and the balanced-scorecard measurement approach have only been encountered a few times, but appear to be useful management practices. As the usage of these approaches expands, they may join the set of best practices in the future.

Best Requirements-Gathering and Analysis Practices for Systems Software

Requirements gathering and analysis in the systems software domain overlaps the approaches used by commercial software. The reason for this is because some of the requirements for systems software projects stem from marketing and competitive studies, rather than being the requests of specific clients. For example, for systems software projects such as telephone switching systems, each major vendor needs to compete with other major vendors, and all need to support similar feature sets. However, systems software requirements are unusual because features are apportioned between hardware and software. Therefore, both hardware and software personnel need to cooperate. Some of the best practices for requirements gathering and analysis in the systems software domain include those presented in the following subsections.

Formal Requirements

Systems software requirements are normally formal documents and average about 0.5 pages per function point. Many systems software producers have standard formats for requirements. The creation of formal requirements is a best practice for new projects and major enhancements in the systems software domain. (Note that overall system requirements include both hardware and software requirements. This discussion is for the software portions only.)

Requirements Inspections

For systems software, requirements inspections are a best practice and occur more often for systems software than for other types. The inspection team for systems software requirements includes hardware engineers, marketing and sales personnel, client representatives, and project technical personnel.

Requirements Tracing

A best practice in both the systems and military software domains is requirements tracing. Each feature in the design and code of an application should be traced back to a specific requirement.

Performance Requirements

Because performance issues are often critical for systems software projects and embedded projects, requirements include performance targets and prototypes that are aimed at judging performance levels.

Quality and Reliability Requirements

A best practice in the systems software domain is to include specific quality and reliability targets in the requirements themselves. Quality can be expressed in terms of incoming defects reported after deployment, defect removal efficiency, or both. Reliability can be expressed in terms of mean time to failure or mean time between failures. Although it has not been encountered enough to be included as a best practice, QFD is becoming a useful tool for expressing the quality requirements of systems software projects.

Requirements Notations

Systems software requirements often utilize formal notations such as the UML, state transition diagrams, Petri nets, and a number of others. This class of notation is deemed a best practice, although the specific notation varies based on the needs of the project.

Requirements Segmentation

A best practice for systems and embedded software requirements includes a formal segmentation of the features to be embodied in hardware, microcode, and software. Also, formal requirements tracing is a best practice for systems software. That is, each feature should be traced back to a specific requirement.

Function Point Size

A best practice for systems software projects is to include function point size derivations from the requirements themselves. Once function point totals are known, they provide a useful baseline for measuring the rate of requirements creep. The systems software domain is somewhat volatile in terms of requirements stability, and changes or additions to requirements can top 3% per calendar month during the design and coding phases. Function point totals are also used for sizing various deliverables, and are a key input to software cost and quality estimates.

Requirements Defects

A best practice in the systems software domain is to measure the numbers and severities of defects or errors found in the requirements themselves. The systems software domain measures requirements defects fairly often, and was the first to note that requirements contribute approximately one defect per function point to overall system totals. The use of formal requirements inspections and requirements tracing makes this task feasible. Much of the empirical data on error rates found in requirements stems from the systems software domain. The systems software domain was the first to realize that approximately 15% of all software errors originate in the requirements themselves. In fact, many of the formal and more powerful software requirements methods originated in the systems software domain.

Best Design and Specification Practices for Systems Software

The systems software domain ranks number two out of all types of software in terms of volume and completeness of specifications. (Military software ranks number one.) The systems software domain is also fairly active in research on specification methods. As a result of research and pioneering studies, the systems software domain uses techniques such as state transition diagrams and Petri nets, which are seldom deployed on projects other than those in the systems and embedded software domains. Best practices noted within the systems software domain include those presented in the following subsections.

Architecture Specifications

A best practice for systems software projects larger than 10,000 function points is the creation of a formal architecture specification, in addition to the more frequently encountered external and internal specification documents. An architecture specification addresses the important topics of how features are to be apportioned across the hardware, microcode, and software portions of hybrid systems projects. The systems software domain may employ architecture specialists for this key activity. Architecture specialists are seldom encountered in other types of software, but are often employed by companies such as IBM and AT&T, which construct large systems software applications.

Specification Segmentation

Because the specifications for large systems software projects are quite large and unusually complete, a best practice is to segment them into a multivolume set, with each volume containing the details of a specific topic. A typical example includes requirements specifications, architecture specifications, external design specifications, internal or logical design specifications, and database specifications. Each specification is under formal change control and goes through multiple iterations.

Prototypes

A best practice for systems software projects is the creation of prototypes for key features and algorithms. The two most common forms of prototype used for systems software are disposable prototypes and time-box prototypes. A time-box prototype has a chronological limit, and must be completed within a specific period, such as one calendar month. The use of evolutionary prototypes is not a best practice because the lack of structure in prototypes makes them unsuited for applications with high quality and reliability targets. Normally, systems software prototypes amount to approximately 10% of the functionality of the finished application. The prototypes concentrate on key algorithms and performance issues.

Design Inspections

A best practice for systems software projects of all sizes, and for enhancements as well as new projects, is the use of formal design inspections on all specification documents. The rationale for this is due to the fact that software designs and specifications contribute roughly 1.25 defects per function point. Worse, design defects are often higher in severity than coding defects. Formal design inspections as used in the systems and embedded domain are derived from the pioneering work on inspections carried out by IBM, and are described in a number of books and articles such as the numerous works of Michael Fagan, Dr. Gerald Weinberg, and Thomas Gilb. Formal design inspections are very effective in defect removal, and average more than 65% efficiency in finding and removing design errors. Some inspections have topped 85% in defect removal efficiency. Inspections also serve as a defect prevention approach too, because participants will avoid problems in their own work that are pointed out during the inspection sessions. The systems software domain uses formal design inspections more often than any other domain, which explains, in part, why systems software quality is better than any other domain.

Performance Analysis

Because performance issues are critical to systems and embedded software applications, several best practices involve performance analysis, models, and prototypes. The systems and embedded software domains often employ "performance specialists." This title refers to software engineers who specialize in all topics associated with accelerating throughput and response time of software applications. The systems and embedded software domains also employ fairly sophisticated performance modeling techniques, and often develop specialized performance prototypes to judge the speed of key transactions.

Reusable Specifications

An interesting best practice in the systems and embedded software domains is that of reusable designs and specifications. Software reuse includes more than a dozen artifacts, with specifications among the most important. What enables reusable specifications in the systems and embedded software domains is often the use of specification methods that support both formalisms and reusability. These approaches include UML and some of the older OO specification approaches as well. Also deployed within the systems software domain are state transition diagrams and several forms of structured design, such as the Yourdon and Stevens structured design approaches.

Best Coding Practices for Systems Software

The systems software domain was among the first to employ formal programming structure techniques. Indeed, many of the pioneers of structured programming, such as Wayne Stevens, Larry Constantine, Edgar Dijkstra, and Dr. Harlan Mills, all worked in the systems software domain. It became obvious in the early 1960s, when software first started to control physical devices, that better methods were needed to ensure necessary levels of quality and reliability. Therefore, the systems and embedded software domains have been among the most active in pursuing research on all aspects of software design and development.

Structured Programming

A definite best practice within the systems and embedded software domains is that of using formal program structure techniques that optimize binding and coupling, and minimize control flow complexity. In fact, most of the common forms of structured programming were invented and first deployed on behalf of systems and embedded programming. The ultimate reason for this is because systems and embedded software need very high levels of quality and reliability. Not only are formal structured coding methods used, but the major systems software companies are among the best in using in-house training for imparting structuring skills to new employees.

Comment Density and Style

It is a best practice for all domains to utilize both module prologs and comments to explain key features and algorithms of programs. Studies performed within IBM found that comments approximately every ten statements was the density at which clarity seemed to peak. Fewer comments made it hard to understand the code. Surprisingly, too many comments also reduced code legibility. The reason that many comments lowered code reading comprehension was because the readers tended to put too much credence in the comments, and some of them may not have been fully accurate. When reading code, it is necessary to read both the code and the comments. The comments serve to explain unusual algorithms or special conditions.

Mnemonic Labels

It is a best practice to use labels for variables and branch instructions that are clear and easy to remember, if possible. Abstract labels such as "routine2" may make it hard for new programmers to understand logic flow. It is a bad practice to use labels that have quirky or private meanings, such as using the names of relatives or movie stars.

Code Inspections

More than any other type of software, the systems and embedded software domains are likely to utilize the best practice of formal code inspections. Not only are formal code inspections used, but the inspections may include 100% of the modules of major systems, as opposed to partial or subset inspections encountered in many other types of software. Formal inspections were first developed in the 1960s within IBM as a method of ensuring the quality and reliability levels of IBM's system software, such as OS/360, which was the precursor to IBM's current MVS operating system. Formal code inspections have the highest defect removal efficiency level of any known removal activity, and they are roughly twice as efficient as most forms of testing. Formal code inspections average 65% in defect removal efficiency, and have approached 90% in some trials. There is no better method for ensuring high quality and reliability levels.

Complexity Analysis

A best practice often encountered within the systems and embedded software domains is the use of complexity analysis tools. Because high levels of code complexity as measured with the common metrics of cyclomatic and essential complexity are known to degrade quality and lower the efficiency of defect removal operations, software that has high reliability criteria should use automated methods of complexity analysis. Once modules are identified as being too complex for safe operation, they can then be recoded or redeveloped.

Error-Prone Module Elimination

A definite best coding practice within the systems and embedded software domains concerns seeking and eliminating error-prone modules. In the 1960s, IBM discovered that coding errors or bugs in large systems were not distributed randomly. They tended to clump in a small number of modules, which were assigned the title of *error-prone modules*. Once discovered, it became imperative to remove or repair these troublesome entities. The method for dealing with error-prone modules is to give them a formal inspection, and then either restructure them, repair them, or redevelop them based on the recommendation of the inspection team.

Module-Level Defect Tracking

Another best practice in the systems software domain is that of defect tracking methods and tools that are granular enough to identify error-prone modules. Indeed, the systems software domain has the best and most thorough defect tracking and measurement tools and methods of any known form of software. Defects are tracked by severity level, origin, and, in particular, are tracked down to the level of specific modules.

Performance Analysis

Because quality and performance are both critical topics within the systems and embedded software domains, another best practice for systems software is the use of sophisticated techniques for predicting, measuring, and improving software performance levels. During the coding phase, systems and embedded applications have their throughputs and response times monitored, and also utilize special kinds of performance test stages. In addition, performance specialists may be called in to tune or refine critical modules or control paths that might be suspected of degrading performance levels.

Programming Languages

Although the choice and use of a programming language is not by itself a best practice, it is significant that the systems software domain has actually developed a number of programming languages aimed at the special problems encountered in systems and embedded software. Among the languages developed specifically for systems and embedded software are C, C++, Objective C, CORAL, CHILL, Forth, and PL/S. Note that many of these languages are object oriented. The systems software domain has been a pioneer in OO programming.

Best Reusability Practices for Systems Software

Because systems software is expensive in terms of cost and lengthy in terms of schedules, major developers have often been pioneers in methods that can improve software productivity without damaging quality and reliability.

Software reuse is a key technology that can benefit cost, schedule, and quality simultaneously. This explains why many major systems software producers such as AT&T, IBM, Motorola, and Hewlett-Packard endorse and support software reusability programs. Indeed, among our clients, software reusability research is more often encountered in the systems software domain than any other. This is a fairly recent phenomenon because our assessment and benchmark studies between 1985 and 1990 did not turn up any significant volume of reuse in systems software projects.

The research efforts into software reusability in the systems software domain were triggered partly by the OO phenomenon and partly by the fact that other avenues of study were turning out to be dead ends, or at least were not as effective as desired. For example, research into software reuse began to accelerate at about the same time that it was realized that CASE was more hype than reality. It was also realized that approaches such as RAD were not really adequate for large software systems with high quality and reliability goals, which are common among systems and embedded software projects.

The systems software domain is in an excellent position to expand the volume of reusable material due to its long tradition of high quality and reliability. Unless reusable material is very close to zero-defect levels, attempts to reuse anything is expensive and hazardous. Only high-quality materials are adequate for successful reuse. This means that the solid tradition of excellence in achieving high quality levels noted in the systems software domain is a good jumping-off place for accumulating libraries of reusable materials that can be reused without excessive recalls for errors or defects.

A complete software reusability program encompasses from six to more than ten software artifacts including

1. Reusable requirements
2. Reusable external specifications
3. Reusable architecture and internal specifications
4. Reusable database designs and data structures
5. Reusable project plans and estimates
6. Reusable source code
7. Reusable quality and test plans
8. Reusable test cases
9. Reusable user documentation
10. Reusable HELP text

In general, the systems software domain has concentrated on four aspects of reuse in which this domain is now better than average:

1. Reusable requirements
2. Reusable architecture and specifications
3. Reusable source code
4. Reusable quality and test plans

Unfortunately the systems software domain has not achieved a leadership position with any of the other potentially reusable artifacts, such as database structures, user documentation, and project plans.

Best practices for software reusability noted within the systems software domain cover four of the major artifacts, although far more research effort has been given to code reuse than to any other artifact.

Reusable Requirements

The use of formal requirements methods and requirements models using techniques such as UML is a best practice that can lead to reusable requirements. In addition, the use of formal requirements inspections raises the probability of reusing successfully some or all of the requirements from one application for other applications.

Reusable Designs

The use of formal design inspections is a best practice that improves the prognosis of reusing specifications and design documents. The frequent use of formal inspections for systems software raises the odds that portions of these specifications can be reused in similar applications.

Code Inspections

The use of formal code inspections is a best practice that improves the prognosis of reusing source code modules and components. Prior to placing a candidate reusable module into a reuse library, it should be subjected to a 100% formal code inspection. The use of code inspections for systems software raises the probability of successful code reuse.

Test Plan and Test Case Inspections

The use of test plan and test case inspections, plus formal regression test libraries and test library control procedures, can raise the probability of successful reuse of test materials in the systems software domain. Prior to being reused, both test plans and test cases should be given a thorough 100% inspection. To date, only the systems software domain has utilized formal inspections for test plans and test cases among SPR's clients. Because uninspected test cases may have serious errors, reusing test cases without subjecting them to inspection is not a best practice and, indeed, is a hazardous practice.

Some interesting reusability practices have not yet been utilized by enough of our clients to determine whether they will become best practices. The most significant practice is *component-based development*. As this book is written, few of our clients use component-based development, few components are actually available, and the results of component development are ambiguous. In fact, failures and problems based on components actually outnumber successes.

Although OO reuse and class libraries are fairly common among our clients, the OO results are not positive enough for definite inclusion of this practice in the set of best practices. For one thing, the failure rate of first-time OO projects is approximately 50%. For another, the productivity and quality levels of the completed OO projects are sometimes no better than ordinary procedural projects. Finally, in spite of the many claims of reusability put forth in the OO domain, the volume of reusable artifacts noted on OO projects actually lags behind the volume noted using other approaches. For example, reusable test materials are rare in the OO domain.

Best Change Control Practices for Systems Software

Change control is a complex and demanding technical challenge for any kind of software project. Fortunately there are tools and approaches available that can ease the difficulties somewhat, although change control is never trivial.

For systems software projects, changes during development can occur for a much wider variety of reasons than those found with internal information systems. Because systems software controls physical devices, many of which are on the commercial market, some late changes in systems software feature sets are due to competitive situations. For example, if a company producing systems software discovers that a competitor is offering a useful new feature, then the marketing or sales group may deem it mandatory to offer the same feature in the next planned release, regardless of whether this is convenient for the software development teams. Best practices in change control for systems software include those presented the following subsections.

Change Control Boards

For all projects larger than 10,000 function points it is a best practice to utilize a formal change control board. This board is usually comprised of three to seven personnel. The representatives include the primary client, the project office, the development team, and the hardware portion of the application. Marketing and sales may participate too, although these organizations are usually the sources of change rather than the final decision makers. The purpose of the change control board is to review suggested changes, prioritize them, and assign them to a specific release.

Automated Change Control

The software artifacts that are subject to change include requirements, architecture, external specifications, internal specifications, database specifications, all quality and test plans, and all user documentation and training materials. Because of the wide variety of changing artifacts, it is a best practice to have fully automated change control systems that can handle all major deliverables. The change control package should facilitate identifying links between artifacts, such as determining what code needs to be changed in response to a requirements or design change. Automated change control tools that support only source code are not adequate for projects larger than 100 function points.

Function Point Metrics for Changes

It is a best practice to estimate and measure the function point totals of all changes to software projects. The function point data can be used for charge-backs and billing, and also to ascertain the monthly rate of requirements creep. However, changes to software applications can exist for several discrete kinds of modification. The most common form of change is adding a new feature. This is called *scope creep* or *requirements creep*. Less common but still a daily event is the removal of a feature, or at least its deferral to a later release because it cannot be finished in time for the current release. A more ambiguous form of change is termed *requirements churn*. This complex topic deals with modifying features in such a way that the function point totals do not increase or decrease. An example of requirements churn is changing the placement of data on an input screen without adding any new kinds of input. Simply moving an input segment from one place to another for aesthetic reasons often occurs.

Cost Estimates for Changes

Cost-estimating changes and cost measurement of changes are both difficult. The best practice for major change estimation is to use automated estimation tools and function point metrics. The best practice for small changes less than 15 function points is to use "backfiring," or Direct conversion from LOC metrics to function point metrics.

Requirements Tracing and Changes

A best practice shared between the systems software and military software domains is that of requirements tracing. That is, each design feature and even each code module can be traced back to a specific requirement, either explicitly or implicitly. Requirements tracking requires fairly sophisticated automation, and also demands a formal change control board.

Best User Documentation Practices for Systems Software

The development and production of manuals, tutorial materials, HELP screens, and "wizards" is a weak link in the software industry. Complaints about poor documents are just as common as complaints about poor software quality, and have as much justification. However, the systems software domain has been fairly energetic in trying to produce excellent user materials, even if these attempts are not totally successful.

Technical Writers

A best practice that was pioneered by the systems software domain as long ago as the early 1960s is the use of professional writers, editors, and graphics personnel for the production of user manuals and tutorial materials. The technical writing, editing, and graphics personnel of some large systems software companies such as IBM can top 5% of overall software employment. Systems software and commercial software have the largest concentration of professional technical writers. Because technical writing is a fairly rare skill, only professional writers can create manuals and tutorials that are clear enough to be effective.

Professional Editors

An obvious best practice that is rare for software is to use professional editors as well as professional technical writers. Although this is a best practice in terms of results, it is only found among a handful of very large corporations. However, professional editors are found more often in the systems software domain than any other, with commercial software taking second place.

Document Inspections

A best practice that is shared among systems software and military software is to utilize formal document inspections, in addition to more conventional copy editing and fact checking. The formal inspections include software engineers and sometimes even clients, and examine the documents page by page.

Document Models

A best practice for new technical writers just joining a company is to provide them with a collection of manuals and tutorial materials voted "excellent" by means of user satisfaction surveys. This approach was pioneered by IBM in the 1960s and has yielded very good results. It works best within large corporations that have scores of manuals and tutorial books available.

Usability Laboratories

A best practice that is found primarily among systems software is that of usability laboratories. Companies such as IBM and AT&T pioneered usability labs in the late 1960s, although the total number of such labs worldwide is probably less than 100 even today. In these usability labs, customer volunteers attempt to exercise software applications for normal business, using only the manuals and tutorial materials to be provided with the application. Their success or failure is monitored by human factors specialists, sometimes supported by one-way mirrors or video cameras. Internal documents such as maintenance manuals can be studied via usability labs, as well as user manuals and external documents.

Reader Suggestions

A fairly minor best practice for systems software is to supply reader comment forms for correcting errors and pointing out problems as part of every published document. On-line reader comments sent in via the Internet or Web are also encompassed under this best practice.

CD-ROM Documents

A very rare best practice is the production of animated or dynamic tutorial materials in the form of CD-ROM, DVD, or videotapes. The purpose is to lead users through the sequence of activities required to use fairly complex applications.

Hypertext Links

A best practice for all user manuals is to include a detailed index with cross-references. Hypertext links for on-line documents should also be included under this best practice.

Graphics and Illustrations

A best practice for all user manuals is the inclusion of a significant volume of graphical materials, as opposed to using pure text. The graphical materials need to be clear and cogent to be effective. Those produced by professional graphics illustrators are often most effective.

Working Examples

A very common best practice found not only in systems software but in all kinds of software is the utilization of actual examples of key features. The examples take a user step by step through the process of invoking a function, using it, and then turning it off or moving to something else when finished.

Best Quality Control and Pretest Defect Removal Practices for Systems Software

Because the requirement for high levels of quality and reliability for complex machinery is older than the software industry, the systems software domain has developed the largest and most sophisticated set of quality control approaches of any software domain. When software began to control complex machinery such as aircraft, switching systems, medical equipment, and computers, the software had to be at least as reliable as the hardware in order for these hybrid machines to operate.

Requirements Inspections

A best practice found in several domains, including systems software, is the use of formal inspections for requirements as well as for other key deliverable items. Requirements inspections can minimize downstream requirements creep. Also, once requirements errors do pass downstream they are remarkably resistant to any other form of defect removal, such as testing. It should never be forgotten that the Y2K problem originated as an explicit requirement from clients to save storage space. Indeed, the two-digit date format was both a formal corporate requirement and a military software requirement from 1965 through 1995.

Design and Code Inspections

The most important best practice for systems software quality is the usage of formal design and code inspections. More inspections are used for systems software than for all other kinds of software put together. More than 80% of systems software projects larger than 1,000 function points among our clients have used formal inspections. Formal inspections were originally created specifically for systems software at IBM's Kingston Programming Laboratory in the early 1970s. Since then, formal inspections have been shown repeatedly to have the highest levels of defect removal efficiency of any known form of removal. Both design and code inspections have averaged more than 65% in defect removal efficiency in repeated trials, and have topped 85% in some cases. Inspections are approximately twice as efficient in removing defects as any form of testing. Formal inspections also serve as a defect prevention method because participants quickly learn what kinds of problems to avoid in their own work. The usage of formal design and code inspections is the only known way for elevating defect removal efficiency levels above 95%. (This is a fact that Microsoft would do well to emulate.)

Software Quality Assurance

Another important best practice in which systems software leads all other types is in the usage of professional software quality assurance personnel. Many of the major systems software producers such as IBM, AT&T, Siemens, and Hewlett-Packard have well-staffed and well-equipped software quality assurance departments. At IBM, for example, the software quality assurance departments represent almost 10% of the total software employment of the major programming laboratories. The functions of the software quality assurance departments include defect estimation, defect measurements, moderating formal inspections, monitoring ISO 9000–9004 practices, and teaching courses in quality topics. Note that these groups are not testing departments, although they do perform some specialized kinds of testing such as standard adherence testing.

Quality Research Laboratories

A fairly rare best practice encountered only in very large corporations such as IBM, AT&T, Lucent, or Hewlett-Packard is that of quality research departments. For example the software quality research group at IBM in San Jose developed IBM's first integrated quality and cost estimation tool in 1973. This group also collected data that proved that complete elimination of error-prone modules could be accomplished. These quality research teams are not large numerically, but may top a dozen software engineers and research specialists in major software laboratories whose overall population is near 1,000 personnel. Although such research groups are neither large nor common, they have been very fruitful in developing innovative approaches. For example, formal design and code inspections, reliability models, software quality estimation tools, defect removal efficiency metrics, clean room development practices, and error-prone module analysis were all pioneered within software quality laboratories.

Error-Prone Module Elimination

A very significant best practice in the systems software domain is prevention and removal of error-prone modules. IBM discovered in the early 1970s that software defects in large systems tended to clump in a small number of very buggy modules. Complexity analysis, module-level defect tracking, formal inspections followed by either repairs or redevelopment, plus assigning numeric quality targets to executives can stamp out error-prone modules and prevent their recurrence.

Quality Measurements

A best practice that originated in the systems software domain in the 1960s is that of formal quality measurements and defect-tracking measurements. The current state of the art of software quality measurement starts the measures early, during requirements. Once the quality measures begin, they are kept up for the entire life of the project so that data is accumulated during development, usage, and many years of enhancements and maintenance. Topics measured include defect numbers, defect severity levels, defect origins, defect removal methods, and complexity of the application and its modules. Other measures include valid and invalid defects, abeyant defects that cannot be replicated, incidents that may or may not be defects, defect repair intervals, and resource and cost data. Quality and defect tracking is highly automated in the systems software domain using either commercial or proprietary defect tracking and quality measurement tools.

Quality Estimation Tools

A best practice pioneered by the systems software domain in the 1970s is the usage of quality and defect estimation tools to predict the probable number of bugs that might be encountered, and the set of defect prevention and removal operations to be used. IBM developed the first software quality estimation tool circa 1973. Quality estimation tools can predict the numbers of bugs or errors in requirements, specifications, source code, user documents, and bad fixes or secondary defects. Severity levels are also predicted. The tools can also predict the specific defect removal efficiency of each review, inspection, or test stage. The final predictions are the numbers of latent defects remaining at delivery, and how many of those will be found by customers.

Reliability Models

Several of the major reliability models such as those of John Musa were created in the systems software domain. For example, John Musa was at AT&T when he published most of his work on reliability models. These models are concerned with mean time to failure and mean time between failures of production systems. Reliability modeling is a best practice for systems and embedded applications for which outages have severe consequences, such as telephone switching systems, medical instruments, or electric power control equipment.

Risk Analysis

A best practice in the systems software domain is the production of a formal risk analysis for the project at or near the completion of the requirements phase. A formal risk analysis considers technical, financial, and schedule risks.

Executive Quality Targets

A best practice found primarily in the systems software domain is setting targets for defect removal efficiency levels and delivered defects. In the 1970s IBM pioneered this approach, and actually included quality targets as part of the bonus plans for software executives. For example, a target might be to achieve more than 97% defect removal efficiency measured during the first 90 days of customer usage. Another target might be to drop below 0.01 valid unique defects per function point in the first 90 days of customer usage.

SEI CMM

A fairly recent quality best practice for systems software, first noted circa 1995, is for systems software companies to achieve level 3 or higher on the SEI CMM. Although the SEI CMM started as a practice for military software, the SEI CMM has been widely utilized within systems software and other civilian types of software. In fact, adoption of SEI principles is now found more widely within the systems domain than any other as of 1999.

Software Quality Standards

It is a best practice for systems software to have a formal standards program in place, and to require that each major project cite the standards that are being followed (or not). However, many international standards are not really complete enough to be the sole guideline for quality purposes. Therefore, standards such as IEEE and ISO quality standards may be followed, but the leading systems software companies also have internal corporate standards that are often better and more complete than international standards. In fact, empirical data on defect removal supports the hypothesis that good corporate standards correlate more closely to high quality levels than adherence to any of the more common international quality standard.

Recall the caveat at the start of this section that to be considered a best practice, a method must have been deployed successfully within ten companies and used on at least 50 projects. This caveat prevents some interesting quality approaches from being deemed best practices as this book is drafted in 1999. In the future, some of these practices will no doubt join the set of best practices if their long-range results are as good as their preliminary results. The emerging candidates for future best practices include the usage of IBM's new "orthogonal" defect classification system, the use of QFD for software projects, and the use of Motorola's "six-sigma" quality targets.

There are several quality practices that are often encountered in the systems software domain that are not included as best practices. The reason for this is that these practices do not appear to improve quality in any tangible way. The most common of these practices is ISO 9000–9004 certification. Many of our clients are certified using ISO standards such as 9001 for software, and their quality is quite good. But similar projects produced by similar companies that are not certified achieve similar quality levels. Achieving ISO certification may be necessary to do business with the European Union, but because the certification is expensive and does not make a tangible improvement in quality, it cannot be considered a best practice in a technical sense.

Another practice for which data is insufficient, at least among our clients, is the usage of IBM's clean room testing approach. Here, too, projects using the clean room method and similar projects not using this method have roughly the same defect levels.

Best Testing Practices and Tools for Systems Software

The systems software domain has long been a leader in software testing. This domain performs more kinds of tests than any other type of software, uses more test tools, and has more professional test personnel.

Test Specialists

A best practice found more often in the systems software domain than any other is the employment of professional testing personnel and the usage of test departments. These professional test personnel normally take over testing after the developers have completed code inspections and unit test. The forms of testing assigned to professional test groups include regression test, performance test, capacity or load test, integration test, lab tests using special equipment, human factors test, and system test. Integration and change control may also be performed by these test departments. The professional test departments also coordinate external beta tests, and work with clients during acceptance test. The total complement of personnel in these test organizations can approach or even exceed 25% of software employment. Professional test groups are approximately 5% more efficient in each test stage than the same stage carried out by the developers themselves.

Test Plan and Test Case Inspections

An additional testing best practice found primarily in major corporations such as IBM and AT&T is to use formal inspections on test plans and test cases. It was discovered in the 1970s, and is still true today, that test cases often contain more errors than the applications they were created to test. An even rarer best practice is to include *test case errors* as a formal defect category of a software quality and defect measurement program.

Automated Test Tools

A best practice that is encountered frequently in the systems software domain is the usage of automated test library tools. Because major corporations have thousands of regression test cases, it is desirable to utilize automated tools for keeping track of these test cases, weeding out redundant tests, and linking tests to applications as needed.

Test Coverage Analysis

A best practice in analyzing the thoroughness of testing is to monitor the number of paths through software that are actually tested. A variety of commercial test monitors are available that can perform this function. Indeed, the overall best practice is to measure the percentage of all code actually tested. In applications with high cyclomatic and essential complexity, there are so many possible paths through the application that 100% testing is essentially impossible. It is a corollary best practice to redevelop or to simplify the complexity of applications that are so complex that complete testing is impossible.

Performance Testing

A best practice found more often in the systems and embedded software domains than any other is that of performance testing. Performance testing is aimed at measuring the throughput of the application and identifying any points that might be degrading performance. Normally, specialists are employed for performance testing, as are specialized test cases and various hardware or software monitoring devices.

Best Maintenance and Enhancement Practices for Systems Software

The systems software domain was among the first to make a sharp distinction between maintenance (defect repairs) and enhancements (adding new features). In general parlance the word *maintenance* can apply to any form of update on deployed software: repairs, new features, cosmetic improvements, mandatory or regulated changes, whatever. Although it is a common practice to use the word *maintenance* for a multitude of activities, it is far from being a best practice. Because updates that add new features are often funded by clients, whereas updates to make repairs often have costs that are absorbed by the vendor, it makes good sense to keep separate records of these two activities.

In all, more than 20 forms of updates have been noted for software applications. The systems software domain, because it is the second oldest type of software (after military software), has experienced more forms of maintenance for more years than almost any other. Some of the best practices for maintenance and enhancement work in the systems software domain include those presented in the following subsections.

Maintenance Departments

A best practice that is common among systems software producers but fairly rare elsewhere is to have separate maintenance departments that handle defect repairs. This practice originated within IBM in the 1960s and has a very long and successful track record. The work of maintenance departments for systems software is primarily that of repairing incoming defects reported from clients or warranty work. The staffing of these specialized maintenance groups sometimes includes customer support, but that function may also be handled by a marketing or sales organization. Enhancements are normally made by the development team. The economic reason for separate maintenance groups is because defect repairs and adding new features are antagonistic and interfere with each other. If the same person tries to fix bugs and add features, then estimating either side becomes messy and difficult. Furthermore, because bug repairs are often less interesting, they tend to be rushed so the programmer can return to development work.

Complexity Analysis

A very common best practice for maintenance of systems software is the use of complexity analysis prior to making major changes or updates. Because high complexity tends to slow down productivity and increase the odds of errors or defects, it is useful to eliminate complex modules before beginning. Both cyclomatic and essential complexity code analyzers are available commercially, and they support many common programming languages such as C, C++, Ada, FORTRAN, Assembly, and many others.

On-line Maintenance Support

A best practice that was pioneered among systems software producers and is now widely used by all types of software is to provide on-line connections between users and the maintenance teams. It is far more efficient and cost-effective for users to be able to report errors and request assistance by means of e-mail or the World Wide Web than it is by telephone or fax. Of course, HELP desks staffed by maintenance experts are also a best practice for systems software maintenance.

On-site Maintenance Support

A fairly rare best practice, found primarily in massive systems software applications (100,000 function points), is full-time, on-site maintenance support at the customer's location. This is considered a best practice only for mission-critical applications that are vital to corporate operations. On-site maintenance has been provided by computer manufacturers primarily, and companies such as IBM, DEC (now Compaq), and Sun have provided such support for major clients. On-site maintenance is quite expensive, but if a client company has dozens of products installed it is justified.

Best Personnel Practices for Systems Software

As noted in previous sections, the systems software domain has been fairly sophisticated in the utilization of software tools and processes. In this section we examine the areas in which the systems software domain is also fairly sophisticated in personnel matters. In fact, within the systems software domain both the use of key specialists and overall compensation levels are among the best for any type of software. There are ten key personnel practices that are examined during assessment and benchmark studies:

1. Staff hiring practices
2. Staff training and education
3. Management training and education
4. Specialists and occupational groups
5. Compensation levels
6. Office ergonomics
7. Organizational structures
8. Morale surveys and results
9. Work patterns and overtime
10. Staff turnover rates

As in the previous section on best technical practices, the personnel practices must have been observed within at least ten companies to be included as best practices. However, the criterion of being noted on at least 50 projects is waived for personnel practices. The reason for this is because personnel practices are normally corporatewide.

Best Staff Hiring Practices for Systems Software

University training in software engineering or computer science in the United States has not been effective in graduating students who can be put to work immediately on systems software projects without some in-house training and mentoring. An ITT vice president once noted that it took about three years of on-the-job training before a graduate software engineer or computer scientist could be entrusted with major software responsibility.

A fundamental weakness of academia as it applies to systems software is the very marginal emphasis on software quality control, and the lack of solid courses in topics such as design and code inspections, performance analysis, and performance testing—all of which are quite critical in the systems software domain.

Another academic weakness in the United States is the lack of specialized courses for key forms of systems software. For example, telecommunications software engineering is not widely taught in the United States. As a result, employers in the systems software domain either look for experienced personnel who have already worked for several years on systems software projects, or they may seek graduates from offshore universities at which technical software engineering is offered. In addition, the larger telecommunications manufacturing companies supplement the limited university curricula with extensive training for new hires, and also very complete curricula of technical and management courses for employees.

Hiring Handicapped Personnel

Software development is primarily a cerebral rather than a physical activity. Thus, software development is one of the best occupations for those with physical handicaps. (Special equipment supporting Braille, or computer controls that can be operated by foot or even by puffs of breath are available.) It is an interesting observation that graduates from schools that teach software development to the physically challenged, such as the Biped school in Connecticut, tend to succeed as software engineers more often than graduates from regular colleges. This is a best practice in every domain, including systems software.

Equal Opportunity Employment

Software development is a difficult human activity. For those who have a proficiency in software, topics such as gender or ethnic origin are irrelevant. It is an interesting observation that commercial software organizations are often very egalitarian in terms of the distribution of employees. For example, software tends to have a more equal distribution of women and minority executives and technical workers than older forms of engineering such as civil engineering or aeronautical engineering. Equal opportunity is a best practice in all domains, and systems software was one of the first to equalize pay for men and women. The systems software domain was also a pioneer in multiethnic hiring, although other domains are now approximately equivalent.

Hiring Experienced Personnel

Due to common academic deficiencies, it is a best practice in the systems software domain to hire technical personnel with at least three years of experience in systems software development and maintenance. It is also a best practice in the systems software domain to seek out potential employees with skills in specific kinds of systems software projects, such as telecommunications, avionics, or manufacturing control. These specialized forms of systems software are not covered in standard academic software engineering or computer science curricula.

Selection Criteria for New Hires

Because systems software tends to be fairly complex and has stringent quality and reliability criteria, it does not lend itself to casual development or to development by the untrained. It is a best practice when hiring new personnel to ensure that they meet the qualifications for this kind of work. Multiple interviews with both managers and other technical staff members is a best practice for hiring technical staff members. Another best practice, but one more rarely encountered, is to give candidates case studies and evaluate their performance. In other words, programming candidates must demonstrate coding proficiency on a known systems software feature. Testing candidates must actually create a test plan and a suite of test cases, and so forth.

Internships

Because of the specialized nature of systems software work, an interesting best practice is to hire software engineering college students during the summer months as interns. This gives the company an ability to judge performance levels on actual systems software work. Suitable interns can be hired as full-time employees on graduation.

Best Staff Training and Education Practices for Systems Software

Because of the marginal performance of U.S. universities in graduating effective software engineering personnel to work in the systems software domain, the major employers of systems software have compensated by establishing perhaps the most sophisticated in-house curricula for key software topics. The in-house software curricula of major systems software companies such as AT&T, BellCore, Lucent, IBM, and Motorola are more extensive and more practical than any university in the United States.

Annual Staff Training Targets

It is a best practice for systems software companies to set targets for the number of days each calendar year that will be set aside for training of technical personnel. Among our systems software clients, the most common target is ten days a year. This target is normally the minimum number of days, but we have noted 15 days occurring fairly often. In calendar years 1998 and 1999, some of these targets were suspended temporarily due to the press of work for Y2K repairs.

External Seminars and Conferences

It is a best practice for systems software clients to fund travel and tuition expenses for external conferences and seminars, such as the annual conferences offered by the SEI or various events on software quality and testing. Among our clients, one external event per year is most common, but two or three external events also occur.

Technical Software Curriculum

Among the courses we have observed (or taught) among our systems software clients, those dealing with design and code inspections are the most common and are an educational best practice. Indeed, every software professional should be well trained in the techniques of design and code inspections because they are the most effective known ways of eliminating software defects. Other courses that can be viewed as best practices for systems software staff include software requirements analysis, software design and specification, software reusability techniques, structured programming techniques, change management and configuration control, testing techniques, performance analysis and tuning techniques, quality measurements, and software maintenance techniques. These are courses noted most commonly as parts of the in-house curricula of major systems software producers.

Because of the caveat that best practices must have been noted among ten companies and used on 50 projects, there are several interesting topics that appear to be useful and beneficial but have not yet accumulated enough empirical data to place them in the category of best practices. Topics that appear to be candidates for future best practices but are not used widely enough to be sure include courses in QFD, IBM's orthogonal defect classification methods, and IBM's clean room development method. Motorola's "six-sigma" quality approach might also be placed in the category of candidate best practices.

There are many courses available on interesting and important topics, but unless these topics have demonstrated empirical results in improving quality, productivity, or schedules there is no justification for viewing them as best practices. This category includes courses in most programming languages and courses in various specific vendor tools. Courses in UML are also in this category because UML has not yet been proved to be effective under field conditions on actual projects.

Best Management Training and Education Practices for Systems Software

Software project management is even more poorly served by universities than software engineering. In fact, very few universities in the world offer courses in some of the more important software management topics such as function point analysis, software cost estimating, and software risk and value analysis. The systems software domain has compensated for this academic gap reasonably well, but not as well as for software engineering topics.

Annual Management Training Targets

It is a best practice for systems software clients to set targets for the number of days each calendar year that will be set aside for training of project management personnel. Among our systems software clients, the most common target for mangers is five days a year. This target is normally the minimum number of days, and we have noted ten days occurring fairly often.

External Management Seminars and Conferences

It is a best practice for systems software clients to fund travel and tuition expenses for external conferences and seminars for managers, such as the annual conferences offered by the SEI or various events on software project management and metrics. Among our clients, two external events per year is most common, but three or four external events also occur.

Executive Training in Key Software Topics

A best practice first encountered in the systems software domain, and still more widely noted here than anywhere else, is the preparation and presentation of *executive briefings* on key software topics. These briefings are offered to executive vice presidents, boards of directors, and chief operating and executive officers. Among our clients, the executives themselves have requested these briefings because software is one of the major assets for which they are responsible, and the asset over which they are least able to exert executive control. Some of the executive topics that are included in a set of best practices are competitive analysis, industry software benchmarks, software economic analysis, software quality costs, Y2K analysis and controls, and Y2K software litigation.

Software Management Curriculum

It is a best practice for systems software managers to understand the economics of software quality control. Therefore, courses on defect estimation, defect prevention, and defect removal are a best practice for systems software managers. Other courses noted among our clients included in the best practice set are software cost estimating, principles of software reuse, software quality estimating, software productivity measurements and metrics, software quality metrics and cost of quality, principles of the SEI CMM, function points for managers, and risk and value analysis. Incidentally, starting in 1996, courses on the Y2K problem began to occur in rather large numbers. Due to the importance of this problem, Y2K analysis was also a best practice for managers.

There are a number of rapidly emerging technologies that may become best educational practices in the near future, but have not yet been encountered among ten clients. The most notable are courses in e-business and Web-based management practices. Although this topic is important, the technology is changing so rapidly and the results are so ambiguous that it is difficult to create an effective course.

Another emerging topic that may become a best practice, but is not there yet, is component-based development.

As always, there are many other courses offered and available, but the topics have not demonstrated any empirical results in improving quality, productivity, schedules, or offering tangible improvements. Some of these topics for managers include courses in ISO 9000–9004 quality standards, courses on ERP tools, and courses dealing with business process reengineering.

Best Practices for Specialization in the Systems Software Domain

The systems software domain was the first to employ specialists in key disciplines such as testing and quality assurance. As the twentieth century ends, the systems software domain remains among the most sophisticated of any software domain in the number and deployment of software specialists.

Software Specialization

There are five key areas in which specialization counts as a best practice, because the results are so much better than when the work is performed by generalists who lack specific training: software testing after unit test, software technical writing, software performance tuning, software quality assurance, and software maintenance in the sense of defect repairs. The systems software domain employs specialists in all five of these key areas in fairly large numbers. In fact, for software quality and testing, more than half of the software quality and testing specialists in the United States work in the systems software domain.

The systems software domain also employs many other kinds of specialists, but there is not enough data to ascertain whether the specialists should be added to the best practice set or not. Some of the many other specialists noted in the systems software domain include cost-estimating specialists, planning and project schedule specialists, function point counting specialists, database administration specialists, ISO 9000–9004 audit specialists, SEI CMM assessment specialists, metrics and measurement specialists, and customer support specialists.

Best Compensation and Salary Practices for Systems Software

In the United States, banking is the industry that pays software personnel and software managers the highest salary levels. Banking employs comparatively few systems software personnel. However, outside of banking, systems software personnel have the best compensation and salary packages for software engineering work.

Compensation Benchmarks

It is a best practice to perform annual compensation benchmark studies for systems software technical and managerial personnel. These benchmarks are normally "blind" studies during which various companies contribute compensation data that is analyzed statistically by a neutral external benchmark company. Each contributing company receives a report on how their compensation packages compare with the group, but the specifics of each company in the group are not included due to both competitive and antitrust reasons.

Compensation Levels

For large companies employing more than 1,000 software personnel it is a best practice to be in the upper quartile of overall compensation including salaries, bonuses, equity, and medical and dental benefits. In large corporations, compensation, quality, productivity, and schedules are more or less correlated. However, for small companies with less than 100 software personnel, and especially for startups with less than 25 software personnel, immediate compensation is less significant and long-range topics such as equity are more significant.

Best Practices in Office Ergonomics for Systems Software

In 1978 when IBM was planning the Santa Teresa Programming Laboratory in San Jose, California, several hundred systems programmers were interviewed by the architect (Dr. Gerald McCue, Dean of Architecture at Harvard University) and his team. IBM then built a state-of-the-art office complex specifically to optimize the development and maintenance of systems software. Approximately 2,000 software professionals work at the IBM Santa Teresa complex.

At the Santa Teresa laboratory, each technical staff member had a full private office of 100 square feet. Project managers had the same offices. Executives at the level of director or vice president had double-size offices. Custom furniture and cabinets were also part of the design. Very large desks, ample storage cabinets, and guest chairs were part of the equipment of every office. Department team members were located in adjacent offices, and each department had access to a small conference room that could hold approximately ten people.

When the Santa Teresa office complex was finished and occupied, the productivity rates of the systems software groups were measured, as they had been prior to moving to Santa Teresa. The productivity at Santa Teresa was almost 11% higher than it had been when the same groups worked in shared cubicles in the San Jose and Palo Alto locations. Indeed, for several years when I was working at Santa Teresa, the lab had the highest productivity levels of any of IBM's 26 software labs at that time.

When the IBM annual morale surveys were completed after occupancy, it was noted that the morale of the technical staff members at Santa Teresa was the highest in the company, and voluntary attrition was the lowest.

More recently, studies by Tom DeMarco and Tim Lister, published in *Peopleware* (DeMarco and Lister 1987), confirmed the findings noted at Santa Teresa. Private office space benefits systems software productivity in a very significant fashion.

In our own assessment and benchmark studies, there are several interesting phenomena that often stand out among clients that turn out to have better than average software performance levels. One of the most visible, which can be noted almost as soon as a consultant enters the building, is the use of private, noise-free office space for software engineers and technical workers.

Another interesting sign of fairly sophisticated software and engineering practices is the presence of a well-stocked research library. Of course, with access to the Web, a research library is no longer absolutely necessary, but it is interesting that productivity and quality levels are likely to be higher in locations that have such libraries. This is probably not a causative factor, but a derivative factor. The companies that fund research libraries also fund other kinds of tools and best practices.

During a typical working day, a software engineer needs quiet and solitude for roughly five hours, and needs to have discussions or meetings for only approximately 1 hour. Roughly two hours are spent on phone calls, using the Internet, or miscellaneous work. From this distribution of effort, it can be seen that private office space is optimal for the major portion of a day's work.

An informal study that I carried out at IBM San Jose prior to the opening of the Santa Teresa office space noted that the mean time to interruption in a three-person cubicle was roughly 11 minutes. The mean time to interruption in a two-person cubicle was roughly 15 minutes.

Private Office Space

It is a best practice to provide private, noise-free office space for software engineers and technical staff members. An area of at least 80 square feet is optimal. This best practice is only encountered within fairly sophisticated companies, but the results support the hypothesis that private office space is optimal for systems software.

Networks and E-Mail

It is a best practice to link all technical employees within a corporation by means of a network that supports e-mail, file transfer, and on-line inspection of key work products.

Meeting Rooms

Because group activities such as design and code inspections, and team meetings are common for software projects, it is a best practice to provide a small meeting room that can hold ten people. Because usage is intermittent, one such meeting room should be able to support roughly 30 staff members.

For software assessments and benchmarks performed in the United States, private, noise-free office space correlates very strongly with productivity and quality levels. However, similar studies in Japan do not show such a correlation. The reason for the difference is uncertain, but it can be hypothesized that social customs in Japan lead to fewer interruptions of colleagues for nonbusiness matters than noted in the United States.

Best Practices in Organizational Structures for Systems Software

For historical reasons outside the scope of this book, the *span of control,* or number of employees reporting to one manager, is generally about eight staff members. This has been true for more than 100 years, and is true for all forms of office work, not just software. (The origin of the span-of-control concept stems from time and motion studies carried out on troop movements after the close of the U.S. Civil War in 1865. Small units, such as squads, could move much faster than larger units, such as companies. Later, the span-of-control concept was picked up by business researchers.)

The average span of control noted among our assessment and benchmark studies is approximately eight technical employees per manager, but the lowest value has been two employees reporting to a manager and the largest value has been 30 employees reporting to one manager.

It is a common belief in the software world that small teams are more productive than large departments. However, many systems software projects are very large and have staffing levels that can top 100 personnel overall. For large projects with more than 50 staff members, small teams are actually not as productive as larger departments with ten to 12 people reporting to one manager. Furthermore, voluntary attrition rates are usually better within companies with a somewhat larger span of control.

The reason for this somewhat surprising finding seems to be that good managers are a fairly scarce commodity. If a company has a small span of control then it will have a large management population. Because bad management is the most common reason why good technical workers change jobs, it can be seen that having fewer but better managers may lead to overall improvements in both performance and morale issues.

In general, productivity levels decline as the number of workers increases. Here, too, this is a general finding from many industries, not just a finding for software projects. However, there is a curious phenomenon within the software domain that was first noted on systems software projects in IBM in the 1970s, and it has been replicated within other companies as well. Productivity levels for software projects tend to decline as the number of managers increases, rather than as the number of technical staff members increases. The implications of this finding are that for large systems (>10,000 function points), small teams are not as productive as departments with ten to 12 employees. The reason seems to be that for large systems, small-team organizational structures put too many managers on the project. As the management count increases, coordination and cooperation between departments becomes difficult due to normal corporate politics.

Optimal Department Size

For large systems software projects (>10,000 function points) it is a best practice to have ten to 15 employees reporting to one manager. Although this is controversial, this is the size at which productivity is highest. Smaller spans of control put too many people in management and raise the difficulty of coordination between departments. Furthermore, a ten-plus staffing complement can handle a fairly large component whereas smaller departments might have to segment the work artificially. In addition, a larger span of control allows backup in case of illness, and encourages mentoring of new team members. It is also easier to handle peer reviews and formal inspections. Needless to say, the managers of these larger departments must be carefully selected, well trained, and very capable.

Optimal Organizational Structures

For large systems software projects (>10,000 function points) a hierarchical organizational structure is a best practice, as opposed to a matrix organizational structure. The hierarchical organization is similar to a military chain of command, in that each manager reports directly to a higher level manager, up to the level of the senior manager responsible for the entire system. The matrix structure tends to raise the management head count for larger projects. Because software productivity declines as the management count goes up, this form of organization can be hazardous for software. (SPR lacks data on the effectiveness of the matrix organization for hardware or other kinds of projects besides software. I have no opinion on the effectiveness of the matrix organization outside the software domain.)

Independent Software Quality Assurance

For large systems software projects (>10,000 function points) it is a best practice to have an independent software quality assurance department outside the control of the project management hierarchy. The reason for this independent group is to protect the integrity of the quality assurance function. If the software quality assurance personnel report to the project manager, they cannot safely point out problems without risking personnel reprisals. The software quality assurance group is distinct from the testing group, which usually does report in the hierarchical project management chain of command. A key role of this organization is to ensure that best practices are followed and dangerous situations, if any, are addressed. The software quality assurance group could not perform this role unless it was independent of the project chain of command.

Specialist Organizations

For large systems software projects (>10,000 function points) it is a best practice to have specialists for several key activities. These specialists may not be employed for the duration of the project, but when working on the project they report within the project management chain of command. The specialist organizations needed for large systems software projects include system-level architecture, system-level design, human factors, database design, quality assurance, technical writing, graphics and illustrations, and testing after completion of unit test.

Virtual Organizations

For large systems software projects involving multiple cities and countries, it is a best practice to support broad-band communication channels so that e-mail, file transfer, and on-line inspection are all possible. Video conferencing among locations is also a best practice for projects that are dispersed geographically. Prior to the availability of the Internet and corporate intranets, projects developed over several geographic regions exhibited sharp productivity declines. In the 1970s, each time a different city was added to the same project, productivity declined by approximately 5%. Since about 1995, virtual teams that are dispersed geographically are just as productive as single-site teams, if communication channels are effective.

In performing benchmark and assessment studies, we have encountered some other organizational issues for which the data is not yet sufficient for rigorous analysis. For example, we have encountered telecommuting in several studies. However, the data on telecommuting among our clients is too sparse to reach overall conclusions as to how this might affect software productivity or quality levels.

Best Practices for Employee Morale in Systems Software

It should not be a surprise that employees who are satisfied with their jobs and their places of employment are more productive and produce higher quality deliverables than employees who are dissatisfied. Productivity data also favors organizations with levels of high morale. Interestingly, one of the critical factors affecting employee morale is the ability of the project managers to whom the technical workers report. Companies that recognize the significance of this finding are very careful about who gets promoted to management, and are careful to weed out managers whose personalities are not suited for this very critical responsibility.

Morale and Opinion Surveys

It is a best practice to perform morale or opinion surveys of all employees, including administrative workers, technical staff members, and project managers. The normal frequency of morale surveys is once a year. Some of our clients conduct two surveys a year. In special situations, such as after a major downsizing, merger, or cancellation of a major project, additional special morale surveys may be needed.

Follow-up to Morale Surveys

It is a best practice to have immediate and formal follow-ups after morale surveys are taken. Asking questions about morale but taking no action based on the responses degrades rather than improves morale. Normally after a morale survey occurs, the results are analyzed statistically within a week, and departmental group meetings are held to discuss the results within two weeks. Within a month, executives and top managers have formulated a plan to deal with any serious morale issues that were encountered. Normally, within approximately six weeks, there is an overall meeting or series of departmental meetings to discuss these action plans.

Open-Door Policy

It is a best practice to have a formal "open-door" policy within large corporations in the systems software domain. The phrase *open door* means that employees who feel that they have been treated unfairly by their manager, or by any other employee, can appeal to any higher level manager and request an investigation. (The appeal could also be made to the human resource department, but an appeal within the chain of command is usually more effective.) To work, the open-door policy must offer a firm promise that there will be no reprisals. That is, if an employee makes a specific complaint about his or her first-line manager, there must be a guarantee that they will not suffer any reduction in appraisals or compensation as a result. Normally, this means that as a result of an open-door appeal, the employee initiating the request is transferred to some other department.

Job Transfer Requests

It is a best practice within large corporations to have a job transfer request system that allows employees to request internal transfers to other cities, or to request a job change to another kind of position. Of course, the employees must have the relevant background and technical skills to perform well in the new situation. Some companies post internal job openings or make this information widely available. In other companies, job information is informal.

Merit Appraisals

In the United States it is a best practice to have annual performance appraisals for both technical staff members and project managers. During the first year of employment in a company, there may be two or more performance appraisals. It is a best practice for employees and managers to agree jointly to performance goals or targets. Note that in some European countries, performance appraisals are forbidden by either national law or union regulations.

Awards and Recognition

It is a best practice to reward outstanding accomplishments. Many companies have a spectrum of awards ranging from local dinner-for-two awards, which are given at the discretion of a supervisor, to major $100,000 awards for some breakthrough that had significant corporate value. Overall, numerous small awards tend to benefit morale more widely than a few very large awards. Although large awards can benefit morale, the odds of receiving one are low. Small awards, on the other hand, can be given to 5% to 10% of the corporate technical staff during the course of a year.

Due to the major shortage of software personnel in the United States and Europe, morale and personnel issues are now extremely important. There are many more topics under this heading that cannot be discussed using assessment and benchmark data, because assessments and benchmarks do not cover every personnel topic. For example, stock option plans and equity may have an affect on employee morale and attrition rates, but we have not been tasked with examining these issues.

Another very strong morale factor is the medical and dental plans offered by employers. Here, too, we have not been commissioned to study this factor. Indeed, if we attempted to study this factor we would probably be asked to stop because human resource organizations regard this kind of information as sensitive.

Best Work Patterns and Overtime Utilization for Systems Software

It was first noted more than 30 years ago that software development and maintenance tends to attract personnel who are fairly intense in their work practices. Within companies such as Microsoft, IBM, Hewlett-Packard, and Motorola, 50-hour weeks are the norm rather than the exception for systems software development. Furthermore, because software personnel are usually salaried workers rather than hourly workers, they are considered "exempt" in the sense that software personnel do not automatically receive overtime pay. Because many corporate time and cost tracking systems exclude unpaid overtime, it is difficult to gather reliable information on this topic. The SPR assessment approach includes questions and interviews about unpaid overtime, but our data is based on reconstruction from the memories of the participants and therefore may have a large margin of error.

Compensatory Time

It is a best practice for systems software personnel to be allowed to take compensatory time during slack periods in return for contributing unpaid overtime during rushed periods.

The issue of unpaid overtime is often encountered during benchmark studies. This topic deserves greater coverage in the software literature because it has a tangible impact on productivity rates.

The topic of unpaid overtime is particularly noticeable in international studies. For example, comparing software projects of 10,000 function points produced in Japan and in Canada often favors Japan by approximately 15% in terms of work hours per function point. The reason for this is that the normal Japanese work week is 44 hours and in addition, approximately 1.5 hours a day are also deployed in the form of unpaid overtime. By contrast, the Canadian work week is roughly 37 hours (it differs in winter and summer), and unpaid overtime is less common than in Japan. Thus if Canadian and Japanese projects of the same size are started on the same day, the odds are that the Japanese project will be finished first and will seem to have higher productivity because the Japanese unpaid overtime is not normally tracked or added to the project's productivity data.

On the whole, the industrialized countries of Western Europe, such as France and Germany, have many more vacation days each year than the United States or Japan. Public holidays vary widely from country to country. This issue is very important for international benchmark analysis.

Best Practices for Minimizing Staff Turnover Rates

Due to the shortage of software personnel in the United States and Europe, software producers are very concerned about losing key personnel. They are also concerned about the high costs for recruiting new personnel. If a company is in financial distress and is downsizing, there are no effective techniques for keeping key personnel. Furthermore, software productivity and quality levels suffer during periods of downsizing. However, if a company is growing rapidly and recruiting actively, it is very useful to pay serious attention to the factors that affect both attracting new hires and minimizing the attrition of existing personnel.

Reducing Voluntary Attrition

To minimize the attrition of key personnel, the set of best practices includes being in the top 50% in terms of compensation and benefits, weeding out less capable managers, and having proactive morale and opinion surveys to identify problems before they grow to a significant magnitude. A very complex issue is also important: Because bad management is the most common reason cited in exit interviews when technical workers quit, it is very important to weed out managers whose personalities are unsuited to management tasks. Thus, very careful management appraisals are a best practice.

Finding New Personnel

Obviously, large companies utilize multiple methods for finding new employees: advertisements, recruiters, and the World Wide Web. However, it is a best practice to also offer incentives or rewards for employees to bring in suitable candidates. The reason for this is because the software community is fairly good at spreading the word regarding interesting opportunities.

Contract Employees

It has been a best practice to utilize contract personnel for a percentage of systems software technical work. The reason for this is because contractors can be brought in fairly quickly, with relevant experience suitable to the projects in need of support. Additionally, when the projects are completed, the contract personnel can be released as quickly as they are brought onboard. However, a number of recent court actions involving contract personnel are raising new issues that we have not yet encountered in our benchmark and assessment studies. As a result, the contracting situation circa 1999 is somewhat ambiguous, even though past results have been favorable.

Systems software outsourcing often occurs, but due to the special skills required the outsource vendors are often specialized companies. For example, the telecommunications industry has developed several international outsource companies that specialize in public and private switching system development. We have not encountered systems software outsourcing often enough to judge whether this should be viewed as a best practice. The results of the outsourced systems software projects we have reviewed have had productivity and quality levels roughly equivalent to those of in-house projects. Some of the outsource vendors have teams in low-cost countries such as the Ukraine or the Czech Republic, so costs have been slightly lower than in-house development in the industrialized countries.

Personnel issues are outside the normal scope of assessment and benchmark studies. However, we have been commissioned to explore some aspects of personnel topics, such as the number of specialists employed and the optimal methods for keeping their skills up to date.

Summary and Conclusions on Systems Software

Systems software controls complex physical devices. Therefore, systems software has long required state-of-the-art levels of quality and reliability. In general, systems software and the embedded subtype are driven by strong needs for very high levels of quality and reliability.

The approaches that have developed within the systems and embedded software domains have led to very good results for large systems in the 10,000-function point and 100,000-function point size plateaus. The systems software domain is more successful and has the highest productivity of any domain at the large end of the spectrum. However, for small applications, the rigor and complete specification sets of the systems software domain have led to reduced productivity, although quality and reliability are usually very good. Overall, the systems software domain is characterized by skilled technical staffs, high staff compensation levels, excellent tool suites, very rigorous development processes, and state-of-the-art quality control.

The weaknesses of the systems software domain are often comparatively minor, and center around a lagging adoption of function point metrics. This in turn has led to faulty research on productivity topics because the older LOC metric is not suitable for economic studies.

In the systems software domain, the larger and more sophisticated companies have been able to build applications successfully in the 10,000-function point and 100,000-function point size ranges. The systems software domain's process rigor and capable quality control are two of the reasons why this domain is more successful than most at building very large systems.

Readings and References for Systems Software

The literature on systems and embedded software has a very significant emphasis on quality control. Many of the best-selling books on testing and inspections were written by authors who work in the systems software domain. Indeed, formal design and code inspections were first invented by IBM for use on systems software.

The literature on software risk analysis and risk abatement also has a strong focus in the systems software domain, as might be expected. In addition, almost all the books on software reliability modeling have been written by authors who work at systems software laboratories such as Bell Labs.

On the other hand, the systems software domain has lagged in books and articles on benchmarking and productivity studies. There was a very notable gap in books and articles that applied function point metrics to the systems software domain, although this gap is starting to be filled. Some of the recent literature on functional metrics in the systems software domain are books dealing with fairly obscure function point variations. It is not clear whether these variations will survive the test of time or will serve a useful purpose. Very little data has been collected on these variant function point metrics, such as 3D function points or full function points. As a result, benchmarks using these metrics are not very complete.

The systems software domain has very active research programs underway. As a result, quite a few inventions and innovations have originated in the systems domain. Much of the literature on the OO paradigm stems from the systems software labs, where the OO concept was pioneered. For example, both C++ and Objective C were created in telecommunications systems software research labs.

Abdel-Hamid, Tarek, and Stuart Madnick. *Software Project Dynamics*. Englewood Cliffs, NJ: Prentice Hall, 1993. (ISBN 013-8220409)

Abran, A., and P. N. Robillard. "Function Point Analysis. An Empirical Study of Its Measurement Processes." *IEEE Transactions on Software Engineering* 1996; 22(12): 895–909.

Austin, Robert D. *Measuring and Managing Performance in Organizations*. New York: Dorset House Publishing, 1996. (ISBN 0-932633-36-6, 216 pages)

Bach, James. "The Immaturity of the CMM." *American Programmer* 1994; 7(9): 13–18.

Beizer, Boris. *Software Testing Techniques*. Boston, MA: International Thomson Computer Press, 1990. (ISBN 1850328803, 550 pages)

Boehm, Barry. *Software Engineering Economics*. Englewood Cliffs, NJ: Prentice Hall, 1981. (ISBN 0-13-822122-7, 900 pages)

Bogan, Christopher E., and Michael J. English. *Benchmarking for Best Practices*. New York: McGraw Hill, 1994. (ISBN 0-07-006375-3, 312 pages)

Briand, Loic, and Daniel Roy. *Meeting Deadlines in Hard Real-Time Systems*. Los Alamitos, CA: IEEE Computer Society Press, 1997. (ISBN 0-8186-7406-7, 300 pages)

Brooks, Frederick. *The Mythical Man-Month*. Reading, MA: Addison Wesley Longman, 1995. (ISBN 0-201-00650-2, 295 pages)

Brown, Norm, ed. *The Program Manager's Guide to Software Acquisition Best Practices*. Version 1.0. Washington, DC: U.S. Department of Defense, (142 pages)

Caputo, Kim. *CMM Implementation Guide.* Reading, MA: Addison Wesley Longman, 1998. (ISBN 0-201-37938-4, 319 pages)

Carmel, Erran. *Global Software Teams: Collaborating Across Borders and Time Zones.* Upper Saddle River, NJ: Prentice Hall, 1999. (ISBN 0-13-924218-X, 269 pages)

Carnegie Mellon University. *The Capability Maturity Model: Guidelines for Improving the Software Process.* Reading, MA: Addison Wesley Longman, 1995. (ISBN 0-201-54664-7, 441 pages)

Charette, Robert N. *Software Engineering Risk Analysis and Management.* New York: McGraw Hill, 1989. (ISBN 0-07-010719-X, 325 pages)

———. *Application Strategies for Risk Analysis.* New York: McGraw Hill, 1990. (ISBN 0-07-010888-9, 570 pages)

Conte, S. D., H. E. Dunsmore, and V. Y. Shen. *Software Engineering.* Menlo Park, CA: The Benjamin Cummings Publishing Company, 1986. (ISBN 0-8053-2162-4, 396 pages)

Curtis, Bill, William E. Hefley, and Sally Miller. *People Capability Maturity Model.* Pittsburgh, PA: Software Engineering Institute, Carnegie Mellon University, 1995.

DeMarco, Tom. *Controlling Software Projects.* New York: Yourdon Press, 1982. (ISBN 0-917072-34-4, 284 pages)

———. *Why Does Software Cost So Much?* New York: Dorset House Publishing, 1995. (ISBN 0-932633-34-X, 237 pages)

———. *The Deadline.* New York: Dorset House Publishing, 1997. (ISBN 0-932633-39-0)

DeMarco, Tom, and Tim Lister. *Peopleware.* New York: Dorset House Publishing, 1987. (ISBN 0-932633-05-6, 188 pages)

Department of the Air Force. *Guidelines for Successful Acquisition and Management of Software Intensive Systems.* Vol. 1 and 2. Hill Air Force Base, UT: Software Technology Support Center, 1994.

Dreger, J. Brian. *Function Point Analysis.* Englewood Cliffs, NJ: Prentice Hall, 1989. (ISBN 0-13-332321-8, 185 pages)

El Emam, Khaled, and Nazim H. Madhavi, eds. *Elements of Software Process Assessment and Improvement.* Los Alamitos, CA: IEEE Computer Society Press, 1999. (ISBN 0 818 685239, 384 pages)

Fetcke, Thomas, Alain Abran, and Tho-Hau Nguyen *Mapping the OO-Jacobsen Approach into Function Point Analysis.* Quebec: Université du Quebec à Montreal, Software Engineering Management Research Laboratory, 1998. (11 pages)

Galea, R. B. *The Boeing Company: 3D Function Point Extensions*. Version 2.0, release 1.0. Seattle, WA: Boeing Information Support Services, June 1995.

Garmus, David, and David Herron. *Measuring the Software Process: A Practical Guide to Functional Measurement*. Englewood Cliffs, NJ: Prentice Hall, 1995. (ISBN 0-13-349002-5)

Gilb, Tom, and Dorothy Graham. *Software Inspections*. Reading, MA: Addison Wesley Longman, 1993. (ISBN 0-201631814, 471 pages)

Glass, Robert L. *Software Runaways: Lessons Learned from Massive Project Failures*. Upper Saddle River, NJ: Prentice Hall, 1997. (ISBN 0-13-673443-X, 259 pages)

Grady, Robert B. *Practical Software Metrics for Project Management and Process Improvement*. Englewood Cliffs, NJ: Prentice Hall, 1992. (ISBN 0-13-720384-5, 270 pages)

———. *Successful Software Process Improvement*. Upper Saddle River, NJ: Prentice Hall, 1997. (ISBN 0-13-626623-1, 314 pages)

Grady, Robert B., and Deborah L. Caswell. *Software Metrics: Establishing a Company-Wide Program*. Englewood Cliffs, NJ: Prentice Hall, 1987. (ISBN 0-13-821844-7, 288 pages)

Gulledge, Thomas R., William P. Hutzler, and Joan S. Lovelace, eds. *Cost Estimating and Analysis: Balancing Technology with Declining Budgets*. New York: Springer-Verlag, 1992. (ISBN 0-387-97838-0, 297 pages)

Howard, Alan, ed. *Software Metrics and Project Management Tools*. Phoenix, AZ: Applied Computer Research, 1997. (30 pages)

Humphrey, Watts S. *Managing the Software Process*. Reading, MA: Addison Wesley Longman, 1989. (ISBN 0-201-18095-2)

———. *Introduction to the Personal Software Process*. Reading, MA: Addison Wesley Longman, 1997. (ISBN 0201548097)

———. *Managing Technical People*. Reading, MA: Addison Wesley Longman, 1997. ISBN 0-201-54597-7; 326 pages.

IFPUG. *IFPUG Counting Practices Manual*. Release 4.1. Westerville, OH: International Function Point Users Group, May 1999. (93 pages)

Jacobson, Ivar, Martin Griss, and Patrick Jonsson. *Software Reuse: Architecture, Process, and Organization for Business Success*. Reading, MA: Addison Wesley Longman, 1997. (ISBN 0-201-92476-5, 500 pages)

Jones, Capers. *Program Quality and Programmer Productivity*. IBM technical report TR07.764. San Jose, CA: IBM Santa Teresa, January 1977. (97 pages)

———. "Measuring Programming Quality and Productivity." *IBM Systems Journal*, 1978; 17(1): 39–63.

————. *Programming Productivity: Issues for the Eighties*. Los Alamitos, CA: IEEE Computer Society Press, 1st ed., 1981; 2nd ed., 1986. (ISBN 0-8186-0681-9, IEEE Computer Society Catalog 681, 489 pages)

————. *Programming Productivity*. New York: McGraw Hill, 1986. (ISBN 0-07-032811-0, 280 pages)

————. *A Ten-Year Retrospective of the ITT Programming Technology Center*. Burlington, MA: Software Productivity Research, 1988.

————. *Assessment and Control of Software Risks*. Englewood Cliffs, NJ: Prentice Hall, 1993. (ISBN 0-13-741406-4, 711 pages)

————. *Critical Problems in Software Measurement*. Carlsbad, CA: Information Systems Management Group, 1993. (ISBN 1-56909-000-9, 195 pages)

————. *Software Productivity and Quality Today: The Worldwide Perspective*. Carlsbad, CA: Information Systems Management Group, 1993. (ISBN -156909-001-7, 200 pages)

————. *New Directions in Software Management*. Carlsbad, CA: Information Systems Management Group, 1994. (ISBN 1-56909-009-2, 150 pages)

————. *Patterns of Software System Failure and Success*. Boston, MA: International Thomson Computer Press, 1995. (ISBN 1-850-32804-8, 292 pages)

————. *Applied Software Measurement*. 2nd ed. New York: McGraw Hill, 1996. (ISBN 0-07-032826-9, 618 pages)

————. *Revitalizing Project Management*. SPR technical report. Burlington, MA: Software Productivity Research, August 1997. (37 pages)

————. *Software Quality: Analysis and Guidelines for Success*. Boston, MA: International Thomson Computer Press, 1997. (ISBN 1-85032-876-6, 492 pages)

————. *The Economics of Object-Oriented Software*. SPR technical report. Burlington, MA: Software Productivity Research, April 1997. (22 pages)

————. *Becoming Best in Class*. SPR technical report. Burlington, MA: Software Productivity Research, January 1998. (40 pages)

————. *Estimating Software Costs*. New York: McGraw Hill, 1998. (ISBN 0-07-9130941, 725 pages)

————. "Sizing Up Software." *Scientific American* 1998; 279(6): 104–111.

————. *The Costs, Schedule, and Value of Software Process Improvement*. SPR technical report. Burlington, MA: Software Productivity Research, January 1998. (27 pages)

————. *The Year 2000 Software Problem: Quantifying the Costs and Assessing the Consequences*. Reading, MA: Addison Wesley, 1998. (ISBN 0-201-30964-5, 303 pages)

————. *Table of Programming Languages and Levels*. Burlington, MA: Software Productivity Research, March 1999. (ten versions from 1985 through July 1999, 77 pages for Version 10)

Kan, Stephen H. *Metrics and Models in Software Quality Engineering*. Reading, MA: Addison Wesley Longman, 1994. (ISBN 0-201-63339-6, 344 pages)

Kemerer, Chris F. "An Empirical Validation of Software Cost Estimation Models." *Communications of the ACM*, 1987;30:416–429.

————. "Reliability of Function Point Measurement: A Field Experiment." *Communications of the ACM* 1993; 36: 85–97.

Love, Tom. *Object Lessons*. New York: SIGS Books, 1993. (ISBN 0-9627477 3-4, 266 pages)

Marciniak, John J., ed. *Encyclopedia of Software Engineering*. New York: John Wiley & Sons, 1994. (ISBN 0-471-54002, two volumes)

McCabe, Thomas J. "A Complexity Measure." *IEEE Transactions on Software Engineering*, 1976: 308–320.

Melton, Austin. *Software Measurement*. London: Chapman & Hall, 1995. (ISBN 1-85032-7178-7)

Mills, Harlan. *Software Productivity*. New York: Dorset House Publishing, 1988. (ISBN 0-932633-10-2, 288 pages)

Moore, James W. *Software Engineering Standards: A User's Road Map*. Los Alamitos, CA: IEEE Computer Society Press, 1998. (ISBN 0-8186-8008-3, 296 pages)

Multiple authors. *Rethinking the Software Process*. CD-ROM. Lawrence, KS: Miller Freeman, 1996. (This is a new CD-ROM book collection produced jointly by the book publisher Prentice Hall and the journal publisher Miller Freeman. This CD-ROM disk contains the full text and illustrations of five Prentice Hall books: *Assessment and Control of Software Risks* by Capers Jones, *Controlling Software Projects* by Tom DeMarco, *Function Point Analysis* by Brian Dreger, *Measures for Excellence* by Larry Putnam and Ware Myers, and *Object-Oriented Software Metrics* by Mark Lorenz and Jeff Kidd.)

Musa, John, Anthony Iannino, and Kazuhia Okumoto. *Software Reliability: Measurement, Prediction, Application*. New York: McGraw Hill, 1987. (ISBN 0-07-044093-X, 619 pages)

Oskarson, Osten, and Robert L. Glass. *An ISO 9000 Approach to Building Quality Software*. Upper Saddle River, NJ: Prentice Hall, 1996. (ISBN 0-13-228925-3, 274 pages)

Park, Robert E., et al. *Software Cost and Schedule Estimating: A Process Improvement Initiative.* Technical report CMU/SEI 94-SR-03. Pittsburgh, PA: Software Engineering Institute, May 1994.

————. *Checklists and Criteria for Evaluating the Costs and Schedule Estimating Capabilities of Software Organizations.* Technical report CMU/SEI 95-SR-005. Pittsburgh, PA: Software Engineering Institute, January 1995.

Perry, William E. *Handbook of Diagnosing and Solving Computer Problems.* Blue Ridge Summit, PA: TAB Books, 1989. (ISBN 0-8306-9233-9, 255 pages)

————. *Effective Methods for Software Testing.* Los Alamitos, CA: IEEE Computer Society Press, 1995. (ISBN 0 471 06097-6, 556 pages)

Pressman, Roger. *Software Engineering: A Practitioner's Approach.* New York: McGraw Hill, 1982.

Putnam, Lawrence H. *Measures for Excellence: Reliable Software On Time, Within Budget.* Englewood Cliffs, NJ: Prentice Hall, 1992. (ISBN 0-13-567694-0, 336 pages)

Putnam, Lawrence H., and Ware Myers. *Industrial Strength Software: Effective Management Using Measurement.* Los Alamitos, CA: IEEE Computer Society Press, 1997. (ISBN 0-8186-7532-2, 320 pages)

Rubin, Howard. *Software Benchmark Studies for 1999.* Pound Ridge, NY: Howard Rubin Associates, 1999.

Schulmeyer, G. Gordon, and James I. McManus, ed. *Handbook of Software Quality Assurance.* New York: Van Nostrand Reinhold, 1992. (ISBN 0-442-00796-5, 562 pages)

Shepperd, M. "A Critique of Cyclomatic Complexity as a Software Metric." *Software Engineering Journal,* 1988; 3:30–36.

Software Productivity Consortium. *The Software Measurement Guidebook.* Boston, MA: International Thomson Computer Press, 1995. (ISBN 1-850-32195-7, 308 pages)

Strassmann, Paul. *The Squandered Computer.* New Canaan, CT: The Information Economics Press, 1997. (ISBN 0-9620413-1-9, 426 pages)

Stukes, Sherry, Jason Deshoretz, Henry Apgar, and Ilona Macias. *Air Force Cost Analysis Agency Software Estimating Model Analysis.* TR-9545/008-2, contract F04701-95-D-0003, task 008. Thousand Oaks, CA: Management Consulting & Research, September 1996.

Symons, Charles R. *Software Sizing and Estimating: Mk II FPA (Function Point Analysis).* Chichester, UK: John Wiley & Sons, 1991. (ISBN 0 471-92985-9, 200 pages)

Thayer, Richard H., ed. *Software Engineering Project Management*. Los Alamitos, CA: IEEE Computer Society Press, 1988. (ISBN 0 8186-80008, 512 pages)

Weinberg, Gerald M. *Quality Software Management. Vol. 2, First-Order Measurement*. New York: Dorset House Publishing, 1993. (ISBN 0-932633-24-2, 360 pages)

Weinberg, Gerald, and Daniel Friedman. *Handbook of Walkthroughs, Inspections, and Technical Reviews*. New York: Dorset House Publishing, 1990. (450 pages)

Wheeler, David A., Bill Brylcznski, and Reginald Meeson. *Software Inspection: An Industry Best Practice*. Los Alamitos, CA: IEEE Computer Society Press, 1996. (ISBN 0-8186-7430-0, 325 pages)

Wiegers, Karl A. *Creating a Software Engineering Culture*. New York: Dorset House Publishing, 1996. (ISBN 0-932633-33-1, 358 pages)

Yourdon, Edward. *Death March: The Complete Software Developer's Guide to Surviving "Mission Impossible" Projects*. Upper Saddle River, NJ: Prentice Hall, 1997. (ISBN 0-13-748310-4, 218 pages)

Zubrow, David, et al. *Maturity Questionnaire*. CMU/SEI-94-SR-7. Pittsburgh, PA: Software Engineering Institute, Carnegie Mellon University, 1994.

Zuse, Horst. *Software Complexity: Measures and Methods*. Berlin: Walter de Gruyter, 1990. (ISBN 3-11-012226-X, 603 pages)

———. *A Framework of Software Measurement*. Berlin: Walter de Gruyter, 1997. (ISBN 3-110 155877)

Zvegintzov, Nicholas. *Software Management Technology Reference Guide*. Release 4.2. New York: Software Maintenance News, 1994. (ISBN 1-884521-01-0, 240 pages)

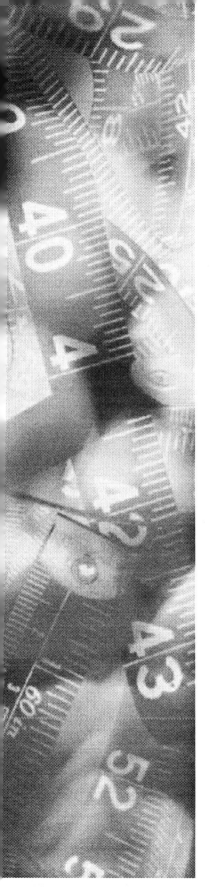

CHAPTER TEN

Benchmarks and Best Practices for Commercial Software

The phrase *commercial software* applies to applications that are produced for large-scale marketing to hundreds or even millions of clients. Examples of commercial software include word processors such as Word Perfect or Microsoft Word, spreadsheets such as Lotus and Excel, project management tools such as Artemis Views, Microsoft Project, KnowledgePlan, COCOMO II, SLIM, and a myriad of other kinds of software. At the large end of the commercial software spectrum can be found ERP applications, such as those from SAP, Oracle, Baan, and JD Edwards. At the low end can be found individual "plug-in" functions, such as Visual Basic controls or JAVA applets.

The commercial software domain overlaps the systems software domain in the arena of operating systems, device drivers, telecommunications, and some "middleware" applications that control physical devices. These applications control physical devices, which makes them systems software. They are also marketed to millions of clients, which makes them commercial software too. However, the commercial software domain also includes thousands of business and technical applications that do not deal with physical devices, such as accounting packages, decision support applications, and day-to-day end user applications such as spreadsheets, word processors, presentation packages, and statistical packages.

The commercial software domain in the United States has become a powerful industry with a favorable balance of trade. Commercial software vendors employ approximately 365,000 software personnel out of a current U.S. total of perhaps 2,400,000. Although there are more than 10,000 companies that produce commercial software in the United States, the major players such as Microsoft and Computer Associates are getting bigger and rapidly acquiring the smaller players. (Small software companies start up and go out of business so often that it is hard to keep track of their numbers.)

The larger commercial software players include both pure software companies and also hybrid companies that market hardware as well. The pure software vendors include companies such as Microsoft, Computer Associates, Oracle, PeopleSoft, Symantec, Platinum, and Sterling. The hybrid companies that build hardware as well as software include companies such as IBM, Compaq, Unisys, Sun, Apple, AT&T, and many others. There are also a host of specialized niches within the commercial software world: accounting software companies, game software companies, medical and legal software companies, and many more.

An interesting and perhaps transient set of commercial software vendors are the thousands of small companies that have only one or a few products on the market, and employ less than 20 personnel. The software business has been very fruitful in creating new companies and thereby creating new jobs too.

Although many small software companies fail, those that succeed have created a number of interesting companies and some significant wealth for many of the founders. The commercial software industry has become a very key part of the overall U.S. economy. Indeed, the balance of trade in the software domain is perhaps the most favorable of any except for food products and defense.

We have not done much work with small companies or with startup companies because they are usually not funded well enough to commission assessments, benchmarks, or baseline studies. However if a startup company survives the critical first two years of operation, or if they receive an infusion of venture capital, they may grow to the size where benchmarks are of interest within a few years. Normally, a company has to employ more than roughly 50 personnel before they are large enough to utilize outside consultants for activities such as assessments and benchmarks.

Although commercial software packages are built throughout the world, the United States is currently the dominant player in global markets. SPR estimates that approximately 85% of the commercial packages running in the United States originated here, and that approximately 40% of the commercial software everywhere in the world has a U.S. origin. This is perhaps the most one-sided balance of trade of any U.S. industry. Even so, the number of commercial software developers outside the United States is large too. SPR estimates the international commercial software companies to employ approximately 350,000 to 500,000 personnel. Some international companies such as SAP AG have global markets, including the United States, but many other international vendors largely serve local markets with software that is tailored for local clients and conditions. The number of international software vendors is growing at the same rapid pace as the current U.S. growth of commercial software producers, such as Microsoft and Computer Associates.

As in the United States, many of the world's commercial software vendors are hybrid companies that build both hardware products and software products. Examples of such hybrids in the international scene include Siemens-Nixdorf in Germany, Tata in India, Bell Northern in Canada, Nippon Telephone and Telegraph in Japan, and Nokia in Sweden.

Special Issues and Technologies for Commercial Software

Because commercial software packages are aimed at thousands or even millions of customers rather than a small group (who may be paying for development), the requirements for commercial software packages are not derived from the users themselves. The normal channels for gathering user requirements for commercial software packages are discussed below.

The ideas of the original inventor of the application is a commonly cited origin for a product. For example, the requirements for our first commercial software cost-estimating product, SPQR/20, were my own and were based on many years of work performing software cost estimates. Other software products that originated from a single person's invention include the first spreadsheet, designed by Dan Bricklin; the APL programming language, developed by Ken Iverson; the Modula programming language, created by Nicklaus Wirth; and the SLIM software estimating tool designed by Larry Putnam.

Once a commercial software product becomes successful in the market, user groups may form around it. User groups are very fruitful sources of new product ideas, and vendors should cultivate such groups and support them fully.

When commercial software companies grow large enough to employ marketing and sales departments, new features are often suggested by marketing and sales personnel, who are in frequent contact with customers of the current release.

Large software companies may perform research studies to gather information about possible future products or about new features for existing products.

These research programs include surveys, focus groups, and even funding for academic research studies.

For commercial products with competitors in the marketplace, the feature sets of the major competitors are a source of new features. All products within the same market niche are more or less constrained to offer similar features to compete. The incidence of "look-and-feel" lawsuits and more standard lawsuits such as copyright and patent violations mean that features cannot be copied directly. However, every market niche has products with similar features, as you can see by examining word processors, spreadsheets, statistical packages, tax preparation packages, accounting packages, and computer-aided design packages.

For specialized and niche products, there may be laws or regulations whose features need to be implemented. For example, it is obvious that tax preparation software packages must support the requirements of the Internal Revenue Service if they are to be sold in the United States.

In any case, the requirements process for commercial software packages is very different from the requirements gathering and analysis for products with specific users whose needs can be expressed to the development team.

For projects with specific users, the technique of JAD is very effective because the clients and the developers meet face to face under the guidance of a JAD facilitator. However, when a software application is being designed for a mass market with millions of possible customers, then the JAD approach is no longer feasible.

The international flavors of commercial software add a significant amount of work to many packages to translate their screens, user manuals, and messages into other national languages. Although some aspects of translation can be automated, the effort needed to translate an application from English into other national languages such as French, German, or Japanese can sometimes approach 20% of the effort and time to create the initial version. Thus, a product translated into five languages can accumulate costs at least equivalent to the costs of building the application initially. Overall, the commercial software domain is the world leader in translation and nationalization of software packages and accompanying materials such as user manuals.

Not only does text require translation, but date and numeric formats require it as well. It is also necessary to check for idioms and nonstandard terms. In general, the changes involved with globalization or nationalization of commercial software packages are complicated enough so that regression testing, system testing, and sometimes external beta testing must be performed on each nationalized version. Thus the translation and testing cycles can run from six to more than 12 calendar months, with testing actually taking more time than the translation itself.

Once the applications are nationalized, they need to be maintained. Thus, customer support, change control, and version synchronization are needed for each version for as long as the product is marketed and supported commercially.

An interesting phenomenon has been noted for commercial software packages. Although the commercial software vendors employ more technical writers than any other software domain, complaints about poor documentation quality are endemic in the commercial software world. As a result, a thriving subindustry has come into existence of book publishers and authors who specialize in tutorial materials in support of commercial software applications. A visit to any large technical bookstore or book Web site will find a whole section devoted to tutorial books for commercial software packages such as Microsoft Office, Lotus Notes, Visio, Quicken, or Adobe products.

There is a great deal of diversity in the commercial software domain, and this is due in part to the need to support diverse operating systems and multiple hardware platforms such as LINUX, UNIX, Windows 98, Windows NT, Windows 2000, OS/2, MVS, VMS, and so forth. Porting applications to multiple platforms and translating applications into multiple national languages are often both performed for the same application. Thus, an application that runs under LINUX, UNIX, Windows 98, and Windows 2000 and is sold in six national languages could have 24 separate versions needing support and maintenance. The existence of so many versions of the same basic software application explains why the commercial software world is usually very effective in dealing with change control, and normally deploys state-of-the-art tools and methods for this purpose.

Another special aspect of marketing software globally deals with piracy protection. Because of widespread customer dissatisfaction with copy protection schemes or special plugs for parallel ports and the like, the commercial software world has adopted fairly stringent legal methods for dealing with unauthorized copies. From time to time both the trade press and even local newspapers and television stations run stories of raids on companies that are reported to be using unauthorized copies of commercial software. The Software Publisher's Association has found such draconian measures to be effective in countries such as the United States. However, software piracy still remains troublesome in countries such as China, although the Chinese government has stated that improvements will be forthcoming.

Because the commercial software domain in the United States has a favorable balance of trade and full employment, it has developed significant political power and some effective lobbying. The passage of the federal Y2K bill, and the approval of draft uniform state laws dealing with commercial software, illustrate the surprising political power of the commercial software industry.

The commercial software domain is also an industry leader in an important but troubling technical area: virus protection. Computer viruses are self-replicating software modules that "hackers" cleverly attach to other software applications. A strange subculture of computer hackers creates viruses either as a so-called protest against commercial software vendors or merely to see if they are clever enough to outwit virus protection methods. Because of the importance of computers and software to police and military services, even more sinister forms of hacking and virus injection may be attempted against government and military software. Indeed, computer and software security have become major fields of endeavor for police and military services.

Viruses can start their transmission by being placed on floppy disks, on CD-ROMs, or by being transmitted over the Internet. Obviously, most viruses are disguised or concealed so that their initial presence is difficult to detect. Once a virus enters a host computer, it is programmed to produce other copies of itself that can be sent to additional computers via e-mail, attached files, or networks. There are many thousands of viruses, and probably at least 100 new ones are created on a weekly basis. Many of them are benign, but many are harmful and can destroy files, lock up computers, or cause screens to display humorous or even obscene messages.

Virus protection has become an important subindustry of the commercial software domain. Several antivirus vendors have full-time virus research laboratories and issue updates of their antivirus software packages almost every week. There are almost as many antivirus packages sold as there are operating systems, because every computer typically runs at least one antivirus application.

The most common programming languages for producing commercial software include Assembly, C, and C++. However, JAVA, Visual Basic, database languages, and many other languages are common too, including FORTRAN, COBOL, LISP, and Pascal. In the DOS era some ten years ago, interpreted languages such as APL and QuickBasic were used for a few commercial packages;

however, the complexity of Windows has necessitated more complete programming environments. In Europe, the Ada83 and Ada95 languages are also used for commercial software packages, and Algol was fairly common before that. Also, the PL/I language was used for commercial software packages in Europe to a much greater degree than in the United States.

A great deal of press coverage is now being devoted to *component-based development*. This phrase implies building software applications from standard, reusable components. Although the idea is good in principle, in practice component-based development is not yet a mature technology. The software industry has two chronic problems that must be solved before component-based development can be fully successful. First, standard interface conventions must be agreed to in order to link components together. Second, software quality control must be capable of building components that approach or achieve zero-defect levels.

The OO approach is very common in the commercial software domain. Here, too, there are many claims being made about the intrinsic ability to reuse OO methods. It has often been stated that OO class libraries provide a very effective strategy for software reusability. However, although some reuse does occur in OO applications, the volume of reusable material remains somewhat less than predicted theoretically. Also, the OO domain has a significant lack of understanding of the importance of software quality control, which is not surprising because poor software quality is endemic throughout most software domains.

A common aspect of the commercial software domain is that the applications are built to appeal to a mass market, rather than built on commission for a specific client or a small number of clients with explicit requirements.

The commercial software domain needs to balance a number of factors to be successful in the marketplace: the feature sets of the products, the quality levels of the delivered software, and the time to reach the relevant market.

Because many small commercial software companies are venture funded, it is significant to note that "failure" in the commercial world often implies failure or bankruptcy of the company itself. It is an unfortunate characteristic of venture funding that the failure rate of venture-backed enterprises approaches or exceeds 50%. This is due in part to the myopia of the venture community in avoiding funding for really new technologies, and a preference to put money into markets that are approaching saturation. Another source of failure is the tendency of venture-backed companies to expand marketing and sales much faster than they expand research and development.

Yet another hazard of the commercial software world is that of litigation. A surprising number of lawsuits occur in the commercial domain dealing with topics such as look-and-feel violations, trade secret infringement, copyright violations, and other assertions of unfair practices.

Quality control in the commercial software domain has ranged from fairly good to very poor. Unfortunately, even major players such as Microsoft, Computer Associates, and Symantec have released products with significant numbers of defects still latent within them.

The most effective sequence of defect removal operations for commercial vendors includes ten discrete stages:

1. Design inspections
2. Code inspections
3. Test material inspections
4. Unit test
5. New function test
6. Regression test
7. Performance or stress test
8. Integration test
9. System test
10. External beta test

This ten-stage sequence would be sufficient to remove more than 96% of software defects prior to delivery of the software to clients and users. However, many smaller software companies tend to bypass the inspections and use a truncated testing sequence that includes unit test, regression test, system test, and sometimes external beta test. This abbreviated sequence can seldom remove more than approximately 70% of latent defects.

The most prominent and unusual form of testing in the commercial domain is that of external beta test. (The term *beta test* dates back to the 1960s, when in-house testing was deemed "alpha" test and external testing was deemed "beta" test, using the first two letters of the Greek alphabet.) Normally, external beta testing occurs after system test, when the vendor thinks that the product is stable enough to be used by at least a sample of courageous users who are willing to put up with some latent bugs to make use of new features. Beta testing is effective, but not all users report defects. Many clients participating in beta tests do not actually make use of the product and hence report no defects. Usually, a small number of very dedicated users exercise the product thoroughly and find most of the problems that beta testing uncovers. It is an interesting phenomenon that if 1,000 clients participate in external beta testing, approximately ten of these clients will submit more than 50% of the total volume of reported defects.

Overall, beta testing itself can top 70% in defect removal efficiency, but only in cases in which thousands of customers use the product and at least 50 of them exercise the product thoroughly. For new products or products with few customers, external beta tests are useful but will probably not find more than approximately 35% of latent defects. Of course, if the product has a large number of really serious bugs still present when beta test begins, the users will tire of its failures and abandon usage. Thus, beta test is best for both clients and vendors if the application is very stable and has few latent bugs at the time beta test commences.

As the twentieth century ended, the commercial software domain faced a significant volume of litigation involving the Y2K problem. Many commercial software packages, including Microsoft's, were not Y2K compliant and caused problems as both fiscal and calendar years changed. Although the commercial software domain spent significant effort in trying to achieve Y2K compliance, the software industry has seldom been 100% efficient in finding and repairing any kind of software defect. Thus, latent Y2K problems still existed, and some of these have been troublesome. Given the normal length of major lawsuits, Y2K litigation can be expected to run out through at least calendar year 2005.

At the end of 1999 and the beginning of 2000, the commercial software domain is at the peak of its power and has enough stature to lobby successfully for two of the most remarkable kinds of protective legislation ever offered to a U.S. industry. The first of these is the Y2K bill, passed by Congress and signed in 1999. This law makes Y2K litigation somewhat more difficult to file and to prosecute. Although this new bill has some virtues, it also has some questionable aspects. The most unusual feature of this legislation is that it provides partial exemption against damages to producers of admittedly flawed products. The second instance of the political prowess of the software industry is the successful lobby to create a uniform set of state laws affecting commercial software packages. This is the proposed Uniform Computer Information Transaction Act (UCITA). If this set of guidelines is turned into state laws, then commercial software vendors will have a unique relationship with their clients. Warranties may become almost meaningless, as indeed many are today.

More significantly, lawsuits against vendors for poor quality or nonperformance of advertised features will become difficult. Furthermore, commercial software vendors will have the right to disable products remotely because they are running on clients' computers. It would be an interesting scenario if customers who complained to software vendors about poor quality or poor service found that their software packages had been disabled remotely as a result, without any ability to take legal action in return.

The UCITA proposal has some merits, of course. It is also clear that uniform state laws governing software products would be useful. However, legislation that favors an industry and places the industry's clients at a disadvantage would appear to be in need of some rethinking.

The political power of the software industry is due to its favorable balance of trade and successful lobbying. From the 1960s through the 1990s, the U.S. computer and software industries have risen from nothing to become major global industries. However, if the impact of the Y2K problem proves to be severe during calendar year 2000, then the software and computer industries could experience a sharp backlash and no doubt would face legislation of a punitive kind. Indeed, if the Y2K problem is severe on a global basis, then punitive legislation in multiple countries might occur.

If Y2K problems should prove to be severe in the United States, then it would not be surprising to see many states introduce licensing requirements for programming personnel. No doubt there would also be a reaction against some of the features of the Y2K bill and the UCITA, although so many organizations and state attorney generals are opposing UCITA that its future is uncertain as this book is written.

Commercial Software Demographics

My data on the commercial software world is less extensive than for other domains. This is due to the fact that many commercial software vendors are fairly small and have cash-flow problems, so they are not likely to commission external assessments, benchmarks, or baselines. The larger commercial vendors such as Microsoft, Computer Associates, Sterling, Oracle, and Platinum are large enough to commission benchmark studies. However, a significant number of small companies are outside the range of our available data in terms of productivity levels, quality levels, or technologies deployed.

I estimate that there are more than 15,000 commercial software applications marketed in the United States at the start of 2000. Approximately 2,500 of these would be the products of the 50 largest software vendors, and the remaining

12,500 would be the products of roughly 10,000 small vendors, each of which has only one or a very few products on the market at any point in time.

Due to the repair and replacement activities associated with the Y2K problem, the years 1998 and 1999 witnessed an unprecedented number of replacements and updates to commercial applications that were not Y2K compliant. These Y2K updates are far too numerous to discuss in this book, but readers are urged to visit the Web sites of all of the vendors whose products they use to ascertain Y2K compliance status. For example, users of Microsoft software can start at the main Microsoft URL of *http://www.Microsoft.com*. Almost all commercial software vendors have sections of their Web sites devoted to Y2K information and to other kinds of update status information.

The unusually large number of updates and releases in 1999 is largely due to the massive efforts associated with Y2K repairs. It should be noted that many commercial applications have been troubled by Y2K date problems, including many Microsoft products such as Excel. Unfortunately Microsoft was a late-comer in disclosing Y2K status, due in part to the fact that as late as 1997 Bill Gates was quoted as denying that PC applications even had Y2K problems. For additional information on commercial software Y2K problems, refer to *The Year 2000 Software Problem: Quantifying the Costs and Assessing the Consequences* (Jones 1998).

Based on demographic studies among SPR's clients extrapolated to national levels, the commercial software domain in the United States contains more than 320,000 professional software personnel and managers, or roughly 14% of the approximate total of 2,300,000 U.S. software personnel. Table 10.1 shows the estimated percentage of total U.S. software personnel working in the domain of commercial software.

The number of U.S. companies that produce commercial software totals more than 15,000 and includes both very large and very small enterprises. Among the large enterprises can be found several of the largest employers of software personnel in the world. Companies such as Microsoft and Computer Associates employ more than 6,000 software personnel. The hybrid companies, such as AT&T and IBM, that build both hardware and software employ even more, and top 25,000 software personnel. (Within IBM, roughly half the software population is in the systems software domain, approximately one quarter builds in-house applications, and roughly one quarter builds commercial packages such as the IMS and CICS database packages, compilers, sorts, industry-specific packages, and the like.) Examples of smaller commercial software vendors include companies

Table 10.1   Estimated U.S. Commercial Software Population circa 2000

Software Occupational Groups	No. Employed	Commercial Software	Percent of Total
Programmer/analyst	400,000	36,000	9.00
Programmer, maintenance	350,000	38,500	11.00
Programmer, development	275,000	30,250	11.00
Project manager, first level	225,000	24,750	11.00
Software engineer, systems	200,000	32,000	16.00
Testing specialist	125,000	25,000	20.00
Systems analyst	100,000	5,000	5.00
Software engineer, real-time	75,000	3,750	5.00
Software technical writer	75,000	18,750	25.00
Software engineer, embedded	70,000	6,300	9.00
Data administration specialist	50,000	5,000	10.00
Project manager, second level	35,000	3,850	11.00
Software quality assurance specialist	25,000	2,500	10.00
Configuration control specialist	15,000	2,400	16.00
Performance specialists	7,500	900	12.00
Project manager, third level	5,000	550	11.00
Software Architect	1,500	180	12.00
Subtotal	2,034,000	235,680	11.59
Support Occupations			
Software sales specialist	105,000	42,000	40.00
Customer support specialist	80,000	22,400	28.00
Systems administration	50,000	4,500	9.00
Software management consultant	45,000	6,750	15.00
Software education specialist	30,000	7,500	25.00
Software librarian	15,000	3,000	20.00
Process auditor/assessor	7,500	375	5.00
Process improvement specialist	5,000	250	5.00

Table 10.1 *continued*

Software Occupational Groups	No. Employed	Commercial Software	Percent of Total
Measurement specialist	3,500	105	3.00
Software marketing specialist	3,000	990	33.00
Cost-estimating specialist	2,000	200	10.00
Human factors specialist	1,000	250	25.00
Certified function point counter	500	25	5.00
Subtotal	322,000	88,345	27.44
Total	2,356,000	324,025	13.75

such as AMS and QS Management, whose technical staffs range from less than 20 to more than 200. These smaller commercial software companies have been important sources of new jobs within the software industry.

Abroad, the countries that produce commercial software in the largest volumes include Germany, Japan, France, and the United Kingdom. Many countries such as Russia, China, India, Brazil, Argentina, Mexico, Taiwan, and South Korea produce some local commercial software packages, but have little or no commercial software for sale in the United States. The non-U.S. total of commercial software personnel ranges from 350,000 to 500,000. Overseas, examples of commercial software producers include SAP AG, Sony, Honeywell-Bull, Alcatel, Nippon Telegraph, Siemens-Nixdorf, LM Ericsson, and Philips.

Some of the industries and SIC codes that produce the greatest amount of commercial software include those presented in Table 10.2.

These industries often produce both commercial packages and some customized systems and applications.

The larger commercial software vendors such as Microsoft and Computer Associates have established some interesting research laboratories. Topics such as human factors, software reusability, and database architectures are among the topics in which exploration is ongoing. Other research topics include quality assurance and testing, requirements analysis, and visual methods. The largest research lab by a pure software company is the Microsoft research lab. This lab is so well funded and has become so prominent that some universities fear a "brain

Table 10.2   Producers of Commercial Software by SIC Code

SIC Code	Industry
3571	Electronic computers
3579	Office machines
3661	Telephone and telegraph apparatus
3845	Electromedical equipment
7371	Custom computer programming services
7372	Prepackaged software
7373	Computer integrated systems design

drain" to the Microsoft facility, which is better equipped and has better compensation levels than universities.

Many hybrid companies that produce both hardware and software also have research divisions and research laboratories. Among the hybrid companies with ongoing research that includes software topics are Apple, IBM, Hewlett-Packard, and Sun.

The larger companies in the commercial software domain are fairly effective in on-the-job training and formal education. From examining some of the curricula within several commercial vendors, some of the courses such as those dealing with change management and maintenance issues appear to be superior to most university courses at both the undergraduate and graduate levels.

The commercial software domain is a major user of high-end development workstations and of PCs in all configurations. The commercial software world in general is well equipped with tools and workstations.

Because the commercial software world has a fairly intense work ethic, both workstations and portable computers may be supplied to key personnel. In fact, the number of computers and workstations in the commercial domain outnumbers technical personnel. This is especially true for vendors whose products operate on multiple platforms, such as Apple, LINUX, and Windows 98. It is not uncommon to see two or three workstations in a development office, so that different versions of the software can be compared and used at the same time.

Another interesting feature of all software domains is the almost universal presence of portable notebook computers. It is now possible for software professionals to be able to work in the office, at home, or even while traveling.

The commercial software domain, like all other software domains, is currently experiencing a shortage of technical personnel. Indeed, this shortage may be more acute for the commercial world than for several other domains. The reason for this is because the thousands of startup companies in the commercial software domain seldom pay high salaries or have outstanding benefits packages. Instead, the startup companies tend to substitute equity, and hope to attract employees who are willing to forgo short-term gain and hope for long-term value should the company succeed and go public. However, due to the shortage of personnel, many large companies are offering excellent salaries, benefits packages, and even signing bonuses. Thus, unless software personnel have an interest in pioneering new product concepts, or regard equity as an important benefit, then small commercial companies may be at a disadvantage in recruiting new staff.

Commercial Software Benchmarks

To provide background for additional discussion, Figure 10.1 illustrates a broad overview of productivity levels in the commercial software domain. Because of fairly effective technologies, capable teams, and lots of unpaid overtime, the commercial software domain is among the most productive of any for applications between 1,000 and 100,000 function points. For major maintenance releases and large enhancements, the commercial software domain is usually the most productive, although some systems software projects are equivalent. A key main point to be derived from Figure 10.1 is the fact that small-project productivity levels vary significantly between "new" projects and "maintenance" projects. This is due to the overhead associated with regression testing of existing software when updates are performed.

Figure 10.1 simplifies the situation and merely provides a general graphical illustration of trends. The reason why new projects are so much more productive than maintenance projects less than 10 function points is due to the fact that maintenance requires regression testing and recompilation of the entire application.

As can be seen from Figure 10.1, the maintenance and new project lines are far apart at the low end, but gradually converge at the large end of the curves. Of course, maintenance releases top out at the 10,000-function point plateau. Small maintenance and enhancement projects are always performed in the context of

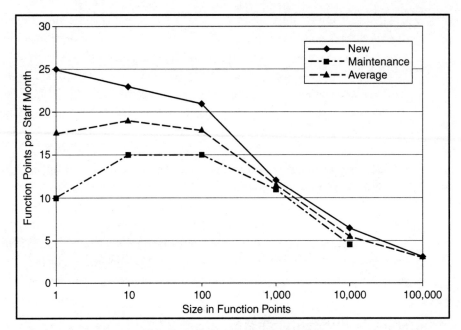

Figure 10.1   Commercial software productivity levels

having to update an existing application. This means that exploration of the application, regression testing, and possibly updating of specifications and user manuals might also occur. From approximately 100 function points in size, new project and enhancements begin to draw together.

The commercial software domain has as great a need for high levels of software quality as the systems software domain. Indeed, these two domains overlap in the case of operating systems such as Microsoft's Windows 98, IBM's MVS, and the like.

However, in general, the commercial software domain is not usually quite as sophisticated in software quality matters as are the older, more established companies in the systems software domain. The commercial software houses are somewhat less likely to have formal software quality assurance departments, although many do have such groups. The commercial domain is not as likely to utilize formal design and inspections, nor are quality measurements as thorough as in the systems software domain.

However, testing and test tools are roughly equal between the systems and commercial domains, and both are much better than average in testing techniques. Both the systems software domain and the commercial software domain are likely to employ trained testing specialists, and to perform the bulk of testing after unit test using well-defined test libraries and formal test plans.

As discussed earlier, the commercial software domain utilizes an interesting form of testing called *external beta test* as a late testing stage. During external beta test, actual customers of the application agree to use it on their own computers at their own sites. Although beta testing is normally a service that clients provide to vendors, Microsoft has changed this equation by actually charging customers for the privilege of finding bugs in its products! This novel approach of charging clients to participate in beta test will, of course, generate revenues. It may also serve to eliminate the idly curious from participating in beta tests, which may be the main purpose of the fees. As all commercial software vendors know, very few beta test customers actually use the software enough to report significant numbers of defects. Many customers simply like to see what features are coming up, and perhaps like the sophistication associated with being part of a beta test group. By charging clients to participate in beta test, Microsoft may be experimenting with a method of screening out those who might not use the product seriously.

However, this new charge structure may also backfire. If charging for beta test participation eliminates any of the small percentage of clients who exercise products thoroughly, then the revenues will not compensate for the loss of useful incoming beta test defect reports.

Overall, the commercial software domain is better than the MIS domain in software quality, but not as good as the traditional systems software domain. The commercial and outsource domains are more or less similar in quality and productivity results. Both tend to employ energetic, hard-working personnel who are willing to provide substantial volumes of unpaid overtime.

The best commercial software projects top 97% in defect removal efficiency, but the average is probably around 90%. However, readers should note the caveat that we have little data from commercial software vendors who employ fewer than 50 software personnel. For the thousands of small commercial shops marketing only one product and employing less than half a dozen software personnel, the results are very sparse. Not only do we lack clients among small companies, but very little of the software quality literature comes from this size domain.

Because I live and work near Boston, I am acquainted with scores of people who work in small software companies. Even though we may not be commissioned to perform formal benchmarks for small companies, we are able to have interesting discussions about productivity and quality matters at events such as the local SPIN meetings, the local IEEE meetings, and other software events in the greater Boston area.

Among the larger commercial software companies employing 100 technical personnel or more, software quality assurance departments are fairly common, and seem to occur in approximately 70% of such companies. For the smaller commercial companies, there may be personnel identified as software quality assurance specialists, but their main focus is often testing rather than other issues such as participating in design and code inspections or running quality measurement programs.

Let us consider some overall benchmark results from the commercial software domain using more recent studies (circa 1995 through 1999). Table 10.3 merely summarizes some of the interesting data points from the SPR studies of systems software.

In general, overall benchmarks are usually interesting; however, such benchmarks do not provide enough information to understand the nature of the work involved. Let us now examine a more detailed activity-level benchmark. As with the other domains, it is useful to consider a specific size application. Because the class of 10,000-function point applications is both common and important within the commercial software domain, let us consider the typical activity patterns for that size of project (Table 10.4). This benchmark shows the activities associated with a commercial software project of 10,000 function points. Assuming that the C programming language is used, this would be about 1,250,000 C statements in size. The C programming language requires approximately 125 statements per function point.

Commercial applications in the 10,000-function point range would include some database packages such as IBM's IMS or customer information control system. Other commercial software in this general size range might include graphical design packages such as AutoCAD, home finance applications, and some language products such as Visual Basic, all with auxiliary features such as Windows CE support.

In Table 10.4 the Assignment Scope column refers to the number of function points normally assigned to one staff member. The Production Rate column refers to the volume of function points that can be completed in a standard time period. Assignment scopes and production rates are key metrics that can be

Table 10.3   Overall Commercial Software Benchmarks

Benchmark	Value
No. of new projects from 1995 through 1999	115
No. of enhancement projects from 1995 through 1999	135
Total no. of projects from 1995 through 1999	250
Average new project size, function points	3,400
Maximum new project size, function points	85,000
Average enhancement size, function points	130
Maximum enhancement size, function points	1,650
Average new development assignment scope, function points	170
Maximum development assignment scope, function points	450
Average maintenance assignment scope, function points	915
Maximum maintenance assignment scope, function points	3,700
Average productivity, function points per staff month	9.2
Maximum productivity, function points per staff month	43.7
Average productivity, work hours per function point	14.35
Maximum productivity, work hours per function point	3.02
Average effort, staff months	31,280
Maximum effort, staff months	391,000
Average new project staff size	20
Maximum new project staff size	714
Average new project schedule, calendar months	25.86
Maximum new project schedule, calendar months	66.00
Average monthly compensation, burdened	$11,500
Maximum monthly compensation, burdened	$18,000
Average cost per function point	$1,250.00
Maximum cost per function point	$5,650.00
Average defect potential per function point	4.8
Maximum defect potential per function point	7.5
Average defect removal efficiency	91.00%
Maximum defect removal efficiency	98.00%
Average monthly rate of requirements creep	2.50%
Maximum monthly rate of requirements creep	6.00%

Table 10.4   Commercial Software Activities and Rates for 10,000 Function Points

Parameter	Value
Application size	10,000 function points
Application size	1,250,000 LOC
Source language	C
Work hours per month	132
Monthly compensation	$11,500

Activities Performed	Assignment Scope, function points	Production Rate, function points	Staff	Effort, months	Schedule, months	Cost	Percent
01 Requirements	1,000	150	10	67	6.67	$766,667	3.17
02 Prototyping	2,000	125	5	80	16.00	$920,000	3.81
03 Initial design	165	75	61	133	2.20	$1,533,333	6.34
04 Detail design	155	60	65	167	2.58	$1,916,667	7.93
05 Design reviews	200	150	50	67	1.33	$766,667	3.17
06 Coding	140	24	71	417	5.83	$4,791,667	19.82
07 Reuse acquisition	2,000	1000	5	10	2.00	$115,000	0.48
08 Code inspections	150	125	67	80	1.20	$920,000	3.81
09 Configuration management	1,500	500	7	20	3.00	$230,000	0.95
10 Formal integration	2,000	500	5	20	4.00	$230,000	0.95

11 Documentation	1,250	90	8	111	13.89	$1,277,778	5.29
12 Unit testing	140	45	71	222	3.11	$2,555,556	10.57
13 Function testing	160	60	63	167	2.67	$1,916,667	7.93
14 Integration testing	160	75	63	133	2.13	$1,533,333	6.34
15 System testing	225	100	44	100	2.25	$1,150,000	4.76
16 Beta testing	500	200	20	50	2.50	$575,000	2.38
17 Quality assurance	1,500	130	7	77	11.54	$884,615	3.66
18 Project management	1,400	55	7	182	25.45	$2,090,909	8.65
Totals/averages	162[1]	4.76[1]	62[1]	2,102[2]	34.10[1]	$24,173,858[2]	100.00[2]

Cost per function point, $2,417; cost per LOC, $19.34.
[1]Average
[2]Total

derived from benchmark studies. The importance of these metrics is that they are fundamental metrics for software cost estimating.

The standard time period in Table 10.4 is a "staff month," which contains approximately 22 working days. Each working day is assumed to be a nominal eight hours in duration, but only six hours a day are devoted to productive work. This totals 132 effective work hours per month. These assumptions are nominal or default values. However, it is quite common among commercial software personnel to have a very intense work ethic. An hour of unpaid overtime per day, plus at least four to six hours of unpaid overtime on weekends (sometimes at home, but sometimes at work) is typical in the commercial domain.

As you can see from Table 10.4, commercial software utilizes a rather complete set of 18 activities, with a significant concentration of resources on quality-related topics such as formal inspections, testing, and quality assurance work. If the application in question has significant performance criteria, then an additional test stage for performance testing might be added.

Because commercial applications in the 10,000-function point range can only be built by fairly large and sophisticated companies, Table 10.4 assumes a formal quality assurance group. It also assumes design inspections, code inspections, and five discrete forms of testing. It is not uncommon for commercial software to utilize between five and nine discrete forms of testing for major projects.

Note that commercial software includes "external beta testing" or tests by clients on their own computers and in their own sites. Although it is too late in the development cycle to use beta testing to find serious errors, the external beta tests are popular with clients and do flush out quite a few errors, including many errors involving interfaces and usability problems.

The list of activities in Table 10.4 is useful when considering only summary or project-level data. Without knowing how many different kinds of work are involved in commercial software, it is difficult to understand why productivity levels for entire projects are so much lower than productivity rates for coding.

When activities from Table 10.4 are aggregated, it is interesting to note that the sum of the work devoted to "defect removal" is by far the largest cost driver of commercial software. As often occurs for large applications, code-related work in the form of prototypes and product programming is only the third largest cost element (Table 10.5).

Note that the production of paper documents shown in Table 10.5 for English documentation. If the commercial product is to be marketed in Canada, France, Japan, Germany, or other countries, then translation of user documents can add substantial costs and effort to the overall project. For example, if the

Table 10.5   Commercial Software Cost Drivers

Commercial Software Cost Drivers	Staff Months	Percent
Defect removal	896	42.62
Paper documents	478	22.73
Code related	547	26.01

product is to be released in other national languages, then each language may add translation and testing costs roughly equal to 20% of the total effort shown in Table 10.4.

Because our clients are interested in "best in class," Table 10.6 contrasts average values with best-in-class results for metrics in the productivity and quality domains. A word of explanation is needed to interpret the table: Commercial software projects range from less than 1,000 function points to more than 100,000 function points. It is necessary to display the sizes in order for the data to be relevant. In Table 10.6 three size categories are used: 1,000, 10,000, and 100,000 function points. There are no complete commercial software projects less than 1,000 function points, although there are many enhancements and features. Also, for projects less than 1,000 function points, individual human variance becomes a major factor, so the results are statistically uncertain. Lastly, the differences between new projects and maintenance projects at the low end really require separate data points.

In Table 10.6 "function point" refers to function points counted using Version 4.1 of the IFPUG counting rules, and LOC refers to logical statements, rather than to physical lines. For the cost items shown in Table 10.6, a constant burdened compensation rate of $11,500 per staff month is assumed. The reason for using a constant value is because the actual difference in monthly compensation is a complex topic. As pointed out earlier, compensation varies by industry, size of company, geographic region, and occupational group.

As you can see from the results in this section, the commercial software domain is quite effective in many ways. The commercial software domain has respectable productivity rates for large systems (>10,000 function points). Although commercial software quality is better than U.S. averages, it is not really as good as it should be. In particular, commercial software often lags behind systems software in quality approaches.

Table 10.6   Average and Best-in-Class Results for Commercial Software

Key Software Topics	100 Function Points	1,000 Function Points	10,000 Function Points
Average staff size	6	59	645
Best-in-class staff size	3	38	455
Average schedule, months	13.80	33.11	74.99
Best-in-class schedule, months	9.77	22.91	63.10
Average function points per staff month	12.68	5.13	2.07
Best-in-class function points per staff month	30.70	11.35	3.49
Average work hours per function point	10.41	25.71	63.86
Best-in-class work hours per function point	4.30	11.63	37.86
Average LOC per staff month in C	1,585	642	258
Best-in-class LOC per staff month in C	3,837	1,419	436
Average effort, staff months	79	1,948	48,380
Best-in-class effort, staff months	33	881	28,680
Average cost per function point	$907.11	$2,240.00	$5,563.73
Best-in-class cost per function point	$456.04	$1,013.27	$3,298.19
Average defects per function point	5.00	5.50	6.60
Best-in-class defects per function point	2.50	4.00	5.20
Average defect removal efficiency	95.00%	91.00%	88.00%
Best-in-class defect removal efficiency	99.50%	98.00%	96.00%
Average delivered defects per function point	0.250	0.495	0.792
Best-in-class delivered defects per function point	0.013	0.080	0.208
Average no. of delivered defects	250	4,950	79,200
Best-in-class no. of delivered defects	13	800	20,800
Average no. of high-severity defects	38	743	11,880
Best-in-class no. of high-severity defects	2	96	2,496

For applications in the 100,000-function point plateau, the commercial software domain is not as good as the systems software domain. Another curious observation is that large companies are better than mid-size companies for building very large systems. Microsoft has been frequently late with major applications compared with larger companies such as IBM. In fairness, bringing out an application of 100,000 function points is challenging for every domain and every company. For smaller applications (<10,000 function points), the capable personnel and intense work ethic noted in the commercial software domain raise productivity rates somewhat.

The next benchmark of interest is how well commercial software meets its anticipated schedules. Table 10.7 includes four columns of data: projects that are early, projects that are on time relative to their formal schedules, projects that are late, and projects that are cancelled and never finished at all.

Much of the work in the commercial software domain has centered around the development of applications between 1,000 and 10,000 function points. For example, many Windows applications are within this size range. The largest and most complex commercial applications are the ERP applications. Some of these, such as SAP R3, with all features installed, can top 250,000 function points.

The nodal point at which commercial software and systems software come together is that of operating systems for computers. The Windows 98 and NT operating systems are in the 100,000-function point domain. This is also the

Table 10.7   Commercial Software Schedule Adherence circa 1999

Size, function points	Early Projects, %	On-time Projects, %	Late Projects, %	Cancelled Projects, %	Total Projects, %
1	9.00	88.00	2.00	1.00	100.00
10	8.00	85.00	5.00	2.00	100.00
100	7.00	75.00	12.00	6.00	100.00
1,000	5.00	65.00	20.00	10.00	100.00
10,000	3.00	35.00	37.00	25.00	100.00
100,000	1.00	30.00	34.00	35.00	100.00
Average	5.50	63.00	18.33	13.17	100.00

approximate size of IBM's MVS mainframe operating system. Interestingly, LINUX and the common UNIX variants are approximately 50,000 function points. Of course, Windows offers many auxiliary features that are not part of the kernel of the operating system, but are useful to clients and users.

Commercial Software Successes and Failures

There are many ways to fail when building large applications and only a few ways to succeed. The commercial software domain often succeeds for projects between 1,000 and 10,000 function points, but has some trouble at the large end of the size spectrum. The construction of large software applications is a high-risk activity in every domain. Every major company that builds software has experienced failures in the large-system domain. To optimize the probability of success for building large applications, project management, process rigor, and quality control must be at state-of-the art levels. Any deficiencies in these three fundamental disciplines can lead to delays or outright failure.

In the commercial software world the terms *success* and *failure* can be applied to either corporations or to specific products, with different meanings. At the corporate level, the term *success* normally implies a company that does well enough to have an initial public offering that makes the founders, shareholders, and some early technical employees wealthy. The term *failure* implies a company that does poorly enough so that eventually bankruptcy and layoffs result.

At the individual product level, *success* implies achieving a significant market share and also profitability. The term *failure* implies a product with few or dissatisfied users, or a product overshadowed by a more successful competitor. Table 10.8 presents the success and failure criteria for commercial software products.

The commercial software world is widely polarized into a rather small set of very successful products, a small set of mildly successful products, and a large number of marginal or unsuccessful products. Some of the more popular and successful commercial products have user associations created among clients. These associations are independent of the vendor, although the vendors often support such associations. User associations can be very helpful to vendors, and are excellent sources of feedback about possible new features that can be added to the product. These associations are also useful sources of complaints about problems that need to be fixed. However, products with too many bugs are seldom popular enough to have a supportive user association.

As a general rule of thumb, roughly 10% of the products in a specific market niche might be classed as very successful, 20% as mildly successful, 40% as mar-

Table 10.8   Commercial Software Success and Failure Factors

Commercial Software Success Factors	Commercial Software Failure Factors
Product achieves significant market share	Product fails to achieve market share
Product is profitable	Product loses money
Product protects unique features	Product is readily imitated
Product prevails in any litigation	Product loses significant litigation
Product leads to follow-on business	Product generates no ancillary business
Customer support is good to excellent	Customer support is poor to marginal
User satisfaction is good to excellent	User satisfaction is poor to marginal
Feature set is better than competitors	Feature set lags behind competitors
Time-to-market is better than competitors	Time-to-market lags behind competitors
Quality levels are good to excellent	Quality levels are poor to marginal
User association forms for product	No organization of product users
Product is fully Y2K compliant	Product is not Y2K compliant

ginal, and 30% as failures. As this book is written, a host of acquisitions, mergers, downsizings, and a sprinkling of bankruptcies are sweeping through the commercial software domain. What may be occurring with software perhaps resembles the automotive industry 60 to 70 years ago, when the number of automobile manufacturers in the United States began to decline from more than 50 to only three. The major software houses such as Microsoft, Symantec, and Computer Associates may be achieving such a strong marketing presence, and acquiring so many smaller companies, that by the middle of the twenty-first century the commercial software market may well be populated by only a few very large companies.

The pure software companies in the commercial domain have been growing rather rapidly for the past 20 years. The hybrid companies that build both hardware and software had a period of decline in the late 1980s and early 1990s: DEC, Wang, Data General, Prime, and several other hybrid companies lost money, were acquired, or reduced staffs by downsizing or selling business units. Some of these hybrid companies such as Apple and Hewlett-Packard have successfully turned around their negative growth and now seem to be healthy companies again.

IBM was also under fire, leading to the replacement of John Akers by Lou Gerstner as chairman. This interesting transition marked the first time in IBM's history that the top executive position was given to an outsider who had not come up through IBM's own executive ranks. Gerstner's fresh approach to IBM's somewhat conservative and introspective style has led to a successful return to growth and profitability.

Other hybrid software and hardware companies have followed another path. AT&T chose to split up into several new companies, such as Bellcore and Lucent. These companies had some awkward moments during the transition, but have now managed to reinvent themselves in their new markets.

Microsoft is the premier pure software company in the world. However, as this book is written, Microsoft is in the midst of an antitrust suit. Although the suit is still in progress, one of the options being discussed should Microsoft lose would be the division of Microsoft into several companies.

A separate lawsuit against Microsoft is also likely to have long-range implications for the software industry as a whole. A number of contract personnel working for Microsoft have received a judgment awarding them some of the benefits usually reserved for Microsoft's full-time personnel. If this judgment is not changed during the appeal process, it can lead to some changes in the use of contract software personnel in the United States.

The technology track record of the commercial software world is mixed, with some notable successes and also some embarrassing failures. The successes in commercial software are often spectacular and make millionaires out of all concerned, as has been the case with Microsoft. The failures are sometimes equally spectacular, and terminate in a burst of personal and corporate bankruptcies often accompanied by litigation.

As this book is written, new commercial software companies focusing on the Internet, World Wide Web, and the topic of e-business are springing up very rapidly. Many of these have already gone through initial public offerings and are now well funded, even if not yet profitable.

As this book is written, the technology sector of the United States stock market has been setting daily records for stock value. In addition, initial public offerings by Internet-related software companies have been returning values far beyond expectations. These trends may not last, but they have certainly provided excitement and are creating wealth at the beginning of the twenty-first century.

There is no question that the Internet and e-business will transform many traditional industries, and also open up many new business opportunities in the commercial software domain. However, the e-business trends are in their infancy, and the way this business will develop cannot be fully understood until sometime in the new century.

Commercial Software Success Factors

The following are some of the areas in which the commercial software domain ranks as best in class, or at least very good compared with other industry segments:

- Development schedules for projects less than 1,000 function points are very short.
- Configuration control of updates and changes is very good to excellent.
- Configuration control of multiple versions and platforms is very good to excellent.
- Nationalization and support for other languages is better than any other domain.
- Software reusability in the commercial world is better than for most industries.
- OO adoption is moving very rapidly among commercial vendors.
- Commercial software is a leader in piracy prevention.
- Standards such as IEEE and ISO are being adopted very rapidly.
- Customer support is good to excellent for most large commercial software vendors.
- User satisfaction surveys rank among the best in class of any industry.
- User associations provide the best source of suggested improvements of any industry.
- Software tool suites are better for commercial software than for most other industries.
- Equity offered to technical workers is more common than in most industries.
- The commercial software world leads in antivirus protection and research.
- The commercial software world leads many industries in political power.

The commercial software world needs short development schedules, high quality levels, and effective configuration control over multiple platforms and releases. Although not every vendor and every product achieves these targets, enough of them have done so to make the commercial software business one of the major favorable components of the United States balance of trade. The commercial software industry is one of the top industries of the United States, and it will be interesting to see whether this situation is maintained in the twenty-first century.

There has been a tendency for U.S. industries to start very strongly and dominate world markets for perhaps 50 years, and then fall behind in quality control, innovation, and product features. Sometimes recovery is possible, and sometimes it is not. The commercial software industry passed its fiftieth anniversary in 1993. So far, the U.S. commercial software business is still expanding, and that is a good sign.

Commercial Software Failure Factors

The commercial software organizations have lagged in some aspects of software development processes and practices:

- Commercial software depends too heavily on massive bursts of unpaid overtime.
- Burnout of software technical personnel is a problem for commercial software.
- Commercial software lags somewhat in software specialization.
- Commercial software lags in quality control methods such as formal inspections.
- Commercial software lags in quality measures and metrics.
- Commercial software lags in productivity measurements and metrics.
- Commercial software vendors lag in adopting function point metrics.
- Commercial software vendors lag in adopting modern software cost-estimating tools.
- Development schedules for large systems (>10,000 function points) run long and late.

The commercial software world is often chided for some other factors that are outside the primary themes of this book, but appear to be important:

- Commercial software tends to announce release dates that are not met.
- Commercial software tends to exaggerate productivity and quality results.
- Commercial software leads in intercompany litigation.
- Commercial software leads in copyright and trade secret litigation.
- Commercial software is a pioneer in look-and-feel litigation.

- Commercial software is in the midst of mergers and acquisitions.
- Commercial software has very powerful political lobbies.
- Commercial software may sometimes lag in customer support.

The commercial software domain tends to have one very bad practice that is professionally unacceptable, and may even be illegal: the practice of making exaggerated claims that using a particular tool or method will improve productivity, schedules, or quality without providing any supporting data. Too many ads placed by commercial software vendors advertise claims such as, "Use tool XYZ and shorten your schedules by 50%." One vendor even advertised a remarkable claim of improving productivity by 1,000%, but would not respond to my queries for supporting evidence.

An anecdote will illustrate the nature of this problem. Several years ago, a marketing vice president from a commercial software vendor called me and requested permission to quote some of my published data in an ad. The data in question did not include any findings from the company's products, which was pointed out to the marketing executive. The response from the executive was, "That doesn't matter, the results look good." When asked whether any similar studies had been performed to ascertain whether the vendor's products actually improved productivity, the response was, "No, that costs too much."

The commercial software industry is too important to be lax in making performance claims. The industry needs empirical studies that can demonstrate the value of tools and practices. Fanciful statements that are hype rather than empirical are harmful to the industry in the long run.

The commercial software domain has been a remarkable success in many ways. It has created thousands of interesting new jobs. The commercial software business in the United States has a very favorable balance of trade with the rest of the world. Because of its success, the commercial software domain also has political power and some very effective lobbying for legislation that favors the industry.

In spite of its usefulness, commercial software is troubled by marginal quality levels. In addition, commercial software warranties are often one sided, and favor the vendor rather than offering any substantial recourse to consumers. The latter issues are troubling to many industry observers.

The Microsoft Pattern

Because Microsoft is such a dominant player in the commercial software world, it is interesting to consider some of the software technology and sociological patterns associated with Microsoft's rapid growth and visible success. By historical accident, Microsoft's business started with fairly small applications with a total size of less than 1,000 function points. This size range is where the original DOS product can be found. Some Microsoft products, such as the early Basic language interpreters, were only a few hundred function points in size, although modern Visual Basic, Version 6.0, approaches 10,000 function points when all features are considered, such as Windows CE support.

Microsoft became one of the most effective enterprises in human history for the development of fairly small PC applications with a size of less than 1,000 function points. Microsoft's success was accomplished in part by hiring very bright people and equipping them rather well. For example, the Microsoft hiring process is extremely rigorous and effective, and includes extensive use of college-level interns, multiple levels of formal interviews, and even having candidates create code, test cases, or some deliverable based on whatever kind of position they are seeking. Once hired, the internal appraisal and motivation systems tend to push capable people along rapidly, while encouraging those who are not so capable to find work elsewhere. On the whole, Microsoft has one of the highest concentrations of really intelligent software people in the world.

However, because the staff was capable, and because early Microsoft products were small enough to be built by small teams, formal methods such as inspections were not used early on. Quality control included extensive in-house testing, daily builds of applications, and early and extensive usage of Microsoft's own products by developers and managers. Also, once Microsoft had established a large customer base, that customer base also gave Microsoft a unique capability: the availability of more than 10,000 customers willing to act as external beta testers for new releases of Microsoft products. This form of high-volume beta testing is more than 80% efficient in finding bugs, and is indeed the only known form of testing to equal or exceed formal inspections in defect removal efficiency.

With the advent of Windows 95, Windows 98, and Windows-based applications such as the newer releases of Microsoft Word, Excel, and PowerPoint, the average size of Microsoft applications expanded from less than 1,000 function points to more than 5,000 function points and even to more than 87,000 function points for Windows 98 (based on "backfiring" Microsoft's source code volumes as published in the *Wall Street Journal*). Windows NT and Windows 2000 are approaching 100,000 function points, making them very large systems indeed. This is roughly the same size category as many older mainframe applications, and is the same size range as the 100,000 function points of IBM's current MVS mainframe operating system.

As the industry has noted, Microsoft did not do as well with large systems as they did with low-end applications. That is to say, schedule overruns, cost overruns, and quality control problems plagued Microsoft just like they plagued everyone else that builds large and complex software systems.

In contrast, IBM's OS/2 operating system came from a company in which quality assurance and inspections had been at state-of-the-art levels for many years, and hence OS/2 was able to achieve stability somewhat before Microsoft's products in terms of chronology.

Although a formal study has not been published, it is interesting that users of the LINUX operating system also report stability and low defect rates as a key virtue, although LINUX is currently less than half the overall size of Windows 98 and probably is less than 40,000 function points as of 1999.

Microsoft has now recognized that building really large systems in excess of 10,000 function points is not the same game as building low-end applications of 1,000 function points or less. As a result, software development practices within Microsoft are beginning to resemble those of AT&T, Motorola, Hewlett-Packard, IBM, and the other successful developers of really large systems. Although Microsoft and IBM are not always on the best of terms, it is interesting that Microsoft is now experimenting with the same kind of formal inspection process that was developed at IBM in the late 1960s and early 1970s, when IBM's operating system, OS/360, also climbed above 10,000 function points.

The essence of the situation is that very bright software generalists like those employed at Microsoft can build low-end applications of less than 1,000 function points in a semiformal way and get away with it most of the time. The same is not true for major systems of 10,000 function points, or when applications approach 100,000 function points, such as Windows 95 and Windows 98. At larger size levels, there is a need to coordinate the work of dozens or even hundreds of different people. Many diverse skills are needed, including quality assurance, testing, configuration control, technical writing, cost estimating, schedule planning, and a host of others.

There are hundreds of successful ways to build small applications, but only a few ways to build large systems successfully. As the average size of PC software creeps up and approaches the average size of mainframe software, the commercial software vendors are beginning to learn that they need more rigorous methods to succeed.

The Emergence of the ISO 9000–9004 Standards

A new factor entered the commercial software world in 1992, when the European Union was created and, as a by-product, the ISO 9000–9004 standards became effective across most of Europe. Pragmatically, to sell products including commercial software to much of Europe, certification to ISO standards became a necessity.

The ISO 9000–9004 standards are nominally quality standards and require certification of various aspects of quality plans. However, a close review of the ISO standards themselves reveals that the authors appear to be perhaps ten years behind the state of the art in understanding software quality control. The basic theme of the ISO standards appears to be "plan and document what you intend to do." Whether what you intend to do is effective, ineffective, or neutral in terms of actually benefiting quality is outside the scope of the ISO standards.

SPR has been doing international research to ascertain whether ISO certification actually improves quality, but to date the empirical results are negligible. The most visible and tangible aspects of ISO certification are the costs of the assessment and a significant increase in the volume of paperwork.

Colleagues working in hardware companies do report some quality success from ISO certification, but so little empirical data is available that the British government directed the British standards organization to stop advertising that ISO certification improved productivity unless actual data demonstrated that improvements did occur.

Some of the U.S. companies that had effective quality control long before the ISO standards were published have chided the ISO organization for taking a step backward rather than forward. The essence of the situation seems to be that for companies such as Motorola and Hewlett-Packard, with effective quality control approaches, ISO certification is fairly easy but irrelevant, except for marketing in Europe. For companies that do not have effective quality control approaches, ISO certification is fairly costly and time-consuming, and insufficient in actually increasing software quality in any tangible way.

Best Technical Practices for Commercial Software

The commercial software domain is the most sophisticated of any kind of software production in two topics: translation of software deliverables into other national languages, and change control of multiple versions and releases. The commercial software domain is better than average in quality control, but not as good as the systems software domain. One of the major weaknesses of the commercial software domain, shared by Microsoft and other large commercial vendors too, are rather primitive quality measurements and a scarcity of data using function point metrics.

The best-practice information derives from our assessment and benchmark studies. Note, however, that SPR's data is derived primarily from larger commercial vendors employing at least 50 personnel. We have done no consulting work for the thousands of small companies with less than ten software personnel (although I have numerous friends and colleagues who work for small software companies, or who have started small software companies, as I did). This section uses the same set of ten key factors that are examined during SPR assessments and benchmarks:

1. Project management methods such as estimating
2. Requirements-gathering and analysis methods
3. Design and specification methods
4. Coding methods
5. Reusability methods
6. Change control methods
7. User documentation methods
8. Pretest defect removal methods such as inspections
9. Testing methods and tools
10. Maintenance methods and tools

As with the other domains, to be cited, the sets of practices termed *best practices for systems software* must have been used on at least 50 successful projects within ten companies. In the views of both project managers and technical personnel, the practices must have been contributors to a successful outcome. Furthermore, to be included in the set of best practices, the practices must not have been cited as contributing to failures, overruns, or litigation for breach of contract. In other words, these are practices that add positive value.

Best Project Management Practices for Commercial Software

In every domain project management is a key technology. Major commercial software producers such as Microsoft, Computer Associates, Oracle, Rational, and Symantec are fairly similar to one another in project management approaches. Standard project management tools such as Microsoft Project or Artemis are often used. Commercial software cost- and quality-estimating tools such as SLIM, SEER, CHECKPOINT, and KnowledgePlan are not used as often in the commercial domain as are proprietary tools or estimating methods.

For what may be sociological reasons, measurements of productivity and quality within the commercial software domain lag behind the systems software domain. Function points are not as widely utilized, nor are activity-based measurements. Quality measurements are also somewhat primitive compared with systems software. The set of commercial software best practices in project management include those presented in the following subsections.

Subscriptions to Special Industry Information Sources

An almost universal best practice among the commercial software domain, or at least among the larger companies, is to subscribe to information about key topics of commercial software importance. Several companies perform studies of market shares, user satisfaction, Y2K issues, and other relevant topics. Some of the companies marketing data to and about commercial software topics include Auerbach, IDC, Gartner Group, Giga Group, and Meta Group.

Project Management Training

All commercial software project managers should be trained in software sizing, cost estimating, quality estimating, milestone tracking, and cost tracking. All project managers should be able to create accurate plans and estimates for projects at least 1,000 function points in size. Entry-level training on promotion to project manager is a common best practice. Setting aside five to ten days a year for project management training is also a best practice, although one that may be suspended for critical issues such as Y2K repairs.

Project Management Tool Suites

All commercial software project managers should be trained in and have available a suite of project management tools, including those that support sizing of key deliverables, cost and resource estimating, quality estimating, standard project management for critical path analysis, cost tracking, and milestone tracking. Personnel management tools for appraisal and job planning support are also a best practice in the United States, but not in Europe, where they may be prohibited.

Activity-Based Cost Estimates

All commercial software cost estimates for projects larger than 1,000 function points should be at the activity or task levels. Project-level or phase-level estimates are inadequate for large projects. Estimation for small projects can be at the phase level, but for large projects this is an unsafe and hazardous practice.

Function Point Analysis

All commercial software project managers should be trained in the basics of function point analysis. Managers do not need to be certified function point counters, however. All productivity and quality studies, and benchmarks, should include function point analysis. LOC metrics are hazardous for cross-language comparisons. It is actually a best practice to utilize both function point metrics and LOC for benchmark studies. It would be useful if commercial software vendors would publish data on the function point totals of their applications and releases. This would help clients in portfolio analysis. However, we have not encountered this practice among any major commercial software vendors.

Empirical Data

All commercial software project managers should know the ranges of quality and productivity levels derived from empirical studies for the kinds of software for which they are responsible. In particular, project managers should know defect removal efficiency levels and productivity levels for similar projects. Otherwise, it is difficult for managers to defend accurate estimates against arbitrary overrides by clients and senior executives.

Milestone Tracking

All commercial software projects larger than 1,000 function points should use formal milestone tracking. This is a best practice that can minimize unpleasant problems such as major schedule delays, or may at least provide an early warning. Major milestones include completion of requirements, external specifications, internal specifications, inspection plans, design inspections, code inspections, test plans, all forms of testing, risk analysis plans, performance analysis plans, user documentation, and installation.

Activity Cost Tracking

All commercial software projects larger than 1,000 function points should use formal cost tracking at the activity level. Examples of activities include requirements analysis, initial and detail design, code development, reusable material acquisition, design and code inspections, quality assurance, all forms of testing, change control, user documentation, and project management. Normalized costs such as "cost per function point" are also a best practice. Costs based on LOC are optional but are not a best practice. Indeed, if LOC metrics are the only productivity measure, this constitutes professional malpractice. Use of both LOC metrics and function points together are also a best practice.

Because of the restriction that best practices need to have been observed in at least ten companies and 50 projects, several interesting practices are not deployed often enough to be included at present. For example, the earned-value cost tracking approach and the balanced-scorecard measurement approach have only been encountered a few times among our commercial software clients, but appear to be useful management practices. As the usage of these approaches expands, they may join the set of best practices in the future.

It is interesting that usage of the SEI CMM has not been observed often enough in the commercial software domain to include it among the set of best practices.

Although ISO certification has passed the requirement of being noted on at least 50 projects in ten companies, the lack of empirical data proving that ISO certification offers tangible improvements in quality means that it is not included among the set of best practices.

Best Requirements-Gathering and Analysis Practices for Commercial Software

Requirements gathering and analysis in the commercial software domain are unique, although they overlap approaches used by systems software, such as operating systems. The reason for this is because some of the requirements for commercial software must meet the needs of thousands or even millions of users, rather than a small number of users whose requirements can be discussed face to face. Thus, commercial software requirements often stem from marketing and competitive studies, rather than the requests of specific clients. For example, for a commercial spreadsheet or word processor, each vendor needs to compete with other vendors in the same market. All need to support similar feature sets. Some of the best practices for requirements gathering and analysis in the commercial software domain include those presented in the following subsections.

Competitive Analysis

It is a best practice in the commercial software domain to analyze the features of competitive products. Of course exact replication of competitive features may lead to look-and-feel litigation, or even charges of copyright or patent violation. In spite of the risks, commercial software companies all tend to offer similar feature sets for similar products.

User Association Recommendations

It is a best practice for commercial software products that have user associations to pay close attention to the suggestions of these associations for possible new features that might be valuable. Most major software vendors have user associations, and in general these associations are valuable sources of new features for existing products.

Focus Groups

It is a best practice for commercial software vendors to invite groups of either possible clients or actual clients to participate in *focus group* discussions about potential new features for commercial products. Focus groups normally comprise six clients to more than a dozen clients, plus a number of marketing and sales personnel employed by the vendor. The purpose of the focus group is to garner user reactions to planned new features and to hear user views on the features they would like to see.

New Inventions

It is a best practice for commercial software vendors to support promising new inventions by employees, should they be offered. This approach is noted most frequently in two situations: (1) startup companies that are founded specifically to build a new commercial product based on the founder's invention and (2) large companies such as IBM that have formal programs for submitting inventions for consideration as possible products. (For example, the APL programming language originated as an invention by Ken Iverson.)

Function Point Size

A best practice for all software projects, including commercial ones, is to include function point size derivations from the requirements themselves. Once function point totals are known, they provide a useful baseline for measuring the rate of requirements creep. The commercial software domain is volatile in terms of requirements stability, and changes or additions to requirements can top 5% per calendar month during the design and coding phases, although 2% is more common. Note that although function point totals for commercial products are used internally, we have not yet encountered any major vendors that publish this information. In the future, it would be very useful if every software product had published data on its size in terms of function points.

Best Design and Specification Practices for Commercial Software

The commercial software domain is not usually as thorough as the systems domain in terms of specifications. Furthermore, prototypes often play a major role in the commercial software domain, in which they are used to prove innovative concepts and to demonstrate features to the development group.

Prototypes

A best practice for commercial software projects is the creation of prototypes for key features and algorithms. The two most common forms of prototype used for commercial software are disposable prototypes and time-box prototypes. A disposable prototype is discarded once it has served its initial purpose. A time-box prototype has a chronological limit, and must be completed within a specific period, such as one calendar month. The use of evolutionary prototypes often occurs, but is not a best practice. The lack of structure in evolutionary prototypes makes them unsuited for applications with high quality and reliability targets. Normally, commercial software prototypes amount to approximately 10% of the functionality of the finished application. The prototypes concentrate on key algorithms and performance issues.

Design Inspections

A best practice for commercial software projects of all sizes, and for enhancements as well as new projects, is the use of formal design inspections on all specification documents. The rationale for this is due to the fact that software designs and specifications contribute roughly 1.25 defects per function point, or approximately 25% of the total. Design defects are often higher in severity than coding defects, and perhaps 35% of severity 2 defects originate in the design itself. Formal design inspections are derived from the pioneering work on inspections carried out by IBM. A number of books and articles discuss inspections, such as the pioneering work of Michael Fagan, Dr. Gerald Weinberg, Daniel Friedman, and Thomas Gilb. Design inspections average more than 65% efficiency in finding and removing design errors. Inspections also serve as a defect prevention approach too, because participants will avoid problems in their own work that are pointed out during the inspection sessions.

Reusable Specifications

An interesting best practice noted in both the commercial and in the systems and embedded domains is that of reusable designs and specifications. Software reuse includes more than a dozen artifacts, with specifications being among the most important. The use of specification methods that support both formalism and reusability is a best practice. These approaches include UML and some of the older, structured specification approaches as well. Our data indicates that use of formal design approaches leads to higher quality and productivity than informal design. However, which formal design approach is used varies with the needs of the project. As an example of reusable specifications, my own company has been able to reuse some of the key algorithms across three of our commercial software estimating tools: SPQR/20, CHECKPOINT, and KnowledgePlan. Of course, the externals of all three products are quite different. Furthermore, KnowledgePlan, the most recent of our products, has many new algorithms that are not part of the older products. However, for common tasks such as estimating coding productivity in procedural languages, reusable specifications have been possible.

Best Coding Practices for Commercial Software

The commercial software domain is among the leaders in requiring the use of structured programming practices. This is due to the practical needs of supporting multiple versions of the same application. It is also due to the need to plan for many years of maintenance after the initial release.

Structured Programming

A common best practice within the commercial software domain is that of using formal program structure techniques that optimize binding and coupling. Minimizing control flow complexity is also an adjunct of structured programming techniques. The structured programming principles of Larry Constantine, Glenford Myers, and the late Wayne Stevens are most often encountered in the commercial domain, as in other software domains as well.

Comment Density and Style

It is a best practice for all domains to utilize both module prologs and comments to explain key features and algorithms of programs. Studies performed within IBM found that comments approximately every ten statements was the density at which clarity seemed to peak. Fewer comments made it hard to understand the code. Surprisingly, too many comments also reduced code legibility. The reason that too many comments lowered code reading comprehension was because the programmers tended to put too much credence in the comments, and some of them may not have been fully accurate. When reading code, it is necessary to read both the code and the comments. The comments serve to explain unusual algorithms or special conditions, but it is necessary to understand the code itself.

Mnemonic Labels

It is a best practice in all domains to use labels for variables and branch instructions that are clear and easy to remember, if possible. Abstract labels such as "routine2" may make it hard for new programmers to understand logic flow. It is a bad practice to use labels that have quirky or private meanings, such as using the names of relatives or movie stars.

Code Inspections

The use of code inspections is beginning to become widely deployed among at least the larger commercial software vendors. Formal inspections were first developed in the 1960s within IBM as a method of ensuring the quality and reliability levels of IBM's system software. When applied to IBM's commercial software, such as the IMS database product, inspections quickly improved the quality of a key commercial product. Formal code inspections have the highest defect removal efficiency level of any known removal activity against coding defects, and are approximately twice as efficient as most forms of testing. Formal code inspections average 65% in defect removal efficiency, and have approached 90%.

Complexity Analysis

A best practice that is somewhat rare within the commercial software domain is the use of complexity analysis tools. High levels of code complexity as measured with the common metrics of cyclomatic and essential complexity can degrade quality and lower the efficiency of defect removal operations.

Module-Level Defect Tracking

A best practice in both the commercial and the systems software domains is that of defect tracking methods and tools that are granular enough to identify error-prone modules. In many large applications, a small percentage of defects accumulate the majority of all bugs or errors, and are known as *error-prone modules*.

It is a best practice in every domain to find and remove error-prone modules. Obviously, quality data must be recorded down to the level of modules for this to occur.

Best Reusability Practices for Commercial Software

Software reuse is a key technology that can, theoretically, benefit cost, schedule, and quality simultaneously. However, to gain positive value, the reusable materials must approach zero-defect levels.

A complete software reusability program in the commercial domain encompasses from six to more than ten software artifacts, including

1. Reusable external specifications
2. Reusable internal specifications
3. Reusable project plans
4. Reusable database designs and data structures
5. Reusable source code ("components")
6. Reusable quality and test plans
7. Reusable test cases
8. Reusable user documentation
9. Reusable translations into other national languages
10. Reusable HELP text

In general, the commercial software domain has concentrated on only two aspects of reuse: source code and user documentation. Source code reuse by itself is not a sufficient technology to make dramatic improvements in schedules or productivity rates. A more extensive and wide-ranging reuse program is more effective. Unfortunately, the commercial software domain has not achieved a leadership position with some of the other potentially reusable artifacts, such as test cases, specification, and even user documentation.

Reusable Interfaces

Reusable interfaces are a definite best practice for commercial software. In spite of the risk of look-and-feel litigation, it can be asserted that reusable interfaces would be valuable across the whole commercial domain. Indeed, if interfaces among competitive products were similar, this would benefit ease of use and reduce the learning curve. After many years of ambiguous interfaces, Microsoft is finally moving toward common interfaces among the applications within their office suite.

Code Inspections

The use of formal code inspections is a best practice that improves the prognosis of reusing source code modules and components. Prior to placing a candidate reusable module into a reuse library, it should be subjected to a 100% formal code inspection. The use of code inspections for systems software raises the probability of successful code reuse by weeding out potentially troublesome segments that might have high recall or failure rates.

Test Plan and Test Case Inspections

The use of test plan and test case inspections, plus formal regression test libraries and test library control procedures, can raise the probability of successful reuse of test materials. Prior to being reused, both test plans and test cases should be given a thorough 100% inspection.

Some interesting reusability practices have not yet been studied enough to determine whether they will become best practices. One example is *component-based development*. As this book is written, few components are actually available, and the results of component development are ambiguous. In fact, failures and problems based on components currently outnumber successes due to the marginal quality of some commercial components.

Although OO reuse and class libraries are common among commercial software vendors, the OO results are not positive enough for definite inclusion of this practice in the set of best practices. For one thing, the failure rate of first-time OO projects is approximately 50%. In spite of the many claims of reusability put forth in the OO domain, the volume of reusable artifacts noted on OO projects lags behind the volume noted using other approaches. For example, reusable test materials are rare in the OO domain. As this book is written, Visual Basic appears to have the most extensive suite of reusable materials available.

Best Change Control Practices for Commercial Software

Change control is a complex and demanding technical challenge for any kind of software project. However, the commercial software domain is very sophisticated in this important technology. There are tools and approaches available that can ease change management difficulties, although change control is never trivial.

Commercial software vendors may market the same application on different hardware platforms. They may offer the same application in different national languages. When major changes occur, they can affect dozens of versions at the same time. Obviously, change control is a key technology for commercial software vendors. Best practices in change control for commercial software include those presented in the following subsections.

Automated Change Control

The commercial software artifacts that are subject to change include marketing requirements, external specifications, internal specifications, source code, quality and test plans, user documentation, and training materials. Because of the wide variety of changing artifacts, it is a best practice to have fully automated change control systems that can handle all major deliverables. The change control package should facilitate identifying links between artifacts, such as determining what code needs to be changed in response to a requirements or design change. Automated change control tools that support only source code are not adequate for projects larger than 100 function points.

Commercial software has more versions that need change control than any other domain. Some applications may be released under a half dozen operating systems, may run on several computer platforms, and may be available in as many as a dozen national versions. The permutations of versions for a single application can often exceed a dozen, and may exceed 50 in extreme cases.

Best User Documentation Practices for Commercial Software

The development and production of manuals, tutorial materials, HELP screens, and "wizards" is a primary concern for the commercial software industry. The commercial software domain employs many professional writers and graphics artists, yet complaints about poor documents are just as common as complaints about poor software quality, and have as much justification.

Although their work is not analyzed in this book in any depth, the documentation picture for commercial software has unique features not associated with any other kind of software. The major technical book publishers such as Addison Wesley Longman, McGraw Hill, Que, and Howard Sams have built a thriving business by writing and selling text and tutorial books to supplement the somewhat elementary books of the software vendors themselves. Any large technical bookstore will have a whole section of books that describe how to use popular software packages such as AutoCAD, Microsoft Word, Quicken, Visual Basic, and scores of other products

Technical Writers

A best practice long used by the commercial software domain is the employment of professional writers, editors, and graphics personnel for the production of user manuals and tutorial materials. The technical writing, editing, and graphics personnel of some large software companies such as Microsoft top 5% of overall software employment. Technical writing is a fairly rare skill, and only professional writers can create manuals and tutorials that are clear enough to be effective.

Professional Editors

An obvious best practice that is rare for software is to use professional editors as well as professional technical writers. Although this is a best practice in terms of results, it is only found among a handful of very large corporations. Professional editors are found much more often in the publishing companies that produce trade books about software products than they are working for software vendors. This explains, in part, why the trade books are often much better than the manuals that are supplied with commercial software packages. However, some of the larger commercial vendors such as Computer Associates, IBM, and Microsoft do employ editors as well as technical writers.

Document Models

A best practice for new technical writers just joining a company is to provide them with a collection of manuals and tutorial materials voted "excellent" by means of user satisfaction surveys. This approach was pioneered by IBM in the 1960s and has yielded very good results. It works best within large corporations that have scores of manuals and tutorial books available.

Usability Laboratories

A best practice that is found in large software vendors is that of usability laboratories. Companies such as IBM and AT&T pioneered usability labs in the late 1960s. Other software companies such as Microsoft also utilize forms of usability labs. The total number of such labs in the world is probably less than 100. In these usability labs, customers exercise software applications for normal business, using the manuals and tutorial materials to be provided with the application. Their success or failure is monitored by human factors specialists, sometimes supported by one-way mirrors or video cameras. Internal documents such as maintenance manuals can be studied via usability labs, as well as user manuals and external documents.

Reader Suggestions

A best practice for commercial software is to supply reader comment forms for correcting errors and pointing out problems as part of every published document. On-line reader comments sent in via the Internet or Web are also encompassed under this best practice.

CD-ROM Documents

A rare but growing best practice is the production of animated or dynamic tutorial materials in the form of CD-ROM, DVD, or videotapes. The purpose is to lead users through the sequence of activities required to use fairly complex applications.

Hypertext Links

A best practice for all user manuals is to include a detailed index with cross references. Hypertext links for on-line documents are also included under this best practice.

Graphics and Illustrations

A best practice for all user manuals is the inclusion of a significant volume of graphical materials, as opposed to using pure text. The graphical materials need to be clear and cogent to be effective. Those produced by professional graphics illustrators are most often effective.

Working Examples

A very common best practice for commercial software is the utilization of actual examples of key features, such as photographs of actual screens. The examples take a user step by step through the process of invoking a function, using it, and then turning it off or moving to something else when finished. It is important that the examples be correct, which implies that the documentation is inspected and tested along with the software.

Documentation Quality Control

It is a best practice among larger software vendors to utilize formal quality control methods on user manuals. This implies inspections of documents, and testing of documents. Document testing is perhaps too strong a phrase. What often happens is that drafts of the user manual are supplied to test personnel, and are used to create test cases and to set up test scripts. In the course of using the manuals for testing, the test personnel often find errors of ambiguity and sometimes errors of fact.

Documentation Outsourcing

Because technical writing is not a common skill, many smaller companies outsource their documentation to freelance professional writers or to companies that specialize in software documentation. Indeed, for software companies with less than 30 personnel, this is a common practice. This is considered to be a best practice primarily because there is no effective alternative.

Best Quality Control and Pretest Defect Removal Practices for Commercial Software

Testing by itself has never been sufficient to remove all errors or defects from large software applications. Therefore, a series of pretest activities such as inspections of design, source code, user manuals, and even test materials are utilized by the more sophisticated commercial software vendors.

Design and Code Inspections

An important best practice for commercial software is the usage of formal design and code inspections. Both design and code inspections have averaged more than 65% in defect removal efficiency in repeated trials, and have topped 85% in some cases. Inspections are approximately twice as efficient in removing defects as any form of testing. Formal inspections also serve as a defect prevention method because participants quickly learn what kinds of problems to avoid in their own work. The usage of formal design and code inspections is the only known way for elevating defect removal efficiency levels above 95%. It is interesting that formal inspections also lead to shorter development schedules for large applications (>10,000 function points). That is, even though inspections are time-consuming, applications that use formal inspections are delivered sooner because testing is quicker.

Software Quality Assurance

Another best practice for larger commercial software vendors is the use of software quality assurance personnel. The functions of software quality assurance departments include defect estimation, defect measurements, moderating formal inspections, monitoring ISO 9000–9004 practices, and teaching courses in quality topics. Note that these groups are not testing departments, although they do perform some specialized kinds of testing, such as standard adherence testing.

Software quality assurance departments begin to show up as best practices for companies with more than 25 employees. The use of these types of departments is a definite best practice for companies employing more than 50 software personnel.

Error-Prone Module Elimination

An important best practice for large commercial applications is preventing and removing error-prone modules. IBM discovered in the early 1970s that software defects in large systems tended to clump in a small number of very buggy modules. Complexity analysis, module-level defect tracking, formal inspections followed by either repairs or redevelopment, plus assigning numeric quality targets to executives can stamp out error-prone modules and prevent their recurrence.

Quality Measurements

A best commercial practice is that of formal quality measurements and defect tracking. The current state of the art of software quality measurement starts the measures early. Once the quality measures begin they are kept up for the entire life of the project so that data is accumulated during development, usage, and many years of enhancements and maintenance. Topics measured include defect numbers, defect severity levels, defect origins, defect removal methods, and complexity of the application and its modules. Other measures include valid and invalid defects, abeyant defects that cannot be replicated, incidents that may or may not be defects, defect repair intervals, and resource and cost data. Quality and defect tracking is highly automated in the commercial software domain using either commercial or proprietary defect tracking and quality measurement tools.

Quality Estimation Tools

A recent best practice in all domains since about 1985 is the usage of quality and defect estimation tools to predict the probable number of bugs that might be encountered, and the set of defect prevention and removal operations to be used. Quality estimation tools can predict the numbers of bugs or errors in requirements, specifications, source code, user documents, and bad fixes or secondary defects. Severity levels are also predicted. The tools can also predict the specific defect removal efficiency of each review, inspection, or test stage. The final predictions are the numbers of latent defects remaining at delivery, and how many of those will be found by customers. Several commercial quality tools are aimed specifically at commercial software, and can predict duplicate defects, abeyant defects, and even user errors or invalid defects.

Software Quality Standards

It is a best practice for large commercial software vendors to have a formal standards program in place, and to require that each major project cite the standards that are being followed (or not). However, many international standards are not really complete enough to be the sole guideline for quality purposes. Therefore, standards such as IEEE and ISO quality standards may be followed, but the large software companies also have internal corporate standards that may be better than international standards. Quite a few companies have very sophisticated quality programs and have developed internal quality standards that are more thorough and complete than either the ISO or IEEE equivalents. Unfortunately, these are proprietary standards that are usually not shared with other companies for competitive reasons. Of course, from the distressingly large numbers of delivered defects in commercial software, not every company has adequate quality standards.

There are quality practices that are often encountered in the commercial software domain that are not included as best practices. The reason for this is that these practices do not appear to improve quality in any tangible way. The most common of these practices is ISO 9000–9004 certification. Many of our clients are certified using ISO standards such as 9001 for software, and their quality is quite good, but similar projects produced by companies that are not certified achieve equal or better quality levels. Achieving ISO certification may be necessary to do business with the European Union, but because the certification is expensive and does not make a tangible improvement in quality, it cannot be considered a best practice in a technical sense.

Best Testing Practices and Tools for Commercial Software

The commercial software domain is an obvious leader in software testing. In spite of this, commercial software quality is not as good as customers demand. Testing by developers alone is not sufficient to remove all defects from large and complex applications. Testing by trained specialists is more effective and efficient. However, formal testing plus formal inspections is the most efficient and cost-effective of all.

Formal Test Plans

A best practice for all new commercial software packages larger than 1,000 function points is to create formal test plans that describe the sequence and nature of the testing to be performed. These plans should also predict the anticipated numbers of defects that will be encountered. If the commercial vendor is very sophisticated, it might also predict the number of defects that are likely to be missed. The tests to be included are the normal sequence for commercial packages, and include unit test, new function test, regression test, stress or performance test, integration test, system test, usability test, and external beta test.

Test Specialists

A best practice found in many commercial software vendors is the employment of professional testing personnel, and the usage of test departments. These professional test personnel normally take over testing after the developers have completed code inspections and unit test. (The test specialists may also participate in formal inspections.) The forms of testing assigned to professional test groups include regression test, performance test, capacity or load test, integration test, human factors test, and system test. The test departments also coordinate external beta test, and work with clients during acceptance test. The total complement of personnel in these test organizations can approach or even exceed 25% of software employment. Professional test groups are approximately 5% more efficient in each test stage than the same stage carried out by the developers themselves.

Automated Test Tools

A best practice that is frequently encountered in the commercial software domain is the usage of automated test library tools. Because major corporations have thousands of regression test cases, it is desirable to utilize automated tools for keeping track of these test cases, weeding out redundant tests, and linking tests to applications as needed.

Test Coverage Analysis

A common best practice in analyzing the thoroughness of testing is to monitor the number of paths through software that are actually tested. A variety of commercial test monitors are available that can perform this function. Indeed, the overall best practice is to measure the percentage of all code actually tested. In applications with high cyclomatic and essential complexity, there are so many possible paths through the application that 100% testing is essentially impossible. It is a corollary best practice to redevelop or to simplify the complexity of applications that are so complex that complete testing is impossible.

Globalization Testing

A testing best practice found primarily among commercial software vendors is that of testing versions of applications that are in other national languages such as Japanese, German, French, and so forth. It is not enough merely to translate the screens and documents into other languages. The other national versions also need testing, such as regression testing, performance testing, system testing, and external best testing.

Multiplatform Testing

A testing best practice found primarily among commercial software vendors is that of testing versions of applications that operate on several platforms, such as Windows 98 and LINUX. Each version requires regression testing and possibly other forms of testing as well, such as performance testing.

Note that the combination of globalization testing and multiplatform testing in the commercial software domain can lead to many complicated situations. If a commercial software product runs on four different platforms and is available in six different national versions, then at least 24 major variants need to be tested and put under formal change control.

Best Maintenance and Enhancement Practices for Commercial Software

The commercial software domain has some special maintenance issues that are distinct from software used by only a small number of clients. If an application is used by millions of individuals, such as Microsoft Windows 98 or Microsoft Word, then customer support and maintenance are, of necessity, major operations. Therefore, the successful commercial software vendors must either expend substantial costs to support their customers or risk losing market shares when customers cannot get problems fixed easily (or even reported).

Balancing effective customer support and minimizing costs is an important topic. Unfortunately, a number of vendors are somewhat one sided and cost conscious. The result is that their customers may abandon them if a better product comes along, or a product with better customer support. Some of the commercial best practices in maintenance and customer support include those presented in the following subsections.

Warranties

It is a best practice, although a rare one, to provide warranties that actually provide useful help for clients in the event of problems. Typical software warranties offer replacements only in the case of defective media. More helpful warranties would include free customer support for a period such as 90 days or six months, and some form of guarantee of fitness for use. Although not enough companies have done this to include it as a best practice, offering a money-back guarantee has occasionally been noted.

Maintenance Agreements

It is a very common best practice among commercial software vendors to offer annual maintenance and support agreements. These agreements are often priced between 10% and 15% of the initial acquisition price of the package. The terms of the agreement include free updates during the contract period, and various kinds of support, including on-site support if needed.

Telephone Support

It is a best practice among commercial software vendors to offer telephone support to clients. In the past, toll-free numbers were offered, but since about 1995, toll-free numbers have almost disappeared for this purpose due to high costs. Commercial software telephone support is a multitier operation. Often the first or bottom tier is contracted out. The first tier consists of telephone operators who are reasonably well trained in the application, and who know the status of common or recently reported errors. If a customer problem is too complex for the first tier, it can be referred to a second tier. The second tier consists of technical personnel who know the application intimately (sometimes developers fill this role). As a rule of thumb, one first-tier telephone support person can handle approximately 500 clients, assuming normal levels of problems. Normally, telephone support is outsourced or contracted to specialized companies, although some software companies provide telephone support using their own employees.

On-line Maintenance Support

A best practice now widely used by all domains is to provide on-line connections between users and the maintenance teams, such as having a customer support section as part of a corporate Web site. It is far more efficient and cost-effective for users to be able to report errors and request assistance by means of e-mail or the World Wide Web than it is by telephone or fax. Of course, HELP desks staffed by live maintenance experts are also a best practice for commercial software maintenance.

User Forums

It is a best practice for successful software vendors whose products have a large number of users to establish user forums on services such as America On Line or CompuServe. These user forums are often linked to corporate Web sites. One of the useful features of such forums are lists of frequently asked questions (FAQs). It often happens that when new users experience problems, they can find the same problem and its solution in the FAQ files of the user forum. Also, the chat rooms or mail lists associated with such forums can often be used to share useful information on workarounds or temporary solutions to software problems.

Maintenance Departments

A best practice for large commercial vendors is to have separate maintenance departments that handle defect repairs. The work of maintenance departments is primarily that of repairing incoming defects reported by clients or performing warranty work. The staffing of these specialized maintenance groups sometimes includes customer support, but that function may also be handled by a marketing or sales organization. Enhancements are normally done by the development team. The economic reason for separate maintenance groups is because defect repairs and adding new features are antagonistic and interfere with each other. If the same person tries to fix bugs and add features, then estimating either side becomes messy and difficult. Furthermore, because bug repairs are often less interesting, they tend to be rushed so the programmer can return to development work.

On-site Maintenance Support

A fairly rare best practice, found primarily for the largest commercial packages (such as SAP R3), is full-time on-site maintenance support at the customer's location. This practice is cost justified only for applications larger than 100,000 function points.

Best Personnel Practices for Commercial Software

The commercial software domain has had one interesting personnel practice that has created some very wealthy individuals. This is the practice, common among software startup companies, of offering equity to key employees in return for fairly marginal salaries and benefits packages. If the company succeeds in having an initial public offering, those employees with equity agreements can become very wealthy indeed. For example Microsoft has created more millionaires than any other corporation of the century. The software industry as a whole has created a number of wealthy individuals due to the growth and importance of software as a business tool.

Of course, if the company does not succeed or goes bankrupt, then the value of the equity is close to zero. Thus employees under equity agreements are highly motivated to help make the company and its commercial products a success. This is the only scenario for which their equity has value, and repays them for the temporary reduction in earnings for which the equity was offered.

In more ordinary personnel issues, the commercial software domain has been fairly sophisticated in recruiting and hiring practices.

As this book is written, Microsoft has been involved in class-action litigation with a number of contractors who were not full-time Microsoft employees. A preliminary judgment has given these contractors some of the benefits of full-time employees, such as stock options. The case is still in progress and it is not certain whether this judgment will be appealed or, if so, whether the appeal will be successful. However, the topic is an important one that can have a major effect on contract work in the United States.

There are ten key practices for personnel issues that are examined during assessment and benchmark studies:

1. Staff hiring practices
2. Staff training and education
3. Management training and education
4. Specialists and occupational groups
5. Compensation levels
6. Office ergonomics
7. Organizational structures
8. Morale surveys and results
9. Work patterns and overtime
10. Staff turnover rates

As with best technical practices, the personnel practices must have been observed within at least ten companies to be included as best practices. The criterion of being noted on at least 50 projects is waived for personnel practices. The reason for this is because personnel practices are normally corporatewide. A personnel practice such as "compensation level" is determined by corporate guidelines and is not set by the project manager for a specific project. True, project managers have some latitude in compensation based on appraisals and bonus policies, but these must be within the overall corporate salary and compensation guidelines.

Best Staff Hiring Practices for Commercial Software

University training in software engineering or computer science in the United States has not been very effective in graduating students who can go to work on commercial software projects without in-house training and mentoring. A common weakness of academia as it applies to commercial software is very limited emphasis on software quality control. Few universities offer solid courses in design and code inspections, geriatric care for aging software, and customer support.

Another gap that is significant to commercial vendors is lack of academic training in either nationalization (in other words, translation of software for other countries) or multiplatform support (applications running under several operating systems or on several kinds of computers).

Hiring Handicapped Personnel

Software development is primarily a cerebral rather than a physical activity. Thus, software development is one of the best occupations for those with physical handicaps. (Special equipment supporting Braille, or computer controls that can be operated by foot, or even by puffs of breath, are available.) It is an interesting observation that graduates from schools that teach software development to the physically challenged, such as the Biped school in Connecticut, tend to succeed as software engineers more often than graduates from regular colleges. This is a best practice in every domain, including commercial software.

Equal Opportunity Employment

Software development is a difficult human activity. For those who have a proficiency in software, topics such as gender or ethnic origin are irrelevant. It is an interesting observation that commercial software organizations are often very egalitarian in terms of the distribution of employees. For example, software tends to have a more equal distribution of women and minority executives and technical workers than do older forms of engineering such as civil engineering or aeronautical engineering.

Selection Criteria for New Hires

Because commercial software tends to be complex, it does not lend itself to casual development or to development by unqualified personnel. It is a best practice when hiring new personnel to ensure that they meet the qualifications for this kind of work. Multiple interviews with both managers and other technical staff members is a best practice for hiring technical staff members. Another best practice, but one that is encountered more rarely, is to give candidates case studies and evaluate their performance. In other words, programming candidates must demonstrate coding proficiency. Testing candidates must actually create a test plan and suite of test cases, and so forth.

Summer Internships

Because of the specialized nature of commercial software work, an interesting best practice is to hire software engineering or computer science college students during the summer months as interns. This gives the company an ability to judge performance levels on actual systems software work. Suitable interns can be hired as full-time employees on graduation. For example, Microsoft uses this practice to such an extent that the parking lots overflow during the summer months. Office space also overflows, and some conference rooms are pressed into service as temporary offices.

Best Staff Training and Education Practices for Commercial Software

Because of the uncertain performance of U.S. universities in graduating effective software engineering personnel to work in the commercial software domain, the major commercial employers compensate by offering in-house curricula for key software topics. The in-house software curricula of large commercial software companies such as Microsoft, IBM, Symantec, Oracle, and Rational are quite extensive and very practical.

Annual Staff Training Targets

It is a best practice for commercial software companies to set targets for the number of days each calendar year that will be set aside for training of technical personnel. Among our clients, the most common target is ten days a year. However, the significant volume of work associated with the Y2K problem and the Euro caused some training targets to be suspended temporarily during calendar years 1998 and 1999.

External Seminars and Conferences

It is a best practice for commercial software companies to fund travel and tuition expenses for external conferences and seminars, such as the annual Pacific Northwest Quality conference. Some vendors also send technical staff members to their own conferences, such as the annual Artemis User Association conference. One external event per year is most common, but two or three external events also occur.

Training and Seminars for Sales and Marketing Personnel

Although we are not commissioned to study software marketing practices, our normal studies bring us in contact with an interesting best practice. The major commercial software vendors are very active in training their sales and marketing personnel. The training includes topics in sales and marketing techniques, and also courses in the tools and technologies themselves.

Customer Training and Seminars

Here, too, although we have not been commissioned to study training of the clients of our own clients, our normal studies bring us in contact with the curricula that software vendors have created to train their own personnel. (In fact, my own company also trains our own clients in software cost-estimating, metrics and other topics.) It is an almost universal best practice for commercial software vendors to create and teach courses to their clients in the products that the vendors market. Often the vendors create additional courses in topics of related interest.

Best Management Training and Education Practices for Commercial Software

Software project management is even more limited in universities than software engineering. Few universities in America offer courses in important software management topics such as function point analysis, measurements, software cost estimating, and software customer support.

Annual Management Training Targets

It is a best practice for commercial software companies to set targets for the number of days each calendar year that will be set aside for training of project management personnel. The most common target for managers is five days a year. Although targets are common, actually being able to reach the target is not always easy.

External Management Seminars and Conferences

It is a best practice for commercial software vendors to fund travel and tuition expenses for external conferences and seminars for managers. Although the conferences attended varies, some of the conferences of interest to the commercial sector include Comdex, and the annual conferences of Gartner Group, Meta Group, and Giga Group. Among our clients, two external events per year is most common, but three or four external events also occur. For startup companies, external conferences sponsored by trade associations or venture capitalists are also popular.

Best Practices for Specialization in the Commercial Software Domain

The commercial software domain is one of the major employers of sales and marketing personnel in the United States. The commercial software domain also employs a number of specialized "systems engineers" who support the sales of software products by providing technical assistance during installation and deployment of major commercial software packages.

Software Specialization

There are several areas of specialization noted in the commercial software domain that are more or less unique. One of these is the "systems engineering" area of specialization. Systems engineers in the commercial software domain assist clients in deployment, installation, tuning, and optimization of software packages. Other key areas in which commercial specialization counts as a best practice include software testing, software technical writing, software quality assurance, software customer support, and software maintenance in terms of defect repairs. Commercial specialists outside software development include marketing and sales personnel in large numbers.

The larger commercial software groups may employ dozens of specialists outside of their software groups, such as corporate attorneys, accountants, and human factors specialists. There are also many kinds of specialization that are not full-time jobs, such as JAD facilitators and certified function point counting specialists. The latter two can be included in the best-practice domain. The non-software specialists may also be best practices, but are outside the scope of our studies.

Best Compensation and Salary Practices for Commercial Software

In the United States, the commercial software domain is not the best in terms of salary levels. (Banking is the industry that pays software personnel and software managers the highest salary levels.) However, the commercial software domain has been a pioneer in offering equity to both technical, managerial, and sales and marketing personnel.

Equity and Stock Options

It is a best practice among small commercial software companies and startups to offer equity and stock options to founders, including technical personnel, managers, and also marketing and sales personnel. The equity is offered in compensation for somewhat below-average levels of salaries and benefits. If the companies succeed and go public, then the equity can be very valuable in the long run. Of course, if the company goes bankrupt the equity will be valueless. The reason equity is a best practice is because it tends to align the goals of the company with the goals of the key employees. Because equity tends to vest over a three- to five-year period, offering equity also helps keep key personnel in the volatile job market. Note that a lawsuit brought by contract personnel against Microsoft may extend equity offers to contract personnel if the suit prevails. The case is undecided as this book is written.

Compensation Benchmarks

It is a best practice to perform annual compensation benchmark studies for commercial software technical and managerial personnel. These benchmarks are normally "blind" studies during which various companies contribute compensation data that is analyzed statistically by a neutral external benchmark company. Contributing companies receive a report on how their compensation packages compare with the group, but the specifics of each company in the group are not included due to both competitive and antitrust reasons.

Compensation Levels

For large commercial software companies employing more than 1,000 software personnel, it is a best practice to be in the upper half of overall compensation including salaries, bonuses, equity, and medical and dental benefits. In large corporations, compensation, quality, productivity, and schedules are more or less correlated. However, for small companies with less than 100 software personnel, and especially for startups with less than 25 software personnel, immediate compensation is less significant, and long-range topics (such as equity) are more significant.

Best Practices in Office Ergonomics for Commercial Software

In our assessment and benchmark studies, there are several interesting phenomena that often stand out among clients that turn out to have better than average software performance levels. One of the most visible, noted almost as soon as a consultant enters the building, is the availability of private, noise-free office space for software engineers and technical workers.

During a typical working day, a software engineer needs quiet and solitude for approximately five hours, and needs to have discussions or meetings for only one hour. Roughly two hours are spent on phone calls, using the Internet, or on miscellaneous work. From this distribution of effort, it can be seen that private office space is optimal for the major portion of a day's work.

Private Office Space

It is a best practice to provide private, noise-free office space for software engineers and technical staff members. An area of at least 80 square feet is optimal. This best practice is only encountered in fairly sophisticated companies, but the results support the hypothesis that private office space is optimal for all domains, including commercial software.

Networks and E-mail

It is a best practice to link all technical employees within a corporation by means of a network that supports e-mail, file transfer, and on-line inspection of key work products.

Meeting Rooms

Because group activities such as design and code inspections and team meetings are common for software projects, it is a best practice to provide a small meeting room that can hold ten people. Because usage is intermittent, one such meeting room should be able to support roughly 30 total staff members.

There are several interesting and probably important topics that we have not been commissioned to study. One of these is telecommuting. Another interesting topic is the presence or absence of day-care centers for children of employees.

Best Practices in Organizational Structures for Commercial Software

The ranges in the commercial software span of control noted among our assessment and benchmark studies averages approximately eight technical employees per manager. The low value has been two employees reporting to one manager and the largest value has been 30 employees reporting to one manager.

It is a common belief in the software world that small teams are more productive than large departments. This is because small teams often build small applications, whereas large departments work on major applications. Many commercial software projects are very large and have staffing levels that can rise to more than 250 personnel overall. For large projects with more than 50 staff members, small teams are actually not as productive as larger departments with ten to 12 people reporting to one manager.

Good project managers are a scarce commodity. If a company has a small span of control then it will have a large management population. Because bad management is the most common reason why good technical workers change jobs, you can see that having fewer but better managers may lead to overall improvements in both performance and morale issues.

In general, productivity levels decline as the number of workers increases. This is a general finding from many industries, not just software projects. However, there is a curious phenomenon within the software domain that was first noted on systems software projects in IBM in the 1970s, and applies to commercial software too. Productivity levels for software projects tend to decline as the number of managers goes up, rather than as the number of technical staff members goes up.

The implications of this finding are that, for large applications (>10,000 function points), small teams of three to six employees are not as productive as larger departments with ten to 12 employees. The reason seems to be that small-team organizations put too many managers on the project. As the management count goes up, coordination and cooperation between departments becomes difficult due to normal corporate politics.

Optimal Department Size

For large commercial software projects (>10,000 function points) it is a best practice to have eight to 16 employees reporting to one manager. Small spans of control put too many people in management and raise the difficulty of coordination between departments. Furthermore, a ten-plus staffing complement can handle a fairly large component whereas small departments have to segment the work artificially. In addition, a large span of control allows backup in case of illness, and encourages mentoring of new team members. It is also easier to handle peer reviews and formal inspections in a large department. Large departments also allow companies to select managers carefully, and to weed out or reassign those who lack management skills.

Independent Software Quality Assurance

For commercial software projects larger than 10,000 function points it is a best practice to have an independent software quality assurance department outside the control of the project manager. The reason for this independent group is to protect the integrity of the quality assurance function. If the software quality assurance personnel report to the project manager, they cannot safely point out problems without risking personal reprisals. This group is distinct from the testing group, which usually *does* report to the project management chain of command. A key role of the software quality assurance organization is to ensure that best practices are followed and dangerous situations, if any, are addressed. This group could not perform this role unless it was independent of the project chain of command.

Virtual Organizations

For large commercial software projects involving multiple cities and countries, it is a best practice to support broad-band communication channels so that e-mail, file transfer, and on-line inspection are all possible. Video conferencing among locations is also a best practice for projects that are dispersed geographically.

Best Practices for Employee Morale in Commercial Software

Our studies indicate that employees who are satisfied with their jobs and their place of employment are more productive and produce higher quality deliverables than employees who are dissatisfied. Interestingly, one of the critical factors affecting employee morale is the ability of the project managers to whom the technical workers report. Companies that recognize the significance of this find-ing are very careful about who gets promoted to management, and are careful to weed out managers whose personalities are not suited for this very critical responsibility.

Morale and Opinion Surveys

It is a best practice to perform morale or opinion surveys of all employees, including administrative workers, technical staff members, and project man-agers. The normal frequency of morale surveys is once a year. Some of our clients conduct two surveys a year. In special situations, such as after a major downsiz-ing, merger, or cancellation of a major project, additional special morale surveys may be needed. Morale and opinion surveys are best practices in larger commer-cial software companies employing more than 50 software personnel. In small companies and startups, formal surveys are not usually performed because everyone knows everyone else.

Follow-up to Morale Surveys

It is a best practice to have immediate and formal follow-ups after morale surveys are taken. After a morale survey occurs the results are analyzed statistically within a week, and departmental group meetings are held to discuss the results within two weeks. Within a month, executives and top managers formulate a plan to deal with any serious morale issues that were encountered. Normally, within approximately six weeks, there is an overall meeting or series of departmental meetings to discuss these action plans.

Merit Appraisals

In the United States it is a best practice to have annual performance appraisals for both technical staff members and project managers. During the first year of employment in a company, there may be two or more performance appraisals. It is a best practice for employees and managers to agree jointly to performance goals or targets. Note that in some European countries, performance appraisals are forbidden by either national law or union regulations.

Awards and Recognition

It is a best practice to reward outstanding accomplishments. Many companies have a spectrum of awards ranging from local dinner-for-two awards, which are given at the discretion of a supervisor, to major $100,000 awards for a breakthrough that had significant corporate value. Overall, numerous small awards tend to benefit morale more widely than a few very large awards. Although large awards can benefit morale, the odds of receiving one are low. Small awards, on the other hand, can be given to 5% to 10% of the corporate technical staff during the course of a year.

Best Work Patterns and Overtime Utilization for Commercial Software

Within commercial software companies such as Artemis, Computer Associates, Microsoft, IBM, Rational, SPR, and Symantec, 50-plus-hour weeks are the norm rather than the exception. The SPR assessment approach includes questions and interviews about unpaid overtime, but our data is based on reconstruction from the memories of the participants and therefore may have a large margin of error.

Compensatory Time

It is a best practice for commercial software personnel to be allowed to take compensatory time during slack periods in return for contributing unpaid overtime during rushed periods.

The issue of unpaid overtime is encountered often during benchmark studies. This topic deserves greater coverage in the software literature because it has a tangible impact on productivity rates.

The commercial software industry has a very intense work ethic. In some of the leading commercial software houses such as Microsoft, Computer Associates, Sterling, Artemis, and SPR, this intense work ethic often leads to weeks with 50-plus hours.

Best Practices for Minimizing Staff Turnover Rates in the Commercial Software Domain

Due to the shortage of software personnel in the United States and Europe, commercial software producers are very concerned about losing key personnel. They are also concerned about the high costs of recruiting new personnel. If a company is growing rapidly and recruiting actively, it is very useful to pay serious attention to the factors that attract new hires and minimize the attrition of existing personnel.

Reducing Voluntary Attrition

To minimize the attrition of key personnel, the set of best practices includes being in the top 50% in terms of compensation and benefits, weeding out less capable managers, and having proactive morale and opinion surveys to identify problems before they grow to a significant magnitude. A very complex issue is also important: Because bad management is the most common reason cited in exit interviews when technical workers quit, it is very important to weed out managers whose personalities are unsuited to management tasks. Thus, very careful management appraisals are a best practice.

Finding New Personnel

Commercial software companies utilize multiple methods for finding new employees: advertisements, recruiters, and the World Wide Web. However, it is a best practice to offer incentives or rewards if employees bring in suitable candidates. The reason for this is because the software community is fairly good at spreading the word regarding interesting opportunities.

Contract Employees

It has been a best practice to utilize contract personnel for a percentage of commercial software technical work. The reason for this is because contractors can be brought in fairly quickly, and have relevant experience suitable to the projects in need of support. Additionally, when the projects are completed, the contract personnel can be released as quickly as they are brought onboard. However, a number of recent court actions involving contract personnel are raising new issues that we have not yet encountered in our benchmark and assessment studies. As a result, the contracting situation circa 1999 is somewhat ambiguous even though past results have been favorable.

Personnel issues are outside the normal scope of assessment and benchmark studies. However, we have been commissioned to explore some aspects of personnel topics, such as the number of specialists employed and the optimal methods for keeping their skills up to date.

There is a major shortage of software personnel in the United States and much of the industrialized world as this book is written. Therefore, personnel issues are unusually important, and will probably stay important for at least the next ten years.

Summary and Conclusions on Commercial Software

The commercial software industry is a great American success story, and a fairly significant success story all over the world. The major U.S. software houses such as Microsoft, IBM, and Computer Associates are the dominant vendors of commercial software applications throughout the world. As the new century begins, the commercial software domain has a very favorable balance of trade among all U.S. industries. As a result, the commercial software domain has achieved a very significant level of political power and some notable lobbying capabilities.

Although the commercial software world has created products that drive the world's computers, many of these critical applications contain more defects than are safe. Indeed, one of the defects found in many commercial applications was the Y2K defect. Quality control in the commercial software domain is better than average, but not as good as it should be.

The great success of the commercial software domain may have led to arrogance and a sense of superiority on the part of major vendors and industry associations. It will be interesting to see whether backlash from the Y2K leap-year problem causes the commercial software domain to be brought under government control in the twenty-first century. If Y2K problems had proven to be severe, then it would not have been surprising to see punitive legislation occurring that would eliminate some of the unique business advantages now enjoyed by software vendors.

Readings and References for Commercial Software

The literature on commercial software overlaps the literature on systems software to a large degree. This is not surprising because systems software and commercial software overlap in the area of operating systems and other mass-marketed applications that control physical devices.

The commercial software domain has developed a literary genre that is more or less unique in the software world. This genre consists of first-hand books of how leading software companies go about their business. The books are obviously aimed at the most successful software companies such as Microsoft, Computer Associates, Symantec, SAP, and the like. This genre includes two interesting subtypes. The first are books by principles in the software companies, such as those by Bill Gates of Microsoft or Charles Wang of Computer Associates. The second subtype are books by researchers or authors who have been invited to study company practices, such as the famous book *Microsoft Secrets* by Michael

Cusumano and Richard Selby. This book has recently become an issue in the Microsoft antitrust suit, or rather the notes taken by the authors in preparing to write the book. The Department of Justice attempted to subpoena the notes and recordings taken during interviews in Microsoft. Fortunately for the research community, the request was denied. If materials gathered under nondisclosure and confidentiality agreements could be used in court for civil cases, then companies would cease to allow academicians or other researchers to have access to executives and employees.

Abdel-Hamid, Tarek, and Stuart Madnick. *Software Project Dynamics*. Englewood Cliffs, NJ: Prentice Hall, 1993. (ISBN 013-8220409)

Austin, Robert D. *Measuring and Managing Performance in Organizations*. New York: Dorset House Publishing, 1996. (ISBN 0-932633-36-6, 216 pages)

Bach, James. "The Immaturity of the CMM." *American Programmer* 1994; 7(9): 13–18.

Beizer, Boris. *Software Testing Techniques*. Boston, MA: International Thomson Computer Press, 1990. (ISBN 1850328803, 550 pages)

Boehm, Barry. *Software Engineering Economics*. Englewood Cliffs, NJ: Prentice Hall, 1981. (ISBN 0-13-822122-7, 900 pages)

Bogan, Christopher E., and Michael J. English. *Benchmarking for Best Practices*. New York: McGraw Hill, 1994. (ISBN 0-07-006375-3, 312 pages)

Briand, Loic, and Daniel Roy. *Meeting Deadlines in Hard Real-Time Systems*. Los Alamitos, CA: IEEE Computer Society Press, 1997. (ISBN 0-8186-7406-7, 300 pages)

Brooks, Frederick P. *The Mythical Man-Month*. Reading, MA: Addison Wesley Longman, 1995. (ISBN 0-201-00650-2, 295 pages)

Brown, Norm, ed. *The Program Manager's Guide to Software Acquisition Best Practices*. Version 1.0. Washington, DC: U.S. Department of Defense, 1995. (142 pages)

Caputo, Kim. *CMM Implementation Guide*. Reading, MA: Addison Wesley Longman, 1998. (ISBN 0-201-37938-4, 319 pages)

Carmel, Erran. *Global Software Teams: Collaborating across Borders and Time Zones*. Upper Saddle River, NJ: Prentice Hall, 1999. (ISBN 0-13-924218-X, 269 pages)

Carnegie Mellon University. *The Capability Maturity Model: Guidelines for Improving the Software Process*. Reading, MA: Addison Wesley Longman, 1995. (ISBN 0-201-54664-7, 441 pages)

Charette, Robert N. *Software Engineering Risk Analysis and Management.* New York: McGraw Hill, 1989. (ISBN 0-07-010719-X, 325 pages)

————. *Application Strategies for Risk Analysis.* New York: McGraw Hill, 1990. (ISBN 0-07-010888-9, 570 pages)

Conte, S. D., H. E. Dunsmore, and V. Y. Shen. *Software Engineering.* Menlo Park, CA: The Benjamin Cummings Publishing Company, 1986. (ISBN 0-8053-2162-4, 396 pages)

Curtis, Bill, William E. Hefley, and Sally Miller. *People Capability Maturity Model.* Pittsburgh, PA: Software Engineering Institute, Carnegie Mellon University, 1995.

Cusumano, Michael A., and Richard W. Selby. *Microsoft Secrets.* New York: Touchstone Books, 1998. (ISBN 0-684-85531-3, 532 pages)

DeMarco, Tom. *Controlling Software Projects.* New York: Yourdon Press, 1982. (ISBN 0-917072-32-4, 284 pages)

————. *Why Does Software Cost So Much?* New York: Dorset House Publishing, 1995. (ISBN 0-932633-34-X, 237 pages)

————. *The Deadline.* New York: Dorset House Publishing, 1997. (ISBN 0-932633-39-0)

DeMarco, Tom, and Tim Lister. *Peopleware.* New York: Dorset House Publishing, 1987. (ISBN 0-932633-05-6, 188 pages)

Department of the Air Force. *Guidelines for Successful Acquisition and Management of Software Intensive Systems.* Vol. 1 and 2. Hill Air Force Base, UT: Software Technology Support Center, 1994.

Dreger, J. Brian. *Function Point Analysis.* Englewood Cliffs, NJ: Prentice Hall, 1989. (ISBN 0-13-332321-8, 185 pages)

El Emam, Khaled, and Nazim H. Madhavi, eds. *Elements of Software Process Assessment and Improvement.* Los Alamitos, CA: IEEE Computer Society Press, 1999. (ISBN 0-818685239, 384 pages)

Galea, R. B. *The Boeing Company: 3D Function Point Extensions.* Version 2.0, release 1.0. Seattle, WA: Boeing Information Support Services, June 1995.

Garmus, David, and David Herron. *Measuring the Software Process: A Practical Guide to Functional Measurement.* Englewood Cliffs, NJ: Prentice Hall, 1995. (ISBN 0-13-349002-5)

Gates, Bill, and Collins Hemingway. *Business @ the Speed of Thought.* New York: Warner Books, 1999. (ISBN 0-446-52568-5, 470 pages)

Gilb, Tom, and Dorothy Graham. *Software Inspections.* Reading, MA: Addison Wesley Longman, 1993. (ISBN 0-201631814, 471 pages)

Glass, Robert L. *Software Runaways: Lessons Learned from Massive Project Failures.* Upper Saddle River, NJ: Prentice Hall, 1997. (ISBN 0-13-673443-X, 259 pages)

Grady, Robert B. *Practical Software Metrics for Project Management and Process Improvement.* Englewood Cliffs, NJ: Prentice Hall, 1992. (ISBN 0-13-720384-5, 270 pages)

———. *Successful Software Process Improvement.* Upper Saddle River, NJ: Prentice Hall, 1997. (ISBN 0-13-626623-1, 314 pages)

Grady, Robert B., and Deborah L. Caswell. *Software Metrics: Establishing a Company-Wide Program.* Englewood Cliffs, NJ: Prentice Hall, 1987. (ISBN 0-13-821844-7, 288 pages)

Gulledge, Thomas R., William P. Hutzler, and Joan S. Lovelace, eds. *Cost Estimating and Analysis: Balancing Technology with Declining Budgets.* New York: Springer-Verlag, 1992. (ISBN 0-387-97838-0, 297 pages)

Howard, Alan, ed. *Software Metrics and Project Management Tools.* Phoenix, AZ: Applied Computer Research, 1997. (30 pages)

Humphrey, Watts S. *Managing the Software Process.* Reading, MA: Addison Wesley Longman, 1989. (ISBN 0-201-18095-2)

———. *Introduction to the Personal Software Process.* Reading, MA: Addison Wesley Longman, 1997. (ISBN 0201548097)

———. *Managing Technical People.* Reading, MA: Addison Wesley Longman, 1997. (ISBN 0-201-54597-7, 326 pages)

IFPUG. *IFPUG Counting Practices Manual.* Release 4.1. Westerville, OH: International Function Point Users Group, May 1999. (93 pages)

Jacobson, Ivar, Martin Griss, and Patrick Jonsson. *Software Reuse: Architecture, Process, and Organization for Business Success.* Reading, MA: Addison Wesley Longman, 1997. (ISBN 0-201-92476-5, 500 pages)

Jones, Capers. *Program Quality and Programmer Productivity.* IBM technical report TR07.764. San Jose, CA: IBM Santa Teresa, January 1977. (97 pages)

———. "Measuring Programming Quality and Productivity." *IBM Systems Journal* 1978; 17(1): 39–63.

———. *Programming Productivity: Issues for the Eighties.* Los Alamitos, CA: IEEE Computer Society Press, 1st ed., 1981; 2nd ed., 1986. (ISBN 0-8186-0681-9, IEEE Computer Society Catalog 681, 489 pages)

———. *Programming Productivity.* New York: McGraw Hill, 1986. (ISBN 0-07-032811-0, 280 pages)

———. *A Ten-Year Retrospective of the ITT Programming Technology Center.* Burlington, MA: Software Productivity Research, 1988.

———. *Assessment and Control of Software Risks*. Englewood Cliffs, NJ: Prentice Hall, 1993. (ISBN 0-13-741406-4, 711 pages)

———. *Critical Problems in Software Measurement*. Carlsbad, CA: Information Systems Management Group, 1993. (ISBN 1-56909-000-9, 195 pages)

———. *Software Productivity and Quality Today: The Worldwide Perspective*. Carlsbad, CA: Information Systems Management Group, 1993. (ISBN 1-56909-001-7, 200 pages)

———. *New Directions in Software Management*. Carlsbad, CA: Information Systems Management Group, 1994. (ISBN 1-56909-009-2, 150 pages)

———. *Patterns of Software System Failure and Success*. Boston, MA: International Thomson Computer Press, 1995. (ISBN 1-850-32804-8, 292 pages)

———. *Applied Software Measurement*. 2nd ed. New York: McGraw Hill, 1996. (ISBN 0-07-032826-9, 618 pages)

———. *Revitalizing Project Management*. SPR technical report. Burlington, MA: Software Productivity Research, August 1997. (37 pages)

———. *Software Quality: Analysis and Guidelines for Success*. Boston, MA: International Thomson Computer Press, 1997. (ISBN 1-85032-876-6, 492 pages)

———. *The Economics of Object-Oriented Software*. SPR technical report. Burlington, MA: Software Productivity Research, April 1997. (22 pages)

———. *Becoming Best in Class*. SPR technical report. Burlington, MA: Software Productivity Research, January 1998. (40 pages)

———. *Estimating Software Costs*. New York: McGraw Hill, 1998. (ISBN 0-07-9130941, 725 pages)

———. "Sizing Up Software." *Scientific American* 1998; 279(6):104–111.

———. *The Costs, Schedule, and Value of Software Process Improvement*. SPR technical report. Burlington, MA: Software Productivity Research, January 1998. (27 pages)

———. *The Year 2000 Software Problem: Quantifying the Costs and Assessing the Consequences*. Reading, MA: Addison-Wesley, 1998. (ISBN 0-201-30964-5, 303 pages)

———. *Table of Programming Languages and Levels*. Burlington, MA: Software Productivity Research, March 1999. (ten versions from 1985 through July 1999, 77 pages for Version 10)

Kan, Stephen H. *Metrics and Models in Software Quality Engineering*. Reading, MA: Addison-Wesley, 1994. (ISBN 0-201-63339-6, 344 pages)

Kemerer, Chris F. "An Empirical Validation of Software Cost Estimation Models." *Communications of the ACM* 1987; 30:416–429.

———. "Reliability of Function Point Measurement: A Field Experiment." *Communications of the ACM* 1993; 36: 85–97.

Love, Tom. *Object Lessons*. New York: SIGS Books, 1993. (ISBN 0-9627477 3-4, 266 pages)

Marciniak, John J., ed. *Encyclopedia of Software Engineering*. New York: John Wiley & Sons, 1994. (ISBN 0-471-54002, in two volumes)

McCabe, Thomas J. "A Complexity Measure." *IEEE Transactions on Software Engineering* 1976: 308-320.

Melton, Austin. *Software Measurement*. London: Chapman & Hall, 1995. (ISBN 0-412-55180-2)

Mills, Harlan. *Software Productivity*. New York: Dorset House Publishing, 1988. (ISBN 0-932633-10-2, 288 pages)

Moore, James W. *Software Engineering Standards: A User's Road Map*. Los Alamitos, CA: IEEE Computer Society Press, 1998. (ISBN 0-8186-8008-3, 296 pages)

Multiple authors. *Rethinking the Software Process* CD-ROM. Lawrence, KS: Miller Freeman, 1996. (This is a new CD-ROM book collection produced jointly by the book publisher Prentice Hall and the journal publisher Miller Freeman. This CD-ROM disk contains the full text and illustrations of five Prentice Hall books: *Assessment and Control of Software Risks* by Capers Jones, *Controlling Software Projects* by Tom DeMarco, *Function Point Analysis* by Brian Dreger, *Measures for Excellence* by Larry Putnam and Ware Myers, and *Object-Oriented Software Metrics* by Mark Lorenz and Jeff Kidd.)

Musa, John, Anthony Iannino, and Kazuhia Okumoto. *Software Reliability: Measurement, Prediction, Application*. New York: McGraw Hill, 1987. (ISBN 0-07-044093-X, 619 pages)

Oskarson, Osten, and Robert L. Glass. *An ISO 9000 Approach to Building Quality Software*. Upper Saddle River, NJ: Prentice Hall, 1996. (ISBN 0-13-228925-3, 274 pages)

Park, Robert E., et al. *Software Cost and Schedule Estimating: A Process Improvement Initiative*. Technical report CMU/SEI 94-SR-03. Pittsburgh, PA: Software Engineering Institute, May 1994.

———. *Checklists and Criteria for Evaluating the Costs and Schedule Estimating Capabilities of Software Organizations*. Technical report CMU/SEI 95-SR-005. Pittsburgh, PA: Software Engineering Institute, January 1995.

Perry, William E. *Handbook of Diagnosing and Solving Computer Problems*. Blue Ridge Summit, PA: TAB Books, 1989. (ISBN 0-8306-9233-9, 255 pages)

————. *Effective Methods for Software Testing.* Los Alamitos, CA: IEEE Computer Society Press, 1995. (ISBN 0 471 06097-6, 556 pages)

Pressman, Roger. *Software Engineering: A Practitioner's Approach.* New York: McGraw Hill, 1982.

Putnam, Lawrence H. *Measures for Excellence: Reliable Software On Time, Within Budget.* Englewood Cliffs, NJ: Prentice Hall, 1992. (ISBN 0-13-567694-0, 336 pages)

Putnam, Lawrence H., and Ware Myers. *Industrial Strength Software: Effective Management Using Measurement.* Los Alamitos, CA: IEEE Computer Society Press, 1997. (ISBN 0-8186-7532-2, 320 pages)

Rubin, Howard. *Software Benchmark Studies For 1999.* Pound Ridge, NY: Howard Rubin Associates, 1999.

Schulmeyer, G. Gordon, and James I. McManus, eds. *Handbook of Software Quality Assurance.* New York: Van Nostrand Reinhold, 1992. (ISBN 0-442-00796-5, 562 pages)

Shepperd, M. "A Critique of Cyclomatic Complexity as a Software Metric." *Software Engineering Journal* 1988; 3: 30–36.

Software Productivity Consortium. *The Software Measurement Guidebook.* Boston, MA: International Thomson Computer Press, 1995. (ISBN 1-850-32195-7, 308 pages)

Strassmann, Paul. *The Squandered Computer.* New Canaan, CT: The Information Economics Press, 1997. (ISBN 0-9620413-1-9, 426 pages)

Stukes, Sherry, Jason Deshoretz, Henry Apgar, and Ilona Macias. *Air Force Cost Analysis Agency Software Estimating Model Analysis.* TR-9545/008-2, contract F04701-95-D-0003, task 008. Thousand Oaks, CA: Management Consulting & Research, September 1996.

Symons, Charles R. *Software Sizing and Estimating: Mk II FPA (Function Point Analysis).* Chichester, UK: John Wiley & Sons, 1991. (ISBN 0 471-92985-9, 200 pages)

Thayer, Richard H., ed. *Software Engineering Project Management.* Los Alamitos, CA: IEEE Computer Society Press, 1988. (ISBN 0 8186-075107, 512 pages)

Wang, Charles B. *Techno Vision.* New York: McGraw Hill, 1994. (ISBN 0-07-68155-4, 198 pages)

Weinberg, Gerald M. *Quality Software Management, Vol. 2, First-Order Measurement.* New York: Dorset House Publishing, 1993. (ISBN 0-932633-24-2, 360 pages)

Weinberg, Gerald, and Daniel Friedman. *Handbook of Walkthroughs, Inspections, and Technical Reviews*. New York: Dorset House Publishing, 1990. (450 pages)

Wheeler, David A., Bill Brylcznski, and Reginald Meeson. *Software Inspection: An Industry Best Practice*. Los Alamitos, CA: IEEE Computer Society Press, 1996. (ISBN 0-8186-7430-0, 325 pages)

Wiegers, Karl A. *Creating a Software Engineering Culture*. New York: Dorset House Publishing, 1996. (ISBN 0-932633-33-1, 358 pages)

Yourdon, Edward. *Death March: The Complete Software Developer's Guide to Surviving "Mission Impossible" Projects*. Upper Saddle River, NJ: Prentice Hall, 1997. (ISBN 0-13-748310-4, 218 pages)

Zubrow, David, et al. *Maturity Questionnaire*. CMU/SEI-94-SR-7. Pittsburgh, PA: Software Engineering Institute, Carnegie Mellon University, 1994.

Zuse, Horst. *Software Complexity: Measures and Methods*. Berlin: Walter de Gruyter, 1990. (ISBN 3-11-012226-X, 603 pages)

———. *A Framework of Software Measurement*. Berlin: Walter de Gruyter, 1997. (ISBN 3 110 155877)

Zvegintzov, Nicholas. *Software Management Technology Reference Guide*. Release 4.2. New York: Software Maintenance News, 1994. (ISBN 1-884521-01-0, 240 pages)

CHAPTER ELEVEN

Benchmarks and Best Practices for Military Software

The phrase *military software* refers to software produced for a uniformed military service such as a nation's air force, army, navy, or coast guard. The term can also include software produced for the DoD (or the equivalent in other countries). Some military software is produced by uniformed military personnel. In the United States, however, the bulk of military software is developed by civilian contractors. Oversight and project management roles are normally the responsibility of military program management offices.

The broad definition of military software includes a number of subclasses, such as software associated with weapons systems; with command, control, and communication systems (usually shortened to C^3); with logistical applications; and with software virtually identical to civilian counterparts, such as payroll applications, benefits tracking applications, and the like.

Our demographic data indicates that the military software domain employs more than 370,000 software professionals in the United States out of a total of approximately 2,300,000 or 16% of the total software employment force. There are more than 5,000 defense contracting companies in the United States, although probably 85% of all defense contract dollars goes to the top 50 of these groups. Examples of major U.S. military contract organizations include AT&T, Boeing, CSC, Hughes, General Dynamics, Grumman-Northrup, IBM, Litton, Lockheed, Logicon, Loral, and Raytheon.

In recent years, since about 1990, the defense contracting subindustry has been undergoing some fairly significant changes in the United States. Waves of mergers and acquisitions are leading to a reduction in overall numbers of defense contractors, but the remaining contractors are growing in size. However, the mergers also are accompanied by "downsizing" (elimination of redundant personnel), so the overall defense sector is not growing in terms of demographics, and may be shrinking.

The DoD and the uniformed military services alone are reported to employ more than 70,000 software personnel, although this number is speculative. (It is interesting that the annual software conferences sponsored by the Air Force's Software Technology Support Center [STSC] attract approximately 3,500 attendees and ranks as one of the largest pure software conferences in the United States.)

The military domain also has funded a number of specialized *think tanks* that do research on a variety of defense-related topics: Mitre Corporation performs research on a variety of subjects, and the SEI is one of the largest software-related research institutions in the world.

There are also research establishments within the military domain itself. For example, the STSC at Ogden Air Force Base, the Naval Post Graduate School in Monterey, and the Air Force Institute of Technology at Wright-Patterson Air Force Base are examples of in-house military research and education facilities. Incidentally, the Air Force's STSC publishes an interesting software journal called *Crosstalk*. This journal is one of the premier software journals in the world. Although many of the articles are on specialized topics of interest to the defense community, *Crosstalk* also publishes many articles by and for the civilian sector. *Crosstalk* tends to publish fairly meaty technical articles that contain more empirical data than many other journals. *Crosstalk* is also available to the software community without charge, which is a rare situation.

There is also the Software Productivity Consortium (SPC), a nonprofit organization sometimes confused with SPR, although the two have no connection. The SPC serves both the defense contract community and civilian companies interested in software topics. The SPC supports a number of research initiatives in topics such as reusability, quality control, and project management.

The United States is far and away the major producer and consumer of military and defense software in the world. The volume and sophistication of U.S. military software is actually a major factor of U.S. military capabilities. All those pictures of cruise missiles, smart bombs, and Patriot missiles destroying Scuds that filled television news during the Gulf War had an invisible force in the background: the software and computers on board that make such weapons possible.

Because the NATO countries tend to use many weapons systems, communication systems, logistics systems, and other software systems produced in the United States, it appears that the volume of U.S. defense and military software may be larger than the volume of the following five countries put together: Russia, China, Germany, the United Kingdom, and France. Many countries produce military and defense software for weapons and communications systems that they use or market, such as Israel, Brazil, South Korea, Sweden, and Japan.

The total of military software personnel outside the United States is estimated by SPR to be approximately 1,000,000. The bulk of these are in Russia, China, and the Ukraine. However, there are also active military software projects and defense contractors in Brazil, Argentina, Mexico, the United Kingdom, Canada, France, Israel, Sweden, Germany, Egypt, India, Pakistan, North Korea, Turkey, Vietnam, Poland, Cuba, Iraq, Iran, and essentially every country with a significant military establishment.

Military Software Technologies and Special Problems

To an outside observer, military software and hardware projects have some very noticeable differences compared with civilian norms. The first noticeable difference is the procurement process itself. The bulk of military projects is acquired by means of competitive bids, with the lowest cost a primary consideration. The bidding process is quite formal and includes rather massive sets of deliverable items on the part of the prospective contractors. Thus, responding to a military request for proposal can be an expensive proposition in its own right.

This form of acquisition (by means of competitive bids) also leads to another difference between civilian and military norms. Military procurement is often accompanied by challenges to the successful bidder, or to litigation. More than half the initial contract awards are challenged by disgruntled vendors. Indeed, a whole body of military contract law, and special courts and arbitrators deal with these challenges.

As a result of frequent litigation challenging the initial contract awards, there is often a delay of six months to 18 months in actually reaching a final decision on military software contracts and starting the work. This means that many large software and hardware projects in the military domain are under immediate schedule pressure because they were delayed in starting due to litigation. Because schedule pressure is one of the major root causes of software failures, many projects that are rushed tend to run late, have poor quality, or end up being cancelled because they cannot meet operational requirements.

Once the contract work begins, a third difference between military and civilian practice is readily apparent. The relationship between the DoD and its contractors tends to be somewhat adversarial. As a result, the oversight and control requirements of military projects are far more extensive and burdensome than civilian norms. For example, the volume of planning and tracking paperwork required for a typical military software project is approximately three times larger than for civilian software projects of the same size. Indeed, software requirements, software specifications, and almost all forms of text-based documents are several times larger for military projects than for equivalent civilian projects.

The enormous volumes of paper documents associated with military software projects is one of the main reasons why military productivity rates lag behind all other domains. It is not easy to be productive when the volume of paper documents is three times larger than civilian norms. Approximately 400 English words are produced for every source code statement in the Ada95 programming language on typical military software projects. These words cost at least twice as much as the code itself. It is not unusual for large defense projects to accumulate roughly 50% of total costs in the area of producing and reviewing paper documents. This is far more than for any other kind of software.

Although every software project needs requirements and specifications, approximately half of the words created for military software projects are due to the very elaborate oversight and status reporting criteria associated with military contract work. Basically, the documents are produced to demonstrate contract compliance rather than to add technical content to the project itself.

The volume of paper documents associated with military software projects is so large that paperwork production is often the most expensive element of large military software projects. For civilian projects, defect removal is the most expensive activity. In the military domain, however, paperwork costs are number one and defect removal costs are number two. (Communication is number three and coding is only number four in the hierarchy of military software cost elements.)

The major programming languages used for military software in the past included Assembly, FORTRAN, and some specialized languages that were seldom used outside of the military domain: Jovial and CMS2. The Ada83 programming language and the newer Ada95 programming language continue the tradition of development of specialized languages for defense software. However, both of the Ada languages have also attracted some civilian users, especially in Europe.

Because of the diversity of software applications under the overall military umbrella, almost all programming languages are used. For example, COBOL is used for more business-oriented military software, such as payroll applications. The C and C++ programming languages are also used. Of the almost 600 programming languages in current use, we have noted at least 75 languages used on various military applications (including JAVA, which is exploding in use).

Over the years, the U.S. defense community has evolved an elaborate set of specialized standards and practices that differ substantially from civilian norms. Although these military practices and DoD standards are not without merit, they have tended to be so cumbersome and baroque that they sometimes serve more as impediments to progress rather than benefiting either the defense contractors or the DoD itself.

Dealing with the DoD and the military services for business and contract purposes is so complex and specialized that the companies that actually do significant amounts of military business usually have special military proposal and contract personnel, who often are retired military officers. It is very difficult for amateurs to bid successfully on a military contract, and the situation is becoming more complicated rather than easier.

Because the United States is the world's largest producer and consumer of military software, the way the United States goes about the production of military software is of global importance. In the United States in 1994, William Perry, the Secretary of Defense at the time, issued a major policy statement to the effect that DoD standards no longer needed to be utilized. Instead, the armed services and the DoD were urged to adopt civilian best current practices. This change in policy is now a little more than five years old as this book is written.

An immediate result of Perry's directive was the convening of several task forces and study groups to explore leading civilian software practices. However, the military community has a strong conservative bent. Many DoD standards such as 2167A or DoD 498 will probably continue to be the de facto standards of the military world for several more years, if for no other reason than because military contractors have used them for so long they are comfortable with the nomenclature and requirements. Also, the defense world does not yet know how civilians do things when they do software well.

Because civilian software fails too (witness the protracted delays associated with the luggage-handling system of the Denver Airport), another challenge for the defense community is to select practices from the civilian sector that truly *do* work, as opposed to practices that are merely fads.

On the whole, the best models for the military domain are the large civilian systems software producers such as AT&T, IBM, and the like. These enterprises build software of similar size and complexity to many large-scale military applications. However, the civilian systems software domain manages to build large applications with shorter schedules, lower costs, and equal or even higher quality than found normally on military projects.

Another aspect of the DoD attempt to move in a civilian direction is increased usage of commercial off-the-shelf (COTS) software. Obviously the use of COTS packages refers to ordinary business and personal software packages such as databases, payroll programs, spreadsheets, and the like. The COTS concept is clearly not aimed at sophisticated weapons systems, for which no civilian packages exist.

Unfortunately, the military domain has no real incentive for adopting civilian best practices. The DoD itself and the military services are not profit-making organizations. If they tend to overspend or develop software in a way that is worse than the civilian sector, so long as the fundamental mission requirements are not compromised, there is no overwhelming reason to improve.

For defense contractors, there are actually tangible business reasons for staying somewhat inefficient compared with civilian norms. For time-and-materials contracts, there is a negative incentive for adopting civilian best practices because increased productivity and shorter schedules reduce the revenues and the profits from major contracts.

For fixed-price contracts, a case might be made that adopting civilian best practices would lower costs and raise the probability of acquiring the contract. However, artificially low bids are common enough so that this strategy might not be effective. The whole process of military procurement and contracting is in need of very careful analysis and some substantial rework.

What is needed is a thorough analysis of all laws, regulations, policies, and related publications that determine the way military software is procured from the outside world and built. This analysis must cover all of the uniformed services and the DoD itself, and possibly related civilian agencies such as NASA, which have contributed to software practices and have some influence in military circles.

The Software Engineering Institute

There are two key facts that should be held in mind regarding software and the defense community: (1) Software is of critical importance to the U.S. DoD and to all U.S. military services, and (2) software engineering in both the civilian and military arenas is a troubling technology with many failures and problems.

Because of these two facts, it is appropriate for the U.S. DoD to invest in research establishments that can add rigor to software development practices, and thereby raise the probability of successful outcomes on software projects. In 1985, the Defense Advanced Research Projects Agency acted on the advice of Dr. Barry Boehm and other software engineering researchers and funded the SEI.

The SEI is located on the campus of Carnegie-Mellon University in Pittsburgh, Pennsylvania. The SEI has become world famous for the creation of an interesting model of software development practices called the *capability maturity model*. It should be noted that the CMM is not static, but is evolving over time, and new concepts are added as the need arises. The first major book on the CMM was Watts Humphrey's *Managing the Software Process* (Humphrey 1989), which has become a best-seller among both civilian and military software specialists. A whole series of books on SEI programs is now in print, making the SEI one of the best-documented research establishments in the entire software world. The SEI also publishes a variety of technical reports on topics such as measurement, quality control, reusability, and other topics of interest to the software domain.

The SEI also created a software assessment method for examining the practices used by companies in building software. The SEI assessment data is collected by means of on-site interviews using both standard questions and observations based on interviews with management and technical personnel. Once collected, the assessment data is analyzed and is used to place a software organization on one of the five plateaus of the SEI CMM. Although the assessment- and maturity-level concepts can be considered separately, most people regard the two as being a linked set.

Because of the importance of very large systems to the DoD, the SEI assessment approach originally dealt primarily with the software processes and methodologies used by very large companies that produced very large systems. The original SEI assessment approach was derived from the best practices used by leading corporations such as IBM and AT&T, which employ from 5,000 to more than 25,000 software professionals, and which could safely build systems in excess of 1,000,000 LOC or 10,000 function points.

Based on the patterns of answers to the SEI assessment questions, the final result of the SEI assessment process is to place the software organization on one of the levels of a five-point maturity scale. The five plateaus on the SEI maturity level are those presented in Table 11.1.

It is obvious that the distribution of software organizations is severely skewed toward the low end of the scale. In 1993 and 1994, the Air Force commissioned several studies to explore the topic of whether moving up the CMM ladder improves software productivity and quality. As data began to be collected, it became evident that there is some overlap among the various SEI maturity levels. For example, in terms of both quality and productivity, the best software projects from level 1 organizations can be equal or superior to the worst developed by level 3 organizations. For some smaller companies that cannot afford some of the infrastructure and special departments assumed by the SEI CMM concept, rather good results are possible even at level 1. Conversely, achieving levels 3, 4, and 5 on the SEI CMM scale do not guarantee that all software projects will be successful.

There is now statistical evidence from a number of studies that software productivity and quality do go up with CMM level. QSM in 1993, and SPR in 1994, examined more than 100 projects and found that when organizations do move from CMM level 1 up to level 3, their productivity and quality levels tend to improve.

The DoD and various military services such as the Air Force are now mandating that the SEI assessment approach be used, and that CMM level 3 is a requirement for receiving some government contracts. Thus, the major U.S. defense contractors have been fairly energetic in moving up the SEI CMM scale.

The investments required to move up the SEI ladder are substantial, and moving from level 1 to level 3 on the SEI CMM can cost more than $20,000 per

Table 11.1　SEI Maturity Levels

SEI Maturity Level	Meaning	Frequency of Occurrence, %
1 = Initial	Chaotic	75.0
2 = Repeatable	Marginal	15.0
3 = Defined	Adequate	8.0
4 = Managed	Good to excellent	1.5
5 = Optimizing	State of the art	0.5

capita. An unanticipated side effect of the SEI level 3 mandate may be to move some defense software offshore. Countries such as India have software development companies with very low labor rates that are achieving fairly high SEI levels. In fact, India has more companies at SEI level 3 (or higher) than any other country besides the United States. Although it is unlikely that weapons systems or classified software could be developed outside the United States, the military applications that are similar to civilian applications (such as payroll or medical benefit processing) have no stringent security barriers.

When first published, it was obvious that the SEI CMM assessment approach concentrated on software development process factors and ignored many other factors. Although software process factors are important, they are not the only factors that influence software projects. The initial SEI CMM approach more or less ignored tools, programming languages, staff hiring practices, appraisal methods, salaries and benefits, office environments, and a host of other important topics. These omissions meant that a company could achieve SEI CMM level 3, 4, or 5 status and still not be totally successful.

More recently, in the mid to late 1990s, the SEI has been broadening the set of factors included under the assessment and CMM umbrella. As the century ends, the SEI is now dealing with a majority of the factors that affect software, including personnel skills and human relations. The SEI has also recognized that small companies cannot afford some of the dedicated departments found in large corporations. Therefore, a subset of overall SEI CMM criteria have been developed for small companies. It is a positive sign that the SEI recognized the early gaps and missing components of the original CMM approach, and has been eliminating them.

Overall, the SEI has performed valuable work for both the military and civilian arenas. The SEI has raised the awareness of the software community to the need for effective development processes. The creation of the CMM has provided a workable (even if not perfect) framework for evaluating the technologies and methods used to develop software applications. Finally, the SEI approach has begun to be adopted globally. The CMM is now being used in many countries, including much of Europe, India, and even in countries such as Russia that do not always agree with U.S. ideas. Thus the SEI has provided a unifying set of principles that software researchers can use to judge relative methods

A very substantial amount of literature has sprung up around the SEI assessment method and the CMM. No less than 30 books and hundreds of articles are now in print on various aspects of software research.

The Airlie Council

In the mid 1990s Dr. Norm Brown was funded by the Navy to form the Software Program Manager's Network (SPMN), which is a group of researchers concerned with identifying and transferring civilian software best practices to the defense community. A mixture of civilian software consultants, academicians, and military personnel have contributed to this work, including Dr. Victor Basili, Dr. Barry Boehm, Dr. Tom McCabe, Ed Yourdon, Larry Putnam, Tim Lister, Tom DeMarco, and myself.

Brown and his staff selected a conference center located approximately 50 miles from Washington, DC, as the site for periodic meetings. Thus the collection of consultants working on transferring civilian best practices to the defense community has come to be called the Airlie Council, taking the name of the conference center where the meetings are held.

After several years of discussion and selection, the Airlie Council has selected a set of 16 key practices that can be considered "best practices" in both the civilian and military software domains. These 16 practices are discussed in depth on a CD-ROM available from the SPMN. The title is *The Road to Performance-Based Management Based on 16 Critical Software Practices*. The sixteen best practices are worthy of discussion because they were selected by some of the top software researchers in the United States:

1. Adopt continuous program risk management
2. Estimate costs and schedules using empirical data
3. Use metrics to manage
4. Track earned value
5. Track defects against quality targets
6. Treat people as the most important resource
7. Adopt full life cycle configuration management
8. Manage and trace requirements
9. Use system-based software design
10. Ensure data and database interoperability
11. Define and control all interfaces
12. Design twice, but code once
13. Assess the risks and costs of reusable material
14. Use inspections of requirements and design
15. Manage testing as a continuous process
16. Compile and build the application frequently

These 16 practices are derived from observations of many successful software projects. It is interesting that when projects that fail are compared with projects that succeed, as discussed later, very few of these 16 show up on the failure side of the picture.

Military Software Demographics

The military software population is divided between the uniformed military services and the civilian defense contract community. Although there is some ambiguity, the civilian population appears to comprise approximately two thirds of the total and the uniformed population roughly one third. These have been the ratios noted among the projects on which we have collected data. (SPR was commissioned by AT&T to study software demographics in large organizations in 1995. The U.S. Air Force was one of the participants. SPR has also done consulting work with the U.S. Navy.)

Military software, like civilian software, has been heavily impacted by the Y2K problem. As a result, a significant proportion of the defense programming community worked on Y2K repairs during calendar years 1998 and 1999. Many applications have either been updated or replaced due to the Y2K problem. For additional information on military software Y2K problems, refer to *The Year 2000 Software Problem: Quantifying the Costs and Assessing the Consequences* (Jones 1998).

Based on demographic studies among SPR's clients extrapolated to national levels, the military software domain in the United States contains approximately 370,000 professional software personnel and managers, or roughly 16% of the approximate total of 2,300,000 U.S. software personnel. Table 11.2 shows the estimated percentage of total U.S. software personnel working in the domain of commercial software.

The number of U.S. companies that produce military software totals more than 5,000 and includes both very large and very small enterprises. Among the large enterprises can be found several of the largest defense employers of software personnel in the world. Companies such as Boeing, Lockheed-Martin, Litton, Grumman-Northrup, and Raytheon employ more than 5,000 software personnel on average.

Many hybrid companies such as AT&T and IBM, which build both hardware and software, serve both the military and civilian domains. Some of these large corporations employ more than 25,000 total software personnel. However, the

Table 11.2   Estimated U.S. Military Software Population circa 1999

Software Occupational Groups	No. Employed	Military Software	Percent of Total
Programmer/analyst	400,000	40,000	10.00
Programmer, maintenance	350,000	56,000	16.00
Programmer, development	275,000	44,000	16.00
Project manager, first level	225,000	31,500	14.00
Software engineer, systems	200,000	36,000	18.00
Testing specialist	125,000	21,250	17.00
Systems analyst	100,000	5,000	5.00
Software engineer, real-time	75,000	26,250	35.00
Software technical writer	75,000	11,250	15.00
Software engineer, embedded	70,000	14,000	20.00
Data administration specialist	50,000	5,000	10.00
Project manager, second level	35,000	4,900	14.00
Software quality assurance specialist	25,000	3,500	14.00
Configuration control specialist	15,000	3,000	20.00
Performance specialist	7,500	1,500	20.00
Project manager, third level	5,000	700	14.00
Software architect	1,500	150	10.00
Subtotal	2,034,000	304,000	14.95
Support Occupations			
Software sales specialist	105,000	21,000	20.00
Customer support specialist	80,000	16,000	20.00
Systems administration	50,000	7,500	15.00
Software management consultant	45,000	6,750	15.00
Software education specialist	30,000	7,500	25.00
Software librarian	15,000	3,000	20.00
Process auditor/assessor	7,500	2,625	35.00
Process improvement specialist	5,000	1,750	35.00

Software Occupational Groups	No. Employed	Military Software	Percent of Total
Measurement specialist	3,500	210	6.00
Software marketing specialist	3,000	750	25.00
Cost-estimating specialist	2,000	700	35.00
Human factors specialist	1,000	150	15.00
Certified function point counter	500	25	5.00
Subtotal	322,000	67,960	21.11
Total	2,356,000	371,960	15.79

military and defense divisions within these large enterprises usually employ only 5,000 or so software personnel.

Examples of smaller software vendors marketing to the defense community include companies such as AMS, SPR, and QSM. These companies sell project management tools that are used on defense projects, as they are on civilian projects. These enterprises have technical staffs that range from less than 20 to more than 200 personnel. There are hundreds of such small and fairly specialized software companies serving both the defense and civilian sectors.

Abroad, the countries that produce military software in the largest volumes include Russia, China, Germany, Japan, France, and the United Kingdom. Other countries such as India, Brazil, Argentina, Israel, Mexico, Taiwan, the Ukraine, and both South Korea and North Korea produce some of their own military software packages. However, a majority of countries depend primarily on military software produced by either the United States or the former Soviet Union, or both. The non-U.S. total of military software personnel tops 1,000,000, with the bulk of these in Russia and China.

Some of the industries and SIC codes that produce the greatest amount of military software include those presented on Table 11.3.

These industries often produce both civilian and military software packages. Modern weapons systems, or at least those produced by the United States, are heavily computerized and contain very large quantities of software:

Table 11.3   Military Software Producers by SIC Code

SIC Code	Industry
3483	Ammunition
3519	Internal combustion engines
3571	Electronic computers
3661	Telephone and telegraph apparatus
3669	Communication equipment
3721	Aircraft
3724	Aircraft engines
3731	Ship building
3761	Guided missiles and space vehicles
3795	Tanks and tank components
4812	Radiotelephone communication
4813	Telephone communication
7371	Custom computer programming services
7373	Computer integrated systems design

- A modern attack aircraft contains more than 20,000 function points or 25,000,000 lines of source code.
- A modern naval vessel such as an Aegis-class ship or a submarine contains more than 500,000 function points or 50,000,000 lines of source code.

When a U.S. infantry soldier advances into combat, he or she is supported by at least 50,000 function points or more than 5,000,000 source code statements of software that actually affect military operations. Some of this software is embedded in communication equipment, some of it controls artillery ranging and targeting, some of it is in radar sets, and some of the software is actually carried into combat. For example, there is software inside night-vision goggles and field radios.

Over and above the software concerned with military combat, each U.S. soldier is also backed up by more than 150,000 function points or 15,000,000 lines of source code that handles logistics, supplies, military payroll, medical and hospital equipment, and military transportation.

The United States military services are effective far beyond their actual numbers due to the deployment of very sophisticated computerized equipment. Almost every U.S. weapons system, including tanks, aircraft, ships, guided missiles, smart bombs, and artillery, is now heavily reliant on computers and software.

The large military software vendors such as Raytheon and Lockheed-Martin have established some interesting research and development laboratories. Of course, much of this research is classified and hence unavailable to ordinary civilians.

The military software domain is a major user of high-end development workstations and also of PCs in all configurations. The military software world in general is well equipped with tools and workstations. Indeed, the military plans to build full life cycle tool suites for software projects actually go beyond anything in the civilian domain.

As with other domains, the military software world has an intense work ethic. However, for classified projects it is not safe to work at home. Although both workstations and portable computers may be supplied to key personnel, the bulk of the work is required to be carried out at secure locations using secure equipment. This is due to the classified nature of some military software. The theft of a notebook computer containing military plans during the Gulf War illustrates the need to use state-of-the-art security methods for all military software and supporting data.

This brings up another important point. Military software is obviously a prime target for espionage. Military software is also becoming a prime target for disruption by enemy "hackers" during combat. Indeed, it was reported in the press that the Serbian government attempted to penetrate and damage U.S. software packages during the recent conflict in Kosovo. The United States also carried out such computer penetrations to Serbian equipment and computers.

The recent history of warfare is interesting. For most of human history warfare was two-dimensional, because it occurred only on the surface. The invention of aircraft, missiles, and submarines made war a three-dimensional undertaking because combat could occur above or below the surface of the world. The invention of radio, computers, and software is adding yet another dimension to warfare. Modern warfare must now be prepared to deal with attacks from cyberspace as well as attacks from the physical world.

The military software domain, like all other software domains, is currently experiencing a shortage of technical personnel. The military shortage is more acute than for any other domain. The reason for this is because military compensation packages have lagged the civilian sector by so much that a "brain drain" may be occurring. Some civilian companies regard the military sector as a choice recruiting ground. Although software technical staff compensation in the defense sector is not the lowest, it is in the lower half of all industries. All industries below the median may give up personnel to industries above the median.

Due to the shortage of personnel, many civilian companies are offering excellent salaries, benefits packages, and even signing bonuses. These practices are rare in the military domain. Unless military software personnel have a pressing need to stay in a particular company (such as an approaching pension), then many are moving toward the more lucrative civilian domains.

Military Software Benchmarks

For a number of reasons, productivity rates for military software projects are lower than any other domain. The low productivity is not because military software personnel are less capable than their civilian counterparts. Indeed, coding productivity is roughly similar between the military domains and others. It simply happens that the residue of military standards has left behind a tradition of massive documents, plus several activities not performed in the civilian sectors. Three major reasons explain the major sources of low productivity on military software projects.

1. Military planning, control, and technical documents such as requirements and specifications are roughly three times more voluminous than civilian averages. The added volume is not because of the technical needs of the projects, but because of the oversight requirements of the DoD and the older military standards.
2. Military software projects perform activities such as IV&V and independent testing by an external company. These activities are seldom utilized on equivalent civilian software projects.
3. Military contract practices tend to encourage fairly low productivity rates. For time-and-materials contracts, low productivity adds to revenues. For fixed-price contracts, being the low bidder means that personnel expenses may be squeezed, so that team experience might not be as high as desirable.

Figure 11.1 illustrates a broad overview of productivity levels in the military software domain. A key point to be derived from Figure 11.1 is the fact that productivity includes more than just coding. The reason for the low productivity is due largely to the huge volumes of paper documents produced for military software projects.

A very interesting aspect of military and defense productivity is the fact that maintenance productivity is often higher than new development productivity. This is because the massive paperwork requirements associated with new military projects are not always encountered on maintenance projects. Figure 11.1 simplifies the overall situation and merely provides an illustration of trends. Note, too, that for very small projects (<100 function points) even military projects relax the massive paperwork requirements that have such an impact on larger applications.

As you can see from Figure 11.1, there is an interesting node at approximately 100 function points. This happens to be the size at which new development projects and enhancement and maintenance projects come together in terms of net productivity rates. Smaller maintenance and enhancement projects

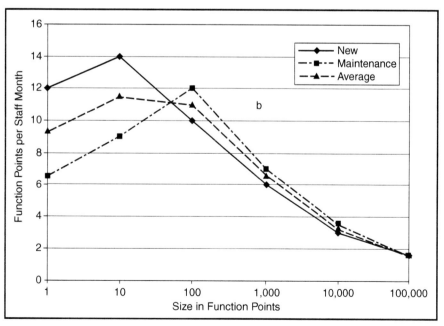

Figure 11.1   Military software productivity levels

have reduced productivity levels due to the overhead associated with regression testing and recompilation of the base application.

Military projects often share common features with civilian systems software projects. One of these features is a need for high quality and reliability coupled with rather sophisticated software quality assurance groups. The military software domain has the second highest levels of defect removal of any type of software SPR has studied. Many military software projects top 95% in defect removal efficiency. (This is true for weapons systems and communications systems, but not necessarily true for ordinary military applications such as payroll and accounting, which do not follow military standards.)

The military domain also ranks number two in the use of software quality assurance departments. On many defense projects, more than 30% of the total work force is involved with testing and quality assurance tasks. Quality control in the military domain for weapons systems is quite sophisticated for obvious reasons. The main reason is because military software controls complicated physical devices such as radar sets and aircraft flight controls. If these don't work as intended, lives and battles could be lost.

The importance of quality control and formal processes within the military software domain explains why, with the exception of systems software, more military software producers can be found at or higher than level 3 on the SEI CMM than other domains. Because many companies that are SEI CMM level 3 produce both military and civilian software, there is some overlap between the systems and military software companies.

Although the U.S. software community is not impressed with the ISO quality standards, it is necessary to be certified in these standards to market many technical products within the European Union. Therefore, many military software producers have been certified under ISO 9000–9004. For companies such as Motorola, ISO certification was not difficult because their quality control practices far exceeded those envisioned by the ISO standards. However, the actual value of ISO certification in terms of improving quality appears to be marginal or none.

A number of fairly sophisticated software quality approaches are quite common in both the military and systems software domains. The quality assurance and control methods used by both systems and military software include

- Use of formal design and code inspections
- Use of quality estimation tools
- Use of quality and defect removal targets for key projects

- Use of QFD
- Use of "six-sigma" quality targets
- Use of complexity analysis tools
- Use of automated defect tracking systems
- Use of test library automation support
- Use of automated change control tools
- Use of trained testing specialists
- Use of formal regression test suites
- Use of full life cycle quality measurements
- Use of the SEI CMM

The military software domain also utilizes two other techniques that are seldom encountered on civilian software projects: (1) IV&V and (2) independent testing by a third party. The phrase *independent verification and validation* implies using a third party or an external company to investigate whether all requirements have been met and whether the design and other documents meet all relevant military standards. The phrase *independent testing* refers to hiring a company other than the prime contractor on a military software project to conduct late-stage testing after internal testing.

Both IV&V and independent testing add significant costs to military software projects that are not encountered on normal civilian projects. Whether these stages actually improve quality is ambiguous. It is true that military software defect removal is among the best of any kind of software project. However, it is no better than the defect removal found on civilian systems software projects.

Adding to the questionable nature of the IV&V activity, it is often a semimechanical task that consists mostly of checking off whether standards and procedures have been followed. The IV&V work is often performed by workers who are not certified quality assurance personnel. Thus, the value of IV&V in finding or removing actual defects is marginal.

The overall results of the military software quality approaches have been generally successful. Defect removal efficiency levels for weapons systems software is higher than U.S. averages. Many military software projects exceed 95% in cumulative defect removal efficiency. Indeed, only systems software and military software have approached or exceeded 99% in cumulative defect removal efficiency levels.

Net productivity levels in the military software domain have been lower than all other types of software, including systems software. The reason for this is because military standards long required enormous plans and specification sets roughly three times bigger than civilian norms when pages per function point are measured. The volume of military planning documents, control documents, requirements, and specifications tends to slow productivity.

Interestingly, coding productivity for military software projects is equal or better than almost any other kind of software except commercial software. The usage of formal structuring methods and code inspections is part of the reason why coding productivity is quite good in the military software domain.

On the other hand, for applications in the 10,000-function point and 100,000-function point domains, the military track record is not too bad. Although productivity rates are low, the number of cancelled projects is below average at the upper end of the military software spectrum. Indeed, for the top size plateau of 100,000 function points, military software is an overall leader in terms of successes and failures, and roughly equal to civilian systems software in success-to-failure ratios. It can be said that the strong emphasis in the military world on rigorous processes, complete specifications, and formal quality assurance controls produce projects that are fairly successful above 10,000 function points in size.

Within all size plateaus, actual coding or programming productivity in the military software domain is quite good. The combination of structured programming, code inspections, and significant volumes of reusable code are all beneficial. However, coding is less than 15% of the total effort devoted to systems software, whereas production of paper documents tops 50%.

Let us consider some overall benchmark results from the military software domain concentrating on more recent studies circa 1995 through 1999. Table 11.4 summarizes some of the data points from the SPR studies of systems software.

General benchmarks do not provide enough information to understand the nature of the work involved. Let us now examine a more detailed activity-level benchmark of 10,000 function points (Table 11.5). The class of 10,000-function point applications is common within the military software domain. The typical activity patterns for that size of project reflect some of the overall practices for military software.

The activities associated with a typical military software project of 10,000 function points are more extensive than any other form of software. Assuming that the Ada95 programming language is used, this would be approximately 800,000 Ada statements. The Ada95 programming language requires roughly 80 statements per function point.

In Table 11.5, the Assignment Scope column refers to the number of function points normally assigned to one staff member. The Production Rate column

Table 11.4   Overall Military Software Benchmarks

Benchmark	Value
No. of new projects	130
No. of enhancement projects	135
Total no. of projects	265
Average new project size, function points	2,800
Maximum new project size, function points	97,000
Average enhancement size, function points	135
Maximum enhancement size, function points	3,750
Average new development assignment scope, function points	140
Maximum development assignment scope, function points	290
Average maintenance assignment scope, function points	475
Maximum maintenance assignment scope, function points	2,350
Average productivity, function points per staff month	4.2
Maximum productivity, function points per staff month	16.5
Average productivity, work hours per function point	31.43
Maximum productivity, work hours per function point	8.00
Average effort, staff months	11,760
Maximum effort, staff months	203,700
Average new project staff size	20
Maximum new project staff size	990
Average new project schedule, calendar months	23.93
Maximum new project schedule, calendar months	73.00
Average monthly compensation, burdened	$15,000
Maximum monthly compensation, burdened	$23,000
Average cost per function point	$3,571.43
Maximum cost per function point	$6,600.00
Average defect potential per function point	6.2
Maximum defect potential per function point	8.3
Average defect removal efficiency	92.50%
Maximum defect removal efficiency	99.10%
Average monthly rate of requirements creep	2.50%
Maximum monthly rate of requirements creep	4.50%

Table 11.5   Military Software Activities and Rates for 10,000 Function Points

Parameter	Value
Application size	10,000 function points
Application size	800,000 LOC
Source language	Ada95
Work hours per month	132
Monthly compensation	$15,000

Activities Performed	Assignment Scope, function points	Production Rate, function points	Staff	Effort, months	Schedule, months	Cost	Percent
01 Requirements	300	40	33	250	7.50	$3,750,000	7.14
02 Prototyping	1,000	100	10	100	10.00	$1,500,000	2.86
03 Architecture	1,000	100	10	100	10.00	$1,500,000	2.86
04 Project plans	1,500	200	7	50	7.50	$750,000	1.43
05 Initial design	170	35	59	286	4.86	$4,285,714	8.16
06 Detail design	135	33	74	303	4.09	$4,545,455	8.66
07 Design reviews	150	50	67	200	3.00	$3,000,000	5.71
08 Coding	125	33	80	303	3.79	$4,545,455	8.66
09 Reuse acquisition	2,000	1,000	5	10	2.00	$150,000	0.29
10 IV&V	750	125	13	80	6.00	$1,200,000	2.28
11 Code inspections	110	75	91	133	1.47	$2,000,000	3.81

12 Configuration management	1,500	500	7	20	3.00	$300,000	0.57
13 Formal integration	1,500	350	7	29	4.29	$428,571	0.82
14 Documentation	600	25	17	400	24.00	$6,000,000	11.42
15 Unit testing	125	50	80	200	2.50	$3,000,000	5.71
16 Function testing	150	60	67	167	2.50	$2,500,000	4.76
17 Integration testing	150	70	67	143	2.14	$2,142,857	4.08
18 System testing	150	60	67	167	2.50	$2,500,000	4.76
19 Independent testing	250	100	40	100	2.50	$1,500,000	2.86
20 Acceptance testing	300	250	33	40	1.20	$600,000	1.14
21 Quality assurance	1,000	125	10	80	8.00	$1,200,000	2.28
22 Installation	2,000	1,250	5	8	1.60	$120,000	0.23
23 Project management	1,000	30	10	333	33.33	$5,000,000	9.52
Totals/averages	133[1]	2.86[1]	75[1]	3,501[2]	46.63[1]	$52,518,052[2]	100.00[2]

Cost per function point, $5,252; Cost per LOC, $65.65.
[1]Average
[2]Total

refers to the volume of function points that can be completed in a standard time period. Assignment scopes and production rates are key metrics derived from benchmark studies. The importance of these metrics is that they are fundamental metrics for software cost estimating. The standard time period in Table 11.5 is the "staff month," which contains approximately 22 working days. Each working day is assumed to be of a nominal eight hours in duration, but only six hours a day are devoted to productive work. This totals 132 effective work hours per month. These assumptions are nominal or default values.

As you can see from Table 11.5, military software performs more activities than any other type of software in the United States. Two activities in particular—independent testing and IV&V—almost never occur on civilian projects.

Military software, like civilian systems software, includes a significant concentration of resources on quality-related topics such as formal inspections, testing, and quality assurance work. In terms of quality-related activities, Table 11.5 includes formal quality assurance teams, design inspections, code inspections, and seven discrete forms of testing.

However, the oversight requirements and the large volumes of specifications required by DoD standards 2167 or DoD 498 lead to the unusual situation that the effort and activities associated with the production of paper documents accumulate more effort and costs than any other aspect of defense software. Among other things, the heavy oversight requirements tend to lead to needing more managers and managerial support staff than civilian projects to keep up with the oversight reports.

Military projects also tend to have larger complements of technical staff members than civilian projects, or at least they did prior to the personnel shortage in 1998 and 1999. Here, too, some of the extra staff are there to fulfill specialized military needs and gather data required by oversight requirement.

The list of activities in Table 11.5 is useful when considering only summary or project-level benchmark data. Without knowing how many different kinds of work are involved in military software, it would be difficult to understand why productivity rates are lower than any other class of software.

When activities from Table 11.5 are aggregated, it is interesting to note that the sum of the work devoted to paperwork is the largest cost driver of military software, followed by defect removal. Code-related work in the form of prototypes and product programming is only the third largest cost element (Table 11.6).

Because best-in-class companies are often of interest, Table 11.7 contrasts average values with best-in-class results for military projects in a number of key

Table 11.6   Major Military Software Cost Drivers

Military Software Cost Drivers	Staff Months	Percent
Defect removal	1,310	37.40
Paper documents	1,505	43.00
Code related	452	12.90

metric areas in the productivity and quality domains. However, an explanation is needed to interpret the table.

Military software projects range from less than 100 function points to more than 100,000 function points. In Table 11.7 three size categories are used: 1,000, 10,000, and 100,000 function points. The function points used in Table 11.7 refer to function points counted using Version 4.1 of the IFPUG counting rules. The LOC metric refers to logical statements, rather than physical lines. For the cost items shown in the table, a constant burdened compensation rate of $15,000 per staff month is assumed. The reason for using a constant value is because the difference in monthly compensation is a complex topic. As pointed out earlier, compensation varies by industry, size of company, geographic region, and occupational group.

The military software domain is handicapped by a number of cumbersome practices that grew up in the days of strict military standards. Although attempts are being made to adopt civilian best practices, the military domain remains somewhat conservative. For applications in the 100,000-function point plateau, the military software domain is not too bad. Success rates are better than average and failure rates are below average. Although it is true that productivity is lower than any other class of software, this is due to project oversight and overhead requirements.

The next benchmark is how well military software meet anticipated schedules. Table 11.8 includes four columns of data: projects that are early, projects that are on time relative to their formal schedules, projects that are late, and projects that are cancelled and never finished at all. The military software domain is the worst in projects finishing early. This is due in part to military contract practices. The military domain is somewhat better than average in on-time completion of 100,000-function point projects, although that is not saying very much because failures and delays outnumber successes at the large end of the size spectrum.

Table 11.7   Average and Best-in-Class Results for Military Software

Key Software Topics	1,000 Function Points	10,000 Function Points	100,000 Function Points
Average staff size	7	77	800
Best-in-class staff size	5	50	571
Average schedule, months	19.50	52.48	141.25
Best-in-class schedule, months	13.80	39.81	100.00
Average function points per staff month	7.69	2.48	0.88
Best-in-class function points per staff month	14.49	5.02	1.75
Average work hours per function point	17.16	53.29	149.16
Best-in-class work hours per function point	9.11	26.28	75.43
Average LOC per staff month in C	962	310	111
Best-in-class LOC per staff month in C	1,811	628	219
Average effort, staff months	130	4,037	113,003
Best-in-class effort, staff months	69	1,991	57,143
Average cost per function point	$1,949.84	$6,055.47	$16,950.45
Best-in-class cost per function point	$1,035.29	$2,985.80	$8,571.43
Average defects per function point	5.25	5.75	6.80
Best-in-class defects per function point	2.50	4.00	5.00
Average defect removal efficiency	95.00%	91.00%	88.00%
Best-in-class defect removal efficiency	99.50%	99.00%	96.50%
Average delivered defects per function point	0.263	0.518	0.816
Best-in-class delivered defects per function point	0.013	0.040	0.175
Average no. of delivered defects	263	5,175	81,600
Best-in-class no. of delivered defects	13	400	17,500
Average no. of high-severity defects	39	776	12,240
Best-in-class no. of high-severity defects	2	48	2,100

Table 11.8   Military Software Schedule Adherence circa 1999

Size, function points	Early Projects, %	On-time Projects, %	Late Projects, %	Cancelled Projects, %	Total Projects, %
1	2.00	92.00	5.00	1.00	100.00
10	3.00	87.00	8.00	2.00	100.00
100	4.00	78.00	12.00	6.00	100.00
1,000	3.00	65.00	22.00	10.00	100.00
10,000	2.00	40.00	33.00	25.00	100.00
100,000	1.00	30.00	36.00	33.00	100.00
Average	2.50	65.33	19.33	12.83	100.00

Much of the work in the military software domain has centered around the development of very large systems between 10,000 and 100,000 function points. To optimize the probability of success for building large military applications, project management, process rigor, and quality control must be at state-of-the-art levels. Any deficiencies in these three fundamental disciplines can lead to delays or outright failure.

Military Software Successes and Failures

Success and failure in the military world is similar to success and failure in the civilian world, but not quite identical. For example, because approximately half of large military procurement contracts are challenged by disgruntled vendors, one attribute of success in the military world is that the contract is awarded based on such a thorough analysis of contractor capabilities that no lawsuits are filed by losing bidders.

Because of military contract practices, military software success does not imply high productivity rates or short schedules. They are not a normal part of military contracts. Running late and exceeding planned budgets is not a sign of success. Military software success does imply that the application meet all requirements. Success also implies that the application perform without serious defects remaining at deployment. Table 11.9 presents the major military software success and failure factors.

Table 11.9   Military Software Success and Failure Factors

Military Software Success Factors	Military Software Failure Factors
Contract let without litigation	Contract challenged in court
Project adheres to relevant DoD standards	Project violates one or more DoD standards
Project adheres to best civilian practices	Project adheres to poor civilian practices
Highly reliable with excellent quality	Very unreliable with poor quality
Project conforms to all requirements	Project fails to meet all requirements
Requirements stable within 15%	Requirements out of control
Schedules predictable within 10%	Schedules out of control
Costs predictable within 10%	Costs out of control
Project passes critical design review	Project fails critical design review
Project actually deployed and used	Project not used or not deployed
Software is fully Y2K compliant	Software is not Y2K compliant

Because military software development practices are slowly being transformed as this book is written, it will be interesting to revisit the military domain from time to time and judge their rate of progress. On the whole, the success-to-failure ratios within the military community have not been outstanding: Failures or delays have tended to exceed successes for many kinds of large military systems such as logistics support and C^3 applications. However, for the subset of military software that actually control weapons and combat systems, the success rates are rather good.

Military Software Success Factors

The military software domain is not without merit. In fact, the military software domain has a few best-in-class attributes:

- Military software is a leader in process assessments and process analysis.
- Military software has excellent research programs for best-in-class practices.
- Military software leads in applications larger than 100,000 function points.
- Military software is among the best in reusability research.

- Military software is among the best in CASE research.
- Military software is a world leader in Ada language research.
- Military software is a world leader in configuration control.
- Military software is a world leader in requirements traceability.
- Military software for weapons systems is among the best in quality control.
- Military software has the highest frequency of usage of cost-estimating tools (although many of these tools are low-end estimating tools that are not widely used by civilians, such as COCOMO and REVIC).

From the perspective of a civilian software researcher who visits the defense software community as well as other software domains, the impression is that the DoD and the military services would like very much to improve software development and acquisition practices. Some of the DoD and military software research programs are creating useful and interesting results. However, the military domain also has a long history of conservatism. This means that new technologies may not move as fast in the military world as they do in the civilian world. For example, the military domain is the last major industry to try and measure software productivity using the obsolete LOC metric. The military software domain is also the farthest behind in the adoption of function point metrics.

Conservatism appears to be widespread in military circles, and not only for software. It is interesting that many military technologies were rejected initially. Some of the technologies that were only adopted after repeated rejections include rifles instead of muskets, armor plate for naval ships, paddle wheels and propellers for naval vessels, self-leveling naval cannons, armored tanks using treads, and aircraft for bombing naval vessels. Not every invention or technology is rejected by the military services, but enough of them are to have established a pattern that is widely cited by military historians.

Military Software Failure Factors

In a number of software topics, the military world lags behind the civilian world by quite a few years:

- Military software lags in the adoption of functional metrics.
- Military software lags in productivity measurement technology.
- Military software exceeds all other industries in the production of huge documents.
- Military software schedules are longer than any other kind of software project.

- Military software productivity is lower than for any other industry.
- Military contracts for software have the highest rates of challenges and litigation.
- Military contractors rank first in layoffs and downsizing.
- Military contractors lag in staff benefits and compensation.
- Military contractors lag in training and education of technical staff.
- Military contractors lag in training and education of project managers.
- Military contract software has the highest growth of creeping user requirements.
- Military contracts associated with SEI maturity levels are much less effective than civilian performance-based contracts.
- Military software in many countries lagged in Y2K repairs.

Between the combination of downsizing the military community, the frequent challenges and litigation associated with military procurement, and the move to adopt civilian practices and COTS software, the military software domain is churning and finding it difficult to achieve any real stability. It will be a few more years before the military software domain stabilizes. Much of the current movement is forward and positive, but there are also some steps backward.

When comparing military practices with civilian systems software, it is interesting to note that the great bulk of the schedule and cost differentials that favor the civilian side are not in the coding phase. The military espousal of the Ada83 and Ada95 programming languages has been surprisingly effective compared with the C and C++ languages, which are often used for civilian systems software.

The initial procurement and startup of a software contract takes 35% to 50% longer on the military side than on the civilian side, and has more than twice the probability of ending up with challenges or litigation by disgruntled vendors.

The precoding analysis, planning, and specification work is approximately two to three times as expensive for military software as for civilian systems software. This is because of the enormous bulk of paper documents created under military standards such as DoD 2167, 2167A, 498, and the like. Although these military standards are no longer required and contractors can adopt civilian practices, the spirit of these standards is still in common usage. The volume of military paper deliverables is between two and three times the size of civilian systems software. The volume of military paper deliverables is three times larger than for MIS projects. By actual count, the volume of English words produced for military software totals approximately 400 English words per Ada83 statement. The cost of the words is more than twice as expensive as the cost of the code!

During the coding phase, the military side actually pulls ahead and is perhaps 15% more efficient with Ada95 than a civilian project using C. Military coding performance can be as good as almost any industry and might not be bad even compared with civilian industry leaders such as Microsoft.

However, the advantages achieved during coding are quickly dissipated. The military side next enters a complex fugue of critical design reviews (CDRs) and IV&V that have no civilian counterparts.

The DoD tendency toward excessive and heavy-handed oversight manages to overcome the tangible technical advantages the military side might have garnered by use of the Ada95 programming language.

The U.S. military world is actively pursuing a program of commercialization of defense contractors. That is, as DoD budgets shrink, the defense community has to turn to civilian work to stay in business. This is not as easy as originally envisioned, and many defense contractors are having trouble building successful civilian business engagements. Moving from defense to civilian life is not easy for managers and technical personnel either. So many defense skills are highly specialized that recruitment of DoD personnel for civilian work is not yet widespread, and may not become widespread.

A more sensitive issue has been the fact that compensation and benefit levels within the defense contractor community have lagged behind the civilian sector for software personnel. This has had the impact of skewing the distribution of top-ranked performers toward the civilian sector, although there are actually quite a few gifted technical workers in the military domain. However, the current shortage of software personnel may be accelerating a "brain drain" out of the military software domain and into the more lucrative civilian world.

One of the more questionable differences between the military domain and the civilian domain is in the area of contract bidding and completion criteria. In the civilian domain, software contracts are starting to move toward performance-based criteria using factors such as cost per function point and delivered defects per function point as the basis for the engagement. In the military domain, contracts are starting to require the achievement of abstract targets such as achieving level 3 on the SEI CMM scale.

The differences between the civilian and military contracting modes lead to very different results. If a civilian contract calls for the production of a software system of 1,000 function points at a cost of $500 per function point, the results are tangible and unambiguous. The same can be said for quality criteria, such as delivering no more than 0.001 defects per function point, or certifying 97% defect removal efficiency. (The function point approach also has an impact on minimizing creeping requirements, and especially so if there is a sliding scale of costs for late requirements.)

If a military contract calls for production of software by a company certified to be at or above CMM level 3, what does that really mean in terms of costs or quality? What does it mean in terms of creeping requirements? Unfortunately, no one knows, including the SEI itself. Although statistically we have noted that companies at level 3 on the CMM outperform companies at level 1, they are not perfect. There are still failures even at level 3.

The point is that being level 3 is not a sufficient guarantee of success for it to be included in software contracts. It would be better for the military domain to adopt some of the modern contractual practices of the civilian outsource community. Including clauses in contracts that require the vendor to demonstrate a defect removal rate of more than 96%, for example, would be useful. It would also be useful to utilize civilian concepts such as "cost per function point" as part of defense software contracts. (Note that using "cost per LOC" would not be a best practice, and especially so in the military world, where coding is barely 15% of the total cost.)

It is technically possible to merge the civilian and military practices by associating average costs per function point with the various SEI CMM levels. However, there is no significant push to do this. In fact, it is currently uncertain whether the military procurement community even knows how civilian contracts are starting to be constructed on the basis of functionality and cost per function point.

I have been involved intermittently with a Navy-hosted study group that the DoD assembled on the adoption of civilian best practices: the Airlie Council. It is interesting that the most common reactions by military and defense personnel to discussions of the way the civilian world is moving in the domain of software procurement contracts are "We don't do it that way" and "We can't do it that way." It will be interesting to see whether the weight of current policies and practices are so heavy that the movement toward civilian best practices is delayed or even prevented from occurring.

Best Technical Practices for Military Software

Because best practice information derives from our assessment and benchmark studies, this section is organized using the same set of ten key factors that are examined during SPR assessments and benchmarks:

1. Project management methods such as estimating
2. Requirements-gathering and analysis methods
3. Design and specification methods
4. Coding methods
5. Reusability methods
6. Change control methods
7. User documentation methods
8. Pretest defect removal methods such as inspections
9. Testing methods and tools
10. Maintenance methods and tools

In the other sections of this book, the sets of practices termed *best practices for systems software* had to have been used within at least 50 successful projects in ten companies. However, because we have done comparatively little military assessment work, in this section the best-practice derivation is reduced by half. In other words, we are using practices noted within five companies or military groups, and only 25 projects.

In the view of the project managers and technical personnel, the practices must have contributed to a successful outcome. To be included in the set of best practices, the practices must not have been cited as contributing to failures, overruns, or litigation for breach of contract. In other words, these are practices that add positive value.

Best Project Management Practices for Military Software

Because so many military projects are large and run for years, project management is a key defense technology. Excellence in project management is associated with almost 100% of successful projects for projects larger than 1,000 function points. Inadequate estimates, careless planning, and inadequate tracking are associated with 100% of project failures, even if other causes occur as well

Formal Risk Management

For all military applications larger than 1,000 function points, a formal risk management analysis should be prepared. This risk analysis should be kept current as the project proceeds. The risks include technical, financial, schedule, and quality risks, and sociological risks such as staff burnout or a need for excessive overtime. Note: Risk management is one of the 16 best practices identified by the Airlie Council.

Process Improvement Programs

Because assessments and benchmarks are diagnostic studies rather than therapies, it is appropriate to follow such studies with planned process improvement programs that can eliminate or minimize the problems that were noted. It is a best practice in the military software domain to implement process improvement programs following assessments and benchmark studies. However, if the organization scores higher than level 3 on the SEI CMM, the process improvement programs may no longer be needed.

Annual Assessments and Benchmarks

Assessments and benchmarks are like snapshots at a moment in time. Once a company undertakes process improvement work, it is useful to have follow-on assessments and external benchmarks. A best practice in the military software domain is to have process assessments on an annual basis, and external benchmark studies approximately every two years, although annual benchmarks are more precise. It is also a best practice to have formal productivity and quality measurements in the intervening periods. Quality data should be summarized and published monthly. Productivity data needs to be reported annually.

Project Offices

For military software applications larger than 10,000 function points a formal *project office* should be established for overall schedule planning, cost estimating, cost tracking, and milestone tracking. The staff of the project office should be well equipped with planning tools, cost-estimating tools, and quality estimating tools. The staff should be experienced with the principles of large-project management. (Less than 1,000 function points, project offices are seldom encountered and are not a best practice. Their value rises with the size of the application.)

Estimating Specialists

For applications larger than 10,000 function points the use of trained software cost-estimating specialists is a best practice in both military and systems software domains. Smaller than this, cost estimates by project managers are the norm.

Estimating specialists are normally equipped with at least two software cost-estimating tools. Some of the cost-estimating tools encountered in the military software domain include COCOMO, COCOMO II, REVIC, CHECKPOINT, KnowledgePlan, Price-S, SEER, and SLIM, because all of these support military software estimation. Note: This is one of the 16 best practices cited by the Airlie Council.

Project Management Training

All military software project and program managers should be trained in software sizing, cost estimating, quality estimating, milestone tracking, and cost tracking. All project managers should be able to create accurate plans and estimates for projects at least 1,000 function points in size. Entry-level training on promotion to project manager is a definite best practice. Setting aside five to ten days a year for project management training is a best practice.

Project Management Tool Suites

All military software project managers should be trained in and have available a suite of project management tools, including sizing of key deliverables, cost and resource estimating, quality estimating, standard project management for critical path analysis, cost tracking, earned-value tracking, and milestone tracking capabilities.

Activity-Based Cost Estimates

All military software cost estimates for projects larger than 1,000 function points should be at the activity or task levels. Project-level or phase-level estimates are inadequate for large projects. Estimation for small projects can be at the phase level, but for large projects this is an unsafe and hazardous practice.

LOC Definitions

The military world continues to utilize the LOC metric in spite of its known hazards. To minimize the risks from this metric, all military software project managers should be trained in the proper and improper uses of this metric. The training should include counting rules for LOC in common military languages such as CMS2, Jovial, and Ada. Counting principles for both physical LOC and logical statements should be included in the training. Conversion logic between physical LOC, logical statements, and function points should be included in the training.

Function Point Analysis

All military software project managers should be trained in the basics of function point analysis. Managers do not need to be certified function point counters. All productivity and quality studies and benchmarks should include function point analysis. LOC metrics by themselves are hazardous for cross-language comparisons. It is a best practice to utilize both function point metrics and LOC for benchmark studies. LOC metrics alone are inaccurate enough to be deemed professional malpractice in situations in which multiple programming languages are used. Function point metrics alone are suitable for benchmarks, but collecting both function point and LOC metrics can demonstrate why LOC metrics are hazardous. Unless LOC metrics are collected too, it may be difficult to explain why they are hazardous. However, the combined use of function points and LOC metrics for similar projects developed using different programming languages can demonstrate why LOC metrics are dangerous for economic analysis.

Empirical Data

All military software project managers should know the ranges of quality and productivity levels derived from empirical studies for the kinds of software for which they are responsible. In particular, project managers should know defect removal efficiency levels and productivity levels for systems software projects. Otherwise, it is difficult for managers to defend accurate estimates against arbitrary overrides by clients and military oversight officers. Note: This is one of the 16 best practices identified by the Airlie Council.

Capability Maturity Model

A best practice in the military software domain is the utilization of the CMM published by the SEI. Not only is the CMM widely used within the military software domain, but approximately 50% of our military software clients have been at level 3 or higher in the sites that commissioned our benchmark studies. The military and systems software domains have more companies at the higher CMM levels than any other class of software.

Milestone Tracking

All military software projects larger than 1,000 function points should use formal milestone tracking. This is a best practice that can minimize unpleasant problems such as major schedule delays, or can at least provide an early warning. Major milestones include completion of requirements, external specifications, internal specifications, CDRs, inspection plans, IV&V, design inspections, code inspections, test plans, all forms of testing, independent testing, risk analysis plans, performance analysis plans, user documentation, and installation. Note: This is one of the 16 best practices identified by the Airlie Council.

Activity Cost Tracking

All military software projects larger than 1,000 function points should use formal cost tracking at the activity level. Normalized costs such as "cost per function point" are also a best practice. Costs based on LOC are optional but are not a best practice. Indeed, if LOC metrics are the only productivity measure, this constitutes professional malpractice. Use of both LOC metrics *and* function points are a best practice.

Earned-Value Tracking

All military software projects larger than 1,000 function points should use earned-value tracking. This is likely to occur because of contractual obligations, but is a best practice in any case. Note: This is one of the 16 best practices identified by the Airlie Council.

Project Postmortems

A best practice for military software larger than 1,000 function points is a postmortem at the end of the project. The purpose of this meeting of the software team is to analyze the processes used and point out areas of strength and weakness. In recent years this practice has often been replaced by a formal assessment and benchmark analysis at the end of the project, which serves the same purpose but gathers additional data.

Best Requirements-Gathering and Analysis Practices for Military Software

The military software domain is a technical leader in requirements tracing. This is due to a legacy from the older DoD standards, but remains a useful activity. Other than better than average tracing, requirements gathering and analysis in the military software domain overlap the approaches used by civilian outsource software. Some of the best practices for requirements gathering and analysis in the military software domain include those presented in the following subsections.

Joint Application Design

The usage of JAD is a standard best practice for both large military projects and large civilian outsource projects. Using the JAD approach, the requirements for an application are the joint responsibility of representatives from the client or user community and from the development organization. A key feature of the JAD approach is the use of a trained JAD facilitator. The JAD team works on the application requirements as a full-time job for a preplanned time period ranging from a few days to more than a month. A key benefit of the JAD approach is more stable requirements with a rate of change that is usually only a fraction of 1% per month, rather than the 1% to 3% noted more commonly for traditional requirements.

Requirements Tracing

It is a best practice for both military and outsource projects to utilize a concept called *requirements tracing*. This concept means that every major feature in a delivered software application can be traced back to a specific user requirement. Requirements tracing is mandatory for many military software contracts.

Prototypes of Key Features

It is a best practice for most military applications between 1,000 function points and 100,000 function points to create working prototypes of key features. These operational prototypes may be a contractual obligation. Less than 1,000 function points, prototypes may not be demanded contractually. More than 10,000 function points, the prototypes become significant projects in their own right and need more formality than prototypes for mid-size applications. Military prototypes are larger than civilian norms. Civilian prototypes are usually no more than approximately 10% of the size of the final application. Military prototypes can top 25% of the size of the final application, but vary with specific applications. Of the three common forms of prototypes—disposable, time-box, and evolutionary—only the disposable and time-box forms are best practices. Evolutionary prototypes are dangerous because prototypes are usually poorly structured and lack safe programming practices. However, evolutionary prototypes are fairly common among military projects.

Requirements Inspections

For military applications larger than 1,000 function points, inspections of requirements are a best practice. The requirements inspection technology is not used as often as desirable. The inspection team for military software requirements includes both client representatives and project technical personnel. Inspections and JAD are complementary, with the inspection stage following the JAD approach. Note: Inspections are one of the 16 best practices identified by the Airlie Council.

Function Point Size

A best practice for military software projects is to calculate initial function point size estimates from the requirements themselves. Once function point totals are known, they provide a useful baseline for measuring the rate of requirements creep. The military domain can be volatile in terms of requirements stability unless JAD sessions, prototypes, and inspections are utilized. In some cases, additions to requirements can top 3% per calendar month during the design and coding phases. Requirements churn, which does not add new features or change function point totals, is also common in the outsource domain. The phrase *requirements churn* refers to things such as changing the placement of data items on a screen based on user preferences. Function point totals are also used for sizing various deliverables and are a key input to software cost and quality estimates.

Requirements Change Control

Even in the best of cases military requirements will change during development. In the worst of cases, the requirements changes can be so extreme as to jeopardize the prospects of completing the project. Therefore, it is a best military practice to utilize formal change control methods for all projects larger than 1,000 function points. Some of the change control methods noted among our military clients include

- Formal change control boards
- Formal change control requests
- Automated change control tools
- Use of JAD sessions for major changes
- Use of requirements inspections for major changes
- Function point sizing and estimating for all changes larger than 15 function points (which is the minimum size for function point counts)
- Application feature planning for several years in the future with a planned evolution of total functionality
- Inclusion of new requirements in requirements tracing tables
- Inclusion of new requirements in earned-value tracking. (Note: This is one of the 16 best practices identified by the Airlie Council.)

Formal Requirements

Military software requirements are normally formal documents and average approximately 0.6 pages per function point. (Note that overall system requirements can include both hardware and software requirements. This discussion is for the software portions only.)

Performance Requirements

Because performance issues are often critical for military software projects, requirements may include performance targets and require prototypes that are aimed at judging performance levels.

Quality and Reliability Requirements

A best practice in the military software domain is to include specific quality and reliability targets in the requirements themselves. Quality can be expressed in terms of incoming defects reported after deployment, defect removal efficiency, or both. Reliability can be expressed in terms of mean time to failure or mean time between failures.

Requirements Segmentation

A best practice for hybrid military systems requirements includes a formal segmentation of the features to be embodied in hardware, microcode, and software.

Requirements Defects

A best practice in the military software domain is to measure the numbers and severities of defects or errors found in requirements themselves. Requirements contribute approximately 1.0 defects per function point to overall system totals. The use of formal requirements inspections and requirements tracing makes requirements defect analysis feasible.

Although military documentation is voluminous, it is often fairly complete. For example, counting function point metrics from military requirements and specifications is usually an easier task than counting function points from civilian requirements and specifications. The reason is because of the similar formats and contents of the military paper documents.

Best Design and Specification Practices for Military Software

In the era of DoD standards 2167, 2167A, 498, and so forth, military software specifications were enormous, rigid in terms of content, and filled with special terms and acronyms. More recently, after the 1994 push to adopt civilian best practices, the rigidity of military software specifications has relaxed somewhat. Military specifications still tend to be larger than civilian norms, and still use a host of specialized terms and abbreviations. This is because there are no convenient alternatives that are widely understood.

The military software domain ranks number one out of all types of software in the volume and completeness of specifications. Military software is also quite good in keeping specifications current, and in managing formal change control.

Architecture Specifications

A best practice for military software projects larger than 10,000 function points is the creation of a formal architecture specification, in addition to the external and internal specification documents. An architecture specification addresses the important topics of how features are to be apportioned across the hardware, microcode, and software portions of hybrid military systems.

Specification Segmentation

Because the specifications for large military software projects are voluminous, a best practice is to segment them into a multivolume set, with each volume containing the details of a specific topic. A typical example includes requirements specifications, architecture specifications, external design specifications, internal or logical design specifications, and database specifications. Each specification is under formal change control and goes through multiple versions.

Prototypes

A best practice for military software projects is the creation of prototypes for key features and algorithms. Indeed, prototypes may be required by contract. The two most common forms of prototype are disposable prototypes and time-box prototypes. A time-box prototype has a chronological limit, and must be completed within a specific period, such as one calendar month. The use of evolutionary prototypes is not a best practice, but remains common for military projects. The lack of structural rigor in evolutionary prototypes makes them unsuited for applications with high quality and reliability targets. Normally, military software prototypes amount to more than 25% of the functionality of the finished application. This is roughly twice the size of prototypes found in the civilian domains.

Design Inspections

A best practice for military software projects of all sizes, and for enhancements as well as new projects, is the use of formal design inspections on all specification documents. The rational for this is due to the fact that software designs and specifications contribute approximately 1.25 defects per function point. Worse, design defects are often higher in severity than coding defects. Note: This is one of the 16 best practices identified by the Airlie Council. (Note that the traditional military CDR is not identical to design inspections. Although CDRs are common, there is not enough data on their value to include them as a best practice. Projects with successful CDRs have been known to fail.)

Performance Analysis

Because performance issues may be critical to military software applications, several best practices involve performance analysis, models, and prototypes. The military software domain may employ "performance specialists." This title refers to software engineers who specialize in topics associated with accelerating throughput and response time of software applications. The military domain also employs fairly sophisticated performance-modeling techniques, and often develops specialized performance prototypes to judge the speed of key response issues. One of the original motivations in the development of digital computers in the 1940s was to accelerate calculations dealing with weapons systems.

Best Coding Practices for Military Software

The military software domain was an early adopter of structured programming practices. It became obvious in the late 1950s, when software first started to affect weapons and communication systems, that better methods were needed to ensure necessary levels of quality and reliability. Therefore, the military domain has been among the most active in pursuing research on all aspects of software structuring.

Structured Programming

A definite best practice within the military software domain is that of using formal program structure techniques for weapons and communication systems. There is no other way of developing software for weapons and communication systems. Even with formal structuring, there still may be latent problems.

Comment Density and Style

It is a best practice for all domains to utilize both module prologs and comments to explain key features and algorithms of programs. Studies performed within IBM found that comments approximately every ten statements was the density at which clarity seemed to peak. Fewer comments made it hard to understand the code. Surprisingly, too many comments also reduced code legibility. The reason that too many comments lowered code reading comprehension was because the programmers tended to put too much credence in the comments, and some of them may not have been fully accurate. When reading code, it is necessary to read both the code and the comments. The comments serve to explain unusual algorithms or special conditions, but it is necessary to understand the code itself.

Mnemonic Labels

It is a best practice to use labels for variables and branch instructions that are clear and easy to remember, if possible. Abstract labels such as "routine2" may make it hard for new programmers to understand logic flow. It is a bad practice to use labels that have quirky or private meanings, such as using the names of relatives or movie stars.

Code Inspections

It is a best practice for weapons and communications software to utilize formal code inspections. The inspections should include 100% of the modules of mission-critical systems, as opposed to partial or subset inspections encountered in many other types of software. Note: This is one of the 16 best practices identified by the Airlie Council.

Complexity Analysis

A best practice sometimes encountered within the military software domain is the use of complexity analysis tools. Because high levels of code complexity, as measured with the common metrics of cyclomatic and essential complexity, are known to degrade quality and lower the efficiency of defect removal operations, software that has high reliability criteria should use automated methods of complexity analysis. Once modules are identified as being too complex for safe operation, then they can be recoded or redeveloped.

Error-Prone Module Elimination

A definite best coding practice within the military software domain concerns seeking out and eliminating error-prone modules. It was discovered in the 1960s by IBM that coding errors were not distributed randomly. They tended to clump in a small number of modules and were called *error-prone modules*. Once discovered, it became imperative to remove or repair these troublesome modules. The method for dealing with error-prone modules is to give them a formal inspection, and then either restructure them, repair them, or redevelop them based on the recommendation of the inspection team. The major defense contractors and the military services are often quite sophisticated in error-prone module prevention and removal.

Module-Level Defect Tracking

A best practice in the military software domain is the use of defect tracking methods and tools that are granular enough to identify error-prone modules. The military software domain is among the best domains, ranking behind systems software, in defect tracking. Defects are tracked by severity level and origin, and are tracked down to the level of specific modules. Defects are also compared against predicted volumes of defects. Note: This is one of the 16 best practices identified by the Airlie Council.

Performance Analysis

Because performance may be a critical topic in the military domain, it is a best practice to use techniques for predicting, measuring, and improving software performance levels. During the coding phase, weapons and communication systems have their throughputs and response times monitored. Performance testing may also be used. In addition, performance specialists may be called in to tune or refine critical modules or control paths that might be suspected of degrading performance levels.

Programming Languages

Although the choice and use of a programming language is not by itself a best practice, it is significant that the military software domain has developed a number of programming languages aimed at the problems encountered with weapons, communications, and logistics software. Among the languages developed specifically for military software are CMS2, Jovial, Ada83, and Ada95. Other languages observed in the military domain include both C and C++, Objective C, COBOL, Forth, PL/I, and both Visual Basic and JAVA in recent years.

Best Reusability Practices for Military Software

Military software is expensive and schedules are lengthy. As a result, the military domain has long been interested in software reusability. At almost every military software conference, such as the annual software technology conferences held in Salt Lake City, software reusability is a featured topic. Software reuse is also a topic of interest to the military think tanks such as the SEI and Mitre. Software reuse is a key technology that can benefit cost, schedule, and quality simultaneously.

Military research efforts into software reusability were triggered partly by the fact that other avenues of study were turning out to be dead ends, or at least not as effective as desired. For example, interest in software reuse began to accelerate at about the same time that it was realized that CASE was more hype than reality. It was also realized that approaches such as RAD were not really adequate for large weapons and communication software systems with high quality and reliability goals.

The military and systems software domains are both in excellent positions to expand the volume of reusable material, due to their long tradition of high quality and reliability. Unless reusable material is very close to zero-defect levels, attempts to reuse anything is expensive and hazardous. Only high-quality materials are adequate for successful reuse.

A complete software reusability program encompasses from six to more than ten software artifacts including

1. Reusable requirements
2. Reusable external specifications
3. Reusable architecture and internal specifications
4. Reusable database designs and data structures
5. Reusable project plans and estimates
6. Reusable source code
7. Reusable quality and test plans
8. Reusable test cases
9. Reusable user documentation
10. Reusable HELP text
11. Reusable applications (COTS software)

In general, the military software domain has concentrated primarily on coding reuse. Although this is certainly important, it is not sufficient. At least six aspects of reuse need to be top priorities in the military domain:

1. Reusable requirements
2. Reusable architecture and specifications
3. Reusable source code

4. Reusable test materials
5. Reusable user documentation
6. Reusable applications (COTS software)

Unfortunately the military software domain has not devoted sufficient attention to many of the other potentially reusable artifacts, such as requirements, database structures, and project plans.

Reusable Applications

Since about 1990, the military domain has made fairly good progress in acquiring and using COTS applications. The use of COTS packages obviously is most common for applications that are not specialized. Payroll applications, inventory and logistics applications, and office tools are the most obvious COTS candidates. The use of COTS for specialized weapons controls is unlikely. Any military application with stringent security requirements or wedded to custom hardware is not a good choice for a COTS application. Given the low productivity of custom military software, any time a COTS alternative is available it will probably be deployed more rapidly and for much less expense that a custom-software solution. COTS software is a best practice if the acquired application is itself of high quality and can be deployed without needing programming modifications. If COTS packages are error prone or need extensive changes, then acquiring such packages would not be a best practice and indeed may be hazardous.

Reusable Designs

Although reusable designs are not uncommon in the military domain, the use of formal design inspections is a best practice that improves the prognosis of reusing specifications and design documents. The use of formal inspections for military software raises the odds that portions of these specifications can be reused in similar applications.

Code Inspections

The use of formal code inspections is a best practice that improves the prognosis of reusing source code modules and components. Prior to placing a candidate reusable module into a reuse library, it should be subjected to a 100% formal code inspection. The use of code inspections for military software raises the probability of successful code reuse, as in all domains. Note: This is one of the 16 best practices identified by the Airlie Council.

Test Plan and Test Case Inspections

The use of test plan and test case inspections, plus formal regression test libraries and test library control procedures, can raise the probability of successful reuse of test materials in the military software domain. Prior to being reused, both test plans and test cases should be given a thorough 100% inspection. To date, only the systems and military software domains have utilized formal inspections for test plans and test cases from among SPR's clients. Because uninspected test cases may have serious errors, reusing test cases without subjecting them to inspection is not a best practice and indeed is a hazardous practice.

Best Change Control Practices for Military Software

The military software community was an early adopter of change control packages. Because changes occur over the complete lifetimes of applications, change control starts during initial development and continues until an application is retired. Change control must support changes to all deliverable items, including requirements, specifications, source code, user documents, and tutorial materials.

Change Control Boards

For all military projects larger than 10,000 function points it is a best practice to utilize a formal change control board. This board is normally from three to perhaps seven personnel in size. The representatives include the primary client, the project office, the development team, and representatives from the hardware portion of the application if the project is hybrid.

Automated Change Control

The software artifacts that are subject to change include requirements, architecture, external specifications, internal specifications, database specifications, all quality and test plans, and all user documentation and training materials. Because of the wide variety of changing artifacts, it is a best practice to have fully automated change control systems that can handle all major deliverables. The change control package should facilitate identifying links between artifacts, such as determining what code needs to be changed in response to a requirements or design change. Note: This is one of the 16 best practices identified by the Airlie Council.

Function Point Metrics for Changes

It is a recent best practice to estimate and measure the function point totals of all changes to military software projects. The function point data can be used to ascertain the monthly rate of requirements creep.

Cost Estimates for Changes

Cost-estimating changes and cost measurement of changes are both difficult. The best practice for major change estimation is to use automated estimation tools and function point metrics. The best practice for small changes less than 15 function points is to use *backfiring,* or direct conversion from LOC metrics to function point metrics.

Requirements Tracing and Changes

A best practice common to both the systems software and military software domains is that of requirements tracing. That is, each design feature and even each code module can be traced back to a specific requirement, either explicitly or implicitly. Requirements tracing requires fairly sophisticated automation and demands a formal change control board.

Because many weapons systems and other military applications are hybrid and include hardware as well as software, change control in the military domain is not limited only to software changes. Some very sophisticated parts lists with extensive cross-references are kept for every component and manufactured part of weapons systems such as the F-115 fighter planes. However, hardware change control is outside the scope of this book.

Best User Documentation Practices for Military Software

User documentation for military software is typically more voluminous than for similar civilian projects. However, user documentation for military applications is no worse than for other domains.

One limiting factor for military software is the absence of third-party commercial books from major publishers. Normally, custom military applications are only documented by technical writers employed by the development group. For many civilian COTS applications, there may be several commercial trade books available. Indeed, there is a whole publishing subindustry that provides better user manuals for COTS packages than those supplied by the vendor.

Technical Writers

A best practice for military software is the use of professional writers, editors, and graphics personnel for the production of user manuals and tutorial materials. Military software contractors have a large concentration of professional technical writers. However, because compensation of technical writers in the military domain is fairly low, the top tier of technical writers may not be present. Technical writing is a fairly rare skill.

Professional Editors

An obvious best practice that is rare for software is to use professional editors as well as professional technical writers. Although this is a best practice in terms of results, it is only found among a handful of very large defense corporations.

Document Inspections

A best practice that is shared among systems software and military software is to utilize formal document inspections, in addition to more conventional copy editing and fact checking. The formal inspections include software engineers and sometimes even users, and examine the documents page by page.

Document Models

A best practice for new technical writers just joining a company is to provide them with a collection of manuals and tutorial materials voted "excellent" by means of user satisfaction surveys.

Usability Laboratories

A best practice that is found primarily among systems and military software is that of usability laboratories. Some of these are fairly sophisticated, such as the training devices used for pilots. The total number of such labs in the world is probably less than 100. In usability labs user personnel attempt to exercise software applications (and hardware) using only the manuals and tutorial materials to be provided with the system, or after normal training. Their success or failure is monitored by human factors specialists, sometimes supported by one-way mirrors or video cameras. For software and hybrid applications for which human safety is at stake (such as aircraft flight instruction), lab tests using simulators is obviously the safest way to learn the initial skills that may be needed.

Graphics and Illustrations

A best practice for all user manuals is the inclusion of a significant volume of graphical materials, as opposed to using pure text. The graphical materials need to be clear and cogent to be effective. Those produced by professional graphics illustrators are often most effective.

Working Examples

A very common best practice found in military software is the utilization of actual examples. The examples take a user step by step through the process of invoking a feature, using it, and then turning it off or moving to something else when finished. It is a best practice to include many such examples.

Best Quality Control and Pretest Defect Removal Practices for Military Software

Weapons systems are often very complex. They also demand high levels of quality and reliability to be used safely without harming operating personnel. When software began to control complex weapons systems, communication equipment, aircraft flight controls, and the like, the software had to be at least as reliable as the hardware in order for these machines to carry out their functions.

Design and Code Inspections

The most important best practice for military software quality is the usage of formal design and code inspections. Inspections are approximately twice as efficient as most kinds of testing in finding defects, and much more efficient in finding defects that might have originated in requirements or design. Formal inspections have been shown repeatedly to have the highest levels of defect removal efficiency of any known form of removal. Both design and code inspections have averaged more than 65% in defect removal efficiency in repeated trials, and have topped 85% in some cases. Note: Use of formal inspections is one of the 16 best practices identified by the Airlie Council.

(Note that military software projects have long utilized an approach called a *critical design review*. This is not the same as a formal design inspection. The CDRs are massive events with scores of participants. Although they may be useful, there is a lack of empirical data on CDR defect removal efficiency levels. CDRs were mandatory for some years and are still common. It is not certain whether CDRs should be included in the set of best practices. On the surface, they seem more expensive than civilian equivalents.)

Software Quality Assurance

An important best practice in which military software is better than average is in the use of professional software quality assurance personnel. Many of the major military software producers such as Raytheon, Motorola, and Lockheed-Northrup have well-staffed and well-equipped software quality assurance departments. The functions of these departments include defect estimation, defect measurements, moderating formal inspections, monitoring DoD standards, and teaching courses in quality topics. Note that the software quality assurance groups are not testing departments, although they do perform some specialized kinds of testing such as standard adherence testing.

Error-Prone Module Elimination

A best practice in the military software domain, and other domains too, is prevention and removal of error-prone modules. It was discovered in the early 1970s that software defects in large systems tended to clump in a small number of very buggy modules. Complexity analysis, module-level defect tracking, formal inspections followed by either repairs or redevelopment, plus assigning numeric quality targets to executives can stamp out error-prone modules and prevent their reoccurrence.

Quality Measurements

A best practice for military software is that of formal quality measurements and defect tracking measurements. The current state of the art of software quality measurement starts the measures early, during requirements. Once the quality measures begin they are kept up for the entire life of the project so that data is accumulated during development, usage, and many years of enhancements and maintenance. Topics measured include defect numbers, defect severity levels, defect origins, defect removal methods, and complexity of the application and its modules. Other measures include valid and invalid defects, abeyant defects that cannot be replicated, incidents that may or may not be defects, defect repair intervals, and resource and cost data. Note: This is one of the 16 best practices identified by the Airlie Council.

Quality Estimation Tools

A best practice used by the more sophisticated defense projects is the usage of quality and defect estimation tools to predict the probable number of bugs that might be encountered, and the set of defect prevention and removal operations to be used. Quality estimation tools can predict the numbers of bugs or errors in requirements, specifications, source code, user documents, and bad fixes or secondary defects. Severity levels are also predicted. The tools can also predict the specific defect removal efficiency of each review, inspection, or test stage. The final predictions are the numbers of latent defects remaining at delivery, and how many of those will be found by customers. Note: Quality estimation is one of the 16 best practices identified by the Airlie Council.

Risk Analysis

A best practice in the military software domain is the production of a formal risk analysis for the project at or near the completion of the requirements phase. A formal risk analysis considers technical, financial, and schedule risks. Note: This is one of the 16 best practices identified by the Airlie Council.

SEI Capability Maturity Model

A best practice for military software, first noted circa 1989, is for military software divisions to achieve level 3 or higher on the SEI CMM.

The military software domain is almost the only domain to utilize a pretest quality activity called *independent verification and validation*. Although we have encountered IV&V practices among our military clients, the data we have collected to date does not indicate that IV&V raises defect removal efficiency in any tangible way. Therefore we cannot place IV&V in the set of best practices.

Best Testing Practices and Tools for Military Software

The military software domain has long been one of the leaders in software testing. Military software projects use more types of testing than any other domain, with the occasional exception of systems software. For example, independent testing is utilized primarily by military projects. However, testing defect removal efficiency in the military domain is not quite equal to civilian systems software.

Test Specialists

A best practice found in both the military and systems software domains is the employment of professional testing personnel. These professional test personnel normally take over testing after the developers have completed code inspections and unit test. The forms of testing assigned to professional test groups include regression test, performance test, capacity or load test, integration test, lab tests using special equipment, human factors test, and system test. Integration and change control may also be performed by these test departments. The total complement of personnel in these test organizations can approach or even exceed 25% of software employment. Professional test groups are approximately 5% more efficient in each test stage than the same stage carried out by the developers themselves. Note that independent testing is not performed in-house, but is subcontracted to a separate company.

Automated Test Tools

A best practice is the usage of automated test library tools. Because major defense contractors have thousands of regression test cases, it is desirable to utilize automated tools for keeping track of these test cases, weeding out redundant tests, and linking tests to applications as needed.

Test Coverage Analysis

A best practice is to monitor the number of paths through software that are actually tested. A variety of commercial test monitors are available that can perform this function. Indeed, the overall best practice is to measure the percentage of all code actually tested. In applications with high cyclomatic and essential complexity, there are so many possible paths through the application that 100% testing is essentially impossible. It is a corollary best practice to redevelop or to simplify the complexity of applications that are so complex that complete testing is impossible.

Performance Testing

A best practice found often for weapons systems and communications software is performance testing. Performance testing is aimed at measuring the throughput of the application and identifying any points that might be degrading performance. Normally, specialists are employed for performance testing, as are specialized test cases and various hardware or software monitoring devices.

Independent testing by a separate company or subcontractor has long been utilized for military software projects. Although we encounter independent testing fairly often, the data we have collected does not indicate that this practice raises defect removal efficiency enough to include independent testing as a best practice. Because civilian systems software projects can equal or exceed military test results without the expense of independent tests, independent testing remains outside the set of best practices. This is not to say that independent testing is of no value, but our data does not merit placing independent testing among the set of best practices.

Best Maintenance and Enhancement Practices for Military Software

Military software is the oldest form of software on the planet. The original impetus for the development of computers, and most applications written during the late 1940s and early 1950s, was military software.

The word *maintenance* applies to any form of update to deployed software: repairs, new features, cosmetic improvements, mandatory or regulated changes, whatever. It is a common practice to use the word *maintenance* for a multitude of activities, but this is far from being a best practice. Because updates that add new features are often funded by clients, whereas updates to make repairs often have costs that are absorbed by the vendor, it makes good sense to keep separate records of these two activities.

In all, more than 20 forms of updates have been noted for software applications. The military software domain, as the oldest form of software, has experienced more kinds of maintenance for more years than almost any other. Some of the best practices for maintenance and enhancement work in the military software domain include those presented in the following subsections.

Maintenance Departments

A best practice is to have separate maintenance departments that handle defect repairs. The work of maintenance departments for military software is primarily that of repairing incoming defects and keeping software operational around the clock, if needed. Enhancements are normally done by the development team. The economic reason for separate maintenance groups is because defect repairs and adding new features are antagonistic and interfere with each other. If the same person tries to fix bugs and add features, then estimating either side becomes messy and difficult. Furthermore, because defect repairs are often less interesting, they tend to be rushed so the programmer can return to development work.

Complexity Analysis

A best practice for maintenance of military software is the use of complexity analysis prior to making major changes or updates. Because high complexity tends to slow down productivity and increase the odds of errors or defects, it is useful to eliminate complex modules before beginning.

On-line Maintenance Support

A best practice now used widely by military and by all types of software is to provide on-line connections between maintenance teams and deployed applications. It is far more efficient and cost-effective for users to be able to report errors and request assistance by means of e-mail or networks than it is by telephone or fax. It is also more secure, which is an important consideration for military software.

On-site Maintenance Support

A best practice found primarily for weapons systems and applications on board naval vessels such as aircraft carriers is on-site maintenance support. This is a best practice only for mission-critical applications that are vital to military operations. On-site support is also commonly provided by vendors at military data centers, such as those used in support of military operations in Vietnam and Kosovo.

Field-Replaceable Units

Because a great deal of military software is embedded in hardware devices, it has long been a best practice to build military equipment in such a way that key components can be replaced with newer versions as updates occur. This is both a best practice and a logical necessity in the world of the twenty-first century.

Best Personnel Practices for Military Software

The military software domain has not been a stellar performer in terms of personnel practices. In fact, fairly marginal compensation packages, some uncertainty about layoffs and downsizing, and rather bleak and cramped office facilities were characteristic of the military software world during the 1960s through the early 1990s.

One of the newer extensions to the SEI CMM regards personnel issues, developed by Dr. Bill Curtis and his colleagues. It is the *People Capability Model*, which deals with how technical personnel should be treated at the various levels of the CMM.

It is also interesting that one of the best practices recommended by the Airlie Council is to "treat people as the most important resource." It is true that software is the most labor-intensive product of the modern world. It is also true that having personnel with high morale often leads to better results than teams with low morale.

However, military software project managers must live within the confines of their somewhat limited budgets. Also, military software project managers have very little ability to deal with a number of issues that raise or lower staff morale. For example, project managers have little control over office space and not a great deal of control over computers and workstations. As the software personnel shortage intensifies, military software personnel are very likely to be lured into civilian companies, where compensation packages are better, and who can blame them?

There are ten key practices for personnel issues that are examined during assessment and benchmark studies, as discussed earlier:

1. Staff hiring practices
2. Staff training and education
3. Management training and education
4. Specialists and occupational groups
5. Compensation levels
6. Office ergonomics
7. Organizational structures
8. Morale surveys and results
9. Work patterns and overtime
10. Staff turnover rates

As in the previous section on best technical practices, the best personnel practices must have been observed within at least five companies. The use of five companies instead of ten is because we have not worked with as many defense companies as we have with civilian companies.

The criterion of being noted on at least 25 projects is waived for personnel practices. The reason is because personnel practices are normally corporatewide. A personnel practice such as "compensation level" is set by corporate or service guidelines and is not set by the project manager for a specific project. Project managers have some latitude in compensation based on appraisals and bonus policies, but these must be within the overall corporate salary and compensation guidelines.

Best Staff Hiring Practices for Military Software

University training in the United States has not been effective in graduating students who can be put to work immediately on software projects without some in-house training and mentoring. A weakness of academia is that there are few courses on software quality control, and there is a lack of solid courses in topics such as design and code inspections, performance analysis, and performance testing, which are quite critical in the systems software domain. In the context of military software, there are no civilian university courses that even deal with topics such as electronic warfare, weapons systems software, or DoD standards.

Another academic weakness in the United States is lack of specialized courses for key forms of military software. For example, weapons systems software engineering is not taught in civilian schools. Also, security is not covered well in academia. As a result, the military software domain looks for experienced personnel who have already worked for several years on military software projects. Because the U.S. defense sector has been shrinking, the pool of experienced personnel has not yet been exhausted.

Hiring Experienced Personnel

Due to common academic deficiencies, it is a best practice in the military software domain to hire technical personnel with at least three years of experience in military software development and maintenance. As long as the defense community is shrinking and layoffs are occurring, a pool of experienced military software personnel may remain available. However, the general shortage of U.S. software personnel is more serious for the military domain than for others due to marginal compensation and benefit packages. Some civilian companies view the military domain as a choice recruiting ground. Indeed, both enlisted software personnel and officers are being solicited actively by civilian companies. Defense contractors have had to increase compensation levels and benefits to stay competitive, but still lag behind many industries such as banking and insurance.

Best Staff Training and Education Practices for Military Software

Because of the marginal performance of U.S. universities in graduating effective software engineering personnel, major employers of software personnel have compensated by establishing in-house curricula for key software topics. The in-house software curricula of major systems defense contractors such as Lockheed, Grumman, Raytheon, Litton, IBM, and Motorola compare favorably with almost any university in the United States.

Annual Staff Training Targets

It is a best practice to set targets for the number of days each calendar year that will be set aside for training of technical personnel. Among our military software clients, the most common target is five days a year, although ten days are sometimes set aside. However, military personnel lag behind the civilian sector by about five days a year in overall training.

External Seminars and Conferences

It is a best practice for the military to fund travel and tuition expenses for external conferences and seminars, such as the annual conferences offered by the Air Force and the software technology conference in Salt Lake City. Among our military clients, one external event per year is most common, but two or more events occur sometimes.

Technical Software Curriculum

Among the courses we have observed among our military software clients, those dealing with design and code inspections are common and are an educational best practice. Every software professional should be trained in the techniques of design and code inspections because they are the most effective known ways of eliminating software defects. Other courses that can be viewed as best practices for military software staff include software requirements analysis, software design and specification techniques, software reusability techniques, structured programming techniques, change management and configuration control, testing techniques, quality measurements, and software maintenance techniques.

There are many courses on interesting and important topics available, but unless these topics have demonstrated empirical results in improving quality, productivity, or schedules there is no justification for viewing them as best practices. Included in this category are courses in programming languages such as Ada, JAVA, CMS, and Jovial. Courses in various specific vendor tools are often interesting, but not necessarily a best practice.

Best Management Training and Education Practices for Military Software

Software project management is even more poorly served by universities than software engineering. In fact, very few universities in the world offer courses in some of the more important software management topics such as function point analysis, software cost estimating, software work breakdown structures, and software risk and value analysis.

Executive Seminars on Software

It is a best practice within the military domain to have intensive seminars for senior military officers and also civilian executives with the DoD and the departments of the Army, Navy, and Air Force. A very good example of executive software seminars for defense personnel is the Bold Stroke program hosted by the Air Force, with sessions held at Air University in Alabama. Military officers from all services above the rank of colonel, and civilian executives above the rank of undersecretary are invited to participate in the Bold Stroke program. Top-ranked civilians and some military specialists are invited to give lectures on both general and specific software topics. Discussions range from flight control software on modern aircraft to the incidence of litigation with software contracts. In more recent events, topics dealing with Y2K and the rollover of dates on the global positioning satellites have been addressed.

Annual Management Training Targets

It is a best practice for military software companies to set targets for the number of days each calendar year that will be set aside for training of project management personnel. A common target for military project managers is five days a year, although we have noted ten-day targets from time to time. However, military targets are somewhat below equivalent civilian targets.

External Management Seminars and Conferences

It is a best practice for military software companies to fund travel and tuition expenses for external conferences and seminars for managers, such as the annual Air Force Software Technology Conference, the conferences offered by the SEI, or various events on software project management and metrics. Among our military clients, two external events per year is most common.

Software Management Curriculum

It is a best practice for military software managers to understand the economics of software quality control. Therefore, courses on defect estimation, defect prevention, and defect removal are best practices. Other courses noted among our clients that are included in the best practice set are earned-value analysis, software cost estimating, principles of software reuse, software quality estimating, software productivity measurements and metrics, software quality metrics and cost of quality, principles of the SEI CMM, function points for managers, and risk and value analysis. Courses on the Y2K problem have also been noted, and are a best practice for managers.

There are a number of rapidly emerging technologies that may become best educational practices in the near future. However, as this book is written they have not been encountered often enough to be added to the best practice set. The most notable are courses in e-business and Web-based management practices. Although these topics are important, the technology is changing so rapidly and the results are so ambiguous that it is difficult to create an effective course. Another emerging topic that may become a future military best practice is component-based development.

Best Practices for Specialization in the Military Software Domain

In 1994 and 1995 we were commissioned by AT&T to explore software specialization in large enterprises. One of the participating organizations was the U.S. Air Force. We noted a total of more than 50 occupational groups overall, and the Air Force was equal to the civilian companies such as AT&T and IBM on overall employment of software specialists.

One interesting aspect of the study was the finding that job descriptions for software specialists who are actually military personnel were much better than job descriptions for civilian employees. In fact, unless we interviewed project managers or the technical personnel themselves, it was not possible to identify specialists among the civilian groups. (Incidentally, software job descriptions inside civilian corporations are ambiguous too.)

Software Specialization

There are six key areas in which specialization counts as a best practice, because the results are so much better than when the work is performed by generalists who lack specific training: software testing after unit test, software technical writing, software performance tuning, software quality assurance, software maintenance in the sense of defect repairs, and software security and encryption. The military software domain employs specialists in the first five of these key areas in proportions roughly equal to the civilian sector. For computer security and encryption, the military community employs a majority of all such specialists in the United States.

The military software domain also employs many other kinds of specialists, but there is not enough data to ascertain whether the specialists should be added to the best practice set. Some of the other specialists noted in the military software domain include cost-estimating specialists, planning and project scheduling specialists, database administration specialists, SEI CMM specialists, metrics and measurement specialists, and specialists in key systems such as the Mark 160 gun control systems, F-115 flight control software, and so forth.

Best Compensation and Salary Practices for Military Software

As this book is written, *ComputerWorld* published their thirteenth annual salary and compensation review. It was interesting to note that the compensation shown for a project manager in the aerospace/defense sector was $75,200 per year. This is not the lowest compensation, but it is quite a bit below several other high-technology sectors:

Computer hardware and software	$108,500 average for project managers
Petroleum products	$96,500 average for project managers
Telecommunications	$93,333 average for project managers

The disparity between the aerospace/defense sector and other high-technology sectors explains why there may be a "brain drain" of software personnel into other domains.

Compensation Benchmarks

It is a best practice to perform annual compensation benchmark studies for military software technical and managerial personnel. These benchmarks are normally "blind" studies during which various companies contribute compensation data that is analyzed statistically by a neutral external benchmark company.

Compensation Levels

For large defense companies employing more than 1,000 software personnel it is a best practice to be in the upper half of overall national compensation including salaries, bonuses, equity, and medical and dental benefits. Otherwise, a net outflow of software personnel might occur.

Best Practices in Office Ergonomics for Military Software

Unfortunately, office ergonomics has not been a major topic of research in the military and defense software domain. From our visits to both military bases and to defense contractors, fairly Spartan cubicles and shared office areas are the norm.

Studies by Tom DeMarco and Tim Lister published in *Peopleware* (DeMarco and Lister 1987) demonstrated that private office space benefits systems software productivity in a very significant fashion. In our own assessment and benchmark studies we have also noted that private, noise-free office space for software engineers and technical workers pays off with higher than average productivity and quality levels. At least this is the case in the United States and Europe. Data from Japan does not indicate a reduction in performance from shared offices.

During a typical working day, a software engineer needs quiet and solitude for approximately five hours, and needs to have discussions or meetings for only one hour. Roughly two hours are spent on phone calls, using the Internet, or on miscellaneous work. From this distribution of effort, it can be seen that private office space is optimal for the major portion of a day's work.

Private Office Space

It is a best practice to provide private, noise-free office space for software engineers and technical staff members. An area of at least 80 square feet is optimal. This best practice is only encountered within fairly sophisticated companies, but the results support the hypothesis that private office space is optimal for systems software.

Networks and E-mail

It is a best practice to link all technical employees within a corporation by means of a network that supports e-mail, file transfer, and on-line inspection of key work products.

Meeting Rooms

Because group activities such as design and code inspections and team meetings are common for software projects, it is a best practice to provide a small meeting room that can hold up to ten people.

Because of security and other issues, military software does not lend itself to working at home via telecommuting. Neither do military projects such as weapons systems lend themselves to offshore development. For classified projects, office ergonomics must be balanced against the needs for very tight security. Because penetration of office space by microwave and electronic means is not impossible, some special precautions are needed. These special needs are outside the scope of this book.

Best Practices in Organizational Structures for Military Software

For historical reasons, the *span of control,* or number of employees reporting to one manager, is generally about eight staff members. This has been true for more than 100 years, and is true for all forms of office work, not just software. (The origin of the span-of-control concept stems from time and motion studies carried out on troop movements after the close of the U.S. Civil War in 1865.)

The range in the span of control noted among our assessment and benchmark studies averaged approximately eight technical employees per manager, with a low of two employees reporting to one manager and a high of 30 employees reporting to one manager.

Many military software projects are very large and have staffing levels that can rise above 200 personnel overall. For larger projects with more than 50 staff members, small teams are actually not as productive as larger departments with ten to 12 people reporting to one manager. Furthermore, voluntary attrition rates are usually better within companies that have a somewhat larger span of control. The reason for this seems to be that good managers are a scarce commodity. If a company has a small span of control, then it will have a large management population. Because bad management is the most common reason why good technical workers change jobs, it can be seen than having fewer but better managers may lead to overall improvements in both performance and morale issues.

The norm among military projects is to have a somewhat smaller span of control than civilian projects, with perhaps five to seven technical personnel reporting to each supervisor. Although the reason for this is uncertain, a hypothesis is that smaller spans of control may be due to "political" issues. That is, higher level managers with many subordinates may have greater status than managers with fewer subordinates.

Project Offices

For military software projects larger than 10,000 function points, or for any military project deemed to be mission critical, it is a best practice to establish a project office. The project office is staffed by trained estimating and measurement specialists who provide support to the project managers in developing plans and cost estimates, and in monitoring progress against those plans. The project office also tracks earned value, and accumulates data from design and code inspections.

Optimal Department Size

For large military software projects (>10,000 function points) it is a best practice to have more than ten employees reporting to one manager. Although this is controversial, this is the size at which productivity is highest. Smaller spans of control put too many people in management and raise the difficulty of coordination between departments. Furthermore, a ten-plus staffing complement can handle a fairly large component. A larger span of control allows backup in case of illness, and encourages mentoring of new team members. Larger teams also facilitate having peer reviews and formal inspections.

Optimal Organizational Structure

For large military software projects (>10,000 function points) a hierarchical organizational structure is a best practice as opposed to a matrix organizational structure. The hierarchical organization is similar to a military chain of command, in that each manager reports directly to a higher level manager, up to the level of the senior manager responsible for the entire system. The matrix structure tends to raise the management head count for larger projects. Because software productivity declines as the management count goes up, this form of organizational structure can be hazardous for software. Unfortunately, the matrix form is fairly common for military software projects.

Independent Software Quality Assurance

For military software projects larger than 10,000 function points it is a best practice to have an independent software quality assurance department outside the control of the project management hierarchy. The reason for this independent group is to protect the integrity of the quality assurance function. If the software quality assurance personnel report to the project manager, they cannot safely point out problems without risking personal reprisals. The software quality assurance group is distinct from the testing group, which usually does report in the hierarchical project management chain of command. A key role of this organization is to ensure that best practices are followed and dangerous situations, if any, are addressed. This group could not perform this role unless it was independent of the project chain of command. Military software has long used IV&V by a subcontractor as another form of quality check. However, the data on IV&V is not sufficient to include it as a best practice.

Test Departments

A best practice is the employment of professional testing personnel, and the usage of test departments. These professional test personnel normally take over testing after the developers have completed code inspections and unit test. The forms of testing assigned to professional test groups include regression test, performance test, capacity or load test, integration test, lab tests using special equipment, human factors test, and system test. Integration and change control may also be performed by these test departments. The total complement of personnel in these test organizations can approach or even exceed 25% of software employment. Professional test groups are approximately 5% more efficient in each test stage than the same stage carried out by the developers themselves. The military domain also utilizes separate subcontractors to carry out independent testing. The data on independent testing is ambiguous and not sufficient to place this practice among the set of best practices. Costs are often higher with independent testing, but defect removal efficiency is not as high as civilian systems software projects that do not use independent testing.

Best Practices for Employee Morale in Military Software

In both combat situations and software projects, good morale can be beneficial. Interestingly, one of the critical factors affecting both troop and employee morale is the ability of the leaders. Companies that recognize the significance of this finding are very careful about who gets promoted to management, and are careful to weed out managers whose personalities are not suited for this very critical responsibility.

Morale and Opinion Surveys

It is a best practice to perform morale and opinion surveys of all employees, including administrative workers, technical staff members, and project managers. The normal frequency of morale surveys is once a year. Some of our clients conduct two surveys a year. In special situations, such as after a major downsizing, merger, or cancellation of a major project, additional special morale surveys may be needed.

Follow-up to Morale Surveys

It is a best practice to have immediate and formal follow-ups after morale surveys are taken. Asking questions about morale but taking no action based on the responses degrades rather than improves morale. Normally, after a morale survey occurs the results are analyzed statistically within a week, and departmental group meetings are held to discuss the results within two weeks. Within a month, executives and top managers have formulated a plan to deal with any serious morale issues that were encountered. Normally, within approximately six weeks, there is an overall meeting or series of departmental meetings to discuss these action plans.

Job Transfer Requests

It is a best practice within large corporations to have a job transfer request system that allows employees to request internal transfers to other cities, or to request a job change to another kind of position.

Merit Appraisals

In the United States it is a best practice to have performance appraisals for both technical staff members and project managers. (These appraisals are termed *fitness reports* in some military units.) During the first year of employment in a company, there may be two or more performance appraisals. It is a best practice for employees and managers to agree jointly to performance goals or targets. Note that in some European countries, performance appraisals are forbidden by either national law or union regulations.

Due to the major shortage of software personnel in the United States and Europe, morale and personnel issues are now extremely important. There are many more topics under this heading that cannot be discussed using assessment and benchmark data, because assessments and benchmarks do not cover every personnel topic. For example, stock option plans and equity may have an affect on employee morale and attrition rates, but we have not been tasked with examining this issue.

Another very strong morale factor is that of the medical and dental plans offered by employers. Here, too, we have not been commissioned to study this factor. Indeed, if we attempted to study this factor we would probably be asked to stop because human resource organizations regard this kind of information as sensitive.

Best Work Patterns and Overtime Utilization for Military Software

It was first noted more than 30 years ago that software development and maintenance tends to attract personnel who are fairly intense in their work practices. This is true for military software as well as civilian projects. Within companies such as Lockheed, Grumman, Raytheon, and Motorola, 50-hour weeks are the norm rather than the exception for systems software development.

Software personnel are usually salaried workers rather than hourly workers. They are considered "exempt" in the sense that software personnel do not automatically receive overtime pay. Because many corporate time and cost tracking systems exclude unpaid overtime, it is difficult to gather reliable information on this topic.

Compensatory Time

It is a best practice for military software personnel to be allowed to take compensatory time during slack periods in return for contributing unpaid overtime during rushed periods.

The issue of unpaid overtime is often encountered during benchmark studies. This topic deserves greater coverage in the software literature because it has a tangible impact on productivity rates. As this book is written, a new United Nations study on international work habits was just published by the *Boston Globe*. This study shows that the United States has one of the longest work years of any industrialized nation (see Table 11.10).

Table 11.10   International Work Habits

Country	Hours per Year
United States	1,966
Australia	1,866
Spain	1,809
United Kingdom	1,731
France	1,656
Sweden	1,552
Norway	1,399

However, software is at the far end of the spectrum in terms of work patterns. It is not uncommon for software professionals to work 50-hour weeks 50 weeks of the year, or 2,500 hours in all.

The same United Nations study also mentioned that some emerging countries such as Thailand and Singapore top 2,300 hours per year. As long as software remains the most labor-intensive commodity, factors such as work hours will continue to play a major role in productivity and schedules.

Best Practices for Minimizing Military Staff Turnover Rates

Due to the shortage of software personnel in the United States and Europe, all software producers are very concerned about losing key personnel. They are also concerned about the high costs of recruiting new personnel.

As the new century begins, the defense community in the United States has been going through waves of mergers, acquisitions, and associated layoffs and downsizing. As a result, the civilian sector has come to regard the defense sector as a potential source for very experienced software personnel. Because compensation and benefits packages may be better in the civilian sector than in the defense sector, military software employers face a serious challenge in terms of keeping their existing technical staffs.

If a company is downsizing, there are no effective techniques for keeping key personnel. Indeed, many of the more capable personnel will look for better options when the downsizing is announced. Furthermore, software productivity and quality levels suffer during periods of downsizing.

However, if a company is growing rapidly and recruiting actively, it is very useful to pay serious attention to the factors that affect attracting new hires and minimizing the attrition of existing personnel.

Reducing Voluntary Attrition

To minimize the attrition of key military software personnel, the set of best practices includes being in the top 50% in terms of compensation and benefits, weeding out less capable managers, and having proactive morale and opinion surveys to identify problems before they grow to a significant magnitude. A very complex issue is also important: Because bad management is the most common reason cited in exit interviews when technical workers quit, it is very important to weed out managers whose personalities are unsuited to management tasks. Thus, very careful management appraisals are a best practice.

Finding New Personnel

Obviously, large companies utilize multiple methods for finding new employees: advertisements, recruiters, and the World Wide Web. However, it is a best practice to offer incentives or rewards if employees can bring in suitable candidates. The reason for this is because the software community is fairly good at spreading the word regarding interesting opportunities.

Contract Employees

It has been a best practice to utilize contract personnel for a percentage of military software technical work. The reason for this is because contractors can be brought in fairly quickly, and have relevant experience suitable to the projects in need of support. Additionally, when the projects are completed, the contract personnel can be released as quickly as they are brought onboard. However, a number of recent court actions involving contract personnel are raising new issues that we have not yet encountered in our benchmark and assessment studies. As a result, the contracting situation circa 1999 is somewhat ambiguous, even though past results have been favorable. If contract personnel are awarded some of the benefits of permanent employees, then the use of contractors will face reevaluation.

Personnel issues are outside the normal scope of assessment and benchmark studies; however, we have been commissioned to explore some aspects of personnel topics, such as the number of specialists employed and the optimal methods for keeping their skills up to date. The new legal issues involving contract personnel have not yet been a factor in any of the assessment and benchmark studies we have performed to date. Because the litigation involving these issues is ongoing, the impact cannot be discussed in full at this time.

Summary and Conclusions on Military Software

The world of military software is complex. Military applications range from ordinary payroll software through very sophisticated and classified weapons systems. The software that controls U.S. weapons and defense capabilities ranks among the best in the world in terms of quality and reliability.

Because of the huge and continual demand for military software, the U.S. Armed Forces and the DoD have justifiably spent millions of dollars in researching state-of-the-art methods. Although military software practices are quite good, they are not as effective as the best civilian systems software practices. Therefore, the DoD has been moving toward adopting civilian best practices.

The state of the art in software development is an elusive topic. Even in the civilian systems software domain, not every project is a success. Therefore, it is necessary to be cautious and to adopt only techniques with a proven value. The software world is given to fads that lack empirical results. Also, many vendors have a tendency to make "silver-bullet" claims without empirical data to back them up. Thus, the military adoption of civilian best practices is, of necessity, somewhat slower than desired.

The approaches that have developed within the military domain have led to very good results for large systems in the 10,000-function point and 100,000-function point size plateaus. The military software domain is more successful in finishing large systems than any other domain except systems software. However, the oversight requirements levied on defense contractors by the DoD has caused productivity problems. Military software plans, specifications, and measurement reports are approximately three times larger than civilian norms. The excess bulk adds little technical value to the projects, but is there primarily due to oversight requirements. For smaller applications ($\leq$1,000 function points), traditional military practices were so rigid and convoluted that productivity rates were lower than any other form of software yet measured.

Overall, the military software domain is characterized by energetic and hard-working technical staffs, below-average staff compensation levels, fairly good tool suites, very strict development processes, and above-average quality control.

The military software domain has some unique and special characteristics that are not a standard part of software assessment and benchmark studies. Among these unique situations is the very frequent litigation when military procurement contracts are first awarded. Because approximately half of the contracts are challenged, the overall effect is to make almost every major project late by at least six months before the work even begins.

Another unique issue, outside the scope of our normal investigations, is the special need for classified projects with very stringent security issues. Such projects are normally not included in the samples we examine during assessment and benchmark studies.

Readings and References for Military Software

The military software literature overlaps the civilian systems software literature to a certain degree. Both domains have a strong interest in software quality and testing. Both the systems and military domains have actively pursued the concepts of the SEI. Indeed, these two domains have more companies or sites at level 3 on the SEI CMM than all other domains put together.

The military software literature also has some unique titles and journals that are circulated primarily to a military audience. For example, the *CrossTalk* software journal published by the Air Force Technology Support Center in Utah is one of the best software journals in the entire industry.

Abdel-Hamid, Tarek, and Stuart Madnick. *Software Project Dynamics*. Englewood Cliffs, NJ: Prentice Hall, 1993. (ISBN 013-8220409)

Austin, Robert D. *Measuring and Managing Performance in Organizations*. New York: Dorset House Publishing, 1996. (ISBN 0-932633-36-6, 216 pages)

Bach, James. "The Immaturity of the CMM." *American Programmer* 1994; 7(9): 13–18.

Beizer, Boris. *Software Testing Techniques*. Boston, MA: International Thomson Computer Press, 1990. (ISBN 1850328803, 550 pages)

Boehm, Barry. *Software Engineering Economics*. Englewood Cliffs, NJ: Prentice Hall, 1981. (ISBN 0-13-822122-7, 900 pages)

Bogan, Christopher E., and Michael J. English. *Benchmarking for Best Practices*. New York: McGraw Hill, 1994. (ISBN 0-07-006375-3, 312 pages)

Briand, Loic, and Daniel Roy. *Meeting Deadlines in Real-Time Systems*. Los Alamitos, CA: IEEE Computer Society Press, 1997. (ISBN 0-8186-406-7, 300 pages)

Brooks, Frederick P. *The Mythical Man-Month*. Reading, MA: Addison Wesley Longman, 1995. (ISBN 0-207-00650-2, 295 pages)

Brown, Norm, ed. *The Program Manager's Guide to Software Acquisition Best Practices*. Version 1.0. Washington, DC: U.S. Department of Defense, 1995. (142 pages)

Caputo, Kim. *CMM Implementation Guide*. Reading, MA: Addison Wesley Longman, 1998. (ISBN 0-201-37938-4, 319 pages)

Carmel, Erran. *Global Software Teams: Collaborating across Borders and Time Zones*. Upper Saddle River, NJ: Prentice Hall, 1999. (ISBN 0-13-924218-X, 269 pages)

Carnegie Mellon University. *The Capability Maturity Model: Guidelines for Improving the Software Process*. Reading, MA: Addison Wesley Longman, 1995. (ISBN 0-201-54664-7, 441 pages)

Charette, Robert N. *Software Engineering Risk Analysis and Management*. New York: McGraw Hill, 1989. (ISBN 0-07-010719-X, 325 pages)

———. *Application Strategies for Risk Analysis*. New York: McGraw Hill, 1990. (ISBN 0-07-010888-9, 570 pages)

Conte, S. D., H. E. Dunsmore, and V. Y. Shen. *Software Engineering*. Menlo Park, CA: The Benjamin Cummings Publishing Company, 1986. (ISBN 0-8053-2162-4, 396 pages)

Curtis, Bill, William E. Hefley, and Sally Miller. *People Capability Maturity Model*. Pittsburgh, PA: Software Engineering Institute, Carnegie Mellon University, 1995.

DeMarco, Tom. *Controlling Software Projects*. New York: Yourdon Press, 1982. (ISBN 0-917072-32-4, 284 pages)

———. *Why Does Software Cost So Much?* New York: Dorset House Publishing, 1995. (ISBN 0-932633-34-X, 237 pages)

———. *The Deadline*. New York: Dorset House Publishing, 1997. (ISBN 0-932633-39-0)

DeMarco, Tom, and Tim Lister. *Peopleware*. New York: Dorset House Publishing, 1987. (ISBN 0-932633-05-6, 188 pages)

Department of the Air Force. *Guidelines for Successful Acquisition and Management of Software Intensive Systems*. Vol. 1 and 2. Hill Air Force Base, UT: Software Technology Support Center, 1994.

Dreger, J. Brian. *Function Point Analysis*. Englewood Cliffs, NJ: Prentice Hall, 1989. (ISBN 0-13-332321-8, 185 pages)

El Emam, Khaled, and Nazim H. Madhavi. *Elements of Software Process Assessment and Improvement*. Los Alamitos, CA: IEEE Computer Society Press, 1999. (ISBN 0-8186-8523-9, 384 pages)

Fetcke, Thomas, Alain Abran, and Tho-Hau Nguyen. *Mapping the OO-Jacobsen Approach into Function Point Analysis*. Quebec: Université du Quebec à Montreal, Software Engineering Management Research Laboratory, 1996. (11 pages)

Galea, R. B. *The Boeing Company: 3D Function Point Extensions*. Version 2.0, release 1.0. Seattle, WA: Boeing Information Support Services, June 1995.

Garmus, David, and David Herron. *Measuring the Software Process: A Practical Guide to Functional Measurement*. Englewood Cliffs, NJ: Prentice Hall, 1995. (ISBN 0-13-349002-5)

Gilb, Tom, and Dorothy Graham. *Software Inspections.* Reading, MA: Addison Wesley Longman, 1993. (ISBN 0-201631814, 471 pages)

Glass, Robert L. *Software Runaways: Lessons Learned from Massive Project Failures.* Upper Saddle River, NJ: Prentice Hall, 1997. (ISBN 0-13-673443-X, 259 pages)

Grady, Robert B. *Practical Software Metrics for Project Management and Process Improvement.* Englewood Cliffs, NJ: Prentice Hall, 1992. (ISBN 0-13-720384-5, 270 pages)

———. *Successful Software Process Improvement.* Upper Saddle River, NJ: Prentice Hall, 1997. (ISBN 0-13-626623-1, 314 pages)

Grady, Robert B., and Deborah L. Caswell. *Software Metrics: Establishing a Company-Wide Program.* Englewood Cliffs, NJ: Prentice Hall, 1987. (ISBN 0-13-821844-7, 288 pages)

Gulledge, Thomas R., William P. Hutzler, and Joan S. Lovelace, eds. *Cost Estimating and Analysis: Balancing Technology with Declining Budgets.* New York: Springer-Verlag, 1992. (ISBN 0-387-97838-0, 297 pages)

Howard, Alan, ed. *Software Metrics and Project Management Tools.* Phoenix, AZ: Applied Computer Research, 1997. (30 pages)

Humphrey, Watts S. *Managing the Software Process.* Reading, MA: Addison Wesley Longman, 1989. (ISBN 0-201-18095-2)

———. *Introduction to the Personal Software Process.* Reading, MA: Addison Wesley Longman, 1997. (ISBN 0201548097)

———. *Managing Technical People.* Reading, MA: Addison Wesley Longman, 1997. (ISBN 0-201-54597-7, 326 pages)

IFPUG. *IFPUG Counting Practices Manual.* Release 4.1. Westerville, OH: International Function Point Users Group, May 1999. (93 pages)

Jacobson, Ivar, Martin Griss, and Patrick Jonsson. *Software Reuse: Architecture, Process, and Organization for Business Success.* Reading, MA: Addison Wesley Longman, 1997. (ISBN 0-201-92476-5, 500 pages)

Jones, Capers. *Program Quality and Programmer Productivity.* IBM technical report TR07.764. San Jose, CA: IBM Santa Teresa, January 1977. (97 pages)

———. "Measuring Programming Quality and Productivity." *IBM Systems Journal* 1978; 17(1): 39–63.

———. *Programming Productivity: Issues for the Eighties.* Los Alamitos, CA: IEEE Computer Society Press, 1st ed., 1981; 2nd ed., 1986. (ISBN 0-8186-0681-9, IEEE Computer Society Catalog 681, 489 pages)

———. *Programming Productivity.* New York: McGraw Hill, 1986. (ISBN 0-07-032811-0, 280 pages)

————. *A Ten-Year Retrospective of the ITT Programming Technology Center.* Burlington, MA: Software Productivity Research, 1988.

————. *Assessment and Control of Software Risks.* Englewood Cliffs, NJ: Prentice Hall, 1993. (ISBN 0-13-741406-4, 711 pages)

————. *Critical Problems in Software Measurement.* Carlsbad, CA: Information Systems Management Group, 1993. (ISBN 1-56909-000-9, 195 pages)

————. *Software Productivity and Quality Today: The Worldwide Perspective.* Carlsbad, CA: Information Systems Management Group, 1993. (ISBN 1-56909-001-7, 200 pages)

————. *New Directions in Software Management.* Carlsbad, CA: Information Systems Management Group, 1994. (ISBN 1-56909-009-2, 150 pages)

————. *Patterns of Software System Failure and Success.* Boston, MA: International Thomson Computer Press, 1995. (ISBN 1-850-32804-8, 292 pages)

————. *Applied Software Measurement.* 2nd ed. New York: McGraw Hill, 1996. (ISBN 0-07-032826-9, 618 pages)

————. *Revitalizing Project Management.* SPR technical report. Burlington, MA: Software Productivity Research, August 1997. (37 pages)

————. *Software Quality: Analysis and Guidelines for Success.* Boston, MA: International Thomson Computer Press, 1997. (ISBN 1-85032-876-6, 492 pages)

————. *The Economics of Object-Oriented Software.* SPR technical report. Burlington, MA: Software Productivity Research, April 1997. (22 pages)

————. *Becoming Best in Class.* SPR technical report. Burlington, MA: Software Productivity Research, January 1998. (40 pages)

————. *Estimating Software Costs.* New York: McGraw Hill, 1998. (ISBN 0-07-9130941, 725 pages)

————. "Sizing Up Software." *Scientific American* 1998; 279(6): 104–111.

————. *The Costs, Schedule, and Value of Software Process Improvement.* SPR technical report. Burlington, MA: Software Productivity Research, January 1998. (27 pages)

————. *The Year 2000 Software Problem: Quantifying the Costs and Assessing the Consequences.* Reading, MA: Addison-Wesley, 1998. (ISBN 0-201-30964-5, 303 pages)

————. *Table of Programming Languages and Levels.* Burlington, MA: Software Productivity Research, March 1999. (ten versions from 1985 through July 1999, 77 pages for Version 10)

Kan, Stephen H. *Metrics and Models in Software Quality Engineering.* Reading, MA: Addison Wesley Longman, 1994. (ISBN 0-201-63339-6, 344 pages)

Kemerer, Chris F. "An Empirical Validation of Software Cost Estimation Models." *Communications of the ACM* 1987; 30: 416–429.

———. "Reliability of Function Point Measurement: A Field Experiment." *Communications of the ACM* 1993; 36: 85–97.

Love, Tom. *Object Lessons.* New York: SIGS Books, 1993. (ISBN 0-9627477 3-4, 266 pages)

Marciniak, John J., ed. *Encyclopedia of Software Engineering.* New York: John Wiley & Sons, 1994. (ISBN 0-471-54002, in two volumes)

McCabe, Thomas J. "A Complexity Measure." *IEEE Transactions on Software Engineering* 1976: 308–320.

Melton, Austin. *Software Measurement.* London: Chapman & Hall, 1995. (ISBN 0-412-55180-2)

Mills, Harlan. *Software Productivity.* New York: Dorset House Publishing, 1988. (ISBN 0-932633-10-2, 288 pages)

Moore, James W. *Software Engineering Standards: A User's Road Map.* Los Alamitos, CA: IEEE Computer Society Press, 1998. (ISBN 0-8186-8008-3, 296 pages)

Multiple authors. *Rethinking the Software Process.* CD-ROM. Lawrence, KS: Miller Freeman, 1996. (This is a new CD-ROM book collection produced jointly by the book publisher Prentice Hall and the journal publisher Miller Freeman. This CD-ROM disk contains the full text and illustrations of five Prentice Hall books: *Assessment and Control of Software Risks* by Capers Jones, *Controlling Software Projects* by Tom DeMarco, *Function Point Analysis* by Brian Dreger, *Measures for Excellence* by Larry Putnam and Ware Myers, and *Object-Oriented Software Metrics* by Mark Lorenz and Jeff Kidd.)

Musa, John, Anthony Iannino, and Kazuhia Okumoto. *Software Reliability: Measurement, Prediction, Application.* New York: McGraw Hill, 1987. (ISBN 0-07-044093-X, 619 pages)

Oskarson, Osten, and Robert L. Glass. *An ISO 9000 Approach to Building Quality Software.* Upper Saddle River, NJ: Prentice Hall, 1996. (ISBN 0-13-228925-3, 274 pages)

Park, Robert E., et al. *Software Cost and Schedule Estimating: A Process Improvement Initiative.* Technical report CMU/SEI 94-SR-03. Pittsburgh, PA: Software Engineering Institute, May 1994.

———. *Checklists and Criteria for Evaluating the Costs and Schedule Estimating Capabilities of Software Organizations.* Technical report CMU/SEI 95-SR-005. Pittsburgh, PA: Software Engineering Institute, January 1995.

Perry, William E. *Handbook of Diagnosing and Solving Computer Problems.* Blue Ridge Summit, PA: TAB Books, 1989. (ISBN 0-8306-9233-9, 255 pages)

——. *Effective Methods for Software Testing*. Los Alamitos, CA: IEEE Computer Society Press, 1995. (ISBN 0 471 06097-6, 556 pages)

Pressman, Roger. *Software Engineering: A Practitioner's Approach*. New York: McGraw Hill, 1982.

Putnam, Lawrence H. *Measures for Excellence: Reliable Software On Time, Within Budget*. Englewood Cliffs, NJ: Prentice Hall, 1992. (ISBN 0-13-567694-0, 336 pages)

Putnam, Lawrence H., and Ware Myers. *Industrial Strength Software: Effective Management Using Measurement*. Los Alamitos, CA: IEEE Computer Society Press, 1997. (ISBN 0-8186-7532-2, 320 pages)

Rubin, Howard. *Software Benchmark Studies for 1999*. Pound Ridge, NY: Howard Rubin Associates, 1999.

Schulmeyer, G. Gordon, and James I. McManus, eds. *Handbook of Software Quality Assurance*. New York: Van Nostrand Reinhold, 1992. (ISBN 0-442-00796-5, 562 pages)

Shepperd, M. "A Critique of Cyclomatic Complexity as a Software Metric." *Software Engineering Journal* 1988; 3: 30–36.

Software Productivity Consortium. *The Software Measurement Guidebook*. Boston, MA: International Thomson Computer Press, 1995. (ISBN 1-850-32195-7, 308 pages)

Strassmann, Paul. *The Squandered Computer*. New Canaan, CT: The Information Economics Press, 1997. (ISBN 0-9620413-1-9, 426 pages)

Stukes, Sherry, Jason Deshoretz, Henry Apgar, and Ilona Macias. *Air Force Cost Analysis Agency Software Estimating Model Analysis*. TR-9545/008-2, contract F04701-95-D-0003, task 008. Thousand Oaks, CA: Management Consulting & Research, September 1996.

Symons, Charles R. *Software Sizing and Estimating: Mk II FPA (Function Point Analysis)*. Chichester, UK: John Wiley & Sons, 1991. (ISBN 0 471-92985-9, 200 pages)

Thayer, Richard H., ed. *Software Engineering Project Management*. Los Alamitos, CA: IEEE Computer Society Press, 1988. (ISBN 0 818680008, 512 pages)

Weinberg, Gerald M. *Quality Software Management. Vol. 2 First-Order Measurement*. New York: Dorset House Publishing, 1993. (ISBN 0-932633-24, 2, 360 pages)

Weinberg, Gerald, and Daniel Friedman. *Handbook of Walkthroughs, Inspections, and Technical Reviews*. New York: Dorset House Publishing, 1990. (450 pages)

Wheeler, David A., Bill Brylcznski, and Reginald Meeson. *Software Inspection: An Industry Best Practice.* Los Alamitos, CA: IEEE Computer Society Press, 1996. (ISBN 0-8186-7430-0, 325 pages)

Wiegers, Karl A. *Creating a Software Engineering Culture.* New York: Dorset House Publishing, 1996. (ISBN 0-932633-33-1, 358 pages)

Yourdon, Edward. *Death March: The Complete Software Developer's Guide to Surviving "Mission Impossible" Projects.* Upper Saddle River, NJ: Prentice Hall, 1997. (ISBN 0-13-748310-4, 218 pages)

Zubrow, David, et al. *Maturity Questionnaire.* CMU/SEI-94-SR-7. Pittsburgh, PA: Software Engineering Institute, Carnegie Mellon University, 1994.

Zuse, Horst. *Software Complexity: Measures and Methods.* Berlin: Walter de Gruyter, 1990. (ISBN 3-11-012226-X, 603 pages)

———. *A Framework of Software Measurement.* Berlin: Walter de Gruyter, 1997. (ISBN 3 110 155877)

Zvegintzov, Nicholas. *Software Management Technology Reference Guide.* Release 4.2. New York: Software Maintenance News, 1994. (ISBN 1-884521-01-0, 240 pages)

CHAPTER TWELVE

Benchmarks and Best Practices for End User Software

The phrase *end user software* refers to small applications that are written for personal use by people who are computer literate. As the twenty-first century begins, computer literacy is rapidly approaching the status of a basic skill in the industrialized nations of the world.

End user applications are, of necessity, small. The great majority are less than 10 function points or 1,000 source code statements in size. The largest almost never exceed 100 function points or 10,000 source code statements. Although it might be technically possible for one person to write an application as large as 1,000 function points or 100,000 source code statements, this might take as long as five years to complete, assuming regular work must continue to be done. Normally, one of the motivations for end user applications is speed. Most end user applications are done in less than a week. This is approximately the greatest amount of time that a working person who is not being paid to program can devote to a software project.

The languages utilized for end user software include spreadsheets such as Excel, several dialects of Basic such as Quick Basic and Visual Basic, and a number of other languages such as JAVA, C++, Realizer, Pascal, Forth, and APL. Spreadsheets and dialects of Basic are by far the most common languages for end user applications.

Although the "mainstream" programming languages such as COBOL, FORTRAN, C, and Ada could be used for personal applications, they usually are not. The reason for this is because a proficiency in the mainstream languages usually requires formal instruction. Learning to use these languages has a fairly steep learning curve.

By the middle of the new century, usage of computers will be as widespread as reading and arithmetic skills are today. Indeed, there is a good chance that computer literacy will actually pull ahead of reading and arithmetic skills, and become the basic human method of acquiring information. It is a widely discussed phenomenon that reading skills are fairly marginal even among high school graduates and indeed among college students. However, usage of computers and enough knowledge to program them is surprisingly common.

Already, usage of computers starts as early as three years of age in homes that have computers available. Many grade schools, and even more high schools, have computer classes available. Many universities not only support campuswide computer networks but actually require computer ownership on the part of all students.

By the time a college student graduates at roughly age 20, many have been using computers for more than 15 years. Although not all children and students learn a programming language or how to program computers, a great many do. Indeed, computer "hacking" or learning enough about programming to penetrate security systems has become something of a high-status cult among both high school and college students.

As computer literacy becomes the norm rather than the exception, many knowledge workers, managers, and other professionals have the technical ability to write software if they choose to do so, or have the time to do so. (For example, I was a corporate chairman and a management consultant, yet I have written dozens of programs in various dialects of the Basic language.)

I estimate that there are approximately 2,400,000 professional software personnel and managers in the United States whose salaries are derived directly from their work associated with software. Yet there are perhaps 12,000,000 managers, engineers, architects, accountants, and other knowledge workers who know enough about programming to build end user applications using tools such as spreadsheets, Quick Basic, Visual Basic, Realizer, and the like.

SPR has never been commissioned to study end user projects as part of our normal assessment and benchmark consulting work. However, in performing our normal work we frequently come across end user applications created by our clients. Also, I have personally developed many end user applications over the years.

There is no exact census of the number of companies in which end users have developed applications, but SPR estimates the U.S. total to be in the range of

50,000 companies, including a host of smaller companies that employ no professional software personnel at all. For example in my company, SPR, several end user financial analysis applications were created in Excel by some of our own financial personnel. Our software quality assurance manager also created an interesting end user application to perform statistical analysis of defect reports.

As an executive of a software company in the greater Boston area, I know more than a hundred managers and workers in scores of companies who have written end user applications. Even in my neighborhood at least a dozen immediate neighbors have home computers and often write interesting applications for personal use.

From our work abroad, we note similar ratios of professional software personnel to end user software personnel in the other industrialized countries. On a global basis, there are perhaps 12,000,000 professional software personnel but probably more than 30,000,000 end users who can develop some form of computer program.

Interestingly, the population of end users seems to be growing at more than 10% per year, whereas the professional software population is now down to single-digit growth rates. The population of end users who can program constitutes one of the largest markets in the world, and a host of vendors led by Microsoft are bringing out tools and products at an accelerating rate.

The software press occasionally runs stories to the effect that end user software will be a "silver bullet" that will bring escalating software costs under control. Unfortunately, the track record of end user software is rather poor. For one thing, successful end user development for projects larger than 100 function points is unlikely and certainly uneconomical. Companies do not want nonprogramming personnel to devote weeks or months of effort to creating personal software applications of uncertain quality and reliability. There are also a number of fairly important legal and technical issues associated with the production of end user software such as:

- Who is the legal owner of software developed by end users?
- How do you apply quality assurance practices to software built by end users?
- If the user who built the software changes jobs, what happens to the software?
- What is the true ROI of end user–developed software?
- In large companies, how do end user applications access corporate applications?
- If you have many users in the same job, how many versions will be built?

- How should end user applications be listed as corporate assets?
- How can end user applications be protected against viruses?
- How can end user applications be checked for harmful functions?
- If end user applications contain serious errors, who is liable?

As this book is written, there are more questions about the quality, value, and economics of end user–developed software than there are answers. Nonetheless, it is a topic of growing importance due to the fact that knowledge of computer programming is becoming a fairly common business skill. In the next century, the world business and government communities will be facing some new and unexpected questions. Before the middle of this century almost every employee will be fully computer literate, and at least half of all knowledge workers will be able to create small computer programs. The most important question for these widespread computer skills is: What is the role of end user programming in corporations and government agencies?

End User Software Demographics

Workers who can write computer programs but whose jobs are something other than programming are not easy to identify. Few companies have personnel records that capture programming skills for nonprogramming workers. Those few companies with skills inventories might record this data, but it is very rare.

Every known occupation now has workers who can write computer programs if they wish. Among my own friends and neighbors I have encountered programming skills in the occupations of law, law enforcement, elected officials, medicine, management, engineering, construction work, real estate sales, retail store clerks, professional golfers, military personnel, teachers, actors, and musicians. Of course, all software personnel can write personal applications too.

Table 12.1 is partly speculative and partly based on observations among our clients extrapolated to national levels. Table 12.1 shows the approximate work force of the United States from 1950 to 2040 in ten-year intervals. This kind of data is available from census reports and commercial almanacs. The speculative portions of Table 12.1 deal with the estimated numbers of workers who could create computer programs and the estimated number of end user programs actually in use.

Although Table 12.1 is speculative, it is based on observations and facts that are probably realistic. Computer literacy is advancing very rapidly, and workers

Table 12.1   **Approximate Number of U.S. Workers Who Can Create End User Software**

Year	Estimated U.S. Work Force	Estimated No. of U.S. Workers who Can Program	Estimated No. of U.S. End User Applications
1950	80,000,000	800	400
1960	85,000,000	8,500	5,950
1970	90,000,000	90,000	72,000
1980	100,000,000	1,000,000	900,000
1990	105,000,000	1,155,000	1,155,000
2000	115,000,000	13,225,000	14,547,500
2010	130,000,000	20,800,000	29,120,000
2020	145,000,000	39,150,000	78,300,000
2030	160,000,000	72,000,000	216,000,000
2040	180,000,000	126,000,000	504,000,000

who can program will soon comprise the majority of all white-collar workers in the United States (and probably blue collar workers too).

From the projected trends in Table 12.1, it appears that businesses and government agencies need to set policies on end user applications fairly soon.

End User Benchmarks

Because my company has not been commissioned to perform benchmark studies of end user applications, the data available for this section is sparse. The data is based on approximately 50 small applications created by my friends, plus a dozen or so I wrote myself. Figure 12.1 shows the overall picture of end user development productivity as noted among personal acquaintances.

The most notable aspect of Figure 12.1 is the fact that it only covers a range that runs from 1 function point to 100 function points. This is roughly equivalent to a range that runs from 100 source code statements to 10,000 source code statements. Although it is possible for individuals to develop applications slightly larger than 100 function points, it is not feasible for one person to

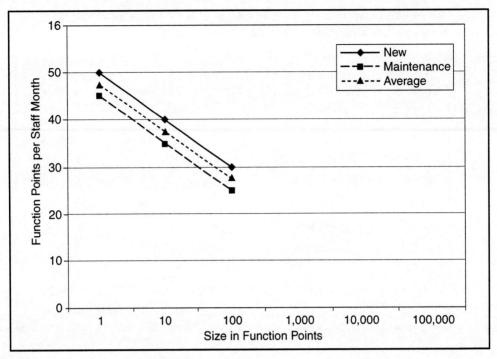

Figure 12.1   End user software productivity

attempt applications much beyond that size limit. Most end user programming is done by people who have jobs to do, so the programming is done at home, at lunch, or during spare time. For one person to attempt large software applications on a spare-time basis would stretch the elapsed time to completion to months, if not years.

Table 12.2 shows rough benchmarks for end user applications. The data is taken from observations of my own personal applications, plus information supplied by colleagues and neighbors. Note that the average size of the personal applications is only 6 function points, which is roughly 600 source code statements in size. The maximum size is only 40 function points. The largest personal application I have developed is roughly 20 function points, or just under 2,000 source code statements. This application took more than two weeks of part-time work. This is not an unusual situation. End user programming is created by people who are not professional programmers. Therefore, we cannot devote more than a few hours a day to programming because we have other work to do.

Table 12.2   Overall End User Software Benchmarks

Benchmark	Value
No. of new projects from 1995 through 1999	56
No. of enhancement projects from 1995 through 1999	6
Total no. of projects from 1995 through 1999	62
Average new project size, function points	6
Maximum new project size, function points	40
Average enhancement size, function points	1
Maximum enhancement size, function points	3
Average new development assignment scope, function points	60
Maximum development assignment scope, function points	60
Average maintenance assignment scope, function points	10
Maximum maintenance assignment scope, function points	10
Average productivity, function points per staff month	26
Maximum productivity, function points per staff month	55
Average productivity, work hours per function point	5.08
Maximum productivity, work hours per function point	2.40
Average effort, staff months	0.23
Maximum effort, staff months	1.54
Average new project staff size	0.10
Maximum new project staff size	0.95
Average new project schedule, calendar months	0.30
Maximum new project schedule, calendar months	2.30
Average monthly compensation, burdened	$8,000
Maximum monthly compensation, burdened	$8,000
Average cost per function point	$307.69
Maximum cost per function point	$750.00
Average defect potential per function point	1.8
Maximum defect potential per function point	2.3
Average defect removal efficiency	90.00%
Maximum defect removal efficiency	99.00%

Table 12.3   End User Software Activities and Rates for 10 Function Points

Parameter	Value
Application size	10 function points
Application size	400 LOC
Source language	Visual Basic
Work hours per month	132
Monthly compensation	$8,000

Activities Performed	Assignment Scope, function points	Production Rate, function points	Staff	Effort, months	Schedule, months	Cost	Percent
01 Coding	15	40	1	0.25	0.38	$2,000	62.06
02 Reuse acquisition	15	1,000	1	0.01	0.02	$80	2.48
03 Unit testing	15	70	1	0.14	0.21	$1,143	35.46
Totals/averages	15, avg.	24.82, avg.	1, avg.	0.40, total	0.60, avg.	$3,223, total	100.00, total

Cost per function point, $322; cost per LOC, $8.06.

End user applications are usually high-speed affairs with requirements that are entirely in the head of the developer. There is usually no formal or written design, although sometimes we may sketch out complex algorithms or screen layouts. Because end user applications involve only one person, group activities such as reviews, inspections, quality assurance, integration, and testing are visibly missing. Also missing is the activity of project management. It is an interesting feature of end user software right now that those who write such applications for our own use at work usually do so without any supervision whatsoever.

The chart of accounts or activities applied to end user projects is about as brief as can be imagined (Table 12.3). Usually only coding and unit test occur, and they are interleaved so tightly that it is hard to distinguish them. The only other activity that is common for end user applications is acquiring reusable code, if any is available. Table 12.3 shows the activities commonly associated with end user development.

In the case of end user software, the concept of best in class does not really apply. Whenever we deal with work carried out by one person, the skill and experience of that person is the dominant factor. The observed range at which individuals can program is at least ten to one. For example, although I have programmed quite a few end user applications myself, I know dozens of colleagues and casual programmers who could do the work much quicker than I did. This assumes we are using the same programming language and the same hardware and tools.

End User Software Successes and Failures

Speaking as an occasional programmer who has written end user applications personally, there are some applications in which we tend to lose interest for one reason or another. Although I've completed more than a dozen small applications, I have also abandoned at least another dozen. Some of these turned out to be harder than I thought. Sometimes I simply put the application aside to do some regular work, and lost interest before I could resume. Table 12.4 presents the success and failure factors for end user software.

There are a number of legitimate business situations in which end user software may be useful and valuable. There are also situations in which end user software can be an expensive mistake. The latter condition is not discussed very often, and is a source of concern. The following are some instances in which end user software has been very troublesome for enterprises:

Table 12.4   End User Software Success and Failure Factors

End User Software Success Factors	End User Software Failure Factors
Legal ownership is clearly established	Legal ownership is ambiguous
Application is of good to excellent quality	Application is of poor to marginal quality
Application is compatible with others	Application is incompatible with others
Application returns positive value	Application returns negative value
Application improves worker capabilities	Application degrades worker capabilities
Application is easily maintained	Application is difficult to maintain
Application can be transferred if needed	Application is difficult to transfer
Application uses standard interfaces	Application uses special interface methods
Application fills a unique, special niche	Application could be replaced by COTS packages
Application is needed by only one user	Application is needed by many users
Application was Y2K compliant	Application contained Y2K errors

- In large companies with multiple end user software applications that deal with common data (such as sales volumes, expenses, and so on), the outputs are often so widely divergent that substantial time is lost trying to figure out why the deviations occur.
- In large companies in which certain kinds of knowledge work may have hundreds of practitioners (for example, accountants and project managers), it is highly uneconomical for such users to build large numbers of more or less similar kinds of software.
- There is a rather low upper limit to the size of applications at which end user development is economical or even possible. As a general rule, any software

application larger than 10 function points or 1,000 LOC should probably be done by professionals rather than amateurs.

There is a shortage of solid empirical data on the success-to-failure ratios of end-user software development, but from my observations of client companies, a preliminary figure of approximately three successes to every one failure can be hypothesized.

End User Software Success Factors

End user software development would not occur if there were no advantages, and the following beneficial results have been noted:

- The schedules are the shortest of any domain for small applications less than 25 function points.
- Many useful applications start as end user prototypes.
- End user applications built using spreadsheet macro languages are very common.
- End user development is satisfying and even enjoyable to those who can do it.

The most effective domains for end user applications are probably those constructed by accounting and financial personnel using various macro languages associated with commercial spreadsheets such as Lotus, Excel, Quattro, and the like. In these specialized domains, end user applications are probably dominant.

End User Software Failure Factors

The downside of end user development is that the results are often so quirky and arcane that only the originator can use the application. The following are some of the hazards observed:

- End user software is impossible for applications larger than 100 function points.
- End user interfaces are often arcane, nonstandard, and even unintelligible.
- End user application maintenance is difficult and sometimes impossible.
- End user quality control is the worst of any kind of software.
- End user reference or user documentation is often nonexistent.
- When users change jobs, the new incumbent can seldom use end user software.

The end user software world is best for prototypes and for truly personal applications for which nothing is available commercially that meets the user's needs. The end user world is not a good choice for high-usage applications for which there are multiple users, nor is it a good choice for any application for which quality and usability are significant.

There are a number of areas in which end user software could be harmful and in some cases even dangerous to human life or safety. The following domains are those in which casual development by end users has no role at all: weapons systems, medical patient monitoring systems, aircraft flight control systems, vehicle propulsion system control, factory process and manufacturing control, and air traffic control.

Best Technical Practices for End User Software

Because end user applications are written for private use, many of the best technical practices for other kinds of software are irrelevant. For example, there are no written requirements and specifications. No formal estimates are prepared. No inspections are used. No one really cares whether schedules are met or run long. Indeed, assuming the work is done at home or during spare time, there are no formal schedules for comparison.

Of course, it is possible to envision a scenario in which an office worker gets so hooked on programming an interesting application that normal work is ignored. This is actually a fairly common occurrence, but outside the scope of this section.

There are only two technical practices for end user software that stand out as being best practices in that they lead to tangible benefits:

1. Use structured programming techniques.
2. Use comments and prologs to explain what the program does.

These two practices are best practices in situations in which the developer may want to make changes after setting aside the program for a month or more. None of us can remember the nuances of code for very long, so if there is any chance at all that the program will be modified, it is a best practice to develop it in such a way that modifications are fairly easy. These two practices also facilitate testing and make defect repairs easier as well.

If the application is written in a language for which reusable materials are plentiful and of high quality, such as Visual Basic, a case can be made that utilizing reusable code might be a best practice too. However, software reuse is not a cut-and-dried proposition. For reuse to be cost-effective, the reused materials must be close to zero-defect status and must also be easy to link and understand.

Best Personnel Practices for End User Software

Because end user development of software applications is outside the normal job descriptions of the developers, it falls into an area in which there may be no formal personnel practices.

Programming is a time-consuming activity at best. This brings up the point that end user applications are either done at home or on personal time, or they are done partly on company time. If they are done on company time, then the developer may be asked to account for some or all of the time utilized.

Another personnel issue with end user software involves the legal ownership of the application when it is finished. Some companies have employment agreements that assign all inventions and technical materials to the company, whether they are produced at home or at work. However blanket agreements of this type are not legal in all states. For example, California and Minnesota do not support employment agreements that are so one sided that they assign all intellectual property to companies regardless of whether it is job related.

Rather than a set of best personnel practices, which do not exist as this book is written, it is useful to list a set of issues that companies and government agencies need to address to establish clear and unambiguous policies for end user software in the future:

- If an end user application is written outside the office without using any company tools or facilities, who is the legal owner of the application?
- If an end user application is written at work, but after working hours or on breaks, who is the legal owner of the application?
- If an end user application is written at work partly on company time, who is the legal owner of the application?
- If an end user application is written at work partly on company time, should the effort and costs be tracked?
- If an end user application is determined to belong to a corporation rather than to the user, should its value be placed on the company books as an asset?
- If an end user application turns out to be so useful that a corporation wishes to convert it to a more general application, should the developer be compensated or rewarded?

- If an end user application has errors or bugs that cause some problem for the company, who should pay for the repairs and recovery?
- If an employee who wrote an end user application leaves the company or changes jobs, who will maintain the application after his or her departure?
- If an employee who wrote an end user application leaves the company, should he or she be asked to create a user's guide before departure?
- If an employee who wrote an end user application leaves the company, should he or she be allowed to take a copy of the application?

As this book is written, there are many questions about end user applications, but not very many answers to the questions.

Readings and References for End User Software

The literature available for end user programming is vast beyond all other domains. This is not to say that books about end user programming are common. However, books on programming languages and tools used by end users, such as Visual Basic, Excel, JAVA, and so forth are too numerous to count. There is no reason to include them here because they are books used by end users, not books about end user applications. However, serious studies of end user applications are in very short supply. In spite of frequent claims by journalists that end user development is becoming common, there is very little hard data on the numbers of end user applications deployed in the United States, or elsewhere.

The software literature that applies to projects developed by multiperson teams of professionals may be of interest to end users, but the bulk of the books and journals on end user practices are specific user guides for actual tools and programming languages. There is very little theory in the end user domain. End user software is outside the scope of corporate control, there is no literature at all on estimating, tracking, measurement, and so forth; therefore these practices are not used for end user applications.

Curtis, Bill, William E. Hefley, and Sally Miller. *People Capability Maturity Model.* Pittsburgh, PA: Software Engineering Institute, Carnegie Mellon University, 1995.

DeMarco, Tom, and Tim Lister. *Peopleware.* New York: Dorset House Publishing, 1987. (ISBN 0-932633-05-6, 188 pages)

Humphrey, Watts. *Introduction to the Personal Software Process*. Reading, MA: Addison Wesley Longman, 1997. (ISBN 0201548097)

————. *Managing Technical People*. Reading, MA: Addison Wesley Longman, 1997. (ISBN 0-201-54597-7, 326 pages)

Jones, Capers. *Patterns of Software System Failure and Success*. Boston, MA: International Thomson Computer Press, 1995. (ISBN 1-850-32804-8, 292 pages)

————. *Software Quality: Analysis and Guidelines for Success*. Boston, MA: International Thomson Computer Press, 1997. (ISBN 1-85032-876-6, 492 pages)

————. *Estimating Software Costs*. New York: McGraw Hill, 1998. (ISBN 0-07-9130941, 725 pages)

————. "Sizing Up Software." *Scientific American* 1998; 279(6):104–111.

————. *The Year 2000 Software Problem: Quantifying the Costs and Assessing the Consequences*. Reading, MA: Addison Wesley, 1998. (ISBN 0-201-30964-5, 303 pages)

Love, Tom. *Object Lessons*. New York: SIGS Books, 1993. (ISBN 0-9627477 3-4, 266 pages)

Marciniak, John J., ed. *Encyclopedia of Software Engineering*. New York: John Wiley & Sons, 1994. (ISBN 0-471-54002, in two volumes)

McCabe, Thomas J. "A Complexity Measure." *IEEE Transactions on Software Engineering* 1976: 308–320.

Pressman, Roger. *Software Engineering: A Practitioner's Approach*. New York: McGraw Hill, 1982.

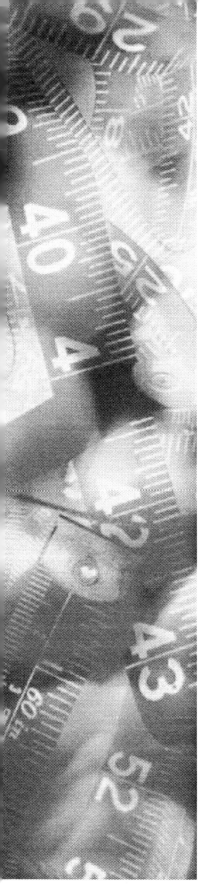

SPR Questionnaire for Assessments, Benchmarks, and Baselines, and Appendix Glossary

Software assessments, benchmarks, and baseline studies need to include similar topics from client to client and project to project. To accomplish this goal, most of the software assessment and benchmark consulting companies utilize scripts or written questionnaires. The following questionnaire is an example of the topics SPR uses when gathering data from clients. Other companies use similar questionnaires.

Note that our questionnaire is used in face-to-face meetings with project managers and technical personnel, rather than being sent by mail or e-mail to the respondents. Because the questionnaire is intended to be used in "live" meetings with trained consultants present, it is not necessary to include written instructions on the questionnaire itself. Questionnaires that are sent by mail must be shorter, and all questions must be either clear or have written instructions to deal with possible answers.

Although this is a large questionnaire, the meetings average just over two hours in duration for each project for which we are gathering data. Copies of the questionnaire are provided to all participants ahead of time, so they have a chance to see the kinds of information that will be asked.

A controversial feature of our questionnaire format concerns the five-point scale for many of the questions. The general meaning of the five values is:

1 Excellent
2 Good or much better than average

3 Average

4 Below average

5 Poor or far below average

We allow two decimal places in answering these five-point questions. When we average the results from all of the projects in a company, we also express the results to two decimal places. Because we use two decimal places so often, when we convert our assessment results into equivalent SEI capability maturity scores, we also use two decimal places. This is at odds with the SEI practice of using only integers. However, our clients like the added information of knowing whether they are toward the front or the rear of a given CMM level.

CHECKPOINT
Questionnaire

Development, Enhancement, Conversion, Package Acquisition, Contract, and Maintenance Projects

Project Name   _____

Project Description   _____

Organization   _____

Location   _____

Manager   _____

Completed By   _____

Current Date (MM/DD/YY)   _____

Platform   _____

Languages   _____

Percent of Reuse   _____

Databases   _____

Notes   _____

    _____

    _____

Notes

_____

_____

_____

_____

_____

_____

_____

_____

_____

_____

Diagram

REQUIRED INPUT

PROJECT CLASSIFICATION

PROJECT NATURE/SCOPE:

1) New Development

    A) Complete stand-alone program   _____

    B) Major system (multiple linked programs or components)   _____

2) Enhancement

    C) Program(s) within a system   _____

    D) Release (current version of an evolving system)   _____

BASE CODE AGE:
(Answer only if Enhancement project.)

1) Less than 1 year old   _____

2) Installed in 1980 or after

3) Installed between 1971–1979

4) Installed in or before 1970

5) Hybrid system with mixed ages for different parts

PROJECT CLASS:

1) Internal program, for use at a single location

2) Internal program, for use at multiple locations

3) Internal program, developed by external contractor

4) Internal program, using military specifications

5) External program, to be put in public domain

6) External program, leased to users

7) External program, bundled with hardware

8) External program, unbundled and marketed commercially

9) External program, developed under commercial contract

10) External program, developed under government contract

11) External program, developed under military contract

FOR MILITARY CONTRACT:

STRICT MILITARY SPECIFICATION (Circle One)   *YES   NO*

PROJECT TYPE:

1) Nonprocedural (generated, query, spreadsheet)   _____

2) Batch application program

3) Interactive applications program

4) Batch database applications program

5) Interactive database applications program

6) Scientific or mathematical program

7) Systems or support program

8) Communications or telecommunications program

9) Process control program

10) Embedded or real-time program

11) Graphics, animation, or image-processing program

12) Robotics or mechanical automation program

13) Artificial intelligence program

14) Hybrid project (multiple types)

FOR HYBRID PROJECTS:

PRIMARY TYPE: _____   SECONDARY TYPE: _____

LIFE CYCLE ACTIVITIES

1. PLANNING AND MANAGEMENT

1.1 Project Planning

    1.1.1 Proposal   _____

    1.1.2 Development plan   _____

    1.1.3 Marketing plan   _____

    1.1.4 Review and inspection plan   _____

    1.1.5 Test plan   _____

    1.1.6 Quality assurance plan   _____

    1.1.7 Documentation plan   _____

    1.1.8 Maintenance and customer support plan   _____

    1.1.9 Training plan   _____

1.2 Development project management

    1.2.1 Personnel management   _____

    1.2.2 Progress and milestone report   _____

    1.2.3 Project cost estimates   _____

    1.2.4 Capital expenditure requests   _____

    1.2.5 Budget variance reports   _____

1.3 Business functions

    1.3.1 Patent or legal reviews   _____

    1.3.2 Import/export license reviews   _____

    1.3.3 Project audit   _____

1.4 Quality assurance

    1.4.1   Review/inspection status reports   _____

    1.4.2   Test status report   _____

    1.4.3   Quality assurance review   _____

1.5 Configuration control

    1.5.1   Configuration control   _____

2. REQUIREMENTS

2.1 Requirements

    2.1.1   Traditional requirements specification   _____

    2.1.2   JAD requirements specifications   _____

    2.1.3   Requirements review   _____

2.2 Prototyping

    2.2.1   Prototyping   _____

2.3 Purchase application acquisition

    2.3.1   Purchase application acquisition   _____

3. EXTERNAL DESIGN

3.1 System architecture   _____

3.2 Functional analysis and design

    3.2.1   Initial functional specifications   _____

    3.2.2   Final functional specifications   _____

3.3 Formal functional design reviews

    3.3.1   Initial functional design review   _____

    3.3.2   Final functional design review   _____

4. INTERNAL DESIGN

4.1 Detail design and specification

    4.1.1   Data design specification   _____

    4.1.2   Program logic specification   _____

    4.1.3   Detail module design   _____

4.2 Formal detail design reviews

    4.2.1   Data structure design review   _____

    4.2.2   Logic design review   _____

    4.2.3   Module design review   _____

    4.2.4   Correctness proofs   _____

5. CODING

5.1 Coding   _____

5.2 Reusable code acquisition   _____

5.3 Unit testing   _____

5.4 Formal code reviews/inspections   _____

6. INTEGRATION AND TEST

6.1 Function testing

    6.1.1   New function testing   _____

    6.1.2   Regression testing   _____

6.2 Integration   _____

6.3 Integration testing   _____

6.4 System testing

   6.4.1   Stress or performance testing   _____

   6.4.2   System testing   _____

6.5 Field testing   _____

6.6 Acceptance testing   _____

6.7 Independent testing   _____

6.8 Independent verification and validation   _____

PERSONNEL

PROJECT MANAGEMENT

PROJECT ORGANIZATIONAL STRUCTURE:
(Defines the type of organizational structure used for this project.)

   1) One-person project   _____

   2) Small-team project (less than four staff members)

   3) Conventional departments, with hierarchical organization

   4) Conventional departments, with matrix organization

   5) Ambiguous or uncertain organization

PROJECT TEAM ROLES AND RESPONSIBILITIES:
(The degree to which project team members are aware of their own responsibilities and the resources represented by their fellow staff members.)

   1) Small project (not applicable)   _____

   2) Very clear and well documented

3) Fairly clear and partially documented

4) Ambiguous and partially documented

5) Ambiguous and frequently changing

PROJECT TEAM MORALE:

(The degree to which project team members are enthusiastic about the project.)

1) Entire team is highly enthusiastic about the project   _____

2) Most team members are enthusiastic about the project

3) Normal project morale and enthusiasm

4) Visible morale problems

5) Very low morale

PROJECT MANAGERIAL AND TECHNICAL COHESIVENESS:

(The degree to which management agrees on project goals, schedule, and methods.)

1) Full agreement on project goals, schedule, methods   _____

2) Partial agreement on project goals, schedule, methods

3) Some agreement on project goals, schedule, methods

4) Uncertain or ambiguous about goals, schedule, methods

5) Sharp disagreement on project goals, schedule, methods

PROJECT MANAGEMENT EXPERIENCE:

(The degree to which management has had prior project management experience.)

1) Expert (implemented many high-priority projects)   _____

2) Extensive (implemented some high-priority projects)

3) Average (implemented some projects)

4) Limited (previous project management experience)

5) Novice (has never managed a project)

PROJECT MANAGEMENT METHODS:
(Describes the type of methods used in support of project management.)

1) Estimates using historical data and automated techniques   _____

2) PERT (Project Evaluation and Review Techniques) charts with CPM (Critical Path Methods), milestones, and delivery dates

3) GANTT or other graphical depiction of major activities

4) Table of major activities with start and end dates

5) Summary schedule

PROJECT MANAGEMENT TOOLS:
(Describes tools used in support of project management methods.)

1) Fully automated, integrated, and effective system   _____

2) Partially automated and generally effective system

3) Manual and effective project management system

4) Manual and cumbersome system

5) No formal system

DEVELOPMENT PERSONNEL EXPERIENCE

DEVELOPMENT PERSONNEL APPLICATION EXPERIENCE:
(Refers to familiarity with the business or technological area addressed by this project.)

1) All experts in the type of program being developed   _____

2) Majority of experts, but some inexperienced personnel

3) Even mixture of experienced and inexperienced personnel

4) Majority of inexperienced personnel, with few experts

5) All personnel are new to this kind of program

DEVELOPMENT PERSONNEL TOOL AND METHOD EXPERIENCE:

(Refers to the development aids provided to project staff to prepare specifications and code.)

1) All experts in the tools and methods for the project   _____

2) Majority of experts in tools and methods

3) Even mixture of experienced and inexperienced personnel

4) Majority of inexperienced personnel in tools and methods

5) All personnel are new to the tools and methods

DEVELOPMENT PERSONNEL ANALYSIS AND DESIGN EXPERIENCE:

(Refers to the levels of experience that the staff has with formal methods.)

1) All experts in formal analysis and design methods   _____

2) Majority of experts in formal analysis and design methods

3) Even mixture of experts and inexperienced personnel

4) Majority of inexperienced personnel in formal analysis and design

5) All personnel are inexperienced in formal analysis and design

DEVELOPMENT PERSONNEL PROGRAMMING LANGUAGE EXPERIENCE:

(Refers to staff facility with the source code language(s) or equivalent used on this project.)

1) All experts in the language(s) used for the project   _____

2) Majority of experts in the language(s) used

3) Even mixture of experts and inexperienced personnel

4) Majority of inexperienced personnel in the language(s) used

5) All personnel are new to the language(s) used

DEVELOPMENT PERSONNEL HARDWARE EXPERIENCE:
(Refers to the development and target platforms for the software.)

1) All experts in the hardware used for the project   _____

2) Majority of experts in the hardware used for the project

3) Even mixture of experts and inexperienced personnel

4) Majority of inexperienced personnel in the hardware

5) All personnel are new to the hardware used for the project

FORMAL REVIEWS AND INSPECTIONS:
(Refers to the knowledge of staff in performing formal design reviews and code inspections. These are quality validation techniques consisting of a group review of a work product, for the purpose of judging its completeness, correctness, consistency, and adherence to guidelines and standards.)

1) All personnel experienced in formal reviews/inspections   _____

2) Most personnel experienced in formal reviews/inspections

3) Even mixture of experienced and inexperienced personnel

4) Most personnel inexperienced in formal reviews/inspections

5) All personnel inexperienced in formal reviews/inspections

FORMAL TESTING EXPERIENCE:
(Refers to the knowledge and practice of staff in software testing techniques and concepts.)

1) All personnel experienced in software test methods   _____

2) Most personnel experienced in software test methods

3) Even mixture of experienced and inexperienced personnel

4) Most personnel inexperienced in test methods

5) All personnel inexperienced in test methods

USER PERSONNEL EXPERIENCE

USER PERSONNEL EXPERIENCE WITH SOFTWARE PROJECTS:

(Concerns the extent to which end users are familiar with the software development life cycle and the expectations regarding their involvement in it.)

1) All users are experts, or user experience with software   _____
    is not a key factor

2) A strong majority of users has software experience

3) Even mixture of experts and inexperienced users

4) Majority of users has no prior software experience

5) All personnel have no prior software experience

USER PERSONNEL EXPERIENCE WITH APPLICATION TYPE:

(Reflects the knowledge of the business or technological area that end users can bring to the gathering of stable and clear requirements.)

1) All users are experts, or user expertise is not a major   _____
    factor for the project

2) A strong majority of users are experts

3) Even mixture of experts, new hires, and novices

4) Majority of new hires and novices, with few experts

5) All personnel are new to this kind of program

USER INVOLVEMENT DURING REQUIREMENTS:

(Refers to the degree of end user involvement in requirements gathering.)

1) All users are heavily involved, or user involvement is not a major factor _____

2) A strong majority of users is heavily involved during requirements

3) Users are somewhat involved during requirements

4) Users are seldom involved during requirements

5) Users are not involved during requirements

USER INVOLVEMENT DURING DESIGN REVIEWS:

(Refers to the degree of end user involvement in design reviews.)

1) All users are heavily involved, or user involvement is not a major factor _____

2) A strong majority of users is heavily involved during design reviews

3) Users are somewhat involved during design reviews

4) Users are seldom involved during design reviews

5) Users are not involved during design reviews

USER INVOLVEMENT DURING ACCEPTANCE TESTING:

(Refers to the degree of end user involvement in acceptance testing.)

1) All users are heavily involved, or user involvement is not a major factor _____

2) A strong majority of users is heavily involved during acceptance testing

3) Users are somewhat involved during acceptance testing

4) Users are seldom involved during acceptance testing

5) Users are not involved during acceptance testing

PERSONNEL

MAINTENANCE PERSONNEL EXPERIENCE

MAINTENANCE PERSONNEL STAFFING:

(Indicates whether the staff that is responsible for fixing bugs is dedicated to maintenance, or if maintenance is performed informally by developers.)

1) All full-time professional maintenance personnel   _____

2) Majority of full-time professional maintenance personnel

3) Some full-time professional maintenance personnel

4) Most maintenance done by development personnel

5) All maintenance done by development personnel

MAINTENANCE PERSONNEL EXPERIENCE:

(Defines the experience of the maintenance staff relative to the project being maintained.)

1) All experts in system being maintained   _____

2) Majority of experts, but some new hires or novices

3) Even mixture of experts, new hires, and novices

4) Majority of new hires, with few experts

5) All maintenance personnel are new to the system

MAINTENANCE PERSONNEL EDUCATION:

(Describes the training given to the maintenance team prior to the start of maintenance. On-the-job training (OJT) is not considered training in this context.)

1) Maintenance training is not required for the project   _____

2) Adequate training in projects and tools is available

3) Some training is available in projects and tools

4) Some training in projects to be maintained is available

5) Little or no training in projects or tools

TECHNOLOGY

SOFTWARE SUPPORT

DESIGN AUTOMATION ENVIRONMENT:

(Implies the use of a computerized tool that integrates text, standard software graphics, and a data dictionary.)

1) Formal design with design-to-code automation   _____

2) Formal design methods and automated text/graphics support

3) Semiformal design with text/graphics support

4) Semiformal design with text automation only

5) Informal design with no automation

CASE INTEGRATION:

(Defines the degree to which the development aids used are able to provide automated transitions between major phases. An example would be a design aid that can update the data dictionary and interface to a source code generator.)

1) Integration across all phases of life cycle   _____

2) Integration across multiple phases

3) Integration between phases

4) Integration within a phase

5) No integration

PROJECT SOURCE CODE LIBRARY:

(Indicates the means for methodically storing and controlling changes to source code components under development.)

1) Full (tracking and mgmt.) project library with automated   _____
   support

2) Partial (tracking and mgmt.) project library with automated support

3) Minimal automated library for source code

4) Manual source code control

5) No formal library control for code

PROJECT DOCUMENTATION LIBRARY:

(Indicates the means for methodically storing and controlling changes to internal and external documentation written during development.)

1) Full (tracking and mgmt.) project library with automated   _____
   support and control

2) Partial (tracking and mgmt.) project library with automated
   support and control

3) Minimal automated library for documentation and control

4) Manual documentation control

5) No formal library control for documentation

SUPPORT SOFTWARE NOVELTY:

(Refers to fundamental development aids, such as the operating system, source code compilers, link editors, text editors, and the like.)

1) All support software is familiar and well understood   _____

2) Most support software is familiar and well understood

3) Mixture of familiar and new or unfamiliar software

4) Most support software is new or unfamiliar to staff

5) Support software is new or experimental or unfamiliar

SUPPORT SOFTWARE EFFECTIVENESS:

(Refers to effectiveness of the fundamental development aids such as operating systems, source code compilers, link editors, text editors, and the like.)

1) All support tools and software are very effective   _____

2) Most support tools and software are effective

3) Support tools and software are usually effective

4) Some tools and support are ineffective or cumbersome

5) Most tools and support are unreliable and unsuitable

PROGRAMMING DEBUGGING TOOLS:

(Refers to type and capabilities of the debugging tools available.)

1) Integrated development, debugging, and automated testing   _____
   environment

2) Traces, multiple breakpoints, and cross-references

3) Adequate source code editing, with traces only

4) Adequate source code editing, but no trace or other flow aids

5) Primitive source code editing and no debug support

HARDWARE SUPPORT

DEVELOPMENT PLATFORM NOVELTY:

(Refers to the staff's knowledge of the computers, peripherals, and other devices on which the project is dependent.)

1) All hardware is familiar and well understood by staff   _____

2) Most hardware is familiar and well understood by staff

3) Mixture of familiar and new or unfamiliar hardware

4) Most hardware is new or unfamiliar to staff

5) Hardware is new or experimental or unfamiliar

DEVELOPMENT HARDWARE COMPATIBILITY/STABILITY:

(Development hardware stability is reflected in the compatibility of the various pieces of equipment used by the development team.)

1) Very stable, with high compatibility   _____

2) Stable with moderate compatibility

3) Single-vendor hardware with some changes and moderate compatibility

4) Mixed-vendor hardware with some changes and moderate compatibility

5) Unstable, changing, or incompatible development hardware

RESPONSE TIME OF DEVELOPMENT ENVIRONMENT:

(Response time refers to the amount of time that passes after a programmer hits the ENTER key when performing a simple on-line function.)

1) Always subsecond response time   _____

2) Subsecond response time is the norm

3) One- to five-second response time is the norm

4) Five- to ten-second response time is the norm

5) More than ten-second response time is the norm

DEVELOPMENT SUPPORT:

(Indicates the quality of support provided to the development team by the operations and technical support groups.)

1) Support is ample, reliable, and effective   _____

2) Support is adequate, reliable, and effective

3) Support is usually adequate and effective

4) Support is sometimes inadequate or ineffective

5) Support is seriously deficient for the project

TOOLS, EQUIPMENT, AND SUPPLIES:

(Indicates the ease and timeliness with which needed devices, aids, and supplies can be acquired for the development team.)

1) Tools and equipment can be acquired as needed   _____

2) Tools and equipment can be acquired with justification

3) Tools and equipment for project are already in use

4) Tools and equipment acquisition is difficult

5) Tools and equipment acquisition is frozen

WORKSTATION ENVIRONMENT:

(Refers to number of terminals, computers, or workstations per staff.)

1) Networked full-powered workstations for all with remote   _____
   support

2) Networked full-powered workstations for most

3) Networked with mixture of full- and underpowered workstations

4) Stand-alone workstations with some unavailability

5) Inadequately powered workstations with significant unavailability

MAINTENANCE SUPPORT

MAINTENANCE COMPUTING SUPPORT:

(Concerns the adequacy of the computing capacity and response time for carrying out maintenance tasks.)

1) Computer support is ample, reliable, and effective _____

2) Computer support is adequate, reliable, and effective

3) Computer support is usually adequate and effective

4) Computer support is sometimes inadequate or ineffective

5) Computer support is seriously deficient

RELEASE CONTROL METHODS:

(Describes the means for assembling, producing, and distributing enhancements and patches to the base software system.)

1) Detailed automated release control system used _____

2) Detailed manual system including problems, logs, staff reports

3) Manual system controlled by naming convention with data and size

4) Informal or ineffective system, not readily available

5) No release control performed

PROBLEM TRACKING AND REPORTING:

(Depicts the method of recording problems reported from the field and following them through to verified fix and communication with end users.)

1) Tools fully integrated with customer support and configuration _____ control

2) Tool use is effective, but does not interface with other systems

3) Partially automated system

4) Manual and generally effective system

5) Ineffective system

REPLACEMENT AND RESTRUCTURING PLANNING:
(Concerns the fact that aging software tends to lose its structure over time as changes are made. Automated restructuring tools can reverse the process.)

1) Automated restructuring service from outside vendor _____

2) Automated code analysis and restructuring tools

3) Aging systems replaced as required

4) Aging systems maintained indefinitely

5) No formal replacement or restructure strategy

PROCESS

DEVELOPMENT METHODS

REQUIREMENTS CLARITY:
(Refers to the degree of clearness and stability of user requirements).

1) Program developers are also users of the program _____

2) Very clear user requirements

3) Fairly clear user requirements

4) Incomplete or ambiguous user requirements

5) User requirements are frequently changing or uncertain

REQUIREMENTS METHODS:
(Refers to the method or style used to gather requirements from the end user.)

1) JAD or equivalent methodology _____

2) Interview-based, formal methods

3) Interview-based, informal methods

4) Limited user involvement

5) No user input to requirements

PROTOTYPING METHODS:

(Refers to the degree that prototyping was used in clarifying requirements.)

1) Prototyping of all major outputs, inputs, and functions   _____

2) Prototyping of some outputs, inputs, and functions

3) Prototyping of major outputs and inputs

4) Prototyping of a few outputs and inputs

5) No prototyping at all

ANALYSIS METHODS:

(The word "clone" means a reusable design derived from similar projects. The word "structured" means one of the standard design methods such as Yourdon or Warnier-Orr techniques. The data analytic method starts with the exploration of the data structure and data flow for the program being designed.)

1) "Clone" data analysis   _____

2) Data and entity modeling

3) Structured data analysis

4) Informal or partial data analysis

5) No data or function analysis

DATA ADMINISTRATION:

(Refers to a group that maintains the integrity of the data and information required for the software systems.)

1) Data administration or data dictionary not needed   _____

2) Data administration and active data dictionary available

3) Data administration and passive data dictionary

4) Partial data dictionary available

5) No data administration or data dictionary

SYSTEM DEVELOPMENT METHODOLOGY:

(Refers to the complex of tasks and deliverables that are organized toward delivering software systems. SDMs predefine the steps that must be taken, the progress reports, the standards for internal and external documentation, the stages of testing, and so forth.)

1) Automated and effective system development methodology   _____

2) Automated but difficult-to-use system development methodology

3) Manual and effective system development methodology

4) Manual but difficult-to-use system development methodology

5) No formal system development methodology

PRODUCTIVITY MEASUREMENTS:

(Indicates the completeness and use of effort, schedule, staff, and deliverable data that can be collected about a project.)

1) Automated and complete life cycle productivity measures   _____

2) Automated but partial life cycle productivity measures

3) Manual and accurate life cycle productivity measures

4) Manual and partial life cycle productivity measures

5) Incomplete or inaccurate productivity measures

CLIENT/SERVER AND OBJECT-ORIENTED FACTORS

CLIENT/SERVER ARCHITECTURE:

(Refers to the number of platforms and the complexity of the coordination between these platforms. For example, a project may focus on the user interface, which is implemented on a single workstation. The user interface logic, however, needs to be aware of and coordinate with the rest of the application, which may be distributed on a mid range for the functional and data access logic and a host system for the database. For this example, the correct choice would be either 4 or 5 depending on the level of complexity.)

1) Single-level architecture   _____

2) Single level with migration to two-level architecture

3) Two-level architecture

4) Three-level architecture with simple coordination

5) Three-level architecture with complex coordination

CLIENT/SERVER STRATEGY:

(Addresses the nature of the distribution of features for the application. In particular, it refers to the distribution of the interface, function, and data logic in the client/server application involved with this project. Answer the question in terms of the relative amount of complexity and risk associated with this project.)

1) Minimal complexity: interface split between client and server   _____

2) Minor complexity: data split between client and server

3) Average complexity: data storage and access only on server

4) Significant complexity: interface only on client

5) Very high complexity: function split between client and server

OBJECT-ORIENTED ANALYSIS AND DESIGN:

(Refers to the nature of the implementation of an object-oriented approach in the requirements, external design, and internal design phases of the project.)

1) Tool-supported, formal and mature OOA and OOD methods in use

2) Formal and mature OO analysis and design methods in use

3) OO analysis and design methods not used to a significant degree

4) Partial and ad hoc use of OO analysis and design methods

5) Unplanned and uncoordinated use of OO analysis and design methods

QUALITY PROCESS

DESIGN DEFECT REMOVAL TRAINING:

(Specify the amount of formal training that has been received by the project team in performing design reviews. Give credit for any training received prior to this project—not for OJT.)

1) Excellent training for design reviews/inspections

2) Adequate training for design reviews/inspections

3) Some training for design reviews/inspections

4) Very limited training for design reviews/inspections

5) No training for design reviews/inspections

CODE DEFECT REMOVAL TRAINING:

(Specify the amount of formal training that has been received by the project team in performing code inspections. Give credit for any training received prior to this project—not for OJT.)

1) Excellent training for code reviews/inspections

2) Adequate training for code reviews/inspections

3) Some training for code reviews/inspections

4) Very limited training for code reviews/inspections

5) No training for code reviews/inspections

PRETEST DEFECT REMOVAL SCHEDULING:

(Indicate the degree to which schedule pressures interfered with the performance of formal design and code reviews.)

1) Always ample time for preparation and sessions   _____

2) Usually ample time for preparation and sessions

3) Satisfactory time for preparation and sessions

4) Some schedule pressure and rushed sessions

5) Severe schedule pressure or cancelled sessions

PRETEST DEFECT REMOVAL FACILITIES:

(Indicate the degree of availability of conference rooms to conduct design and code reviews.)

1) Excellent availability of rooms/facilities for reviews   _____

2) Good availability of rooms/facilities for reviews

3) Somewhat limited availability of rooms/facilities for reviews

4) Very limited availability of rooms/facilities for reviews

5) No availability of rooms/facilities for reviews

TESTING FUNCTION:

(Specify the degree to which specialists perform formal testing.)

1) Formal test department, plus development and user tests   _____

2) Formal test department, plus development testing

3) Formal testing with results compared with known criteria

4) Informal testing with no predefined goals or criteria

5) Hasty or casual testing due to schedule pressures

TESTING METHODS:
(Indicate the degree of automation available for constructing test scripts and data.)

1) Fully automated test bed facilities   _____

2) Partially automated test bed used

3) Effective scripted manual test bed used

4) Nonscripted or partial manual test bed used

5) No test bed available

TESTING TRAINING:
(Specify the amount of formal training that has been received by the applicable staff in planning and executing test steps. Give credit for any training received prior to this project—not for OJT.)

1) Excellent training for testing   _____

2) Adequate training for testing

3) Some training for design testing

4) Very limited training for testing

5) No training for design testing

TEST PLANNING:
(Specify when test plans were written and reviewed.)

1) Test plans developed and formally reviewed during design   _____

2) Test plans developed during design but not formally reviewed

3) Test plans developed during coding and informally reviewed

4) Test plans developed during coding but not reviewed

5) No formal test plans developed

QUALITY ASSURANCE FUNCTION:

(Specify the degree to which the QA function is implemented.)

1) Formal QA group with adequate resources   _____

2) Formal QA group, but understaffed

3) QA role assigned to development personnel

4) QA role performed informally

5) No QA function exists for the project

QUALITY ASSURANCE PROCESS:

(Specify the degree to which QA activities take place. Active QA denotes the existence of a quality planning process with some centralized facilitation of quality activities and standards maintenance. Passive QA implies a group whose job is to monitor performance of reviews and tests.)

1) Formal QA activities are planned and executed   _____

2) Most QA activities are planned for the project

3) QA activities performed informally

4) Formal sign-off procedures

5) No QA activities distinct from testing

QUALITY AND DEFECT MEASUREMENT:

(Specify when in life cycle defect tracking starts.)

1) Quality and defect measurement from requirements on   _____

2) Quality and defect measurement from design on

3) Quality and defect measurement from testing on

4) Partial or intermittent quality and defect measurements

5) No measures of quality and defects

FORMAL REVIEWS AND INSPECTIONS

(Refers to the effectiveness of the formal reviews and inspections performed for the project. These are quality validation techniques consisting of a group review of a work product, for the purpose of judging its completeness, correctness, consistency, and adherence to guidelines and standards. Formal reviews and inspections are more effective than peer to peer.)

1) All reviews and inspections are formal and very effective   _____

2) Majority of reviews and inspections are formal and effective

3) Reviews and inspections are informal but effective

4) Reviews and inspections are informal and tend to be ineffective

5) Reviews and inspections are not normally executed

TESTING EFFECTIVENESS

(Refers to the effectiveness of the various testing techniques employed for the project. Formal testing by test specialists is more effective than testing by development personnel.)

1) Testing is formal, automated, and very effective   _____

2) Testing is formal and very effective

3) Testing is formal and usually effective

4) Testing is informal but effective

5) Testing is informal and tends to be ineffective

MAINTENANCE PROCESS

CENTRAL MAINTENANCE:

(Depicts the nature of the defect repair process once software has been delivered.)

1) Formal defect repairs with 24-hour staffing   _____

2) Formal defect repairs and update distribution

3) Informal defect repairs and update distribution

4) On-line communications between users and maintenance

5) No central maintenance for project

FIELD MAINTENANCE:

(Concerns the dispatch of maintenance personnel to user locations to assist in defect repairs and problem identification.)

1) Permanent on-site field maintenance personnel   _____

2) Field maintenance at customer site

3) Field maintenance for special and rare situations

4) On-line communication between users and maintenance

5) No field maintenance for project

SOFTWARE WARRANTY COVERAGE:

(For commercial software, describes the form of explicit or implicit warranty.)

1) Limited warranty, with penalties for nonperformance   _____

2) Limited warranty, with substantial guarantees

3) Limited warranty, but additional support for good will

4) Limited explicit warranties

5) No explicit or implicit warranties on software

CUSTOMER SUPPORT:

(Describes the postinstallation assistance, such as telephone hot-lines, provided to users.)

1) Full telephone hot-lines with adequate support   _____

2) Telephone hot-lines that are sometimes overloaded

3) Informal telephone support; normal write-in support

4) No telephone support; limited write-in support

5) Limited or no customer support

DELIVERY SUPPORT:

(Describes the explicit help that is provided to users in installing software on their computers.)

1) On-site support for all deliverables   _____

2) On-site support for special cases

3) On-site support for early customers

4) On-site support during field test only

5) No on-site customer support at delivery

ENVIRONMENT

PRODUCT RESTRICTIONS

LEGAL AND STATUTORY RESTRICTIONS:

(Relates to the effort required to make the system requirements and performance comply with statutory constraints.)

1) No known legal or statutory restrictions   _____

2) Minor legal or statutory restrictions

3) Some statutes or government regulations impact project

4) Numerous legal or statutory regulations impact project

5) Stringent legal or government regulations on project

SECURITY RESTRICTIONS:

(Relates to the effort required to make the system requirements and performance comply with security considerations.)

1) No known security restrictions   _____

2) Minor security restrictions

3) Some security restrictions

4) Numerous security restrictions

5) Stringent security restrictions

PRODUCT PERFORMANCE OR EXECUTION SPEED RESTRICTIONS:

(Relates to the effort required to make system requirements and performance comply with performance or execution speed restrictions.)

1) No performance or execution speed restrictions   _____

2) Minor performance or execution speed restrictions

3) Performance and execution speed restrictions

4) Significant performance and execution speed restrictions

5) Severe performance and execution speed restrictions

PRODUCT MEMORY UTILIZATION RESTRICTIONS:

(Relates to the effort required to make system requirements and performance comply with memory utilization restrictions.)

1) No memory utilization restrictions   _____

2) Minor memory utilization restrictions

3) Normal memory utilization restrictions

4) Significant memory utilization restrictions

5) Severe memory utilization restrictions

TARGET HARDWARE NOVELTY:

(Denotes the experience the development staff has with the hardware to be used with the finished software product.)

1) All hardware is familiar and well understood by staff   _____

2) Most hardware is familiar and well understood by staff

3) Mixture of familiar and new or unfamiliar hardware

4) Most hardware is new or unfamiliar to staff

5) Hardware is new, experimental, or unfamiliar

FUNCTIONAL NOVELTY:

(Describes the nature of the type of program being developed.)

1) Conversion or functional repeat of a well-known program   _____

2) Functional repeat, but some new features

3) Even mixture of repeated and new features

4) Novel program, but with some well-understood features

5) Novel program, of a type never before attempted

PHYSICAL ENVIRONMENT

INDIVIDUAL OFFICE ENVIRONMENT: (if cubicles, add .5)

(Denotes the amount of space available for each staff member.)

1) More than 100 square feet of enclosed space per worker   _____

2) 80 to 100 square feet of enclosed space per worker

3) 60 to 80 square feet of enclosed space per worker

4) Less than 60 square feet of enclosed space per worker

5) Open office environment

OFFICE NOISE AND INTERRUPTION ENVIRONMENT:

(Denotes the typical amount of noise and interruption levels experienced by the development staff.)

1) Low background noise and few interruptions   _____

2) Low background noise and frequent interruptions

3) Some background noise and few interruptions

4) Some background noise and frequent interruptions

5) Significant background noise and frequent interruptions

DEVELOPMENT GEOGRAPHY:

(Describes the development staff location.)

1) Single department, single-site development project   _____

2) Multiple development departments within same site

3) Multiple development sites or multicompany project

4) International development within same company

5) International multicompany development

NUMBER OF DEVELOPMENT LOCATIONS: _____

MAINTENANCE ENVIRONMENT

CURRENT SYSTEM STATUS:

(Describes the overall system stability and user satisfaction.)

1) System is stable, with good customer satisfaction _____

2) System is stabilizing, with fair customer satisfaction

3) System is new, with few current customers

4) System is unstable, with some customer dissatisfaction

5) System is error prone, with severe customer dissatisfaction

LONG-RANGE PROJECT STABILITY:

(Concerns the volatility of the software over time and the frequency with which new functions, data types, or hardware platforms might be needed.)

1) Few or no changes to code, data, or new hardware _____

2) New functions and new data types will sometimes occur

3) New functions, data types, and new hardware may occur

4) Frequent changes in functions and data types

5) Frequent changes in functions, data types, and hardware

PROGRAM EXECUTION FREQUENCY:

(Specifies how often the software will be executed.)

1) Quarterly or annual runs _____

2) Monthly or weekly runs

3) Daily or hourly runs

4) Continuous runs or availability

5) Run frequency is not defined

INSTALLATION AND PRODUCTION GEOGRAPHY:

(Describes the number of locations where the software is installed.)

1) Single production site, in a single city _____

2) Multiple production sites, in a single city

3) Multiple production sites, in multiple cities

4) International installation and production

5) Installation and production not defined

NUMBER OF SYSTEM INSTALLATION SITES: _____

ANNUAL PERCENT GROWTH IN INSTALLATION SITES: _____%

NUMBER OF SYSTEM MAINTENANCE SITES: _____

SPECIAL FACTORS

RISK/VALUE ANALYSIS

PROJECT RISK (This is the risk going into the project)

	N/A	VERY HIGH	HIGH	AVERAGE	LOW	VERY LOW
1) Risk of high project novelty	0	5	4	3	2	1
2) Risk of unstable user requirements	0	5	4	3	2	1
3) Risk of change in project architecture	0	5	4	3	2	1
4) Risk of change in development hardware	0	5	4	3	2	1
5) Risk of inadequate speed/memory capacity	0	5	4	3	2	1
6) Risk of inadequate functionality	0	5	4	3	2	1
7) Risk of poor quality and reliability	0	5	4	3	2	1
8) Risk of significant usability problems	0	5	4	3	2	1
9) Risk of significant schedule overruns	0	5	4	3	2	1
10) Risk of significant cost overruns	0	5	4	3	2	1
11) Risk of insufficient project staffing	0	5	4	3	2	1
12) Risk of insufficient project skill levels	0	5	4	3	2	1
13) Risk of excessive schedule pressure	0	5	4	3	2	1
14) Risk of high staff turnover and attrition	0	5	4	3	2	1
15) Risk of major management disagreements	0	5	4	3	2	1

PROJECT VALUE

	N/A	VERY HIGH	HIGH	AVERAGE	LOW	VERY LOW
1) Project is mandatory due to law or policy	0	1	2	3	4	5
2) Value to human life or safety	0	1	2	3	4	5
3) Value to security or national defense	0	1	2	3	4	5
4) Value to morale and human relations	0	1	2	3	4	5
5) Value to enterprise prestige	0	1	2	3	4	5
6) Value to competitive advantage	0	1	2	3	4	5
7) Value to market share	0	1	2	3	4	5
8) Value to quality and reliability	0	1	2	3	4	5
9) Value to direct revenues from project	0	1	2	3	4	5
10) Value to indirect revenues from project	0	1	2	3	4	5
11) Value to enterprise strategic plans	0	1	2	3	4	5
12) Value to enterprise tactical plans	0	1	2	3	4	5
13) Value to enterprise operating costs	0	1	2	3	4	5
14) Value to enterprise operating speed	0	1	2	3	4	5
15) Value to related or future projects	0	1	2	3	4	5

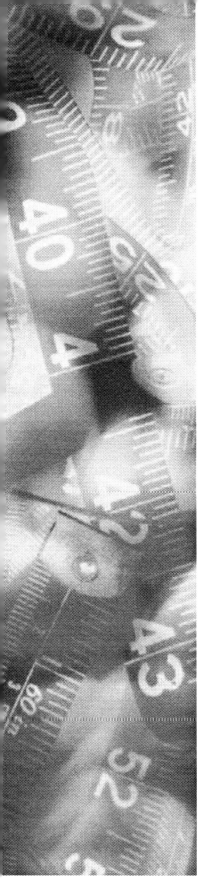

Glossary

acceptance testing (**activity and task**): *Acceptance testing* refers to a special test by the users or customers of an application that is used to determine whether the software meets their needs and expectations. If *acceptance testing* is successful, then the software will be acquired and utilized by the customer. If unsuccessful, then the developers must normally make corrections. *Acceptance testing* is very common for management information systems.

annual deleted code (**percent**): *Annual deleted code (percent)* is an optional field that defines the average annual amount of code deleted from a software application. Real-world data indicates that software is not stable, and that from time to time code is both deleted and added.

audio training cassettes (**task**): *Audio training cassettes* are produced primarily for commercial software such as word-processing programs. They are tutorial devices that allow users to listen to a cassette while performing exercises or drills with the associated software.

automated restructuring (**task**): *Automated restructuring* is a new technology that can analyze the control flow of a program or system and then restructure the software selectively to make future changes easier. Restructuring is very common for COBOL applications, and possible but infrequent for FORTRAN and PLII. Most other languages lack restructuring tools.

budget variance reports (**task**): *Budget variance reports* are normally monthly reports that compare expenses against planned budgets. Such reports are normal in large enterprises that have formal budgets and automated project tracking and accounting systems.

business functions (activity): *Business functions* consist of those planning and management efforts that support the accounting or legal aspects of a software development project.

capital expenditure requests (task): *Capital expenditure requests* are normally created when a project requires new equipment, such as a mainframe or supercomputer. Large enterprises usually have formal capital expenditure planning and approval cycles.

central maintenance (activity and task): *Central maintenance* refers to the tasks of fixing user-reported bugs at a primary maintenance facility. The tasks include analyzing defect reports, analyzing the system or application, making updates, testing the updates, integrating the fix, and preparing the distribution copies of the new version or fix for the users.

code added annually (percent): *Code added annually (percent)* is an optional field that defines the average annual amount of new and modified code that will affect an existing software application. Real-world data indicates that most software applications will range between 2% and 10% of new and changed code per year, for an indefinite period.

code reviews (activity and task): *Code reviews* refers to a methodical and formal critique of application source code carried out in a rigorous manner. The review or inspection team includes a moderator, a recorder, the person whose code is being inspected, and sometimes other inspectors as well. All discovered defects are recorded and are fixed offline after the review or inspection is over.

coding (activity and task): *Coding* refers to the suite of tasks carried out by the programmers who are part of the application team. The normal tasks included with coding are coding, debugging, and desk checking.

coding (phase): *Coding* refers to the set of activities revolving around the production of source code, including coding, unit testing, reusable code acquisition, and code inspections.

configuration control (activity and task): *Configuration control* refers to the formal maintenance of the requirements, specifications, documentation, and code of a software application. Military specifications require full backward traceability of all features and functions to the original requirements. Therefore, military projects normally have automated configuration control support to ensure that all documents match, and that updates to any document or code that causes changes to any other document are reflected correctly.

correctness proofs (task): *Correctness proofs* are attempts to apply mathematical proof techniques to software algorithms. *Correctness proofs* are expensive and not very effective because errors in the proofs themselves are sometimes more plentiful than in the algorithms.

customer support (activity and task): *Customer support* refers to a complex of tasks that includes answering telephone inquiries, providing some form of training for new users, and relaying user defect reports to the central maintenance facility.

data design specification (task): *Data design specification* is sometimes included in the application's functional specifications, although it is often a separate document. Such specifications are normal in large data-oriented systems built around database technology. They include the logical and physical database design.

data structure design review (task): A *data structure design review* looks at the file structure and the logical and sometimes physical data organization selected for the project.

detail design and specifications (activity): *Detail design and specifications* refers to the design document that is produced at a very granular level. The detail design is the implementation-level documentation necessary to begin coding, and often concentrates on the internal structure, control flow, and data organization of the application. The detail design is usually performed either by analysts or by programmers themselves.

detail design reviews (activity): *Detail design reviews* refers to a methodical and formal critique of application specifications carried out in a rigorous manner. The review or inspection team includes a moderator, a recorder, the person whose work is being inspected, and sometimes other inspectors as well. All discovered defects are recorded and are fixed offline after the review or inspection is over.

detailed module design (task): *Detailed module design* is the set of materials prepared by the programmers themselves prior to coding. Such materials are normal for large systems and those that use formal system development methodologies. For small programs and for software developed by experts who have built similar programs before, they may not be produced at all.

development plan (task): A *development plan* is a formal statement of milestones, deliverables, required resources, and schedules. Development plans sometimes include detailed work plans for individual staff members. Such plans are common for military and commercial software, but unusual for information systems.

development project management (activity): *Development project management* refers to the supervisory tasks associated with running software projects. Some of the tasks include supervision of staff, hiring, appraising, budgeting, tracking, and reporting on project milestones.

documentation (phase): *Documentation* comprises all efforts to produce external documentation of the application, including user and maintenance manuals.

documentation plan (task): A *documentation plan* defines the set of user and maintenance documents that will be produced for a program or system. Formal documentation plans are usually produced only for large commercial and military projects, for which as many as 100 different documents may be required.

documentation reviews (activity): *Documentation reviews* is comprised of inspection tasks aimed at specific external documents.

end user training manual (task): An *end user training manual* is organized for teaching purposes and is not necessarily for reference or quick usability. It often includes case studies, examples, and other tutorial devices. Such manuals are normally produced for commercial and end user applications such as spreadsheets, word-processing software, and the like.

error-prone module analysis (task): *Error-prone modules* have been discovered in most large systems. Software bugs do not tend to be scattered randomly through code, but clump in a small number of discrete locations, often in the most complex modules.

external design (phase): *External design* produces a functional design for the application. Working from the user requirements specifications, a functional analysis is performed and then translated into a complete set of procedural and data specifications from the user point of view.

field service (activity and task): *Field service* refers to the on-site assistance given to customers at their own locations. *Field service* is normal only for very large com-

mercial software packages such as operating systems, databases, and the like.

field testing (activity and task): *Field testing* refers primarily to commercial software for which selected early customers try out the application in their own environments. Sometimes the term *beta test* is used as a synonym for field test.

final functional design review (task): *Final functional design review* refers to a methodical and formal critique of application specifications carried out in a rigorous manner. The review or inspection team includes a moderator, a recorder, the person whose work is being inspected, and sometimes other inspectors as well. All discovered defects are recorded and are fixed off-line after the review or inspection is over.

final functional specifications (task): *Final functional specifications* are normally produced after joint review of the initial specifications with the users, and define the complete set of features and functions that the project will implement and the data that the project will utilize.

functional analysis and design (activity): *Functional analysis and design* refers to the first set of specifications produced in response to user requirements. Normally this set of tasks focuses on the external or user view of the application and deals with the major functions and data flows of the application. Often the initial analysis and design is performed by user specialists or by systems analysts.

functional design reviews (activity): *Functional design reviews* look at the design deliverables that specify the external aspects of the software that affect the users directly. Formal *functional design reviews* use a methodology that specifies roles and responsibilities, budgets preparation time for inspectors, uses a moderator to facilitate the process, establishes a rework verification procedure, and records all discovered defects.

functional testing (activity): *Function testing* refers to the test of sets of modules or programs that collectively perform some generic function of the application. Because the work of several programmers may be involved, *function testing* is often carried out by testing specialists.

HELP screens (task): *HELP screens* are special screens that contain information useful for solving problems with an application. The most sophisticated *HELP screens* are context sensitive and give information based on exactly what the user was trying to accomplish. Such screens are normally produced for commercial applications such as spreadsheets, word-processing packages, and the like.

icon and graphic screens (task): *Icon and graphic screens* are those in which the information is presented visually rather than in textual form. Such screens are normally produced for graphics packages, computer-aided design packages, and other applications in which visual representation is useful and appropriate.

import/export license reviews (task): *Import/ export license reviews* are normally only needed for commercial software or military software that is intended for use outside the United States or must pass some form of customs barrier. Increasingly stringent U.S. security policies may extend the need even to internal software, if it is developed by international companies.

independent testing (activity and task): *Independent testing* refers to a formal test of an application by an external enterprise such as a testing contractor. *Independent testing* is normal for military software projects and is required by U.S. military specifications. It is seldom found outside the military domain, although some enterprises may use external testing contractors.

independent verification and validation (activity and task): *Independent verification and validation* refers to a formal review of an application by an external enterprise such as a testing or quality assurance contractor. IV&V is a normal part of military software development, but is very seldom used outside the domain of military specifications.

initial functional design review (task): *Initial functional design review* refers to a methodical and formal critique of application specifications carried out in a rigorous manner. The review or inspection team includes a moderator, a recorder, the person whose work is being inspected, and sometimes other inspectors as well. All discovered defects are recorded and are fixed off-line after the review or inspection is over.

initial functional specifications (task): *Initial functional specifications* are normally produced in response to user requirements and contain the basic description of the functions the project will implement.

installation (activity and task): *Installation* refers to the tasks associated with putting a new application onto its production computers.

installation and training (phase): *Installation and training* refers to the tasks associated with putting a new application onto its production computers, and training new users in how to utilize the software.

installation guide (task): An *installation guide* defines the sequence of steps needed to put a program or system onto a host computer and make it operational. Such manuals are normally produced for medium to large products and for commercial software for which there may be no direct installation assistance available.

integration (activity and task): *Integration* refers to the assemblage of modules, programs, and components of an application into the complete system. *Integration* is normal for large systems but may not be performed for small applications. Two forms of integration are common: discrete builds that occur at specified time intervals, and continuous integration during which updates are made as needed.

integration and test (phase): *Integration and test* comprises the assemblage of application components and all test activities through installation of the application.

integration testing (activity and task): *Integration testing* refers to the testing of an application after the integration process. In applications constructed in a series of discrete builds, each build is followed by an integration test. For those applications integrated continuously, *integration testing* is normally performed as needed.

interactive video training disks (task): *Interactive video training disks* are produced primarily for very complex commercial and military software. Video disks allow alternate results to be illustrated based on user responses, and are quite effective as training mechanisms.

internal design (phase): *Internal design* produces a detailed description of an application used to implement in code the features and functions specified in the functional design.

introduction (task): An *introduction* defines the overall features and concepts of systems. Such manuals are normally produced only for large and complex projects, for which they serve to introduce the overall concepts of the product.

JAD requirements specification (task): *JAD* (joint application design) defines a new way of dealing with software requirements by having user representatives and software representatives create the requirements as a joint deliverable, with the effort mediated by a facilitator. This is an effective technique for information systems. JAD is usually a replacement for the traditional requirements specification.

logic design review (task): A *logic design review* looks at the internal aspects of software such as calling sequences and internal interfaces.

maintenance (phase): *Maintenance* comprises all activities after installation aimed at detecting and repairing defects, surveying user satisfaction, and restructuring software.

maintenance and customer support plan (task): A *maintenance and customer support plan* defines the kinds of update policies, warranty repairs, defect reporting, and support service that will be provided for a program or system. Formal maintenance plans are usually produced only for large commercial and military projects, although some distributed internal software in large corporations may also create these plans.

maintenance defect repairs (task): *Maintenance defect repairs* refers to the tasks of fixing user-reported bugs at a primary maintenance facility.

maintenance documentation review (task): A *maintenance documentation review* is an extended form of edit that looks at the clarity, completeness, and style of the maintenance manuals. Reviews are normal for commercial and military software, but infrequent for information systems projects, which seldom have any maintenance documentation at all.

maintenance management (activity and task): *Maintenance management* refers to the normal supervisory tasks associated with managing technical staff, including hiring, appraising, handling budgets, expense tracking, and the like.

maintenance manual (task): A *maintenance manual* defines the structure and control flow of a program or system, and supplemental data useful for maintenance purposes such as what actions typically trigger certain error conditions, which modules may be involved in specific error conditions, and the like. *Maintenance manuals* are normally produced only for large commercial and military projects.

maintenance years: *Maintenance years* defines the probable life expectancy of the software created by the project. Entering zero disables maintenance and enhancement estimation and measurement.

marketing plan (task): A *marketing plan* is appropriate only for commercial software and defines the distribution channels, target markets, and other aspects associated with commercial products.

message and return code reference manual (task): A *message and return code reference manual* defines all program-generated error messages and action codes. Such manuals are normally produced only for large systems that might create large numbers of messages.

module design review (task): A *module design review* looks at the control flow and modularization of individual program modules prior to the commencement of coding.

new function testing (task): *New function testing* is defined as the test of a set of individual modules that add new capabilities to a system that is under development. Such tests are normal for large commercial and military projects, and for large information systems as well.

on-line error messages (task): *On-line error messages* are screens that provide useful information when user or system errors occur.

on-line tutorial (task): An *on-line tutorial* is a teaching method that users can invoke from the software itself, rather than using paper manuals. Such tutorials are normally produced for commercial applications such as spreadsheets and word-processing packages.

operator's guide (task): An *operator's guide* is aimed at computer operators, and defines how to load a program or system and what specific tape or disk files are needed. Such guides also define error messages and operator actions needed in response to those messages. *Operator's guides* are normally created only for mainframe software intended for use in computers with formal operators.

patent or legal reviews (task): *Patent or legal reviews* are normally required only for commercial software that has financial or commodity trading constraints and may be subject to audit trail requirements by an agency such as the SEC or the IRS.

personnel management (task): *Personnel management* is comprised of those project management efforts directed at supervision, hiring, and appraising of staff.

planning and management (phase): *Planning and management* comprises the planning, management, and accounting functions of development, and those activities that specifically support the project, such as marketing, personnel, and educational services.

postdelivery defect reports (task): *Postdelivery defect reports* are bug reports based on errors users discover after software delivery. Such reports usually identify the number of bugs by month or quarter, the severity, and other information such as bugs by geographic region.

principles of operation (task): A *principles of operation* manual defines the overall protocols that govern the invocation, execution, and termination of a system, and the methods for adding or deleting functions. These manuals are normally produced for systems software such as operating systems to facilitate the development of applications that will work with the system.

product input/output screens (task): *Product input/output screens* are those created for interactive and on-line applications. They comprise the normal screens seen by users when operating the software as well as special screens that might appear only during installation or troubleshooting.

program logic specification (task): *Program logic specification* defines the structure, data organization, flow of control, and data flow through a program or system. The logic specifications are for the use of the developers rather than the users.

programmer's guide (task): A *programmer's guide* is normally produced for systems software to define how to tailor the software to meet local conditions, and how to connect and operate local applications in conjunction with the system.

progress and milestone reports (task): *Progress and milestone reports* are monthly reports produced by project managers and supervisors, highlighting both accomplishments and trouble spots in ongoing development. Such reports are normal in large enterprises and for large systems.

project audit (task): Typical *project audit* tasks include determining the adequacy of measurement activities to be performed on the project, assessing the cost/benefit study independently, reviewing the project organization, and performing a risk/ value assessment.

project cost estimates (task): *Project cost estimates* are created several times for a project. Three common points are at requirements, when design is finished, and when coding is finished. Estimates include both labor and equipment costs as well as special costs, such as moving, external fees and services, and so forth. Formal cost estimates are normally produced for large systems and by large enterprises.

project planning (task): *Project planning* refers to the construction of detailed work breakdown structures and staff loading plans. Formal project plans are normal for large systems and most military software projects for which project planning is a standard task supported by specialists and many tools. Smaller applications and management information systems are often planned informally.

project postmortems (task): *Project postmortems* are reports produced after a project is finished (or cancelled) that describe what went right and what went wrong during development. Postmortems are useful in preventing future problems, and are common for large commercial software projects as well as some military and information systems.

proposal (task): A *proposal* is a formal suggestion that a program or system is needed to meet a particular set of user requirements. For military and commercial software, proposals are normally solicited by a formal request for proposal. Information systems and internal software are usually less formal, and proposals are sometimes omitted.

prototyping (activity and task): *Prototyping* refers to building a partial replica of an application to demonstrate inputs, outputs, and sometimes kernels of functions. Normally prototypes comprise approximately 6% of the functionality of the finished application. Two forms of prototyping occur: disposable prototypes, which are discarded after serving their purpose, and evolutionary prototypes, which grow into final software applications.

purchase application acquisition (activity and task): *Purchase application acquisition* refers to the tasks associated with evaluating and leasing or buying a package from an external source such as a vendor or software house. The tasks involved include matching the characteristics of the application to those of the package, validating package reliability and quality, and assessing package performance and usability as well as the administrative tasks associated with leases or purchases.

quality assurance (activity): *Quality assurance* refers to the formal certification of the deliverables of a software project by a group or person authorized to judge whether acceptable levels of quality have been met. Formal quality assurance departments are normal for commercial, military, and systems software projects. Informal or no quality assurance at all would be normal for personal and management information systems.

quality assurance plan (task): A *quality assurance plan* lays out the sequence of tasks to be carried out by a QA organization, including which deliverables and documents it will review as well as how it monitors or performs tests, validates proof of advertising claims, and carries out other QA functions.

quality assurance review (task): A *quality assurance review* is a written evaluation by the responsible QA manager as to whether a software project meets the relevant standards for quality and can be delivered safely. Such reports are normal for commercial and military software but rare for internal and information systems.

quick reference card (task): A *quick reference card* defines the basic commands and functions of a program or system. It is intended as a convenient prompting device for users. Such cards are normally produced for end user applications such as spreadsheets, word-processing software, graphics packages, and the like.

read-me file (task): A *read-me file* is produced almost exclusively for personal computer applications such as spreadsheets and word-processing programs. *Read-me files* are special text files on the software disk describing last-minute changes and information that occurred after the user manuals were printed.

reference manual (task): A *reference manual* is normally produced as a companion to a user guide, and differs from a user guide in several respects. Reference manuals are often organized in alphabetic rather than task sequence, tend to contain more information than user guides, and are normal in large systems as well as military and commercial software. They are uncommon in small programs and internal information systems.

regression testing (task): *Regression testing* is the test of a software product to ascertain whether the addition of new functions accidentally damaged any prior functions.

requirements (phase and activity): *Requirements* are tasks associated with exploring and documenting the users' needs, which will be embodied in a software application. Requirements are normally the first set of tasks connected with building a new application and are also part of major enhancements.

requirements review (task): *Requirements review* is the first formal step in the defect removal cycle. Reviews normally occur for military and large information systems projects, but only infrequently for systems and small projects.

restructure interval (years): *Restructure interval (years)* is an optional field that defines the periods at which the software will be completely restructured (in other words, run through a commercial restructuring tool). If no restructuring occurs, the structure of the software will slowly degrade over time, matching the real-world experiences of actual software projects whose structures decay as enhancements and repairs accumulate.

reusable code acquisition (activity and task): *Reusable code acquisition* refers to the tasks associated with bringing in code for use in the current application. The source of reusable code can be a formal reusable code library, informal or personal library, borrowed code from a prior application, or code written for the current application but suitable for multiple usage.

review and inspection plan (task): A *review and inspection plan* lays out the sequence of key reviews, approximate timing, locations, and personnel involved.

review/inspection status reports (task): *Review/inspection status reports* are normally monthly or quarterly reports that define how many reviews have been held, total defects found to date, and other similar information. Such reports are normal in large enterprises and for large systems.

sales and marketing brochures (task): *Sales and marketing brochures* define the highlights of a program or system to aid in customer selection. Such materials are produced exclusively for commercially marketed software.

stress or performance testing (task): *Stress or performance testing* is defined as the test of a software product under full-load conditions, such as the test of a telephone switching system with several thousand simultaneous calls. Such tests are normal for performance-sensitive applications such as real-time software, but rare for information systems.

system architecture (activity and task): *System architecture* refers to the effort to design the overall structure of an application. Formal architecture tasks are usually associated with large systems or with systems for which new hardware and software are being built concurrently, such as new operating systems or telecommunication systems.

system documentation review (task): A *system documentation review* is an extended form of edit that looks at the clarity, completeness, and style of the maintenance manuals. Reviews are normal for commercial and military software but infrequent for information systems projects, which seldom have any system documentation at all.

system programmer's guide (task): A *system programmer's guide* defines how to customize, tune, and adjust a program or system for optimum performance, minimum storage, or some other factor. Such manuals are normally produced only for systems software such as operating systems.

system testing (activity): *System testing* refers to the test of a complete application with all its features and functions fully integrated. This is normally the last stage of testing prior to delivery of an application to users.

Sometimes, the phrase *alpha test* is used to refer to the final internal testing stage.

system testing (task): *System testing* is defined as the final test of a full system, with all features and capabilities installed.

test plan (task): A *test plan* lays out the sequence of key tests to be carried out, nature of the tests, origin of the test cases, timing of the tests, and other matters of importance.

test status reports (task): *Test status reports* are either produced monthly for large systems or at the completion of individual test steps. They define the number of tests run, number of bugs found, severity of bugs, origin of bugs, and other similar information. Such reports are normal in large enterprises and for large systems.

traditional requirements specification (task): *Traditional requirements specification* defines what the software is going to do for users and why it will be useful. Requirements specifications are normal for information systems and military projects for which users typically have known needs. For commercial software aimed at large numbers of users, requirements are often constructed artificially based on market studies or the insights of software inventors themselves.

training plans (task): *Training plans* define the needs for user education in how to utilize the application resulting from the project. *Training plans* typically include an outline of the course offerings, the curricula, and the target audiences.

unit testing (activity and task): *Unit testing* refers to the test, normally carried out by the programmers themselves, of individual modules or programs. *Unit testing* is often informal and freely intermixed with the basic tasks of code development.

user and maintenance documentation (activity): *User and maintenance documentation* refers to the tasks associated with producing user guides, reference manuals, programmer guides, messages, HELP screens, and on-line tutorials; in other words, all materials that enable users to learn how to use an application and all materials produced to enable future programmers to maintain the application.

user documentation review (task): A *user documentation review* is an extended form of edit that looks at the clarity, completeness, and style of the user documents. These are normal for commercial software and military projects, but infrequent for small information systems projects.

user guide (task): A *user guide* defines the basic information that an end user needs to start using a software package, carry out basic and extended functions, and shut the package down when finished with a session. User guides are the most common form of manuals for software and occur for almost all programs and systems.

user satisfaction survey (task): A *user satisfaction survey* is a periodic interview or questionnaire intended to discover whether users like the functions, reliability, and ease of use of programs and systems. Such surveys are common for commercial software but are rare elsewhere.

user training (activity and task): *User training* refers to the tasks associated with training new users in how to utilize the software and with teaching existing users how to utilize new features.

video marketing tapes (task): *Video marketing tapes* are produced primarily for commercial software. Such tapes highlight the features and advantages of the product, and may illustrate aspects of the product for sales purposes.

video training tapes (task): *Video training tapes* are produced primarily for commercial software such as database programs. They are tutorial devices that allow users to watch the videotape while performing exercises or drills with the associated software.

Complete List of
Readings and References

Abdel-Hamid, Tarek, and Stuart Madnick. *Software Project Dynamics.* Englewood Cliffs, NJ: Prentice Hall, 1993. (ISBN 013-8220409)

Abran, A., and P. N. Robillard. "Function Point Analysis. An Empirical Study of Its Measurement Processes." *IEEE Transactions on Software Engineering* 1996;22(12):895–909.

Albrecht, Allan. "Measuring Application Development Productivity." Presented at the proceedings of the Joint Share/Guide/IBM Application Development Symposium. Monterey, April, 1979 (10 pages)

———. *AD/M Productivity Measurement and Estimate Validation.* Purchase, NY: IBM Corporation, May 1984.

Andrews, Dorine C., and Susan K. Stalick. *Business Reengineering: The Survival Guide.* Englewood Cliffs, NJ: Prentice Hall, 1994. (ISBN 0-13-014853-9, 300 pages)

Applehans, Wayne, Alden Globe, and Greg Laugero. *Managing Knowledge: A Practical Web-Based Approach.* Reading, MA: Addison-Wesley, 1999. (ISBN 0-201-43315-X, 115 pages)

Austin, Robert D. *Measuring and Managing Performance in Organizations.* New York: Dorset House Publishing, 1996. (ISBN 0-932633-36-6, 216 pages)

Bach, James. "The Immaturity of the CMM." *American Programmer* 1994; 7(9):13–18.

Beizer, Boris. *Software Testing Techniques.* Boston, MA: International Thomson Computer Press, 1990. (ISBN 1850328803, 550 pages)

Boar, Bernard H. *Application Prototyping*. New York: John Wiley & Sons, 1984. (ISBN 0-471-89317-X, 210 pages)

Boehm, Barry. *Software Engineering Economics*. Englewood Cliffs, NJ: Prentice Hall, 1981. (ISBN 0-13-822122-7, 900 pages)

Bogan, Christopher E., and Michael J. English. *Benchmarking for Best Practices*. New York: McGraw Hill, 1994. (ISBN 0-07-006375-2, 312 pages)

Briand, Loic, and Daniel Roy. *Meeting Deadlines in Real-Time Systems*. Los Alamitos, CA: IEEE Computer Society Press, 1997. (ISBN 0-8186-7406-7, 300 pages)

Brooks, Frederick P. *The Mythical Man-Month, Anniversary Edition: Essays on Software Engineering*. Reading, MA: Addison Wesley Longman, 1995. (ISBN 0-201-00650-2, 295 pages)

Brown, Norm, ed. *The Program Manager's Guide to Software Acquisition Best Practices*. Version 1.0. Washington, DC: U.S. Department of Defense, 1995. (142 pages)

Caputo, Kim. *CMM Implementation Guide: Choreographing Software Process Improvement*. Reading, MA: Addison Wesley Longman, 1998. (ISBN 0-201-37938-4, 336 pages)

Carmel, Erran. *Global Software Teams: Collaborating across Borders and Time Zones*. Upper Saddle River, NJ: Prentice Hall, 1999. (ISBN 0-13-924218-X, 269 pages)

Carnegie Mellon University. *The Capability Maturity Model: Guidelines for Improving the Software Process*. Reading, MA: Addison Wesley Longman, 1995. (ISBN 0-201-54664-7, 464 pages)

Charette, Robert N. *Software Engineering Risk Analysis and Management*. New York: McGraw Hill, 1989. (ISBN 0-07-010719-X, 325 pages)

———. *Application Strategies for Risk Analysis*. New York: McGraw Hill, 1990. (ISBN 0-07-010888-9, 570 pages)

Chidamber, S. R., and C. F. Kemerer. "A Metrics Suite for Object Oriented Design." *IEEE Transactions on Software Engineering* 1994;20:476–493.

Chidamber, S. R., D. P. Darcy, and C. F. Kemerer. *Managerial Use of Object Oriented Software Metrics*. Working paper no. 750. Pittsburgh, PA: Joseph M. Katz Graduate School of Business, University of Pittsburgh, November 1996. (26 pages)

Conte, S. D., H. E. Dunsmore, and V. Y. Shen. *Software Engineering Models and Metrics*. Menlo Park, CA: The Benjamin Cummings Publishing Company, 1986. (ISBN 0-8053-2162-4, 396 pages)

Crosby, Philip B. *Quality Is Free.* New York: Mentor Executive Library, 1979. (270 pages)

Curtis, Bill, William E. Hefley, and Sally Miller. *People Capability Maturity Model.* Pittsburgh, PA: Software Engineering Institute, Carnegie Mellon University, 1995.

Cusumano, Michael A., and Richard W. Selby. *Microsoft Secrets.* New York: Touchstone Books, 1998. (ISBN 0-684-85531-3, 532 pages)

Davis, Alan M., and Marilyn D. Weidner. *Software Requirements.* Englewood Cliffs, NJ: Prentice Hall, 1993. (ISBN 0-13-805763-X, 521 pages)

DeMarco, Tom. *Controlling Software Projects.* New York: Yourdon Press, 1982. (ISBN 0-91702-32-4, 284 pages)

————. *Why Does Software Cost So Much?* New York: Dorset House Publishing, 1995. (ISBN 0-932633-34-X, 237 pages)

————. *The Deadline.* New York: Dorset House Publishing, 1997. (ISBN 0-932633-39-0)

DeMarco, Tom, and Tim Lister. *Peopleware.* New York: Dorset House Publishing, 1987. (ISBN 0-932633-05-6, 188 pages)

Department of the Air Force. *Guidelines for Successful Acquisition and Management of Software Intensive Systems.* Vol. 1 and 2. Hill Air Force Base, UT: Software Technology Support Center, 1994.

Dreger, J. Brian. *Function Point Analysis.* Englewood Cliffs, NJ: Prentice Hall, 1989. (ISBN 0-13-332321-8, 185 pages)

El Emam, Khaled, and Nazim Madhavji, eds. *Elements of Software Process Assessment and Improvement.* Los Alamitos, CA: IEEE Computer Society Press, 1999. (ISBN 0-8185-8523-9, 384 pages)

Fenton, Norman, and Shari Lawrence Pfleeger. *Software Metrics: A Rigorous and Practical Approach.* 2nd ed. Los Alamitos, CA: IEEE Computer Society Press, 1997. (ISBN 0-534-95600-0, 416 pages)

Fetcke, Thomas, Alain Abran, and Tho-Hau Nguyen. *Mapping the OO-Jacobsen Approach into Function Point Analysis.* Quebec: Université du Quebec à Montreal, Software Engineering Management Research Laboratory, 1996. (11 pages)

Galea, R. B. *The Boeing Company: 3D Function Point Extensions.* Version 2.0, release 1.0. Seattle, WA: Boeing Information Support Services, June 1995.

Garmus, David, and David Herron. *Measuring the Software Process: A Practical Guide to Functional Measurement.* Englewood Cliffs, NJ: Prentice Hall, 1995. (ISBN 0-13-349-002-5)

Gates, Bill, and Collins Hemingway. *Business @ the Speed of Thought.* New York: Warner Books, 1999. (ISBN 0-446-52568-5, 470 pages)

Gilb, Tom, and Dorothy Graham. *Software Inspections.* Reading, MA: Addison Wesley Longman, 1993. (ISBN 0-201-63181-4, 471 pages)

Glass, Robert L. *Software Runaways: Lessons Learned from Massive Project Failures.* Upper Saddle River, NJ: Prentice Hall, 1997. (ISBN 0-13-673443-X, 259 pages)

Grady, Robert B. *Practical Software Metrics for Project Management and Process Improvement.* Englewood Cliffs, NJ: Prentice Hall, 1992. (ISBN 0-13-720384-5, 270 pages)

———. *Successful Software Process Improvement.* Upper Saddle River, NJ: Prentice Hall, 1997. (ISBN 0-13-626623-1, 314 pages)

Grady, Robert B., and Deborah L. Caswell. *Software Metrics: Establishing a Company-Wide Program.* Englewood Cliffs, NJ: Prentice Hall, 1987. (ISBN 0-13-821844-7, 288 pages)

Gulledge, Thomas R., William P. Hutzler, and Joan S. Lovelace, eds. *Cost Estimating and Analysis: Balancing Technology with Declining Budgets.* New York: Springer-Verlag, 1992. (ISBN 0-387-97838-0, 297 pages)

Hansen, Kirk. *Data Structured Program Design.* Topeka, KS: Ken Orr & Associates, 1983. (ISBN 0-9605884-2-6, 414 pages)

Howard, Alan, ed. *Software Metrics and Project Management Tools.* Phoenix, AZ: Applied Computer Research, 1997. (30 pages)

Humphrey, Watts S. *Managing the Software Process.* Reading, MA: Addison Wesley Longman, 1989. (ISBN 0-201-18095-2, 512 pages)

———. *A Discipline for Software Engineering.* Reading, MA: Addison Wesley Longman, 1995. (ISBN 0-201-54610-8, 816 pages)

———. *Introduction to the Personal Software Process.* Reading, MA: Addison Wesley Longman, 1997. (ISBN 0-201-54809-7, 304 pages)

———. *Managing Technical People: Innovation, Teamwork, and the Software Process.* Reading, MA: Addison Wesley Longman, 1997. (ISBN 0-201-54597-7, 352 pages)

IFPUG. *IFPUG Counting Practices Manual.* Release 3. Westerville, OH: International Function Point Users Group, April 1990. (73 pages)

IFPUG. *IFPUG Counting Practices Manual.* Release 4. Westerville, OH: International Function Point Users Group, April 1995. (83 pages)

IFPUG. *IFPUG Counting Practices Manual.* Release 4.1. Westerville, OH: International Function Point Users Group, May 1999. (95 pages)

Inmon, W. H. *Developing Client/Server Applications in an Architected Environment.* Boston, MA: QED Technical Publishing Group, 1991. (ISBN 0-89435-389-6, 199 pages)

Jacobson, Ivar, Martin Griss, and Patrick Jonsson. *Software Reuse: Architecture, Process, and Organization for Business Success.* Reading, MA: Addison Wesley Longman, 1997. (ISBN 0-201-92476-5, 528 pages)

Janulaitis, Victor M. *Information Systems, Communication and Data Processing Metrics HandiGuide.* Santa Monica, CA: Positive Support Review, 1993.

Jones, Capers. *Program Quality and Programmer Productivity.* IBM technical report TR07.764. San Jose, CA: IBM Santa Teresa, January 1977. (97 pages)

————. "Measuring Programming Quality and Productivity." *IBM Systems Journal* 1978;17(1):39–63.

————. *Programming Productivity: Issues for the Eighties.* Los Alamitos, CA: IEEE Computer Society Press, 1st ed., 1981; 2nd ed., 1986. (ISBN 0-8186-0681-9, IEEE Computer Society Catalog 681, 489 pages)

————. *Programming Productivity.* New York: McGraw Hill, 1986. (ISBN 0-07-032811-0, 280 pages)

————. *A Ten-Year Retrospective of the ITT Programming Technology Center.* Burlington, MA: Software Productivity Research, 1988.

————. *Assessment and Control of Software Risks. Englewood Cliffs, MJ:* Prentice Hall, 1993. (ISBN 0-13-741406-4, 711 pages)

————. *Critical Problems in Software Measurement.* Carlsbad, CA: Information Systems Management Group, 1993. (ISBN 1-56909-000-9, 195 pages)

————. *Software Productivity and Quality Today: The Worldwide Perspective.* Carlsbad, CA: Information Systems Management Group, 1993. (ISBN 156909-001-7, 200 pages)

————. *New Directions in Software Management.* Carlsbad, CA: Information Systems Management Group, 1994. (ISBN 1-56909-009-2, 150 pages)

————. *Patterns of Software System Failure and Success.* Boston, MA: International Thomson Computer Press, 1995. (ISBN 1-850-32804-8, 292 pages)

————. *Applied Software Measurement.* 2nd ed. New York: McGraw Hill, 1996. (ISBN 0-07-032826-9, 618 pages)

————. *Table of Programming Languages and Levels.* Burlington, MA: Software Productivity Research, 1996. (eight versions from 1985 through July 1996, 67 pages for Version 8)

————. *Revitalizing Project Management.* SPR technical report. Burlington, MA: Software Productivity Research, August 1997. (37 pages)

————. *Software Quality: Analysis and Guidelines for Success.* Boston, MA: International Thomson Computer Press, 1997. (ISBN 1-85032-876-6, 492 pages)

————. *The Economics of Object-Oriented Software.* SPR technical report. Burlington, MA: Software Productivity Research, April 1997. (22 pages)

————. *Becoming Best in Class.* SPR technical report. Burlington, MA: Software Productivity Research, January 1998. (40 pages)

————. *Estimating Software Costs.* New York: McGraw Hill, 1998. (ISBN 0-07-9130941, 725 pages)

————. "Sizing Up Software." *Scientific American* 1998;279(6):104–111.

————. *The Costs, Schedule, and Value of Software Process Improvement.* SPR technical report. Burlington, MA: Software Productivity Research, January 1998. (27 pages)

————. *The Year 2000 Software Problem: Quantifying the Costs and Assessing the Consequences.* Reading, MA: Addison-Wesley, 1998. (ISBN 0-201-30964-5, 368 pages)

————. *Table of Programming Languages and Levels.* Burlington, MA: Software Productivity Research, March 1999. (ten versions from 1985 through July 1999, 77 pages for Version 10)

————. *Function Points, Data Points, Service Points, and Value Points.* Burlington, MA: Software Productivity Research, June 1999. (40 pages)

Kalakota, Ravi, and Marci Robinson. *e-Business: Roadmap for Success.* Reading, MA: Addison Wesley Longman, 1999. (ISBN 0-201-60480-9, 400 pages)

Kan, Stephen H. *Metrics and Models in Software Quality Engineering.* Reading, MA: Addison Wesley Longman, 1995. (ISBN 0-201-63339-6, 368 pages)

Kelly, Sean. *Data Warehousing: The Route to Mass Customization.* New York: John Wiley & Sons, 1996. (ISBN 0-471-96328-3, 200 pages)

Kemerer, Chris F. "An Empirical Validation of Software Cost Estimation Models." *Communications of the ACM* 1987;30:416–429.

————. "Reliability of Function Point Measurement: A Field Experiment." *Communications of the ACM* 1993;36:85–97.

Keys, Jessica. *Software Engineering Productivity Handbook.* New York: McGraw Hill, 1993. (ISBN 0-07-911366-4, 651 pages)

Lacity, Mary C., and Rudy Hirschiem. *Information Systems Outsourcing.* New York: John Wiley & Sons, 1993. (ISBN 0-417 938823, 273 pages)

Love, Tom. *Object Lessons.* New York: SIGS Books, 1993. (ISBN 0-9627477 3-4, 266 pages)

Lozinsky, Sergio. *Enterprise-Wide Software Solutions: Integration Strategies and Practices.* Reading, MA: Addison Wesley Longman, 1998. (ISBN 0-201-30971-8, 224 pages)

Marciniak, John J., ed. *Encyclopedia of Software Engineering.* New York: John Wiley & Sons, 1994. (ISBN 0-471-54002, in two volumes)

McCabe, Thomas J. "A Complexity Measure." *IEEE Transactions on Software Engineering* 1976; 308–320.

McMenamin, Stephen M., and John F. Palmer. *Essential Systems Analysis.* New York: Yourdon Press, 1984. (ISBN 0-91702-30-8, 392 pages)

Melton, Austin. *Software Measurement.* London: Chapman & Hall, 1995. (ISBN 0-412-55180-2)

Mertes, Karen R. *Calibration of the CHECKPOINT Model to the Space and Missile Systems Center (SMC) Software Database (SWDB).* Thesis AFIT/GCA/LAS/96S-11. Wright Patterson AFB, OH: Air Force Institute of Technology, September 1996. (119 pages)

Mills, Harlan. *Software Productivity.* New York: Dorset House Publishing, 1988. (ISBN 0-932633-10-2, 288 pages)

Moore, James W. *Software Engineering Standards: A User's Road Map.* Los Alamitos, CA: IEEE Computer Society Press, 1998. (ISBN 0-8186-8008-3, 296 pages)

Muller, Monika, and Alain Abram, eds. *Metrics in Software Evolution.* Munich: R. Oldenbourg Vertag GmbH, 1995. (ISBN 3-486-23589-3)

Multiple Authors. *Rethinking the Software Process.* CD-ROM. Lawrence, KS: Miller Freeman, 1996. (This is a new CD-ROM book collection produced jointly by the book publisher Prentice Hall and the journal publisher Miller Freeman. This CD-ROM disk contains the full text and illustrations of five Prentice Hall books: *Assessment and Control of Software Risks* by Capers Jones, *Controlling Software Projects* by Tom DeMarco, *Function Point Analysis* by Brian Dreger, *Measures for Excellence* by Larry Putnam and Ware Myers, and *Object-Oriented Software Metrics* by Mark Lorenz and Jeff Kidd.)

Musa, John, Anthony Iannino, and Kazuhia Okumoto. *Software Reliability: Measurement, Prediction, Application.* New York: McGraw Hill, 1987. (ISBN 0-07-044093-X, 619 pages)

Oman, Paul, and Shari Lawrence Pfleeger, eds. *Applying Software Metrics.* Los Alamitos, CA: IEEE Computer Society Press, 1996. (ISBN 0-8186-7645-0, 336 pages)

Orr, Ken. *Structured Requirements Definition.* Topeka, KS: Ken Orr & Associates, 1981. (ISBN 0-9605884-0-X, 235 pages)

Oskarson, Osten, and Robert L. Glass. *An ISO 9000 Approach to Building Quality Software.* Upper Saddle River, NJ: Prentice Hall, 1996. (ISBN 0-13-228925-3, 274 pages)

Park, Robert E. "Software Size Measurement: A Framework for Counting Source Statements." Technical Report CMU/SEI 92-TR-020. Pittsburgh, PA: Software Engineering Institution, June 1992.

———. *Software Cost and Schedule Estimating: A Process Improvement Initiative.* Technical report CMU/SEI 94-SR-03. Pittsburgh, PA: Software Engineering Institute, May 1994.

———. *Checklists and Criteria for Evaluating the Costs and Schedule Estimating Capabilities of Software Organizations.* Technical report CMU/SEI 95-SR-005. Pittsburgh, PA: Software Engineering Institute, January 1995.

Perlis, Alan J., Frederick G. Sayward, and Mary Shaw, eds. *Software Metrics.* Cambridge, MA: MIT Press, 1981. (ISBN 0-262-16083-8, 404 pages)

Perry, William E. *Data Processing Budgets.* Englewood Cliffs, NJ: Prentice Hall, 1985. (ISBN 0-13-196874-2, 224 pages)

———. *Handbook of Diagnosing and Solving Computer Problems.* Blue Ridge Summit, PA: TAB Books, 1989. (ISBN 0-8306-9233-9, 255 pages)

———. *Effective Methods for Software Testing.* Los Alamitos, CA: IEEE Computer Society Press, 1995. (ISBN 0 471 06097-6, 556 pages)

Pressman, Roger. *Software Engineering: A Practitioner's Approach.* New York: McGraw Hill, 1982.

Putnam, Lawrence H. *Measures for Excellence: Reliable Software On Time, Within Budget.* Englewood Cliffs, NJ: Prentice Hall, 1992. (ISBN 0-13-567694-0, 336 pages)

Putnam, Lawrence H., and Ware Myers. *Industrial Strength Software: Effective Management Using Measurement.* Los Alamitos, CA: IEEE Computer Society Press, 1997. (ISBN 0-8186-7532-2, 320 pages)

Roetzheim, William J., and Reyna A. Beasley. *Software Project Cost & Schedule Estimating.* Upper Saddle River, NJ: Prentice Hall, 1998. (ISBN 0-13-682089-1)

Rubin, Howard. *Software Benchmark Studies For 1998.* Pound Ridge, NY: Howard Rubin Associates, 1999.

Schulmeyer, G. Gordon, and James I. McManus, eds. *Handbook of Software Quality Assurance.* New York: Van Nostrand Reinhold, 1992. (ISBN 0-442-00796-5, 562 pages)

Shepperd, M. "A Critique of Cyclomatic Complexity as a Software Metric." *Software Engineering Journal* 1988;3:30–36.

Software Productivity Consortium. *The Software Measurement Guidebook.* Boston, MA: International Thomson Computer Press, 1995. (ISBN 1-850-32195-7, 308 pages)

Software Productivity Research. *Quality and Productivity of the SEI CMM.* Burlington, MA: Software Productivity Research, 1994.

St-Pierre, Denis, Marcela Maya, Alain Abran, and Jean-Marc Desharnais. *Full Function Points: Function Point Extensions for Real-Time Software, Concepts and Definitions.* TR 1997-03. Quebec: University of Quebec, Software Engineering Laboratory in Applied Metrics (SELAM). March 1997. (18 pages)

Strassmann, Paul. *The Politics of Information Management: Policy Guidelines.* New Canaan, CT: The Information Economics Press, 1995. (ISBN 0-9620413-4-3, 523 pages)

―――. *The Squandered Computer.* New Canaan, CT: The Information Economics Press, 1997. (ISBN 0-9620413-1-9, 426 pages)

―――. *Information Productivity: Assessing the Information Management Cost of US Industrial Corporations.* New Canaan, CT: The Information Economics Press, 1999. (ISBN 0-9620413-8-6, 157 pages)

Stukes, Sherry, Jason Deshoretz, Henry Apgar, and Ilona Macias. *Air Force Cost Analysis Agency Software Estimating Model Analysis.* TR-9545/008-2, contract F04701-95-D-0003, task 0008. Thousand Oaks, CA: Management Consulting & Research, September 1996.

Symons, Charles R. *Software Sizing and Estimating: Mk II FPA (Function Point Analysis).* Chichester, UK: John Wiley & Sons, 1991. (ISBN 0 471-92985-9, 200 pages)

Thayer, Richard H., ed. *Software Engineering Project Management.* Los Alamitos, CA: IEEE Computer Society Press, 1988. (ISBN 0818680008, 512 pages)

Wang, Charles B. *Techno Vision.* New York: McGraw Hill, 1994. (ISBN 0-07-68155-4, 198 pages)

Weinberg, Gerald M. *Quality Software Management. Vol. 2, First-Order Measurement.* New York: Dorset House Publishing, 1993. (ISBN 0-932633-24-2, 360 pages)

Weinberg, Gerald, and Daniel Friedman. *Handbook of Walkthroughs, Inspections, and Technical Reviews.* New York: Dorset House Publishing, 1990. (ISBN 0932633196, 450 pages)

Wheeler, David A., Bill Brylcznski, and Reginald Meeson. *Software Inspection: An Industry Best Practice.* Los Alamitos, CA: IEEE Computer Society Press, 1996. (ISBN 0-8186-7430-0, 325 pages)

Whitmire, S. A. *"3-D Function Points: Scientific and Real-Time Extensions to Function Points."* Presented at the Proceedings of the 1992 Pacific Northwest Software Quality Conference. June 1, 1992.

Wiegers, Karl A. *Creating a Software Engineering Culture.* New York: Dorset House Publishing, 1996. (ISBN 0-932633-33-1, 358 pages)

Yourdon, Edward. *Death March: The Complete Software Developer's Guide to Surviving "Mission Impossible" Projects.* Upper Saddle River, NJ: Prentice Hall, 1997. (ISBN 0-13-748310-4, 218 pages)

Zells, Lois. *Managing Software Projects: Selecting and Using PC-Based Project Management Systems.* Wellesley, MA: QED Information Sciences, 1990. (ISBN 0-89435-275-X, 487 pages)

Zubrow, David, et al. *Maturity Questionnaire.* CMU/SEI-94-SR-7. Pittsburgh, PA: Software Engineering Institute, Carnegie Mellon University, 1994.

Zuse, Horst. *Software Complexity: Measures and Methods.* Berlin: Walter de Gruyter, 1990. (ISBN 3-11-012226-X, 603 pages)

———. *A Framework of Software Measurement.* Berlin: Walter de Gruyter, 1997. (ISBN 3-110 1555877)

Zvegintzov, Nicholas. *Software Management Technology Reference Guide.* Release 4.2. New York: Software Maintenance News, 1994. (ISBN 1-884521-01-0, 240 pages)

Index

Index

Index

SQL (Structured Query Language), 70, 78
SQM, 31
Squandered Computer, The (Strassman), 52
Staff turnover rates, 389–391, 463–465, 540–541
State transition diagrams, 354
Sterling, 173, 400, 408
Stevens, Wayne, 205, 357, 439
Stock equity programs, 89
Stock option plans, 388, 458
STRADIS, 151
Strassman, Paul, 52, 243
Structured programming, 205, 357–358
    commercial software and, 439
    military software and, 514–515
STSC (U.S. Air Force Software Technology Support Group), 474
Subscriptions, to special industry information sources, 434
Sun Life Insurance, 183
Sun Microsystems, 327, 374, 400
Surveys, 223–224, 312, 386, 537
Sweden, 91, 105, 241
    commercial software and, 401
    military software and, 475
    systems software and, 327
Switzerland, 91, 339
Symantec, 400, 406, 425, 433, 455, 463, 465
Symons, Charles, 75
System 12, 347
Systems engineering, 457
Systems software, 17, 321–322, 329–341
    analysis practices for, 353–355
    basic description of, 321
    benchmarks and, 59, 64–67, 94–95, 349
    best practices for, 321–398
    change control practices for, 363–364
    classification factors and, 116–117
    coding practices for, 357–360
    cost drivers, 338–339

demographics, 323–329
design practices for, 355–357
diverse origins of, 174–177
enhancement practices for, 372–374
ergonomics and, 381–382
formal requirements for, 353
history of, 322
maintenance practices for, 372–374
morale and, 386–387
organizational structures for, 383–384
overtime utilization and, 388–389
personnel practices for, 374–390
producers by SIC code and industry, 327–328
productivity rates for, 64–67
project management practices for, 140, 349–350
quality control practices for, 366–371
requirements-gather practices for, 353–355
reusability practices for, 360–362
schedule adherence and, 340–341
specification practices for, 355–357
successes and failures, 341–348
technical practices for, 348–372
testing practices for, 371–372
unifying theme of, 59
user documentation practices for, 364–366
work patterns and, 388–389

Taiwan, 327, 411, 485
Tata, 327, 401
Taxes, 89, 90, 220–221
    dual employment and, 235
    outsourced projects and, 266
Taxonomy, of software projects, 12–19
Technical practices
    commercial software and, 432–453
    end user software and, 562–563
    military software and, 505–527
    outsourced projects and, 280–284
    systems software and, 348–372
Technical support, 60, 451–452

Index

Index